A Game of Our Own
Camogie's Story
1904-2010

Mary Moran

© Mary Moran.

All rights reserved.

Permission is granted to reproduce materials from this publication for educational purposes.

First published in 2011.
The Camogie Association
Croke Park
Dublin 3
www.camogie.ie
info@camogie.ie
00 353 1 8658651

Any views in this publication are the author's and not necessarily those of the Camogie Association. While every effort has been made to ensure that the information in this publication is accurate, no legal responsibility is accepted by the author or the Camogie Association for any errors or omissions.

Design and layout: Seán Ó Mainnín, *Grafaicí*
Cover design: Mark Dignam, Knockout Graphics:
Editing: Claire Rourke
Printed in Ireland by W &G Baird

ISBN 978-1-908591-00-5

Contents

Acknowledgments	i
Preface by Joan O'Flynn	iii
1 Camogie's Story	1
2 Crokes to the Rescue	15
3 Tailteann Games	29
4 A Huge Step Forward	39
5 Decline and Controversy	55
6 Cork out in the Cold	71
7 Dublin's Phenomenal Run	83
8 Antrim's Hour	99
9 No Stopping Dublin	115
10 New Champions	133
11 Cork Bridge 29-Year Gap	149
12 Kilkenny Breakthrough	169
13 Limerick's Day in the Sun	187
14 First Full-time Official	205
15 Dublin's Return	223
16 Kilkenny on a Roll	241
17 Kilkenny Motor On	251
18 Cork on Points Spree	277
19 Step Closer to the GAA	297
20 New Dawn for Tipperary	319
21 Preparing for the Centenary	343
22 Let the Celebrations Begin	369
23 Into the Second Millennium	387
24 Growing Staff	409
25 Changing of the Guard	433
26 We've Come a Long Way	473

Sections

Roll of Honour	481
Servants of the Game	489
Appendix	504
Index	522

A Game of Our Own

'A Game of Our Own' charts the journey of the Camogie Association from its foundation in the Keating Branch of the Gaelic League in 1904, through its first century, to the vibrant organisation that it is today. Its evolution is a fascinating story.

Many people have helped me along the way. My appreciation and thanks are due to the members of the History Committee: Joan O'Flynn, Eoghan Corry and Alan Aherne. Their commitment, enthusiasm and advice were a source of encouragement.

A large number of people gave of their time to assist me in a variety of ways. Many shared their memories and knowledge of the past. Every contribution is deeply appreciated. I sincerely thank Lily Spence, Lil O'Neill, Séamus McAleenan, Eileen O'Mahony, Sr. Mairéad Fearon, John Moran, Frank O'Grady, Anne Ashton, Eileen Naughton, Sheila Wallace, Eithne Conway, Donal McAnallen (Cardinal Tomás Ó Fiach Memorial Library and Archive), Eamon McMahon, P. J. And Maureen Fulham, Jane Beatty, Kathleen Quinn, Eileen Hogan, Eithne Leech, Patricia Woods and friends, Máire Uí Scolaí, Brídín Uí Mhaolagáin, Brighid Brennan Brown, Eileen O'Brien, Maeve Gilroy, Barbara Ryan, Ailish Kavanagh, Jim and Eileen Blayney, John Cassidy, Albert Farrell, Frank Kearney, Geraldine McGrath, Seán Geraghty, Miriam Higgins, Glen Rovers ladies, South Presentation P.P. ladies, Sinéad O'Connor and Claire Egan.

A few words

While still a schoolgirl, I started collecting camogie material and, over fifty odd years, I have accumulated a considerable hoard. My collection (1955-2011) comprises of cuttings from national and provincial newspapers; Gaelic games books, magazines and annuals; Camogie Association publications; annual reports of various sections of the Camogie Association; hand-outs issued and notes taken at camogie meetings; match programmes, photographs, memorabilia and personal diaries. I have drawn heavily on my collection for this book which includes cuttings from the Cork Examiner, Irish Examiner, Irish Press, Irish Inde-

Acknowledgments

of thanks...

pendent, Irish Times, Gaelic Weekly, Irish News, Sunday Press, Sunday Independent, Southern Star, Limerick Leader, Tipperary Star, Clare Champion, Nenagh Guardian, Kilkenny People, Enniscorthy Echo, Wexford People, Evening Echo, Evening Press, Evening Herald and Connacht Tribune. G.A.A. annuals and yearbooks, An Camán, An Cúl, Gaelic Sport, Gaelic World, Our Games, Hogan Stand, High Ball, Gaelic Stars and Solo have provided information. I have also made use of research and interview notes undertaken for my previous publications.

Valuable material was gathered from minute books of the Camogie Association; Seán O'Duffy's scrapbooks; the Camogie Association's archives and the writings of Agnes O'Farrelly, Seán O'Duffy, Jean McHugh, Maureen Smyth, Paddy Purcell, Agnes Purcell, Kathleen O'Duffy, P. J. Fulham, Máire Uí Scolaí and Ríona Ní Congáil, Paul Rouse, Mike Cronin, Donal McAnallen, Marcus de Búrca, Jim Cronin, Brendan Fulham, Raymond Smith, Jack Mahon, Tom Ryall, Martin Bourne, Seamus P. O Ceallaigh, Tom Keith and Jim Brophy.

Photographs have been supplied by Caroline Quinn Photography, Sportsfile, Phyllis Breslin and the Camogie Association's archives (held at the GAA Museum). The remainder were drawn from my own collection, including a number gathered over the years and those taken by myself.

Finally, I wish to thank the Camogie Association for trusting me with this work and hope that the finished product lives up to their expectations.

Réamhrá/Preface

Tá an-áthas orm cúpla focal a scríobh ar fhoilsiú an leabhair thábhachtaigh seo. Cé go mbaineann an leabhar seo le stair na Camógaíochta san am atá caite, táim cinnte go spreagfaidh sé daoine chun ár gcluiche a neartú agus seans a thabhairt do níos mó ban agus níos mó cailíní spraoi, spórt agus sult a bhaint as Camógaíocht sna blianta atá amach romhainn.

When the Camogie Association was founded there were many challenges facing women, let alone women in sport. Our pioneering founders turned challenges into opportunities and were the first to establish a women's Gaelic game.

Today, the tradition they started remains vibrant and expansive. There are more Camogie players, teams, competitions and supporters than ever before. Our game reaches into more communities and homes than ever before with a budding international dimension in Britain, Europe, North America, Canada, Australia and most latterly Asia.

The publication of *A Game of Our Own, Camogie's Story* documents, for the first time, a distinctive and national narrative of the players, teams and games that have absorbed generations.

I have no doubt that the compendium of match results, team lists, honours won, captains, referees and so on will prove to be an extremely valuable reference for future students of Camogie history. Each date or name will recall many memories and moments for its readers and will surely settle a few table quizzes too!

The book publishes, also for the first time, unique and beautiful photographs of people, events and artefacts from the formative years of the Association. These reflect back to us an era of fundamental social change from the start of the 20th century.

At that stage of our history, a cultural nationalist revival, that involved the Irish language movement and Gaelic sport, inspired the emerging emancipation of middle class women to create something new and original – a women's national game. In the context of the time, this was a remarkable and courageous effort. The social significance of the newly named Camogie is wider than the game itself. The development of a popular female Gaelic game changed women's role in sport in Ireland. At a time when women's role in Gaelic games was deemed to 'decorate the jerseys for the boys'[1], Irish women needed to no longer remain passive. We could actually *play*, as well as referee, train and coach, organise and administer a game of our own.

In 1904/05, sports women were not commonplace. Sport was 'manly' and not for females. While women's economic and social advancement has been significant since then, echoes of that viewpoint are still heard. Even so, the progressive role of women in Gaelic games is evidenced by many more Camogie players and increasing numbers of women taking up administrative and leadership roles not just in Camogie but also in the wider Gaelic games family. Reflecting these developments, there is a strengthening synergy

Réamhrá

A Game of Our Own is an outstanding testament to the integrity, commitment, encyclopaedic knowledge and detailed record keeping of its author, Mary Moran. Mary loves and cherishes Camogie. This combined with her meticulous application to the task, no small amount of patience and a strong sense of stewardship of the history of the game characterised Mary's approach to the work. It is a great pleasure to offer Mary deep and sincere gratitude for her service to us through this work and for the many roles that she has served in Camogie, including that of former National President (1979-1982).

To bring the work from concept to fruition, Eoghan Corry and Alan Aherne joined, with Mary, in a history sub group of the Camogie Association's National Communications Committee. They too gave most generously of their time and expertise in meetings, in conversations and debates in the task of overseeing the production and publication process of the book. I thank them wholeheartedly for the important contributions they made to the project.

between the Camogie Association, the GAA and Ladies Gaelic Football.

In recent years, and particularly since the Camogie Association's centenary in 2004, several local club and county histories are being published. The national Camogie story was a missing piece and something that required to be remedied at the earliest opportunity. This work fulfils that.

The publication of the first national history is a central and most important element in the narrative that binds our sporting past, present and future. Taking a retrospective look does not make us prisoners of history, but shines an important light on the journey we have travelled.

The journey to promote Camogie is never over and the best days are always ahead. I am absolutely confident that Camogie's best days will be inspired by the knowledge and understanding we will gain from this book of the wonderful game we inherit and the wonderful passion for the game that we share with past, present and future generations of Camogie players and supporters.

Joan O'Flynn
Siobhán Ní Fhloinn
Uachtarán
2011

[1] Cronin, Mike, William Murphy and Paul Rouse. (2009). 'Michael Cusack: Sportsman and Journalist' in *The Gaelic Athletic Association* 1884-2009. Dublin: Irish Academic Press.

The Author

Mary Moran has had a long involvement with Camogie. She fielded with St. Aloysius School, Old Aloysians, U.C.C., Celtic and Cork. She won an All-Ireland senior medal with Cork and an All-Ireland club championship medal with Celtic.

Mary chaired the Cork Camogie Board and Munster Council. She was a member of Central Council for almost thirty years and served as President of the Camogie Association (1979-1982).

Previous titles by the author include *Gymfrocks to Headbands* (a history of Munster Colleges Camogie), *A Resounding Success* (a history of All-Ireland Colleges Camogie), *Camogie Champions* (a record of All-Ireland competitions), *Cork's Camogie Story* and *Munster's Camogie Story*.

Chapter One

CAMOGIE'S STORY

WOMEN'S LIVES DIFFER so much today from the time of the founding of the Camogie Association in 1904, when a woman's life expectancy was 48 years. Irish women from both rural and urban backgrounds lived out their lives within the social and economic boundaries of the class into which they were born. Life was a continuous struggle at the lower rung of the class ladder. It was somewhat easier for the better off but, here too, social customs and economic priorities dictated their options.

Very few women in Ireland, irrespective of their ability, received recognition at the time. Arranged marriages were common. Frequently, the bride married into a household where there were more people than just her new husband. She had to fit in with elderly parents and unmarried siblings. Caring for the family was the expected priority of women.

Even though infant mortality rates were high, families were large and housework was an overwhelming burden for women. The majority of households, particularly in rural areas, had no piped water and a great deal of physical labour was required for every single domestic task. Laundry, with no electrical aids, was strenuous work. The rich employed servants to do their household work. Many women from the lower classes left school at 13 or 14 years of age to work, and a considerable number were unable to read or write. Women had not yet been granted the right to vote. Failure to recognise

Right: Women playing hockey in the 1890s

A Game of Our Own

the value of women was common. Women were not considered for the top jobs in any walk of life. The first woman in either Ireland or Great Britain to take up an appointment as university professor was Mary Ryan who was named Professor of Romance Languages at UCC in 1910. It took a further eight years before a woman was elected to parliament.

Sport and Leisure

The public participation of women in team sports was unheard of until the late 1880s and was considered "socially undesirable". Hockey made an appearance in Dublin in 1894. The number of girls with sufficient leisure time to indulge in any organised outdoor sport was very limited until almost the turn of the 20th century. Admission of women to the civil service and a rapid increase in the number of young female students entering the universities and teacher training colleges began to provide a pool of potential players.

Many of these girls had come up to Dublin from areas where the nationalist tradition and the GAA were both strong. A number of them, quite naturally, joined the Gaelic League, then in the first flush of its youthful vigour and enthusiasm and the focal point of all things national.

The Gaelic League

The Gaelic League was founded in 1893 by Douglas Hyde, Eoin McNeill and Eugene O'Growney to ensure that the Irish language would be spoken in Ireland. The members sought to promote Irish culture and encourage a spirit of nationalism amongst the people of Ireland. The movement was initially confined to urban-based intellectuals but it grew in popularity in the early years of the 20th century. The league also promoted hurling and football. The Keating Branch of the Gaelic League, based at 8 North

Cuchulainn's Camogie Team 1904. (Names on photo).

The lower stick was used in a match in Cork in 1905. It is compared with a stick in use in 1984 in the photo.

Camogie's Story

Frederick Street, Dublin, was formed in 1901 by Risteard Ó Foghlú, Shán Ó Cuiv, Tadhg Ó Donnachadha ('Torna') and Seán Ua Ceallaigh ('Sceilg'). The branch was named in memory of Seathrún Céitinn (Geoffrey Keating), the Tipperary-born historian whose chief work was Foras Feasa ar Éirinn (History of Ireland). Young enthusiastic people of both sexes affiliated to the new branch. The boys won the Dublin hurling and football championships in 1901. The girls were great supporters of the branch Gaelic teams, but soon began to ask, "What about us? We want a game of our own."

A New Game

Early in 1903, a group led by Máire Ní Chinnéide, and including Seán Ó Ceallaigh (Sceilg), Tadhg O'Donoghue and Séamus Ó Braonáin, drew up a set of rules based on hurling but modified to suit girls. The name 'Camóguidheacht' was proposed for the new game. Who were those people whose courageous and enterprising approach gave the girls and women of Ireland a game of their own?

Máire Ní Chinnéide (May Kennedy) was born in Dublin to Munster parents. Her father, John H. Kennedy from Nenagh, ran a drapery shop in South Great George's Street. Her mother was Margaret O'Dwyer from Co. Clare. Máire was educated by the Dominicans at Muckross Park. She graduated with a BA in modern literature from the Royal University and was awarded the first travelling studentship in Irish from the university. Máire was fluent in Irish, French, Italian and German and took up the position of professor of Irish in Ard Scoil Mhuire, Donnybrook.

She was President of Keating's Camogie Club and its leader for many years. At the age of 26, she was elected President of An Cumann Camóguidheacht, a daunting task for one so young, but she set about the job with energy and vigour. Máire played in the first camogie match between Keating's and Cuchulainns and had the distinction of scoring the first goal in competitive camogie.

Drama, in particular, caught her interest. She played the part of Una in Douglas Hyde's Casadh an tSúgáin in the Gaiety Theatre. Máire wrote a number of plays herself, which she produced in the old Peacock

Máire Ní Chinnéide

Article written by Máire Ní Chinnéide on the state of fledgling sport which appeared in 'Banba' the magazine of the Keating Branch of the Gaelic League.

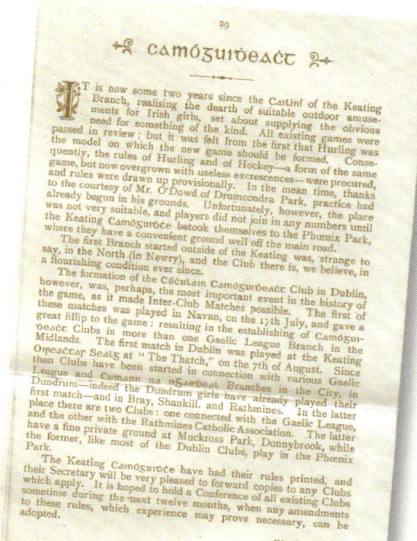

Theatre and took a prominent part in the founding of An Comhar Drámaíochta. She was the first woman to be President of An tOireachtas, having served the Gaelic League in a variety of roles for 50 years. Held in high esteem in Irish society, she was a member of the board of Trustees of the National Library, sat on the Film Censorship Appeal Board and was appointed a member of the Council of the Royal Dublin Society.

Máire married John Fitzgerald, who was Accountant General of the Civil Service at the height of his career. She died on April 25th, 1967 at the age of 88.

Tadhg O'Donoghue ('Torna') was born in Carrignavar, Co. Cork, an area steeped in Irish folklore and poetic tradition. The oldest of six children, Tadhg grew up on a farm. His father, Donncha, was an Irish speaker and Tadhg and his siblings became fluent in the language. As an adult, he lectured in St Patrick's College, Drumcondra and was deeply involved in the Gaelic League. It was Tadhg who provided the name 'Camóguidheacht' for the new game. 'Torna' was a pseudonym he used when he became editor of the Gaelic Journal.

Tadhg O'Donoghue ('Torna') pictured with his sister, Cáit, the first organiser of the Camogie Association.

He studied old Irish under Professor Mulhausen of Heidelberg University and mastered French, German, Welsh and Breton from which languages he produced many translations. His academic output was enormous. He returned to Cork to take up the position of Professor of Irish Studies at UCC. His brother, Eamonn, already lectured in Irish at UCC, while his young brother, Donncha, entered the priesthood and served as parish priest of Bandon. A gentle man, Tadhg puffed quietly on his pipe and listened to what others had to say. He married Nora Foley from Killeagh in East Cork.

Seán Ó Ceallaigh ('Sceilg') A native of Valentia Island, Seán was a politician, author and publisher. He served as Minister for Education in the Second Dáil and was President of the Gaelic League (1919–1923). He was a prolific author on the Irish language and historical topics, and editor of Banba, The Catholic Bulletin and An Camán.

His daughters, Máire and Iney, figured prominently in camogie circles. Máire won All-Ireland medals with Dublin in 1932 and 1933 but, sadly, died in her prime. Iney served as Chairperson of the Leinster Council and was a Trustee of the Camogie Association.

Seán died on March 26th, 1957 at the age of 85.

Séamus Ó Braonáin (Jimmy Brennan) was a native of Ballyouskill, near Ballyragget, Co. Kilkenny. He played hurling and football with Keating's and was their outstanding player. A talented footballer, he won four All-Ireland senior medals with Dublin. He married Bridget Dillon who played for Keating's in the first match at Navan. Séamus served in the Department of Education and, later, as Director of Radió Éireann.

First Set of Rules of Camogie

The first set of rules provided for:
- 12 players on a team
- Pitch size of 40–60 yards wide and 60–100 yards long
- Duration of match was 40 minutes
- Recommended weight of hurley was not to exceed 32ozs
- Weight of ball was to be between 4 and 5ozs
- Circumference of ball was to be between 7 and 9 inches
- Goalposts were to be 10 feet apart with a crossbar 7 feet from the ground
- Skirts to be worn not less than 6 inches from ground
- Intentionally stopping the ball with the skirt was a foul.

The rules of camogie were first printed in Banba, the magazine of the Keating Branch of the Gaelic League, in 1904.

In a hand-written set of playing rules forwarded to the Newry club in 1903, Points' Posts are positioned 10 feet on either side of the goalposts, similar to those used in Australian Rules football. A point was scored when the ball was driven by either side between the goalposts and over the crossbar or over the goal line between the Points' Posts and the goalposts at any height. This rule was not included when the rules were circulated in 1905.

The camogie stick, or hurley, is cut from ash with an easily visible curved grain in it. To suit female players, the stick is shorter and lighter than those used by men. Individual preferences decide the weight of the stick and the amount of spring in it. Traditionally, defenders tend to use a heavier stick than attacking players.

The players lined out in the following positions: goalkeeper, full-back, two wing-backs, centre-back, three midfield players, centre-forward, two wing-forwards and full-forward. A parallelogram was not used in the early days.

Camóguidheacht

The name of the new game, 'camóguidheacht', is roughly translated as 'junior hurling' (the English-language version, 'camogie' is more often used). Early rule books included lists of Irish words and phrases in an effort to encourage players to

Notice above in The Irish Independent, May 20, 1905 of the first camogie league matches

speak Irish. The more commonly used words were: 'camóg' (camogie stick or hurley); 'sliothar' (ball); 'cúl báire' (goalkeeper); and 'poch soar' (free stroke). To foster Irish conversation on the field, the following phrases were suggested: 'Buail an liathróid cugamsa' (Pass the ball to me); 'Is mór an luct leanamhna atá agaibhse' (You have a good many supporters); 'Is deacair dúinn imirt i gcoinne na gaoithe (It is hard to play against the wind) and 'Ba dheas an poch é sin' (That was a nice shot).

First Practice

With the rules in place, it was time for practice to commence. The girls took their first lessons from members of the men's committee, Bill Allen, Tadhg Murphy, Mick Hayes, Jimmy Brennan and others. The girls were shy and hesitant to appear in public – with prejudice so strong, the girls carried their hurleys to the practice pitch wrapped in brown paper or neatly hidden under their coats.

The first fixed practice took place in Drumcondra Park – the space between Binn's Bridge and Croke Park owned by Mr O'Dowd and long since built upon. The area was small and became congested as numbers grew. Progress was slow as the girls built up their physique.

Keatings Camogie Team 1904. Back Row: Back Row: S. Roche, M. Foley, N. Mulcahy, M. Roche, M. Ryan and A. Power. Third Row: I. Nic Concarraige, A. Keogh, E. Kirivan, S. Keogh, N. Dillon and E. Doyle. Second Row: M. Sheehy, E. Gibbons, N. Roche, M. Curtin, M. Kennedy, M. O'Sullivan, E. O'Donovan and E. Hayes. Front Row: M. Coughlan, B. Dillon, B. Foley and S. O'Keeffe.

Second Club

The ladies of Newry were already active in the Gaelic League and they, too, sought an Irish game to play. In May 1903, the Fág-an-Bealach Club was formed. It was the second club in Ireland and the first in Ulster. The inaugural committee was Miss M. Lavery (president), Miss Rose McAnulty (secretary) and Miss L. Lavery (captain).

The girls of the Keating's Club took over the running of their own affairs in 1904 and the following were elected: Máire Ní Chinnéide (president), Margaret Curtain (vice-president), Nora Roche (secretary), Anastasia Rafferty (treasurer), Cáit O'Donoghue, the sister of 'Torna' who had come up from Cork to act as housekeeper to her brother 'Torna' (captain) and Mary O'Sullivan (vice-captain. As the evenings grew

Camogie's Story

longer, they sought a more suitable venue for practice. They made their way to the Phoenix Park where they found a secluded spot off the main road. The ground they selected was later Dublin Camogie Board's pitch No. 2.

A second Dublin Gaelic League branch, Cuchulainns, formed a camogie club in 1904 and the way was clear to commence competition. As one of the main attractions at a Gaelic League Aeridheacht at the Meath Agricultural Society Grounds (later Páirc Tailteann), Keating's met Cuchulainns on July 17th, 1904. Both teams lined out in graceful attire – Cuchulainns wore light blue blouses and red sashes; Keating's were clad in their branch colours, light blue with yellow ties.

At the start of the game, the players occupied their allotted positions on the field and the ball was thrown in by Mr Bartley. Play was fast throughout with Keating's doing most of the pressing. However, it was five minutes to full-time before a score was registered. It fell to Máire Ní Chinnéide the honour of scoring the first goal in competitive camogie. A feature of the game was the splendid defensive play of Cuchulainns' full-back Nellie Lombard. The final score was Keating's 1–0, Cuchulainns 0–0.

Handshakes at the first camogie practice in Drumcondra in 1904

Keating's team: Cáit O'Donoghue (captain), Alice Gibney, Anastatia Rafferty, Mary O'Sullivan, Nora Roche, Sheila Reilly, Sheila O'Keeffe, Eileen Donovan, May Kennedy, Shevaun Clery, Bridget Dillon, Bridget Foley.

Cuchulainns team: Maggie Morgan, Nellie Lombard, Mollie Hogan, J. Monks, Madge O'Sullivan, M. K. Hogan, J. Hayes, Nellie Corless, Ciss Corless, M. Kenny, M. Collins, Annie Morgan.

The match gave a great fillip to the game and resulted in more than one Gaelic League branch in the Midlands forming a camogie club. The first game played in Dublin was at The Thatch, Drumcondra on Sunday, August 7th, 1904. Staged on the final day of Oireachtas Week, the 'novelty' attracted several hundred spectators, despite being played between two sides selected from the Keating's Club.

The newspapers of the day made no reference to the quality of the play in the early games but it is reasonable to assume that the standard was not very high, something that could be accounted for because the players were adults before they took up the game. It was not the accepted thing for women to participate in sport, so a field game would have been new to these girls.

The style of dress of those early players did not lend itself to athletic activity. Long hobble skirts frequently tripped up the wearers. Footwear was also rather restrictive. Laced or buttoned boots, which often came well up the leg, tended to hamper movement, whereas the alternative consisted of canvas shoes that held no grip on a wet pitch.

The majority of the players confined their efforts to ground camogie. A few used all their energy just to show how far they could puck the ball. The longer the shot, the more satisfaction the wielder of the stick got from her exertion. Whether the ball landed to the advantage of her teammates or outside the playing area did not seem to matter. Scoring a point was beyond the ability of camogie's first players. In fairness to the players, the condition of the playing pitches was a far cry from today's manicured grounds.

Another match was played at The Thatch on October 8th, 1904 as one of the highlights of Oireachtas Week. Many delegates from rural areas were present and remained on to view the match. The hope was expressed that, as a result of what they saw, they would endeavour to introduce the game to their native districts.

Expansion

Within three months of the first match in Ireland, the game had spread to Glasgow. The Gaelic League was strong in the city and had a large membership from the Irish community. A club to be known as Emer was formed in October 1904 and was open to members of all branches of the Gaelic League. Twenty-four girls handed in their names and subscriptions. The following officials were elected to run the club: Áine Ní Aodhagain (president), Eibhlin Bean Mac Aodhagain (treasurer) and Máire Ní Daithe (secretary). A successful league was run in Glasgow as Irish girls took to the new game at a phenomenal rate.

The game continued to spread in the Dublin area. By the end of 1904, five clubs were playing in league competition – Keating's, Cuchulainns, Dundrum Volunteers, Rathmines and Drumcondra. The inaugural league was won by Cuchulainns. Dominican College, Muckross Park, where first president, Máire Ní Chinnéide, had been educated, was the first school to take up the new game.

A camogie club was formed in Arklow in the spring of 1904 and the team was trained by Catherine O'Toole. Amongst the players was Julia Russell-Lynch whose daughter, Nancy Lynch, represented Wicklow from 1949 to 1964. The original Arklow club was active until 1908 and was then revived in 1913 and remained for many years.

An Cumann Camoguidheachta

An association called An Cumann Camoguidheachta was formed at the Keating Branch at 8 North Frederick Street, Dublin, on February 25th, 1905. The constitution drawn up provided for:

- A Central Council for the management of championships and as a court of appeal in all club disputes
- Quarterly meetings of delegates
- An annual meeting of delegates from clubs with power to make laws for the Association, control its funds and

elect the Central Council which was to consist of a president, vice-president, treasurer, secretary and committee of eight.

No club was permitted to have more than two representatives on the body. Provision was made for league competitions and the formation of committees in counties having three or more affiliated clubs. The colours (blouse and ties) worn by players were to be of Irish manufacture. Championship medals were to be made in Ireland, of national design and with the inscription in Gaelic. Máire Ní Chinnéide was elected president. The playing rules were printed and made available to all who requested them.

The Dundalk club Emer's. Formed in 1905 it quickly became one of the most prominent sides in the game.

Dundalk

The Dundalk club Emer's was formed in 1905 and quickly became one of the most prominent and successful sides in the game.

Their first team included Angela, Lizzie and Claire Ward, Kathleen and Mary Nolan, Annie and Kate Gogarty, Mary F. O'Hara, Ciss Carragher, Mary K. Smith and Annie Fearon.

Opposition from Clergy

A small number of the clergy opposed camogie and considered that playing the game harmed the morality and the purity of women.

The United Irishman related that, in 1905, the parish priest of Rathmines, Canon Fricker, had been shocked and horrified to meet six or eight young girls on the bridge carrying sticks which looked like hurling sticks under their arms.

He was greatly shamed and pained and hoped he would never see such an awful sight again crossing that bridge and he certainly would not like to think that any of his parishioners would do such a thing.

Cork Takes to Game

A letter was received by Central Council in September 1905 from Cork stating that three or four clubs were in the process of formation and requesting two teams to travel down from Dublin to play an exhibition match. The request did not meet with a favourable response, but the Cork girls got on with establishing the game.

The first Cork club was formed in the Blarney Street area of the city in the summer of 1905 and was named Fainne an Lae. Tadhg Barry, author of Hurling and How to Play It, and Seán Condon, secretary of Lee Gaelic Football Club, introduced the girls to the basics of the game. The club was captained by Kate Conlon (aunt of Íde Bean Uí Shé, later President of Cork County Board). Cork's second club, Clan na nGael, was formed in the Blackpool area and Eilis Walsh was its first captain. She later married Tomás MacCurtain, the first republican Lord Mayor of Cork who was murdered by the British forces in his home in 1920.

The way was now clear for Cork's first camogie match. The eagerly awaited challenge was staged at the O'Neill Crowley Grounds at Victoria Cross before a large, enthusiastic crowd. The victors, Fainne an Lae, were presented with a set of camogie sticks specially manufactured by C. O'Connell & Co., Leitrim Street. The triumphant team returned to the city amidst much jubilation in a wagonette, with the players waving their sticks in the air. This is in stark contrast to the Dublin girls who wrapped their sticks in brown paper or hid them under their coats. A camogie stick used by Kate Conlon in this match is in the Cork Public Museum.

Clan Eimear, Cork's third club, was formed in the Lough area by Mary Agnes Sheehan and Katie Dooley. The fourth club to mushroom was Clan Eanna with Daisy Murphy, Aggie O'Connor, Mary Madden, Angela Lombardi and Norah Murphy as prominent players. They wore long hobble skirts and were trained by Liam Ruiséal whose bookshop on the corner of Oliver Plunkett Street and Marlboro Street still bears his name.

Growth in Ulster

A camogie match was part of the programme at an Aeridheacht in Derry city on June 23rd, 1905. By the summer of 1906, girls could be seen practising at Seaghan's Park, Belfast. Clubs were

Cork ladies take to the new game around 1907.

formed in Omagh (Tyrone), Moville (Donegal) and Clones (Monaghan).

Two Dublin clubs, Keating's and Ard Craobh, were invited to play in an exhibition game in conjunction with a hurling tournament at Nenagh in 1906. The match had the desired effect of encouraging the locals to take up the game. In May 1907, Nenagh fielded senior and juvenile teams in a tournament at Birr against Keating's. The number of clubs continued to grow in Dublin. As the standard varied between the clubs, it was decided to organise a senior and a junior league. Four teams entered for the senior competition and ten in the junior grade. Irish Industries presented a cup and medals for the winners. In 1906, the league was won by Dundrum Volunteers.

Three teams existed in Athlone in 1906 – Athlone Ladies, Athlone Woollen Mills and Athlone Town – all had been set up and were organised by Clareman, Patrick Markham. A tournament, consisting of football, hurling and camogie matches, in aid of Multyfarnham Franciscan Bazaar was successfully staged at the Horse Show Grounds on August 12th, 1906. The camogie game, which was advertised as 'Ladies Hurling' resulted in a win for Athlone over Mullingar by 2-3 to 0-0.

In 1906, the Crokes Hurling Club set up a camogie section, the first GAA club to do so. This development was to have far-reaching effects. The Kevin's and Colmcille's GAA clubs followed suit. Dundalk Emer's proved their worth when they overcame Crokes (Dublin) by 2-9 to 0-1 on September 9th. Scoring nine points in a match was a huge achievement. In a curtain-raiser to a football match between Dublin and Tipperary at Jones's Road on August 13th, Cuchulainn's defeated Rathmines by 2-3 to 1-1.

Enthusiasm Begins to Fade

The early enthusiasm for camogie began to fade in the Dublin area and there was no competition in the summer of 1907. Some friendly contests were arranged and the game was kept alive in this way. A number of matches were played north of the River Boyne during the year. On July 14th, Latton overcame Castleblayney at the Monaghan Aeridheacht by 0-2 to 0-1. On the same date, Dublin Cuchulainns played Emer's at the Dundalk Feis before a large gathering. This game brought the standard of play to a new level. The excited spectators applauded the skill and endeavour of the players. Emer's won the day by 2-4 to 1-4. Emer's were a very active club and they staged their own tournament in Dundalk on September 15th where they disposed of the challenge of Whitecross (Armagh) by 1-8 to 0-2.

The Banba Club, Belfast, came into existence in 1908 through the efforts of Seaghan an Diomas. Sisters of the Shaun's hurlers and footballers and daughters of the Shaun's officials provided a panel of players. They played their first game on June 7th, 1908 at the Dundalk Feis. The local Emer's proved too strong for the newcomers and won by 4-5 to 2-1.

The Banba team comprised: K. O'Leary, M. Nicholl, R. Ward, A. Ward, E. Dobbin, E. Murphy, K. Murphy, J. Sheehan, N. McIlvenny, S. Ward, A. O'Neill.

The Emer's team was: Mary Nolan, A. Fearon (captain), B.

Smith, Ciss Carragher, M. Hughes, A. Gogarty, A. Ward, K. Lennon, K. Gogarty, A. Hanratty, A. Gorman, S. Ward.

The Banba team hoped that other camogie clubs would be organised in Belfast but that did not happen. The pioneer Antrim club enjoyed a brief existence mainly due to lack of opposition for matches.

A club existed in Cavan town in 1908 and held their practice sessions at Killymooney. The first officers of the club were Mrs Anne Kirwan (captain); Kathleen Marron (secretary) and Mary McGuinness (treasurer). A friendly match was played against a team from Belturbet. Again, the lack of competition proved crucial and the club folded in little over a year. A second club, Clan Ulagh, was formed in Co. Down. Lissummon and Ballymoyer fielded teams in Co. Armagh. Oughterard was mentioned in the Galway newspapers as an area that had taken up the game.

The Leinster Leader carried an advertisement from the Athy Ladies Hurling Club stating that they wished to play other clubs. In July 1909, the newspaper displayed a further advertisement announcing that the club planned to hold a reunion.

Seán O'Duffy

Seán O'Duffy, a young Mayo man, came to Dublin in 1900. He was to play an immense role in the growth and development of the Camogie Association. He had acquired a love of Irish culture from his mother and had joined the Crokes Gaelic Club and became immersed in the activities of the club. When the Crokes Camogie Club was formed in 1906, Seán O'Duffy and other Crokes hurlers lent a hand to train the camogie players. From their involvement, they were in a good position to see the precarious position that the game was in. The novelty effect associated with the new game in 1904 had worn off. Players now realised how difficult it was to master the new game and only those with strong determination persisted. The game needed to be taught at a young age rather than be taken up in adulthood.

Seán O'Duffy

Need to Improve

The Crokes hurlers were well aware of the need to raise the standard of the game. The girls needed to gain satisfaction from playing so that they would continue. With this in mind, the Crokes trainers put an intensive training programme in place when they met at a special meeting on April 10th, 1910 at 115 James Street. The large attendance of girls learned that they would be required to attend practice sessions on Sunday evenings from 4 to 6 and on Mondays, Wednesdays and Fridays from 7 to 9. S. O'Callaghan was elected captain for the coming season.

Belfast Revival

Between 1910 and 1911, interest in camogie in Belfast was revived to some extent thanks to the great efforts of the O'Neill Crowley's, John Mitchel's and Ardoyne GAA clubs. A very large crowd turned up to view a contest between Mitchel's and Crowley's at MacRory Park. The teams were accorded an ovation on entering the pitch. The match was a grim struggle in wet and slippy underfoot conditions and there were some humorous moments as players lost their balance on the muddy pitch and came crashing down on all fours to the amusement of the crowd. The winning Mitchel's team was well served by Nan Harte, Nellie McCormack, Rose McAuley, Maggie Devlin, Minnie Watson and Jeannie Watson. The Crowley's stalwarts were Lily McCorry, Susie McCorry, Lizzie O'Neill, Maggie Grant, Minnie Graham, Mary Nolan, Lizzie Taggart, Teasie Reid, Agnes Kennedy, Lizzie Totton and Minnie Neeson.

These three clubs carried on playing challenge matches between themselves. Occasionally, they visited places in the county or outside it. Hopes that other clubs would appear on the horizon were doomed to disappointment. The outbreak of the First World War in August 1914 put an end to camogie activities in so far as Antrim was concerned until 1927. A camogie challenge match between Greenan's Cross, Co. Monaghan, and Ardoyne, Belfast, was played as a curtain-raiser to the Ulster hurling championship semi-final at Monaghan on April 10th, 1910.

Crokes played Colmcille's for a set of silver medals at an Aeridheacht under the auspices of the Crokes Gaelic Club at Richmond Hill, Rathmines, on September 4th, 1910. A thrilling contest was witnessed by a large crowd and the occasion helped to reawaken interest in the Dublin area.

Progress in London

While the game was struggling in Ireland, it was making steady progress in London. Between 1910 and 1913, four clubs were active in the city. The longest established was Ethna Carbery's, named after an Irish suffragette who had died in 1902. They played their home matches at Wormwood Scrubs. Róisín Dubh, Eoghan Ruadh and Gráinne Maol clubs followed and practised at Clapham Common, Parliament Hill Fields and West Ham Park, Forest Gate, respectively.

Where We're At

Eight years on from the initial meeting, what was the state of play? A new Irish game had been established with a set of rules which would stand the test of time. A small pool of players, more or less from similar backgrounds, was available in Dublin to play the game, though playing facilities were meagre where they existed at all. Prejudice hung like a cloud over the early players. Participating in field sport was not the thing for women to do, and the fear of being seen not to confirm to public opinion forced some players to conceal their camogie sticks.

For the first two years, the novice players were swept along on a wave of enthusiasm. Then reality set in. The new game was very difficult to master. The Gaelic League embraced an array of activities including Irish-language classes, debating, music and drama. It is reasonable to assume that some of the girls joined to take part in other activities and that sport held little attraction for them. For some, it would have been their first attempt to play a field game and it proved to be more strenuous than they expected, so they drifted away.

Early photographs show that the standard of play and field conditions were not good. Players were anxious to get on the ball and tended to hunt in packs, leaving large areas of the pitch empty. The basics of team play had not been acquired and scores were few and far between.

The administrators of the game were based in Dublin and were preoccupied with the advancement of the game in the capital. There was talk of spreading the game nationwide but no plans were put in place as to how this might be achieved. Areas outside Dublin were left to their own devices to organise the game. It is to their credit that at least fifteen counties, Glasgow and London, adopted camogie and no surprise that the rules were interpreted differently from place to place.

In hindsight, it is easy to ask why the game was not introduced at a younger age when girls could adapt more easily. Only one school, Dominican College, Muckross Park, where founder member Máire Ní Chinnéide was educated, took up the game in the early years and played in the Dublin League against adult teams. Generally speaking, the Camogie Association was slow to realise the benefits of underage and schools camogie.

As things stood, camogie was in danger of dying out. Players needed to play at a higher standard to gain satisfaction from the game and make a long-term commitment to it. Proper training was required. A wider player base was called for with the universities and secondary schools being obvious targets. The spread of the game to the girls of rural Ireland required attention and plans needed to be drawn up to cater for their situation.

Chapter Two

CROKES TO THE RESCUE

The Crokes Gaelic Club, noted for its Gaelic, athletic and cultural activities, took up the dying embers of the Camogie Association. What Keating's did in the earlier years, Crokes did in 1910 and afterwards. It is probably true to say that were it not for the intervention of Crokes Gaelic Club, the game would not have survived.

The Crokes Gaelic Club issued a circular inviting all interested parties to a meeting of An Cumann Camoguidheacht at the Gaelic League Hall, 25 Rutland Square, on April 21st, 1911, to re-establish the game. Seán O'Duffy and Cáit O'Donoghue also wrote letters to the newspapers drawing attention to the forthcoming meeting.

The meeting took place before a large and enthusiastic audience. The following Dublin clubs were represented: Ard Craobh, Keating's, Colmcille's, St Margaret's, Crokes, Inghinidhe na hEireann, Drumcondra, Kevin's, Emmet Choir and Fianna. Mrs E. C. Hamilton (Foxrock) chaired the meeting.

Elizabeth, Countess of Fingall, President of Camogie Association 1911-1923

Letters of Support

Several letters were read, warmly commending the idea of forming an association that would have for its primary object the promotion of a pleasant pastime for girls.

The Countess of Fingall wrote: "I will be delighted to do anything I can to help what I consider a splendid work, for I believe if we could make the boys' and girls' lives in Ireland more happy and cheerful, we would keep many more of them at home. I will gladly be President of the Association and do all that I can to further the objects for which it is being founded. I regret it will be impossible for me to attend tonight's meeting."

A Game of Our Own

Máire de Buitléir, the Irish Revival writer, expressed her views: "It was with great pleasure and interest I heard that some patriotic women and girls were taking steps to organise open-air games and other recreations for themselves and their fellow countrywomen. The old classic ideal of a 'healthy mind in a healthy body' should be aimed at in modern Ireland. Perhaps in the stress of intellectual work entailed by the Gaelic Revival, we have been hitherto led to overlook the need for physical culture. As the majority of our women spend most of their time at sedentary work, outdoor exercise, combined with pleasant companionship is very desirable."

Mrs Anita Lett, founder member of the Society of United Irishwomen (name later changed to Irish Countrywomen's Association), wrote: "I am very glad to hear that the subject of games for girls is again being taken up. I think if only girls could be induced to play more games we would not see so many, as we do now, unable to work, run, or even walk with ease or grace. Besides this, I feel their health would be vastly improved with healthy outdoor exercise. I hope, however, that should games amongst girls be developed to any great extent, that they will not fall into the error which has become the curse of football among men – that is, that while 15 play, 15,000 look on. I wish the Association every success."

Action from a club match at O'Neill Crowley grounds in Cork in 1912.

For her own part, Mrs Hamilton thought it an admirable idea that ladies should have some form of recreation of their own that would, while giving healthy enjoyment, counteract the evil effects of town life, and make them physically and otherwise better and nobler women. She believed it was a great pleasure and boon to be able now and again to cast aside the cares and worries of everyday life and throw oneself wholeheartedly into some entertaining and delightful pastime.

An Cumann Camoguidheachta Re-Established

During the meeting, an Cumann Camoguidheachta was re-established. The election of officers resulted as follows:

- President: Elizabeth, Countess of Fingall

Crokes to the Rescue

- Vice-Presidents: Mrs E.C. Hamilton and Máire de Buitléir
- Secretary: Tomás Mac Aodha (Crokes)
- Treasurer: George Hughes (Crokes)
- Organiser: Cáit O'Donoghue (Keating's)

The Countess of Fingall was a notable figure in Irish society and her relationship with the fledging Camogie Association lent it recognition and status. Through her work with many charitable committees and the co-operative movement, she was thought of very highly and was well-known. At a time when the Camogie Association was yearning for acceptance, her public utterances on the sport were welcome. However, she was not a hands-on president and merely gave her name to the Association.

It was decided that the committee should consist of the officers listed above, together with one delegate from each affiliated club. An affiliation fee of five shillings was agreed upon. Because of the lack of organisation in many of the clubs, it was decided to defer the start of the competitive league and to concentrate all energies on developing and popularising of the game itself. The role of the organiser was to work with the Gaelic League branches and encourage them to form camogie clubs. In reality, though, the Association's committee concentrated on the Dublin area and no thought or consideration was given to the clubs that existed in other parts of the country. They were left to their own devices.

Coincidentally, the 1972 Annual Congress was held in the same room as the historic 1911 meeting. By then, the building was occupied by Coláiste Mhuire and the room had been renamed the '1916 Room'. Seán O'Duffy felt that there was something familiar about the place before realising that he had been there 61 years previously.

Revised Rules

Revised rules were drawn up at a further meeting held on May 5th, 1911 with a view "to rendering the game less boisterous and more fascinating for women". Many, who were previously pessimistic about camogie, now assumed the role of enthusiastic followers. It was reported that girls were beginning to develop a little initiative and were less sensitive.

The goal was widened from 10 to 15 feet and a parallelogram was introduced and a 25-yard free when the ball was played wide by a defender.

The meeting heard from two teams that had been invited to Enfield to play for a dress length of Irish linen. Permission was declined as it was not considered prudent to permit teams to travel. However, the following meeting agreed to permit three teams to travel to Castlebellingham.

Organiser Cáit O'Donoghue wrote to Agnes O'Farrelly, then lecturer in Modern Irish Poetry in UCD, inviting her to become involved with the Camogie Association and asking her to use her influence to have teams formed in the universities. Cáit interviewed Dr Douglas Hyde who expressed favourable opinion regarding the game and offered to use the first opportunity to speak in its favour to the lady students of the National Universities. The girls of the National University (Dublin) met in June and agreed to form a club. In a series of letters to the newspapers, Cáit O'Donoghue did much to engender interest in the game.

An application was sent to the Board of Works asking for grounds for general practice and matches to be allocated in the Phoenix Park, Dublin. The board replied that camogie could use any of the five pitches allocated for hurling and football any day of the week, except Saturday and Sunday.

Teams were established in Kilmessan and Dunsany through the good offices of Lady Fingall. She showed a genuine interest in the sport and assigned a fine playing pitch on her land, as well as ordering two dozen hurleys and two balls at her own expense.

More than Two for Tea

Mrs Hamilton invited the North Dublin and South Dublin teams to play at the Foxrock Aeridheacht. Furthermore, she issued an invitation to representatives of the teams to join her for tea at her home after the match. But nobody sends representatives to tea in camogie circles. They all arrived, teams, officials, referee, umpires and supporters. The attendance caused consternation in the household but the kitchen staff coped heroically.

Travel

Travel was rather restrictive in the early days of camogie but the distances covered were relatively short. The options were walking, cycling and horse-drawn vehicles. In those days, girls would not flinch at a five-mile walk or ten-mile cycle on the way to a match. A horse-drawn vehicle and a pair of horses would have to be obtained if the team was to travel together. Side-cars, wagonettes, charabancs and long carts were popular in different parts of the country.

None of these modes of transport provided any shelter from the elements and road surfaces left a lot to be desired, particularly in rural areas. But the enjoyment of the day out was unlikely to be affected by hitches of that nature.

Abbeyleix Club Disbanded

Concern was expressed at the October 1911 meeting of the committee when a letter was read from Fanny Kelly of Abbeyleix. It outlined how the Abbeyleix Camogie Club had been disbanded at the express wish of the parish priest. However, at the same meeting, an enquiry was received from a priest in Mullingar seeking assistance in setting up a club.

Jones' Road

In February 1912, F.B. Dineen, owner of Jones's Road (later Croke Park), consented to place the grounds at the disposal of the Dublin League on Sundays after 4 o'clock. Nine teams took part in the league which was won by Kevin's. Dublin was making great strides with teams springing up in all parts of the city. St Angela's College, Patrick's Hill, was the first Cork school to take up camogie in 1912. They were joined shortly by their sister school, Ursuline Convent, Blackrock.

Annual Convention

1912 Annual Convention took place in the Oak Room of the Mansion House with Mrs E.C. Hamilton presiding. A large number of delegates were present from Dublin clubs together with representatives from Cork, Louth, Wexford, Kerry, Roscommon and London. The meeting heard that there were six clubs in New York.

The following counties were classified as active: Laois, Wexford, Louth, Meath, Dublin, Wicklow, Westmeath, Kilkenny, Cork, Limerick, Tipperary, Clare, Kerry, Waterford, Roscommon, Galway, Monaghan, Antrim, Down and Cavan. However, the level of activity varied from getting a team together to compete in an Aeridheacht to a number of clubs participating in regular competition.

The first Tipperary club was formed in the Lattin area and was quickly joined by Fethard and Mullinahone. St Aidan's, Ferns, were the front-runners in Wexford. Bree, Davidstown, Enniscorthy, Newtown and Ballyoughter swelled the numbers, resulting in a Wexford County Committee being set up in June 1912. In Roscommon, Boyle, Athleague, Kilbride, Roscommon Town, Kiltoom and Strokestown led the way. Camogie was played in Kilkenny City, Ballycloven, Threecastles, Mooncoin and Piltown. The game was up and running in Rosenallis, Abbeyleix, Mountmellick and Mountrath in Co. Laois.

First Inter-County Match
The first inter-county match was staged at the Crokes' Aeridheacht at Jones's Road on July 7th, 1912 between Louth and Dublin. The report on the game made the following observations: "While play was predominantly on the ground, the beautiful rising and striking by Miss Reilly and Miss Cleary won great acclamation. Louth, with an almost overwhelming rush, came from midfield down on the Dublin goal. Falls were pretty frequent owing to players not wearing studs on their shoes."

The Louth team was comprised almost exclusively of players from Dundalk Emer's. The side was captained by A. Fearon who had led her club side to victory on 33 occasions. A very large attendance turned out to see the game which ended in a win for Dublin by 2–2 to 0–0.

Skirts Raised
The 1913 convention returned the outgoing officers and added a third vice-president, Bertha Byrne (Wexford). A general council was formed comprising Miss Ward (Louth), Ms Stritch (Louth), Ms O'Hare (Dublin), Ms Dunbar (Wexford) and the organiser, Cáit O'Donoghue. The length of players' skirts was raised to eight inches above the ground. During the meeting, Cáit O'Donoghue spoke of the problems of overcoming prejudice and unreasonable opposition.

UCC Camogie Club
Camogie was introduced to University College Cork in 1913. The beginnings of the club were closely linked with the Irish Ireland Movement and the founders were lady members of the Gaelic Club in the college. Among the first officers was Margaret McKenna, an aunt of actress Siobhán McKenna. Margaret joined the Mercy Order and became Sr Bonaventure, principal of St Aloysius School, Cork, where camogie flourished under her wing. Hannah O'Donovan was another member of the initial committee. Later,

she filled the role of principal at Drishane Convent, Millstreet, another camogie-playing school.

Lack of Pitches

The Dublin League ran into difficulties procuring playing pitches for their fixtures. Richmond Hill, Rathmines, was no longer available as a venue, with the result, the 1913 league was not completed. Apart from the odd tournament or Aeridheacht, matches were few and far between for the next few seasons. Meetings were held and matches arranged but the lack of a venue left fixtures unfulfilled.

Cork v. Kilkenny

Kilkenny travelled to play Cork in an inter-county challenge at the O'Neill Crowley Grounds, Victoria Cross, on July 20th, 1913. The gate receipts amounted to £60, a massive sum at that time. At 6d a head for adults, 2,400 paid to view the game. As children were admitted free, the actual attendance would have been considerably more. Cork overcame Kilkenny by 2–2 to 1–0. Misses Lombard, Fitzpatrick, Cox and Joyce figured prominently for Cork. Ms Reid scored from a free for Kilkenny.

The Cork team that defeated Kilkenny at the O'Neill Crowley grounds, Cork in 1914.

Progress in Liverpool

Camogie had developed sufficiently in Liverpool that they could pose a real challenge to a Kevin's-selected side from Dublin at Greenwich Park on August 4th, 1913. Playing under the banner of Lancashire, the Liverpool exiles were not out of their depth and put up a good show while conceding defeat by 4–0 to 2–0. This match was played as a curtain-raiser to the All-Ireland hurling semi-final between Kilkenny and Lancashire.

A return match between Lancashire and a Laurence O'Toole's selection opened the 1914 season on April 19th as part of a high-profile programme at Croke Park. The teams were evenly matched in general play but the Dublin girls were more proficient at finishing their chances and ran out winners by 3–2 to 0–0. Lancashire team: Misses Tobin, Holmes, O'Driscoll, Donohue, Kennedy, Lanigan, O'Neill (Exiles), Twomey, Ryan, Kehoe and Murphy (Clan na hEireann). O'Toole's Selection: Misses Lawless, Delahunty, O'Rourke, Smith, Carey, McDonnell, Kelly, Drumm, McDonald, O'Carroll, Lynch, Mackey, Colgan and Redmond. Lancashire made a second trip across the Irish Sea to participate in the Dundalk Feis on June 24th.

Crokes to the Rescue

Cork Schools Championship

Cork Schools competitions commenced in 1914. Drishane Convent, Millstreet, and South Presentation Convent, Douglas Street, joined St Angela's and the Ursuline Convent, Blackrock. St Angela's were the first holders of the Cork Schools' Champions title. Two years later, they were joined by Scoil Ité, an Irish-speaking school run by Mary MacSwiney, sister of Terence MacSwiney, Lord Mayor of Cork, who died on hunger strike in Brixton Prison. Second-level schools camogie has continued in Cork without a break from 1914 to the present day.

The First World War

The outbreak of the First World War brought camogie in Belfast to a halt from 1914 to 1927. Camogie activities also ceased, or were severely curtailed, in the UK. Some members turned their attention to national organisations, such as Inghinidhe na hÉireann and Cumann na mBan.

In 1915, three members of Na Fianna Camogie Club, Eileen Conroy (mother of Eileen Hogan of Kilmacud Crokes), Nellie Kelly and May Chadwick, carried hurleys as they walked in O'Donovan Rossa's funeral, something for which they were arrested and held for three nights. Fr Albert, a Capuchin from Cork, intervened to have them released. Eileen Conroy ran dispatches in the St Stephen's Green area during Easter Rising.

The UCD team with the Ashbourne Cup in 1915

Agnes O'Farrelly

UCD Camogie Club

The UCD Camogie Club was founded at a meeting presided over by Agnes O'Farrelly on May 11th, 1914. She was elected president of the new club, a position she held until her death in 1951. In 1915, she prevailed on her friend, Edwin Gibson, Lord Ashbourne, a Trinity graduate, to present a cup bearing his name. He obliged with the unique and impressive Ashbourne Cup despite the fact that he had never seen the game. Lord Ashbourne was the son of the first Baron Ashbourne, Lord Chancellor of Ireland and was President of the Gaelic League where camogie had its roots. A fluent linguist, he spoke French, German, Irish, Scottish Gaelic, Welsh, Breton and Polish. He frequently attended the Ashbourne finals, colourfully attired in a saffron kilt.

However, the fledgling club at UCD met with the disapproval of the college authorities.

First Ashbourne

As camogie clubs existed in UCD and UCC, the way was clear for competition to begin. From the start, the Ashbourne Cup competition proved to be a winner. Players prepared diligently and looked forward with great anticipation to the competition. College life for camogie players revolved around the Ashbourne. UCD, captained by K. King, claimed the first Ashbourne Cup title when they overcame UCC by 0–7 to 0–3 at Terenure in April 1915.

UCD retained the cup in 1916. However, the cup was destroyed during the disturbances of Easter Week, but was subsequently replaced. The early years of the Ashbourne Cup were dominated by UCD and UCC and these colleges produced wonderful contests and talented players.

Edwin Gibson, Lord Ashbourne, who gifted the cup bearing his name.

West Cork

The clubs in Cork city had become sufficiently proficient in the game to stage exhibition matches at venues around the county. Clan Emer and Clan na nGaedhal accepted an invitation to display the new game at Dunmanway Aeridheacht in June 1914, and their arrival was awaited with great interest. The *Southern Star* report on the fixture stated: "The ladies can double and swing, puck and save just as well as their brawny heroes and are credited with having more judgement when the ball gets within the scoring area." The correspondent added "it is hoped that the ladies of Carbury may be enticed to prefer the invigorating national game to suffragette demonstrations".

In conjunction with an Aeridheacht held at Bealed on June 30th, 1916, a camogie match between the pick of the Letter and Kilbree girls and the more experienced Clonakilty women was staged on Matt Donovan's splendid lawn. The *Southern Star* report continued: 'Where as fine a muster of womanhood of West Cork had been seen for a dozen years. The Silver Band gave great satisfaction and played a number of classical Irish pieces throughout the proceedings."

Eleven clubs – Clonakilty, Dunmanway, Canovee, Lislevane, Kilkerranmore, Barryroe, Scart, Letter, Kilbree, Bantry and Kilumney – entered for the West Cork Championship in September 1917, where a set of silver medals was the prize on offer. Some of the matches were played in conjunction with local Aeridheacht and others as stand-alone fixtures. An impressive gathering assembled at Árd Mór, near Clonakilty, on August 12th, 1917 to compete for the Long Puck championship of West Cork.

Crokes to the Rescue

Championship Honour

Described in the preview as the four best teams in Ireland, Meath, Louth, North and South Dublin met in a tournament for 'championship honour' at Jones's Road on September 19th, 1915.

Meath were represented by players from Killeen and Dunboyne, while the pick of Dundalk Emer's and Drogheda Emerald's formed the Louth team.

Such was the interest in the fixture that a special train left Navan at 10.30 a.m. carrying fans to Broadstone. The admission ticket was priced at 4d and entitled the holder to participate in a draw for prizes.

South Presentation Convent, Cork, winners of Cork Schools League in 1915.

Cleaver

In July 1915, a new club named Cleaver affiliated to the Association. Euseby Digby Cleaver was a Church of Ireland clergyman whose grandfather had been Archbishop of Dublin and who himself was vice-president of the Gaelic League. It can be seen that camogie, by its courageous and independent spirit, contributed to the freedom enjoyed by the modern woman.

Seán Answers the Call

Seán O'Duffy was one of those who believed in the full restoration of his country's rights. When the Rising came, Seán answered the call alongside members of the Crokes Gaelic Club. The club's record must be unique as 32 of the 40 affiliated men took part in the Rising. Seán said, "Never follow a man or a leader simply because he is a leader. Follow a cause, an ideal, or a principle, and you will never go wrong."

Seán served in the North King Street area under Limerick man, Commandant Ned Daly, and took part in what was one of the fiercest fights of that proud and terrible week. For almost the entire five days, they were under constant fire, night and day. Following the insurrection came the executions and imprisonments, and Seán found himself in Stafford Gaol where Michael Collins was among his fellow prisoners. Months passed and, eventually, Seán and his companions were released.

He was able to resume his services to his country and to its native games. He continued to work in collaboration with such men

Camogie and the Irish Revolution

Within the membership of camogie, there were women who had a desire for Irish self-determination and who wished to have a role in the nationalist movement. From the beginning, the Camogie Association was non-political and to reinforce that view the following rule was passed: "The Association shall be strictly non-political and non-sectarian. No club shall be named after a living person, and no member of the Association shall, under penalty of suspension, endeavour to identify the affairs of the Association with those of any organisation of a political character."

However, a number of camogie members became involved in their private capacity. They joined Cumann na mBan or Inghinidhe na hÉireann and took part in the struggle in varying degrees. The decision to keep the Association out of politics prevented a likely split in the years to come.

Merriman Cup

Mollie Riordan joined the teaching staff of St Aloysius School in 1916 and brought with her the enthusiasm of the newly formed UCC Camogie Club. St Aloysius School was to dominate the Cork colleges scene for several decades. Dr Merriman, Professor of History and, later, President of UCC, presented a silver cup for senior competition among the Cork secondary schools. The first name to be engraved on the trophy was St Aloysius School.

UCG Camogie Club

The UCG Camogie Club was established early in 1916 and won the Ashbourne Cup in 1917 under the captaincy of M. O'Dowd. It is an Ashbourne tradition that the names of the winning team are

As Michael Collins and Austin Stack. There was little time now for camogie, but Seán never forgot the game. When troubled peace did come, he returned with all his vigour and enthusiasm to the spreading of camogie.

U.C.G. team that won the Ashbourne Cup in 1917. Included are M. O'Dowd, C. O'Farrell, C. Doherty, E. Tennant, U. Leader, M. Joyce, B. Martin, M. Hanley, N. McSherry, R. Ryan, M. Byrne and S. Connery.

engraved on the base of the cup. However, controversy broke out in UCG when certain members of the winning 1917 team refused to have their names engraved in the Irish language, something that brought their future selection into doubt.

Equal Rights Demand
Inter-faculty competitions in a variety of sports took place on a piece of waste ground known as The Quarry in UCC. Students lined the banks shouting and cheering at the players below. Because of the confined playing area and the atmosphere created by the supporters, things got out of hand now and then.

Margaret McKenna and Hannah O'Donovan, members of the newly formed UCC Camogie club, decided to organise an inter-faculty camogie competition at The Quarry. A match was in progress, much to the entertainment of the lads in the gallery, when a member of staff arrived and halted proceedings. Many of the players scurried indoors but the two organisers held their ground and refused to leave.

Following much activity, they were summoned to the president's office, where a compromise was reached. Approval was given for an inter-faculty camogie competition but not at The Quarry – the matches had to be played at the Mardyke. The ladies in question had planned to enter the convent on graduation but because of the stand they took, a question was raised as to their suitability to become nuns. Years later, both filled the role of principal in two camogie nurseries, St Aloysius School and Drishane Convent.

The UCC team playing in 1916

Dublin League Reformed
Seven clubs were represented at a meeting held on June 11th, 1917 to reform the Dublin League and arrangements were made to get the competition underway. Mollie Gill took over as chairman of the league, a position she held until 1935. An offer to manage the financial matters of the Dublin League and to organise the competition was made by the Dublin GAA Board. However, the league declined the proposition, wishing to remain independent. Another step forward was taken with the approval of lady referees.

A Game of Our Own

Permits Required

A declaration was made by the British Army in July 1918 that all gatherings required a special permit, otherwise they would be pronounced illegal. On July 13th, 1918, Inspector Siddley of the RIC, backed by a large force of military, ordered a camogie match at Kilbeacanty, Co. Galway, to be stopped. The players and referee ignored the order and completed the match. Afterwards, the spectators were baton-charged by police and dispersed. The names of the teams were not recorded.

The Dublin League Committee decided not to apply for permits. When matches were stopped, the fixture was re-scheduled for the following Sunday. The GAA announced a full programme of fixtures for 'Gaelic Sunday' on August 4th, 1918. Over 500 football, hurling and camogie matches were arranged as a protest against the restrictions placed on Irish pastimes. Large numbers of spectators turned up at all venues. Only in Dublin was any attempt made to stop the games. When the entrance to Croke Park was barred by armed police, girls played an impromptu camogie match on the road outside.

On the same afternoon, a hurling match was fixed for Turloughmore, Co. Galway. Local organisers moved the match to a field across the river from where they could observe the comings and goings at the Turloughmore grounds. When the RIC were seen approaching the pitch, the hurlers withdrew and were replaced by camogie players. The RIC moved on when they saw that girls were playing.

Action from the U.C.D. v U.C.C. Ashbourne Cup final at the O'Neill Crowley grounds on March 1st, 1916.

Game Curtailed

Camogie was curtailed from 1919 to 1921 because the situation pertaining in the country. The game, however, continued in educational establishments. UCC captured the Ashbourne Cup for the first time. Dublin completed their championship and league programmes with Faughs and Gaelic League the respective winners. A Presentation Céili, which was to become a popular event on the Dublin calendar, was held to distribute the medals to the winners of the various competitions.

Wicklow showed expansion with clubs in Arklow, Rathnew, Conary, Glenealy, Bray and Wicklow Town. Much good work was done to promote the game in Cavan by Dr Martin Comey and Fr Michael McLaughlin, with teams being formed in Cavan Town, Ballinagh, Lavey, Belturbet, Killygarry, Drumbo and Tullycoe. Cavan staged a county championship for the first time, with Belturbet defeating Lavey 0-1 to 0-0 in the final.

The Game in Britain
The game in Britain continued to expand throughout this time, with clubs being set up through the Gaelic League in Woolwich, Wigan and Manchester. Camogie continued to be played in parts of London, Liverpool and Glasgow. The London County Board held its first meeting on February 12th, 1922. Liam MacCarthy, who had donated the All-Ireland senior hurling cup, presented a Shield for the London Camogie Championship.

U. C. D. team that won the Ashbourne Cup in 1918. Included are B. Brady (Capt), E. Cleary, E. Shannon, J. Walsh, B. Power, E. Greene, M. McGrath, A. Cullen. B. Farrell, N. Dalton, U. O'Farrelly, C. White and S. Cleary.

Preparation Work
The subcommittee in charge of the organisation of camogie for the 1924 Tailteann Games met in June 1922 and appointed officials who would be responsible for preparation work in the various centres. The officials were: Esther Ryan (Dublin), Mary Sheehan (Cork), Martina O'Loughney (Galway), Josephine McKenna (Monaghan), Eileen McCarthy (England) and M. O'Sullivan (Scotland). Clubs anxious to participate in elimination games were to apply direct to the officials named.

Mary (Peg) O'Keeffe, who later married Paddy O'Keeffe, Secretary General of the GAA, captained the UCC team that won the Ashbourne Cup in 1922. The Roche Cup, for senior competition, continued in Cork right through the Civil War. Clan Eimear, Carrig Dubh, Emmets (Monkstown) and Midleton were among the strongest sides contesting the trophy. The junior clubs competed for the Crawford Cup.

A Game of Our Own

Mollie Gill Elected President

Mollie Gill was elected President of the Camogie Association in January 1923. A member of the Crokes Club, she chaired the Dublin League Committee and was employed by the Cuala Press in Baggot Street. She was a fine camogie player and captained Dublin to their first All-Ireland success in 1932. Mollie was the longest serving president of the Camogie Association, holding office from 1923 to 1942. Kathleen Ryan was elected Vice-President and Áine Ryan filled the post of Ard Runaí. The meeting voted to ban metal bands on hurleys as they were considered dangerous.

Seán O'Duffy informed a meeting on May 23rd, 1923, that the president, Mollie Gill, and Esther Ryan had been arrested the previous Saturday at the Cuala Press. In an attempt to break the Republican organisation, women began to be arrested from the end of 1922.

The Phoenix Park

The Board of Works responded to an application from the Dublin Camogie Board and made a pitch in the Phoenix Park available for camogie and this acquisition proved to be a tremendous boon to the promotion of the game in Dublin. Some years later, a second pitch was acquired. At that time, Clann Eadair, Emmet-Tones, Colmcille's, Eire Óg, St Molaga's, Keating's, St Mary's, O'Toole's, Clann na Gaedeal, Parnell's, The Harps, Lady Geraldine's and Crokes participated in the Dublin League.

Mollie Gill: elected President of the Camogie Association in January 1923

Where We're At

The timely intervention by the Crokes Gaelic Club was vital to the revival and advancement of the Camogie Association. They knew how to organise sport and they attracted girls with a keen interest in the game. Around this time, individuals of national standing lent their support to the revitalisation of camogie which afforded much-needed publicity for the game and eased the pressure of negative opinion.

The introduction of schools competitions and the inter-varsity championship were major steps forward. Dublin, Galway and Cork, where this progress was made, were the front-runners when the All-Ireland championship commenced in the thirties. The standard of play improved and the game continued to fan out from Dublin, albeit at a slow pace.

Activity on the playing fields halted in most areas during the years of political unrest in the early 1920a and it took time to catch up when play resumed. While the Association still faced many obstacles, the atmosphere created by the announcement of the Tailteann Games and the election of a 'hands-on' president, Mollie Gill, raised spirits and gave hope for the future.

Chapter Three

TAILTEANN GAMES

Aonach Tailteann was originally an annual assembly instituted about 800 BC by Lugh Lamh Fada, the second of the Tuatha De Dannaan kings of Ireland, in commemoration of his foster-mother, Queen Tailte. The festival was primarily a gathering of the youth and manhood of the nation to participate in memorial games which honoured the dead and fortified the living.

The Olympic Games, the games of ancient Greece, had been successfully revived in 1896. The Free State government wished to promote its independence and boost the self-confidence of the country. With this in mind and taking into account the Greek experience, it was decided to revive the Tailteann Games. The importance and the significance of the rebirth of the Games were immense.

A number of inter-county challenge matches were played in the build-up to the 1924 Tailteann Games. However, on July 9th, 1924, a mere month before the opening of the games, Central Council of the Camogie Association decided to withdraw for financial reasons. The programme of the Tailteann Games included a number of camogie matches which would have necessitated the teams from the provinces and Britain remaining in Dublin for the duration of the competition.

As the provincial councils were not formed at this time, the responsibility for covering the accommodation, meals and transport costs fell to Central Council who did not have funds to cover outlay of that nature.

Action from the 1924 Tailteann Games

A Game of Our Own

Considerable funds were made available by the government to the Tailteann Games Committee to stage the event. Central Council had expected that a grant would be made to assist with the funding of the teams but none was forthcoming.

Ard Runaí, Miss A. Ryan, notified J. J. Walsh, Director of the Tailteann Games, that, owing to financial difficulties, the Camogie Association had withdrawn from the games as they found it impossible to bring off the five-day competition as planned. Mr Walsh replied through the national newspapers. He refused to accept that the lack of financial support was the reason for camogie's withdrawal and accused the Camogie Association of being politically motivated in their decision. This viewpoint was strongly rejected by Miss Ryan. Letters continued to and fro in the newspapers as relations between the two sides deteriorated.

The players were naturally very disappointed with the news of the camogie teams' exit from the games. Mr Walsh was determined to have a camogie match on the programme and left the way open for teams to enter. London-Irish and Wicklow responded and, on August 6th, 1924 at University Park, Terenure, and playing under the banners of Ireland and Britain, Wicklow defeated London-Irish by 8–0 to 0–0. The Wicklow ladies were presented with gold medals. The Wicklow team was: Rose Cannon, Aggie Cunningham, May Porter, May Kelly, Martha Cullen, Babs McDonald, Norah Byrne (captain), Judith Kearns, Alice Thackberry, Liz Bowden, Sheila Glynn and Maureen O'Brien.

Two weeks later, a letter appeared in the *Wicklow People* bearing the name A. Ní Riain, Ard Runaí, stating that all the Wicklow players and officials, including a future President of the Camogie Association, Mrs Lucy Byrne, were expelled from the Camogie Association. None of the London-Irish players were included as they were not affiliated to the Central Council. Wicklow were furious at the decision. They were not afforded an opportunity of being heard in their own defence. On behalf of the Wicklow

St. Aloysius School, Cork, winners of Merriman Cup in 1920. Back Row: Miss Mollie Riordan, H. Gamble, E. Harris, E. Sheehan, M. Murphy and V. Hegarty. Seated: K. Murray, R. O'Sullivan, P. Callanan (Capt), K. McCarthy and T. Hegarty. In Front: A. Gamble and P. Deasy.

> The Irish Camoguidheacht Association has, we learn from Miss Ní Ryan, hon. sec., withdrawn from the Tailteann Games. She states that owing to financial difficulties it was found impossible to bring off the five days' competition entered.
>
> Miss Ryan, on behalf of the Association, wishes to deny the rumour which is being circulated that the withdrawal has a political motive. The Camoguidheacht match listed for Aug. 3 has not been sanctioned by her Association. She adds, always has been and remains strictly non-political and is open to all denominations. From the outset the Association has been handicapped for want of funds, as gates on matches are practically nil. The game has, however, made steady progress during the past eight years, and it is of vital importance for the future of the game that the above rumour should not be allowed to go uncontradicted.
>
> All members of the Association are warned not to receive or countenance any correspondence in connection with Camoguidheacht other than from the Hon. Sec.

County Board, Mrs Byrne stated: "It is farcical that Ms Ryan and a couple of people in Dublin should have the power of expelling players who took part in the great national festival." A major bone of contention was that the decision to expel the Wicklow players and officials was taken by the Dublin-based Steering Committee rather than Central Council.

Wicklow received support from many quarters including the majority of the Dublin clubs. A new Dublin County Board was formed. The UCD club tried to effect a settlement but without avail. On April 26th, 1925, the rival sections held their conventions. UCD and Bray United affiliated to the Dublin League in 1926 and, by 1927, all Dublin clubs had returned to the fold. The main loser in this affair was Wicklow camogie and the game was not played in the county for a number of years.

Over 100 Delegates

Over 100 delegates gathered in Conarchy's Hotel, Parnell Square, on April 25th, 1925 for the Annual Congress. The Central Council officers were re-elected with the exception of the position of organiser. Seán O'Duffy replaced Cáit O'Donoghue, who had held the post for 14 years. Cáit had returned to her native Cork and, on her arrival in the southern capital, she had set about forming a club in the Glasheen Road area of the city called Cara Cliodhna. The new club attracted players who had learned the game at secondary school or university level and challenged the more established Cork clubs within a short time.

The Éire Óg club from Armagh and the Betsy Gray Club from Warrenpoint were newcomers to the scene in 1925, while the Maids of Mourne (Kilkeel) and Craobh Ruadh (Newry) joined in the following season.

Dublin travelled to play Kilkenny in the Ossory Feis on June 29th, 1925 and won comfortably. Teams now existed in Wexford Town, Enniscorthy and Campile, to add to the teams that had already formed in the county. A Wexford selection made the trip to

Dublin League delegates pictured on 19, May, 1928. Camogie President Mollie Gill is seated sixth from left. Dr. Agnes O'Farrelly is seated seventh from left. Sean O'Duffy is standing on left.

Dublin to take on the home county on July 2nd, 1926. However, they were unable to match the more experienced Dublin girls and were defeated by 3–1 to 0–0.

Athletic Meetings

In the twenties, the Camogie Association went under the name of the Irishwomen's National Athletic and Camoguidheacht Association and the Association promoted athletic meetings amongst its members. The first of these took place on June 28th, 1926 at St James's Park, Dublin. The programme included sprint, hurdle and relay races and events of a fun nature. The Sports Day was a popular date on the Dublin calendar for several decades. In other parts of the country, it was usual for camogie players to enter athletic events at a Feis or Aeridheacht in addition to playing a match. Guidelines for staging athletic and sports meetings were included in the early Rule Books.

1929 Camogie Convention

Clann United, winners of 1930 Dublin Championship and League. Seated front left is Molly Fitzgerald-Murphy and front right is Eileen Conroy-Cronin, mother of Eileen Hogan (Kilmacud).

Your Party Piece

On Saturday, May 19th, 1928, the delegates of the Dublin League were entertained to tea by Miss Agnes O'Farrelly, President of the UCD Camogie Club, at her residence, 21 Brighton Road. In all, 40 delegates were present representing 20 clubs. After tea, the delegates rendered some exquisite vocal and instrumental items. Miss O'Farrelly presented a perpetual cup for the Dublin Senior League. A senior championship was started in 1927 with Crokes claiming both the new title and the O'Farrelly Cup.

Women's Reserve

The idea of girls playing field games in public continued, in certain quarters, to be considered little short of sinful. Pope Pius XI declared in 1928 that sport was "irreconcilable with women's reserve". Such was the influential position of the Catholic Church that announcements like this posed problems for the Association and frustrated efforts to spread the game in convent schools. Mary Immaculate College, Limerick, initiated its 'Modest Dress and Deportment Crusade' to eliminate immodest dress among prospective primary teachers. The college fielded a camogie team at the time.

Significant Progress

By 1927, significant progress had been made in Galway. Four teams – Galway Town, UCG, Taylor's Hill and Technical College – in the city, along with Currandrum, Ballinasloe, Tuam, Headford, Derrydonnell and Prospect from the county fielded in regular competition. These fixtures were played at The Sportsfield, Renmore Army Grounds and College Road.

An attempt was made in 1927 to establish an inter-county competition. However, there was a belief within some camogie circles that the game should be played as a leisure activity and not be competitive. A few matches were played but some counties were not sufficiently organised to field inter-county sides.

Camogie also prospered in County Limerick in the late twenties and early thirties, enabling two divisional boards, West Limerick and East Limerick, to be formed. Teams usually played challenge and tournament matches. West Limerick received affiliations from Adare, Ardagh, Askeaton, Ballingarry, Ballysteen, Croagh, Foynes, Glin, Kildimo, Killoughteen, Monegea, Newcastle West, Pallaskenry, Shountrade, Templeglantine and Tournafulla. The East Limerick Board looked after Ballylanders, Bruree, Fedamore, Pallasgreen, Castleconnell, Kilteely, Doon and Kilmallock. The game was not popular in Limerick City.

1928 Tailteann Games

The rift between the Tailteann Games Committee and the Camogie Association had been patched up before the 1928 event came around. Central Council was much better prepared on this occasion. The Tailteann Games brought much-needed publicity to camogie with many people viewing the game for the first time and being pleasantly surprised by the standard of play. On August 27th, Connacht played Leinster at Croke Park. Players from Dublin, Kilkenny, Louth and Wexford made up the Leinster team while Connacht was represented by Galway players. Leinster outscored Connacht by 5–1 to 1–0 to claim the coveted Tailteann medals.

The Leinster panel: Mollie Gill (captain) (Dublin), K. Boylan (Dublin), Kathleen O'Byrne (Dublin), I. Carolan (Dublin), B. Bergin (Dublin), Eileen Windsor (Dublin), E. O'Reilly (Dublin), Queenie Dunne (Dublin), Rose Quigley (Louth), S. Hopkins (Wexford), T. Walsh (Kilkenny), Eileen Davis (Dublin), M. McCarthy (Dublin), Molly Fitzgerald (Dublin), K. Ryan (Dublin), Nan Boyle (Louth) and Bríd Kenny (Dublin).

The Connacht panel: N. Elwood (captain), F. Geoghegan, S. Belton, S. McDonald, M. Tonry, E. Crowe, N. Walsh, N. Jennings, N. Greaney, R. Hession, T. Glynn, P. Morris, M. Curran, C. Reynolds, N. Cooke and J. Wallace.

Famous Clubs

In 1928, the first two of the celebrated clubs that would stand the test of time were founded. Celtic, on the northside of Dublin, was founded by the Keegan sisters and Brigid Lynch; while Jim Johnson set up the Deirdre club in Belfast. These clubs faced one another in the first All-Ireland Club Championship final at Croke Park 36 years later. Deirdre joined O'Connell's, St Mary's Training College, McKelvey's, Ardoyne, Gael Uladh and Countess Markievicz to commence a league in south Belfast. In the following season, St Malachy's, Moran's and Wolfe Tones swelled the numbers. With a large number of girls available to them, many from hurling areas, the Civil Service Camogie Club took to the field in 1928.

Meanwhile, Ballycastle, Glenarm, Dunloy, Carnlough, Cushendun and Glenariffe came under the banner of North Antrim. St Olcan's (Creggan), Tir-na-nÓg (Randelstown), St Brigid's (Antrim), Toomebridge and St Trea's (Newbridge) registered with South-West Antrim. The South Antrim League got underway in 1930. The three divisions sat down a year later to work out the logistics and to pave the way for county championships.

Galway County Board

Seán O'Duffy, national organiser, was invited to a meeting in Galway in 1928 at which a county board was formed. Mr S. A. O'Callaghan, principal of the Technical College, was elected chairman. The remaining officer positions were filled by Mick King, Tom Farrell and Violet Bodkin, who captained UCG to win the Ashbourne Cup. Eight clubs affiliated and a competition on a league system was agreed upon.

UCD Fail to Travel

As they considered the date unsuitable and had insufficient practice, UCD did not make the trip to Galway for the 1929 Ashbourne Cup. Two hundred couples attended the Ashbourne dance in the Town Hall in Galway and, on the stroke of 12 o'clock, Mrs Anderson, wife of the UCG President, presented the cup to Kathleen Lonergan, captain of the successful UCC team. Dancing continued to five o'clock in the morning, demonstrating the staying power of the players of the time.

Points' Bar

The most controversial rule in the history of camogie was introduced in 1929 and remained in the rule book until 1980. It provided for a bar joining the top of the goalposts. This created a "'points' space". Some counties, particularly those in hurling areas, were strongly opposed to it and did not use it. Those in favour, however, considered that it made the game distinctive and promoted accurate shooting. Some players felt intimidated by the top bar and shied away from attempting a point. The small number of points scored in those days vis-à-vis today is linked with the use of the top crossbar. A challenge match between Louth and Dublin at Croke Park on September 29th, 1929 saw the top crossbar in use for the first time.

Kerry County Board

A Kerry County Board was formed on June 8th, 1929 at the meeting in the Gaelic Rooms in Tralee. The game had made considerable progress in the county since 1926 and representatives of seven clubs were present at the meeting. Miss Kate Breen (Castlegregory), who was a member of Kerry County Council, was elected to the position of chairman. Brother Ryan (Cahirciveen),

Tailteann Games

Miss Dolly Kelter (Tralee), Miss B. Gorman (Tralee) and Liam Skinner (Tralee) filled the remaining positions. A Kerry Selection drew with Cork in Mallow on August 25th, 1929. Cork travelled to Tralee for the replay which was won by Kerry.

A stronghold of the game existed in Darver, near Dundalk, under the guidance of Fr Soraghan. The club side was so strong that it represented Louth in the Leinster and All-Ireland championships. The level of skill acquired by the Darver players was not surpassed by any of the Dublin clubs. The girls in light blue counted a number of star performers in their ranks. Kathleen Hanratty was an exceptional player and her sister Nan was a fine full-back. Brigid Lawless played ducks and drakes with opposing defences and Sarah McGuinness was an outstanding goalkeeper. Darver, who were very hospitable to all visitors, found it difficult to find opponents as many clubs fell shy of such engagements.

Camogie was well supported in Donegal for a number of years with clubs flourishing in Letterkenny, Bundoran, Ballybofey, Buncrana and Ballyshannon.

Kerry's camogie team in 1929

Nellie Remembers

"A camogie team was formed in Ballinacree, near Oldcastle, Co. Meath, in 1930 and remained in existence for almost ten years. The team practised their skills in Kit Reilly's field at the bridge of Tubrid and used Willie Hennessy's house as dressing rooms and tea rooms. Dressed in black gym frocks and yellow blouses, we played memorable matches against Belaney and were treated to tea and cake in Jack Hand's house after the exertions on the field. I have great memories of the chat and banter in the cars and lorries full of players and spectators travelling to Clonifad and Dulane to play Oldcastle. Dances were held in Ballinrink Hall to raise much-needed funds for the club. The dances and the matches were great social gatherings for the young men and women of the area. These young men came to the matches to cheer us on and, sometimes, to protect us. We were a great team and I enjoyed every minute of it." Nellie Brown (Farrelly), Ballinacree.

The memories recalled by Nellie could be replicated in many parts of the country where a group of girls grew up together. Camogie was more than a healthy exercise, it was their social outlet. Girls trained, played matches and enjoyed each other's company from their teenager years to the time of their marriage, after which a number moved from the area to live with their new husbands. Starting a family was not deferred in those days.

One by one, the players became unavailable to the team and the club folded when they were insufficient players for form a team. When the daughters of the original players were old enough to play camogie, the club was revived and the tradition continued.

Seán O'Duffy presents the O'Duffy Cup to Camogie President, Mollie Gill, for inter-county competition.

there is great credit to those who worked to promote the game that it reached the standard and spread as widely as it did by the early thirties.

Camogie provided the opportunity to Irish girls and women to play an Irish game. It gave them a social outlet and a new pastime. Through playing the game, they developed aspects of their personality and athleticism, and learned to depend and support one another as members of a team. Their confidence, independence and general health all improved.

Slow Progress

Progress in the years 1904 to 1930 had been slow for a variety of reasons: a lack of players with leisure time to play; a dearth of funds; difficulties in obtaining use of playing pitches; absence of public support; problems with transport and communication; no previous experience of organisation; girls moving on marriage; child bearing and rearing; the burden of work in rural areas; and public opinion against women's participation in sport. Indeed,

America

Seán O'Duffy's work with the Tailteann Council brought him to America in 1930. While in New Jersey, he saw a notice advertising a camogie match at Inisfail Park between Cork and Offaly. On his arrival at the grounds, he was delighted to find two teams ready to play. Seán was recognised by acquaintances from the home country and was ushered to the centre of the pitch, handed a whistle and the game was left in his charge.

Seven teams were affiliated in the United States at the time.

Tailteann Games

They played under the names of Cork, Tipperary, Offaly, Roscommon, Leitrim, Cavan and Stanford. P. J. Grimes headed the American Board and his secretary was Nancy Kennedy.

Wexford and Monaghan

Thomas Forde, a prominent figure in the GAA and Gaelic League, formed a club in Gorey in 1931. Wexford Town, St Ibar's, St Mary's, Clann Gabriel, St Fintan's, Clann Senan, Bunclody Insurgents and Gorey all provided players for an exhibition match at Gorey Feis that was witnessed by many thousands of supporters. The match proved more interesting and exciting than the hurling shield final which followed it.

A young Cavan girl, Julia Muldoon, came to work in Tydavnet, Co. Monaghan, in 1931. She set about organising camogie and before long clubs had mushroomed in the area. Teams taking part in competitions at the time included: Goland; Monaghan; Emyvale, Glaslough; Moybridge; Mullan Mills; Truagh; Ballyoisin; Scotstown; and Griggy. The latter team was made up of nurses from St Davnet's Hospital. Legnakelly, Castleshane, Rockcorry and Inniskeen joined over the following three years and, by the end of the decade, Monaghan could boast of 30 clubs and a thriving league.

New Publications

Two new publications, *The Irish Press* and *An Camán*, appeared in 1931. *The Irish Press* immediately recognised the value of covering Gaelic games and allotted significant space to them. Seán Ó Ceallaigh, who helped to draw up the original rules of camogie, edited *An Camán*. These two outlets for camogie coverage were very welcome, however, they concentrated their attention on the Dublin scene and paid little attention to the remainder of the country.

Murphy Cup

From 1931 to 1945, the Murphy Cup, a very successful competition, was organised between the Brigidine convents in Goresbridge, Mountrath, Tullow and Abbeyleix. The cup itself had been donated by Mrs Martin Murphy, a former Colmcille's player. .

Many clubs had sprung up around the country and counties became active and set up competitions. A club named An Tiolar Dubh (Black Eagles) was formed in Newry. They dressed in black, including black berets, and travelled to their matches in a side car.

Where We're At

Instead of being a wonderful occasion to exhibit the game to the public at large, the 1924 Tailteann Games ended in chaos as far as camogie was concerned. With no proper planning, camogie was shown up in a very poor light. The controversy, which led to the suspension of Wicklow, was badly handled and set the Association back in the eyes of the public. However, lessons were learned from the debacle and officials got it right for the 1928 games. Aonach Tailteann gave impetus and confidence to camogie and convinced members that the Association was ready for inter-county competition.

Camogie spread its wings to embrace athletics adding a

welcome dimension to its activities. This period witnessed the establishment of large clubs which were to stand the test of time and reach a very high standard, for example Celtic (Dublin) and Deirdre (Belfast). It is notable that these clubs were formed by individuals and without the influence of the Gaelic League or GAA clubs.

By the thirties, the full-length skirt and long-sleeved blouse had been replaced by the gym frock and a less-decorative blouse. Many players were soon to adopt a shirt which lent itself to activity rather than the more tight-fitting blouse. Canvas boots, with rubber studs, became the fashionable footwear. It was usual for gym frocks to be home-made and, therefore, the set worn by a team was not identical. When a player retired, she passed her gym frock down the line to a younger player and the garment was fully worn out and faded before it was discarded. The early custom of wearing hats or berets while playing the game was diminishing, although a few ladies maintained the habit.

From 1927 onwards, significant growth was noticeable throughout the country, Britain and America. Additional clubs sprouted up in areas where the game was already played and clubs were also formed in regions where camogie was hitherto unknown. County boards were formed and more structure was brought to the Association. Increased publicity was afforded to camogie. At last, we had a national game.

Chapter Four

A HUGE STEP FORWARD

1932 was a milestone year in the history of camogie, during which the haphazard approach to competitions in most counties became more structured. A spate of new clubs was formed and county boards were established, as well as an increase in the number of women involved in administration and refereeing. The rules of the game were brought into line throughout the country and the All-Ireland Championship was inaugurated.

Clubs outside Dublin, particularly in the south, were reluctant to accept the authority of Central Council as it was then constituted, because a number of officials sat on both the Central Council Steering Committee and the Dublin League Committee. An examination of minute books of the time shows that matters dealing with the affairs of the Dublin League and those of the national body were handled at the same meeting. Taking into consideration that the Dublin clubs could have 35 to 40 delegates present at these meetings, it was not surprising that others were unhappy with the situation.

Until 1932, the clubs and counties outside Dublin generally did their own thing – what happened in Dublin did not gravely concern them. But with an All-Ireland Championship looming, the time had come to put camogie's administrative house in order. A preliminary conference was called for St Patrick's Day to bring all units of the Association together and to see what was necessary to streamline the Association's structure and prepare for the All-Ireland Championship.

1932 Tailteann Games medal won by Molly Fitzgerald-Murphy.

Congress 1932

On April 25th, 1932, 60 delegates attended congress. Reporting on developments from the foundation of the Association, Seán O'Duffy stated that: "The founders were a few enthusiastic members of the Keating Branch

39

of the Gaelic League whose idea it was to have a national game for girls which would provide them with healthy open air exercise suitable to Irish girls and that it should be of a distinctively Irish character. The game was similar to hurling but in a modified form. Progress had been slow due to the amount of prejudice which had to be overcome against girls playing games. But the game was making steady progress. Teams were being formed in new areas, even outside the country in London, Manchester, Liverpool and America."

Congress confirmed the rules and regulations for the new All-Ireland Championship.

Matches would be played on pitches of 60–70 yards in length and 45–60 yards wide. The duration of play would be 40 minutes and the top crossbar would be used. The four forwards would line up in the centre of the field for the throw-in. A substitute would only be allowed to replace an injured player and not more than one player could tackle an opponent in possession of the ball. The meeting considered it unsafe to permit two players to challenge a sole opponent. For the first time, regrading was introduced. Play-

Mollie Gill (President of Camogie Association) watches Professor Agnes O'Farrelly cut the tape at the opening of the Phoenix Park camogie pitch in October, 1933. Dublin captain, Mary Walsh, and Seán O'Duffy are behind Mollie Gill.

ers, who were unable to hold their places on their club senior team, were eligible to field in a lower division where, it was hoped, they would impart the experience gained in the upper division to the juniors with beneficial results.

A rule was passed to control representation at congress. Two delegates were permitted for a county with up to ten clubs, and an additional delegate for each subsequent ten clubs. Dublin had 36 delegates present at the congress and claimed that each club was entitled to be represented. Over the years, Dublin had sought and effected the same representation at congress as they were entitled to at their own annual convention. However, the new rule settled the matter.

All counties with more than three clubs were requested to form a county board and affiliate to Central Council. It was recommended that county boards should be controlled as far as possible by women. In the elections for the board of the Association, Mollie Gill (Dublin) was elected president, Professor Agnes O'Farrelly (Cavan) and Kate Breen (Kerry) became vice-presi-

A Huge Step Forward

dents, Esther Ryan (Dublin) became secretary/treasurer and Seán O'Duffy (Dublin) was elected the national organiser.

Workplace Clubs

Many businesses and factories formed camogie teams in the early thirties. The most famous of these were GSR (CIÉ) in Dublin and Lee Hosiery (Cork) – both won their respective county senior championship – but there were many more, including: Jacobs, Hospital Trust, Imperial Tobacco, Players and Macintosh's (all in Dublin); Sunbeam Wolsey and Dunlop's (in Cork); Rosco Leather (in Roscommon); Irish Ropes (in Kildare); and Goodbody's (in Clara).

The Tailteann final between Connacht and Leinster in 1932. The caption states "The ups and downs of Camogie during the Leinster Connacht match at Croke Park.

An inter-departmental competition was also set up between the various departments of the civil service. An Post defeated the Department of Agriculture in the Phoenix Park on September 29th, 1932 to become the first holders of the McCall Trophy.

GSR (whose name was changed to CIÉ in 1945) Camogie Club was established by Tom Brady in 1931 for the company's workers or members of their families. The players wore a wine-coloured gym frock, green blouse and white sash. When Dublin were 'outside' the Association in 1948, the CIÉ Club affiliated directly to Central Council. They successfully participated in the All-Ireland Championship under the name of Dublin and could truly be said to be the first All-Ireland club champions. Amongst their ranks were some of the best players ever to represent Dublin, including Kathleen Mills, Kathleen Cody, Sophie Brack, Jean Hannon, Betty Hughes and Carmel Walsh.

The employees of O'Dwyer & Company in Cork, manufacturers and retailers in the clothing industry, formed their own camogie club, Lee Hosiery. The company provided a sports ground at Tivoli where the club played its home games. Lee Hosiery travelled to play many friendly matches as well as competing in the Cork senior league and championship. When they went to Killarney to take on a Dick Fitzgerald selection, they had to hire a special train to accommodate their supporters.

1932 Tailteann Games

Warm applause greeted the camogie teams as they walked past the stand in the Grand Opening Ceremony at the Tailteann

Games in Croke Park on June 29th, 1932, with the music from the Army Band together with a massed Pipers' Band rendering a sense of occasion. The Irish hurling team played the Scottish shinty team in the opening match. Leinster and Connacht camogie teams took the field and entertained the crowd with a fine display. The home side was the fitter and better trained side and finished in front.

The Leinster team which won the camogie competition at the 1932 Tailteann Games.

Ulster were due to meet Munster on July 3rd but they did not travel. Connacht lined out in their place and defeated Munster, who were represented by Tipperary, by 3–4 to 2–1. Connacht lined out for the third time in the final on July 10th against Leinster. Kathleen Hanratty, the Louth forward, gave a brilliant exhibition of attacking play, scoring 4–1 to secure a win for Leinster by 7–1 to 2–0.

Leinster team: (all Dublin except where stated) Bríd Kenny, Mary Walsh, Kathleen O'Byrne, Mollie Gill (captain), Essie Forde, Eileen Windsor, Eileen Davis, Máire O'Kelly, Dillon Bowden, Kathleen Hanratty (Louth), Nan Boyle (Louth) and Queenie Dunne.

Connacht team: (all Galway) Kathleen Higgins, M. Fitzgerald, Kitty Hynes, Madge Tonry, Nellie Ellwood, Peg Morris, Una O'Riordan, Sheila Belton, N. Greaney (captain), Dell Kearney, S. Kavanagh and J. Higgins.

Teams from Manchester and Liverpool also made the trip to Dublin and played under the banner of Britain. They fielded against Ireland, represented by the Darver Club (Louth), in the junior final, where the combined play of Kathleen Hanratty and Nan Boyle ensured victory for the home side by 4–5 to 0–0.

1932 All-Ireland Championship

Ten counties entered the inaugural All-Ireland Championship, organised on an open draw basis. The start of the competition was delayed until the autumn because of the Tailteann Games, consequently, the matches dragged on into the following season. Few counties donned the same colours as their GAA teams. Money was very tight and a new set of playing gear was beyond most budgets. Instead, the county team took the field in the colours of the county champions or in the uniform of a club that

A Huge Step Forward

had a respectable set of gym frocks. Cork regularly borrowed gym frocks from UCC who, very conveniently, did not use them during the summer months. Players took the field wearing gym frocks that covered the knee, long black stockings, black canvas boots, white blouses and belts or sashes.

Dublin proved too strong for Wexford in the semi-final and advanced on the score of 8–1 to 1–1. The second semi-final between Galway and Louth was a close exciting affair with the Connacht side emerging winners by 4–3 to 4–2.

The 1932 All-Ireland final was played as a double-header with a senior hurling challenge between Galway and Cork at The Sportsfield, Galway, on July 30th, 1933. After ten minutes, the hurling match was abandoned because of the appalling conditions. However, the girls were not put off by the muddy field and driving rain. J. J. McDonnell (Meath) was appointed to referee the match but did not officiate, instead Stephen Jordan (Athenry), the well-known GAA referee, took the whistle and became the first person to referee All-Ireland senior hurling and camogie finals.

Dublin won the toss and tore into attack. The first score was registered by Jean Hannon (Dublin). The highlight of the game was the exciting tussle between the Galway captain, Peg Morris, and Dublin's Eileen Windsor. Dublin's attack combined well and was the deciding factor in their 3–2 to 0–2 victory. Bríd Kenny, Mary Walsh and Essie Forde excelled in the Dublin defence. Máire O'Kelly (daughter of founder member 'Sceilg'), Queenie Dunne and Eileen Windsor formed a strong midfield line. Ita McNeill and Jean Hannon were dangerous in front of goal. Galway had quality players in Bríd O'Beirne, Peg Morris, Dell Kearney and Una O'Riordan. The Dublin team contained four Wicklow girls, Eileen Windsor, Jean Hannon, Dillon Bowden and Queenie Dunne. They were members of the Bray club which participated in Dublin competitions at the time.

Dublin team: Bríd Kenny, Mary Walsh, Essie Forde, Mollie Gill (captain), Kathleen O'Byrne, Máire O'Kelly, Queenie Dunne (2–2), Eileen Windsor, Maura McGuinness, Ita McNeill, Dillon Bowden and Jean Hannon (1–0).

Galway Team: Bridie Murray, Kitty Hynes, Peg Lahiffe, Nora Henahan, Una O'Riordan, Nora Conroy, Peg Morris (captain), Dell Kearney, Sheila Belton, Bríd O'Beirne (0–1), Kathleen Walsh (0–1) and Rita Cosgrave.

Seán O'Duffy donated a silver cup for the championship, to be known as the O'Duffy Cup, which was hand-crafted by silversmiths in Weirs of Dublin. As Mollie Gill was both President of the Camogie Association and captain of the winning team, Seán O'Duffy presented his cup to her after the game.

Earlier Start

Delegates at the 1933 congress in Jury's Hotel were adamant that the All-Ireland Championship should start in May and be completed by the end of October. Motions were passed to set up provincial councils and recommend that county boards should be controlled as far as possible by girls. Tipperary sought to have the All-Ireland final and the Ashbourne Cup final played in Thurles as part of the GAA Golden Jubilee celebrations in 1934. However, no decision was made on this proposal.

Ban on Foreign Games

A ban on foreign games was debated at the Cork Convention. When a vote was taken, the majority opposed the introduction of the ban. The outcome was raised at the subsequent meeting of the Cork GAA Board where disapproval of the Camogie Board's decision was voiced and the feeling was that the Camogie Board should have followed the ideals of the GAA Board. This difference of opinion put the use of GAA facilities by camogie in doubt.

The camogie clubs in Cork were divided on the issue, and both camps formed their own county board and affiliated to Central Council. The GAA Board announced that they were cutting their links with the Camogie Board.

When the time came to make the draw for the All-Ireland Championship, Central Council found itself with a dilemma – they had two entries from Cork. They decided that until the two opposing county boards came together, Cork's name would not go into the hat for the draw.

The saga dragged on to September, leaving the Cork players sidelined as far as the All-Ireland championship was concerned. The players felt let down and disappointed and rumblings of discontent were widespread. The seeds of antagonism towards male officials, which was to become a major issue in the coming years, were sown during this dispute.

Appeal for Assistance

Central Council appealed to the GAA for assistance to promote camogie. One of the first to respond was Michael Hennessy, Secretary of the Clare GAA Board, and he set about establishing camogie clubs in the county. He started in his own parish of Clooney where he received great response and put a juvenile team together. He used his GAA contacts throughout the county and encouraged them to follow his lead. By 1934, eight clubs existed in Clare – Clooney, Doolin, Ennis, Kilshanny, Ballynacally, Meelick, Newmarket and Tulla. A county board was formed with Michael Hennessy as chairman and Martina Griffin as secretary. All eight teams paraded through the streets of Ennis in the Golden Jubilee celebrations of the GAA in 1934.

Great progress was also evident in Tipperary in the early thirties. Many new clubs were formed with Boherlahan, Coolmoyne, Cashel, Clonmel, Cappawhite, Moycarkey, Roscrea,

1933 All-Ireland match report

A Huge Step Forward

Two-Mile-Borris, Killenaule, Nenagh, Toomevara, Drom, Moyle Rovers and Thurles all up and running by 1933. A Tipperary County Board was formed with Seán Ryan N.T. as chairman and the well-known athlete, Tommy Ryan, as secretary.

Fermanagh have come and gone from the camogie scene many times over the years. In 1933, Dr J. P. Cassidy spearheaded the county board which legislated for seven clubs – Clonmaullin, Lisnaskea, St Matthew's, Cavanacross, Enniskillen, Belcoo and Teemore.

A second pitch in the Phoenix Park was made available to the Dublin League by the Board of Works. Colourfully dressed in club uniforms, 600 players, representing 85 teams and headed by the O'Rahilly Band, marched from Parnell Square to the Phoenix Park for the official opening on October 29th, 1933. Agnes O'Farrelly officially opened the new pitch and an exhibition match between two selected sides from the Dublin League was staged. To mark the occasion, Paddy O'Keeffe presented a set of sideline and umpire's flags on behalf of the GAA.

1933 All-Ireland Championship

Dublin, Galway, Louth and Kildare were the last four standing from an entry of 16 in the 1933 All-Ireland Championship. Dublin outscored Louth by 9–1 to 5–3 while Galway overcame Kildare by 3–2 to 1–0 in the semi-finals.

Galway travelled to meet Dublin at the New Ireland Park, Killester, on December 17th. The Dublin midfield trio of Mollie Gill, Máire O'Kelly and schoolgirl Emmy Delaney dictated the game. Galway stayed in the match until half-time, but were swept away in the second period. The versatile Peg Morris overshadowed the remaining Galway players. She received most assistance from Martha O'Connor, Bríd O'Beirne, Nora Conroy and Monica Duggan, sister of hurling star, Jimmy Duggan. Polished stylist, Ita McNeill, and clinical finisher, Jean Hannon, shared seven goals between them in the Dublin attack. Dublin retained the O'Duffy Cup by the comfortable margin of 9–2 to 4–0.

Dublin team: Bríd Kenny, Mary Walsh, Queenie Dunne, Kathleen Mayne, Essie Forde, Mollie Gill (captain), Emmy Delaney, Máire O'Kelly, Dillon Bowden (1–1), Maura McGuinness (1–0), Ita McNeill (4–0) and Jean Hannon (3–1).

Galway team: Bridie Murray, Martha O'Connor, Peg Lahiffe, Nora Conroy, Monica Duggan, Una O'Riordan, Peg Morris (captain), Dell Kearney, Bríd O'Beirne (2–0), Kathleen Maguire (2–0), Kathleen Walsh and Maureen Lawless.

Queen's University

From 1915 to 1933, the Ashbourne Cup was confined to the three national universities – Galway, Dublin and Cork. UCC, hosts of the 1934 competition, wrote to Lord Ashbourne enquiring if he had any objection to Queen's University participating in the competition. He replied "Belfast is in Ireland" and went out of his way to be at Kingsbridge Station to wish the Queen's players every success as they headed south.

Students from St Mary's Training College attended lectures at Queen's and so were eligible to turn out for the university team.

Queen's camogie team was the first Ulster side to compete in All-Ireland competition. Veronica Laverty, May McCarroll, Una and Grace McClafferty, Frances McNabb, Madeline McKenna and Eileen O'Kane, all past pupils of St Louis, Kilkeel, were members of the first Queen's side.

That Ban Again

Twenty-two counties were represented at the 1934 Annual Congress, where delegates voted to extend the duration of a match to 50 minutes, play the All-Ireland championship on a provincial basis and introduce a ban on foreign games, as existing in the GAA. The ban motion was passed by 26 votes to 17 and met with very strong opposition from Dublin and Cork.

An annoyed Brighid Ní Mhaoileóin, captain of the Athy camogie club, expressed the following views in a letter to *The Irish Press* on March 15th: "[The ban] has come as a shock to the majority of camogie players and to the public in general.

Why, in the name of common sense, has this narrow-minded and retrograde step been taken? An association which has to use coercion to exist is not worth supporting, and in view of the amazing strides the game has made since its inauguration 30 years ago, and that it is now well on its way to the zenith of success, it is difficult to see the need for such coercion, and, in truth, there is none." She accused the supporters of the ban of making "a hypocritical and self-glorifying attempt to create a halo of patriotism around their own heads".

It is no surprise that members or the general public knew little of what went on at congress, as coverage by the media was particularly sparse. Counties found it difficult to send delegates to congress as Saturday was a full working day for the vast majority of the workforce and there was little chance of getting a day off to attend a camogie meeting.

The foreign games ban was a huge issue in Ulster where advocates argued that it was necessary to preserve Ireland's national culture from the forces of Anglicisation. They saw it as an expression of a player's exclusive loyalty to camogie.

Provincial Councils

Three provincial councils were formed in May 1934. Mrs Maggie Dunne (Wexford) and Ms Kay Hyland (Laois) were elected to the key positions of chairman and secretary of the Leinster Council. Galway captain, Peg Morris, chaired the new Connacht Council with Ms M. McGough (Mayo) as her secretary. Sinéad Crotty

Camogie players taking part in the G.A.A. Golden Jubilee celebrations in 1934 at Croke Park.

A Huge Step Forward

(Cork) sat in the Munster chair with Mary Donnellan (Clare) by her side. Later in the year, Ulster also organised itself and Agnes O'Farrelly (Cavan) took the chair for the first year but was replaced by Rosemary Marron at the following convention, when Ms O'Farrelly moved to the position of president. Vera Campbell (Tyrone) was the first Ulster secretary, a position that she held for six years.

The game was now on a sound footing with 318 clubs affiliated.

GAA Jubilee

The GAA celebrated its Golden Jubilee in 1934 and camogie players joined in the festivities at many venues, including the hundreds who marched in the main parade through O'Connell Street in Dublin. Cork organised a special competition to mark the occasion in which Lee Hosiery pipped Mayfield for the Jubilee Cup. Later in the season, Lee Hosiery visited London and the Gaumont Film Company made a special picture of their match against Tara at Catford.

John Charles McQuaid

John Charles McQuaid, President of Blackrock College and, later, Archbishop of Dublin, wrote to *The Irish Times* in February 1934 expressing his strong reservations towards women's participation in sport. He was particularly forceful in his condemnation of athletic meetings where both men's and women's events were staged, calling them "un-Irish and un-catholic". Seán O'Duffy reacted to this statement by advising camogie players not to appear at any sports meeting in case their actions would appear repulsive to the national or Catholic ideals of the people of this country.

Agnes O'Farrelly did not agree with the stand taken by the Very Rev. McQuaid. She was saddened that his opinions would do harm to the progress which had been made to date by the Camogie Association. She reacted to the threat by obtaining a statement from the ecclesiastical authorities to quash negative publicity, preventing significant damage being done to the progress of the game, particularly in convent schools.

Cork, in darker uniforms, led by Kate Dunlea, and Louth, headed by Rose Quigley, parade before the 1934 All-Ireland final at Croke Park.

1934 All-Ireland Championship

Galway, Antrim, Louth and Cork were the first provincial champions. Impressive victories over Limerick, Kerry and Waterford in the Munster championship convinced Cork that they had a good chance of making an impact in the All-Ireland championship and they knuckled down to training. For captain, Kate Dunlea, it meant cycling 22 miles to the city, participating in the training session and cycling home afterwards. The reward for Cork was a 4–1 to 2–0 win over Antrim at Croke Park in the semi-final.

The Darver club side, supplemented by two players from Knockbridge, accounted for Dublin, Kilkenny and Meath for Louth to claim the Leinster title. They then shaded the verdict over Galway by 2–3 to 2–1 in the second semi-final at Darver.

In the final at Croke Park on October 28th, 1934, Cork were stronger on the ball and faster in striking than Louth . Cork played as a team and capitalised on their chances. Louth had outstanding performers in Kathleen Hanratty, Rose Quigley and goalkeeper, Sarah McGuinness, but they were unable to prevent Cork winning by 4–3 to 1–4.

Cork team: Nora Clarke, Monica Cotter, Essie Staunton, Lena Delaney, Kitty McCarthy (1–2), Monie O'Hea, Lil Kirby, May McCarthy, Kate Dunlea (captain) (2–0), Mary Kenneally, Betty Riordan (1–1) and Josie McGrath.

Louth team: Sarah McGuinness, Nan Hanratty, Mary McArdle, Bridget McKeown, Aggie McCluskey, Kathleen Johnson, Mary McKeever, Rose Quigley (captain), Nellie McDonnell, Kathleen Hanratty (0–3), Bridie Donnelly (1–0) and Mary Murtagh (0–1).

At 15 years of age, Betty Riordan was the youngest player to win an All-Ireland senior medal. Monica Cotter (Cork) was the first player to win an All-Ireland medal and represent her country in another sport. Under her married name Monica 'Girlie' Hegarty, she played golf for Ireland many times and, later, became President of the ILGU. Cork forward Mary Kenneally is a sister of John Kenneally who won an All-Ireland senior hurling medal in 1929.

Monica Cotter-Hegarty, the first All-Ireland medal-holder to represent Ireland in sport. She won an All-Ireland medal with Cork in 1934 and played golf for Ireland on several occasions.

Lord Ashbourne at Queen's

Queen's University hosted the Ashbourne Cup in 1935, the first inter-varsity Gaelic event to be held in Belfast. The matches were played at Corrigan Park. Lord Ashbourne added colour when he arrived wearing a saffron kilt with his French wife, Marianne. Harry Diamond, member of Northern Ireland Parliament, refer-

A Huge Step Forward

eed the final. In excess of 600 guests attended a Gala Céilí at the Belfast Plaza to round off the Ashbourne weekend.

The Ulster Convention, which was held in Derry on January 13th, 1935, voted to suspend any club which held a dance other than céilí for a six-month period. Seán O'Duffy, who was present, stated that "when girls took up a native game, they ought all to see that everything connected with the game should be both native and national".

Professor Agnes O'Farrelly, Life President of Camogie Association presenting the Sean O'Duffy trophy to Ita Hynes in 1936.

Ten Thousand Players

Delegates to the 1935 congress listened to impressive figures from national organiser, Seán O'Duffy. The Association had 423 teams, which totalled 10,000 players. The game had spread to 28 of the 32 counties, as well as London, Liverpool, Manchester, Glasgow and the United States. Ulster succeeded in extending the ban on foreign dances to the remainder of the country. Motions were passed to permit men act on county boards (in a one-year trial) but only female delegates could attend congress, Central Council and the provincial councils.

During the debate on the motion to exclude men, a telegram was read from the vice-president, Kate Breen (Kerry), who was "greatly disturbed to be missing such important meeting". She went on to say she was: "Utterly opposed to giving men delegates status or any voting power whatsoever in women's association. They are source of constant strife in every country." Remembered as a rather formidable lady, Kate Breen was vice-chairman of Kerry County Council and unlikely to have any difficulty dealing with men.

A news report in 1934 regarding the disputed gender of a player and a ruling on skirt length.

> recently have been brought to light which show that there is need of reform in the world of camogie. The first was the outcome of a camogie county league final. After the match was over the beaten team formulated a protest to the effect that one of their opponents was a man. This would have been irregular, as the teams were supposed to be composed of women. In the second case the regulations as to gender were observed, but the skirts worn by one of the teams were so long that they constituted an additional hazard for the opposition. The ruling on this point is strict. Skirts may descend no farther than one inch below the knee; anything in excess of that is not allowed by the rules of the game. An interesting match might be

Agnes O'Farrelly

Congress elected Agnes O'Farrelly Honorary Life President, a position that she held until her death in 1951. The Cavan lady was a noted Gaelic scholar, educationalist, writer and upholder of women's rights. She was drawn to the Camogie Association because there was a mixture of the old culture and the new world right to its very roots and it tried to create belief and a new status for the women of Ireland. She saw camogie as promoting the unity of women, giving them a common aim which was non-political as well as providing a new pastime for women so that they would want to stay in Ireland instead of emigrating.

She believed that the support of the Gaelic League was needed by the Camogie Association because of the excellent methods of publicity it had. The league had branches established in every part of the country and this would help to promote camogie all over Ireland. She adopted the thinking and the aims of the Camogie Association and, before long, came to the understanding that camogie was a necessary part of the process of the re-Gaelicisation of Ireland and would also add to the new self-confidence of the women of the country.

Fingal League

Expansion continued in Dublin. The number of junior clubs had grown and it was considered prudent to set up a Junior Board. The Fingal League was formed in north County Dublin as a separate organisation from the Dublin Board. Fingal catered for ten teams, including Balrothery, Lusk, Man-o-War, Rush, Donabate, Oldtown and Swords, all of which competed for the Duke Cup.

Naomh Aoife

Naomh Aoife, a club to reach its Golden Jubilee, was formed in the parish of St James, Inchicore, in 1935 by Fr V. Steen. He thought that there was nothing for the young girls to do and he tried to get them interested in camogie. He called on John Timmins, the well-known cross-country athlete, to assist him in getting the club up and running. Enjoyment through camogie was the club's mantra over the years.

Teenager Kathleen O'Neill was involved from the beginning and devoted her life to her club, Dublin Board, Leinster Council and the game of camogie. Kathleen married John Timmins who supported her camogie activities and their daughter, Patricia, went on to win five All-Ireland senior medals with Dublin.

1935 All-Ireland Championship

The All-Ireland senior championship semi-finals were staged together at Croke Park on November 10th. Cork were severely tested by Antrim who were dour battlers but survived on the score of 4–1 to 2–4, whereas Dublin had a comfortable passage over Galway by 8–5 to 2–1. Seventeen-year-old schoolgirl, Josie McGrath, led Cork in the parade in the final against Dublin at the Cork Athletic Grounds on November 24th.

St Aloysius School had won the Cork Schools Championship so easily that they sought a stiffer challenge and so were permitted to enter the Cork Senior Championship, which they also won, twice. As a result, the school could nominate the captain of the Cork team and the honour went to Josie, who was joined on the Cork team by two schoolmates, Peggy Hogg and Kitty Buckley – though goalkeeper, Peggy Hogg, was a late withdrawal from the starting team. She was replaced by May Kelleher, a grand-aunt of Joanne O'Callaghan, the All-Ireland winning captain in 2006.

Dublin had a great defence which quelled the frequent raids of the Cork forwards. The play swept up and down the field at a hectic pace in what was easily the best final played to date. Exciting moments abounded in both goalmouths. Cork were marginally in front by 2–2 to 2–0 at the break.

Angela Egan, Bríd Kenny, Jean Hannon, Queenie Dunne and Emmy Delaney played superbly for Dublin. Cork had exceptional performers in Essie Stanton, Lil Kirby, Dolly Quirke, Joan Cotter and Kitty Buckley. Cork held out to win by 3–4 to 4–0 in a heart-stopping finish.

Cork team: May Kelleher, Joan Cotter, Essie Stanton, Lena Delaney, Dolly Quirke, May McCarthy, Lil Kirby (0–3), Margaret Delaney, Kitty Buckley (2–1), Josie McGrath (captain), Sheila Brennan (1–0) and Maura Cronin.

Dublin team: Bríd Kenny, Mary Walsh, Eileen Windsor, Emmy Delaney, Louise Doran, Angela Egan, Mollie Gill, Máire O'Kelly, Nuala Sheehan (1–0), Queenie Dunne, Ita McNeill and Jean Hannon (3–0).

Dolly Quirke's brother, John, won four All-Ireland senior hurling medals with Cork, though the family originally came from Milltown, Co. Kerry.

Signs of Decline

1934 and 1935 were regarded as peak years of the Association when the struggle to attain an All-Ireland organisation had succeeded. The advance made in such a short period was remarkable. While appreciating the progress made, it was disappointing to note that Monaghan had not participated in the Ulster championship and Kilkenny were not affiliated to Leinster Council.

The combined Dublin and Cork teams photographed before the 1935 All-Ireland final at the Cork Athletic Grounds. Dublin are in the lighter uniforms.

Before the end of 1935, however, there were signs of decline in Munster. Camogie in Kerry disappeared, mainly because emigration hit the development of the game in the county. The girls who remained at home often found summer jobs in the tourist industry where long hours and weekend work left little time for camogie. Kerry also suffered from isolation as the county was far from the hub of activity and every trip was a long journey.

Clare suffered a heavy defeat to Cork and withdrew from the Munster championship (they would rejoin in 1944). Within a short space of time, the number of clubs in Tipperary fell from 16 to five and the county did not compete at inter-county level for the next six years. This scenario was repeated in various parts of the country from time to time and gave rise to the question of whether the structure of the clubs was adequate. Was the fact that organisation of the clubs was left to one or two people mean that, when they moved on, the clubs folded?

The players of that time played for the love of the game – seeking honour and glory was not a priority. Camogie was their social outlet and their teammates were their close friends. Players lived for camogie.

1936 All-Ireland Championship

Galway, who defeated Sligo in the Connacht final, played very well in the first-half of the All-Ireland semi-final against Louth at Killester and carried a comfortable margin into the second-half. However, a remarkable rally by Louth saw them snatch victory by 3–6 to 2–3.

The clever Cork attack worked good scores in the second semi-final against Antrim at Killester. Antrim regretted missed chances and made a tame exit by 5–2 to 0–0.

The Cork girls were invited to a Siamse Mór in the Mansion House on the night before the All-Ireland final and the night's activity did them no harm. The final at Croke Park on October 11th was played at an unrelenting pace from beginning to end. Cork had the speedier forwards who combined cleverly and shot accurately. There were no weak links on the Cork side that was

A Louth attack is repelled by Cork in the 1936 All-Ireland final in Croke Park

A Huge Step Forward

regarded as the best team to claim the O'Duffy Cup in its short history. Louth, who were noted for their sporting approach to the game, had dangerous inside forwards in Kathleen Hanratty, Bernie Donnelly and Kathleen Johnson. The score at the final whistle was Cork 6–4 Louth 3–3.

Cork team: Nora O'Sullivan, Lena Delaney, Essie Stanton, Mollie Higgins, Maura Cronin, Kitty Cotter (captain), Lil Kirby (0–2), May McCarthy, Kitty Buckley (1–2), Josie McGrath (1–0), Sheila Brennan (1–0) and Anne Barry (3–0).

Louth team: Sarah McGuinness, Nan Hanratty, Mary McArdle, Bridget McKeown, Aggie McCluskey, Rose Quigley (captain), Bríd Sharkey, Mary McKeever, Nellie McDonnell, Kathleen Hanratty (0–3), Bernie Donnelly (2–0) and Kathleen Johnson (1–0).

Cork's Joan and Kitty Cotter became the first sisters to win All-Ireland medals.

"Perplexed"

Writing under the name "Perplexed", a spectator at the All-Ireland final wrote to the newspaper expressing his/her amazement at finding "… the players attired in skirts. One would have thought that this form of 'athletic' costume would have been long since relegated to the limbo of forgotten things, where it belongs". S/he had to wait a further thirty-six years before the gym frock was hung up for good.

Fleet-Footed Kay

The time registered by Kay Mannion (Colaiste San Dominic) for the 100 yards sprint at the 1935 Dublin Sports raised eyebrows. People wondered if she had really run that fast. Was the distance properly measured? Was the timing accurate? When the 1936 Sports Day, staged at Croke Park, came around every care was taken to record the time of the event and experienced timekeepers from athletics were brought in to ensure accuracy.

Kay took off down her lane at the gun leaving the remainder of the field watching her heels. The official timekeeper called 11 seconds as the winning time. A few months earlier, Ms H. Stephens of the United States had won the 100 yards at the Berlin Olympics in a time of 11.5 seconds. What time would Ms Stephens have re-

Camogie players who took part in a sprinting contest at the 1935 All-Ireland. On right is a press report.

turned if she had run in a gym frock, long black stockings and a pair of rubber dollies?

Where We're At

The 1932 Tailteann Games did much to popularise the game and whet the appetite for the inaugural All-Ireland Championship. The playing rules, which up to that point had varied from county to county, were brought into line. County representation at congress was decided in a fair manner, leading to the recognition of the top body by counties which previously had taken little heed of its rulings. It was all systems go for the opening round of the championship.

One-third of the counties entered for the first inter-county championship. The remaining counties felt that they were not strong enough or sufficiently prepared to challenge for honours. The dismal weather and underfoot conditions did not deter Galway and Dublin at the Sportsground, Galway, in the decider. The *Connacht Tribune* reporter commented: "The game was good throughout. Many scores were lost on both sides. A few of the girls have not the camogie temperament and placings on the field were ignored."

With scores of women employed, all of the hard-working type, it was no surprise that teams were formed by some of the manufacturing companies that competed very favourably with the established clubs. A well-organised and eagerly contested league was set up for the ladies of the civil service. The provincial councils were established, bringing identity and organisation to the regions and paving the way for provincial competitions.

More and more, the names of the top players became known and talked about. Kathleen Hanratty (Louth), Peg Morris (Galway), Jean Hannon (Dublin), Angela Egan (Dublin), Lil Kirby (Cork) and Kitty Buckley (Cork) were recognised by sports followers. Camogie reached a peak in 1935 with a very commendable figure of 10,000 players and in excess of 400 clubs.

However, camogie remained vulnerable to the opinions and remarks of the clergy as evident by the impact of a letter of John Charles McQuaid in 1934. It took a person of the stature of Agnes O'Farrelly to take a stand and defend the Association. Not all the hindrances to progress came from external sources. The decision to impose a ban on foreign games proved fateful and had very serious consequences in the years that followed.

In the latter stages of 1935, signs of decline started to emerge. Was an All-Ireland championship too ambitious? It was for some counties. Massive defeats in the opening round – e.g. Dublin 11–3 Longford 0–0, Antrim 9–0 Down 1–1 and Cork 10–0 Clare 1–0 – deflated the weaker counties. County organisation was not strong enough to carry the clubs. Women were not used to being in charge and struggled in positions of responsibility. In rural areas, long working hours remained an obstacle to playing camogie.

Chapter Five

DECLINE AND CONTROVERSY

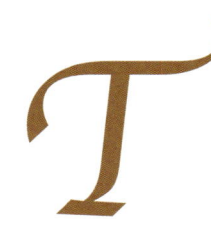

The Munster Council was disbanded in September 1937 when the number of affiliated counties fell below the required minimum of three – only Waterford and Cork participated in the Munster championship. It was hoped that when the mandatory number of counties registered, the council would be reinstated. In the meantime, Jean McHugh, Secretary of Central Council, carried out the work of the Munster Council.

A definite falling off in the number of teams affiliated was evident all over the country. It was suggested in some quarters that the decline was due to the premature exclusion of male officials. Girls, particularly in rural areas, did not have the time to organise and travel about. Kilkenny did not enter the Leinster championship for a number of years and Donegal withdrew from the Ulster championship as a result of failure to reach agreement with Cavan over arrangements for an inter-county fixture.

1937 All-Ireland Championship

Galway and Antrim took part in an epic struggle in the All-Ireland semi-final at Killester. It was score for score with neither side being able to exert authority. The Connacht side edged in front to win by 5–0 to 3–3. In the second semi-final at Croke Park, Cork persistently attacked the Dublin goal, but poor shooting saw many chances go to waste. Dublin played as a team and drew the rewards but Cork had the more stylish camogie players. Angela Egan played brilliantly and set up goal chances for Jean Hannon and Doreen Rogers. Cork lost their first championship game by 3–2 to 2–1.

Following the excitement of the two semi-finals, the decider between Dublin and Galway at Croke Park on November 28th was something of an anticlimax. Dublin, who were not called upon to raise their game to the same heights as the semi-final, were in command from start to finish.

The Dublin forwards swung the ball about, completely bewildering the Galway defence. Josie Melvin, in the Galway goal, drew frequent rounds of applause with save after save. Jean Hannon and Angela Egan had Dublin two goals up within three minutes of the start. Eileen O'Beirne did pull a goal back for Galway but, after that, their attack faded. Galway apparently resigned themselves to defeat and concentrated on keeping Dublin's score down.

Peggy Griffin and Mary Walsh were watertight in the Dublin defence. Emmy Delaney was authoritative in midfield and Angela Egan delighted the crowd with her characteristic runs down the wing. Life President, Agnes O'Farrelly, presented the O'Duffy Cup to Mary Walsh following Dublin's 9–4 to 1–0 victory.

Dublin team: Mary Lahiffe, Mary Walsh (captain), Patty Kenny, Peggy Griffin, Rose Fletcher, Sheila Hodgins, Emmy Delaney, Angela Egan (1–0), Eva Moran (2–0), Nuala Sheehan (0–2), Doreen Rogers (2–0) and Jean Hannon (4–0).

Galway team: Josie Melvin, Monica Duggan, Peg Morris (captain), Frances Coen, Nora Conroy, Kathleen Cosgrave, Mary Lyons, Nora O'Connell, Mary Joyce, Nora Kavanagh, Celia Mulholland and Eileen O'Beirne (1–0).

Dublin winger, Angela Egan, married Jimmy Cooney who won an All-Ireland senior hurling medal with Tipperary in 1937. They were the first of a special band of husbands and wives to hold All-Ireland senior medals.

Radio Talk

In a talk on Radio Athlone in 1937, Life President, Agnes O'Farrelly, expressed her wishes for the advancement of the game: "The raising of the standard of physical fitness among women will react inevitably on the whole race so that it is no exaggeration to say that the future of Ireland is bound up with the success of this camóguidheacht movement. As a national game for women, camóguidheacht has had a rapid growth. The first camóg meeting was held rather as a national gesture against foreign games for women, and few foresaw the nationwide appeal the new game was destined to make."

Dr O'Farrelly exhorted the delegates at the 1938 Annual Congress to make a big effort to organise the youthful players in schools and colleges. She called for the national game of camogie to be introduced to preparatory and training colleges, for teachers in primary schools to take an interest in the game and for playing

Fr. Micheál O.F.M. Cap. Starts the 1938 All-Ireland final at the Cork Athletic Grounds on October 31st, 1938

Decline and Controversy

facilities to be provided. She concluded: "'More camogie in all our primary schools and colleges' should be our slogan for the coming year."

Player Power

All-Ireland players, Lil Kirby and Josie McGrath, took over the pivotal positions of chairman and secretary of the Cork County Board, ending the dominance of male officials. In fact, the entire list of officers was comprised of prominent players with Lena Delaney, Renee Fitzgerald, Maura Cronin and Kathleen Coughlan filling the remaining positions.

Celtic Congress

A novel feature of the Celtic Congress held in Douglas, Isle of Man, was a camogie match for a silver cup between two selected sides representing UCD and Scoil Brighde (Dublin) on July 2nd, 1938. The congress delegates were enthralled with the camogie exhibition and were particularly taken with the skill of Kathleen Cody. The richly ornamented cup was presented to the winners and the day ended with a giense, or Manx, céile.

Speaking at the presentation ceremony, Professor Agnes O'Farrelly said that there, among their Gaelic friends, they were planting the seed of their national game. She added that it would not be sufficient to develop the physical side of men alone. "If we wish to have a healthy race, we must also develop the physical side of women."

On returning to Dublin, the cup was handed over to the Dub-

UCD team in 1938. Celtic Congress delegates were enthralled with a camogie exhibition given by them and Scoil Brighde on the Isle of Man in July of that year. The picture features Iney O'Kelly-Leonard (fourth from left), Agnes Hourigan-Purcell (sixth from right) and Josie Kelly-Stuart (second from right) who were to become prominent in camogie in the years ahead.

lin Board. A new knockout competition was organised at the beginning of future seasons to prepare clubs for the established competitions and was known as the Isle of Man Cup.

1938 All-Ireland Championship

Cork recorded an easy win over Galway at the Sports Field in the semi-final of the All-Ireland Championship. Cork captain, Kathleen Coughlan, was invincible at centre-back. Renee Fitzgerald, Kitty Buckley and Betty Riordan shared 5–1 between them. Galway's reply was a point from Frances Coen.

GAA president, Paddy McNamee, threw in the ball at the second semi-final between Antrim and Dublin at MacRory Park. Nuala Sheehan was the Dublin star on the day. She opened the Antrim defence and created good opportunities for Eva Moran (2–1) and Jean Hannon to finish. Antrim put delightful passages of play together but fell short by 3–1 to 2–1.

Two late goals by Doreen Rogers snatched victory for Dublin over Cork in the All-Ireland final at the Cork Athletic Grounds on November 30th. With five minutes remaining, the scores were level, but Dublin stormed the Cork goal and slammed home the winning scores. Lil Kirby and Emmy Delaney fought a tremendous duel in midfield. Angela Egan, Nuala Sheehan and Ita McNeill left their stamp on the game. Kathleen Coughlan was outstanding for Cork and received most help from Bríd Cronin, Kitty Buckley and Josie McGrath. Dublin regained the O'Duffy Cup on the scoreline of 5–0 to 2–3.

Dublin team: Mary Lahiffe, Rose Martin, Patty Kenny, Peggy Griffin, May Fletcher, Sheila Hodgins, Emmy Delaney (captain) (1–0), Angela Egan, Agnes Hourigan, Nuala Sheehan (1–0), Doreen Rogers (2–0) and Ita McNeill (1–0).

Cork team: Eileen Lyons, Kathleen Coughlan (captain), Bríd Cronin, Nan O'Dowd, Essie Staunton, Lil Kirby (0–3), Maura Cronin, Chrissie Cashman, Josie McGrath, Kitty Buckley (1–0), Renee Fitzgerald (1–0) and Betty Riordan.

Dublin forward, Agnes Hourigan, became one of the best-known figures in camogie under her married name, Agnes Purcell.

Ballinacree Camogie team, Co. Meath. Players who lined out for club from 1930 to 1940 included Mary Muldoon, Kathy Muldoon, Peg Briody, Bridie Gilsean, Teresa Brown, Lilly Reilly, Nellie Brown, Delia Heery, Rosie Butler, Rosie Hennessy, Biddy Kevin, Peggy Kevin, Rosie Kevin, Sissy Coyle, Maggie Smith, Julie Smith and Molly Smith.

Decline and Controversy

She had a long association with UCD and served as President of the Association (1976–1978).

No Money for Replacement

A girl, who was due to play for Cork in the All-Ireland final on the Sunday, went out for a few pucks on the Friday night. Tragedy struck as she broke her hurley. She had begged, borrowed and done overtime to make the amount she had to contribute towards the cost of travel and accommodation. Tears filled her eyes at the predicament she found herself in. She had to get a stick before Sunday or risk losing her place on the team. Living in a strong hurling area, she set out to beg for one. The lad in the first house said he had a championship match on Sunday and needed his stick. The next hurler called on had two sticks, and, though he was not willing to lend his new stick, she could borrow his old one. However, it had been repaired several times and was held together with nails and prohibited banding. Her luck changed at the third house. A young man handed over his stick and wished her well.

She cared for the stick over the weekend as if her life depended on it and never let it out of her sight for a moment. As the train pulled into Kent station, she saw him standing on the platform and was delighted to hand it back safe and sound.

Marriage Ban

The belief was held in some quarters that it was not in the best interests of married women to participate in sport. A lack of healthcare services, the poor health and inadequate diet of mothers, poor housing and frequent pregnancies led to high mortality rates during childbirth. Problems during pregnancies were not identified and led to major complications at childbirth. In contrast to the care and attention afforded to pregnant women in modern times, a large number of Irish women bore children without the services of a doctor. Instead, they were often attended by unqualified midwives.

If the birth was normal, the midwives were able to cope; if something went wrong, however, it was easy to point the finger at the physical exertion of sport and conclude that the victim had suffered an injury which was responsible for the complication.

> Cork 6-1   Galway 1-1
> CORK won the first All-Ireland Camoguidheacht Championship of the National Camoguidheacht Association, when, at Croke Park yesterday, they defeated Galway in the final by 6-1 (19) to 1-1 (4).
> The large crowd witnessed a spectacular struggle which, even allowing for the fact that the result was a foregone conclusion shortly after half-time, never lost interest. An early lead of four points by Cork was soon wiped off the boards, and for a long time it seemed as if Galway were on the road to their first title.
> In the second half, however, the effortless style and wonderful combination of the Cork team took its toll and they piled on the scores.

1939 Galway-Cork final match report

It is not surprising, therefore, that a 'marriage ban' on players was introduced in certain areas. Old Aloysians (Cork) was one of the clubs that imposed a marriage ban on its playing members so that a player automatically retired on getting married, irrespective of whether she wished to continue or not. This rule was not deleted by the club until 1968. While it was not a written rule, Leinster Council did not select married players for the Gael-Linn Cup competition for many years.

A Game of Our Own

Tragic Year

1939 was a tragic year for camogie. A Dublin motion to congress to have the ban on hockey lifted caused considerable controversy. The motion was strongly opposed by Ulster, Galway and Cork. A vote on the decisive motion was deferred to a special delegate meeting on April 15th. Ulster issued an ultimatum stating that only one delegate from each county would be entitled to vote at the special meeting. When this was refused, the Ulster counties announced that they would not attend and would withdraw from the Central Council if the ban was lifted. Only Leinster delegates attended the special delegate meeting – Dublin had 15 representatives. Together with Kildare, they out-voted the remaining counties present and the ban was rescinded.

Ulster issued an invitation to counties which were in sympathy with the retention of the ban to attend a meeting in Jury's Hotel in Dublin on August 26th, which Rosemary Marron (Antrim) presided. It was their intention to establish a truly national organisation for the promotion of camogie. Delegates from Wexford, Meath and Cork were present as well as those from the Ulster counties. Letters of support were read from Galway, Louth and a few Dublin clubs that were in favour of the retention of the ban. A resolution "that an organisation be formed to promote camogie for all Ireland" was passed.

A new body known as The National Camógaíocht Association was set up with the following officers: patron, His Eminence Cardinal MacRory; president, Mrs Maggie Dunne (Wexford); chairman, Mrs Condon (Meath); secretary/treasurer, Jean McHugh (Antrim); and director of organisation, Mr T. O'Connor (Carlow).

Agnes O'Farrelly, who held the position of Life President of the Camogie Association, had been appointed President of Ulster Council at their AGM at Portadown the previous January and this placed her in an awkward position with a foot in both camps.

Although she did not agree with the ban, she was sympathetic to the Ulster stand, as she considered that they were showing a determination to be Irish at all costs. She stood down temporarily from the position of Life President and adopted the role of intermediary between the two sides of the dispute.

Seán O'Duffy was very distressed over the split. He was in the unhappy position of being in sympathy with the Ulster ideal while, at the same time, maintaining the policy of discipline which is the keynote of any properly conducted organisation. Dublin was the county to which he owed his allegiance and Dublin was the county that carried the ban vote.

A report on the row over the removal or retaining of the ban on hockey

Decline and Controversy

At the first meeting of the new National Camogie Association, it was made clear that they intended to seek the help of the GAA to further their objectives and hoped to stage the All-Ireland final at Croke Park on the first Sunday that the ground was available in November.

Marjorie Dwyer of the Civil Service Club pointed out that the ban would be circumvented time after time. She believed that it had an undesirable effect. It converted girls into "sneaks and spies". Dublin clubs decreased in strength over the period that the ban was enforced, but their internal competitions went ahead.

Britain

Birmingham was slow to take up the game, but, in 1939, three clubs – Kevin Barry's, Granuaile and Inisfáil – were formed. Most of the original players were daughters of Gaelic League members.

The outbreak of the Second World War in September 1939 focused the attention of people to more relevant issues of the day, such as food rationing and how to feed and clothe their families. The result was decline in the interest of all sports, including camogie, and clubs found it difficult to function. Transport was practically at a standstill.

1939 All-Ireland Championship

Cork were unable to fund the trip to Darver for the All-Ireland semi-final against Louth and offered a walkover. Louth refused to accept the free passage to the final, sent Cork their travelling expenses and offered to accomodate the team and officials. Many of the Cork players completed a long day's work before setting off on their journey by car. It was late and pitch dark as the convoy of Cork cars approached Drumisken. As the cars descended the hill into the village, the lights went on and the crowd, who had stayed up into the small hours, ran to welcome their visitors. They

The Galway and Cork teams march behind a girls' pipe band en route from Parnell Square to Croke Park for the 1940 All-Ireland final. Galway are led by their captain, Peg Morris. Lil Kirby heads the Cork team while referee, Vera Campbell (Tyrone), is in the centre.

enjoyed a brilliant game of camogie the following afternoon when Cork won their way to the final by 6–2 to 2–3.

Galway contained the Antrim attack in the second semi-final at MacRory Park, but wasted many chances in front of goal themselves. In a low-scoring game, Galway did enough to advance to the decider by 2–1 to 1–1.

In the All-Ireland final against Galway at Croke Park on November 12th, Cork played in the grey, green and white colours of county champions, Old Aloysians, which provided ten of the starting 12 players. The game was won and lost in midfield where Nan O'Dowd, Lil Kirby and Maura Cronin held sway. Peggy Hogg's faultless display in goal and the excellent cover that she received from full-back Joan Cotter kept the Galway forwards at bay.

The over-worked Galway defence had barely cleared one Cork attack when they were under siege again. Eileen Casey had a hand in all the Cork scores and proved a real thorn in Galway's side. Renee Fitzgerald at full-forward benefited most from Eileen's openings and finished four opportunities to the net. Josie Melvin was heroic in the Galway goal. Peg Morris and Hilda Murphy worked extremely hard for the Connacht side. Cork became the first holders of the National Camoguidheacht Association's championship on the score of 6–1 to 1–1. However, they did not receive the O'Duffy Cup as Dublin, the 1938 winners, failed to hand it over.

Cork team: Peggy Hogg, Joan Cotter, Bríd Cronin, Kathleen Coughlan, Mary Fitzgerald, Nan O'Dowd, Lil Kirby (0–1), Maura Cronin, Kitty Buckley (1–0), Josie McGrath, Eileen Casey (1–0) and Renee Fitzgerald (captain) (4–0).

Galway team: Josie Melvin, Kathleen Keyes, Monica Duggan, Catherine Griffin, Nora O'Connell, Nora Kavanagh, Kathleen Cosgrave, Frances Coen, Hilda Murphy (1–0), Eileen O'Beirne, Peg Morris (captain) (0–1) and Celia Mulholland.

No Foreign Dances

In his address to the 1940 Antrim Convention, the chairman, Seán McKeown, said that 1939 had been a memorable year in the history of the Association. A revolution in the character and control of the national game had taken place and there was an immediate and enthusiastic response from every affiliated county committee in support of their action.

Antrim put the ball in motion to have the ban extended so that any member of the Association known to attend foreign dances would be expelled. The new Association was further boosted when Kildare changed allegiance and came on board. Dublin was then left in isolation.

1940 All-Ireland Championship

Despite travel restrictions caused by the war, the All-Ireland championship was completed. In the only championship match played in Munster, Cork proved too strong for Waterford by 5–3 to 1–4. The match was refereed by dual All-Ireland medallist and future Taoiseach, Jack Lynch.

Cork conceded the venue to their All-Ireland semi-final opponents, Louth, as a gesture to Louth's generosity in the previous

Decline and Controversy

year. Once again, it was Cork goalkeeper, Peggy Hogg, who stood between Louth and a place in the final. She thwarted the Louth sharpshooter, Kathleen Hanratty, on many occasions. Cork's goal scorers, Eileen Casey, Renee Fitzgerald and Kathleen Barry-Murphy carved a 4–3 to 1–5 win.

Cavan were no match for Galway in the second semi-final at the Sports Field. Their positional play and combination were weak. Celia Mulholland, Eileen O'Beirne, Peg Morris and Frances Coen steered Galway to the final by 4–4 to 0–3. Nancy Reilly, Mary Meehan, Mollie Donoghue and Bridie Clarke were the pick of the Cavan side.

Loose marking by Galway and splendid combination by Cork allowed the champions to build up a lead of 4–1 to 0–1 by half-time in the All-Ireland final at Croke Park on October 12th. However, Galway rallied admirably in the second-half. They kept Cork scoreless for the remainder of the game and piled on pressure at the other end. Goals from Peg Morris and Celia Mulholland had Cork's back to the wall but they held out to win by 4–1 to 2–2.

Every Cork player had a hand in the ultimate victory but none more so than Kathleen Coughlan, Mary Fitzgerald and Lil Kirby. Josie Melvin, Kathleen Keyes, Peg Morris, Frances Coen and Kathleen Cosgrove were prominent for Galway. The players were numbered for the first time in an All-Ireland final but, as there was no programme, it did not serve much purpose.

Cork team: Peggy Hogg, Kathleen Coughlan, Maura Brennan, Joan Cotter, Mary Fitzgerald, Kitty Buckley (1–0), Lil Kirby (captain) (1–1), Nan O'Dowd, Patty Hegarty (1–0), Eileen Casey, Renee Fitzgerald (1–0) and Maureen Cashman.

Galway team: Josie Melvin, Kathleen Keyes, Monica Duggan, Catherine Griffin, Nora Conroy, Kathleen Cosgrove (0–1), Frances Coen, Hilda Murphy, Peg Morris (captain) (1–1), Eileen O'Beirne, Nora O'Connell and Celia Mulholland (1–0).

Cork's Kathleen Coughlan was a sister of Eudie Coughlan who captained the Cork hurlers to win the All-Ireland in 1931. Eudie had also won All-Ireland senior medals in 1926, 1928 and 1929. Their father, Pat, was also an All-Ireland senior medal-holder. Mary Fitzgerald was a daughter of Cork hurling goalkeeper, Andy Fitzgerald. Maureen Cashman was a sister of Mick, who played in goal for Cork and Munster and an aunt to hurling All-Stars, Tom and Jim Cashman.

Wedding Bells

In October 1940, the wedding of Seán O'Duffy and Kathleen McKeown took place at Haddington Road church. Kathleen was a native of Omeath, Co. Louth, and had won an All-Ireland with Dublin in 1933. Employed in the Department of Finance, Kathleen became a most respected and much sought-after referee.

Well Done Myself

Speaking at the 1941 Leinster Convention, president, Maggie Dunne (Wexford), said that those present had every reason to congratulate themselves on the progress they had made during the year. Nine counties took part in the championship. The chairman, Mrs Condon (Meath), believed that, "Girls who play camogie should be fit enough to take to the road on their bicycles. Now is the time to show real spirit." A Meath motion was passed giving authority to the referee to stop play when a defender fell while her goal was being rushed.

Ulster expressed delight at the progress in every department and the improved attendances reported at their convention. All nine counties were affiliated. It was decided to place a levy of £2 on clubs for the funds of the Ulster Council.

Paddy O'Keeffe Mediates

In October 1941, Paddy O'Keeffe, General Secretary of the GAA, wrote to both camogie associations stating that, as a result of a wish expressed by some members of his council, he had been asked to try to bring them both together. Mollie Gill and Esther Ryan, officers of the 'old' association, felt that it was not a matter for any outside body to interfere with. Agnes O'Farrelly pointed out that, as the attempts already made had failed, it would be wise to avail of the suggestion. Seán O'Duffy backed her viewpoint and Paddy O'Keeffe was accepted as a mediator by both associations. Mr O'Keeffe and President of the GAA, Pádraig McNamee, met the representatives of both sides.

An agreement was reached at a meeting held on October 26th and ratified at a general meeting on December 7th, 1941. The settlement provided for one body to control the game, with the finances and property of the previously existing bodies being handed over to the new association. Tributes were paid to Agnes O'Farrelly and Seán O'Duffy for their persevering efforts in the cause of unity over the previous two years. Agnes O'Farrelly was re-affirmed as Life President of the Camogie Association. Lil Kirby (Cork) was elected president, Jean McHugh (Antrim) as secretary/treasurer

Dublin, represented by G.S.R. team, and Cork await the signal to commerce the pre-match parade at the 1941 All-Ireland final at Croke Park. Dublin, on left, are headed by their captain, Josie Dempsey and Cork are led by Kitty Buckley.

Decline and Controversy

and Paddy Higgins (Galway) as the director of organisation.

Two long-serving officials, Mollie Gill, who had acted as president since 1923, and Esther Ryan, who filled the role of Ard Runaí from 1932, stepped down. Lil Kirby, the new president, captained UCC to win the Ashbourne Cup. She would go on to win six All-Ireland medals with Cork and was the first woman to chair the Cork Camogie Board.

Cork All-Ireland Winning Teams 1939-41. Back Row: Mary Tuohy, Mary Morris, Kathleen Coughlan, Eily Lyons and Hilda Dempsey. Second Row: Maureen Cashman, May Sheehan, Nan O'Dowd, Joan Cotter, Sheila O'Leary, Maura Cronin, Maura Brennan and Bríd Cronin. Seated: Maureen Hegarty, Peggy Hogg, Renee Fitzgerald, Lil Kirby, Kitty Buckley, Mary Fitzgerald and Patty Hegarty. Front Row: Kathleen Barry, Eileen Casey, Mona Hobbs and Mary Vallelly.

Jean McHugh was a member of the Deirdre Club, Belfast and chaired the Antrim County Board and served as Ard Runaí from 1941 to 1953. Employed by YP Pools, she had a business-like approach to her duties. Paddy Higgins was a brother of Mick Higgins who had captained the Galway footballers to All-Ireland success in 1934. Paddy worked in the printing business and trained the Galway camogie teams for many years. He always addressed the players in his care as 'Miss'.

1941 All-Ireland Championship

Dublin were represented by the GSR club in the 1941 All-Ireland championship. They drew with Cavan 3-3 to 4-0 in the semi-final at Breffni Park but won the replay at Inchicore by 3-4 to 1-1. Cork had an easy passage over Galway at the Mardyke, winning by 8-3 to 0-2.

In the final at Croke Park on October 12th, Cork built up an early lead, rested on it and, when danger threatened, came again to show their strength. Kathleen Coughlan, Kitty Buckley, Lil Kirby, Mona Hobbs and Peggy Hogg stood out on a star-laden Cork side. Kathleen Cody, Mary Bergin and Kathleen Lanigan produced exciting moments for Dublin. Kitty Buckley was in a class of her own and put Cork firmly on the road to victory with six goals. Cork took their sixth All-Ireland title on the score of 7-5 to 1-2.

Cork team: Peggy Hogg, Joan Cotter, Maureen Hegarty, Lil Kirby, Mary Fitzgerald, Kathleen Coughlan (0-3), Mary Vallelly, Mona Hobbs, Patty Hegarty, Kitty Buckley (captain) (6-0), Eileen Casey (1-0) and Kathleen Barry (0-2).

Dublin team: Mary Bergin, Tess Leahy, Eileen Stack, Dolly Byrne, Queenie Hackett, Josie Dempsey, Kathleen Cody (0–2), Kathleen Mills, May Neville, Kathleen Lanigan (1–0), Sheila Cunningham and Laura Blunn.

Maureen and Patty Hegarty were the first twins to win All-Ireland medals. Tess Leahy, the Dublin full-back, was the first Kilkenny girl to play in an All-Ireland final. Her brother, Terry, scored the winning point for Kilkenny in the 1947 All-Ireland hurling final.

Peg Could Not Let the Sides Down

Peg Morris from Headford was an iconic figure on the sports fields of County Galway. Her inter-county career stretched from 1928, when she took part in the Tailteann Games, to 1945. She captained Galway in five All-Ireland finals but finished her career without a coveted medal.

Peg was appointed to referee the 1941 All-Ireland in Croke Park. She learned on the Friday evening that no public transport would run over the weekend because of restrictions caused by The Emergency.

Unwilling to let the teams down, she rose early on the Saturday morning and cycled to her sister's home in Kells, Co. Meath. After a night's rest, she set off for Croke Park early on Sunday and arrived in good time to officiate at the game.

Ulster Colleges' Council

Ulster was the first province to set up a Colleges' Council and inaugurate a provincial, second-level colleges championship. At a meeting in Portadown, an enthusiastic gathering formulated the competition structure, elected Fr John Murphy as president and Maureen Harbinson (Ballynahinch) as secretary. Agnes O'Farrelly donated a beautiful trophy, known as 'Corn Una', for the senior competition. Dominican Convent, Portstewart, played Sacred Heart, Armagh, in the first final at MacRory Park, Belfast. Teams from Ballycastle, Coleraine, Newry, Portstewart, Armagh, Omagh, St Dominic's, Belfast, Dungannon and Kilkeel competed in the early years.

1942 All-Ireland Championship

The coverage of sport in the newspapers was drastically reduced during the war years and the reporting of camogie affairs was practically non-existent. An inter-county championship match might attract a paragraph, but no teams would be listed and, on occasions, only the result was printed.

The appointed Dublin referee for the Cork v. Galway semi-final at the Mardyke failed to put in an appearance so a would-be spectator was cajoled into refereeing the match. An unimpressive start by Galway allowed Cork to build up a big score and Cork were well on the road to victory after 15 minutes play. With their midfield trio in control, the home side ran out winners by 7–4 to 2–0.

Dublin were too slick for Antrim in the second semi-final at Dolphin's Barn. Kathleen Cody provided a splendid service to the Dublin attackers which Doreen Rogers, Kay Mills and Maura

Decline and Controversy

Moore converted into goals. The Antrim defence was unable to cope with the marauding Dublin forwards and saw the game finish with Dublin 12-0 and Antrim 1-0 on the scoreboard.

There was a dramatic ending to the 1942 All-Ireland final between Dublin and Cork at the Mardyke on October 25th. A late goal by Cork's Renee Fitzgerald levelled the scores. The cheers of the home followers had not died down when Renee had the ball back in the Dublin net. Thinking that victory was theirs, delighted Cork fans raced onto the pitch to carry their heroines shoulder high. However, at the far end of the pitch, the Dublin players cheered and hugged one another after Referee J.F. Gleeson (Tipperary) had confirmed to them that he had blown the final whistle before Renee Fitzgerald had put the ball past the Dublin goalkeeper for the second time.

The replay at Croke Park on November 15th was marked by two firsts. Central Council issued a match programme and Radio Éireann broadcast the match with Riobard Bramham as commentator. The Dublin GAA Board cancelled all their fixtures to enable fans to support the girls and, despite travel restrictions, a record crowd attended.

The athleticism and sharp reflexes of the two goalkeepers, Maura O'Carroll (Dublin) and Peggy Hogg (Cork), drew gasps and cheers from the crowd. Mona Hobbs (Cork) had an excellent game and curbed the threat of Kathleen Cody who had made such an impression in the drawn game. However, other Dublin players were on their game, notably Peggy Griffin, Rose Martin, Kathleen Mills and Doreen Rogers. The excellent Dublin defence hooked, blocked and hassled the Cork forwards and severely curtained their effectiveness. Dublin were full value for their 4-1 to 2-2 win.

Dublin team: Maura O'Carroll, Rose Martin, Patty Kenny, Peggy Griffin (captain), Kathleen Kearns (0-1), Eva Moran, Kathleen Cody, Kathleen Mills, Íde O'Kiely, Rose Fletcher (1-0), Doreen Rogers (2-0) and Maura Moore (1-0). Sub used: Josie Kelly.

Cork team: Peggy Hogg (captain), Joan Cotter, Maureen Cashman, Mary Fitzgerald, Maureen Hegarty, Mary Vallely, Kathleen Coughlan, Kathleen Barry, Kitty Buckley (1-2), Patty Hegarty, Eileen Casey (1-0) and Renee Fitzgerald. Sub used: Mona Hobbs.

1942 All-Ireland programme

Congress 1943

At the 1943 Congress, Liam Dynan (Cork) defeated Seán O'Duffy (Dublin) for the post of director of organisation. An inspector with the New Ireland Assurance Company, Liam Dynan proposed to bring out a newspaper devoted entirely to camogie under the name Gaelic Echo, with the first issue being published to coincide with the 1943 All-Ireland final.

Advertisements to the value of £40 were required to meet the cost involved, but he was unable to achieve this goal and the paper was not published. Central Council was willing to back the proposed publication to the figure of £15, but £40 was beyond what their budget would allow.

The playing time of club matches was extended to 50 minutes. A motion to permit a team which commenced a match with only nine players, to finish the game with only nine players was successfully tabled. Prior to that, if the absent players did not arrive before the start of the second half, the team had to concede a walkover.

Dublin and Cork Schools

Íde Bean Uí Shé, the Cork chairman, made contact with Mary Walsh, who was associated with the camogie teams while Íde was a boarder in Eccles Street in Dublin and the two set up a home and away challenge between the Dublin schools and the Cork schools. This event was soon to become the highlight of the schools' year with players looking forward to the trip with great anticipation. The competition ran from 1943 to 1969 when the setting up of the All-Ireland Colleges Championship made this annual challenge redundant.

1943 All-Ireland Championship

Cork were unchallenged in Munster and met Galway in the All-Ireland semi-final at the Mardyke. They had an easy passage over a poor Galway side and won by 6–7 to 1–0. In a low-scoring semi-final at MacRory Park in Belfast, Dublin displayed great appetite for hard work which was necessary to open the tight-marking Antrim defence. However, the Antrim attack made little impression and Dublin recorded a 1–4 to 0–0 victory.

Dublin and Cork provided the most exciting final to date when the sides met at Croke Park on October 17th, with the title being won by the Dublin forwards. Star goalkeeper, Peggy Hogg, was forced to withdraw through illness on the morning of the match. Elizabeth Mulcahy, who was to become one of Ireland's leading fashion designers, scored a goal in the opening minute.

Cork had nobody to match Peggy Griffin, Kay Mills, Kathleen Cody, Íde O'Kiely and Doreen Rogers, and Kathleen Cody showed flashes of brilliance which had the Dublin supporters up on their toes.

Long accurate shots from Kay Mills found her forwards whose marksmanship was deadly. Cork were not equal to the challenge presented by Dublin and had to concede by 8–0 to 1–1.

Dublin team: Maura O'Carroll, Rose Martin, Patty Kenny, Peggy Griffin (captain), Kathleen Kearns, Josie Kelly, Kathleen Cody, Kathleen Mills (1–0), Íde O'Kiely (2–0), Elizabeth Mulcahy (1–0), Doreen Rogers (3–0) and Maura Moore (1–0).

Cork team: Eily Lyons, Mary O'Leary, Maureen Cashman, Mary Fitzgerald, Maureen Hegarty, Kitty Buckley, Kathleen Coughlan (captain), Mona Hobbs, Kathleen Barry, Patty Hegarty (0–1), Eileen Casey (1–0) and Sheila Kelleher.

Decline and Controversy

Rumours Quashed

The question of whether or not camogie was a suitable game for girls raised its head again but Agnes O'Farrelly reacted to nip the issue in the bud. In a statement delivered on March 3rd, 1944 on games for girls, she declared: "While varied views have been expressed, the predominating feeling is that women's games have come to stay, particularly our national game of camogie. The controversy, I believe, will clear the air of misapprehensions and put an end to unauthorised rumours. The real facts that now emerge are that the ecclesiastical authorities are not opposed to camogie. Some of our most distinguished doctors – particularly the gynaecologists – are enthusiastically in favour of the game and energetic boards and councils see that the game is played under strict rules and never to excess."

Dr O'Farrelly emphasised that the utmost precaution was taken by the directors and committees of the camogie organisation to prevent any harmful development of the game. "They are opposed to over strenuousness or to a rigorous course of training for finals such as prevails in the boys' games. The Association has a well-organised system of watchful boards and councils who see to it that the game is not overdone and who suspend, if necessary, players or clubs, who break the rules or indulge in rough behaviour." She used the occasion of the presentation of All-Ireland medals to Dublin players to expand her views. "This national game of ours of which the Cardinal (MacRory) is patron, cannot by any stretch of the imagination be called unwomanly or in any way unsuited to the dignity of our sex."

Agnes O'Farrelly: strong defence of camogie.

The uniform, she said, was becoming and suitable to its purpose. "We have had, time and again, the best medical opinion on the game, and it has been decidedly favourable. We are, besides, convinced from long experience that camogie, properly played, is a boon to Irish womanhood. We have now second generation camogie players – girls whose mothers played the game and who were so convinced of its benefit that they were eager to have their daughters follow in their footsteps. This game had taken root in Irish soil simply because it suited the need of their time and their people. It had nothing to fear if judged by the canons of good taste and suitability."

Dr O'Farrelly's utterances brought a close to the argument. The benefit of having an official of her standing in the Association cannot be overstated.

Where We're At

A move by Dublin to repeal the controversial ban on foreign games reignited the contentious issue and evoked strong feelings in different parts of the country. Many were saddened that the Association, which had made great strides in the previous 30 years, was being ripped apart. Ulster reacted to what they perceived as a perilous position and objected to those who resented their action to protect Gaelic games. Others held that the Association was strong enough to stand on its own two feet and was not endangered by outside influences. They argued against the use of coercion to exist – but, as far as Ulster were concerned, there could be no compromise.

Considerable confusion reigned and the Association was crippled for a decade. Progress made in spreading the game was thrown back 20 years, with some of the greatest players and hardest workers were lost to the game.

Unfavourable comment to competitive sport for girls by a distinguished cleric did nothing to raise spirits and showed how vulnerable the Association was criticism. Once again, prompt action by Agnes O'Farrelly prevented the situation from getting out of hand. Expert medical opinion was sought which proved that there was no foundation to the allegations made.

It was not all doom and gloom during this period. Lovers of the game were thrilled to witness classic exhibitions of camogie by Dublin and Cork. New stars made the headlines: Peggy Griffin, Doreen Rogers, Emmy Delaney, Íde O'Kiely and two youngsters, Kathleen Cody and Kathleen Mills, delighted Dublin fans. While Cork supporters sang the praises of Peggy Hogg, Kathleen Coughlan, Josie McGrath, Joan Cotter and Eileen Casey.

Chapter Six

CORK OUT IN THE COLD

As Tipperary, Waterford and Clare had affiliated to Central Council, the Munster Council was reformed on September 17th, 1944 at a meeting at Cappoquin. Ard Runaí, Jean McHugh, who had attended to Munster business since the council was dissolved in 1937, presided. Cork chairman, Íde Bean Uí Shé outlined the conditions that she required to be fulfilled, including an all-female Munster Council, before she would hand over the cheque for the Cork affiliations.

When her demands were refused, she and Cork secretary, Alice Quigley, left the meeting. Sheila Horgan, the vice-chairman of the Cork Board, who was also at the meeting, did not agree with the actions of her chairman and remained. She submitted affiliations on behalf of Mid-Cork (the Muskerry Divisional Board).

Seán Gleeson (Tipperary) was elected Munster chairman, and Sheila Horgan (Mid-Cork) and Mary Montayne (Waterford) filled the posts of secretary and treasurer. Mid-Cork, which comprised five junior clubs, went into the hat for the championship draw and was paired with Clare.

Delegates at the following meeting of the Cork County Board were shocked to learn about what had happened at Cappoquin. Íde Bean Uí Shé had not been instructed by the Cork County Board to withhold Cork's affiliations and nobody had been aware of her planned action. She considered what she had done to be in the best interests of camogie and that missing out on a championship season was a small price to pay.

The club scene continued as normal in Cork. The full range of leagues and championships were played. The Cork Schools Board carried on as usual. However, it would be eight long years before Cork competed in the Munster or All-Ireland championships.

1944 All-Ireland Championship

Clare, who had defeated Waterford 3–1 to 3–0 in the Munster final, were overwhelmed by Dublin in the All-Ireland semi-final at Inchicore. The Banner County was unable to cope with the superior play of the Dublin girls and conceded by 8–7 to 0–0. The second semi-final between Galway and Antrim at the Galway Sports

Field produced some excellent passages of play. Sheer persistence paid off for Antrim. A late rally yielded a goal by Bridie O'Neill and a place in the final by 3–2 to 2–2.

Dublin had not been tested in the Leinster Championship or against Clare in the semi-final so, to prepare for the final, they travelled to Cork the weekend before the match and took on the home side. Cork won a great match by 3–0 to 1–3. Dublin enjoyed most of the play but found Peggy Hogg in inspired form in the Cork goal. This game put a question mark over the legality of the Dublin team as Cork were not affiliated.

The Bishop of Down and Connor, Dr Daniel Mageean threw in the ball between Dublin and Antrim in the All-Ireland final at Corrigan Park on November 5th. At £111, the gate was only one-third of the previous year's final. The accurate shooting of the Dublin forwards together with the all-round brilliance of Kathleen Cody proved too much for Antrim. However, even though they were well beaten in every sector, Antrim deserved credit for the way they fought – even if their forwards scorned gilt-edged chances. Dublin were never in danger of losing their title and won impressively by 5–4 to 0–0.

> By Our Special Representative.
> **Dublin, 5-4; Antrim, 0-0.**
>
> THE accurate shooting of the Dublin forwards, coupled with the all-round brilliance of K. Cody, proved too much for Antrim in the All-Ireland Camogie final at Corrigan Park, Belfast, yesterday, and the Leinster champions scored 5 goals and four points without reply to retain the trophy.
>
> Though beaten badly in practically every sector, Antrim deserve credit for the manner in which they fought to the final whistle. The shooting of their forwards was poor, however, and had they availed of a few gilt-edge chances which came their way the score might have been vastly different.

1944 match report

Dublin team: Bríd Kenny, Rose Martin, Patty Kenny, Rose Fletcher, Sheila McMahon, Carmel Keogh, Kathleen Cody (2-2), Kathleen Mills, Íde O'Kiely (1–0), Elizabeth Mulcahy (0–2), Doreen Rogers (2–0) and Maura Moore.

Antrim team: Patsy Smith, Marcella Quinn, Betty Stafford, Moya Branigan, Bridie Murray, Marie O'Gorman, Claire McDermott, Winnie Storey, Bridie O'Neill, Mavis Madden, Claire Marshall and Sue McKeown.

Censorship Officer

Ard Runaí, Jean McHugh, reported to the October Central Council meeting that the Minute Book had been taken from her by the Censorship Officer on the train from Belfast. When she explained to him that she required the minutes of the previous meeting, he tore out the relevant pages, handed them to her but retained the Minute Book without giving any specific reason.

Cork Suspended

At a meeting of the Central Council held on January 21st, 1945, a proposal to suspend Cork until such time as they affiliated to the Munster Council was passed by six votes to two. The meeting also decided to regularise the position of Dublin and Antrim, even though both counties had played against illegal or unaffiliated teams.

Mrs Agnes Hennessy (Cavan) defeated Miss Esther Ryan (Dublin) for the position of president at the 1945 Congress. Jean McHugh (Antrim) was opposed for the post of secretary by Eilish Keegan (Dublin) but she held off the challenge. Patrick Higgins

Cork out in the Cold

(Galway) ousted Seán O'Duffy from the role of organiser.

Agnes Hennessy was from Drumgoon, Cootehill, Co. Cavan. She had served as Chairman of the Ulster Council and had been vice-chairman of Cavan County Board from 1935 to 1940 when she became chairman, a post she held until 1948.

Leinster Withdraw

Delegates at a Central Council meeting on May 11th, 1945 learned that the Leinster Council had withdrawn from the Camogie Association. They listed their grievances as: no proper procedure at Central Council meetings; no confidence in Central Council officials; the presence of men at meetings; the Rule Book being out of date; and Liam Dynan (Cork) officiating at matches under the auspices of Central Council while suspended.

Leinster demanded a new constitution, a complete change of officers and a ban on men holding administrative posts at county board, provincial or central council level. Leinster were informed that only congress could make such changes and that the decision of congress would be final.

To complicate matters further, the Combined Universities team travelled to play Cork for the Cronin Cup. Having wiped the slate clean earlier in the year as regards illegal players, many colleges, clubs and counties slipped back into the quagmire.

Ashbourne in Belfast

Noreen Wrenne, niece of founder member, Tadhg O'Donoghue, recalls a visit to Belfast with her UCC colleagues for the 1945 Ashbourne Cup. President Alfred O'Rahilly was reluctant to grant permission to the team to travel over the border into a dangerous war zone. Eventually, however, after a good deal of persuasion, he agreed. The team set off on the long and arduous journey by train which seemed to be powered by turf. The Cork party stayed in Dublin overnight and crossed the border into a grey and sparse landscape the following morning. The first station at which the train stopped was deserted except for soldiers. One of the Cork girls jumped out to investigate and was immediately approached by two Canadian soldiers who enquired if her stick was a "stocking-stretcher".

Many of the Cork girls, prompted by tales of scarcity, brought provisions for the weekend. The abiding memory of the weekend was the céilí with all traditional Irish dances, some of which they had never heard of before. When she remarked to her dancing partner that at home a few old-time waltzes would be on the programme, he replied that in their situation, they have to be completely dedicated to survive. The outstanding impression which she retains from the visit was of the warm hospitality shown to all the visitors by the host committee.

In those days, and for many years afterwards, travelling college teams were chaperoned by middle-aged ladies bearing the title of 'Lady Dean of Residence', or other archaic name, who supervised the activities of the weekend and saw to it that the behaviour of the players was irreproachable and that the good name of the university was upheld at all times.

A Game of Our Own

1945 All-Ireland Championship

With Dublin and Cork, the only two counties to win the All-Ireland title, out of the running, the way was clear for a new champion. Waterford won the Munster championship for the first time when they overcame Tipperary 4–1 to 2–1. They then received a bye to the All-Ireland final as Leinster counties were ineligible to participate. Antrim defended very effectively against Galway in the All-Ireland semi-final at Corrigan Park on September 16th. Celia Quinn, Marie O'Gorman and Marjorie Griffin denied possession and territory to the Galway attack. Bridie O'Neill and Winnie Storey slotted home the scores to register a 3–1 to 1–0 victory for Antrim.

John McCormack, Ireland's world famous tenor, died the week of the final and tributes to him commandeered the newspapers, leaving no coverage for the camogie final. Five cars left Belfast at six o'clock on the Saturday morning and travelled the length of the country. The Antrim girls were mesmerised by the magnificent scenery of the Knockmealdown Mountains as they approached their destination.

Five thousand spectators cheered Antrim and Waterford onto the pitch at Cappoquin for the 1945 All-Ireland final on September 30th. Antrim showed better combination and relied wholly on ground play. The Waterford girls preferred to lift the ball and were dispossessed time and again by the determined tackling of the Antrim players. The speedy Antrim forwards outstretched the home defence in the second-half to add three goals to their half-time tally. Kathleen Rainey, Patsy Smith and Celia Quinn excelled in the Antrim defence. Peg Dooey and Winnie Storey won a lot of ball in midfield. A brace of goals from both Bridie O'Neill and Róisín McCamphill helped Antrim to claim their first All-Ireland title by 5–2 to 3–2.

Bríd McGrath was the outstanding Waterford player on view, while Nellie Breen, Angela Spencer, Maura Curran and Mamie O'Meara all made significant contributions to the game. There was no presentation of the O'Duffy Cup because, despite several requests, Dublin did not return the cup.

Antrim team: Patsy Smith, Celia Quinn, Kathleen Rainey, Marie O'Gorman (captain) (0–1), Marjorie Griffin, Peg Dooey, Claire McDermott, Winnie Storey, Sue McKeown (1–0), Mavis Madden (0–1), Roisin McCamphill (2–0) and Bridie O'Neill (2–0).

Waterford team: Cáit Flynn, Maura Curran, Mamie O'Meara, Nellie Breen, Nora Hennessy, Kitty O'Sullivan (0–1), Bríd McGrath (1–1), Josie McNamara, Teresa Hynes, Angela Spencer, Noreen Healy and May Kennedy (2–0).

Bríd McGrath married Nicholas McGrath, who served as Chairman of the Munster GAA Council. Mamie O'Meara is the only Waterford player to win an All-Ireland senior medal. While working in Dublin, she played for CIÉ and won a coveted medal in 1948.

CAMOGIE NOTES

ANTRIM'S STRONG FINISH SECURES TITLE

Antrim, 5-2; Waterford, 3-2.

The All-Ireland Camogie Final between Antrim and Waterford attracted a record attendance in the Cappoquin Sports Field on Sunday last. Under ideal weather conditions and on a splendidly prepared pitch, the spectators were treated to a fine display, which kept them thrilled during the first half. Remarkable speed and stamina were displayed by both teams, but Antrim showed better combination. The half-time score found them level at 2-2 each, with a disallowed goal for Antrim. Antrim showed up to better advantage in the second half and kept the Waterford defenders under great pressure, in the course of which several fine saves were effected by K. Flynn, the Waterford goalie; but the Northern colleens continued to hold the mastery and were deserving winners of a brilliant game on the final score of 5-2 to 3-2. Mr. Frank Gleeson, Chairman, Tipperary Co. Board, refereed.

1945 match report

Cork out in the Cold

Unofficial All-Ireland Final

The suspended players were not short of match practice. A Leinster selected side made a trip to the Mardyke when they took on but lost to Cork on June 24th, 1945. Cork and Dublin drew in Croke Park in an unofficial All-Ireland final on October 14th. The match was replayed at the Mardyke on November 18th when Dublin came out on top. The winners received a set of hurleys presented by Denis Guiney, Managing Director of Clery & Co. Ltd. Dublin's second string, with Nell McCarthy, future president of the Association, at full-back, took on the Fingal League (North Dublin) in a curtain-raiser to the Croke Park finals.

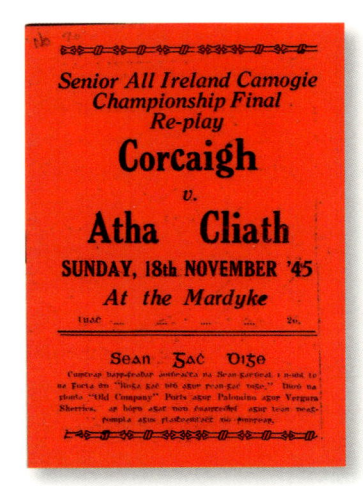

Unofficial 1945 All-Ireland programme

Congress 1946

The 1946 Congress saw several changes in personnel. Shortly after her election as president, Agnes Hennessy's husband died suddenly and she did not seek re-election. Sheila Horgan (Mid-Cork) was elected in her place. The positions of secretary and treasurer were separated, with Jean McHugh retaining the former and Mary Montayne (Waterford) holding the purse strings. Seán Gleeson (Tipperary) was elected organiser.

Sheila Horgan in her playing days

From Ballinora, Co. Cork, Sheila Horgan kept Mid-Cork affiliated to the Camogie Association during the years that the Cork County Board was on the outside. She held many positions in Cork and Munster. Mary Montayne was a gifted music teacher and choir conductor. She set up a School of Music and produced musicals in Mitchelstown where she settled with her husband, Jack Keane. A native of Clogheen, Co. Tipperary. Seán Gleeson taught in the local Vocational School. He was a founder of Féis na Suire and regional secretary of Muintir na Tíre. He married Marie O'Shea, a native of Bantry, who played camogie while at school at St Louis, Monaghan.

Fundraising

Raising funds has always been a problem in camogie circles. Before the advent of sponsorship, funds had to be raised to cover all outgoings. There were the hardy annuals – raffles, church door collections, flag days and cake sales. The church door collection was more effective in rural areas where neighbours would have to pass the table manned by hand-picked club members. On the other hand, the constant flow of shoppers on a busy street made the Flag Day a better choice in the cities and large towns.

'Guest Teas' were popular in Belfast. A club would secure the use of a hall and fit in as many tables with chairs as possible. The morning was spent making tea cakes. Each club member was assigned to a table. She invited her family, friends, neighbours or anyone she could drag along to fill the table and charged them two shillings, or two shillings and six pence if she could get away with it. When all were seated and fully paid up, plates of cakes and pots of hot tea were produced. Was that the forerunner of corporate lunches?

Rallying Song

A new Gaelic rallying song for the national women's game was written by 'Una Uladh' (Dr Agnes O'Farrelly, Life President of the Camogie Association) and set to a marching air by Professor J. F. Larchet, was sung for the first time by Idé Ní Cadhlaigh, the well-known Dublin player. She performed it at a reception for university players at the UCD Club at St. Stephen's Green where inter-faculty medals were presented.

1946 All-Ireland Championship

Very few teams entered the All-Ireland Championship in 1946. Because of the defection of Leinster, Antrim received a bye at the semi-final stage. In the other semi-final it looked like Clare would win a historic appearance in an All-Ireland final, when a late rally by Galway snatched victory from their grasp. Had Clare more players of the calibre of Chris Markham, Theresa McNamara and Nora Glynn, they would have been regular visitors to Croke Park.

The well-known hurling referee, Mick Hennessy (Clare) got the 1946 All-Ireland final going between Antrim and Galway at Corrigan Park on September 29th. This young, fit Galway side was considered the best to represent the county. Seven of the team were aged between 16 and 18 and were the future of Galway camogie.

The conditions at Corrigan Park were not up to standard for an All-Ireland final. Thick grass, four to five inches long, covered the pitch and a second set of posts stood close to those in use. Even with that, the game was full of thrills and exciting passages of play. The fast-covering Antrim defenders tackled resolutely and cleared to safety. Winnie Storey was moved to midfield where she played the game of her life. Sue McKeown, Mavis Madden, Kathleen Dooey and Nancy Milligan fought heroically for Antrim who were two points ahead at the break.

Annie McDermott and Rita Clinton were excellent in midfield for Galway. Monica Duggan and Patsy Noone tackled decisively but up front only Celia Mulholland was effective for the Connacht side. Interest in the game never flagged and the outcome lay in the balance until the final whistle when the score stood at Antrim 4–1, Galway 2–3.

Galway sent a letter of protest to the Central Council con-

Antrim, 4-1; Galway, 2-3.

A CROWD represented by a £250 "gate" was delighted by the series of thrilling exchanges in the All-Ireland camoguidheacht final at Corrigan Park, Belfast, yesterday, in which Antrim beat Galway 4-1 to 2-3 to retain the title.

Galway, the stronger side at close quarters, were more decisive in the tackles on the heavy grass-coated pitch but Antrim's speed and forward combination swayed the game in the champions favour in the closing stages. Galway opened like winners, striking in facile fashion but finding the Antrim defenders putting up a stout resistance. For a period the Antrim forwards could not get the ball to run for them on the slow surface and they missed several chances by trying to raise the ball.

Galway dominated at centre-field, where A. McDermott and R. Clinton lifted and hit almost at will. However, in the second half, W. Storey came back to strengthen the Antrim centre-field, and, playing brilliantly, initiated the attacks that won Antrim the match.

The Galway backs—M. Duggan, B. Glynn, and F. Moore tackled and cleared decisively, but were often outpaced by M. Madden and S. McKeown, extremely fast Antrim forwards.

Only C. Mulholland, Galway's best forward, and J. Melvin could evade the fast covering Antrim backs, K. Dooey, C. Quinn, M. Griffen and K. Rainey.

THE SCORERS

Goals by S. McKeown and M. Madden in reply to a point by A. McDermott and a goal by C. Mulholland gave Antrim an interval lead of 2-0 to 1-1.

W. Storey (1-0), S. McKeown (1-0) and E. Henry (0-1) completed Antrim's total in the second half, whilst R. Clinton (1-0), J. Melvin (0-1) and A. McDermott (0-1) scored for Galway.

1946 match report in The Irish Independent

cerning the condition of the pitch, requesting the council to put up a set of medals for a challenge match between the two counties at Croke Park. The council agreed for Galway's demand but Croke Park was not available.

Antrim team: Mary Ann Donnelly, Celia Quinn, Kathleen Rainey, Kathleen Dooey, Marjorie Griffin (captain), Nancy Milligan, Patsy Smith, Ita O'Reilly, Mavis Madden (1–0), Winnie Storey (1–0), Sue McKeown (2–0) and Eithne Henry (0–1).

Galway team: Kathleen McGinn, Catherine Griffin, Monica Duggan (captain), Patsy Noone, A. Glynn, M. Lohan, Annie McDermott (0–2), Rita Clinton (0–1), Kitty Greally, K. P. Greally, Josie Melvin and Celia Mulholland (2–0).

Another New Organisation

A new body, Coltas Camógaíochta na hÉireann, was formed in Dublin on April 21st, 1947. Mrs Lucy Byrne (Wicklow) was elected president and Alice Quigley (Cork) became secretary. The new association attracted affiliations from Wicklow, Meath, Laois,

Antrim's exploits celebrated in a local magazine.

Louth and Cork who believed that the existing body had not exercised proper control.

Later in the year, Coltas Camógaíochta na hÉireann organised an All-Ireland Championship. The final, between Meath and Cork, was staged at Ashbourne on November 2nd. Following a keen and interesting struggle, the game ended in a draw, two goals apiece. There is no record of a replay.

Frustrated by lack of inter-county action and the ongoing squabbling, the CIÉ club formed an alternative Dublin County Board on September 30th, with club members filling the key positions. Inter-county star, Kathleen Cody took the chair and her deputy was another Dublin player, Sophie Brack. Joan Cosgrave and Brenda Neville filled the roles of secretary and treasurer. However, the expected flow of affiliations from other Dublin clubs did not take place. Not wishing to see another splinter group, the Central Council advised the CIÉ club to affiliate directly to them and to drop the idea of a second Dublin County Board. This advice was accepted and CIÉ represented Dublin in the 1948 All-Ireland Championship.

The Leinster Council was disbanded and an entirely new one

formed on September 6th. It started with Kildare, Kilkenny and one Dublin club, CIÉ. However, it shortly attracted affiliations from Laois, Carlow and Wexford. William Fisher (Kildare) led the new council and had strong supporters in P. Tuite (Carlow), Bill Keogh (Kilkenny) and Patrick O'Donovan (Wexford).

1947 All-Ireland Championship

The Tipperary players and officials paid their own expenses to Belfast for the All-Ireland semi-final against Antrim at Corrigan Park. The county board was already burdened by debt and could not afford to go deeper into the financial mire. In a see-saw game, the pendulum swung from side to side with Antrim having the final say by 5–2 to 4–1. Eileen Walsh (Tipperary) and Bridie O'Neill (Antrim) were major players with three goals apiece.

The CIÉ club team represented Dublin in the 1947 All-Ireland Championships. The semi-final, between Dublin and Galway at Ballinasloe, ended in disorder with hundreds of spectators rushing onto the field to voice their displeasure at the referee, Mr. B. McDonnell (Wicklow). The gardaí restored order and escorted the referee away by car. Disagreements with the referee's decisions started early in the game and developed into the angry protests seen at the end. Galway led by 2–1 to 0–1 at the interval but scores from Kathleen Cody and Kathleen Mills swung the game in Dublin's favour to win by 2–3 to 2–1.

The CIÉ team representing Dublin in 1948

In the closing minutes of the All-Ireland final between Dublin and Antrim at Corrigan Park on November 9th, Kathleen Cody raced through the Antrim defence and sent a pile-driver goalwards. The ball sank in the sea of mud that filled the goal area before the Antrim goalkeeper, Kathleen Madden, fished out the ball and cleared it to safety. Dublin appeals that the ball had crossed the line were not entertained and Antrim retained their title.

Antrim had got off to a great start and had 1–1 on the scoreboard within five minutes. Tremendous play by those two greats of the game, Kathleen Cody and Kathleen Mills, brought Dublin back into contention, but neither side was able to dominate the game. Antrim, who had been well prepared by Dublin man, Charlie McMahon, held out to win by 2–4 to 2–1 and achieved a hat-trick of All-Ireland titles.

Antrim team: Kathleen Madden, Celia Quinn (captain),

Nancy Milligan, Kathleen Dooey, Marjorie Griffin, Kathleen Rainey, Mavis Madden (0–4), Mary McGarry, Mary Keenan, Rita McGarry, Sue McKeown and Bridie O'Neill (2–0).

Dublin team: Rita Manifold, Teresa O'Donoghue, Catherine Bowler, May Fitzpatrick, Carmel Nulty, Thelma Tighe, Kathleen Cody, Kathleen Mills, Brenda Neville, Joan Cosgrave (1–0), May Neville and Sophie Brack (1–1).

Emigration

In the aftermath of the Second World War, America opened up for immigration. England, too, looked for workers to rebuild their cities, industries and services. Ireland had the highest rate of female emigration between 1945 and 1960 of any country in Europe.

The 1948 Down team

Girls, particularly in rural areas, who had seen their own mothers prematurely worn out by constant physical work, thought that there must be a better life somewhere else. The son inherited the farm, leaving nothing for the girls so many had to emigrate. These conditions affected camogie and clubs that could not field teams folded.

It was no surprise that the game flourished in Britain and America from 1948 onwards. The new arrivals from Ireland joined the established Irish communities. London, Lancashire and Warwickshire got a new lease of life and applied to Central Council for permission to set up a provincial council and organise inter-county competitions. This council was formed on July 11th, 1948 with Mr T. Ryan (Tipperary) as chairman.

A number of teams were also formed in New York. They practised in Van Courtland Park and played against each other on Saturday evenings or before the regular GAA matches on Sundays at Gaelic Park. The most successful club was Pride of Erin and the most outstanding player was Bridie O'Neill, who had won three All-Ireland medals with Antrim. The team was trained by Tom Flynn (Waterford) and included Margaret Logue (Donegal), Hannah Dowling (Kerry), Nancy Morley (Clare), Terry O'Hanlon (Clare), Nellie Coughlan (Westmeath), Ann Sharkey (Mayo), Phyllis O'Grady (Roscommon), Myra Kennedy (Galway), Josie Flynn (Carlow), Mary Tarpey (Mayo) and Kathleen Quain (Cork).

Deep-Rooted Views

The idea of women taking part in sport was still frowned upon.

The benefits to be derived from physical exercise were ignored. When Fannie Blankers-Koen, a superbly talented athlete from Holland, won four gold medals at the 1948 Olympics, Pope Pius XII deplored the participation of women in athletics.

Dublin and Cork still remained outside the Camogie Association. A crying need for unity existed and unity meetings, aimed at bringing all counties back into the Association, were organised. However, progress was slow as the various parties clung to their own point of view.

1948 All-Ireland Championship

Kathleen Cody carved gaps in the Tipperary defence and struck some glorious points in the All-Ireland semi-final against Dublin at Roscrea. Tipperary were limited in attack and conceded by 1–5 to 1–1. Down, who had defeated Derry by 4–5 to 1–0 at Kilclief to win their first Ulster title, caused something of a shock against Galway in the second semi-final at Renmore. Galway ran out of steam against a much faster and fitter Down side and were beaten by 1–4 to 1–1.

As Croke Park was not available for a Sunday fixture, the All-Ireland final between Dublin and Down was played on Saturday night, October 23rd. Down were badly affected by nerves in what was their first appearance in Croke Park. With superior skill and combination, Dublin were comfortably placed, 5–1 to 1–2, at the break. Down made a much better go of it in the second-half but could not catch up and Dublin, represented by the CIÉ club team, won impressively by 11–4 to 4–2. Subsequently, London challenged Dublin for their title at Croke Park but were heavily defeated by 9–3 to 2–2.

Dublin team: (CIÉ) Rita Manifold, Mamie O'Meara, Catherine Bowler, May Fitzpatrick, Carmel Nulty, Jean Hannon (0–1), Kathleen Cody (3–1), Kathleen Mills (0–1), Brenda Neville (2–0), Joan Cosgrave (3–0), May Neville and Sophie Brack (3–1).

Down team: Bernie Kelly, Anna Kerr, Rosaleen Denvir, Peg Dooey (2–2), Kathleen Mallon, Jean McGrath, Sheila Keary (1–0), Anna Hollywood, Una Kelly, Mary Foy (1–0), Betty Curran and Angela Denvir.

Where We're At

Readers must wonder how an individual could withdraw Cork from the Association and get away with it. I have put that question to camogie people of the time and the usual reply was 'we were unable to challenge her'. Íde Bean Uí Shé lectured in Irish at UCC, whereas many of the delegates that attended the Cork County Board had left school in their early teens. If someone disputed the point with her, she immediately switched to speaking Irish, leaving the delegate at a disadvantage. On the other hand, some delegates were happy to let Íde lead the way and they followed without question. The situation dragged on for years. Eventually, Old Aloysians came up with the idea of making her Life President of the Cork Board. She was delighted with the honour. A new chairperson was elected and Cork affiliated.

The Leinster counties withdrew from the Association in May 1945, listing a catalogue of grievances. This was the darkest hour

Cork out in the Cold

in the history of the Association. Between the counties that had withdrawn and those which had fallen by the wayside, only a few remained to contest the All-Ireland championship. There was no entry from Leinster, Tipperary and Waterford played in Munster, Galway received a bye in Connacht and a few Ulster counties participated.

1947 saw another new camogie body formed and the Leinster Council disbanded. A completely new Leinster Council was formed but it was only able to attract two counties to affiliate. Distrust and lethargy held sway and there was a crying need for strong leadership.

My earliest memories are of holidays in my grandmother's farmhouse in the midlands in the late forties. The place was a hive of activity, indoors and outdoors, with every job time-consuming and labour-intensive. Neither electricity nor running water had reached that part of the country and the women were in the kitchen before seven o'clock in the morning, stoking the range and putting on pots of water to boil in preparation for the day's work. They remained on their feet all day, attending to a never-ending list of chores. It was nine o'clock in the evening before the day's work was done and they could sit down.

Giving a commitment to any outside leisure pursuit was not a reality during the week. There was only free time on Sundays when, because of religious observance, only essential work was carried out. Where an event like a fete was on, which attracted all members of the household, the pony and trap was taken out and all travelled together. Occasions like this provided an opportunity to play a match. There was no organised training but those women were strong and constantly active and the exertions of a match would have presented no problems to them.

A Game of Our Own

Happy Camogie Players!

Chapter Seven

DUBLIN'S PHENOMENAL RUN

A lady, who was to have an immense impact on the direction and development of the Camogie Association, was elected president at the 1949 Congress. From Warrenpoint, Co. Down, Sheila McAnulty led the Association in a professional manner. With foresight, acumen and idealism, she guided the path of camogie for 50 years.

Managing Director of A. E. Arthur Walker & Co., she served the Camogie Association at many levels, including as Secretary of the Down County Board, Chairman of the Ulster Council, Ard Runaí (1953–1975), President of All-Ireland Primary Schools and a trustee (1985–2004). In 1999, she was honoured with the title Life President of the Camogie Association. Sheila immediately set about bringing all sides together with the aim of complete unity in the Association. The Leinster Council held an informal meeting with the unaffiliated counties with Sheila acting as chairman and, within a short space of time, all counties with the exception of Cork were affiliated to the Camogie Association.

Sheila McAnulty

Suspension of University Players

The Galway, Antrim and Dublin county boards suspended for six months the university players who had taken part in the Ashbourne Cup as they had played against UCC, which was unaffiliated at the time.

An application made by Fidelma Byrne and Frances Owens of the Deirdre Club in Belfast, for a reduction of the sentence was not entertained by Central Council.

Consideration was given to the idea of using a full-length hurling pitch and 15-a-side teams at the Central Council in February 1949.

Counties were asked to discuss the matter and form an opinion. However, 50 years elapsed before the change was made.

1949 All-Ireland Championship

With Dublin back in the fold, a full representative side, which only included Kathleen Cody and Sophie Brack of the CIÉ team that had played in the 1948 final, took the field against Down in the All-Ireland semi-final at Kilclief. Dublin's greater skill and experience stood them in good stead as they defeated Down by 3–4 to 1–3. Tipperary and Galway met in a well-contested semi-final at Roscrea. Mary Ann O'Brien was outstanding at centre-back for Tipperary and instrumental in their 3–2 to 1–3 victory.

Even though the 1949 All-Ireland final at Roscrea on October 30th was played in a constant downpour, the standard of play was high. The Tipperary defence was unable to cope with the penetrating runs and lethal finish of Kathleen Cody and she proved the difference between the sides. Mary Ann O'Brien, Terry Griffin and Joan Maher strove tirelessly to turn the tide in Tipperary's favour, but the failure of the Tipperary forwards to finish some good movements was costly. In addition to Kathleen Cody, Rose Fletcher, Doreen Rogers and Sophie Brack made a major contribution to Dublin's 8–6 to 4–1 victory.

Dublin team: Eileen Duffy, Anna Young, Patricia O'Connor, Rose Fletcher, Mona Walsh, Nancy Caffrey, Kathleen Cody (6–7), Mary Kelly, Kathleen O'Keeffe (1–0), Pat Raftery, Doreen Rogers (captain) (1–0) and Sophie Brack.

Tipperary team: Marie Flanagan, Terry Griffin, Mary Ann O'Brien (1–1), Madeline Bowers (captain), Kitty Gleeson, Kitty Callanan, Mary Power, Joan Maher, Eileen Walsh (2–0), May Hynes, Maura Curran and Margaret Walsh. Sub used: Lizzie Aherne (1-0).

London's Challenge

Less than 18 months after the revival of camogie in Britain, the British champions, London, challenged Dublin at Croke Park on December 4th. The London side was drawn from three clubs – Cuchulainn's, Sarsfield's and St Monica's – and the players had the additional handicap of adapting to the smaller space as matches

Group of Camogie Officials 1949. Seated: Seán O'Duffy, Inez O'Kelly, Jean McHugh and Sheila McAnulty. Included at back are: Maureen Smyth, Noreen Murphy, Maura Nicholson, Eileen Keating, Lily Spence, Patricia McGeough, Eilish Redmond, Riobard Bramham, Nell McCarthy, Peggy McGee, Kathleen O'Duffy, Molly Murphy, Muriel Munnelly and Sophie Brack.

Dublin's Phenomenal Run

Tipperary and Galway in the 1949 semi-final.

in London were played on a full-sized hurling pitch. Dublin had a comfortable win by 9–3 to 2–2. The London team comprised N. Waters, B. Ennis, J. Keohane, K. O'Reilly, K. Waters, N. Collins, B. Kelly, A. Lee, M. Ward (captain), M. Kelly, I. Cotter and L. Ward.

Financial Loss

The sequel to the 1949 All-Ireland final was the main topic of discussion at the 1950 Congress. Croke Park was not made available to stage the Dublin v. Tipperary decider. The gate receipts at Roscrea had been wiped out by the expenses incurred in staging the event, the most disconcerting being a large bill submitted by local stewards. The Dublin supporters, who regularly flocked to Croke Park to cheer their favourites, did not venture to Roscrea, with the result that the admission returns were way down on other years. They were not the only ones to stay at home. The Radio Éireann broadcast unit remained at base, leaving the country in the dark about what was happening at Roscrea.

Central Council ruled that all teams taking part in the Ashbourne Cup competition must be affiliated and that UCD, as hosts, would be responsible for conveying the directive to the remaining universities. However, the universities ignored the order, and each college played the unaffiliated UCC in turn. A side captained by Eileen Bourke brought the much-coveted trophy to UCD. In due course, UCD, UCG and Queen's University were suspended by their county boards.

1950 All-Ireland Championship

Galway opened their All-Ireland semi-final against Dublin at Parnell Park in impressive fashion and, inside a minute, had 1–1 on the scoreboard. However, Kathleen Cody and Kathleen Mills took command of midfield and monopolised the play, leading to

1949 All-Ireland match report

a comfortable 9–7 to 2–1 win for Dublin. Antrim had an easy assignment at Corrigan Park in the second semi-final. They were in no danger at any time from a Tipperary side that struggled to find form. Goals from Madge Rainey, Sarah O'Neill and Mary Rua McGarry reserved a place for Antrim in the final.

The final at Croke Park on December 3rd exceeded all expectations. Antrim matched Dublin puck for puck. Level at half-time and finely balanced for three quarters of the contest, it was only in the closing minutes that Dublin's superiority began to show. A brace of goals from Sophie Brack and another major by Patsy Cooney put a gloss on the scoreboard, 6–5 to 4–1 in Dublin's favour.

Dublin team: Eileen Duffy, Nan Mahon, Anna Young, Sadie Hayes, Mona Walsh, Nancy Caffrey, Kathleen Cody (0–4), Kathleen Mills (0–1), Patsy Cooney (2–0), Joan Cosgrave (1–0), Pat Raftery (captain) and Sophie Brack (3–0).

Antrim team: Betty McFaul, Peg Dooey (captain), Moya Forde, Kathleen Dooey, Geraldine Swindles, Sue McMullan, Mary McGarry, Ethna Dougan, Sarah O'Neill, Madge Rainey (2–0), Mary McKeever (2–0) and Mary Rua McGarry (0–1).

Dublin, subsequently, crossed the Irish Sea to play London at

The victorious 1950 Dublin team

Mitcham. The ball was thrown in by Mrs Frances Boland, wife of the Irish ambassador. Without having to perform to their full potential, the champions won readily by 8–2 to 1–2.

Trustees Appointed

Congress appointed trustees for the first time in 1951; Iney O'Kelly (Dublin) and Paddy Higgins (Galway) were the first holders of the posts. Kathleen Cody (Dublin) was elected treasurer and her father, Michael Cody (Dublin), filled the position of national organiser.

Counties and clubs continued to suffer as emigration limited the number of players. Limerick conceded a walkover to Tipperary in the Munster championship. The only game played in the competition was a runaway win by Tipperary over Kerry. The number of counties competing in the provincial championships was reduced to seven for Leinster, five for Ulster and three for Connacht.

Camogies' best year in a decade

THIS was camogie's best year in a decade. New clubs sprang up in every province, and so high was the standard of play that the game grows steadily in popularity.

Five counties took part in the Munster championship. In a fast final Tipperary proved too strong and clever for Limerick and retained the title which they held in 1949.

SEVEN COUNTIES

Competition in Ulster was never so keen and seven counties played in the Senior Championship. The final was reached by the old rivals— Down (holders) and Antrim. This time Antrim won

MORE CLUBS

The number of affiliated teams in Leinster was doubled. In Dublin half-a-dozen new clubs were affiliated.

The first all-Ireland Camogie Semi-Final proved a big surprise. Tipperary travelled to Corrigan Park, Belfast, with abundant confidence, but were beaten by a fine Antrim side.

TITLE FOR DUBLIN

In the second semi-final, played at Parnell Park, Dublin, Galway, the Connacht champions, fully extended Dublin for 25 minutes before the home county won. In the final, played at Croke Park, Dublin, on December 3rd, Dublin beat Antrim by 6-5 to 4-1

The view of 1950

Dublin's Phenomenal Run

The gap in standards between Dublin and the remaining Leinster counties led to a motion being tabled at the Leinster Convention to divide Dublin into two counties for camogie purposes. Needless to say, the Dublin delegates were not happy at the suggestion and, following some discussion, it was withdrawn.

Cork Back in the Fold

Following a series of meetings involving officials of the Central Council, the Munster Council and the Cork County Board, a cheque for Cork's affiliations was handed over to the Munster Council in November 1951. The cloud that had hung over Cork for eight years was lifted and it was all systems go as Cork directed all their energy to getting things moving again. All the players who brought glory to the county in the early forties had retired. Indeed, some players missed out on the honour of representing their county in championship camogie because they had peaked and hung up their boots before the rift was healed. A five-point defeat to the Combined Universities highlighted the amount of work that Cork had to make up.

1951 All-Ireland Championship

London entered the All-Ireland Championship at the quarter-final stage and created something of a shock by defeating Galway, 3–4 to 2–2 at The Sportsground. Although well beaten by a better Antrim combination, London never gave up trying in the semi-final at New Eltham. Deirdre O'Gorman, Moya Forde and Peg Dooey were at their best for the Antrim side and were hugely instrumental in their county's 5–1 to 0–1 win. However, in Nora Scully, London had one of the best performers on view and she was well supported by Kathleen Waters, Noreen Collins and Bridie Ennis.

Tipperary opened the scoring in the second semi-final against Dublin at Roscrea but were under constant pressure for the remainder of the match. Dublin's forward play was incisive and accurate and propelled them to a comprehensive 6–6 to 0–1 victory.

Eileen Duffy performed heroics in the Dublin goal as her keen anticipation and lengthy clearances foiled Antrim in the All-Ireland final at Croke Park on August 19th. Time and again, Kathleen Cody raced through the Antrim defence in awesome fashion to set up scoring opportunities for her inside-forwards. Kathleen spelled a kind of magic. She was responsible for the introduction of a new style of play. While her Dublin colleagues played predominately on the ground, Kathleen popularised the quick lift, solo run and powerful striking.

With accuracy from Sophie Brack, Eileen Bourke and Annie Donnelly, the scores started to flow. On the other side, Antrim

1951 final report

fell below expectations. They seemed overawed in the opening quarter when Dublin laid the foundations to their 8–6 to 4–1 victory. The Northerners fought back with tenacity, none more so than Geraldine Swindles, Sarah O'Neill and Ethna Dougan, however, a three-goal blitz by Dublin midway through the second-half sealed Antrim's fate.

Dublin team: Eileen Duffy, Nan Mahon, Carmel Walsh, Deborah Dunne, Mona Walsh, Joan Cosgrave, Kathleen Cody (0–3), Kathleen Mills (0–1), Patsy Cooney (1–0), Annie Donnelly (1–0), Eileen Bourke (2–0) and Sophie Brack (captain) (4–2).

Antrim team: Pat Rafferty, Nancy Murray, Moya Forde, Deirdre O'Gorman, Geraldine Swindles, Ethna Dougan (0–1), Sue McMullen, Mary McGarry, Madge Rainey (1–0), Sarah O'Neill (1–0), Mary McKeever (2–0) and Mary Rua McGarry.

Death of Agnes O'Farrelly

Following a long illness, Agnes O'Farrelly, Life President of the Camogie Association, died on November 5th, 1951. In a tribute to her, Sheila McAnulty referred to the great loss her death caused the Association.

> "Her name was revered and honoured by every member. Agnes was a guide, philosopher and personal friend to everyone with whom she came in contact. On many occasions, she saved us when we were apt to make rash decisions. She was one of that band of gallant workers who kindled the flame of nationality when it was but a flickering ember. No one can replace her and the greatest tribute we can pay her is to keep alive the high ideals of the Association for which she unselfishly lived and worked."

Sheila's Term Extended

Sheila McAnulty had been very involved in meetings aimed at bringing together all counties under the one umbrella. While she had made significant progress, a tiny minority had strayed again and the early fifties remained a critical time for the Association. A period of consolidation was necessary. In the circumstances, the term of office of Sheila McAnulty as President of the Camogie Association was extended to a fourth year. National organiser, Michael Cody, did not seek re-election, owing to illness, and was replaced by Seán O'Duffy.

Cualacht Camógaíochta na hÉireann, the last of the fringe associations, held what was to be its final congress in 1951, where a motion to permit players to declare for the county of their choice was passed. However, before any player availed of this permission, the association folded.

Motorised Transport

Horses, wartime petrol shortages and trains running on turf were dim and distant memories to the camogie teams of the fifties. Cars and buses were the way to go. But what had not changed was the attitude to spending money. If possible, no outlay was incurred. Players were packed into cars and vans and if transport had to be hired, the cheapest option was sought. A lorry could be hired for £2 and, with the cribs in place, could hold 35 standing. At two shillings a head for supporters, it did not cost the club too much to get the team to the venue.

New cars and buses were few and far between. What was available was old and unreliable. Overheated engines, punctures, snapped fan belts and malfunctioning fuel gauges causing the driver run out of petrol were all part and parcel of getting to a match. Stranded on the side of the road watching black smoke gush from the engine with no means of contacting anybody is a memory shared by many camogie players. Somebody always came to the rescue, though, and got the vehicle going again.

1952 All-Ireland Championship

A national newspaper strike that spanned the period of the All-Ireland championship impinged on the interest in the competition and curtailed attendances. Following an eight-year absence from the inter-county scene, Cork returned to take the Munster title in emphatic fashion. Over 3,000 followers turned up at Casement Park to witness a marvellous contest between Antrim and Cork in the All-Ireland semi-final. Not yet up to the speed of inter-county camogie, Cork were spreadeagled by the speedy Antrim forwards and lost by 3–2 to 1–6. Galway, who had overcome Mayo by 3–2 to 3–0 in the Connacht final, failed to find any sort of form in the second semi-final against Dublin. The statistics show that Galway lost the match by the substantial margin of 9–5 to 0–1.

Kathleen Cody, who for many years had been a tower of strength on the Dublin side, had retired and was replaced by a young UCD student, Annette Corrigan, who would also make a considerable impact on the team. Dublin were lucky to emerge with two points to spare, 5–1 to 4–2, from a great final on August 10th. The Celtic Club supplied the entire Dublin defence. Goalkeeper Eileen Duffy, her sister Pauline, Carmel Walsh, Doretta Blackton and Deborah Dunne all denied the Antrim forwards goal

Antrim and Dublin react to the throw-in at the 1952 All-Ireland final.

chances. Ita O'Reilly, Sue McMullan, Maeve Gilroy, Madge Rainey and Anne McGarry were outstanding in everything they did in the colours of Antrim. Neither side was able to impose themselves on the game and the margin between the teams was rarely more than a single score. The experienced Dublin captain, Sophie Brack, slipped through the Antrim cover in the last minute for the winner. The score stood at Dublin 5–1, Antrim 4–2 as Celia Mulholland (Galway) blew the final whistle.

Dublin team: Eileen Duffy, Doretta Blackton, Carmel Walsh, Deborah Dunne, Pauline Duffy, Nancy Caffrey, Annette Corrigan (0–1), Kathleen Mills, Eileen Bourke (1–0), Nan Mahon (1–0), Marie Price and Sophie Brack (3–0).

Antrim team: Anne McGarry, Moya Forde, Peg Dooey, Mary McGarry, Deirdre O'Gorman, Sue McMullan, Ita O'Reilly, Maeve Gilroy (0–2), Sarah O'Neill, Mary McKeever, Madge Rainey (2–0) and Fionnuala Forde (1–0).

Lucy Byrne New President

In her final address as President of the Camogie Association, Sheila McAnulty said that she was pleased at the progress made by the schools and colleges, but deplored that some schools considered only foreign games to be fashionable. She projected a true image when she admitted: "Women were gradually assuming control of the organisation but this would have to come gradually as, in several parts of the country, women were not quite ready to assume control." She lamented the sparse publicity afforded the game.

Dublin and Tipperary come together in the 1953 All-Ireland.

Lucy Byrne

Lucy Byrne (Wicklow) was elected as the new President of the Camogie Association. She came from a strong Gaelic games background and was the guiding light in Wicklow camogie circles for over 30 years. Held in high respect, she was an enthusiastic and whole-hearted worker for the Association.

Following 13 years as Ard Runaí, Jean McHugh

Dublin's Phenomenal Run

(Antrim) stepped down. However, there were no nominations to replace her as no one was willing to take on the onerous position. Sheila McAnulty volunteered and filled the office with distinction for 22 years. This happening caused Seán O'Duffy to express the view that the Association was not making sufficient progress because people were not prepared to take off their coats and work.

Girls, who played and resided outside their native counties, now had the opportunity to complete a Declaration of Intention and assist their native county. The first to avail of this new permission were Susan Smith (Cavan), Bernadette King (Armagh), Sally Blake (Tipperary), Peggy Hogan (Tipperary) and Eithne Neville (Limerick).

No Lost Balls

There was a time when a lost ball meant an abandoned match. The ball, always referred to in the singular, was minded and cared for until it was beyond repair. Players were expert at looking for and finding balls that had been struck out of the playing area. High grass, nettles, clumps of gorse, hedges, woods, gullies and drains presented no problem to the experienced ball finder and the art of throwing stones to get a ball floating in a river to come to the riverbank had been well mastered. Training sessions were confined to running or a match when only one ball was available.

1953 All-Ireland Championship

No Connacht county entered for the 1953 All-Ireland championship. London were due to play Tipperary in the All-Ireland semi-final at Roscrea, but four of their team were unable to take holidays for the journey over. Consequently, they conceded a walkover.

In the semi-final at Mayobridge, the Down defenders were unable to cope with the demands imposed upon them by the fast-moving Dublin forwards. For long periods of the game, Dublin literally owned the ball and ran out easy winners by 9–2 to 2–0.

Two goals by Dublin in the opening three minutes rattled Tipperary in the All-Ireland final at Croke Park on August 2nd. Tipperary were powerless to climb back up and were forced to yield to a runaway 8–4 to 1–3 win by Dublin. The score was a trifle unfair to Tipperary who played with spirit. Dublin were faster to the ball and played it to the advantage of their front players. Loose marking allowed the Dublin forwards carve a path to goal which they pursued repeatedly.

Dublin team: Eileen Duffy, Doretta Blackton, Carmel Walsh, Pauline Duffy, Sheila Donnelly, Nancy Caffrey, Annette Corrigan, Kathleen Mills, Una O'Connor (4–1), Sheila Sleator (1–0), Eileen Bourke and Sophie Brack (captain) (3–3).

Tipperary team: Maura Treacy, Kitty Callanan, Kitty Kirwan, Mary Ann O'Brien (captain) (0–1), Mary Morris, Nancy Foley, Mary England (0–2), Kathleen England, Kathleen Griffin (1–0), Terry Griffin, Kathleen Downes and Tess O'Meara.

Golden Jubilee Year

The Camogie Association celebrated its Golden Jubilee in 1954. In her report to congress, Sheila McAnulty posed a question: "Camogie has an intrinsic value as a game which cannot be denied, but it has a much higher value as part of our Irish-Ireland movement and that is an aspect which we should keep before our minds. We have come a long way in organisation and strength since 1904 but are we as sincere in our motives, as clear in our ideals as those who formed the Association? They gave Irish women camogie to keep them close to the traditions of their race at a time when the only games in which women could participate were those introduced by people whose allegiance was to England and whose eyes and ideals were firmly fixed on the other side of the Irish Sea. In keeping close to tradition, those who played camogie must be conscious of their proud heritage and so the spirit of nationality was kindled."

It was a timely reminder to the members to remain steadfast to the ideals and aims of the Association.

First Interprovincial Match

To mark the Golden Jubilee of the Association, Central Council planned to stage an inter-provincial contest between Leinster and Ulster at the Agricultural Grounds in Navan, which had been the venue of the first competitive camogie match. It is extraordinary that the main event of the Jubilee celebrations involved only Leinster and Ulster and ignored the two other provinces. The teams paraded through the town of Navan as torrential rain poured. Eileen Duffy remembers wrapping the Tóstal flag around her in an effort to protect herself from the unseasonal elements.

Not surprisingly, the Leinster team, selected to play Ulster on September 19th, was built around the Dublin All-Ireland team. The champions provided seven of the 12 players with Wicklow and Meath each supplying a set of sisters. Only a point separated the sides at the break. On the resumption, Leinster knuckled down to the serious business of winning the match. Ahead by 8–3 to 5–3 at the finish, Leinster were presented with special medals while runners-up, Ulster, received brooches.

Leinster team: Eileen Duffy (Dublin), May Kavanagh (Dublin), Ettie Kearns (Meath), Sheila Donnelly (Dublin), Aggie

Nell McCarthy, Inez O'Kelly, Molly Murphy, Seán O'Duffy and Clare Gaynor pictured at the Golden Jubilee celebrations in 1954.

Dublin's Phenomenal Run

Kavanagh (Wicklow), Aileen Kearns (Meath), Annette Corrigan (Dublin) (0–1), Kathleen Mills (Dublin) (2–1), Una O'Connor (Dublin) (3–0), Sheila Sleator (Dublin), Eileen Bourke (Dublin) (2–0) and Kay Douglas (Wicklow) (1–1).

Ulster team: Bernie Kelly (Down), Moya Forde (Antrim), Teresa Halferty (Derry), Carrie Rankin (Derry), Bernadette King (Armagh), Maeve Gilroy (Antrim) (1–0), Nancy Danagher (Cavan), Ita O'Reilly (Antrim) (1–0), Patsy McCloskey (Derry) (2–1), Deirdre O'Gorman (Antrim) (1–1), Chris Hughes (Antrim) and Patsy O'Brien (Derry) (0–1).

1954 All-Ireland Championship

The Dublin v. Cork All-Ireland semi-final at Croke Park had everything, and is considered to be one of the best camogie matches ever played. There were marvellous individual displays, brilliant scores, near misses, daring saves and the woodwork acting as a second Dublin goalkeeper. Every score was hard earned. Dublin were better at finishing and that was the deciding factor. Annette Corrigan, Una O'Connor, Kathleen Mills, Eileen Duffy, Carmel Walsh and Sheila Sleator earned the repeated cheers of the Dublin fans. It was no fault of Sheila Cahill, Betty Walsh, Peg Lucey, Noreen Duggan or Teresa Murphy that Cork finished on the wrong side of the 5–3 to 3–1 scoreline.

Derry surprised Antrim in the Ulster final at Clady by 5–3 to 2–2 and travelled to Newport to take on Mayo in the All-Ireland semi-final. The Derry girls were astounded by the resounding welcome accorded to them by the friendly people of Mayo. From the moment they arrived until their departure, they were royally treated. The seaside town was decorated in the colours of both teams and, as the Derry cars pulled into the town, a battery of fireworks lit up the sky. On the Sunday morning, the townspeople turned up in cars, decorated in Derry colours, to take the visitors on a tour of the scenic areas. They arrived back shortly before the start of the match. In the square of the town, the teams were formally introduced to each other. A band led the parade of the teams to the playing field as the locals lined the way, clapping generously. Derry won the match 5–2 to 0–0.

In 1954, London were allowed entry to the championship after the semi-finals had been played and were drawn against Derry. The village of Greenlough was alight with bunting and flags for

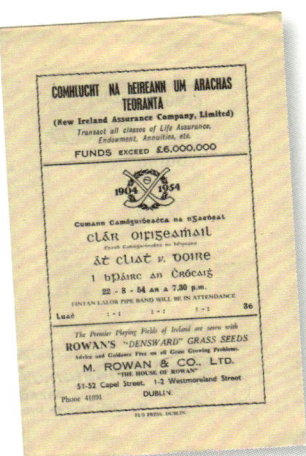

1954 programme

DUBLIN DOMINANT STILL IN CAMOGIE

Dublin........ 10-4   Derry........ 4-2

DUBLIN won their sixteenth All-Ireland camogie title at Croke Park last evening, scoring the easiest of victories over Derry, in the final. In the first half the Derry girls were so outplayed that they only crossed the half-way line three times, getting a solitary point against Dublin's six goals and two points. The score sheet took on a better appearance for the losers when Dublin eased up in the last quarter.

The Dublin scorers were Misses S. Brack 3-1, S. Slater 2-0, W. O'Connor 3-1, E. Burke 1-0, M. O'Connor 1-0, and A. Corrigan 0-2. For Derry—Misses M. McCluskey, T. O'Brien, R. McAllister and Bryson had a goal each, and Messrs. McCluskey and D. O'Brien a point each.

Junior All-Ireland Area hurling semi-final—At Limerick: Limerick, 6-8; Galway, 2-8.

1954 report

the visit of London. The Derry hosts laid on a spectacular welcome for the exiles. Once the ball was thrown in, Derry were the masters. The first time doubling on the ball, snappy passes and accurate shooting of the home side were too much for London who trailed 3–11 to 0–3 at the final whistle.

The vastly experienced Dublin team, to whom winning was a habit, faced a Derry side making their first appearance in Croke Park on August 22nd. Derry acquitted themselves well by scoring 4–2 against their highly rated opponents. The real difference between the sides was Dublin's understanding within the team. Their players passed the ball around with no sign of selfishness and their finishing was lethal. Una O'Connor, Sophie Brack and Sheila Sleator shared ten goals while Rose McAllister, Patsy McCloskey, Anna Bryson and Patsy O'Brien replied with Derry majors. Cork referee, Noreen Murphy, awarded only one free in the match which must be a record in its own right.

Dublin team: Eileen Duffy, Doretta Blackton, Betty Hughes, Carmel Walsh, Sheila Donnelly, Nancy Caffrey, Annette Corrigan (0–3), Kathleen Mills, Una O'Connor (4–0), Sheila Sleator (2–0), Eileen Bourke and Sophie Brack (captain) (4–1).

Noreen Murphy (Cork), Sean O'Duffy and Crios O'Connell (Limerick) at Congress in 1955

Derry Team: Anna McPeake, Theresa Clarke, Teresa Halferty, Carrie Rankin, Margaret Dorrity, Mary McSwiggan, Patsy McCloskey (captain) (1–2), Kathleen McCloskey, Kathleen Madden, Patsy O'Brien (1–0), Anna Bryson (1–0) and Rose McAllister (1–0).

Presidential Challenge

Prior to 1955, it was unheard of to challenge an incumbent president, up to that point each president had been allowed to complete her term of office without having to face a second contest. However, Teresa Davis (Armagh) threw her hat in the ring against Lucy Byrne in 1955. Despite having missed a number of meetings through illness, the majority of delegates did not wish to see Lucy ousted and she was returned by a comfortable margin.

Warwickshire tabled a motion to replace the traditional gym frock with a divided skirt, but the Association was not ready for such drastic change and voted heavily against it.

Emigration continued to eat into camogie numbers. Clubs folded because of players moving abroad or because of the loss of the personnel who organised and held the club together. The secretary's report to congress highlighted the falling off: only Armagh, Antrim, Down and Derry participated in the 1954 Ulster

Dublin's Phenomenal Run

championship. There was further slippage when organised camogie ceased in Co. Down because of a friendly match getting out of control. Kilkenny, Carlow, Offaly, Westmeath, Sligo and Kerry were not affiliated and Clare had only one club, Killaloe. On the other hand, camogie was making progress in Wexford where Mr J. J. Corry presented a silver cup for a county league competition.

1955 All-Ireland Championship

The most amazing scoreline of the 1955 season was the Connacht final result which read Mayo 6–1 Galway 0–0. Boosted by this performance, Mayo made the trip to Parnell Park for the semi-final against Dublin full of confidence – but found the champions in no mood to abdicate. Mayo's hopes of creating a second surprise were dashed long before the end of an 11–5 to 1–0 drubbing.

The Cork defence contained the Antrim forwards in the second semi-final at the Cork Athletic Grounds. With a generous supply of ball to work with, the Cork attack prised open the Antrim backline and the inevitable outcome was a 4–1 to 0–3 home win. London withdrew from the All-Ireland series.

The final between Dublin and Cork was fixed for Croke Park on Sunday evening, August 21st, at seven o'clock. With a thunder storm and torrential rain pouring, the teams huddled under the old Cusack Stand looking out at the pitch that had been badly cut up by the Dublin v. Mayo football semi-final earlier in the day. About 200 brave souls waited patiently for news of the fixture outside the stadium. At 7.30 the match was called off. The cancellation caused considerable financial loss to the Association. The final was rescheduled for August 28th, at Croke Park.

This was a wonderful game of camogie. The teams served up 14 goals in a feast of attacking play. Cork had excellent individual players in Noreen Duggan, Anna Crotty, Angela Lane and Peg Lucey. Their stylish play yielded 5–6, a score which would have won many All-Irelands. But it was the clever combined play of the Dublin attack that won the day. Captain Sophie Brack led the forward line superbly. She scored three goals and laid on perfect passes to those around her to complete the job. Una O'Connor, Fran Maher, Kathleen Mills and Annette Corrigan availed of Sophie's deft touches to register scores.

Dublin team: Eileen Duffy, Eileen Kelly, Betty Hughes, Eileen Cronin, Sheila Donnelly, Bríd Reid (1–0), Annette Corrigan (0–1), Kathleen Mills, Fran Maher (3–0), Eileen Bourke, Una O'Connor (2–1) and Sophie Brack (captain) (3–0).

Cork team: Sheila Cahill, Betty Walsh, Bridie Lucey, Teresa Murphy, Joan Clancy, Anna Crotty (captain) (0–3), Lily McKay, Peg Lucey, Angela Lane (1–1), Noreen Duggan (3–2), Mona Joyce and Maura Hayes (1–0). Sub used: Maura O'Connell.

Sophie Brack captained Dublin to win six All-Ireland championships. Eileen Duffy's brother, Billy, played first team soccer for Arsenal. Eileen Cronin married Paddy Hogan, who hurled for Laois in the 1949 All-Ireland final. Eileen Bourke is a sister of GAA historian, Marcus Bourke. Cork goalkeeper, Sheila Cahill, married Donie O'Donovan who won Railway Cup medals with Munster and coached Cork to win the 1973 All-Ireland senior football title. West Ham soccer player, Jackie Morley, married

A Game of Our Own

Joan Clancy. Their son, Pat, was a prominent League of Ireland soccer player. Angela Lane's brother, Mick, and her son, Michael Kiernan, were Irish rugby internationals.

Dublin's Success

Dublin set off on an amazing championship run that saw them only lose one match between 1948 and 1967. Why were Dublin so much better than the remaining counties? Dublin were well organised, there were no club matches were played during the inter-county season, they had a large pool of players to choose from, including players from other counties who were working or studying in the city, their players were disciplined and played as they were instructed to do and they had tremendous pride in wearing the blue gym frock. Throughout that period, Dublin had a core of top-class players. Above all, Dublin had an excellent coach in Nell McCarthy.

Dublin 1959 team. The county lost only one championship match between 1948 and 1967. Back: Kay Ryder, Kay Mills, Una O'Connor, Kay Lyons, Concepta Clarke, M. Crowley, Annette Corrigan, Joan Kinsella and Ally Hussey. Front: Anne Twamley, Doreen Brennan, Mary O'Sullivan, Bríd Reid (Capt), Betty Hughes, Eithne Leech, Annie Donnelly and Nuala Murney.

Nell McCarthy

Nell was born into a hurling family in Carrigtwohill, Co. Cork. Her uncle, Jimmy 'Major' Kennedy, captained Cork to win the 1919 All-Ireland hurling title and her brother, Dan, wore the red jersey. Every Sunday, the men folk of the family went to a hurling match, when they returned, they sat around the table and analysed the game in every detail.

The young Nell sat with them taking it all in. When she was old enough, she went along to the matches and tried to anticipate what the verdict of the panel would be later on. It was here that she learned how to read the game, how to place a team and how to counteract the opposition.

Nell had the ability to spot talent and bring the best out of everyone. She gave a player the confidence to face any task. Excellent to pass on skill, Nell set standards and everybody kept them. She talked and lived for hurling and camogie. A civil servant in the Department of Education, she played a huge part in the Dublin camogie scene.

Dublin's Phenomenal Run

Where We're At

The timely arrival of Sheila McAnulty on the scene made an immediate and significant impact. She set the unity of the Association as her primary aim. With her Ulster background, she had to win the confidence of the other regions, especially Dublin. She treaded her way, with skill and impartiality, through a series of unity meetings and succeeded in winning over opposing sides with the exception of Cork. That took a little longer.

Each time Cork's demands were met, they came up with a fresh set to test her patience. When the Cork Board had removed Íde Bean Uí Shé from the position of chairperson, in the guise of promoting her to the role of Life President, the new incumbent, Eileen Keating, quickly made peace. The bleakest chapter in the history of the Association was closed. As the ageing Agnes O'Farrelly slipped into the background, Sheila McAnulty donned the mantle of leader. Clear-thinking and articulate, Sheila commanded attention and served the Association admirably for several decades.

On the playing fields, Dublin's supremacy was unmatched. Other teams lacked the organisation, teamwork and discipline of the Dublin sides – they operated from a smaller pool of players and did not always pull together. The availability of camogie pitches in the Phoenix Park allowed Dublin to choose the timing of their season. Play commenced in late September and finished in early May, giving a free run to the Dublin coach in the preparation of the team for the All-Ireland championship. In most counties, local championships and inter-county competitions were inter-twinned with resultant complications. Players had to travel long distances to county training in the large counties and, often, had to rely on others to bring them or thumb a lift on roads with little traffic. Above all, they lacked a coach of the calibre of Nell McCarthy. Counties were inhibited by Dublin's prolonged winning run and placed more importance on their own county championships than inter-county contests.

The choice of an inter-provincial match as the main event of the Golden Jubilee celebrations in 1954 was warmly welcomed by the players. It was no surprise that the inter-provincial competition was made permanent two years later. In contrast to the present time, players looked forward to the announcement of the provincial teams and the chance to display their talent in top-class company. It must be remembered that, in those days, only a select few played third-level camogie. The national leagues or the All-Ireland club championship had not commenced and, for many, inter-county camogie was confined to one or two matches a season.

A Game of Our Own

SKIRMISH IN THE SQUARE

Chapter Eight

ANTRIM'S HOUR

Lily Spence, a member of the St Teresa's Club in Belfast, was elected President of the Camogie Association at the 1956 Congress. Lily received the presidency at a young age and continued to work for camogie for many years after her term of office was complete, giving a lifetime of service to camogie.

Roscommon's Return

Following a lapse of 20 years, the Roscommon County Board was revived with the Kilmurry, Ballinagare, Castlerea and Knockcroghery clubs affiliating. Phil Gannon (Castlerea), J. T. Kemmitt (Kilmurry), Teresa Keenan (Portahard) and Martha Finan (Kilmurry) filled the officer positions.

Ulster introduced a junior championship in 1956. The first name to be engraved on the cup was Cavan.

Pay to Play

The Cork County Board rented a pitch at Church Road for the 1956 season and it was all hands on deck to pick the stones from the pitch and remove the stubble from a crop of mangles that still dotted the site. The annual rent was £60 – huge money in those days – and to meet this outlay, everybody had to pay at the gate; supporters one shilling and six pence and players one shilling. When the grass started to grow, the need of a mower became urgent so one was purchased on the 'never-never', with a weekly instalment of two shillings and six pence. A collection was made at the weekly county board meeting and the figure of two shillings and six pence had to be met irrespective of how many were present.

The early arrivals at Church Road on match day were delegated to go for the keys, collect and erect the posts, hunt out the cows, get shovels and remove cows' pancakes. Others were dispatched to fill bottles of water or take the gate. It was usual for players to arrive already togged out in gym frock and black stockings

Lily Spence: elected President in 1956

but if anybody had to change, coats would be held around the player to afford privacy. Toilet facilities were over the ditch and mind the nettles. The duties of the line-judge included keeping an eye on the baby in the pram. When the match was over, the posts were carried from the field to the back garden of a supporter's house for safe keeping.

1956 All-Ireland Championship

Mayo were paired with Cork at the semi-final stage of the All-Ireland championship on August 26th. However, during the summer, a serious outbreak of polio hit Cork and Mayo asked the Central Council to postpone the fixture indefinitely. The Central Council sought the advice of the Mayo County Medical Officer in making its decision and he had no objection to the match going ahead. However, the Cork Medical Officer recommended that the match be deferred to September 16th, and, initially, all parties agreed with this compromise.

Antrim – All-Ireland champions 1956. Back: Grace Connolly, Eithne Dougan, Winnie Kearns, Marion Kearns, Moya Forde, Deirdre O'Gorman and Maeve Gilroy. Front: Ita O'Reilly, Eilish McCamphill, Chris Hughes, Teresa Kearns and Madge Rainey (Capt).

A further request from the Mayo County Board to defer the match was discussed at an emergency meeting of the Central Council on September 12th. Medical advice held no reservations about Cork travelling and, consequently, the fixture was confirmed. Mayo refused to field and Cork were awarded a walkover. Mayo contacted the press, both in Ireland and Britain, and widespread publicity of an adverse nature was afforded to the case.

A wonderful display by Antrim toppled long-standing champions Dublin in the second semi-final of the All-Ireland championship held at Casement Park. It was thrilling stuff from start to finish with the lead switching from one side to the other. A point ahead at the interval, Antrim stayed with the champions. With a minute to go, Sophie Brack scored what seemed to be the winner but one last attack by Antrim saw Marion Kearns engineer a goal to leave the final score at Antrim 6–2, Dublin 6–1 and Dublin released their grip on the cup. The *Irish Independent*

Antrim's Hour

'Sports Star of the Week' award went to the Antrim team.

Fran Maher had been the reserve goalkeeper for the Dublin team when they had set out to retain their All-Ireland title in 1955. In the final, Dublin had found themselves short a forward and had asked Fran to fill in. She did, and had gone on to score three goals. She repeated the feat in the 1956 semi-final against Antrim, showing that she could score goals as well as stop them.

The Silver Jubilee of the first All-Ireland final was decided between Antrim and Cork at Croke Park on September 30th. With Dublin out of the running, Cork carried high hopes of taking the title for the first time since 1941. However, it was not to be, as Antrim continued where they left off against Dublin. Teresa Kearns, the 14-year-old Antrim goalkeeper, made a huge contribution to victory, stopping an array of shots from the Cork attack, including a memorable save from Noreen Duggan. Antrim responded to this match-winning block by sweeping the ball up the field and making an opening for Gertie Connolly who placed the ball beyond the reach of Sheila Cahill.

The Antrim attack moved the ball quickly, creating problems for the Cork defence. Chris Hughes, Moya Forde, Maeve Gilroy, Marion Kearns and Madge Rainey played great camogie and provided the platform for an Antrim victory. Noreen Duggan was Cork's brightest star. She was well supported by Angela Lane, Mona Joyce and Maura Hayes. Cork were handicapped by injuries to their captain, Lil Coughlan, and Teresa Murphy, both of whom had to be replaced. A delighted president, Lily Spence, presented the O'Duffy Cup to Madge Rainey at the close of the game which ended Antrim 5–3, Cork 4–2.

Antrim team: Teresa Kearns, Moya Forde, Ethna Dougan, Winnie Kearns, Deirdre O'Gorman, Eilis McCamphill, Ita O'Reilly (0–1), Maeve Gilroy (0–1), Marion Kearns (2–0), Madge Rainey (1–0) (captain), Chris Hughes (1–1) and Grace Connolly (1–0).

Cork team: Sheila Cahill, Bridie Lucey, Betty Walsh, Joan Clancy, Teresa Murphy, Lil Coughlan (captain), Lily McKay, Anna Crotty (1–0), Angela Lane (2–0), Noreen Duggan (0–2), Mona Joyce and Maura Hayes (1–0).

Low-Key Celebrations

Grace Connolly recalls her memories of the 1956 All-Ireland weekend:

> "I was a student nurse in the Royal Victoria Hospital and the rules were that everyone had to be in by ten o'clock or be locked out. Having to travel to Dublin for the final meant that I required a late pass. Fr McBride, who was involved with the county board, eventually got it for me. Since I had never travelled farther than Belfast, I felt the trip to Dublin was very long. I felt petrified by the size of Croke Park and felt very nervous in the pre-match parade. Nevertheless, we settled down when the match started. We played well to beat Cork. There was no wild fuss, no big invasion of spectators on to the pitch to clap our backs. A meal was provided and we were instructed not to order anything costing more than two shillings and six pence. We made a safe journey home and I was on the ward at ten to seven on Monday morning."

A Game of Our Own

1956 Gael-Linn Cup

The reaction to the inter-provincial match played at Navan, as part of the Golden Jubilee celebrations, was enthusiastic. The competition allowed players from weak counties to display their talent in top-class company. Many players, who were not lucky enough to reach an All-Ireland final, were thrilled to represent their province. The announcement of provincial teams was eagerly awaited in the early days of the competition. Gael-Linn donated a splendid trophy for the new Inter-provincial Championship.

Leinster finished ahead of Munster, 6–4 to 4–2, in the first game played at Cahir. Connacht did not enter a team, leaving Ulster through to the final. Four goals separated Leinster and Ulster, 7–1 to 3–1, in the decider at Knockbridge. Dublin star, Una O'Connor, gave a polished performance with five well-crafted goals. At the end of the match, Leinster captain, Annette Corrigan, lifted the Gael-Linn Cup.

Leinster team: Kathleen Woods (Louth), May Kavanagh (Wicklow), Claire Monaghan (Kildare), Kay Ryder (Dublin), May Kavanagh (Dublin), Lily Parle (Wexford), Annette Corrigan (Dublin) (captain), Kathleen Mills (Dublin), Fran Maher (Dublin), Mary O'Sullivan (Dublin), Una O'Connor (Dublin) and Kay Douglas (Wicklow).

Ulster team: Teresa Kearns (Antrim), Moya Forde (Antrim), Mona Kelly (Down), Winnie Kearns (Antrim), Deirdre O'Gorman (Antrim), Ita O'Reilly (Antrim), Margaret Dorrity (Derry), Maeve Gilroy (Antrim), Marion Kearns (Antrim), Madge Rainey (Antrim), Chris Hughes (Antrim) and Grace Connolly (Antrim).

A Camogie Heroine

Cass McCarthy was a key figure in London camogie. Born in Drumcollogher, Co. Limerick, she emigrated to England in the early twenties. She settled in London where she formed a camogie club known as The Exiles. Far more than a camogie organiser, she was always willing to help anyone and was a true friend to scores of girls who came across the Irish Sea, helping them to adjust to their new surroundings through camogie. When London participated in the All-Ireland Championship in the forties and fifties, Cass was the team manager.

Past v. Present

The annual Past v. Present match was eagerly looked forward to. We sat on a bench in the school gym awaiting the arrival of the opposition. Clad in hats and costumes, high-heeled shoes and handbags, they entered and displayed great welcome for one another. A few pounds heavier than in their playing days, they squeezed into gym frocks and stretched black stockings to the limit. According to tradition, the oldest had first choice of position on the team and so forth down the line. Those who had recently left school had no hope of making the starting 12. However, substitutes were very important as lungs and legs gave out. We giggled at the thought of those old dears running and convinced ourselves that they would pose no problems.

Armed with the school bell, the referee got the match underway. A little leniency was shown to the old girls as they warmed to the task. It did not take long for us to realise that we were in

Antrim's Hour

trouble. The skills perfected in their playing days began to surface. Shooting at the rather large goalkeeper proved a waste of time. The Past controlled the middle of the field and placed the ball to the advantage of their attackers. The experienced inside-forwards steered the ball out of the reach of the young defenders and goalkeeper. We did all the running whereas their neat touches were far more effective.

Back in the gym, we headed for the tea and cakes and sat chastened while they chatted noisily. To add insult to injury, the Past captain encouraged us to keep on practising and said we might come good.

1957 All-Ireland Championship

In the best Leinster final in years, Dublin found themselves a point in arrears with six minutes remaining against Wicklow. A goal by Una O'Connor and points from Phyllis Campbell and Mary O'Sullivan saved the day for the long-standing champions.

Apart from a period midway through the second half, Cork

Dublin and Antrim in the 1957 All-Ireland. Antrim led with two minutes to go.

struggled against Dublin in the All-Ireland semi-final at Parnell Park. Bríd Reid, Annette Corrigan and Kathleen Mills secured any ball that came into the midfield sector and starved Cork of possession. The Cork rearguard was under constant pressure. As soon as they cleared the ball, it was back in their area again. Dublin advanced by 5–4 to 1–3.

Antrim were decidedly lucky to emerge from McHale Park with a 2–1 to 1–2 win over Mayo in the second semi-final. With time running out and trailing by a point, Antrim moved Maeve Gilroy to centre-forward and she responded with a goal to ensure a place in the final.

Fielding practically the same side that won the 1956 title, Antrim led Dublin in the All-Ireland final at Croke Park on October 6th with two minutes left on the clock. Then, Eilis McCampbell suffered a head injury which necessitated her departure from the field, something that appeared to unsettle her team-mates. With their concentration broken, Una O'Connor, who the Dublin selectors had omitted in favour of Annie Donnelly, came on to set up the winner for Bríd Reid.

Eileen Duffy was brilliant in the Dublin goal. She timed her advances to perfection, bringing off many crucial saves. May Kavanagh and Doris Nolan shone in defence. Annie Donnelly marked her return to the Dublin side after a six-year absence with a well-taken goal.

Teresa Kearns and Moya Forde maintained their high standard in the Antrim defence. Madge Rainey, Maeve Gilroy and Marion Kearns troubled Dublin but could not prevent them from regaining the O'Duffy Cup by 3–3 to 3–1.

Dublin team: Eileen Duffy (captain), May Kavanagh, Doris Nolan, Doreen Brennan, Kay Lyons, Bríd Reid (1–0), Annette Corrigan (0–2), Kathleen Mills (0–1), Maura Murphy (1–0), Mary O'Sullivan, Annie Donnelly (1–0) and Betty Hughes. Subs used: Una O'Connor and Brid Shannon.

Antrim team: Teresa Kearns, Moya Forde, Agnes Dillon, Winnie Kearns, Deirdre O'Gorman, Eilis McCamphill (1–0), Madge Rainey, Maeve Gilroy (captain) (1–1), Marion Kearns (1–0),

1957 All-Ireland champions Dublin. Back: Bríd Shannon, Phyllis Campbell, Kay Mills, Una O'Connor, Doris Nolan, Kay Lyons, Doreen Brennan, Annette Corrigan and May Kavanagh. Front: Maureen Brennan, Eithne Neville, Bríd Reid, Carmel Kennedy, Eileen Duffy, Betty Hughes, Mary O'Sullivan and Annie Donnelly.

(Dublin) (0–1), Annette Corrigan (captain) (Dublin), Anna May Brennan (Laois), Mary O'Sullivan (Dublin) (1–0), Annie Donnelly (Dublin) (2-0), Una O'Connor (Dublin) (1–0) and Jean Hannon (Wicklow) (1–0).

Munster team: Catherine Carroll (Tipperary), Betty Walsh (Cork), Bridie Lucey (Cork), Teresa Murphy (Cork), Josie McNamara (Waterford), Terry Griffin (Tipperary), Anna Crotty (Cork), Mary Nugent (Waterford), Noreen Duggan (Cork) (2-0), Mary Margo Kane, Chris Hughes and Frances Forde.

1957 Gael-Linn Cup

Munster had a close call, 2–1 to 1–2, over Connacht, and Leinster had a two-goal winning margin, 4–0 to 2–0, over Ulster at Parnell Park to reach the final of the Gael-Linn Cup. Then, on a miserably cold and wet afternoon in Cahir, Leinster retained their title by 5–1 to 3–1.

Leinster team: Kathleen Woods (Louth), May Kavanagh (Wicklow), Vera Lee (Kildare), Agnes Kavanagh (Wicklow), May Kavanagh (Dublin), Bríd Reid

Antrim's Hour

England (Tipperary), Mona Joyce (Cork) (1–1) and Kathleen Griffin (Tipperary).

Leinster midfielder, Anna May Brennan, is better known as Anna May McHugh, Managing Director of the National Ploughing Championships.

No Support for Motions

An All-Ireland Club Championship was first mooted at Congress in 1958. It was suggested that it would be organised on similar lines to the soccer Champions League with the top 16 clubs in the country taking part. The proposer envisaged that the entrants to the competition would be four Dublin clubs, three Cork, two from Galway, Antrim, Tipperary and Mayo and one from Derry. However, the counties that were not mentioned were completely opposed to the suggestion and the idea was dropped.

The same West of Ireland delegate, Mrs Nora Hanrahan, who had proposed the club competition, also proposed that prominent clubs adopt weak neighbouring counties and take them under their wing. The plan included friendly matches in the summer months and demonstration training sessions.

1958 All-Ireland Championships

Galway's top player, Chris Conway, played herself to a standstill in an effort to curb Dublin's Kathleen Mills in the semi-final of the All-Ireland championship at Pearse Park. She succeeded, but it was other Dublin players who caused problems for the home side.

Eileen Duffy: brilliant in the Dublin goal

Dublin's main strength lay in their forward line and their return of 5–4 to 0–1 secured a place in the final.

Many people were surprised to see Antrim yield to Tipperary in the second semi-final at Roscrea, but Tipperary's win was merited. In a match of 13 goals, Tipperary's forwards came out on top by 8–0 to 5–1. National organiser, Seán O'Duffy, had bought a sliothar for the match at a cost of seven shillings. After the game, he sold it for five shillings.

It was becoming more and more difficult to secure Croke Park for the All-Ireland final. The only slot available in 1958 was an evening fixture on August 10th. Many of the spectators who had watched Tipperary's hurlers defeat Kilkenny in the afternoon remained on to view the camogie match.

The Tipperary players were not as well prepared as their opponents. In fact, some of the players did not know one another. Financial restraints prevented Tipperary from booking into a hotel and so players had made their own way to Dublin and some had stayed overnight with relatives.

Dublin made a late change to the team listed in the programme. Full-back May Kavanagh was positioned in goal in place of Carmel Kennedy, and Doris Nolan was called upon to fill the vacancy in defence. Tipperary put up gallant resistance and Dublin were made to fight harder than the final score of 5–4 to 1–1 suggests. Thanks to a brilliant display by Tipperary goalkeeper, Catherine Carroll, the teams were level at the break. As the game wore on, Dublin's combined attacking play opened the Tipperary defence, leading to 4–3 without reply.

Dublin team: May Kavanagh, Betty Hughes, Doris Nolan, Doreen Brennan, Kay Lyons, Bríd Reid, Annette Corrigan (0–2), Kathleen Mills (captain) (2–0), Mary O'Sullivan, Kay Ryder (1–0), Annie Donnelly (0–1) and Una O'Connor (2–1).

Tipperary team: Catherine Carroll, Kitty Flaherty, Peg Moloney, Kathleen England, Bridie Scully, Terry Griffin, Alice Hanley, Mary England (0–1), Edie Merrigan, Mary O'Neill, Kathleen Downes (1–0) and Kathleen Griffin.

1958 Gael-Linn Cup

In the semi-finals of the Gael-Linn Cup, Ulster had a point to spare over Munster, 4–1 to 2–6, whereas Leinster hammered Connacht, 6–7 to 0–2. Free-scoring Leinster cruised to victory over Ulster in the final at Parnell Park by 8–2 to 3–3.

Leinster team: May Kavanagh (Dublin), Betty Hughes (Dublin), Vera Lee (Kildare), Kay Ryder (Dublin), Rose Woods (Louth), Bríd Reid (Dublin), Annette Corrigan (captain) (Dublin), Kathleen Mills (Dublin), Anna May Brennan (Laois) (1–0), Mary O'Sullivan (Dublin) (1–0), Una O'Connor (Dublin) (6–1) and Annie Donnelly (Dublin).

Ulster team: Teresa Kearns (Antrim), Moya Forde (Antrim), Eithne Carabine (Antrim), Winnie Kearns (Antrim) (0–1), Irene Maguire (Antrim), Margo McCourt (Antrim), Margaret Dorrity (Derry) (1–1), Madge Rainey (Antrim), Chris Hughes (Antrim), Claire Kearns (Antrim) (0–1), Maeve Gilroy (Antrim) (2–0) and Marion Kearns (Antrim) (0–1).

Eilish Redmond Elected President

Seven candidates were nominated for the post of President of the Camogie Association at Congress 1959: Iney O'Kelly (Dublin), Agnes Purcell (Dublin), Crios O'Connell (Limerick), Maureen Smith (Antrim), Nancy Murray (Antrim), Eilish Redmond (Dublin) and Mrs McKiernan (Galway). However, not all allowed their names to go forward. When the votes were counted, Eilish Redmond (née Keegan) was elected. A founder member of the Celtic camogie club, Eilish had filled the role of club chairman for many years. Sincere and concerned, Eilish attended to her duties in a ladylike way.

Congress voted to allow university players line out with their home clubs during holiday time. It was felt it was important to maintain the link between the player and her home club, otherwise she might be lost to the game on graduation. The college season was short and, unless this permission was granted, a player would experience very little action on the playing fields.

In her report to congress, Sheila McAnulty warned against apathy towards or a watering down of the Association's ideals and traditions: "I feel that it is not inopportune to stress again the national aspect of our organisation and, indeed, I have been somewhat disappointed on occasions at the apparent apathy in this regard by some of our members. If the spirit of the founders of the Camogie Association ceases to inspire its members, then, whatever our numerical strength, it represents no progress.

Antrim's Hour

In these days when television opens new vistas and brings the outside world to many of our firesides, we must be wary that in the new spirit of internationalism that is abroad we do not lose our own identity as one of the oldest nations in Europe with a proud heritage of learning, of sanctity and of endeavour. Let us not think that the organisation of camogie alone is sufficient for our national effort. Promotion of our own games is but one facet of the Irish-Ireland movement. We should take an interest in our country's history and music, speak our own language wherever possible and encourage support for our traditional Irish dances.

Mayo goalkeeper, Mary McGuire, comes out to save a shot in the 1959 All-Ireland final at Croke Park. Mary O'Sullivan (Dublin) and Margaret Kelly (Mayo) await developments.

Because these are our own we should love them and honour them and this is something which should be put before the younger members of the Association. Besides this support of the spirit for things Irish, on the practical side, we should help to provide greater employment and better conditions for our people by whenever possible buying Irish-made goods."

1959 All-Ireland Championship

History was made at Casement Park when a BBC television crew covered the All-Ireland semi-final between Antrim and Dublin. The players were thrilled to see camogie make its first appearance on the small screen. The teams rose to the occasion to display the game at its best and the fast, exciting and skilful contest ended Dublin 3–3, Antrim 2–4.

The unlikely pairing of Mayo and Waterford met in the second semi-final at Newport. Mayo had surprised Galway, but Waterford had made banner headlines by defeating Cork, Clare and London to qualify for the penultimate stage. After extra-time, Mayo and Waterford were all square and both captains refused to play further extra-time. The referee was critical of the Newport pitch, which she claimed was entirely unsuitable for an All-Ireland semi-final. The All-Ireland final was put back and a replay arranged for Roscrea where Mayo snatched a last-minute victory – 3–4 to 2–6 – with a long-range point from centre-back, Josie Ruane.

Dublin captain, Bríd Reid, returned from her honeymoon to lead her side in the All-Ireland final against Mayo at Croke Park on September 13th. Mayo failed to exert a serious challenge on

Action from the Mayo Dublin final.

the champions. Dublin's superiority stemmed from midfield where Annette Corrigan, Kathleen Mills and Bríd Reid held sway. They supplied the attack with a regular supply of good possession. The clever, fast-striking Dublin forwards accumulated a winning score of 11–6 to 1–3.

Mayo was not the first team to be over-awed on their inaugural visit to Croke Park. Josie Ruane, the only Mayo player to match Dublin's standards, did Trojan work at centre-back. Margaret Kelly, Margaret Clarke, Florrie Clarke and Teresa Hoban played their hearts out for a side guided by P.J. Hennelly of Manulla.

Dublin team: Eithne Leech, Betty Hughes, Nuala Murney, Doreen Brennan, Kay Lyons, Bríd Reid (captain), Annette Corrigan (0–1), Kathleen Mills (1–1), Mary O'Sullivan (2–1), Kay Ryder (2–0), Annie Donnelly (2–0) and Una O'Connor (4–3).

Mayo team: Mary Maguire, Margaret Kelly, Kathleen Staunton, Josie Ruane (0–3), Margaret Clarke, Marcella McDonnell, Vera McDonnell, Carmel McHugh, Eileen Clarke (1–0), Bríd Moran, Teresa Hoban and Bridie Kilroy. Subs used: Peggy Coughter, Rose Conway and Mary Daly.

Dublin Forwards

Nell McCarthy had a massive influence on the way the Dublin teams performed. She set down tactics and strategies for the forwards who were the key players in her overall plan. Each forward was keenly aware of where the rest of the attackers were at all times. Because the forwards were constantly on the move, open spaces were always there and it was into these open spaces that the ball was played. They moved to leave space for the ball to be played into and returned at pace to collect and use the ball. How do you mark forwards, who are constantly on the move, continuously changing places and positions, crossing the ball in and out, close passing one moment, then suddenly all moving outfield and bringing the defence with them?

The Dublin forwards received an excellent service from their celebrated midfield players. Coming up against a forward line of this quality, particularly for the first time, left opposing defences bewildered and resulted in runaway wins for Dublin.

1959 Gael-Linn Cup

Two close semi-finals produced narrow victories, Leinster 7–2 to Munster 6–3 and Ulster 3–4 to Connacht 3–3. Five goals from Una O'Connor placed Leinster on the road to a 6–0 to 1–3 victory over Ulster.

Leinster team: Lily Tobin (Kilkenny), Betty Hughes (Dublin), Susan Lennon (Louth), Doreen Brennan (Dublin), Rose Woods (Louth), Chris Whitty (Laois), Annette Corrigan (Dublin) (captain), Betty Green (Wexford), Mary O'Sullivan (Dublin) (1–0), Kay Ryder (Dublin), Annie Donnelly (Dublin) and Una O'Connor (Dublin) (5–0).

Ulster team: Eileen Gormley (Antrim), Alice Mackle (Armagh), Carrie Rankin (Derry), Chris Hughes (Antrim) (0–1), Sue Ward (Antrim), Margo McCourt (Antrim), Margaret Dorrity (Derry), Brigid Downey (Derry), Marion Kearns (Antrim), Bernadette McCluskey (Derry), Maeve Gilroy (Antrim) (1–2) and Lily Reynolds (Armagh).

Minister for Education

President Eilish Redmond and Ard Runaí, Sheila McAnulty, were delegated by congress to call on the Minister for Education, Paddy Hillery, to seek playing facilities for national schools and the inclusion of camogie to the curriculum of teacher training colleges. They met with a pitiful response. Mr Hillery stated that he had no direct control over the national schools and that it was not usual for him to interfere with the curriculum of teacher training colleges.

Progress in Leinster

Also in 1959, the Leinster Council introduced a Junior Championship and Smiths of Balbriggan donated the Smyco Cup for the competition. A Midland League, involving Longford, Westmeath, Cavan and Roscommon, was organised.

The Leinster Colleges Council was set up in 1960. Nine colleges competed for the Stuart Cup, donated by Dr J. J. Stuart, former President of the GAA, whose wife Josie was long-time President of the UCD Camogie Club. Holy Faith, Clontarf, won out from

The Mayo team that played in the 1959 All-Ireland.

Holy Faith, Glasnevin; Clarendon Street; King's Inns Street; St Clare's, Harold's Cross; Sion Hill, Maryfield College; Mercy, Callan; and Mercy, Athboy.

New York

In 1960, New York Young Irelands' Camogie Club was founded by Kathleen O'Dwyer McDonagh from Tipperary and Terry O'Brien Dolan from Galway. The club has stood the test of time, being a home from home for many Irish girls. The New York/Connecticut League was organised from 1960–1966. Young Irelands have hosted many Irish clubs and colleges over the years.

1960 All-Ireland Championship

Annette Corrigan won seven All-Ireland medals as a key player in the engine room of the Dublin team. While still at the height of her career, she stood aside to "give someone else a chance". Bríd Reid, who had gone to live in Cork, and Mary O'Sullivan were also missing from the Dublin lineout for the All-Ireland semi-final against Tipperary at Parnell Park. In what was considered to be the best showing of a Tipperary side to date, the Premier County took Dublin to extra-time. A hard, fast and exciting contest was highlighted by a wonder goal from Kathleen Mills before finishing on the score of Dublin 5–1, Tipperary 3–3.

In the second semi-final, Galway shocked Antrim at Casement Park by 3–1 to 2–3. Antrim, who were confidently expected to advance to the final, led until three minutes from the end, when Chris Conway dropped a high lobbing ball into the Antrim goalmouth. The ball struck the in-rushing Emer Walsh on the top of the head and was deflected out of the reach of the Antrim goalkeeper for the winner.

Because the All-Ireland Football final ended in a draw, the original date for the All-Ireland Camogie decider was withdrawn by the GAA and the participating teams were left idle for almost three months. November 13th was a bleak, wintry day at Croke Park as the Dublin and Galway teams took the field. The long wait had killed off much of the interest in the fixture and the attendance was the lowest in years. Because of the revised date, the match was not broadcast.

Dublin's monopoly was not seriously threatened by Galway. Ten points ahead after ten minutes' play, Dublin carried real menace in every attack. Though, most of the Dublin goals came from rebounds, Eileen Naughton having saved the original shot. When Galway got moving, they battled gamely but, with three 16-year-olds in their lineout, this Galway team was one for the future. Dublin won by 6–2 to 2–0.

Dublin team: Eithne Leech, Betty Hughes, Nuala Murney, Doreen Brennan (captain), Anna Nulty, Colette Nolan, Ally Hussey, Kathleen Mills, Joan Kinsella (3–0), Kay Ryder, Annie Donnelly (1–0) and Una O'Connor (2–2)

Galway team: Eileen Naughton, Patsy Colclough, Evelyn Niland, Ronnie Heneghan, Sheila Tonry, Chris Conway, Kathleen Higgins (1–0), Kathleen Corcoran (captain), Frances Fox (1–0), Kathleen Clancy, Kathleen Flaherty and Emer Walsh.

Antrim's Hour

1960 Gael-Linn Cup

Leinster registered a clear-cut win over Ulster by 10–5 to 3–1 while Munster advanced by 6–6 to 4–0 at the expense of Connacht. The final at Cahir was a close affair with Leinster hanging on to win by 4–1 to 3–2.

Leinster team: Lily Tobin (Kilkenny), Betty Hughes (Dublin), Teresa Nolan (Carlow), Doreen Brennan (captain) (Dublin), Susan Lennon (Louth), Chris Whitty (Laois), Ally Hussey (Dublin), Mary Kehoe (Wexford), Geraldine Callanan (Laois), Claire Hanrahan (Kilkenny) (1–1), Annie Donnelly (Dublin) (2–0) and Una O'Connor (Dublin) (1–0).

Munster team: Catherine Carroll (Tipperary), Peg Moloney (Tipperary), Teresa Murphy (Cork), Bridie Scully (Tipperary) (1–1), Joan Clancy (Cork), Terry Griffin (Tipperary), Pat Doyle (Waterford), Lil Coughlan (Cork), Carrie Gillane (Limerick), Geraldine Power (Waterford), Tess Moloney (Tipperary) (2–1) and Kathleen Griffin (Tipperary).

Wexford girl, Doreen Brennan, was the first player to captain All-Ireland and Gael-Linn winning teams. Her brother, Ray, had played in goal for Wexford in the 1951 All-Ireland hurling final. Munster's Geraldine Power is a sister of Seamus Power, who had won an All-Ireland senior hurling medal with Waterford in 1959.

Congress on Sunday

Congress 1961 was held on a Sunday instead of Saturday, but the experiment was not successful and only nine counties were represented. Dublin moved a motion to include old-time and céili dancing at camogie functions. The idea met with strong opposition from Ulster who felt that Dublin should be ashamed of themselves. The meeting favoured a Cork motion which stated that registered members should not have to take orders from those who were not members of the Association. An attempt to make coloured stockings an option to the regulation black failed to get sufficient support.

Medals at Last

In 1961, Kerry were welcomed back into the fold, a move that saw all six Munster counties affiliated. The Munster final yielded a very satisfactory gate at Clonmel, leaving the Council in a healthy financial state. Players who had won Munster Championship titles from 1952 to 1961 received no medals. Empty boxes were presented when the players came forward to receive their medals. Now that there was money in the kitty, those who were due three or more medals were presented with a silver brooch in the shape of a hurley.

1961 All-Ireland Championship

With Antrim's highly efficient full-back, Moya Forde, unavailable, Tipperary found the route to goal easy to negotiate in the All-Ireland semi-final at Casement Park. Kathleen Downes and Tess Moloney took full advantage to build up a final score of Tipperary 6–3, Antrim 3–3. In the second semi-final at Pearse Stadium, Eithne Leech, Betty Hughes and Ally Hussey were excellent in the Dublin defence against Galway. Judy Doyle, a player who was to strike up a lethal partnership with Una O'Connor, scored three

Tess Moloney scores a goal for Tipperary in the 1961 All-Ireland final at Croke Park. The other players in picture are from left, Bríd McGrath (Tipperary), Betty Hughes (Dublin), Nancy Timmins (Dublin) and Eithne Leech (Dublin).

goals on her inter-county debut. Dublin won by 5–2 to 0–5.

Dissatisfaction abounded that no date for the All-Ireland final had been offered by the GAA despite several requests. Team coaches were handicapped in planning their training programme, not knowing when to peak. From a financial point of view, it was particularly difficult for Tipperary as their players were drawn from the four corners of a large county. The Association also lost out on the publicity angle as interest had died away. The counties waited from the semi-final date of July 19th to October 8th to secure a Croke Park fixture. At this stage, Radio Éireann was unable to alter the schedule and no match broadcast was made.

However, the excitement was rising in the Dublin camp. Kathleen Mills had indicated that the All-Ireland final would be her last match in the blue of Dublin. As the pre-match parade started to move off, Dublin captain, Betty Hughes, stood back to let Kathleen lead the Dublin team. The move was met by a standing ovation from the Dublin fans who showed their appreciation for the wonderful service Kathleen had given.

Kathleen Downes got Tipperary off to a flying start with a well-taken goal. Tipperary matched Dublin in the opening half and were only a point behind at the changeover. Dublin were determined that Kathleen Mills should finish on a winning note and upped their work rate. Kathleen signed off with a trademark goal from midfield as Dublin won by 7–2 to 4–1.

Bridie Scully gave a commanding performance at centre-back for Tipperary and was well supported by Honor O'Flynn, Kitty Flaherty and the Griffin sisters, Terry and Kathleen. With another three goals, Judy Doyle underlined what a valuable asset she was to Dublin. On receiving the O'Duffy Cup, Betty Hughes handed it to Kathleen Mills who was carried shoulder high by her colleagues. The Dublin County Board obtained permission to have a small replica of the O'Duffy Cup made and presented it to Kathleen Mills in recognition of her awesome achievement in winning 15 All-Ireland medals.

Tall, slight and fair-haired, Kathleen Mills was camogie's first superstar. She had a natural aptitude for the game and an amazing turn of speed that did not diminish with time. She possessed a competitive spirit that was roused to its greatest when defeat threatened. A left-handed player, she struck the ball with power and accuracy, sending many a ball from midfield to her opponent's net to the consternation of backs and goalkeeper.

Kathleen's glittering inter-county career stretched from 1941 to 1961. In that time, she collected 15 All-Ireland, 20 Leinster and three Gael-Linn medals. She was honoured with a Cuchulainn Hall of Fame Award and selected on the Team of the Century. Kathleen possessed a gentle nature and a passion for camogie.

Dublin team: Eithne Leech, Betty Hughes (captain), Nuala Murney, Ally Hussey, Nancy Timmins, Colette Nolan, Kay Ryder, Kathleen Mills (1–0), Mary Ryan (1–0), Joan Kinsella (1–1), Judy Doyle (3–0) and Una O'Connor (1–1).

Tipperary team: Honor O'Flynn, Kitty Flaherty, Peg Moloney, Bridie Scully, Kathleen England, Terry Griffin, Terry Cummins, Phyllis Ryan, Tess Moloney (2–0), Kathleen Griffin, Kathleen Downes (2–1) and Bríd McGrath.

1961 Gael-Linn Cup

Leinster suffered their first defeat in the competition at the hands of Connacht by 7–3 to 5–1 at Pearse Park. While, at Roscrea, it took a dramatic late goal by Kathleen Downes for Munster to see off the challenge of Ulster by 4–1 to 2–6. Munster used the ball shrewdly to claim the title for the first time by 5–2 to 1–0 against Connacht at water-soaked Pearse Park.

Munster team: Honor O'Flynn (Tipperary), Josie McNamara (Waterford), Peg Moloney (Tipperary), Pat Doyle (Waterford), Joan Clancy (Cork), Bridie Scully (Tipperary) (0–2), Terry Griffin (Tipperary), Lil Coughlan (Cork), Tess Moloney (Tipperary) (2–0), Kathleen Griffin (Tipperary) (1–0), Kathleen Downes (Tipperary) (1–0) and Eithne Neville (Limerick) (1–0).

Connacht team: Eileen Naughton (Galway), Josie Ruane (Mayo), Ronnie Heneghan (Galway), Margaret Kelly (Mayo), Sheila Tonry (Galway), Kathleen Higgins (Galway), Kathleen Quinn (Galway), Chris Conway (Galway) (captain), Frances Fox (Galway), Eileen Niland (Galway), Carmel McHugh (Mayo) and Frances Clarke (Mayo).

Kay Mills holds the O'Duffy Cup while Tipperary captain, Honor O'Flynn congratulates Dublin's Betty Hughes after the game. President, Eilish Redmond looks on.

A Game of Our Own

Where We're At

From 1948, Dublin ran away with the All-Ireland championship and, in the interests of the competition and the remaining counties, their monopoly needed to be halted. Counties were losing heart and wondered if the effort expected to prepare for the championship was worthwhile. Antrim had come within striking distance more often than others. When the opportunity of hosting the champions in Casement Park presented itself, they made the most of it and edged out Dublin by a single point. Their victory was hailed throughout the country. Antrim, who could raise their game for the special occasion, finished the job at the expense of Cork in the final. Any ideas that this was the end of the great Dublin team were without foundation. With renewed vigour, they set off on a ten-in-a-row winning streak.

From the early days of the Camogie Association, volunteers afforded sterling service to the game which they loved. Duty and dedication were bywords. Senior officials fostered newcomers and passed on the tradition. No job was too difficult or too small for these camogie heroines who made themselves available for duty at all times. Many spent the best years of their lives advancing the game and managed to accommodate a full-time job and/or family commitments. The length of service, loyalty and generosity afforded was exceptional. People, who fit into this category, are found in every county and have forged life-long friendships which sustained them in their work. The Association would not have survived without them.

I spent my last holiday on the farm in the midlands in 1957. Rural electrification had come to the area by then and the scene had changed totally, with a bathroom, electric light and appliances having been installed. A car was parked at the door while the bikes rusted in the shed. The work horses had been replaced by a tractor. They called it progress. For me, the place had lost its magic – even though, the working day finished earlier, work had become easier and there was free time. Rural camogie clubs faced a new problem. Many of the women who worked in the big houses and farms were no longer required. and, with no alternative employment for them in rural Ireland, they moved to the cities or took the boat to England. Consequently, clubs found it difficult to field teams.

Chapter Nine

NO STOPPING DUBLIN

Belfast woke up to a carpet of snow, six to eight inches deep, on the morning of the Ashbourne Cup final. Teams of volunteers, comprising students, staff, supporters and even passers-by were commandeered to clear the pitch. In true Ashbourne form, the match went ahead with UCD defeating Queen's 6–0 to 2–2.

Crios O'Connell Elected President

Crios O'Connell was elected President of the Camogie Association at Congress 1962. She was the first Limerick lady to be chosen for the top office. A very capable chairperson, Crios served Limerick and Munster well.

Even though congress attracted a poor turnout that year – only Antrim travelled from Ulster and Connacht had no representative– 226 clubs were now affiliated, an increase of 43 in ten years. Munster, Leinster and Connacht showed improvement, but Ulster had gone backwards. The issue of whether or not the Association should permit live television coverage of matches and how the new medium could be used to camogie's advantage received considerable airing.

Seán O'Duffy, National Organiser, Sheila McAnulty, Árd Runaí, Crios O'Connell, President and Seán Ó Siocháin, G.A.A. pictured at the Camogie Association's Diamond Jubilee Celebrations in 1964.

Off the Menu

Fr Liam Murray turned to go into the hall to put on the kettle as the match drew to a close in Whitegate, Co. Clare. Coming out against him was a red setter wagging his tail. Sandwiches were off the menu.

Fr Murray was a great man to work for his community. Realising that there was very little for girls in rural areas, he formed a camogie club in every parish in which he worked. He set up clubs in Whitegate and Killanena (Co. Clare), Ahane (Co. Limerick) and Cloughjordan (Co. Tipperary).

In the days before telephones became common, Fr Murray read out the camogie fixtures and times of training from the pulpit at Sunday masses. If he noticed that a player was not at mass, he surveyed the congregation for someone who lived near her and asked him/her to pass on the message.

Family Life

It was not unusual for Lily Spence, Nancy Murray and Mary McMahon to set off from Belfast on a Saturday morning for a Central Council meeting in Dublin and to go home via Galway or Mayo on the Sunday, where Lily or Nancy would have refereed a match and the other two would have been umpires.

Mary would leave a note on the fridge with instructions for her children. Family life was organised around camogie and everybody just got on with it and did what had to be done.

Una O'Connor (Dublin) shoots for goal in the 1962 Dublin-Galway All-Ireland final.

1962 All-Ireland Championship

Antrim played wonderful camogie for two thirds of the All-Ireland semi-final against Dublin at Parnell Park, but faltered when victory loomed. Dublin were a shadow of their usual selves and only exceptional work by Betty Hughes and Kay Ryder kept them in the game. The magic touch of Una O'Connor created a series of chances to save the day for Dublin on the score of 6–4 to 6–2. Cork won enough possession in their semi-final against Galway in Fermoy to win the game but shot so wildly that they blew any chance of victory. The Galway attack made good use of the ball that came their way to deservedly advance to the final by 3–1 to 1–4.

The All-Ireland final between Dublin and Galway was played at Croke Park on August 12th, a beautiful summer's day. Fans took off to the seaside, leaving the camogie final with its lowest attendance in years. A small snippet on the match was included on the Sunday night television sports' programme but no radio broadcast was made.

The game fell well below expectations. Dublin held a pronounced superiority in midfield and the majority of play was between the Galway defence and the Dublin attack. The Galway forwards were starved of possession, but made the most of the two good opportunities that came their way. Galway were unfortunate to lose their centre-back, Ronnie Heneghan, early in the game. Eileen Naughton, in the Galway goal, drew rounds of applause as she saved at least ten potential goals. Dublin were 5–5 to 2–0 ahead at the final whistle.

Dublin team: Eithne Leech, Betty Hughes (captain), Nuala Murney, Ally Hussey, Kay Lyons, Kay Ryder, Mary Sherlock, Mary Ryan (0–2), Patricia Timmins (1–0), Bríd Keenan (0–1), Judy Doyle (3–1) and Una O'Connor (1–1).

Galway team: Eileen Naughton, Patsy Colclough, Rita Flaherty, Ronnie Heneghan, Sheila Tonry (captain), Kathleen Higgins, Kathleen Quinn, Chris Furey, Frances Fox, Kathleen Clancy (1–0), Kathleen Flaherty (1–0) and Emer Walsh.

Gerry or Betty

Small in stature but big in heart, Betty Hughes is known to many people as Gerry Hughes. Her father, Gerry, worked in CIÉ and, as a tiny tot, she had competed in the CIÉ Sports, challenging girls much bigger than herself. Her father's co-workers wished to support the plucky little one but did not know her Christian name. So they called her 'Gerry' and the name stuck.

1962 Gael-Linn Cup

The quality of the games in the Gael-Linn series was everything that one would wish for. Ulster overcame Connacht by 2–9 to

Kathleen O'Duffy presenting Dublin Colleges Cup to Maryfield College in September, 1962.

3–4 at Carrickmacross. Leinster got the better of Munster in a highly entertaining contest by 7–3 to 5–5. In the final, confusion reigned when the final whistle sounded at Casement Park with the score standing at Leinster 7–2, Ulster 5–3. Referee Kathleen Griffin had played 20 minutes in the second-half instead of the regulation 25 minutes. A hastily convened meeting of the Central Council members who were present allowed the result to stand.

Leinster team: Anne Brennan (Louth), Mary Sinnott (Wexford), Nuala Murney (Dublin), Susan Lennon (Louth), Betty Hughes (Dublin), Kay Ryder (Dublin), Margaret Hearne (Wexford), Joan Murphy (Wexford), Geraldine Callanan (Laois) (3–0), Una O'Connor (Dublin) (1–2), Judy Doyle (Dublin) (2–1) and Lily Parle (Wexford) (1–0).

Ulster team: Teresa Jordan (Armagh), Mary Mallon (Armagh), Patricia McKeever (Derry), Chris Hughes (Antrim), Margo Kane (Antrim), Mairéad McAtamney (Antrim) Sue Ward (Antrim) (1–0), Leontia Carabine (Antrim), Marion Kearns (Antrim) (1–1), Mary Phil Jameson (Antrim) (1–0), Maeve Gilroy (1–1) and Lily Reynolds (Armagh) (1–0).

Slow but Steady Progress

1963 saw a county board established in every Munster county. Ten of the 12 Leinster counties took part in the provincial championship, the only exceptions being Wicklow and Carlow. The return of Fermanagh, Cavan and Donegal was awaited in Ulster. Galway and Mayo continued to promote the game in Connacht. The Cork Schools Team routed their Dublin counterparts with a wonderful exhibition of camogie at the Phoenix Park. Following a lapse of 11 years, the Dublin Sports were revived and Teresa Walsh (Austin Stacks) won the trophy for the best individual athlete from a full programme of 38 events.

Mistaken Identity

Maureen Smyth, the Antrim PRO, was being interviewed by a Belfast radio station. Much to Maureen's annoyance, the interviewer kept addressing her as "Missus". He said it once too often and she replied, "I am Miss not Missus and I haven't missed much."

Wexford camogie players marched in the St Patrick's Day Parade wearing gym frocks and black stockings. A lady in the crowd was heard to say, "Look at the little girls out of the orphanage."

1963 All-Ireland Championship

A fast and brilliant game of camogie between Cork and Dublin in the semi-final of the All-Ireland championship at the Mardyke had the crowd on their toes. Trailing by 3–2 to 1–0 with less than 15 minutes remaining, Dublin were lucky to survive. A goal by Una O'Connor breathed new life into Dublin and their attack motored on to snatch a draw.

It was a different story when the sides met again some weeks later. The train carrying the Cork team on the morning of the match broke down at Ballybrophy en route to Dublin. Tension mounted as time passed. Cork, who were unable to make contact with the organisers, togged off on the train and eventually reached Parnell Park some minutes after the scheduled starting time. Without being afforded time to draw breath, they were rushed on to the pitch and the ball was thrown in.

The Cork players, who were still in an agitated state, failed to settle and play their normal game, which allowed Dublin to dominate the game and win comfortably by 8–4 to 1–0. Deirdre Sutton, in the Cork goal, was under constant pressure from Una O'Connor and Judy Doyle in the Dublin attack. All three were top class. Antrim were self-assured and displayed a great appetite for work in the second semi-final against Galway at Craughwell and were rewarded with a 4-6 to 1-3 victory.

It was evident from the early stages of the All-Ireland final between Dublin and Antrim at Croke Park on September 8th that the influence of the Dublin forwards would have a significant impact on the outcome of the game.

Una O'Connor roamed from her full-forward position to gain valuable possession, which she cleverly distributed to her lethal wing-forwards, Judy Doyle and Brίd Keenan. Deficiencies in the Antrim defence were patently clear as seven goals were conceded over the hour.

At the other end, the Antrim forwards were pitted against a defence that was not in the mood to concede. Mairéad McAtamney was majestic in midfield, Betty Smith, Sue Ward and Leontia Carabine were always in the picture for Antrim but Concepta Clarke, Una O'Connor, Judy Doyle, Betty Hughes and Brίd Keenan proved match-winners for Dublin. The final score was

Dublin 7-3, Antrim 2-5.

Dublin team: Concepta Clarke, Betty Hughes, Sheila Ware, Ally Hussey, Kay Lyons, Maureen McEvoy, Mary Sherlock (0-2), Mary Ryan, Brίd Keenan (3-0), Kay Ryder, Judy Doyle (2-1) and Una O'Connor (captain) (2-0).

Antrim team: Teresa Kearns, Moya Forde, Margo Kane, Chris Hughes, Mairéad McAtamney, Betty Smith, Sue Ward (captain) (0-2), Leontia Carabine (0-1), Marion Kearns (1-0), Mary Phil Jameson (1-1), Maeve Laverty and Maeve Gilroy (0-1).

Dublin – All-Ireland Champions 1963. Back: Maureen McEvoy, Brίd Keenan, Mary Ryan, Patricia Timmons, Kay Lyons, Mary Sherlock and Concepta Clarke. Front: Cora Crowe, Sheila Ware, Judy Doyle, Kay Ryder, Una O'Connor (Capt), Eithne Leech, Betty Hughes and Ally Hussey.

1963 Gael-Linn Cup

Munster were lively and inventive against Connacht in the semi-final of the Gael-Linn at Pearse Park and made good use of their opportunities to win by 5-10 to 1-3. Leinster made no mistake in a their high-scoring semi-final at Carrickmacross. Once they got into their stride, they powered ahead to win by 9-3 to 6-0.

In an exciting and often brilliant final at Gorey, Munster

defeated Leinster. The standard of play was first class and the verdict was in doubt up to the end. Ann Carroll, Lilian Howlett, Deirdre Young, Deirdre Sutton and Rena Manley engineered a 3–2 to 2–2 win for Munster.

Munster team: Deirdre Sutton (Cork), Kitty Barry-Murphy (Cork), Bridie Giltenane (Limerick), Peg Moloney (Tipperary), Josie McNamara (Waterford), Terry Geaney (Tipperary) (1–0), Lilian Howlett (Waterford) (0–1), Deirdre Young (Cork) (0–1), Ann Carroll (Tipperary) (1–0), Rena Manley (Cork) (1–0), Stephanie O'Connell (Cork) and Kathleen Griffin (Tipperary).

Leinster team: Eileen Ellard (Wexford), Mary Sinnott (Wexford), Joan Murphy (Wexford), Mary Sherlock (Dublin), Kay Lyons (Dublin), Kitty Murphy (Dublin), Kay Ryder (Dublin), Margaret Hearne (Wexford), Claire Hanrahan (Kilkenny) (1–2), Una O'Connor (Dublin) (captain), Judy Doyle (1–0) and Bríd Moran (Kildare).

Kitty Barry-Murphy's father, Dinny, had captained Cork to win the All-Ireland senior hurling title in 1929. Deirdre Young is a daughter of Josie McGrath, who had captained Cork to win the 1935 All-Ireland Camogie title. Lilian Howlett's five sons – Billy, Rory, Daragh, Patrick and Shane O'Sullivan – have played senior hurling for Waterford and her two daughters, Gail and Clara, have played camogie with the county team.

For the first time in the history of camogie, individual awards were made to the top players. Una O'Connor (Dublin) and Deirdre Sutton (Cork) were honoured with Gaelic Stars Awards.

Celtic (Dublin) – Winners of Jubilee Cup 1964. Back: Dorothy O'Boyle, Ally Hussey, Claire Heffernan, Mary Casey, Una O'Connor, Mary Moran, Alison McGarry and Jean McNally. Front: Cora Crowe, Angela Gill, Bríd Hanbury (Capt), Mary O'Keeffe, Dervil Dunne and Eithne Leech.

Permission to Play Hockey

In November 1963, the Central Council meeting considered a request from Sion Hill to permit their PE students to play both hockey and camogie matches. A deputation was sent to explain the camogie rules to the principal. The matter was aired at the following Congress 1964. A prolonged discussion took place in which divergent views were expressed. Many delegates felt that to accede to the request would create a dangerous precedent while others thought that agreeing to such a decision would be justified because of the good that could come to the game by having trained coaches in the schools. The proposal to allow the PE students of Sion Hill to play both games was lost on the president's casting vote.

The Diamond Jubilee of the Camogie Association was celebrated in 1964. In his report to congress as national organiser, Seán O'Duffy reviewed the progress of the Association and expressed disappointment that camogie was no longer strong in some counties where it had been played for many years.

He felt that the Association in its 60 years of existence had not made the impact in the country which such an organisation should have made. The Association came through from the period of foreign rule to the era when we had our own government but while other games had made tremendous strides since the twenties, Camogie had not grown at the same pace or indeed at any great pace.

He was not despondent. However, he felt that if all the members of the Association got down to the job of working for it, the Association would go forward and progress and would contribute much to the life of the country.

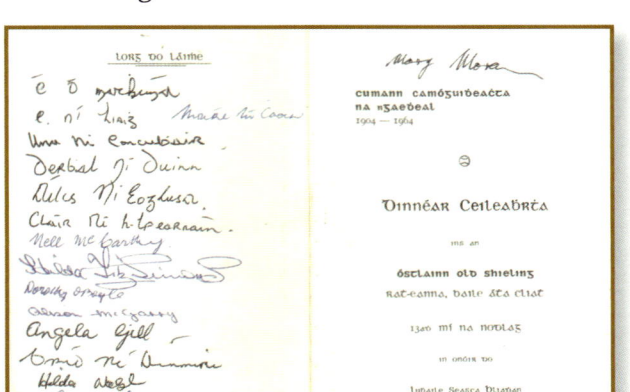

50th Anniversary Dinner Programme, autographed by members of the Celtic team which won the first All-Ireland Club Championship that day (13 December, 1964).

Jubilee Cup

To mark the Diamond Jubilee of the Association, Central Council organised an All-Ireland Club Championship. A most unusual silver cup, known as the 'Jubilee Cup', was presented for the competition by an anonymous donor. Clubs that had won their county championship were eligible to enter the provincial club championship. The four provincial club champions were paired at the All-Ireland semi-final stage.

Deirdre (Belfast), Glen Rovers (Cork), Celtic (Dublin) and Newport (Mayo) emerged from the provincial finals. Newport failed to travel to Belfast much to the annoyance of the organisers. Celtic arrived at Ballinlough (Cork) to find that no camogie goalposts were available. The match eventually went ahead on the full-sized hurling pitch. An epic battle that was brimful of incident and excitement ended all square. Ahead by four points in the closing stages of the replay at Parnell Park, Glen Rovers seemed destined to advance to the final. When Una O'Connor retired with a head injury, there seemed to be no way back for the Dublin side. Substitute Kit Kehoe signalled her arrival in the game by first-timing the ball in the direction of her own goal. Luckily for Celtic, Eithne Leech was alert and coped with the unexpected shot. Kit ran onto the dropping puck out and doubled on the ball to the Glen Rovers net to throw the game open. She struck again with a powerful drive. Deirdre Sutton got her stick to the ball but could not prevent it crossing the line. Celtic advanced to the final by 5–1 to 4–1.

Following the drama of the semi-final and replay, the All-Ireland Club final between Celtic and Deirdre at Croke Park on December 13th was an anti-climax. Polished performances by Una O'Connor, Ally Hussey and Eithne Leech proved too much for a Deirdre side that was over-dependent on Sue Ward. Celtic claimed the Jubilee Cup by 5–2 to 1–0 and were allowed to keep it permanently.

Celtic team: Eithne Leech, Hilda Walsh, Angela Gill, Ally Hussey, Dervil Dunne, Mary Moran, Mary Casey, Claire Heffernan, Bríd Hanbury (captain), Mary O'Keeffe (2–1), Cora Crowe and Una O'Connor (3–1).

Deirdre team: Kathleen McCartan, Nancy Murray, A. O'Hare, Maura McKenna, Kathleen Byrne, Babs McCabe, Sue Ward (captain) (1–0), Eileen McGrogan, L. Lanigan, Ita Sheridan, Pat Lalor and Vera Corscadden.

Angela Gill is a daughter of Mick Gill who won All-Ireland hurling medals with Galway and Dublin. Mary Casey is a sister of Bill Casey, who had won an All-Ireland football medal with Dublin in 1963. Claire Heffernan is a sister of star footballer and Dublin coach, Kevin Heffernan.

The Celtic Club was formed in the Coolock area of Dublin's northside by the Keegan sisters in 1929. Six presidents of the Camogie Association wore the famous black, red and blue colours – Eilish Keegan-Redmond, Mary Kelly-Lynch, Nell McCarthy, Mary Moran, Mary Fennelly and Liz Howard. Eilish was the only Dubliner, all the rest were working in Dublin at the time that they fielded with the club. Una O'Connor, Eileen Duffy, Ally Hussey, Betty Hughes, Eithne Leech, Kit Kehoe, Kitty Murphy, Deirdre Lane, Una Crowley and Ann Colgan are a sprinkling of the stars that won many Dublin championship medals with Celtic.

1964 All-Ireland programme

Jubilee Banquet

Dignitaries of the GAA and camogie worlds attended a banquet at the Old Shieling to mark the Diamond Jubilee of the Camogie Association on the night of the All-Ireland Club final, during which Seán Ó Síocháin and Micheál O'Hehir amused the large attendance with witty speeches. A presentation of a television was made to Seán O'Duffy set and a bouquet of flowers to his wife Kathleen. When Seán rose to speak, he posed the question, "What would I want with a television?" and referred to the bouquet of flowers as a "wreath".

Making one's own entertainment was the order of the day. Paddy Murphy gave a boisterous rendition of 'Biddy Mulligan'" and Seán Ó Síocháin sang 'Boolavogue' in his distinctive baritone voice. Nancy Murray set aside the disappointment of the afternoon to do justice to 'Roddy McCorley' with her rich velvet tones, while Nell McCarthy, Maureen Hoey, Crios O'Connell and Eileen Bourke performed their party-pieces.

1964 All-Ireland Championship

Following Paddy O'Keeffe's death in May 1964, Seán Ó Síocháin took over the role of General Secretary of the GAA. The affable Corkman was a great friend to camogie and one of the first things he did in his new role was to write to Ard Runaí, Sheila McAnulty, offering Croke Park for the All-Ireland Camogie final on October 4th. His gesture was very well received.

In the semi-final of the All-Ireland Championship at Parnell Park, Galway suffered a cruel blow before the throw-in against Dublin when their excellent goalkeeper, Eileen Naughton, had to cry off. Clever distribution of the ball resulted in six Dublin forwards finding the Galway net in a flawless exhibition to win by 10–2 to 0–0.

Tipperary were unable to match the pace and stick work of Antrim at sunny Glenarriffe in the second semi-final. Margo Kane, Teresa Kearns, Maeve Gilroy, Mary Phil Jameson and Sue Ward thrilled the home fans with their attractive play. Antrim won by 6–8 to 3–3.

Antrim and Dublin had served up magnificent exhibitions of camogie in previous years and followers of the game expected to see another classic at Croke Park on October 4th. However, Dublin's Judy Doyle hit a purple patch in the opening seven minutes and shot three goals before the Ulster girls had settled. Lesser sides might have succumbed at that stage but Antrim re-jigged their team bringing Lily Scullion to midfield and Maeve Gilroy to centre-forward. They fought back tenaciously. Una O'Connor, who had contributed to Judy Doyle's goals, added another as did Bríd Keenan.

Nell McCarthy had brought the work of team preparation to a fine art. She produced a succession of champion sides that moved so smoothly no matter what individuals came and went over the years. The Dublin teams played to the same successful pattern.

Sue Ward played a captain's part at centre-back and set up attack after attack. Mary Phil Jameson, Betty Smith and Maeve Gilroy scored goals to raise Antrim's hopes but further goals by Judy Doyle and Bríd Keenan sealed the outcome in Dublin's favour. Despite the scoreline of 7–4 to 3–1, the game produced some excellent passages of play.

Dublin centre-back Ally Hussey was a classy player. Unlike the vast majority of players, the less she trained, the better she performed. Ally could lie in the sun for two weeks, fly back to Dublin hours before the match and play the proverbial blinder. Dublin selector, Anne Ashton was directed to have a lighted cigarette ready at half-time and block Nell McCarthy's view while Ally took a few puffs.

Dublin team: Concepta Clarke, Mary Ryan, Rose O'Reilly,

Ally Hussey, Kay Lyons, Patricia Timmins, Mary Sherlock, Orla Ní Síocháin, Bríd Keenan (2–0), Kay Ryder, Judy Doyle (4–1) and Una O'Connor (captain) (1–3).

Antrim team: Teresa Kearns, Moya Forde, Chris O'Boyle, Sue Ward (captain), Mairéad Carabine, Betty Smith (1–0), Maeve Gilroy (1–0), Mairéad McAtamney (0–1), Marion McFetridge, Lily Scullion, Kitty Finn and Mary Phil Jameson (1–0).

1964 Gael-Linn Cup

Connacht were unable to scrape together sufficient funds for the trip to meet Leinster in the semi-final of the Gael-Linn Cup and withdrew from the competition. In the other semi-final, all counties but Kerry were represented on the Munster team that proved too good for Ulster by 7–3 to 2–4 at Roscrea. Peggy Dorgan registered 3–1 but an injury kept her out of the final against Leinster at Cahir. The Griffin sisters, Terry and Kathleen, withdrew from the Munster team owing to the death of their father. Kitty Murphy, Lilian Howlett, Ann Carroll and Rena Manley stepped up to the mark to defeat Leinster by 2–6 to 3–2 and retain the trophy.

Munster team: Deirdre Sutton (Cork), Peg Moloney (Tipperary), Bridie Giltenane (Limerick), Bridget Ryan (Limerick), Anne Graham (Tipperary), Deirdre Young (Cork), Lilian Howlett (Waterford) (0–2), Teresa Murphy (Cork), Ann Carroll (Tipperary) (0–2), Bernie Moloney (Tipperary) (1–0), Kitty Murphy (Clare) (0–2) and Rena Manley (Cork) (1–0).

Leinster team: Concepta Clarke (Dublin), Mary Sinnott (Wexford), Joan Murphy (Wexford), Ally Hussey (Dublin), Kay Lyons (Dublin), Mary Walsh (Wexford), Pat Higgins (Kildare), Kay Ryder (Dublin), Kitty Murphy (Louth) (1–0), Una O'Connor (Dublin) (2–0), Judy Doyle (Dublin) (0–1) and Claire Hanrahan (Kilkenny) (0–1).

Girl or Boy

Nan Lynch, widely regarded as Westmeath's best player, still fielded with her club, Tang, at the age of 68. Many years before, Nan was collected by car on the way to a championship match between Tang and Cullion at Moate. There was an individual in the back of the car with her face covered by a headscarf and wearing heavy make-up. Nan did not recognise who it was. This person played in the match and allegations were made that he was a boy. Afterwards this mysterious person made a quick getaway through the crowd as soon as the game was over. The newspapers picked up the story and gave it considerable coverage. Central Council were not pleased to read about the incident and instructed the Westmeath County Board to withhold the championship medals.

Lil Elected President

Lil O'Grady (Old Aloysians, Cork) succeeded Crios O'Connell as President of the Camogie Association at the 1965 Congress in Dublin. A very capable and impartial chairperson, Lil enhanced the profile of camogie during her presidency.

Congress voted to make the All-Ireland Club Championship a permanent fixture on

Lil O'Grady

the Camogie calendar. The Antrim County Board imposed a six-month suspension on Queen's University Camogie Club because they staged a dance in conjunction with the Ashbourne Cup. According to rule at the time, any club that organised foreign dances under its auspices was liable to such a penalty.

Financial Control

Women used to managing on tight household budgets applied the same controls when it came to handling camogie finances. Their strategy was not to spend if at all possible and going into debt was to be avoided at all costs. An end-of-year treasurer's statement which showed a credit balance after all liabilities had been met was considered very satisfactory. The proverb 'speculate to accumulate' was not for them.

A glance at the 1965 treasurer's statement shows how the Association managed on very meagre income. Affiliation fees of £32.15.0, representing 262 clubs, and profit of £211 from the All-Ireland senior and club championships were the only sources of income. Expenditure covered routine items such as postage, officials' expenses, medals and an audit fee. Grants amounting to £105 were made to travelling teams. A once-off subsidy of £56 to the Jubilee Banquet and a loss of £29 on the Gael-Linn series reduced the bank balance to £106. The recurring loss on the Gael-Linn was a matter of real concern.

Tipperary – 1965 All-Ireland finalists. Back: Monica Ryan, Honor O'Flynn, Anna Carson, Bernie Moloney, Alice Long, Sally Long, Margaret Phelan and Mary Graham. Front: Anne Graham, Margo Loughnane, Maureen Hally, Terry Griffin, Ann Carroll, Peg Moloney, Kathleen Griffin and Peggy Graham.

1965 All-Ireland Championship

Tipperary had little difficulty in outsmarting Galway in the All-Ireland semi-final at Tuam. Fitter and faster than their opponents, the Tipperary girls had the job done by half-time when they led by 6–5 to 0–0. The Galway forwards were unable to penetrate the Tipperary defence. Not for the first time, goalkeeper Eileen Naughton saved Galway from a total annihilation. The final score was Tipperary 8–5, Galway 0–0.

Mairéad McAtamney, a wonderful artist of the game, gave an exhibition of striking in the picturesque surroundings of

Glenariffe in the All-Ireland semi-final against Dublin. The large attendance thoroughly enjoyed a fast, open game of camogie that produced 17 goals. Una O'Connor and Judy Doyle played cat and mouse with the Antrim defence with clever positioning, changes of pace and direction, great ball control and clinical finishing. Some brilliant scores were executed at the other end by former goalkeeper, Teresa Kearns, Mary Phil Jameson, Mairéad McAtamney and Lily Scullion. The goal feast ended at Dublin 10–1, Antrim 7–5.

The ability to convert their chances was the only difference between Dublin and Tipperary in the All-Ireland final at Croke Park on September, 19th. Una O'Connor opened up the Tipperary defence with incisive passes to which Judy Doyle and Kit Kehoe applied the finishing touch. Kay Ryder, Mary Sherlock, Eithne Leech and Mary Ryan got through a lot of hard graft to earn a 10–1 to 5–3 victory. Tipperary made a brave bid for their first All-Ireland title and, individually at least, were as good as their opponents. But in craft and combination, they fell short of Dublin's standards. Ann Carroll, Honor O'Flynn, the Griffin and the Graham sisters worked extremely hard for Tipperary.

Dublin team: Eithne Leech, Mary Ryan, Bríd Keenan, Ally Hussey, Kay Lyons, Mary Sherlock, Patricia Timmins, Orla Ní Síocháin, Kit Kehoe (3–0), Kay Ryder (captain) (1–0), Judy Doyle (5–0) and Una O'Connor (1–1).

Tipperary team: Sally Long, Peg Moloney, Anne Graham, Margaret Phelan, Mary Graham, Ann Carroll (captain) (2–1), Peggy Graham (1–0), Bernie Moloney, Margo Loughnane (0–1), Kathleen Griffin (1–0), Honor O'Flynn (0–1) and Terry Griffin (1–0). Subs used: Maureen Hally and Monica Ryan.

The Dublin team sported 48 All-Ireland medals between them, an average of four each in those 12-a-side days. Orla Ní Síocháin was a daughter of Seán Ó Síocháin, former Director General of the GAA. She married Jack Ryan, son of Seamus Ó Riain, former President of the GAA and her son, Shane, is a prominent Dublin hurler and footballer.

Fran Whelan picked up All-Ireland medals with Dublin in 1965 and 1966. Her brother, Mickey, had won an All-Ireland football medal with Dublin in 1963.

St. Patrick's, Glengoole – All-Ireland Club champions 1965 and 1966. Back: Ann Carroll, Alice Long, Monica Ryan, Mary Brennan, Rita Scott, Lucy Scott, Maura Maher and Kathleen Griffin. Front: Bernie Moloney, Margo Loughnane, Ann Graham, Peggy Graham, Mary Graham and Sally Long.

1965 All-Ireland Club Championship

Bill Carroll, father of Tipperary star Ann Carroll, donated a cup for the All-Ireland Club Championship. Celtic, who had won the Jubilee Cup the previous year, qualified as Dublin champions but decided not to enter the competition. St Patrick's (Munster), Deirdre (Ulster), St Ibar's (Leinster) and St Rita's (Connacht) contested the All-Ireland semi-finals. St Patrick's trounced St Rita's by 12–4 to 1–2 at Carramore, while Deirdre enjoyed a comfortable outing against St Ibar's at Wexford Park and won by 4–4 to 1–2.

St Patrick's became the first holders of the Bill Carroll Cup when they narrowly defeated Deirdre by 3–3 to 2–3 at Casement Park. Right through the field, Deirdre matched their opponents. Ann Carroll was hugely effective in midfield for the winners and contributed 1–3 of the final score. Nancy Murray and Sue Ward performed to a very high standard for Deirdre who were unfortunate to lose out in a tight finish.

St Patrick's team: Sally Long, Ann Graham, Monica Ryan, Maura Maher, Mary Graham, Ann Carroll (captain) (1–3), Peggy Graham (1–0), Kathleen Griffin, Bernie Moloney, Margo Loughnane, Alice Long (1–0) and Lucy Scott.

Deirdre team: Kathleen McCartan, Nancy Murray, Briege Gilmore, Maura McKenna, Babs McCabe, Kathleen Byrne, Sue Ward, Eileen McGrogan, Ita Lanigan, Kathleen McManus, Eileen Doran and Christine Wheeler.

Two small clubs, Ballingarry and Glengoole, had joined forces to form St Patrick's in 1964. Alice Graham, Statia Dunne, Annie Langton and Ann Carroll were the first officers of the club. Tipperary champions in 1964, 1965 and 1966, St Patrick's won Munster and All-Ireland honours in 1965 and 1966 and attracted many players from other clubs. Following victory in 1966, the club disbanded and the players returned to their original clubs.

1965 Gael-Linn Cup

Connacht offered little by way of resistance to a superior Ulster outfit at Castlebar and paid the heavy price of a 7–13 to 1–0 defeat. In the second semi-final, Leinster turned in a sterling performance to overcome Munster by 4–9 to 2–1 at Fermoy. Wind-assisted Leinster had a hand on the cup when they led by 3–3 to 1–0 at the break in the final at Casement Park, but Ulster

Phyllis Campbell, Pat Irvine, Teresa Foy and Sheila McEvoy who played members of Cumann na mBan in the 1916 pageant in Croke Park by Bryan McMahon: Seacht Fear: Seacht Lá.

mounted a late rally that yielded two goals to leave the final score at Leinster 4–3, Ulster 4–1.

Leinster team: Eithne Leech (Dublin), Mary Sinnott (Wexford), Susan Dooley (Offaly), Ally Hussey (Dublin), Margaret O'Leary (Wexford), Mary Sherlock (Dublin), Kay Ryder (Dublin) (captain), Orla Ní Síocháin (Dublin) (0–1), Kit Kehoe (Dublin) (1–0), Claire Hanrahan (Kilkenny) (0–2), Judy Doyle (Dublin) (1–0) and Una O'Connor (Dublin) (2–0).

Ulster team: Kathleen Kelly (Antrim), Moya Forde (Antrim), Angela Kennedy (Down), Maeve Gilroy (Antrim), Sue Ward (Antrim) (3–1), Marion McFetridge (Antrim), Mary McKenna (Monaghan), Mairéad McAtamney (Antrim), Madeline Sands (Down) (1–0), Betty Smith (Antrim), Lily Clarke (Monaghan) and Mary Phil Jameson (Antrim).

Kathleen Kelly (Antrim) and Kit Kehoe (Dublin) contest the ball in the 1966 All-Ireland final at Croke Park.

Easter Week Golden Jubilee Celebrations

The Camogie Association participated in the Easter Week Golden Jubilee Commemorations at many levels. At a reception given by Central Council on the night of the All-Ireland final, a Commemoration Pageant, The Walk of a Queen, devised by Sheila McAnulty, was presented by a cast from the four provinces.

One hundred camogie players took part in the GAA commemorative pageant *Seachtar Fear – Seacht Lá*, by Bryan McMahon in Croke Park, filling the roles of Cumann na mBan and James Connolly's workers. Many more participated in commemorative ceremonies at local level.

See-Saw Position

The see-saw position of camogie in the country continued. New clubs were formed in some areas while others folded elsewhere. In 1965, Donegal, Derry, Leitrim, Longford and Carlow all failed to affiliate. While some measure of progress was being made in Munster, Leinster and Ulster, Connacht had slipped back with the Mayo club numbers reduced to two and Galway's almost halved.

Munster initiated a Secondary Championship in which players who held Munster senior medals were ineligible to participate. The result saw very evenly matched sides provide close and exciting games. Limerick emerged as the first winners of the Kenneally Cup and took their first Munster title.

No Stopping Dublin

Her Hour

Typical of many young women of her day, Eileen lived with her husband Joe and three small children in one of Dublin's new suburbs. It was her responsibility to look after the children and attend to the chores of the day. Joe left for work early in the morning and did not return until late. Life was lonely at times as she had left her parents' home and the community where she grew up on the other side of the River Liffey.

On Sundays, Eileen cycled to the Phoenix Park to play with her club or puck around if they had no fixture. She looked forward to greeting friendly faces, participating in healthy exercise and chatting with like-minded company. It was 'her hour'. The visit to the park released the frustrations of everyday life and she returned home refreshed, happy to face the challenges and responsibilities of the coming week.

Una O'Connor

1966 All-Ireland Championship

Confusion reigned at the finish of an exciting encounter between Tipperary and Dublin in the semi-final of the All-Ireland championship at Cahir. The referee called it a one-point win for Dublin but many people, including neutrals, believed the match ended in a draw. Some of the Tipperary supporters acted in an unruly manner for which the county received a six-month suspended sentence. Tipperary appealed against the result but their objection failed and the referee's score of Dublin 5–0, Tipperary 3–5 was confirmed.

Sue Ward powered Antrim to victory over Galway in the second All-Ireland semi-final at Ballinasloe. The superior striking of the northern girls, particularly Kathleen Kelly, Betty Smith, Maeve Gilroy and Anne Marie Finn, in addition to the non-stop action of midfielder, Sue Ward, proved too much for the home side and resulted in a 4–4 to 3–0 win for Antrim.

Dublin have defenders Mary Ryan, Kay Lyons, Kitty Murphy and Bríd Keenan to thank for a hard-earned 2–2 to 0–6 victory over Antrim in the All-Ireland final at Croke Park on September 18th. The Dublin rearguard kept the Antrim attackers at bay and their goal intact, while, for Antrim, Teresa Kearns brought off a series of outstanding saves, denying Dublin more goals.

Moya Forde, Ethna Dougan and Maeve Gilroy put in sterling work to curtail the highly rated Dublin forward line. Mairéad McAtamney excelled in midfield and accounted for all but two points of her team's score. Goals from Una O'Connor and Kit Kehoe gave the holders a narrow lead.

With only a goal separating the sides in the closing minute, Mairéad Carabine drew on a high dropping ball which flew inches over the bar and Antrim's chance was gone. Antrim had reason to rue their 16 wides over the 50 minutes.

Dublin team: Eithne Leech, Mary Ryan, Bríd Keenan, Kitty Murphy, Kay Lyons, Mary Sherlock, Kay Ryder, Orla Ní Síocháin, Kit Kehoe (1–0), Anne McAllister, Judy Doyle and Una O'Connor (1–2).

Antrim team: Teresa Kearns, Moya Forde, Ethna Dougan, Maeve Gilroy, Kathleen Kelly, Betty Smith, Mairéad Quinn, Mairéad McAtamney (0–4), Mairéad Carabine (0–2), Margaret Finn, Eileen McGrogan and Mary Phil Jameson.

Caltex Award

For the first time in the history of the game, camogie was included in the list of Caltex Sports Awards, the most coveted tribute for sports ability in the country. The recipient, Una O'Connor (Dublin), was a player of exceptional talent. A born forward, Una possessed a special body swerve which allowed her pass her opponent and make room for her shot. Una read the play at a glance, distributed the ball with telling effect and took her own scores with rare accuracy.

The blue-eyed, fair-haired forward holds a record of ten All-Ireland medals in-a-row and 13 in all. The happiest night of her life is how she described the function at the Gresham Hotel when Taoiseach, Jack Lynch, presented her with her trophy. Una's father was her greatest fan and was extremely proud of her achievements. Unfortunately, he had passed away in the previous year and did not live to join her on the special occasion.

1966 All-Ireland Club Championship

Deirdre (Belfast) were cast on the back foot from the start against St Patrick's in the semi-final of the All-Ireland Club Championship at Holycross and never looked like getting into the game. Showing some delightful touches, St Patrick's completely outplayed their rivals by 11–5 to 0–0.

In the second semi-final at Kilkenny, St Paul's were more accurate in attack than Oranmore, and tested them with a series of attacks. Claire Hanrahan, Mary Fennelly, Nuala Duncan and Rosaleen Vennard stamped their presence on the game to ensure a 5–3 to 2–0 win for the Kilkenny side.

St Patrick's, who had scored 36 goals and 37 points on the way to the final, were not going to be stopped at the last hurdle in St John's Park on October 30th. St Paul's gave it their best shot and contained the champions to a certain degree. In effect, St Patrick's were a County Tipperary selection and ten of the starting team

The Munster team which defeated Ulster in the Gael-Linn Interprovincial at Carrickmacross. Back: Ann Carroll, Bunty Guiry, Anna Crotty, Bridie Giltenane, Lilian Howlett, Stephanie O'Connell, Kathleen Griffin and Mel Cummins. Front: Peggy Dorgan, Margo Loughnane, Ann Graham, Bernie Moloney, Peggy Graham, Monica Ryan and Sally Long.

held Munster senior championship medals. Their free-scoring forwards kept the cup in Tipperary by 5–5 to 2–1.

St Patrick's team: Sally Long, Ann Graham (capt), Maura Maher, Ann Carroll, Mary Graham, Alice Long, Kathleen Griffin, Monica Ryan, Bernie Moloney, Lucy Scott, Margo Loughnane and Peggy Graham.

St Paul's team: Teasie Brennan, Nuala Duncan, Mary Holohan, Ann Gargan, Mary Connery, Carmel O'Shea, Mary Fennelly, M. Butler, Claire O'Hanrahan, Olive O'Neill, Rose Vennard and Nuala Grace.

Bernie Moloney's brother, Donie, captained Roscrea to win the first All-Ireland Club hurling championship in 1971.

1966 Gael-Linn Cup

In the first semi-final of the Gael-Linn Cup as Naas, a good start and a strong finish were sufficient for Leinster to dispose of the Connacht challenge by 3–6 to 1–0. With a sharper and more focused set of forwards, Munster were good value for their 7–3 to 1–4 win over Ulster at Carrickmacross.

With all the Dublin players, except Kay Ryder, making themselves unavailable for the Gael-Linn final at Ballinlough, Munster made good use of the opportunity to regain the cup. Stephanie O'Connell, Bernie Moloney, Lilian Howlett and Kathleen Griffin were outstanding in everything they did and ensured a Munster win by 4–2 to 1–3.

The team which brought the tenth consecutive title to Dublin in 1966. Back: Sheila Creevy, Kay Lyons, Claire Heffernan, Fran Whelan, Concepta Clarke, Anne McAllister, Mary Ryan, Patricia Timmons, Bríd Keenan and Mary Sherlock. Front: Orla Ní Siocháin, Kitty Murphy, Kit Kehoe, Una O'Connor, Kay Ryder (Capt), Judy Doyle, Eithne Leech and Josie Quinn.

Munster team: Sally Long (Tipperary), Mel Cummins (Cork), Bridie Giltenane (Limerick), Ann Graham (Tipperary), Bunty Guiry (Limerick), Ann Carroll (Tipperary), Lilian Howlett (Waterford), Peggy Dorgan (Cork), Margo Loughnane (Tipperary) (1–0), Stephanie O'Connell (Cork) (0–2), Bernie Moloney (Tipperary) (2–0) and Kathleen Griffin (Tipperary) (1–0).

Leinster team: Joan Cullen (Wexford), Mary Holohan (Kilkenny), Joan Murphy (Wexford), Margaret O'Leary (Wexford), Mary Connery (Kilkenny), Peg Cash (Wexford), Margaret Hearne (Wexford), Monica Malone (Kildare), Barbara Magee (Kildare), Kay Ryder (Dublin), Carmel O'Shea (Kilkenny) and Claire Hanrahan (Kilkenny).

Where We're At

The Association had been established over 60 years, but how secure was it? In 1964, 32 clubs were affiliated to the Cork County Board. Two years later, the number was down to 19. This situation was not confined to Cork. Most clubs were vulnerable because there were no young players coming on-stream. Clubs catered for adult players and had no underage teams so when a player retired, married or moved away to take up employment, there was no ready-made replacement to fill her shoes. Lack of attention to underage was undermining progress. Where a few players left at the same time, the club was unable to continue.

Schools camogie remained under-developed. At convention time and at annual congress, pious words were spoken concerning the need to foster the game in the schools, but no practical steps were taken to do anything positive about it. There it rested until the next annual gathering. Queen's University had entered the Ashbourne Cup in 1934, bringing the number of participants to four, and, 30 years on, the number was still four. The competition was organised by the host university, who was more interested in making arrangements to suit itself than developing the third-level sector. Both the second and third levels were crying out for a national council to be formed to take ownership of the area and develop it.

Television had come to the homes of Ireland and was proving to be a great novelty and topic of conversation. Congress talked of preparing for the arrival of the new medium so that camogie would portray a good image on the screen. But the newly established RTÉ was not interested in camogie and ignored the game.

On the positive side, the new All-Ireland Club Championship was an instant success. Clubs improved and became stronger through their efforts to prepare for the competition. It was, and still is, the most difficult championship to win as it incorporates three competitions, county, provincial and All-Ireland championships. Clubs, which reach the latter stages, undergo eight to ten months of serious training, bringing the side to a higher plane.

The granting of a Caltex award to Una O'Connor was a major shot in the arm for camogie. It placed camogie's top star on an equal footing with the celebrities of other sports. Female recipients of the honour were few and far between and the publicity afford to Una, on the occasion, was welcome and very pleasing.

Chapter Ten

NEW CHAMPIONS

Congress 1967 passed an Antrim motion which read: "Any member who plays hockey or football thereby incurs suspension from membership of the Association for a period of at least 12 months." The new rule included indoor football which was gaining popularity at the time. Louth clubs and officials were the first to fall foul of the new rule. The introduction of this rule brought ridicule on the Camogie Association and certainly did not draw girls to the sport. Ulster, in particular, believed that it was anti-national to play foreign games.

Congress also increased the dimensions of the playing pitch to 105–120 yards in length and 65–75 yards in width. It was decided that the ball should be thrown in by the referee between the midfield players to commence play, with all other players to be in their position in advance. A motion to modernise the playing uniform failed by a mere two votes.

Máire Ní Chinnéide

A vote of condolence was passed to the relatives of the late Máire Ní Chinnéide, founder member and first President of the Association.

Antrim captain, Sue Ward receives the O'Duffy Cup from President, Lil O'Grady.

Coaching at Orangefield

A major breakthrough took place at Orangefield, Belfast, in August when a weekend residential coaching course was organised by the Ulster Council with assistance from the Belfast Educational Authority. The basic skills of the game, both theory and practice, were expertly taught by Nell McCarthy, coach to the successful Dublin teams, and top Antrim player, Maeve Gilroy. The course attracted almost 60 students who responded enthusiastically to their teachers and were very keen to learn and improve. The warm personality of Ulster Chairman, Rosina Mc-

Manus, ensured that all worked efficiently in a spirit of friendship.

Rosie's Big Moment

Like every Friday, Rosie ran her eye over the school notice board. Her heart missed a beat. Yes, her name was there – OK she was number 19, but her name was there. She could not eat with excitement on Saturday and got to the venue in good time. While not expecting her name to be read out when the team was announced, she felt a twinge of disappointment. "Mind the coats and don't let them get wet," shouted the captain. The match wore on with no sign of her getting a chance. "Peel the oranges," was the next instruction.

The match was well into the second-half and Rosie had almost given up hope of making an entrance. Patsy let a roar and went down in a heap. Rosie held her breath. Half a bottle of water was poured on Patsy's leg. Believing that she had done enough for one day, she hobbled off. "Hey, young one, get your coat off," shouted the captain. It was Rosie's big moment. She fumbled with the buttons, threw her coat on top of the pile and ran onto the field. "Where's your stick?" Armed with her stick, she took up position ten yards from goal and won-

Obituary for Máire Ní Chinnéide that appeared in The Irish Independent

dered what she was supposed to do.

The opposing centre-forward bore down on goal and unleashed a shot. Rosie closed her eyes. A stab of pain in her leg told her what happened. No way was she going to come off even though her leg was stinging. She was delighted with the attention as the remainder of the bottle of water was poured over her leg. Rosie felt very happy as she limped to the bus stop. St Brigid's had won and she had stopped a certain goal.

Camogie in Toronto

Madge Galligan from Meath was the chief organiser behind the Shamrock Camogie Club in Toronto. Formed in 1967, the club frequently played against Young Ireland's, New York. The Toronto girls held the upper hand from 1968 to 1970 but lost the Molson Shield to New York in 1972. The club folded in 1974. Sheila and Elizabeth Costello revived the game in the 1980s but there was no opposition to play against.

Players of Toronto's glory years were Liz O'Grady (Offaly), Agnes McGlade (Tyrone), Frances Keely (Dublin), Kitty O'Toole (Offaly), Kitty Daley (Offaly), Joan and Marie Hamill (Antrim), Bernadette McMahon (Belfast), Joyce Martin (Dublin), Ann Mul-

New Champions

vanney (Cavan), Trudy Reelis (Mayo), Nuala McNamara (Dublin), Bridie Costello (Galway), Alice Jordan (Kilkenny), Maura Leahy (Dublin), Joan Caulfield (Dublin), Anne and Bonnie Coyle (Tyrone), Clare Carty (Offaly), Sylvia Bonnie (Dublin), Patricia Egan (Meath), Dympna McGuinness (Wexford), Margaret Dwyer (Kilkenny), Maureen Walsh (Kilkenny), Bernadette and Sheila Kilcawly (Sligo), Chris McMahon (Clare), Liz Dolan (Meath), Kitty, Hannah and Mary Murphy (Kilkenny). The team was captained by Kitty Freely-Murphy and coached by Chris Kirby (Limerick) and Teddy Hurley (Cork).

1967 All-Ireland Championship

Mayo got off to a good start against Dublin in the All-Ireland semi-final at Parnell Park and led briefly. Before long, however, Dublin settled into their stride and pulled away. Both Una O'Connor and Judy Doyle scored a hat-trick of goals to put Dublin on the road to a 7–7 to 2–0 victory.

Lily Scullion enjoyed her greatest hour at the Mardyke when her five-goal blitz eliminated Cork from the championship and shot Antrim into the final. Strong in defence and attack, Antrim were never in trouble and won comfortably by 5–7 to 2–2.

Anne McAllister (Dublin) chases Mairéad McAtamney (Antrim) in the 1967 All-Ireland final at Croke Park. Patricia Timmins (Dublin) and Maeve Gilroy (Antrim) look on.

Sheets of rain poured down at Croke Park on September 17th, as Dublin and Antrim made their way from the dressing rooms for the 1967 All-Ireland final. Kitty Murphy was called into the Dublin side at short notice as Bríd Keenan was unable to play. Antrim had lost the 1966 final by two points. Sue Cashman (née Ward) and Marion McFetridge (née Kearns) were missing on that occasion. The return of the brilliant midfielder and the sharp-shooting forward was expected to swing the pendulum in Antrim's favour.

A wonderful game of camogie, full of skill and drama, ensued. Dublin burst into the lead and looked destined for an easy win. Eileen Collins was switched to left wing where her inspiring play got Antrim moving. The concluding stages were fought out in a welter of excitement as Antrim cut Dublin's lead and forged ahead with minutes remaining. Una O'Connor carved her way through the Antrim defence to set up Judy Doyle for a Dublin goal. Antrim missed two scoreable chances before Sue Cashman broke through. Eithne Leech got her hand to Sue's fierce drive. She prevented a winning goal but the ball flew over the bar to draw the match at 4–2 apiece.

A Game of Our Own

The replay was staged as a curtain-raiser to the Oireachtas Hurling Final between Kilkenny and Clare at Croke Park on October 15th. Both counties fielded unchanged sides with Kitty Murphy retaining the number 3 position for Dublin. Antrim played with great spirit and commitment and gave a remarkable display of camogie which drew round after round of applause from the appreciative hurling crowd. It was the first time that camogie was seen by such a large audience and, to a man, the hurling fans got behind Antrim.

Unlike the drawn game, Antrim put their possession to much better use. The players raised their game and treated the attendance to a brilliant game of camogie. While Dublin played well, Antrim were superb. Teresa Cassidy (née Kearns), Moya Forde, Mairéad McAtamney, Lily Scullion, Eileen Collins and Sue Cashman were in brilliant form. At the end of a thrilling encounter, Antrim were ahead on the scoreboard by 3-9 to 4-2.

Nancy Murray, holder of three All-Ireland medals, became the first lady both to win an All-Ireland medal and to coach a winning team. Dressed in the Antrim colours, ten-month-old Paula McFetridge proved to be a lucky mascot. Her mother Marion, Maeve Gilroy and Mairéad Carabine had decided to make the final their last game for Antrim. What a way to finish! Antrim captain, Sue Cashman, was honoured with a Caltex award. As Dublin trooped off the field, who would have believed that none of the 1967 team would appear in a final again. Other counties had caught up on Dublin and were soon to pass them out.

Dublin forward, Judy Doyle, grabs the ball against Antrim in 1967 All-Ireland final. Players from left are Kay Lyons (Dublin), Moya Forde (Antrim), Anne McAllister (Dublin), Maeve Gilroy (Antrim), Kit Kehoe (Dublin) and Teresa Cassidy (Antrim).

Antrim team: Teresa Cassidy, Moya Forde, Ethna Dougan, Maeve Gilroy, Kathleen Kelly, Mairéad Carabine (1-0), Sue Cashman (captain) (0-1), Mairéad McAtamney (0-4), Marion McFetridge (0-2), Mairéad Quinn (1-0), Eileen Collins (1-0) and Lily Scullion (0-2).

Dublin team: Eithne Leech, Mary Ryan, Kitty Murphy, Ally Hussey, Kay Lyons (captain), Mary Sherlock, Patricia Timmons, Orla Ní Síocháin, Kit Kehoe (2-1), Anne McAllister (1-0), Judy Doyle and Una O'Connor (1-1).

New Champions

Mairéad Quinn married Derry and Ulster footballer, Larry Diamond, who captained Bellaghy to win the All-Ireland club football title. Mairéad McAtamney's brother, Tony, won a Railway Cup medal with Ulster.

1967 All-Ireland Club Championship

Eoghan Ruadh from Dublin battled back against Glen Rovers from Cork in the semi-final of the All-Ireland Club Championship after playing second fiddle for the first-half at Togher. The superb goalkeeping of Deirdre Sutton enabled Glen Rovers to maintain their advantage for three-quarters of the match. The superior fitness of Eoghan Ruadh and the outstanding play of Margaret O'Leary seized the initiative. Goals by Eilish Toner, Jean Foley and Connie Lyons sealed a 4–4 to 2–4 victory for Eoghan Ruadh.

Deirdre, Ulster champions since 1964, were surprisingly ousted by Oranmore in the second semi-final at Belfast. Powered by three sets of sisters, Divillys, O'Flahertys and Quinns, the Galway side reached the final with a good brand of skilful and determined camogie by 4–1 to 2–4.

Scores were even, 3–4 to 4–1, at the finish of 50 minutes' hectic play between Eoghan Ruadh and Oranmore in the final of the All-Ireland Club Championship at Parnell Park. When the pitch was cleared, only one team remained. Despite being informed by referee, Bernie Byrne, that extra-time would be played in the event of a draw, the Oranmore contingent had made their exit.

Five months later, following much boardroom discussion, the final was re-scheduled for Ballinasloe. On this occasion, there was no fear of Eoghan Ruadh being caught. Backed by a strong breeze, they set about their task in an industrious manner and opened up a gap of 6–2 without replay by half-time. Margaret O'Leary was a towering figure at centre-back and swept the ball forward continuously. She received excellent support from team

Antrim – 1967 All-Ireland champions. Back: Mairéad Carabine, Mairéad McAtamney, Sheila Maguire, Sue Ward (Capt), Lily Scullion, Mary Phil Jameson, Moya Forde, Eileen McGrogan and Ethna Dougan. Front: Maeve Gilroy, Marion McFetridge, Eileen Collins, Mairéad Quinn, Teresa Cassidy and Kathleen Kelly.

captain Ailish Toner, Maureen Murphy, Kay Lyons, Anne Ashton and Jean Foley. Did Oranmore lose out by not playing extra-time in Dublin? They were short three of their original team for the replay.

Eoghan Ruadh team: Anne Carey, Maureen Kearns, Pat Rafferty, Margaret O'Leary, Anne Ashton, Maureen Murphy, Ailish Toner (captain), Kay Lyons, Phyllis Breslin, Connie Lyons, Jean Foley and Delores Barber.

Oranmore team: Joan Cosgrove, R. Linnane, Rita O'Flaherty, Grace Divilly, Kay Quinn, Rosemary Divilly, Ann Dillon, Kathleen O'Flaherty, Sheila Quinn, Mary Mahon, Kay McGrath and M. Forde.

Eoghan Ruadh was founded in 1937 by Muriel Munnelly, Annie Hogan, Elsie Hickey and the O'Briens in Aughrim Street Parish, Dublin. The club was promoted to the senior grade in 1939 and has remained in the top level since. They won their first Dublin senior championship in 1953 and a three-in-a-row from 1967 to 1969. Two presidents of the Camogie Association, Pat Rafferty and Phyllis Breslin, and Dublin chairperson, Anne Ashton, played on the winning 1967 team.

1967 Gael-Linn Cup

Fresh from their All-Ireland success, an Antrim-dominated Ulster team showed no mercy to Connacht at Cavan. While the Connacht girls battled as best they could, they were overwhelmed by superior and much fitter opponents and Ulster advanced by 9–14 to 3–0. In the second semi-final at Naas, Leinster lasted the pace better and there was little between the sides in play or on the scoreboard. The game finished Leinster 2–5, Munster 3–0.

Ulster captured the Gael-Linn Cup for the first time when they defeated Leinster by 5–4 to 5–1 at Parnell Park on October 29th. Passages of brilliant play kept both sides in the game before a flurry of late scores sealed the issue in Ulster's favour.

Ulster team: Teresa Cassidy (Antrim), Moya Forde (Antrim), Moira Caldwell (Down), Maeve Gilroy (Antrim) (captain) (0–3), Kathleen Kelly (Antrim), Mairéad McAtamney (Antrim), Sue Cashman (Antrim) (1–0), Pat Crangle (Down) (1–0), Marion McFetridge (Antrim), Mairéad Quinn (Antrim), Eileen Collins (Antrim) (2–0) and Lily Scullion (Antrim) (1–1).

Leinster team: Eithne Leech (Dublin), Mary Sinnott (Wexford), Mary Holohan (Kilkenny), Margaret O'Leary (Wexford), Kay Lyons (Dublin), Mary Sherlock (Dublin) (0–1), M. Milne (Offaly), Margaret Hearne (Wexford), Nuala Duncan (Kilkenny) (2–0), Una O'Connor (Dublin) (1–0), Judy Doyle (Dublin) (1–0) and Mary Fennelly (Kilkenny) (1–0).

Rosina McManus Elected President

A native of Kilkeel, Co. Down, Rosina McManus (née Hughes) was elected President of the Camogie Association at Congress 1968. She moved to Belfast to take up an appointment in the Northern Ireland civil service and rendered outstanding service to her adopted county. Rosina approached every task with drive and enthusiasm and was an exceptional worker for camogie.

Louth, Dublin, Mayo and Galway made an attempt to have

New Champions

the rule forbidding hockey and football deleted. The Connacht delegates spoke passionately against the ban which they considered to be detrimental to the progress of the Association in the west. The motion to rescind the ban was lost. The meeting accepted a proposal to introduce an All-Ireland Junior Championship for which counties were graded individually: some counties were permitted to field their first-choice players, other counties had to select their second-best side and the top counties were limited to players from their intermediate and junior clubs.

An Taoiseach, Jack Lynch, throws in the ball to start the Cork Schools final between St. Aloysius School and Drishane Convent at the Cork Athletic grounds in April, 1968.

Policy Commission

Congress 1968 appointed a Special Policy Commission to consider how to advance the interests of the Association. The members of the Commission were P. J. Toner (Armagh), Maureen Smyth (Antrim), Mary Moran (Cork), Crios O'Connell (Limerick), Mary Travers (Roscommon), Eileen Naughton (Galway), Nell McCarthy (Dublin), Ann Carroll (Tipperary), Sheila McAnulty (Ard Runaí) and Eithne Neville (Munster secretary). Their brief was to examine the Association under certain headings, obtain the views of a wide cross-section of members, formulate recommendations and present them to a special congress in due course.

Colleges Camogie

The Munster Council attracted entries from all counties except Tipperary for the inaugural Munster Colleges Championship. St Aloysius (Cork) overcame Coláiste Muire (Ennis) in the final. Later in the year, a Munster Colleges' Council was formed under the guidance of Crios O'Connell from Limerick to which 15 colleges affiliated. Connacht followed and organised a provincial colleges' competition.

A decision that was to have far-reaching effects on the promotion of camogie was taken by the government in 1968 when free education and school buses were introduced. These measures allowed girls, particularly from rural areas, to continue their education and complete second level. Provincial colleges' competitions were up and running and the All-Ireland Colleges Championship was soon to be inaugurated.

People qualified in the teaching profession coached the game at second level. Their ability to impart the basics of the game to young players was invaluable. Many teachers came from a hurling background and the number of qualified PE teachers was on the increase. They brought knowledge and expertise to the game. Over the following years, the number of talented camogie players leaving secondary school and entering third-level colleges grew with obvious benefits to the game.

Taoiseach throws in the Ball

The final of the Cork Schools Championship between St Aloysius School and Drishane Convent took on special significance when St Aloysius captain, Honor Lynch, asked her uncle to come along and see her play. Her uncle was An Taoiseach, Jack Lynch, and he duly accepted. When the news of his intended presence got abroad, interest in the fixture grew sharply and the Cork Athletic Grounds was made available. The Lord Mayor and other dignitaries attended and nuns and parents with limited or no interest in camogie turned out for the occasion. Jack Lynch did the honours of throwing in the ball. St Aloysius won the match comfortably and the coffers of the Cork Schools Board were also enhanced by the occasion.

1968 All-Ireland Senior Championship

The Dublin selectors dropped a bombshell when they omitted Una O'Connor from their team to meet Kilkenny in the Leinster Championship at Parnell Park. Without their talented playmaker, Dublin failed to ignite and were defeated for the first time within the province since 1936. The Kilkenny bus had broken down on the way to Croke Park for the Leinster final and some of the players inhaled fumes and felt sick as they took the field. Wexford, who like Kilkenny had lived in the shadow of Dublin over the years, saw their opportunity. They scored three goals in the first five minutes and, inspired by Margaret O'Leary, drove on to realise their ambition.

Cork moved effortlessly into the All-Ireland final by virtue of a 2–11 to 1–2 victory over Galway at Ballinasloe. Liz Garvan, Nuala Humphries and Sheila Dunne won the lion's share of possession in midfield. Peggy Dorgan and Anna Crotty translated it into scores.

All-Ireland champions, Antrim were taken by surprise by the intensity of the Wexford challenge in the second semi-final at Glenarriffe. In what was essentially a team victory for Wexford, every girl played to her potential to earn a 4–6 to 4–4 win.

Cork opened impressively with two goals in seven minutes in their first All-Ireland final for 12 years at Croke Park on September 15th. Wexford battled back magnificently, with Mary Sinnott

Wexford – All-Ireland senior champions 1968. Back: Bridget O'Connor, Mary Walsh (Capt), Phyllis Kehoe, Josie Kehoe, Mary Sinnott, Eileen Lawlor and Eileen Allen. Front: Joan Murphy, Bridget Kehoe, Teresa Sheil, Mary Shannon, Carmel Fortune, Mary Doyle, Margaret O'Leary and Bernadette Murphy.

and Joan Murphy excelling in defence. They used the handpass to great effect to move the ball to a free player whose long clearance put them on the attack. Bridget O'Connor, Margaret O'Leary and Bridget Doyle took a grip on midfield and contributed handsomely to victory. Wexford finished strongly to earn a 4–2 to 2–5 win and their first All-Ireland title.

Action from the Wexford-Cork final. From left Teresa Sheil (Wexford), Carmel Fortune (Wexford), Peggy Dorgan (Cork) and Joan Murphy (Wexford).

Wexford team: Teresa Sheil, Mary Sinnott, Phyllis Kehoe, Joan Murphy, Carmel Fortune, Bridget O'Connor, Margaret O'Leary, Bridget Doyle (0–2), Josie Kehoe (1–0), Mary Walsh (captain) (1–0), Mary Doyle (1–0) and Mary Shannon (1–0).

Cork team: Mel Cummins, Teresa Murphy, Hannah Dineen, Mary Jo Ryan, Sheila O'Sullivan, Liz Garvan, Sheila Dunne, Nuala Humphries, Peggy Dorgan (1–1), Anne McAufiffe, Anne Comerford (0–3) and Anna Crotty (captain) (1–1).

Wexford's full-back, Mary Sinnott was also a top-class badminton player and represented her country 59 times in international competition. Her uncle, Mick O'Hanlon, had won All-Ireland senior medals with Wexford in 1955 and 1956.

1968 All-Ireland Junior Final

The new All-Ireland junior final was staged as a curtain-raiser to the senior final at Croke Park. Down and Cork qualified for the decider by virtue of two outstanding individual performances. Cork's Kathleen Healy scored 3–2 to see off the challenge of Galway at Ballinasloe while Pat Crangle with 2–2 was Down's star against Wexford at Clonduff in the semi-finals.

The new championship was an instant success. An open and skilful game was enjoyed by supporters. Down, who fielded more experienced players, were quickly into their stride. Pat Crangle, Barbara Sands, Moira Caldwell and Carmel Reid gave Down a decided advantage throughout the field and the Ulster county was ahead by 2–2 to 0–0 at the break. Cork played their best camogie early in the second-half and reduced the deficit by 1–1. Down regained control and ran out deserving winners by 2–3 to 1–1. The winning team was prepared by Peg Dooey, the former Antrim All-Ireland medal holder.

Down team: Nuala McKenna, Patsy McGrady, Róisín McCann, Eileen Coulter, Nollaig Sands, Rita Walsh, Moira Caldwell (captain), Barbara Sands (0–2), Carmel Reid (1–0), Pat Crangle (0–1), Ann Marie Kelly and Eucharia Turley (1–0).

Cork team: Mary Heelan (captain), Peg O'Brien, Julia Buckley, Betty Burke, Nuala Collins, Pat O'Sullivan, Josie Pyne,

Margaret Mee, Anne O'Sullivan (1–0), Kay Ryan (0–1), Breda O'Sullivan and Kathleen Healy. Sub used: Anne Kirby (sister of Ned Kirby who had won All-Ireland football medal in 1973).

1968 All-Ireland Club Championship

Ahane (Limerick) seemed set for their first All-Ireland Club Championship final when they led Ballinasloe (Galway) by 3–3 to 1–1 with only minutes remaining in the semi-final, but they had to endure a single-minded rally from the home side which yielded 2–1 before securing their place.

St Paul's (Kilkenny) made hard work of disposing of the Antrim champions, Deirdre, in the second semi-final at Casement Park. They enjoyed the majority of the play but had difficulty in reflecting their supremacy on the scoreboard. The St Paul's defence, notably Jo Golden, Anne Phelan and Mary Holohan, provided the platform for victory. Deirdre were foiled by 3–4 to 2–2 in pursuit of a place in the final.

St Paul's scooped the biggest prize in club camogie at the expense of Ahane by 7–2 to 1–2 in the final at St John's Park. The Kilkenny side showed good combination, ball skills and striking ability, whereas Ahane relied on a few good individual players, with Carrie Clancy, Joan Hayes and Helen Roche battling bravely as the game faded away. St Paul's did not have a weak link and were deserving winners. Four goals from Ann Carroll, who had transferred from St Patrick's (Tipperary), and three from Maura Cassin were the match-winning scores. Ann Carroll became the first player to win All-Ireland Club Championship medals with two different clubs.

St Paul's team: Jo Golden, Mary Holohan, Joan Kelly, Anne Phelan, Bríd Fennelly, Mary Conway, Carmel O'Shea, Liz Neary, Maura Cassin, Breda Cassin, Teasie Brennan (captain) and Ann Carroll.

Ahane team: Helen Roche, Bridget Ryan, Mary Hayes, Margaret Madden, Kitty Ryan, Kathleen Richardson, Carrie Clancy, Betty O'Leary, Teresa Fennessy, Joan Hayes, Mary Barry and Peggy Duffy.

Down – All-Ireland Junior Champions 1968. Included are: Moira Caldwell (Capt), Nuala McKenna, Patsy McGrady, Róisín McCann, Eileen Coulter, Nollaig Sands, Rita Walsh, Barbara Sands, Carmel Reid, Pat Crangle, Ann Marie Kelly, Eucharia Turley, J. Nelson, B. Turley, R. Braniff, J. Rodgers, D. Doherty and C. Swail.

New Champions

The St Paul's Club had been formed in 1963 by John Fennelly, Mick Kenny, Jimmy Morrissey and Dick Cassin. Most of their players were products of Presentation, Kilkenny. St Paul's won eight All-Ireland Club Championship titles. Five St Paul's girls – Angela Downey, Liz Neary, Bridie Martin, Ann Downey and Breda Holmes – won National Player of the Year awards. Mary Fennelly was elected President of the Camogie Association in 1982 and Jo Golden served as Ard Runaí.

1968 Gael-Linn Cup

Leinster scored an easy victory over Connacht by 7–9 to 3–1 at Pearse Park and had Judy Doyle to thank for shooting five goals. Munster had to bow to a superior Ulster side at Fermoy. The vigilance of goalkeeper, Mel Cummins, kept the margin from being more than 8–4 to 4–4.

Ally Hussey gave a classy display for Leinster in the final of the Gael-Linn Cup against Ulster at Croke Park. She dominated the game from the centre-back position and kept Leinster going forward. Margaret O'Leary, Mary Walsh, Carmel O'Shea and Teresa Sheil played confidently for the winners who finished with a comfortable margin of 7–0 to 2–5.

Leinster team: Teresa Sheil (Wexford), Mary Holohan (Kilkenny), Joan Murphy (Wexford), Ally Hussey (Dublin), Carmel O'Shea (Kilkenny), Mary Sherlock (Dublin) (1–0), Margaret O'Leary (Wexford), Bríd Kinsella (Kilkenny), Kit Kehoe (Dublin) (1–0), Mary Walsh (Wexford) (captain) (2–0), Judy Doyle (Dublin) (3–0) and Mary Doyle (Wexford).

Ulster team: Teresa Cassidy (Antrim), Moya Forde (Antrim) (captain), Moira Caldwell (Down), Eileen Coulter (Down), Kathleen Kelly (Antrim), Mairéad McAtamney (Antrim) (0–1), Sue Cashman (Antrim) (0–2), Barbara Sands (Down), Pat Crangle (Down) (1–0), Mairéad Quinn (Antrim), (0–2), Eileen Collins (Antrim) and Lily Scullion (Antrim) (1–0).

Armaments Seizure

An announcement on the BBC television news programme gave details of an armaments seizure on the outskirts of Newry: 14 hurleys and eight golf sticks were listed as the offensive weapons. The RUC had impounded the sticks and deposited them in Newry Barracks. The news item was picked up by other stations and repeated many times over the next few hours.

It later emerged that Rosina McManus, President of the Camogie Association, was driving to a Central Council meeting in Dublin when she was stopped at a road block by the RUC. They asked her to open the boot of her car where they found the 'offensive weapons'. Rosina coached the juveniles at the club and carried a supply of spare sticks in her car. Having listened to a detailed explanation from Rosina and her travelling companion, Lily Spence, the officer allowed them to continue the journey to Dublin.

Recommendations of Commission

Traditionally, motions seeking something new fail at the first attempt. It takes a few years before the majority view things in a different light and approve changes. This was the case with some of the commission's recommendations. Less contentious suggestions, such as holding seminars for administrators and referees, staging coaching courses, increasing affiliation fees, issuing instructive pamphlets and efforts to get camogie on the curriculum of PE and teacher training colleges, were accepted immediately, but more far-seeing ideas had to wait for another day.

Inaugural Colleges' Championship

Excitement within camogie circles built up as April 19th, 1969 approached. Seán Ó Síocháin, a great friend to colleges camogie, made Croke Park available for the inaugural All-Ireland Colleges Championship final. Presentation (Kilkenny) and St Aloysius (Cork) won the honour of being the contestants.

Members of the O'Kelly family presented Corn Sceilg as a perpetual trophy for the All-Ireland Colleges Championship. It commemorated the late Seán Ó Ceallaigh ('Sceilg') who was one of the members of the Keating Branch of the Gaelic League who founded the Camogie Association in 1904. The shape of the cup is on the lines of the Ardagh Chalice and is beautifully designed and engraved in Celtic tracery. Medals depicting 'The Sword of Light' were designed and made by John Miller from Dublin.

Hundreds and hundreds of youthful supporters, singing songs specially composed for the occasion, armed with flags, scarves, teddy bears and hats in school colours, added to the day. Parents, siblings, grannies, aunties and past-pupils chatted noisily in the stand as they awaited the throw-in. Over-excited nuns issued orders to bus drivers, stewards and anyone else in range.

Excitement was at fever pitch as Nancy Murray threw in the ball. Cheers grew louder and louder as play swung from end to end. Lovers of camogie were delighted with the high standard of play and the sporting attitude of the players, a number of whom went on to become established senior inter-county stars, notably Liz Neary, Helena O'Neill, Anne Phelan, Teresa O'Neill and Carmel Doyle of Presentation and Liz Garvan and Rosie Hennessy of St Aloysius.

The Kilkenny girls claimed Corn Sceilg by 3–2 to 1–2. In a spirit of sportsmanship, the Cork players threw their arms round the Kilkenny victors at the final whistle and, later, lined up to clap the champions as they entered the after-match reception. The All-Ireland Colleges Championship was an instant success.

All-Ireland Colleges Council

A meeting was called for Bru na nGael, Dublin, on November 8th, 1969 for the purpose of setting up an All-Ireland Colleges Council. A constitution for colleges' camogie was agreed and the following officers elected: president, Lily Spence (Belfast); vice-president, Agnes Purcell (Dublin); secretary, Mary Moran (Cork); and treasurer, Maeve Clissman (Sligo). Maeve withdrew after a few months but Lily Spence and Mary Moran remained as colleges' officers for 36 years.

1969 All-Ireland Senior Championship

There was a time when consideration of the All-Ireland senior championship was confined to speculation about which team would qualify to meet Dublin in the final. By 1969, those days had gone. Five counties – Wexford, Antrim, Kilkenny, Cork and Dublin – could be classified as serious contenders with Tipperary and Galway not far behind. The success of the All-Ireland Junior and Colleges championships raised hopes of other counties being able to step up to the mark in coming seasons.

In the All-Ireland semi-final at Wexford Park, and for the first time in an inter-county match, a player from each side was sent to the line. Mary Graham (Tipperary) and Josie Kehoe (Wexford) were dismissed by referee Nancy Murray for rough play. Tipperary threw caution to the wind and hurled with abandon. They matched the champions in a close, tense game. The outcome was only decided in the last minute when Margaret O'Leary struck a free to the Tipperary net for the winning score. Wexford advanced by 4-4 to 3-3.

In the second semi-final at Glenariff, Galway trailed Antrim by seven points at the break. They came back with a storming finish, but failed by a single point to catch Antrim. Mona Flaherty, Pat Feeney and Margaret Kilkenny played great camogie for Galway. Mairéad McAtamney, Mairéad Quinn and Nuala Havelin earned a 2-6 to 3-2 win for Antrim.

It took a great goal by Cathy Power, 90 seconds from time, to save the day for Wexford in the All-Ireland final against Antrim at Croke Park on September 21st. The lead changed hands twice in the closing minutes as Antrim made a remarkable comeback and they were within touching distance of snatching an unexpected victory. The political situation in Northern Ireland had prevented Antrim from preparing for the final as they would have liked. In the circumstances, their performance was all the more praiseworthy. Mairéad McAtamney gave a five-star exhibition and Kathleen Kelly, Mairéad Quinn, Eileen Collins, and Kathleen McManus shared brilliant moments for Antrim. Margaret O'Leary, Bridget Doyle, Joan Murphy, Bridget O'Connor and Mary Shannon outshone all others and were the backbone of Wexford's 4-4 to 4-2 win.

Wexford team: Teresa Sheil, Joan Murphy, Anne Foley, Bridget Doyle (captain), Bridget O'Connor, Mary Walsh, Margaret O'Leary (0-2), Bernie Murphy, Cathy Power (1-0), Annie Kehoe (0-1), Mary Doyle (1-1) and Mary Shannon (2-0). Sub used: Peg Moore.

Antrim team: Kathleen Kelly, Moya Forde, Ethna Dougan, Maeve Gilroy, Kathleen McManus, Eileen Collins, Mairéad McAtamney (1-1), Nuala Havelin (1-0), Mairéad Quinn (0-1), Marion McFetridge (1-0) Lily Scullion (1-0) and Christine Wheeler.

1969 All-Ireland Junior Championship

The Kildare v. Cork All-Ireland junior semi-final at Naas was progressing nicely when a loud voice announced that there was a car on fire in the car park. Belfast referee, Lily Spence, took off to check her vehicle, leaving the players to their own devices. When she established that it was not her car, she returned to finish the job. Cork had a two-point win 1-5 to 2-0 to reach Croke Park for the second successive year. In the second semi-final at Bellaghy,

Derry earned a 3–2 to 2–1 win over Galway in a game that produced some decent passages of camogie.

Derry ensured that the New Ireland Cup remained in Ulster when they converted the opportunities presented to them in the All-Ireland junior final at Croke Park on September 21st. Two speculative balls crawled into the Cork goal early in the first-half. Cork struggled to recover but the damage was done. They came more into the game in a competitive second-half but the experienced Derry players were not going to be denied and won by 4–2 to 2–4.

Derry team: Brigid McCann, Kathleen McDonald, Mary McNally, Isobel McErlean, Philomena Downey, Sheila McErlean, Kathleen O'Hagan (captain) (0–1), Carmel Kelly, Kathleen McPeake (1–0), Aileen McGurk (2–0), Eileen McErlean (0–1) and Martina McPeake (1–0).

Cork team: Mary Barron, Mary Crowley (captain), Mary Whelton, Mary A Murphy, Miriam Higgins, Maisy Murphy, Blanche Gibbons, Marion McCarthy, Mary Ita O'Sullivan, Joan Fitzpatrick (0–1), Angela Cronin (1–2) and Rosie Hennessy (1–1).

Cork's Mary Barron is the mother of current Waterford hurling goalkeeper, Clinton Hennessy. Mary A. Murphy's brother, Simon, had won an All-Ireland hurling medal with Cork in 1966 as well as All-Ireland minor and under-21 medals in both hurling and football.

1969 All-Ireland Club Championship

Ahane (Limerick) won the right to have a second shot at the All-Ireland Club title when they defeated Antrim side, Ahoghill, in the semi-final at Castleconnell. The visitors opened sensationally when Moya Forde struck a 30-yard free to the net. Lily Scullion immediately followed up with a hand-passed goal. Ahane responded with goals from the in-form Joan Hayes and Marjorie Doohan to win by 5–0 to 3–2. In the second semi-final at St John's Park, when St Paul's had recovered from an early Oranmore goal, they motored on to victory by 7–7 to 2–1.

The players of Ahane and St Paul's had to contend with absolutely miserable weather for the final at Castleconnell. With the gale and driving rain to their backs, St Paul's were winning on a score of 1–6 to 0–1 by half-time. Goals from Peggy Duffy and Marjorie Doohan gave Ahane some hope but their scoring spree was short-lived and St Paul's came again to secure the title by 3–7 to 2–1.

St Paul's team: Jo Golden, Mary Conway, Nuala Duncan, Joan Kelly, Liz Neary, Carmel O'Shea, Ann Carroll, Maura Cassin, Helena O'Neill, Rose Vennard, Breda Cassin and Ann Phelan.

Ahane team: Helen Roche, Kitty Ryan, Bridget Ryan, Mary Hayes, Carrie Clancy, Betty O'Leary, Kathleen Richardson, Margaret Madden, Marjorie Doohan, Peggy Duffy, Mary Tierney and Joan Hayes.

1969 Gael-Linn Cup

Evenly matched sides, Munster and Connacht, met in the semi-final of the Gael-Linn Cup at Athenry, where well-taken goals by Ann Comerford and Beatrice Lawrence decided the issue in

Munster's favour, 2–2 to 0–4.

Ulster caused little trouble to a strong Leinster outfit at Croke Park in the second semi-final. Brigid McCann in the Ulster goal had a torrid time from the sharp-shooting Leinster forwards. She made many courageous saves to keep the score down to 7–5 to 1–4 in Leinster's favour.

Munster struggled to make any headway against a multi-talented Leinster side in the final of the Gael-Linn Cup at Cahir. Leinster had the sharper and more focused set of forwards who built up a commanding lead. Although Munster reduced the gap, Leinster made it home by 5–4 to 2–2.

Leinster team: Teresa Sheil (Wexford), Joan Murphy (Wexford), Mary Ryan (Dublin), Margaret O'Leary (Wexford), Ally Hussey (Dublin), Ann Carroll (Kilkenny) (0–2), Kitty Murphy (Dublin), Orla Ní Síocháin (Dublin) (0–1), Mary Doyle (Wexford) (1–0), Mary Walsh (Wexford) (1–0), Judy Doyle (Dublin) (3–0) and Una O'Connor (0–1).

Munster team: Sally Long (Tipperary), Mel Cummins (Cork), Josephine Marshall (Tipperary), Anne Graham (Tipperary), Mary Jo Ryan (Cork), Liz Garvan (Cork) (0–1), Margaret Cleary (Tipperary), Anne Comerford (Cork) (captain), Beatrice Lawrence (Tipperary), Carrie Clancy (Limerick), Anne McAuliffe (Cork) and Bridie Conroy (Tipperary) (2–1).

Where We're At

Real progress was made between 1967 to 1969: the first coaching course; the inaugural All-Ireland Junior Championship; the setting up of the All-Ireland Colleges' Council and championship and the findings of the commission were all positive steps. People came to the first coaching course who did not know how to take a training session and needed guidance and direction in the basics of the game. They picked up knowledge and confidence over the weekend and returned home equipped to do a better job.

The new All-Ireland Junior Championship produced an excellent standard of play and opened up the possibility of attaining All-Ireland honours to a range of additional counties. A realistic chance of success is necessary to motivate counties to prepare diligently and improve the standard of their game and organisation.

The establishment of the All-Ireland colleges' championship and the setting up of the All-Ireland Colleges' Council were the outstanding highlights and had major long-term benefits. This was an area of great potential where young players, in their formative years, were taught the basic skills, shown the value of teamwork and tutored in planning their approach to the game. The invaluable spin-off was a flow of players from the schools to the clubs.

Central Council administered the affairs of the Camogie Association with four to five meetings a year. Matters arising between meetings were left until the following get-together, which resulted in opportunities for progress being missed. Meetings were taken up with routine matters and no time was made available to explore development. The commission suggested the setting up of sub-committees to handle standard work like making fixtures, but some members of the Central Council saw this as a diminution of their powers, and the recommendation was rejected. The commission found the level of organisation at club and county levels to be weak in many instances and highlighted the need for administration seminars and instruction pamphlets.

Antrim had run Dublin close in 1965 and 1966 and, consequently, it was no real surprise that the Ulster girls caught their great rivals in the 1967 replay. What proved a shock was Dublin's inability to regroup and fight back in the following year's competition. A group of Kilkenny players, unknown outside their province, caused a sensation when they lowered Dublin's colours in Leinster for the first time in over 30 years. Waiting in the long grass were the Wexford players who did not allow Kilkenny much time to enjoy their new-found fame. In turn, they picked off Kilkenny, Antrim and Cork to engrave a new name on the O'Duffy Cup. Tall, strong and athletic, Wexford introduced a host of new names to the camogie world. Bridget Doyle, Margaret O'Leary, Mary Sinnott, Joan Murphy, Teresa Shiel and Mary Walsh had arrived and would adorn the stage for years to come.

Chapter Eleven

CORK BRIDGE 29-YEAR GAP

A competition for advanced colleges in the Dublin area was set up under the auspices of the Dublin County Board. The four entrants were: Carysfort Training College; Domestic Economy College, Cathal Brugha Street; St. Raphael's PE College, Sion Hill; and UCD. As UCD, with a long tradition in the game, were considerably stronger than the other three colleges, the Belfield students were represented by players other than their Ashbourne side.

Rosina McManus presided over a heavy agenda at Congress 1970, where 47 motions were tabled. Among the motions presented, Galway were successful in having the ban on foreign dances lifted and it was agreed that the semi-finals and final of the All-Ireland Club Championship should be staged between the previous year's provincial champions in March.

Cork's motion to allow a substitute to replace a player was also approved. Prior to 1970, a player had to be injured and unfit to continue in the eyes of the referee before she could be substituted, though this rule was not always adhered to. Players were known to receive the signal to lie down and put on academy award-winning performances as they faked injury.

A selector gave Margo the cue to come off but she chose to ignore it. A second selector joined in and the gestures became more animated. Soon all the selectors were running up and down the sideline, waving their arms and shouting but to no avail. Margo finished the match but was dropped for the next game.

Teresa got the signal. Carefully, she put her two hands to the back of her head and eased herself slowly to the ground to protect her hairdo as she was going to a function later on. Her acting was so impressive that the referee enquired about her state

Séamus Ó Riain, President G.A.A. and Kay Mills admire Tommy Moore's Gaelic All-Star award. Note Kay's bracelet which is made from All-Ireland medals.

of health afterwards.

Government Grant

Accustomed to living on its own meagre resources and within limited means, the Camogie Association were pleased to receive £1,000 in the first allocation of grants to sporting organisations. A special meeting of Central Council was summoned to decide how best to spend the money. Having thrown many ideas around, the gathering decided on: 1) a coaching film; 2) a stick-subsidy scheme; and 3) a national coaching course. Ard Runaí, Sheila McAnulty, was appointed to COSAC, the Sports Council set up by the government.

National Coaching Course

It was only a matter of time before the Central Council reacted to the success of the Ulster Council's coaching course at Orangefield and the demands for specialised tuition for potential coaches. The first National Coaching Course was held at Gormanston College over the weekend of July 17th–19th, 1970. The chief instructors were Dessie Ferguson, former Dublin dual star and the GAA's top hurling coach, and Christy Hayes, who had fielded at centre-back for Dublin in the 1961 All-Ireland hurling final.

Group pictured on occasion of former Cork goalkeeper, Peggy Hogg, receiving Hall of Fame Award in 1970. Front: Nell McCarthy, Séamus Ó Riain, President G.A.A., Kathleen O'Duffy, Molly Murphy, Seán O'Duffy and Inez Leonard. Behind: Agnes Purcell, Sheila McAnulty, Ann Purcell, Josie Stuart, Rosina McManus, Rita Carragher, Lily Spence and Peggy Hogg.

Across the expansive playing fields of Gormanston College in excess of 100 students, representing 25 counties, practised newly acquired skills with determination and enthusiasm. All of them were happy to give up a weekend to equip themselves to teach, coach and organise camogie throughout the country. They came from all walks of life, young and not-so-young, top-class players, rising stars and relative beginners. No one lost sight of the social side of things and new friendships were made over the weekend that was meticulously organised by Rosina McManus and her committee. The weekend was an outstanding success and the National Coaching Course became a regular feature on the camogie calendar.

Leitrim Shapes Up

A County Board was formed in Leitrim in July 1970. Three clubs – Seán Mac Dhiarmada (Carrick-on-Shannon), Shee Mór (Leitrim) and Gortletteragh – affiliated. Ollie Mitchell (chair), Stella Nagle (vice-chair), Mary O'Rourke (secretary), Elizabeth Molloy (treasurer) and Nuala McGreevey (registrar) were elected to run the new board. All five Connacht counties were now playing camogie.

Cork Bridge 29-Year Gap

Roscommon won their first Connacht title when they defeated Galway in the junior championship at Athleague.

1970 All-Ireland Senior Championship

Kilkenny won the Leinster Championship for the first time when they defeated Dublin 5-3 to 4-3. Then Galway handed them a passage to the final when they scratched from the competition, but received a three-month suspension for failing to fulfil the fixture. Cork owed their passage to the final to three youngsters, Pat Moloney, Liz Garvan and Rosie Hennessy. Playing with skill and confidence, the trio held no fear of their experienced opponents from Antrim at the Mardyke. They showed delightful touches as they shared Cork's total between them. Antrim did not give in easily and Marie Costine, Hannah Dineen and Mary Jo Ryan had to tackle tenaciously to keep Antrim at bay. Cork won a sparkling game by 3-5 to 3-2.

Cork bridged a 29-year gap when they overcame Kilkenny by 5-7 to 3-2 in the All-Ireland final at Croke Park on September 20th. Ann Carroll scored a great goal in the first minute. But such was the confidence and spirit instilled in the Cork side by former Blackrock hurler, Jack Dempsey, that they brushed aside this setback. Teenager Liz Garvan stole the show. In a magical display of style and class, she scored 3-6 from play. She had a clever partner in Peggy Dorgan who added 2-1.

Kilkenny were handicapped by the loss of full-back, Nuala Duncan, early in the game but remained in step with Cork for three-quarters of the game. The Cork defence, in which Marie Costine, Hannah Dineen, Mel Cummins and Mary Jo Ryan played to a very high level, was unbeatable in the last quarter. Over the hour, Ann Carroll, Helena O'Neill, Liz Neary, Peggy Carey and Anne Phelan put in tremendous work for Kilkenny but some members of the team seemed overawed by the occasion.

Cork team: Mel Cummins, Marie Costine, Hannah Dineen, Mary Jo Ryan, Sheila Dunne, Betty Sugrue, Anne McAuliffe, Anne Comerford (captain), Pat Moloney, Liz Garvan (3-6), Peggy Dor-

Kilkenny goalkeeper, Jo Golden, and Cork forward, Peggy Dorgan concentrate on the ball in the 1970 All-Ireland final at Croke Park.

A letter of congratulations to the Cork team from Taoiseach Jack Lynch

gan (2–1) and Rosie Hennessy. Sub used: Anna Crotty.

Kilkenny team: Jo Golden, Nuala Duncan, Anne Phelan, Mary Kennedy, Joan Kelly, Liz Neary, Carmel O'Shea, Peggy Carey (1–1), Helena O'Neill, Ann Carroll (2–1), Breda Cassin and Maura Cassin. Sub used: Mary Conway.

Cork annexed All-Ireland hurling and camogie titles in 1970. Tomás Ryan, right-half-forward on the hurling side, married Cork's midfielder, Anne McAuliffe.

1970 All-Ireland Junior Championship

An Ulster side got the better of Cork for the third year running in the All-Ireland Junior Championship. Armagh's Angela Toal scored 3–3 and was the best player on the field in the semi-final at the Mardyke which ended Armagh 3–4, Cork 1–3. Dublin carried too much scoring power for Roscommon in the second semi-final and were clear winners at Athleague by 5–5 to 1–3.

In the final at Croke Park, Dublin established a stronghold and were cruising to victory with four goals to spare over Armagh, when, suddenly, Armagh sprang to life and might have snatched

Cork players celebrate their All-Ireland victory in September, 1970. Front: Marion McCarthy, Betty Sugrue, Anne Comerford (Capt), Anna Crotty and Peggy Dorgan. Back: Liz Garvan, Mary Moran, Mel Cummins, Rosie Hennessy, Pat Moloney, Nuala Guilly and Marie Costine.

a victory that would not have reflected the general play. Tension and excitement filled the air as Armagh surged forward in search of the winner in the closing minutes. Dublin held out to win by 4–2 to 3–3.

Dublin team: Anne Carey, Ann Marie O'Loughlin, Claire Harrington, Vera Sullivan, Rita Whyte, Veronica Fingleton (0–1), Vera Feely (captain) (0–1), Muireann Hayes, Nora McDonald, Pauline Brennan (2–0), Rita Halpin (2–0) and Marian Coogan.

Armagh team: Kathleen Fearon, Elizabeth Scullion, Sheena McKeown, Anne McCone, Marian Courtney, Angela Toal (0–1), Marion Delaney (0–1), Isene Patterson, Alice Beagan (0–1), Patricia McLaughlin, Anne McGuinness (1–0), Ann Cairns (1–0) and Joan Austin (1–0).

1970 All-Ireland Club Championship

South Presentation Past Pupils (Cork) made a determined effort to dethrone the All-Ireland champions, St Paul's (Kilkenny), but fell a little short. The winners led from the start but had to survive a late rally at St John's Park before advancing by 3–4 to 3–3.

Cork Bridge 29-year Gap

Bellaghy (Derry) lined out at Castlebar with seven Derry county players together with Teresa Cassidy, the former Antrim goalkeeper. The combination proved too strong for the Breaffy (Mayo) challenge by 6–2 to 0–1.

St Paul's recorded a hat-trick of All-Ireland Club titles when, before a large home following at Bellaghy on March 28th, they created their own bit of history. With Helena O'Neill, Carmel O'Shea and Maura Cassin the key influential players, St Paul's outsmarted Bellaghy by 6–5 to 2–0. Goals from P. Molloy and Kathleen Diamond gave temporary hope to Bellaghy, but St Paul's quickly slammed the door.

St Paul's team: Teresa O'Neill, Nuala Duncan, Anne Phelan, Carmel O'Shea (0–2), Kathleen Brennan, Breda Cassin, Liz Neary, Maura Cassin (2–1), Carmel Doyle, Helena O'Neill (3–0), Mary O'Neill (0–2) and Mary Conway (captain) (1–0).

Ballaghy panel: Mary Lee, Philomena Molly, Kathleen Diamond, Annie McNally, Mary McNally, Eta McNally, Noeleen McNally, Breege Mackle, Evelyn Mackle, Rosemary McPeake, Martina McPeake, Patricia McPeake, Kathleen Marron, Teresa Cassidy, Josephine Mawhinney and Celine Scullion.

1970 Gael-Linn Cup

Two UCD players, Jo Golden and Ann Carroll, did most to deny Munster in the Gael-Linn Cup at Gorey. Ann scored 2–3 while Jo played brilliantly in goal to earn a 3–5 to 1–2 victory for Leinster. Connacht did not field a team and allowed Ulster to advance to the final.

The inevitable outcome of the Gael-Linn Cup final at Carrickmacross was a clear-cut win for Leinster over Ulster by 12–2 to 4–1. The Leinster attack exerted enormous pressure on the Ulster goal and proved somewhat of a nightmare for the Ulster rearguard.

Leinster team: Jo Golden (Kilkenny) (captain), Mary Ryan (Dublin), Joan Murphy (Wexford), Margaret O'Leary (Wexford), Bridget O'Connor (Wexford), Liz Neary (Kilkenny), Ann Carroll (Kilkenny) (1–1), Orla Ní Síocháin (Dublin) (2–1), Helena O'Neill (Kilkenny) (4–0), Annie Kehoe (Wexford) (1–0), Judy Doyle (Dublin) (3–0) and Maura Cassin (1–0).

Ulster team: Teresa Cassidy (Antrim), Moya Forde (Antrim)

Goalmouth action in the 1970 All-Ireland junior final between Armagh and Dublin at Croke Park.

(captain), Anne McCone (Armagh), Moira Caldwell (Down), Kathleen Kelly (Antrim), Angela Toal (Armagh), Kathleen Diamond (Derry), Mairéad McAtamney (Antrim) (1–0), Patricia McGreevey (Monaghan) (1–0), Anne McIvor (Antrim) (1–0), Chris O'Boyle (Antrim) (1–1) and Lily Scullion (Antrim).

Nell McCarthy Elected President

Before stepping down at Congress 1971, outgoing president, Rosina McManus, stressed the need for professionalism within the Association, called for greater drive and initiative from members, sought support from non-participating counties for the All-Ireland final and expressed satisfaction at the growth of the colleges sector.

Nell McCarthy

Her successor, Nell McCarthy, grew up in a hurling family in Carrigtwohill, Co. Cork. She joined the civil service and worked in the Department of Education and, later, in the National College of Art. Nell chaired the Dublin County Board from 1952–1970 where she was held in high respect. Best known for her coaching ability, she guided the great Dublin teams of the fifties and sixties.

Congress made some changes: the closing stages of the All-Ireland Club Championship reverted from the spring to November and goalkeepers and referees were permitted to wear tracksuits in adverse weather conditions rather than the regulation gym frock.

Gretta Kehoe and Betty Sugrue lead the Wexford and Cork teams in the pre-match parade at the 1971 All-Ireland final at Croke Park.

Camogie Magazine

Eleven Dublin-based players got together to produce an excellent magazine aptly entitled *Camogie*. All voluntary workers with no previous experience in publishing, they brought out a magazine that could stand side by side with any commercially produced title on the bookstands. Edited by Jo Golden, the team comprised Kitty Murphy, Blánaid Ní Annracháin, Ann Carroll, Vera Sullivan, Orla Ní Síocháin, Muireann Hayes, Sheila Murray, Anne Sheehy, Ann Marie O'Loughlin and Pat Morrissey. It is to the eternal shame of camogie followers that they did not give their own magazine the backing that it deserved. Due to lack of support, the publication went from a quarterly to an annual and finally ceased publication.

Cork Bridge 29-year Gap

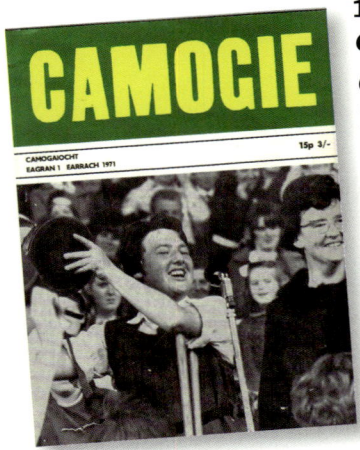

1971 All-Ireland Senior Championship

Cork were not tested in the All-Ireland senior semi-final by Galway at the Mardyke. Galway had not played a match for two years and were decidedly ring-rusty. Unable to cope with the demands placed upon them, the Galway defence floundered at the hands of a free-scoring Cork side and conceded by 3–14 to 0–3.

Wexford qualified for their third All-Ireland final in four years at the expense of Antrim at Croke Park on the score of 6–3 to 3–3. In a sensational start, three scores were registered in under two minutes, leaving Antrim 1–1 to 1–0 in front. Josie Kehoe nipped in for a goal to give Wexford the lead which they never released.

Having accounted for Dublin, Kilkenny and Antrim, it was believed that Wexford would not be stopped in the All-Ireland final at Croke Park on September 19th. It certainly looked that way in the opening quarter of the game as they forged ahead but Cork came back like true champions and, by half-time, had the game won.

Keeping the best performance of the season for the final, Cork put on something of a show. Their defence was a brick wall. Mel Cummins, Marie Costine, Hannah Dineen and Anne McAuliffe

Marie Costine (Cork), Josie Kehoe (Wexford) and Hannah Dineen (Cork) seen under the dropping ball at the 1971 All-Ireland senior final at Croke Park

closed all avenues to goal and Marion McCarthy, Betty Sugrue and Pat Moloney dominated the middle of the field. Rosie Hennessy, Anne Comerford and Liz Garvan took their scores with aplomb. Margaret O'Leary, Anne Kehoe and Mary Walsh did all in their power to reverse the trend of the game but it was not their day. Cork won by 4–6 to 1–2.

Cork team: Mel Cummins, Marie Costine, Hannah Dineen, Anne McAuliffe, Mary Whelton, Marion McCarthy, Betty Sugrue (captain), Pat Moloney, Anne Comerford (2–1), Liz Garvan (0–3), Nuala Guilly and Rosie Hennessy (2–2).

Wexford team: Teresa Sheil, Joan Murphy, Peggie Doyle, Bernie O'Dwyer, Bridie Jacob, Annie Kehoe, Margaret O'Leary,

Elsie Walsh, Mary Shannon, Mary Walsh (1–0), Mary Sheil and Josie Kehoe (0–1). Sub used: Maggie Hearne (0–1) .

1971 All-Ireland Junior Championship

Dublin's 4–2 to 1–2 victory over Armagh in the semi-final of the All-Ireland Junior Championship at Croke Park was due to a magnificent team effort. Armagh had excellent individual players but, tactically, they were not as good as their opponents.

Cork had an easy passage against Roscommon in the second semi-final. Their forwards were more dynamic and registered 5–6 as against 1–2 for the Connacht side.

Dublin were obliged to field a completely new team, having won the trophy in the previous year. The newcomers survived the early skirmishes and grew in stature against Cork in the final at Croke Park. The winning margin would have been much wider in Dublin's favour but for the brilliant goalkeeping of Deirdre Sutton. Evelyn Sweeney, Marion Conroy, Pat Morrissey and Mary Raymond proved their pedigree and guided Dublin to a 2–2 to 1–2 victory.

Dublin team: Mary Raymond, Jennie Dooley, Pat Morrissey (captain), Sheila Wallace, Pat Rafferty, Christine Dignam, Marian Conroy, Anna McManus, Evelyn Sweeney (2–1), Sheila McEvoy, Miriam Higgins (0–1) and Dympna Caldwell. Sub used: Fiona Murray.

Cork team: Deirdre Sutton (captain), Mary Salter, Rosie O'Sullivan, Marion O'Leary, Nuala Jennings, Anne Keane, Mary A Murphy (0–1), Angela Higgins, Mary Humphries, Marion Sweeney (0–1), Mary Mahon and Kay Spillane (1-0). Subs used: Phil Walsh, Pat Mortell and Marie Mackey.

1971 All-Ireland Club Championship

The miserable conditions at Thurles reduced the All-Ireland club semi-final between Ballinasloe and Thurles to an endurance test. The standard of play suffered as the players tried to cope with cold hands, driving rain and the mud. Not surprisingly, scores were kept to a minimum. Margo Loughnane (0–3) and Marion Moynihan (1–0) were on target for the home side while Jane Murphy replied with 1–1 for Ballinasloe.

Dublin club, Austin Stacks, made a successful debut in the All-Ireland Club Championship at Randelstown and qualified for the final at the expense of Portglenone (Antrim). Bríd Keenan, Orla Ní Síocháin, Anne Sheehy and Dympna Caldwell did most to achieve victory for Stacks. Mairéad McAtamney was the top performer for Portglenone and, despite displaying her exceptional array of skills in midfield, Stacks won comfortably by 5–2 to 1–0.

Austin Stacks reached a major milestone when they overcame Thurles at Croke Park by 5–4 to 2–1 in the final. The winners were better prepared and displayed superior teamwork. Thurles had some fine strikers, but they were too anxious to lift the ball even when a ground stroke would have yielded a better result.

Goals from Pauline Brennan, Anne Sheehy and Rita Halpin put Stacks ahead at the interval. The Tipperary girls had their best period after the break when they cut Stacks' margin to four points. Stacks recovered, added further goals and dominated the

Cork Bridge 29-year Gap

closing stages of the game. Sally Long was a gallant figure in goal for Thurles and saved her side from a heavier defeat.

Austin Stacks team: Sheila Murray, Mary Ryan (captain), Bríd Keenan, Vera Sullivan, Fiona Murray, Sheila McEvoy, Lucy McEvoy, Orla Ní Síocháin, Pauline Brennan, Anne Sheehy, Rita Halpin and Dympna Caldwell.

Thurles team: Sally Long, Mary Graham, Margaret Murphy, Bernie O'Dowd (captain), Alice Perry, Beatrice Lawrence, Ann Ralph, Kit Boland, Marion Moynihan, Kay Bermingham, Margo Loughnane and Marion Troy.

Austin Stacks Camogie Club was formed in 1930 by Molly Heron, Violet Forde, Molly Tubbert, Rose Kelly, Rita Blake and the Fallon sisters. Their best-known administrator, Molly Murphy (née Fitzgerald) chaired the Leinster Council and the Dublin County Board. She trained Stacks teams for many years in Herbert Park. The club won the Dublin Senior Championship on 11 occasions and produced many outstanding players, including Doreen Rogers, Bríd Reid, Pat Cooney, Mary Sherlock, Bríd Keenan, Mary Ryan and Orla Ní Síocháin.

1971 Gael-Linn Cup

Leinster had a runaway win over Connacht in the semi-final of the Gael-Linn Cup at Parnell Park, scoring 7–4 without reply. In contrast, the Ulster v. Munster semi-final was a tit-for-tat affair at Carrickmacross with the final whistle sounding with Ulster a point in front, 4–3 to 3–5. There was nothing between Leinster and Ulster in the first-half of the final at Parnell Park, but Leinster pulled away in the second half to win by 5–4 to 0–5.

Leinster team: Teresa Sheil (Wexford), Mary Ryan (Dublin), Joan Murphy (Wexford), Margaret O'Leary (Wexford) (captain), Carmel O'Shea (Kilkenny), Annie Kehoe (Wexford) (0–1), Anne Sheehy (Dublin), Elsie Walsh (Wexford) (0–1), Helena O'Neill (Kilkenny), Mary Walsh (Wexford) (0–1), Orla Ní Síocháin (Dublin) (2–0), Josie Kehoe (Wexford) (3–1).

Ulster team: Teresa Cassidy (Antrim), Kathleen McCann (Down), Anne McCone (Armagh), Mairéad Diamond (Antrim), Kathleen Kelly (Antrim), Kathleen Fee (Tyrone), Sue Cashman (Antrim) (captain) (0–1), Mairéad McAtamney (Antrim) (0–2), Pat Crangle (Down), Chris O'Boyle (Antrim), Marion Delaney (Armagh) (0–2) and Lily Scullion (Antrim).

New Look for Camogie

Two significant decisions were made at Congress 1972. The ban on hockey and football was deleted and a new playing uniform was introduced. While the ban on football had only been applied recently, the boycott of hockey had been in existence for over 30 years. The withdrawal of the ban cleared the way for schools and colleges at all levels to play both games, with obvious benefits.

The gym frock and black stockings were replaced by divided skirts, sports shirts and bobby socks. The new clothing allowed players more freedom and looked smarter. While the vast majority of players welcomed the latest camogie fashion, some members were loath to discard the gym frock and some clubs, and a few counties, continued to dress in the old style for several years. Dublin proposed that an assistant be appointed to the Ard Runaí. The debate came to a sudden halt, when Miss McAnulty stated emphatically that she did not require an assistant.

CCIA

The Camogie Council for Colleges of Higher Education was formed in March 1972. Up to that point, only the universities had been catered for, with no consideration for the non-university colleges. The fact that 14 colleges were represented at the meeting highlighted the need and the demand for such a council. The new body commenced a successful league, which attracted entries from seven universities and seven institutes of advanced learning.

A fresher's competition was added shortly after as the committee worked to break new ground and build tradition. Agnes Purcell (UCD) headed up the new council.

The remaining officers, all newcomers to administration, were: vice-president, Geraldine Cummiskey (Trinity); secretary, Jane Murphy (UCG); treasurer, Emer Bell (Garnaville); and registrar, Mary O'Brien (UCC). Trinity College, NUI Maynooth and the University of Ulster, Coleraine brought the number of teams competing in the Ashbourne Cup to seven and necessitated the holding of preliminary round matches.

Dublin captain, Pat Morrissey, lifts the New Ireland Cup following Dublin's success in the 1971 All-Ireland junior championship at Croke Park.

Off to USA

Thurles was the first camogie club to visit the United States. Formed only six years previously, the club went from strength to strength in a short time. The current Tipperary champions travelled with a hurling selection that included Tipperary star, Jimmy Doyle. The Thurles girls defeated a North American selection at Gaelic Park and, in a return game, a week later at Prospect Park. Young Ireland's Club, New York, visited Ireland in 1973 when they played Thurles at Bansha.

From Camogie to Olympics

Margaret Barry was an all-rounder. A superbly fit player, she collected Cork and Munster senior championship medals. Her husband, Paud Murphy, encouraged her to concentrate on athletics and, within a few short years, she was representing Ireland. The highlight of her career was walking into the Olympic Stadium in Munich wearing the Irish colours for the opening ceremony. The XXth Olympiad was famous for good and bad events: it signalled the arrival of diminutive Soviet gymnast Olga Korbut and the multi-medal swimmer Mark Spitz, but it was also where eight Arab commandos broke into the Olympic village and killed two Israeli team members before being killed in a shootout with German police.

Margaret competed in the pentathlon, which includes shot-putt, long jump, high jump, 100m hurdles and 200m flat. She did

Cork Bridge 29-year Gap

Cork – All-Ireland senior champions 1972. Back: Betty Sugrue, Pat Moloney, Liz Garvan, Anne McAuliffe, Marion Sweeney, Marian McCarthy, Deirdre Sutton and Rosie Hennessy. Front: Anne Keane, Anne Phelan, Nuala Guilly, Hannah Dineen (Capt), Mary Whelton, Sheila Dunne and Marie Costine.

not feature in the medals but was pleased with a personal best. The event was won by Belfast girl, Mary Peters.

Match Analysis

In the days when RTÉ ignored the All-Ireland final, match analysis took a different form. When the post-match function was over and the cheering had died down, the Cork players would congregate in a bedroom to listen to Hannah Dineen replay the match. Her ability to recall the play was exceptional. Scores were traced back through several moves to a missed tackle or a badly taken sideline. The build-up to a Cork score had to be replayed over and over again and was always met by a resounding cheer. Some players agreed that the game had passed them by and were delighted to hear Hannah bring it to life.

1972 All-Ireland Senior Championship

With Galway graded as juniors for 1972, Leinster champions, Kilkenny, had no opposition at the semi-final stage and advanced to the final. Contrasting fortunes awaited Antrim and Cork in the second semi-final at Croke Park. Antrim started promisingly but faded. On the other hand, Cork were sluggish in the opening half but thundered into the game to progress to the final by 5–5 to 3–1.

The Kilkenny players ran onto Croke Park for the All-Ireland final against Cork on September 17th looking very smart in their new camogie uniforms. The game took time to open up as tension and nerves gripped the players. Deirdre Sutton, who had replaced the retired Mel Cummins in goal, brought off a number of spectacular saves. As the match progressed, Betty Sugrue and Pat Moloney came into their own in midfield. Liz Garvan, Anne Phelan and Marion Sweeney found scores hard to come by with the brilliant defending of Kilkenny's Teresa O'Neill, Ann Phelan and Carmel O'Shea. Liz Garvan blasted a free to the net to cancel out a great shot from Angela Downey. The deciding score came from Anne Phelan who was left unmarked long enough to unleash a powerful drive to the Kilkenny net.

Without reaching their best, Cork were good enough to win by 2–5 to 1–4. A small 15-year-old, Angela Downey, made her All-Ireland final debut and was soon to become the most talked about player in the history of the game.

Shortly after the final, Liz Garvan travelled to Zambia to take up a teaching job and her wonderful talent was lost to the game. One can only speculate on the heights that her career would have reached if she had remained.

Cork team: Deirdre Sutton, Marie Costine, Hannah Dineen (captain), Anne McAuliffe, Mary Whelton, Marion McCarthy, Betty Sugrue, Pat Moloney, Anne Phelan (née Comerford) (1–1), Liz Garvan (1–2), Marion Sweeney (0–2) and Rosie Hennessy.

Kilkenny team: Teresa O'Neill, Phil O'Shea, Mary O'Neill, Carmel O'Shea, Ann Phelan, Breda Cassin, Ann Carroll (0–3), Liz Neary (0–1), Bridie Martin, Maura Cassin, Helena O'Neill (captain) and Angela Downey (1–0).

1972 All-Ireland Junior Championship

A fitter and more nippy Galway side secured a place in the All-Ireland junior final at Lurgan at the expense of Armagh. Forwards were on top in the high-scoring game that generated 12 goals. Pat Feeney put her name on five of the Galway goals and Marion Delaney replied with 3–2 for Armagh. The final whistle blew with the score at Galway 7–3, Armagh 5–2.

Wexford were in a different class to Limerick in the second semi-final at Castleconnell and caused the home side endless trouble. Brigid Higgins (3–0) and Bridie Tobin (2–3) put the game out of Limerick's reach and the teams stood at Wexford 6–8, Limerick 1–6 at the finish.

Galway, who had been regraded from senior to junior earlier in the year, were too experienced for a youthful Wexford side at Croke Park. There was little between the sides in the opening half. Galway used craft, combination and know-how to shut Wexford down while scoring 3–6 to 2–1 to claim the New Ireland Cup. Centre-back Kathleen Quinn, Jane Murphy and Nono McHugh were very prominent for Galway.

Galway team: Margaret Killeen, Mary Kilkenny, Claire Collins, Kathleen Quinn, Rosemary Divilly, Grace Divilly (1–1), Josie Kelly, Catherine Ward, Nono McHugh (captain) (0–1), Jane Murphy (1–3), Sheila Crowe and Pat Feeney (1–1).

Wexford team: Margaret Kelly, Mary Boggan, Breda Finn, Gretta Kehoe, Geraldine Duggan, Mairéad Darcy, Eileen Hawkins (captain) (0–1), Breda Murphy, Brigid Higgins, Bridie Tobin (1–0), Breda McCleane (1–0) and Mary Murphy. Sub used: Sheila Redmond.

Breda McCleane is the mother of current Wexford stars, Ursula and Helena Jacob.

1972 All-Ireland Club Championship

Sheila Murray, the Austin Stacks goalkeeper, was the player of the match in the All-Ireland club semi-final against Oranmore at Athenry. She saved a wide variety of shots including a rasper from a 15-yard free. The Dublin club were the better-balanced side, whereas Oranmore depended heavily on Nono McHugh and Josie

Cork Bridge 29-year Gap

Kelly. Austin Stacks finished ahead by 4–5 to 1–4.

Portglenone had a clear-cut win over Ahane in the second semi-final. Led by their highly rated star, Mairéad McAtamney and well-supported by Sue McLarnon, Teresa McAtamney and Brigid Graham, Portglenone were well in control against an Ahane side that disappointed their travelling supporters.

Champions, Austin Stacks, were considerably strengthened by the acquisition of Liz Neary, who had already won three All-Ireland Club medals with St Paul's, and the return of Sligo-born Mary Sherlock, holder of five All-Ireland senior medals. They were now a very formidable outfit with seven interprovincial players in their ranks.

The final at Croke Park contained some very entertaining passages of play. There was not a great deal between the sides but the teamwork and support play of the champions told. Mairéad McAtamney was an inspirational figure on the Portglenone team and received most assistance from her sister Teresa, Olive Webb, Sue McMullan and the Graham sisters. Anne Sheehy, Mary Ryan, Lucy McEvoy, Bríd Keenan and Vera Sullivan were key figures in Stacks' 4–2 to 2–0 win.

Austin Stacks team: Sheila Murray, Mary Ryan (captain), Bríd Keenan, Vera Sullivan, Dympna Caldwell, Liz Neary (0–1), Lucy McEvoy, Orla Ní Síocháin (0–1), Pauline Brennan, Anne Sheehy (2–0), Rita Halpin (2–0) and Mary Sherlock.

Portglenone team: Sue McLarnon, Teresa McAtamney, Brigid Graham, Olive Webb, Sadie McMullan, Brenda Dillon, Mairéad McAtamney, Ann Kelly, Frances Graham, Patricia O'Doherty, Enda Webb and Sheena McAtamney.

1972 Gael-Linn Cup

With 11 Cork players all fresh from their All-Ireland triumph on the team, Munster were expected to do well against Leinster in the semi-final at St Finbarr's (Cork), but they failed to reproduce their Croke Park form and wilted before the Leinster challenge by 4–2 to 1–0. Sheila Murray, Margaret O'Leary, Orla Ní Síocháin and Maura Cassin were in excellent form for Leinster.

The Connacht selectors placed their faith in the 12 Galway players who won the All-Ireland junior title for the Gael-Linn semi-final against Ulster in Sligo. Their trust was repaid with a lively display that earned a place in the final by 6–6 to 5–5. However, the junior champions found the pick of Kilkenny, Wexford and Dublin too difficult to cope with and were forced to concede by 7–7 to 4–2.

Leinster team: Sheila Murray (Dublin), Rita Whyte (Dublin), Joan Murphy (Wexford), Margaret O'Leary (Wexford), Carmel O'Shea (Kilkenny), Breda Cassin (Kilkenny), Miriam Miggan (Kildare), Orla Ní Síocháin (Dublin) (1–3), Anne Sheehy (Dublin) (2–0), Ann Carroll (Kilkenny) (captain) (1–1), Elsie Walsh (Wexford) (1–1) and Maura Cassin (Kilkenny) (2–2).

Connacht team: (all Galway) Margaret Killeen, Mary Kilkenny, Claire Collins, Kathleen Quinn, Rosemary Divilly, Grace Divilly, Josie Kelly, Catherine Ward, Nono McHugh (captain) (1–0), Jane Murphy (1–2), Sheila Crowe and Pat Feeney (1–0). Sub used: Catherine O'Grady (1–0).

Nancy Murray Gets the Top Job

The term of office for a President of the Camogie Association is three years. However, Nell McCarthy chose to step down after two years. Nancy Murray (née Milligan) from the Deirdre club, Belfast, was elected president. Knowledgeable and experienced in administration and the game, she slipped into the demanding role easily. Nancy left her mark on many facets of the game.

Group taken at the first National Coaching Course at Gormanston College in July, 1970.

Congress on the Move

Galway was the venue for Congress 1973, the first time that it had been held outside of Dublin. Armagh's call for an All-Ireland minor championship met with approval, with an age limit of under 16 being agreed for the new competition. Dublin sought to introduce an open draw system for the All-Ireland senior championship. With only one senior county in both Ulster and Connacht, it was unrealistic to continue the championship on a provincial basis.

In her secretary's report, Sheila McAnulty called for the restructure of the Association. She considered the existing set-up and the volume of work completed at Central Council level to be unsatisfactory. Too much time was taken up with trivial matters which could be best dealt with by sub-committees.

Into Europe

University College Cork and Old Aloysians, Cork, brought camogie to Holland in March 1973. The first match to be played on mainland Europe took place at Bussum and the return fixture at Leiden University. Fresh from their Ashbourne success, UCC claimed the trophy, a delft musical windmill, on their aggregate score. The locals were mesmerised by the skill of Liz Garvan and what she could do with the stick and ball. Several members of the local rugby club were anxious to try our game and got on the spot personal tuition. Dutch national television broadcast the first match and showed part of it later that evening.

Girls Take Over

Central Council looked to GAA coaches to get the National Coaching Course up and running. Although excellent tuition had been

Cork Bridge 29-year Gap

provided by Dessie Ferguson, Donie Nealon, Christy Hayes and Fr Maher at different times, it was always the intention that those in the camogie community would supply their own coaches as soon as they felt confident to do so. That time came earlier than expected when almost 150 students were booked into Gormanston College in 1973 and none of the recognised GAA coaches were available.

The first choice camogie coaches approached to do the job declined. So, with their backs to the wall, Central Council settled on Kilkenny star, Ann Carroll, and Mary Moran, who had coached Cork to All-Ireland titles. They grew into the job following a tentative start. Shortly afterwards, Ann, whose enthusiasm for any task knew no bounds, completed a Master's degree in Recreation Management at Loughborough University. For many years, Ann and Mary directed the National Coaching Course at Gormanston College and many courses at venues around the country.

Another step forward was the appointment of Eithne Neville to take students for camogie sessions at the National College of Physical Education in Limerick.

Bernie Dixon (Antrim) arrives too late to block Marie Costine's (Cork) clearance in the 1973 All-Ireland senior final at Croke Park.

1973 All-Ireland Senior Championship

The new open draw threw up a representative from each province for the semi-final stages of the All-Ireland senior championship. Antrim scored a hard-earned but merited 1–8 to 1–4 win over Wexford at Wexford Park, having combined more successfully than their opponents to engineer vital scores.

Galway, by virtue of their success in the All-Ireland Junior Championship, returned to the senior ranks. Cork had to battle hard to earn a narrow 3–2 to 2–3 victory at Ballinasloe. Both sets of players were guilty of squandering chances from play and placed balls.

The All-Ireland final at Croke Park on September 16th had everything – top-class camogie, goalmouth thrills and no more than a single score separating the sides at any time. Full credit went to Antrim, who were severely hampered in their preparations, to be able play with such skill and flair. The neutrals in the attendance got behind Antrim and cheered their every move.

Chris O'Boyle threaded the ball along the ground through the Cork defence and shot a brilliant goal to get Antrim off to a great start. From then on, they picked and drove high balls into the heart of the Cork defence. Time and again, Marie Costine caught the ball and sent it back with interest and this waste of possession proved costly for Antrim. The play swung from end to end with both sides shooting narrow wides.

The last few minutes were heart-stopping. Sue Cashman equalised with a point from far out. Ann Phelan got on the end of a diagonal ball and crashed it to the net. Marion McCarthy pointed a free. The ball was swept down the field where Deirdre Sutton saved at the expense of a 30-yard free. Up stepped Mairéad McAtamney and drove the ball past a packed Cork goalmouth. The game entered the final minute with a single point between the sides. Another Antrim raid was cleared to touch. Mairéad cut the sideline ball and it skimmed the outside of the Cork post to leave the score Cork 2-5, Antrim 3-1. Cork had achieved a four-in-a-row. Cally Riordan, who came on in the senior game, made her own bit of history by winning two All-Ireland medals in the same afternoon.

Cork team: Deirdre Sutton, Marie Costine (captain), Hannah Cotter, Sheila Dunne, Mary Whelton, Marion McCarthy (0–3), Pat Moloney, Betty Sugrue, Anne Phelan (2–1), Marion Sweeney (0–1), Nuala Guilly and Rosie Hennessy. Sub used: Cally Riordan.

Group pictured at first Colleges Coaching Course at Gormanston College in 1973.

Antrim team: Sue McLarnon, Kathleen Kelly, Josephine Maguire, Mairéad Diamond, Jo McClements, Rita McAteer, Sue Cashman (0–1), Mairéad McAtamney (captain) (1–0), Chris O'Boyle (1–0), Bernie Dixon, Nuala Havelin and Lily Scullion (1–0).

1973 All-Ireland Junior Championship

The Galway team that had won the 1972 All-Ireland Junior Championship was promoted to the senior grade for 1973, so for their semi-final against Wexford at Ballinasloe, Galway fielded a different group of players. It was obvious that the selectors had unearthed some real talent. Midge Poniard, Phil Foye and Ann O'Donoghue were instrumental in Galway's 4–4 to 3–3 victory.

The Cork team relaxed in a Dundalk hotel on the morning of their semi-final against Armagh when a telephone call from president, Nancy Murray, conveyed the tragic news that Armagh centre-forward, Marion Delaney, had lost both parents in a car accident the previous night. They had been returning from holiday to see the match. The Armagh team were devastated and in no

Cork Bridge 29-year Gap

condition to play a match. Armagh offered Cork a walkover but, in the circumstances, Cork did not accept it.

The Cork party returned on the following Sunday to Knockbridge. Armagh failed to produce the form that brought them the Ulster title. Marion Delaney lined out but the events of the previous weekend had taken their toll and she was unable to play her usual inspiring game. Good approach play by Nancy O'Driscoll, Mary Canavan and Elizabeth Higgins provided good ball for Cally Riordan to convert three goals. Angela Toal, Marian Courtney and Marion Delaney fought courageously in Armagh's cause but could not prevent Cork advancing by 4-2 to 0-2.

September 16th, 1973, was a special day in the history of Cork camogie. The county claimed the first All-Ireland championship double on the same afternoon. Narrowly defeated on three previous occasions, the Cork juniors finally made the breakthrough and lifted the New Ireland Cup at the expense of Galway at Croke Park. With the advantage of a strong wind in the first-half, Cork played an attractive brand of fast, skilful camogie and led by 4–4 to 0–3 at the break.

Galway returned to the fray in determined mood. Mary Kelly, Midge Poniard and Phil Foye gained a grip in midfield. Great defensive work by Elizabeth Higgins, Bríd McAuliffe and Rosie O'Sullivan confined Galway to two scores and enabled Cork to win by 4–4 to 1–4.

Cork team: Elizabeth Higgins, Bríd McAuliffe, Marie Mackey, Rosie O'Sullivan, Nuala Jennings, Marion McCarthy, Mary Canavan, Angela Higgins, Mary Mahon, Mary O'Leary (1–3), Nancy O'Driscoll (captain) (2–0) and Cally Riordan (1–1).

Galway team: Kathleen Moore, Bernie Larkin, Rita Jordan, Alma Dwane (0–1), Mary Kelly, Midge Poniard (0–1), Phil Foye (1–1), Ann O'Donoghue (0–1), Margaret Murphy, Teresa Duane, Fionnuala Walsh and Kathleen Coughlan. Sub used: Anne Kilkenny.

Rosie O'Sullivan's father, Ted, won All-Ireland senior hurling medals with Cork in 1941 and 1943.

1973 All-Ireland Club Championship

The losing scoreline – 1–6 to 0–2 – of the All-Ireland semi-final between St Paul's and Thurles does not reflect the huge effort put in by the Tipperary club. The difference between them was that the winners had more finishing power. The vital score, a goal from Helena O'Neill, came midway through the second half. Oranmore survived the late challenge of Creggan (Co. Antrim) to qualify for the All-Ireland club final. The Galway side were coasting to victory when hit by a purposeful late rally and had to call on their experience to see them through.

The Bill Carroll Cup crossed the Shannon for the first time when Oranmore came away with the spoils at the finish of a very exciting encounter against St Paul's at Nowlan Park. Oranmore raced into the lead with goals by Josie Kelly and Pat Feeney. A number of St Paul's raids on the Oranmore goal came to nothing until Angela Downey soloed through to score late in the half. Teresa Carroll collected the puck-out and scored directly to leave Oranmore in front by 3–0 to 1–0.

St Paul's went straight into attack as play resumed and were rewarded with a goal from Helena O'Neill. The home players sensed victory and attacked furiously in an attempt to equalise and go in front. But Oranmore were not to be denied. Points were exchanged but Paul's could not find the goal needed to give them victory. The final score was Oranmore 3–2, St Paul's 2–3.

Oranmore team: Margaret Burke, Bridgie Henley, Mandy Cosgrave, Ann Dillon, Rosemary Divilly, Margaret Murphy, Nono McHugh (0–1), Grace Divilly, Teresa Carroll (1–0), Josie Kelly (captain) (1–1), Pat Feeney (1–0) and Marian Forde.

St Paul's team: Teresa O'Neill, Nuala Bolger, Mary O'Neill, Carmel O'Shea, Mary Kavanagh, Liz Neary, Ann Downey, Helena O'Neill, Ursula Grace, Carmel Doyle, Angela Downey and Mary Conway.

1973 Gael-Linn Cup

Connacht and Munster drew at Castleconnell 3–7 to 4–4 in the Gael-Linn Cup despite 20 minutes of extra-time being played. Connacht fully deserved their five-point win, 1–6 to 1–1, in the replay at Ballinasloe. The Leinster v. Ulster semi-final was also a very close affair at Naas, with Leinster fashioning a two-point win, 4–3 to 3–4. Connacht won the Gael-Linn Cup for the first time at Parnell Park. Their speedy forwards outpaced the Leinster defence to snatch vital scores in a 4–4 to 3–3 victory.

Connacht team: (All Galway) Margaret Killeen, Mary Kilkenny, Claire Collins, Kathleen Quinn, Rosemary Divilly, Nono McHugh (captain) (1–2), Josie Kelly, Catherine Ward, Ann O'Donoghue, Phil Foye (1–0), Jane Murphy (0–1) and Margaret Murphy (2–1).

Leinster team: Anne Carey (Dublin), Joan Murphy (Wexford), Rita Whyte (Dublin) (captain), Bridget Doyle (Wexford) (1–0), Carmel O'Shea (Kilkenny) (0–1), Elsie Walsh (Wexford), Margaret Leacy (Wexford) (1–0), Peggy Carey (Kilkenny), Helena O'Neill (Kilkenny) (1–0), Marion Conroy (Dublin), Orla Ní Síocháin (Dublin) (0–2) and Angela Downey (Kilkenny).

Where We're At

The seventies witnessed a shift in attitude and a willingness to embrace change: amongst the most prominent changes congress saw reason and brought the era of bans to a close and teams were allowed to substitute players.

I never saw the sense in prohibiting the replacement of a player – anything that both teams are entitled to do is fair. Under the system whereby the referee had to be satisfied that a player was injured before she could be inter-changed was unfair on the teams' substitutes who turned up match after match and rarely saw any action. The ban on football and hockey was outdated and, in fact, detrimental to the Association. It attracted adverse comment and was an obstacle to progress.

Women's fashions constantly change and there was a need for a more feminine, colourful and comfortable playing outfit. The new uniform created a better appearance, gave freedom of movement and bestowed a more youthful image.

Social contact was at a premium in camogie circles, with players and officials having little or no contact with their counterparts from other parts of the country. Moving congress out of Dublin was a step in the right direction. When the annual meeting was held in the capital, the delegates made their own arrangements with regard to meals and accommodation and went their own way as soon as the meeting ended. However, with the entire attendance staying in the same hotel, at venues around the country, the opportunity presented itself to meet other delegates at meal times and to socialise when the business of the day was complete.

The National Coaching Course had a lively social side too. In fact, it could be a bit too frolicsome for those who wished to get a night's sleep. The enthusiasm and dedication of the students, who tried to absorb as much knowledge as possible, was exceptional. Everyone tried so hard to master the skills on the field, particularly those whose playing days were over. New friends were made. The courses were a huge take in the early days. The GAA coaches led the way and the students responded leading to a very beneficial weekend.

Great credit was due to the group of Dublin-based players who took it upon themselves to improve the communication and image of the Association. They found time and energy to undertake the daunting task of compiling and producing camogie's first national magazine – an excellent publication that stimulated interest in camogie. The magazine allowed members keep in touch with one another, feel part of the Association and relive the highlights of the season.

With no senior side to represent Connacht, a change to an open draw system for the All-Ireland senior championship was inevitable. Only six counties – three in Leinster, two in Munster and one in Ulster – were good enough to be rated senior. The first two counties to take the All-Ireland junior crown, Down and Derry, cut no ice on the senior scene. A number of suggestions were put forward as to how an open draw might operate. A 'losers' group' and a league system were among the recommendations put forward to provide extra matches, but a straight-forward knockout competition was agreed. However, the real problem, presented by such a small entry, remained.

Playing a refreshing brand of camogie, Cork established themselves as kingpins of the game with an impressive four-in-a-row series of senior titles. New stars were launched on the camogie scene: Pat Moloney and Marie Costine contributed immensely and would be named on the Team of the Century in 2004. Liz Garvan, Rosie Hennessy, Mel Cummins, Betty Sugrue and Hannah Dineen also ranked with the best.

A Game of Our Own

CHAMPIONS

Chapter Twelve

KILKENNY BREAKTHROUGH

The unqualified success of the introduction of camogie to second-level colleges led to calls for a similar body to be set up to cater for the game in the primary schools. Sheila McAnulty was appointed to steer the new national body, the Primary Schools Council, in 1974 and Mary O'Brien (Clare) filled the role of secretary. Mary Lynch, Sr Mairéad, Vera Mannion, Kitty Flaherty, Joan Bourke, Breda McCleane, Sr Sarah and Bríd Donnellan made up the council.

Primary schools camogie was played in certain counties where teachers or individual officials promoted it, and where rules were adapted to suit local circumstances.

It was considered that most of the children in primary schools would be too young to participate in serious competition, therefore, the emphasis was on teaching the children how to play the game.

County boards were requested to set up a sub-committee that would encourage the schools to take up the game. The role of the Primary Schools Council was one of encouraging and fostering those working at ground level.

Seán and Kathleen O'Duffy watching the inaugural Kilmacud Sevens at Glenalbyn in 1974

First Administration Course

With the Camogie Association expanding at different levels, the workload of administrators was increasing. New officials were required and needed to be trained in the procedures and best practice of the organisation. It was equally important that the best use was made of existing officials. With these concerns in mind, the first National Administration Course was planned to take place in Howth on May 3rd–5th, 1974.

Lectures on the internal workings of the Association were given by experienced administrators, including Nancy Murray, Lily Spence, Eithne Neville, Anne Ashton and Iney Leonard.

Prominent GAA officials spoke on broader issues. Dr Donal Keenan, Seán Ó Síocháin, Paddy Purcell, Michael O'Callaghan, Maurice Prenderville and Tom Loftus covered: co-operation between the two associations; club development; communication; fund-raising and publicity; and social and cultural activities. The programme was interesting and informative and appreciated by those present.

Ceol, Caint agus Damhsa

On the social side, the Ceol, Caint agus Damhsa competition, which had been successfully run in Ulster, was extended to an All-Ireland competition. It was run on similar lines to the GAA Scór with solo singing, ballad groups, novelty acts, question time, set dancing and figure dancing, and instrumental music on the programme. Ulster were great supporters of this event and flocked to the finals in their hundreds. In the remainder of the country, only individual clubs gave backing.

National PRO

Jo Golden (Kilkenny), editor of *Camogie* magazine, was appointed National PRO in June 1974. She immediately set about upgrading the All-Ireland programme. Always excellent with the pen in her hand, Jo produced a 16-page souvenir worthy of the occasion.

Mary Conway left, KK tussling for the ball with Sheila Dunne, Cork in the 1974 Final

Later in the year, she edited the first *Camogie Annual*.

Colleges Double for Presentation, Athenry

1974 saw the introduction of an All-Ireland Colleges Junior Championship. Presentation, Athenry, enjoyed a wonderful outing in Croke Park when they claimed both the All-Ireland senior and junior colleges titles, with four Athenry girls – Bernadette Duffy, Noreen Treacy, Olive Coady and Eileen Hynes – played on both winning teams.

RTÉ sent a camera to the finals and transmitted excerpts from the games.

Kilmacud Sevens

The Kilmacud Crokes All-Ireland Sevens is very much part of the All-Ireland weekend, providing a very enjoyable day in pleasant surroundings. It attracts teams to Dublin from all over the country and beyond, many of whom go along to Croke Park to view the All-Ireland finals on the following day. It offers an opportunity for players to enjoy a novel brand of camogie, renew friendships and meet camogie folk from all over the country. For many the competitions are not important.

The entry has expanded considerably over the years. Recent

Kilkenny breakthrough

Camogie

CORK HOLD ON FOR DRAW

Cork 4-5 (17)
Kilkenny 3-8 (17)

CORK and Kilkenny finished all level in the All-Ireland senior camogie final at Croke Park yesterday, the holders, Cork, surviving a great challenge from the opposition.

Kilkenny had the opening two points, Cork replied with a "thirty". This was followed by a goal from a free and a further goal. Kilkenny replied with a similar score. The Kilkenny girls then took command and ran up a lead of three points. Cork rallied and led at the interval by 3-3 to 2-5.

Resuming, Cork had a free but a wide resulted. They continued to attack but failed to raise a flag. Kilkenny improved and a good goal by Carmel Doyle put them in the lead by two points. H. O'Neill pointed from a free, but Cork steadied up and returned to the attack and in the 18th minute, T. Maloney pointed. Two minutes later M. Sweeney notched a goal on the move, but Cork held fast and B. Considine went over for a point. In a dramatic finish H. O'Neill equalised with a point.

Scorers: Cork—M. Sweeney (2-1), N. O'Driscoll (1-0), M. McCarthy (1-2), P. Maloney (0-1), B. Considine (0-1). Kilkenny—Carmel Doyle (2-0), H. O'Neill (0-6), A. Downey (0-1), N. Conway (1-1).

Irish Times report on the 1974 Cork-Kilkenny drawn game

statistics read: 500 players; 96 matches; 56 clubs; 10 pitches and a Puc Fada competition. The hard-working organising committee deserve the congratulations and gratitude of the Camogie Association and of the scores of players for hosting this prestigious event on the camogie calendar. There are clubs who take the competitions very seriously and strain muscle and limb in pursuit of honours. The Prionnsias Ó Cróinín (father of Club President, Eileen Hogan) Memorial Cup and the Seán Flynn Shield are the trophies for the two competitions. And there are those who come every year, like Danny Bowe and his team from Ardkeen, just to be part of a great day.

Coaching Film

An instructional film, *Camogie*, was organised and completed under the direction of the Coaching Committee. It covered the basic skills of the game and included excerpts from matches to show the particular skills in play. Copies of the film were deposited in the Film Institute and could be hired out by schools and clubs. RTÉ used the film in their *Sports Club* programme.

1974 All-Ireland Senior Championship

Cork had a convincing win over Antrim in the All-Ireland semi-final at Glenariff by 8–2 to 3–1. Following a close first-half, Cork opened up and played a superior brand of attacking camogie to which Antrim had no answer.

Wexford were caught by a last-minute point from a free by Helena O'Neill in the second semi-final at Wexford Park. Kilkenny should not have had to rely on a late score to advance as they had most of the play and should have had the game won before then.

It took two days to decide where the O'Duffy Cup would rest for 1974. In a match of high standard, Kilkenny drew the final against Cork at Croke Park on September 15th, with the last puck of the match – Helena

Camogie: All-Ireland final replay

Kilkenny emerge from a thriller

KILKENNY .... 3-3 (12)   CORK 1-5 (8)

KILKENNY, who broke Dublin's stranglehold in Leinster for the first time in 1968, and who were beaten by Cork in their two All-Ireland finals since then, finally won the All-Ireland senior camogie championship for the first time at Croke Park yesterday, depriving Cork of their eleventh title in all and their fifth in a row.

There are many who still believe that this game is a weak, delicate version of hurling. Those not converted to the merits of camogie in its own right among the attendance of approximately 5,000 at headquarters yesterday must none surely be, for this match provided as much excitement, skill, and scoring effort as any I have seen in hurling this year, and, with the exception of Kilkenny's tense victory over Wexford in the penultimate stages of the championship.

—BY—
AIDAN McCARTHY

The programme's short history on camogie in Kilkenny notes that, in 1923, Alice McCormack was reputedly "as good as any man." Many of the players on both teams yesterday would justify the same observation, and Angela Downey, showed more adeptness with stick and sliothar than many of the players on Kilkenny's victorious senior hurling team.

Those close to the game admit that the standard has been considerably higher in recent years, mainly because of the new coaching schemes at schools' level. It is likely that there is much scope for further improvement, but if the quality of yesterday's game could be repeated every year there would be no cause for complaint.

While Angela Downey's inevitably successful dummies and quick acceleration past the defence, a benefit of her association with athletics, provided the highlights of the game, there were many other individual and collective movements to keep the partisans of both camps on their toes.

An indication of the game in store came before five minutes elapsed. Ursula Grace finding Angela Downey with an astute pass, and the latter turning and sending a snappy shot to the roof of the net. This goal left Kilkenny 1-1 ahead, Carmel Doyle having pointed in the first minute.

DECISIVE MOMENTS

Three minutes later, it seemed that Cork were in for a severe drubbing, for their defence was wilting under the speed and penetration of the four Kilkenny forerunners, and had conceded another goal, Helena O'Neill's free from 50 yards being allowed to reach the net through a crowded goalmouth.

After ten minutes, however, the Kilkenny goalkeeper, Teresa O'Neill, was injured, requiring almost five minutes attention to a head wound before recovering, and the play had just resumed when Bernie Costine racing in to score a fine goal, reducing the Cork deficit.

There were no more scores before half-time, Kilkenny, although not gaining a decisive territorial advantage, had by far the more chances, notably Miss O'Neill's free from 50 yards being allowed to reach the net through a crowded goalmouth.

After ten minutes, however, the Kilkenny goalkeeper, Teresa O'Neill, was injured, requiring almost five minutes attention to a head wound before recovering, and the play had just resumed when Bernie Costine racing in to score a fine goal, reducing the Cork deficit.

There were no more scores before half-time, Kilkenny, although not gaining a decisive territorial advantage, had by far the more chances, notably Miss Downey, but the Cork defence, gaining in composure, stood resolute and at the break, Kilkenny were ahead by 2-1 to 1-0.

The second half saw Cork exert severe pressure for lengthy periods and although Kilkenny lost points were scored, Kilkenny never always able to score a quick retaliatory blow and on the 22nd minute, Miss Downey again doing the ground work with a searing run through, and Miss Grace finishing the ball to the net from a bunch of players.

While Miss Downey was unquestionably the player of the game, Liz Neary, Helena O'Neill, Mary Fennelly, Mary Conway and Carmel Doyle also caught the eye frequently for Kilkenny, while Marion McCarthy, in particular, Máire and Bernie Sweeney were most prominent for Cork, who must be commended for the heart they put into the game right up to the final whistle.

Irish Times report on the 1974 Cork-Kilkenny replay

A Game of Our Own

O'Neill held her nerve to slot over a free from an acute angle. Marion McCarthy, Nancy O'Driscoll and Marion Sweeney scored goals for Cork in the first-half while Carmel Doyle and Angela Downey replied for the Noresiders. Kilkenny rearranged their defence and afforded little space to Cork to add to their score.

A number of the Cork team did not play up to form, but they still remained in contention to the finish. The Cork attack was the most disappointing sector and missed the class of Liz Garvan and Rosie Hennessy. Carmel Doyle and Marion Sweeney swapped goals as tension mounted. A long-range point by substitute Bernie Costine put Cork ahead with time almost up. Then, referee Jane Murphy awarded Kilkenny a free 40 metres from goal and up stepped Helena O'Neill to earn a second bite of the cherry for Kilkenny by 3-8 to 4-5 for Cork.

Kilkenny led from start to finish in the replay at Croke Park on October 6th. The game contained brilliant passages of play and, only for the outstanding goalkeeping of Deirdre Sutton, Kilkenny would have won by more. With cool heads and expert marksmanship, Kilkenny dictated the play. Liz Neary, Ann Carroll and Bridie Martin snuffed out the threat posed by the Cork attack. Young Angela Downey caused panic in the Cork defence with searing solo runs. Cork were not as sharp as they had been over the previous four years. Deirdre Sutton, Hannah Cotter (née Dineen), Marion McCarthy and Pat Moloney played their hearts out but could not prevent Kilkenny winning by 3-3 to 1-5.

In a sporting gesture, Cork, led by Hannah Cotter, carried Ann Carroll, now in her 12th inter-county season, off the field.

The Kilkenny camogie team which beat Cork by 3-3 to 1-5 in the 1974 All-Ireland final replay on October 6. Back (from left): Ann Carroll, Carmel Doyle, Mary Conway, Teresa Brennan, Liz Neary, Peggy Carey, Annie Bowden, Mary Kennedy, Mary Purcell. Front (from left): Angela Downey, Marie Kavanagh, Bridie Martin, Teresa O'Neill (capt.), Mary Fennelly, Helena O'Neill, Ursula Grace, Anne Downey. Mascots are Bernadette Tracey and Maria Glendon.

Kilkenny team: Teresa O'Neill (captain), Ann Carroll, Liz Neary, Bridie Martin, Mary Kavanagh, Helena O'Neill (1-1), Peggy Carey, Mary Fennelly, Ursula Grace (1-0), Mary Conway, Angela Downey (1-1) and Carmel Doyle (0-1). Subs used: Mary Purcell and Mary Kennedy.

Cork team: Deirdre Sutton, Marie Costine, Nuala Jennings, Sheila Dunne, Hannah Cotter, Marion McCarthy (0-2), Betty Sugrue, Pat Moloney, Marion Sweeney (captain) (0-2), Anne Ryan, Bernie Costine (1-0) and Nancy O'Driscoll (0-1). Subs used: Nuala Guilly and Mary Canavan.

Peggy Carey is an aunt to All-Star Kilkenny hurler, D. J. Carey.

Kilkenny breakthrough

Ursula Grace is a daughter of Paddy Grace who had won All-Ireland hurling medals in 1939 and 1947 and was long-time Secretary of the Kilkenny GAA Board.

1974 All-Ireland Junior Championship

Clare's superiority throughout the field was not reflected on the scoreboard at the finish of their All-Ireland semi-final against Galway at Ballinasloe. Margaret O'Toole played a commanding role at centre-back and her long clearances provided plenty of opportunities for her forwards, but most were squandered. Goals by Maureen Davoren and Maureen Saunders booked a place in the final by 2–1 to 0–3.

Dublin and Antrim treated the large attendance at Glenariff to an entertaining game of camogie in the second semi-final, with little between the sides. Dublin's Maura Sutton, Lucy McEvoy and Helen Roche helped themselves to goals and a place in the final by 4–1 to 3–0.

Appearing in their first All-Ireland final, Clare snatched victory from Dublin in a most exciting contest at Croke Park. Both teams played the ball on the ground which accounted for the fact that there were no points scored from play. Dublin held a goal advantage at half-time and increased their lead on the resumption. Clare stormed the Dublin goal and were rewarded with goals from Maureen Davoren and substitute Mary Griffin shortly before the referee sounded the final whistle. Many believed that the second-half had lasted only 20 minutes, but she was adamant that she played the regulation 25 minutes. The final score stood at Clare 3–2, Dublin 3–0.

Clare: 1974 All-Ireland junior champions after defeating Dublin.

Clare team: Maureen Kelly, Ann Marie O'Loughlin, Rose Kelleher, Margaret O'Toole (captain), Claire Harrington, Teresa McDonagh, Kitty McNicholas, Maureen Davoren (1-2), Mary Dolan (1-0), Mary Mahon, Pauline Ryan and Eleece Fitzgibbon. Subs used: Mary Griffin (1-0) and Maureen Saunders.

Dublin team: Phyllis Breslin, Phil Barry, Bridget Kennedy, Ann Whelan, Mary Murphy, Marion Kenny, Liz Howard, Anne Redmond, Maura Sutton (1-0), Lucy McEvoy (captain), Margaret McMahon (1-0) and Helen Roche (1-0). Sub used: Anne Tallon.

Clare players, Ann Marie O'Loughlin and Claire Harrington, were the first players to win All-Ireland junior medals with two different counties. They had both collected medals with Dublin in 1970 before returning to their native county.

1974 All-Ireland Minor Championship

From the time, congress passed a motion to inaugurate an All-Ireland Minor Championship, followers of the game looked forward to seeing what the competition would produce and they were not disappointed. Emerging talent stepped on to the inter-county stage for the first time and the backers of the motion were delighted with the standard. Players, who up to then were only known in their own counties, were given an opportunity to shine and make the first rung up the ladder of their inter-county careers. Picking out the players likely to make it to the top in the years ahead became an added diversion for followers.

Patricia Mackey got Cork off to a great start in the semi-final against Galway at the Mardyke. Patricia's early goal was followed by similar scores from Ellen McCarthy and Margo Sugrue to leave Cork 3–4 to 0–0 ahead at the break. Galway came into the game in the second-half but excellent goalkeeping by Kathleen Costine kept them at bay.

Down and Kilkenny drew in the second semi-final at Nowlan Park 5–0 to 4–3. With a strong home backing, Down edged in front in the replay at Hilltown. Sheila McCartan, Susan Lively and Rita Neeson shone as Down won by 2–4 to 1–4.

The first All-Ireland minor final was played at Croke Park as a curtain-raiser to the replay of the All-Ireland senior final between Kilkenny and Cork. Down deservedly became the first All-Ireland minor champions, scoring a hard-earned victory over Cork. Down played direct and decisive camogie and their efficient defence coped with the Cork attack. Susan Lively, Teresa Gilchrist, Stephanie Kelly and Sheila McCartan played with maturity for their age and were key performers in Down's 3–0 to 0–1 win.

The last Tailteann Games took place in 1932 and the Tailteann Committee, of which Seán O'Duffy was a member, was wound up in 1974. A sum of money remained and part of it was given to the Camogie Association. Out of this money, a new cup was purchased for the All-Ireland Minor Championship which was engraved Corn Tailteann.

A set of silver medals, bearing the image of Queen Maeve, symbol of the Tailteann Games, remained from an unfinished Tailteann competition and this set, which was of great sentimental value and of far greater financial value than any set that the Camogie Association would have purchased, was presented to the winning Down team.

Down team: Christina Rooney, Teresa Gilchrist, Stephanie Kelly, Carmel Courtney, Sheila McCartan, Maria Finnegan, Susan Lively (captain) (1–0), Margaret Montgomery, Bernadette Malone, Rita Neesan (1–0), Mary McGrath (1–0) and Cathy O'Hare.

Cork team: Kathleen Costine, Claire Harris (captain), Betty Joyce, Margo Twomey, Jane O'Brien, Cathy Landers, Patricia Riordan, Gay Desmond (0–1), Eileen Kavanagh, Margo Sugrue, Patricia Mackey and Ellen McCarthy. Subs used: Anne O'Connor and Eileen Walsh.

Kilkenny breakthrough

Ellen McCarthy, sister of Cork's dual All-Ireland hurling and football medallist, Teddy McCarthy, was tragically injured in a car accident and died some years later (RIP).

1974 All-Ireland Club Championship

With 11 of the Kilkenny senior panel available to them, St Paul's looked potential champions from their first outing. Angela Downey shot 4–3 in the semi-final against Portglenone at Nowlan Park despite many excellent saves by Sue McLarnon. Antrim star, Mairéad McAtamney did her best to get her team going, but they were up against a better side.

A week following success in the Ashbourne Cup, Munster champions, UCC, looked a bit off colour in the second semi-final against Oranmore at the Mardyke. The Galway girls were crisper strikers and were capable of converting their chances. Nono McHugh, Grace Divilly and Josie Kelly dominated the middle of the field and set up many good opportunities for the forwards. Mary Roche, Pat Moloney, Ger Butler and Nuala Jennings did their best to stem the tide for UCC, Oranmore advanced by 6–5 to 2–2.

The final, a repeat of the previous year's decider, opened at a cracking pace at Ballinderreen. St Paul's were first to score with a well-worked goal by Mary Conway. Pat Feeney finished an accurate pass from Josie Kelly to leave it all square at the break. After the restart, St Paul's tore into attack and engineered 1–1, dominating the remainder of the match and adding 1–2. They ran out winners by 3–3 to 1–1.

St Paul's team: Teresa O'Neill, Ann Carroll, Liz Neary, Ann Downey, Mary Kavanagh, Helena O'Neill, Hanora Fogarty, Mary Fennelly, Angela Downey, Carmel Doyle, Ursula Grace and Breda Coonan.

Oranmore team: Margaret Burke, Rita Jordan, Mandy Cosgrave, Ann Dillon, Rosemary Divilly, Grace Divilly, Josie Kelly, Nono McHugh, Marion Forde, Anne Finn, Margaret Murphy and Teresa Carroll.

1974 Gael-Linn Cup

There was only one team in the running when Munster and Ulster met in the semi-final of the Gael-Linn Cup in Shannon: Munster 10–4 and Ulster 1–3 is a fair reflection of the relative merits of the teams. In the second semi-final at Ballinasloe, holders Connacht had a decisive and well-earned win over Leinster by 6–3 to 1–2.

Connacht retained the Gael-Linn Cup in a hugely entertaining contest at Ballinasloe. The outcome was balanced on a knife-edge until a flurry of points won the game by 3–7 to 3–0.

Connacht team: (all Galway) Margaret Killeen, Mary Kilkenny, Claire Collins, Rita Jordan, Marion Forde, Nono McHugh (1–5), Ann O'Donoghue, Catherine Ward (0–1), Midge Poniard (0–1), Josie Kelly, Jane Murphy and Margaret Murphy (2-0).

Munster team: Deirdre Sutton (Cork), Marie Costine (Cork), Sheila Dunne (Cork), Margaret O'Toole (Clare), Claire Harrington (Clare), Deirdre Lane (Tipperary), Pat Moloney (Cork), Bríd Stokes (Limerick), Marian Sweeney (Cork) (1–0), Anne Ryan

(Cork), Marion McCarthy (Cork) (1–0) and Nancy O'Driscoll (Cork) (1-0).

Ashbourne Diamond Jubilee

The Diamond Jubilee of the Ashbourne Cup was celebrated on the playing fields of St Patrick's College, Maynooth. Ten years previously, the idea of playing an Ashbourne series in Maynooth would have been beyond the wildest stretch of anybody's imagination, but that was before female students were admitted to the college. The number of potential players available to Maynooth fell way short of the larger universities and, while Maynooth College had yet to win the Ashbourne Cup, they had come very close when Angela Downey had worn the college colours.

Sheila McAnulty Steps Down

Sheila McAnulty stepped down from the position of Ard Runaí at Congress 1975, which was held in Limerick. For 22 years, Sheila steered the Association with clear thinking, sound judgement and foresight. Jo Golden (Kilkenny) was elected to replace her, gaining 17 votes to 16 for Pat Rafferty (Dublin). Kitty Murphy (Clare) filled the post of National PRO.

Sheila signed off with a plea to the members to remain faithful to the beliefs and aspirations of the founders: "Our Association was built on taking a stand in identifying itself with our distinct nationality. Lose that and we lose what is particularly ours, the heart and core of Cumann Camógaíochta na nGael. The members of our Association 'are bound together and must stay together' to ensure in this generation the retention of the consciousness of that identity."

Congress in Limerick was more than just a meeting. It was excellently organised in pleasant surroundings, with the entertainment put on by the Rathkeale Comhaltas Group on the Saturday night, being particularly memorable.

For a trial period of three years, it was decided to confine the Gael-Linn interprovincial series to junior players. Congress appointed a number of new sub-committees, including ones for fixtures and finance. Ann Carroll and Mary Moran were appointed national coaches and were asked to draw up: a programme for the National Coaching Course, a format for coaching examinations, and a system for grading coaches and the awarding of coaching badges.

1975 All-Ireland Senior Championship

With four newcomers – Mary O'Leary, Bernie Costine, Nuala Jennings and Cally Riordan – in the team, there was freshness about Cork in the All-Ireland semi-final against Kilkenny at Nowlan Park. They played with enthusiasm which was not matched by the home team. Cork advanced by 4–4 to 3–2.

Dublin were no test for a revitalised Wexford in the second semi-final at Na Fianna grounds. The home side could only muster two points in the first-half when they had the benefit of a stiff breeze.

Kilkenny breakthrough

Wexford kept Dublin scoreless for the remainder of the match to ensure a place in the final by 3-4 to 0-2.

Wexford created a major surprise in the All-Ireland final at Croke Park on September 21st by not only beating Cork, but by brushing them aside. The win provided a welcome wedding present for the Wexford captain, Gretta Quigley, who had got married the day before. Wexford were faster to the ball, crisper in their striking and more determined than their opponents, though the Cork defence was resolute in the opening half and confined their opponents to two scores.

On the change of ends, Wexford turned up the pressure and pulled away from Cork. The Rebels disintegrated in a most uncharacteristic fashion and few can reflect on the occasion with satisfaction. Kathleen Tonks, Bridget Doyle, Elsie Walsh, Margaret Leacy, Bridie Doran and Kit Codd were in big players in Wexford's 4-3 to 1-2 victory.

Wexford team: Kathleen Tonks, Margaret Leacy, Gretta Kehoe (captain), Bridget Doyle, Dorothy Walsh, Breda Murphy, Eileen O'Gorman (0-1), Elsie Walsh, Kit Codd (1-0), Bridie Doran (1-1), Margaret Hearne (0-1) and Peg Moore. Sub used: Mairéad Darcy (2-0).

Cork team: Deirdre Sutton, Marie Costine, Nuala Jennings, Sheila Morgan (née Dunne), Mary Whelton, Marion McCarthy, Pat Moloney (0-1), Bernie Costine, Mary O'Leary (captain) (1-1), Cally Riordan, Nancy O'Driscoll and Marion Sweeney.

Wexford's Elsie Walsh married Brian Cody, who would win a total of four All-Ireland senior hurling medals and would go on to coach several successful Kilkenny teams. Elsie's sister, Dorothy, was left-back on the team. Gretta Kehoe and Bridget Doyle became the first sisters to captain All-Ireland winning senior teams.

Gretta married Ray Quigley who served as Chairman of Leinster Camogie Council. Kit Codd, sister of captain Gretta, became the first player to win All-Ireland senior medals with two counties – Dublin (1965 and 1966) and Wexford (1975).

Five Kehoe sisters from Clonleigh, Co. Wexford – Bridget, Kit, Josie, Annie and Gretta – won All-Ireland senior medals. Bridie Doran is a sister of Mick Jacob, the first Wexford man to win an All-Star. She married Bill Doran who won an All-Ireland Intermediate hurling medal, brother of All-Ireland hurlers, Tony and Colm.

Wexford's 1975 team

1975 All-Ireland Junior Championship

Dublin qualified for their fourth All-Ireland junior final in six years when they ended Limerick's interest at the semi-final stage at the Phoenix Park. Phyllis Breslin in the Dublin goal and her four defenders kept Limerick at bay while their forwards made good use of their chances to win by 4–2 to 2–5. In the second semi-final, Down travelled to Athleague where they readily disposed of Roscommon by 4–9 to 0–5.

Down were unable to cope with the formidable challenge of Dublin in the All-Ireland junior final at Croke Park. Dublin outplayed their opponents in every sector of the game and their teamwork carved gaps in the Down defence. The Dublin forwards sought the direct route to goal which proved profitable. Down fielded some fine individual players but, as a unit, could not match Dublin and had to concede by 5–0 to 0–3.

Dublin team: Phyllis Breslin, Mary Brennan, Bridget Kennedy (captain), Ursula Flynn, Mary Murphy, Aileen Gleeson, Mary Mernagh, Barbara Redmond, Maura Sutton (2–0), Ann Byrne (1–0), Margaret McMahon (1–0) and Helen Roche (1–0).

Down team: Lil Kane, Stephanie Kelly, Kathleen King, Brigid Morgan (captain), Sheila McCartan, Joan Hamilton, Susan Lively, Margaret Montgomery, Mary McGrath, Marian McGarvey (0–3), Bernie Brown and Cathy O'Hare. Subs used: Marian McGrattan and Rita Neeson.

1975 All-Ireland Minor Championship

The small attendance at Ballinasloe was treated to a first-class display of camogie by Galway and Kilkenny in the semi-final of the All-Ireland Minor Championship. Galway went in front with a well-taken goal after five minutes and were never overtaken. The final score stood at Galway 3–7, Kilkenny 1–1. The second semi-final between Cork and Monaghan at Carrickmacross was a much closer affair than the score suggests. Eleanor Hughes was Monaghan's star performer and she created problems for the visitors. Cork brought on Clare Cronin to put a rein on Eleanor Hughes and released Ann Connolly to the forward line. Both players benefited from the switch

Croagh-Kilfinny – All-Ireland club champions 1975. Back: Margie Neville, Mary T. Hannon, Bernie O'Dea, Margaret Hickey, Eileen O'Keeffe and Margie O'Sullivan. Middle: Ann O'Flynn, Sheila Murphy, Margaret O'Neill, Esther Sheehy and Breda Hannon. Front: Helen Sheehy, Anne Sheehy, Bríd Stokes, Mary Fitzgerald and Helen Mulcair.

and Cork won by 8–1 to 2–2.

A brilliant first half by Cork left Galway reeling in the All-Ireland minor final at Na Piarsaigh Grounds, Cork, on September 14th.

Clare Cronin, who started on this occasion, split the Galway defence with searing solo runs as she helped herself to 2–1 and provided opportunities for her forwards.

Galway upped their game in the second-half but could make little headway against a strong Cork defence. Cork had stars in Clare Cronin, Claire Hackett, Anne Delaney, Marie Coughlan and Janet Davis. Noreen Treacy, Anne Burke, Mary Daly and Olive Coady never stopped trying for Galway who conceded by 6–2 to 0–3.

Cork team: Kathleen Costine, Claire Harris (captain), Betty Joyce, Marie Coughlan, Jane O'Brien, Cathy Landers (0–1), Anne Delaney, Claire Hackett (1–0), Clare Cronin (2–1), Anne Connolly, Eileen Kavanagh (1–0), Margo Sugrue. Sub used: Janet Davis (2–0).

Galway team: Agnes Haverty, Mary Murphy, Maureen Hynes, Noreen Treacy, Carmel Bracken, Olive Coady (0–1), Anne Burke, Angela Broderick (0–1), Una Jordan, Mary Daly (0–1), Mary Kelly and Kathleen Connell. Subs used: Bridie Glynn and Christine Cannon.

Cork Minor team 1975

1975 All-Ireland Club Championship

Eleven wides, five from very scoreable frees, cost Buffers Alley dearly in the semi-final of the All-Ireland Club Championship against Athenry at Monamolin, Co. Wexford. Athenry made better use of the ball and led by four points at the break. Both sides created tremendous excitement in the second-half in their pursuit of advancement, however, a superb Athenry defence held firm to earn their ticket to the final by 0–5 to 0–3.

Croagh-Kilfinny (Limerick) had a close call before their own supporters when, after leading 5–3 to 1–1 at the break in the second semi-final against Newry Shamrocks at Adare, they nearly let it slip. The Down side were a different outfit with the wind behind them. Marian McGarvey aimed several long shots at the posts but they drifted in the wind. Good work by Sheila Turley, Monica McPartland and Marion Finnegan clawed Croagh-Kilfinny's lead back to 5–4 to 4–4.

The first national title ever to come to Limerick was achieved by Croagh-Kilfinny at Kenny Park against Athenry. Amid scenes of wild excitement, Croagh-Kilfinny came from behind in extra-time to snatch the trophy. The miserable conditions were not conducive to good camogie but, nonetheless, there were passages of good play and some fine individual displays. The winners, who had stars in Bríd Stokes, Marion Doyle, Margie Neville, Anne Sheehy and Helen Mulcair, won by a single point, 4–6 to 4–5.

Croagh-Kilfinny team: Helen Sheehy, Margaret Hickey, Margie Neville, Anne O'Flynn, Eileen O'Keeffe, Anne Sheehy, Mary T. Hannon, Helen Mulcair, Mary Fitzgerald, Marion Doyle (1–6), Margie O'Sullivan and Bríd Stokes (captain) (3–0).

Athenry team: Breda Coady, Madeline Coady, Josephine Coen, Ann Duane, Noreen Treacy, Midge Poniard, Sarita Coady, Ann O'Donoghue, Mary Daly, Olive Coady, Bernie Poniard and Teresa Duane.

Croagh-Kilfinny was formed in 1953, but, after a few years the club lapsed before being reformed in 1960. The club has captured 13 Limerick Senior Championship titles. Croagh-Kilfinny opened their own playing pitch on August 26th 2001 and the playing field is dedicated to the memory of Helen Sheehy Fitzgerald whose vision had initiated the development. Club members Eithne Neville, Bríd Stokes and Bernie O'Dea have all served Limerick and Munster in several capacities and were also top-class referees.

Officers and delegates pictured at 1975 Annual Congress at Limerick

1975 Gael-Linn Cup
Many new faces were seen in the inter-provincial series as the selectors chose from junior-graded players. In the semi-final of the Gael-Linn Cup at Gowran, Co. Kilkenny, Munster raced into a five-goal lead against Leinster, and though Leinster hauled back 1–1, they could get no further.

Marion McGarvey, Susan Lively, Anne McCone and Anne McCaffrey did most to secure a 3–1 to 1–5 win for Ulster against Connacht in the second semi-final at Carrickmacross.

Nine Limerick girls lined out in the blue of Munster against Ulster in the final and won comfortably by 5–1 to 2–0. Margie Neville, Susan Burke, Brigid Darcy and Frances Barry-Murphy led the way for Munster and captured the first inter-provincial junior title.

Munster team: (all Limerick except where stated) Helen Butler, Ann Meaney, Margie Neville, Geraldine O'Brien (captain), Mary Walsh (Cork), Dolores O'Brien, Marion Doyle, Susan Burke (Cork), Brigid Darcy, Carrie Clancy, Bríd Stokes and Frances Barry-Murphy (Cork).

Kilkenny breakthrough

Ulster team: Eleanor Hughes (Monaghan), Anne McCone (Armagh), Eileen McAvinney (Monaghan), Patsy Toal (Armagh), Ann McCaffrey (Fermanagh), Susan Lively (Down), Mary Ogle (Tyrone), Margaret Moriarty (Armagh), Breda Sherry (Monaghan), Marian McGarvey (Down), Josephine Hands (Tyrone) and Pauline Vallelly (Armagh).

Frances Barry-Murphy is a sister to dual All-Ireland senior medallist, Jimmy. She married Dinny Allen who would go on to captain Cork to win the All-Ireland senior football title in 1989.

Agnes Purcell Chosen as President

A native of Ballingarry, Co. Limerick, Agnes Purcell was elected President of the Camogie Association in 1976. Agnes filled many senior positions in Leinster Council, All-Ireland Colleges, CCIA and Treasurer of the Association. She was a kind and gentle lady who worked enthusiastically for camogie and supplied camogie copy to the national newspapers for many years.

Congress 1976 set up the National Senior League to provide an opportunity to inter-county sides to prepare for the championship. The Association also decided to introduce metric measurements, however, a motion proposing that umpires should raise a red flag to indicate a 'square ball' failed to obtain the required number of votes.

Hardy Annuals

Congress brings together delegates from all parts of the country. Many make the trip on a regular basis and have a dozen or more congresses behind them. There are those who question, give their opinion and take careful notes. Another group listen but do not break their silence. The clickedy-clack of knitting needles was always a part of congress. Experienced hands at the job could complete the back of the garment at the first session and add the sleeves in the afternoon. If Congress ran to a second day, the finished garment was brought home. However, the modern trend of buying clothes rather than making them has seen the end of the knitters.

The meeting usually coincided with the Grand National and there were always those ready to organise a sweep – but the serious gambling was left to later when the poker schools assembled.

1976 All-Ireland Senior Championship

It was the purpose and sharpness of the Kilkenny attack that marked it apart in the semi-final of the All-Ireland

Down captain Marian McGarvey celebrates her team's 1976 Junior championship victory.

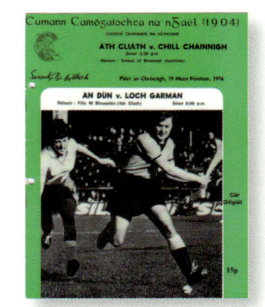

Senior Championship against Cork at Thomastown. Reaching their sixth successive final proved a step too far for Cork who found themselves on the back foot early in the game. Helena O'Neill and Angela Downey were deadly accurate and had opened a six-point gap by half-time. Cork needed goals to survive, but Teresa O'Neill defended her goal brilliantly and Kilkenny won by 1–10 to 2–4.

Dublin were well in command against Galway in the second semi-final at Ballinasloe. The opportunism of Maura Sutton and the goalkeeping of Sheila Murray were key factors in Dublin's 6–1 to 3–2 win.

The two Leinster teams contested the All-Ireland final at Croke Park on September 19th. In the lowest-scoring All-Ireland final, Dublin and Kilkenny competed in a game where defences dominated. The closeness of the score kept the spectators interested, but the game did not reach any great heights. Kilkenny's strength lay in a dominant midfield trio of Helena O'Neill, Peggy Carey and Mary Fennelly. Many of the chances they created were uncharacteristically sent wide by their forwards or brilliantly saved by Dublin goalkeeper, Sheila Murray. It was fitting that the accurate Helena O'Neill should strike the winner to leave the score Kilkenny 0–6 Dublin 1–2 at the final whistle.

Kilkenny team: Teresa O'Neill, Liz Neary, Ann Downey, Bridie Martin, Mary Canavan, Helena O'Neill (0–4), Peggy Carey, Mary Fennelly (captain), Jo Dunne, Carmel Doyle, Angela Downey (0–1) and Ann Carroll (0–1).

Dublin team: Sheila Murray, Rita Whyte, Sheila Wallace (captain), Bernie Conway, Mary Murphy, Anna McManus, Felicity Sutton, Barbara Redmond, Maura Sutton (1–0), Mary Mernagh (0–2), Noreen Fleming and Anna Byrne. Sub used: Ann Lindsey.

1976 All-Ireland Junior Championship

Limerick were thwarted at the penultimate stage for the second year in succession in the All-Ireland Junior Championship at Adare. With Marian McGarvey, Mary McGrath, Joan Hamilton and Susan Lively on their game, Down comfortably advanced by 3–4 to 0–6. While Galway put up a good fight in the second semi-final against Wexford at Monamolin, they found scores at a premium. A resolute Wexford defence emerged as the heroines of the hour and secured a win by 2–4 to 1–1.

The final between Down and Wexford held the interest of spectators from start to finish at Croke Park, with neither side being able to draw clear of the other. Marian McGarvey, at centre-field, was the player of the match and had a hand in all Down's scores. Wexford worked extremely hard to wipe out Down's 2–3 to 1–1 half-time lead. However, taking the game as a whole, Down just about deserved their one-point victory, 3–4 to 3–3.

Down team: Eileen Hamill, Brigid Maginn, Elizabeth Gibson, Joan Hamilton, Stephanie Kelly, Bernie Brown, Marian McGarvey (captain) (1–4), Anne Rooney (1–0), Kathleen Rice (1–0), Susan Lively, Mary McGrath and Lil Kane.

Wexford team: Ann Butler, Mary Boggan (captain), Geraldine Duggan (0–1), Martina Cousins, Deirdre Cousins, Fiona Cousins, Josephine Millar, Teresa Hobbs, Eileen Kehoe (1–2), Monica

Kilkenny breakthrough

O'Leary (2–0), Mary O'Connor and Brigid Higgins. Subs used: Rita Flynn, Josephine Kehoe and Patricia Higgins.

1976 All-Ireland Minor Championship

A last-gasp goal by Margaret Murphy gave Cork a second chance in the semi-final of the All-Ireland Minor Championship against Kilkenny at Thomastown. Cork had come from 2–1 down at half-time to force a late, but well-deserved, equaliser. Cork raised their game for the replay at the Mardyke. Goals from Rose Desmond, Margaret Murphy and Clare Cronin had Cork 3–5 to 0–2 ahead at the break and there was no way back for Kilkenny. Cork ran out easy winners by 4–8 to 1–2.

The advantage of the breeze was significant in the second semi-final between Down and Galway at Leitrim. Galway were in the happy position of having a 3–2 to 0–1 cushion at the turnaround. With the wind at their backs, Down got to work and soon wiped out Galway's advantage and added the winning scores to finish by 4–2 to 3–3.

Cork minors made the long journey to Mayobridge to meet Down in the All-Ireland final on August 29th. The heavens opened in the first-half, making good camogie very difficult. Moving the ball on the heavy pitch provided problems for both sides and, not surprisingly, it was all square 0–3 to 1–0 at the interval. As conditions improved, Cork pressed forward and were rewarded with some good scores. Martha Kearney sent a steady stream of good ball forward which was put to good use by the inside players. Down fought back gamely to the final whistle but they were unable to overtake Cork who won by 4–6 to 2–1.

Cork team: Kathleen Costine (captain), Anne Moore, Anne O'Sullivan, Anne Delaney, Ber McDonnell, Martha Kearney, Catherine McCarthy, Claire Hackett, Clare Cronin (2–2), Ger Murray (0–1), Margaret Murphy and Rose Desmond (2–3).

Down team: Josephine McCrickard, Julia Madden, Margaret McCombe, Noreen O'Prey, Debbie Torney, Bronagh Crilly, Oonagh McKnight, Maureen McCartan, Pauline McAvera, Maura Arterton, Veronica McGreevey (1–1) and Joan Doran (1–0).

1976 All-Ireland Club Championship

Athenry made history before a ball was pucked in the semi-finals of the All-Ireland Club Championship, when the Galway club travelled by air to fulfil the fixture against Creggan (Antrim) – the first camogie team to do so. It was a wise decision as they were able to survive the miserable and trying conditions. Athenry took the initiative in the second-half and built up a creditable score. Noreen Treacy, Anne Duane, Midge Poniard and Mary Daly rarely put a foot astray for the visitors. Creggan's better performers were Mairéad Diamond, Rita McAteer and Josephine Maguire. Athenry proceeded to the final by 7–2 to 3–3.

St Paul's, Kilkenny, qualified for the final by virtue of a seven-point win over Ahane at Castleconnell. A vital goal by Carmel Doyle was the turning point. When Ursula Grace increased St Paul's tally with a well-taken goal, the game was over and St Paul's won by 3–4 to 1–3.

St Paul's were ahead by 2–2 to 1–1 at the interval of the final at Nowlan Park against Athenry. A goal by Angela Downey on the resumption broke the hearts of the Athenry players and St Paul's motored on to win by 6–3 to 1–3.

St Paul's team: Teresa O'Neill, Liz Neary, Ann Downey, Bridie Martin, Mary Kavanagh, Helena O'Neill, Hanora Fogarty, Mary Fennelly (captain), Angela Downey, Carmel Doyle, Ursula Grace and Breda Coonan.

Athenry team: Breda Coady, Noreen Treacy, Gretta O'Brien, Anne Duane, Anne Delaney, Olive Coady, Midge Poniard, Ann O'Donoghue, Marion Freaney, Mary Daly, Anne Morris and Teresa Duane.

1976 Gael-Linn Cup

Munster, the stronger overall team, defeated Connacht by 3–1 to 1–3 at Roscommon, whereas a late rally by Leinster secured a place in the final against Ulster at Mayobridge. Leinster, who were very effective in front of goal, won by 4–5 to 1–3.

Leinster snatched a late winner when a draw seemed to be inevitable in the final against Munster at Adare. Kay Barry got the all-important score two minutes from time. Leinster took the trophy by 2–6 to 2–3.

Leinster team: Ann Butler (Wexford), Terry Lynch (Kildare), Geraldine Duggan (Wexford), Martina Cousins (Wexford), Bernie Whistler (Dublin), Fiona Cousins (Wexford), Mary O'Loughlin (Wicklow), Miriam Miggan (Kildare), Ann O'Neill (Wicklow), Monica O'Leary (Wexford), Kathleen O'Neill (Wicklow) and Kay Barry (Wicklow).

Munster team: Helen Butler (Limerick), Mary Roche (Cork), Betty Joyce (Cork), Geraldine O'Brien (Limerick), Margie Neville (Limerick), Vera Mackey (Limerick), Marion Doyle (Limerick), Bernadette O'Brien (Limerick), Brigid Darcy (Limerick), Carrie Clancy (Limerick), Ger Ring (Cork) and Brid Stokes (Limerick).

Where We're At

With structures in place to cater for second-level and third-level colleges, the next area to require attention was the primary schools. The remit of the new council was to introduce children to camogie at an earlier age. Where the simple skills of the game were taught, an all-round improvement in standards resulted which was of tremendous help when the children moved on to second level. Considered too young for serious competition, the young players participated in small-sided games using a sponge or tennis ball.

With the assistance and co-operation of GAA administrators, the Association conducted a very worthwhile national administration course. It provided a platform for sharing ideas, discussing problems and broadening horizons. Uniformity and clearly defined procedures are essential to the efficient running of an organisation and additional administrators were required to meet the needs of the growing Association, with existing officials benefiting from the exchange of views.

Camogie's Ceol, Caint agus Damhsa (CCD) programme offered an opportunity to members, the young and the not-so-young, to become involved and make their own entertainment while active-

Kilkenny breakthrough

ly supporting the aims and ideals of the Camogie Association in relation to Irish traditions. The competitions were a tremendous success in Ulster where they proved to be an enjoyable source of winter activity for the clubs. The All-Ireland finals produced a high standard and provided good entertainment. The CCD did not meet with universal support, however, and many clubs made no effort to participate.

The addition of an All-Ireland Minor (Under-16) Championship, the election of a National PRO and the setting-up of the Kilmacud Crokes Sevens were steps in the right direction. Following a long drawn-out struggle, the Association succeeded in getting camogie included on the curriculum of the National College of Physical Education in Limerick. Former Limerick player, Eithne Neville, lectured on the subject.

Hot on the heels of Wexford's breakthrough, Kilkenny hit the big-time. Like their hurlers, the Kilkenny girls played a skilful and economic type of game that was attractive to watch. The game's collection of stars expanded quickly, as the black-and-amber-clad players proved themselves, and the names of Angela Downey, Liz Neary, Ann Carroll, Mary Fennelly, Bridie Martin and the O'Neill sisters, Teresa and Helena, were added to the list of stars.

CHASE FOR POSSESSION

Chapter Thirteen

LIMERICK'S DAY IN THE SUN

Castlerea, Co. Roscommon, was the venue for Congress 1977. Delegates were not in the mood for approving motions and only matters of minor significance received the required votes. However, some new ideas received an airing, including: the appointment of a full-time officer, the holding of a Youth Convention, the use of synthetic hurleys and the writing of the Association's history.

The playing strength of the Association had expanded to 29,000, with 26 counties were affiliated (the absentees were Longford, Westmeath, Carlow, Offaly, Sligo and Leitrim, though there were reports of some camogie being played in these counties). The All-Ireland Colleges Council had 130 units under its wing and 14 higher institutes were affiliated to the CCIA, which catered for four competitions.

Progress was being made at primary-school level where counties showed an interest. Sadly, there was apathy towards this level in certain areas.

In her secretary's report, Jo Golden was pleased to relate that a flow of ideas emanated from the new sub-committees to Central Council, with many proposals being approved and awaiting implementation. While noting that the Ceol, Caint agus Damhsa (CCD) provided entertainment of a high standard, she was disappointed to observe that many counties made no effort to participate.

Coaching Manual and Badges

A camogie coaching manual was launched in August 1977. The manual, which was published with the help of the Department of Education, was written by Ann Carroll and Mary Moran, who had been in charge of the National Coaching Course for the previous five years. It was a concise guide for coaches and teachers and the initial print run of 2,000 sold out. At the same function in Croke Park, 30 coaches received their official badges, the first to qualify under the national coaching scheme. The recipients of the Grade C Badges were accommodated at a higher level course at Gormanston College to prepare for a Grade B badge.

Cherished Memories

Former players were asked to recall memories of their playing days. The majority of the answers related to friendship and varied from the cup of tea and the chat after the match, the craic in the bus going to the game, being part of something and not wanting it to end, to the nights preparing for Ceol, Caint agus Damhsa events. Nobody mentioned winning championships and medals.

North American Board

November 1977 saw the formation of the North American Camogie Board in Pittsburgh. The first President of the NACB was Mary O'Dea (Clare), founder of Boston Éire Óg, who served from 1977 to 1981. The remaining officers were: Eileen Minnock (Pittsburgh's Cailini-Cu-Cullainn); Mary O'Leary (Cleveland Emerald's); Mary Boland (Detroit Na Fianna); Patricia Murphy (New York Young Ireland's) and Kathleen McDonagh (New York Young Ireland's).

A championship was organised in 1978 between the following clubs: Tyrone, Cavan and Mayo from Philadelphia; St Bridget's and Erin Rovers from Chicago; Éire Óg, Keltics and Cladagh from Boston; Na Fianna from Detroit; Emerald's from Cleveland; Cailíni-Cu-Cullainn from Pittsburgh and New York Young Ireland's. Éire Óg (Boston) defeated New York Young Ireland's by one point in the first final at Gaelic Park.

Group pictured at the launch of the Camogie Coaching Manual at Croke Park in August, 1977. From Left: Angela Rogers, Mary Moran, Rosina McManus, Lily Spence and Ann Carroll.

National League

Prior to the commencement of the open draw in 1973, counties competed in the provincial championships. As these were organised on a knockout basis, defeat signalled the end of the season, therefore weaker teams had no chance to gain experience and improve through competition. As well as this, selectors were unable to experiment and try new players as every match was a do-or-die affair. Many a player came to the attention of county selectors with a good performance in a club game and this led to an outing with the county side for a championship fixture. Should a player find herself out of her depth and her team lost, the season was over and she had no opportunity to redeem herself.

The National League brought new hope. The matches were more low-key with less pressure on players and they gave teams a chance to prepare for the championship. Monica Butler led Tipperary to success over Wexford, 4–2 to 1–3, to claim the inaugural National League title.

Limerick's Day in the Sun

1977 All-Ireland Senior Championship

By 1977, Kilkenny star, Angela Downey, had stepped up to the status of superstar. She notched 6–3 to defeat Tipperary single-handedly in the opening round of the championship and four goals came from her stick to dispatch Dublin in the All-Ireland semi-final at Russell Park. Dublin tried desperately to win back the initiative, but Kilkenny were playing too well and advanced by 5–3 to 2–4. Wexford earned a place in the final when they overcame Clare by 6–4 to 1–3 in the second semi-final at Monamolin. Clare were rarely in the game and only for the excellent goalkeeping of Maureen Kelly, they would have suffered a heavier defeat.

The sheer brilliance of Angela Downey presented Wexford with insurmountable problems in the All-Ireland final at Croke Park on September 18th. While Angela was the most talented player on the field, Kilkenny were the better all-round team. Teresa O'Neill, Liz Neary, Anne Holden, Ann Downey, Helena O'Neill and Bridie Martin seriously curtailed Wexford's best efforts and, midway through the second-half, the Wexford challenge faded against the unyielding pressure. Goalkeeper Kathleen Tonks and full-back Margaret Leacy saved Wexford from a heavier defeat than 3–4 to 1–3. Maggie Hearne, Breda Murphy and Kit Codd toiled very hard with little reward. The *Irish Independent* 'Sports Personality of the Week' was awarded to Angela Downey.

Teresa O' Neill, Kilkenny, Bernie Murphy, Wexford, Mary Canavan, Kilkenny and Eileen O'Gorman, Wexford during the 1977 All-Ireland

Kilkenny team: Teresa O'Neill, Liz Neary, Anne Holden, Bridie Martin, Mary Canavan, Helena O'Neill (0–1), Ann Downey, Mary Fennelly, Jo Dunne (1–0), Mary Purcell, Angela Downey (captain) (2–3) and Carmel Savage (née Doyle).

Wexford team: Kathleen Tonks, Margaret Leacy (captain), Mairéad Darcy, Bridget Doyle (1–1), Dorothy Walsh, Breda Murphy, Elsie Walsh, Maggie Hearne (0–2), Kit Codd, Bridie Doran, Bernie Murphy and Eileen O'Gorman. Sub used: Annie Kennedy.

1977 All-Ireland Junior Championship

At half-time in the All-Ireland junior semi-final at Adare, Galway led by 1–3 to 0–2 over Limerick and may have harboured thoughts of playing in the final. However, Limerick were a vastly improved side in the second-half. They stormed into the attack and scored 6–4 without reply.

For the second time in weeks, Monaghan lost out on the chance of playing in an All-Ireland final. A better balanced Wexford team soaked up the early pressure and deservedly progressed to the final by 5-4 to 3-0.

Limerick's day in the sun finally came. Led by Carrie Clancy, who had given 21 years of committed service to the county team, Limerick claimed the New Ireland Cup at the expense of Wexford by 2-7 to 3-1. The Shannonsiders stamped their authority on the game from the outset and were 2-3 to 0-0 ahead after 20 minutes, but they were rocked back to reality by two splendid goals from Eileen Kehoe. Following an exchange of points, Eileen Kehoe soloed past Limerick defenders to equalise. The final minutes produced drama and excitement before Marion Doyle sealed the outcome. Geraldine O'Brien was brilliant at centre-back for Limerick. She received most help from Margie Neville, Vera Mackey, Carrie Clancy and Bernie O'Brien. Wexford's big performers, Eileen Kehoe, Carmel Higgins, Ann Butler and Teresa Hobbs were forced to stand and watch the presentation of the cup for the second year running.

Limerick team: Helen Butler, Anne Meaney, Margie Neville, Geraldine O'Brien (0-1), Liz Hayes, Bernie O'Brien, Vera Mackey, Helen Mulcair, Brigid Darcy (1-1), Carrie Clancy (captain) (0-4), Pauline McCarthy (1-0) and Bríd Stokes. Sub used: Marion Doyle (0-1).

Wexford team: Margaret Kelly, Mary Boggan, Geraldine Duggan, Deirdre Cousins, Bridget O'Connor, Fiona Cousins, Martina Cousins, Bernie Doyle, Josephine Kehoe, Teresa Hobbs, Eileen Kehoe (captain) (3-1) and Ann Butler. Subs used: Carmel Higgins and Monica O'Leary.

Limerick's Vera Mackey is a daughter of John 'Tyler' Mackey, a niece of the legendary Mick Mackey and mother of present-day Limerick players, Claire and Niamh Mulcahy. Geraldine and Bernie O'Brien are sisters of Jim O'Brien who had won an All-Ireland senior hurling medal in 1973. Bernie Doyle, one of the Kehoe sisters of Clonleigh, is the mother of Irish soccer international, Kevin Doyle.

1977 All-Ireland Minor Championship

Dublin were fortunate to get the better of Monaghan in the semi-final of the All-Ireland minor championship at Carrickmacross, relying on a last-minute goal from Edel Murphy to secure their advancement to the final by 2-4 to 2-1.

In a low-scoring semi-final at Ballinderreen, Galway's first-half performance placed them on the road to the final. Scores from Madge Hobbins and Mary Kelly went unanswered by Limerick. The home side maintained their superiority in the second-half when Una Jordan, Anne Delaney and Anne Burke controlled the middle of the field to secure victory 1-5 to 1-1.

The All-Ireland minor final between Dublin and Galway was played before the largest crowd to view a camogie match. It was staged as a curtain-raiser to the replay of the All-Ireland football semi-final between Armagh and Roscommon at Croke Park. When Galway turned over with a three-point lead having played into the teeth of a gale, the writing was on the wall for Dublin.

Limerick's Day in the Sun

They added 2–3 without reply to underline their superiority.

Galway had several highly skilled players on view. Bridie Cunniffe at centre-back and the three Presentation, Athenry, girls – Anne Morris, Una Jordan and Anne Burke – impressed. Goalie Cathy Hickey, Imelda Lambert, Nora Maguire and Edel Murphy worked hard for Dublin, but Galway ran out deserving winners by 5–4 to 2–1. Monsignor Tomás Ó Fiach, later Cardinal Ó Fiach, was present as an Armagh supporter and was very taken by the skilful play of the young camogie players and clapped enthusiastically. He came over to the presentation area after the game to congratulate the girls individually.

Galway team: Kathleen Daly, Eileen Howley, Patricia O'Connor, Bridie Cunniffe, Patricia Creaven, Anne Delaney, Anne Burke (1–0), Una Jordan (1–0), Mary Kelly (0–1), Anne Morris (captain) (1–0), Madge Hobbins (1–2) and Mary Rooney (1–1).

Dublin team: Catherine Hickey, Deirdre Hogan, Imelda Lambert, Anne Heavey (1–0), Maria Kerr, Aileen Redmond (0–1), Miriam Crawford, Nora Maguire (captain), Geraldine Hughes, Edel Murphy, Gwen Reddy and Joan Gormley (1–0). Subs used: Geraldine Brady and N. Noone.

1977 club champions Athenry

1977 All-Ireland Club Championship

Athenry squandered many scoreable chances in the semi-final of the All-Ireland Club Championship against Ballyagran at Kenny Park. Their inaccurate shooting was adequately compensated by teamwork and good defensive play. Ballyagran found it very difficult to make progress against a tight-knit and efficient backline.

Five times champions, St Paul's from Kilkenny, were surprisingly eliminated from the club championship by Portglenone at the north Antrim venue. Moving the ball quickly on the ground, Portglenone were more effective. Mairéad McAtamney proved a match-winner with four points and she received great support from her nieces, Jackie and Siobhán. Portglenone advanced by 1–4 to 0–3.

Before their own supporters at Kenny Park, Athenry banished the memories of the two previous finals with a three-star performance against Portglenone in the final. There really was only one team in the contest. Athenry had all the ingredients of a winning outfit and Olive Coady, Midge Poniard and Madge Hobbins pumped balls forward from midfield to give the forwards a host of opportunities. They turned over with a lead of 5–4 to 1–0 and continued to pile on the pressure on Portglenone who were unable to halt the one-way traffic. Teresa Duane and Anne Morris shared eight goals between them for Athenry to finish with a total of 10–5 against 1–1.

Athenry team: Breda Coady, Noreen Treacy, Gret O'Brien, Ann Duane, Anne Delaney, Olive Coady, Midge Poniard, Madge Hobbins, Marion Freaney, Mary Daly, Anne Morris and Teresa Duane.

Portglenone team: Sue Dillon, Ann Kelly, Enda Webb, Jackie McAtamney, Vera McAleese, Mairéad McAtamney, Siobhán McAtamney, Claire McIlvenna, Ann Marie O'Neill, Sheena McAtamney, Briege Kelly and Patricia O'Doherty.

Athenry Club was founded in 1973 by Gilbert McCarthy, a teacher at Presentation, Athenry, Christy Kelly and Anthony Poniard, and enjoyed success from the beginning. The club fed off the very successful Presentation School sides and many of the players who won All-Ireland senior and junior championships in 1974 had been the backbone of the club teams. Considerable time and effort have been invested in underage players leading to 13 Galway senior titles. Over the years, the club has been able to call on dedicated and committed people who work tirelessly to promote the game.

1977 Gael-Linn Cup

Holders Leinster were ousted by a late Connacht goal in the semi-final of the Gael-Linn Cup at Russell Park, Blanchardstown. Connacht shaded the verdict by 2–3 to 1–5. In the other semi-final, Munster were not flattered by a comprehensive 6–4 to 1–3 win over Ulster at Carrickmacross. Relying heavily on the Limerick players who had won the All-Ireland junior championship, Munster were too strong in all departments.

Munster got the upper hand in the second-half of the Gael-Linn final against Connacht at Adare. Playing with the wind advantage, Munster edged ahead and led by five points at half-time. Connacht fought back but were thwarted by a tight-marking Munster defence, and the final score was 3–7 to 3–1 in Munster's favour.

Munster team: (all Limerick except as stated) Helen Butler, Margie Neville, Betty Joyce (Cork), Geraldine O'Brien, Marie Coughlan (Cork), Bernie O'Brien, Marion Doyle, Vera Mackey, Brigid Darcy, Carrie Clancy (captain), Eileen Kavanagh (Cork) and Bríd Stokes.

Connacht team: (all Galway except as stated) Breda Coady, Catherine Gannon (Roscommon), B. Glynn (captain), Bridie Cunniffe, Bernie Barrett, Una Jordan, Anne Burke, Anne Morris, Mary Kelly, Marion Freaney, Madge Hobbins and Bernie Condron (Roscommon).

Full-Time Officer

Following a decision taken at Congress 1977 to examine the possibility of appointing a full-time officer, the Finance Committee was asked to explore ways and means by which this could be made possible. The committee reported that considering the continuing growth of the Association, more progress could be made under direction from a full-time officer.

At this stage, it was envisaged that the full-time post would combine the offices of Ard Runaí, PRO and fixtures secretary and the expenses would be funded from a government grant and increased affiliation fees. A small number of members were hesitant to accept the reality of a full-time official and deemed it preferable to run the organisation with voluntary workers.

Congress 1978 at Kilkenny reviewed the trial period of three years in which the Gael-Linn Cup was contested by junior players. It was considered unfair to deprive senior players of the opportunity to represent their provinces but as the junior counties had gained immensely from their participation in the competition, it was also believed that it would be a backward step to discontinue the junior competition. Congress took the sensible approach and voted to organise both senior and junior competitions.

The original Gael-Linn Cup was awarded to the winners of the senior interprovincial series and a new Gael-Linn Trophy was to be obtained for the junior competition.

Féile Skills

Féile na nGael moved to Kilkenny in 1978 where 24 under-14 teams prepared to welcome their visitors. Camogie had expanded considerably within Féile and Kilkenny brought it to a new level. The organisation was first class and the playing pitches were immaculate. A skills competition was added for the first time where the champions from each participating county completed a number of skill tests to find the overall winner. The first Féile Skills Star was Deirdre O'Shea (Na Piarsaigh, Cork) whose father, Christy O'Shea, had hurled for Cork.

Armagh History

Armagh County Board launched *Armagh Camogie Story*, the first county to compile and publish its history. The book recalled the early days of camogie within the county, the progress of the county team, individual club histories, songs and poems, and had an ample selection of photographs. Armagh blazed a trail in this regard but other counties were very slow to follow their example.

1978 All-Ireland Senior Championship

Cork took a firm grip on the All-Ireland senior semi-final against Clare at Páirc Uí Chaoimh. With an attack that showed remarkable ability and skill, they ran out easy winners by 5–15 to 3–1 over Clare, who had no answer to the power of their opponents.

Dublin's superior ground play proved decisive in their semi-final against Wexford at Russell Park. Once Dublin had wiped out an early Wexford lead, they pushed ahead through a fine opportunist goal by Mary Mernagh. Dublin, who were best served by Sheila Murray, Bernie Conway and Noreen Fleming, fought off a determined rally by Wexford to win by 2–4 to 2–3.

Cork shot out of the traps in the All-Ireland final against Dublin at Croke Park on September 17th and were 3–2 ahead after 20 minutes. Marion McCarthy, who had won four All-Ireland medals

Camogie—All-Ireland finals

Early Cork blitz leaves Dublin with no hope of victory

CORK 6-4   DUBLIN 1-2

THE CELEBRATIONS, which had just begun to wane in Cork after that county's great hurling three-in-a-row, will probably be sparked off again by the return to the Lee of Cork's girls, with the O'Duffy Cup, the all-Ireland senior camogie trophy, their brilliant, if somewhat one-sided, victory over Dublin at Croke Park yesterday. It was a performance of great power and skill and was a fine advertisement for the game of camogie itself.

The Dublin girls were left with a completely hopeless task after only 20 minutes, by which time Cork had scored three goals and two points, without reply. By half-time, Cork had added another goal and two points, while Dublin were still scoreless.

BY **SEAN KILFEATHER**

However, in the second half too, Dublin ran up a plucky fight and we were left wondering why they had been so ineffective earlier. Yet still they could never really dominate the game which, towards the end, Cork put on another spurt to leave, in two more goals and a couple of points, to leave the issue completely beyond doubt.

Had Dublin adopted different tactics from the start, they would scarcely have been outscored to the extent of 17 points. Their tactics were to play the ball on the ground first time and it seems to me that this way, playing into the hands of Cork girls and did not suit the less physical Dublin team either.

Had the Dublin players slowed down the pace of the game by bringing the ball to hand, or by trying to lob it over the Cork defence, things might have been closer, but the Cork backs simply revelled in the girl-to-girl marking and they were adept and nimble in lifting the ball and in driving the Dublin girls back time and again in loose clearances.

In this respect, none was more impressive than Cork's full back, Marie Costine, whose catching and clearing were heartbreaking for Dublin.

DEADLY ACCURACY

As if that were not enough, Cork had their forwards of such deadly accuracy and skill that the Dublin defence was always at full stretch. In that department, Patricia Maloney was the outstanding player on the field and it was her contribution, particularly early in the match, which left Dublin without any hope.

Dublin attack was broken up by a brilliant burst by Cork with the ball travelling from Miss Moloney to Miss Geaney to Miss O'Leary for a goal. A minute later, Miss O'Leary returned the compliment to Pat Miss Geaney in for another goal. Dublin had no answer and, even though two sides were called into action, they could not make any impression.

CORK: M. McCarthy; ... ...

Even more devastating in terms of scores was Mary Geaney, who hit the back of the Dublin net three times, while Mary O'Leary also needed constant watching. Her clean striking of the ball and unselfish contribution to the team effort was a constant worry to the bewildered Dublin defence.

All through, however, Sheila Murray in the Dublin goal remained defiant, even though she had little protection from her defence. Bernie Conway and Barbara Redmond tried valiantly to turn the tide and Evelyn Sweeney and Noreen Fleming did much to save Dublin's pride in the closing stages, but with Cork in such marvellous form there was little anyone could do. Miss Moloney ran through the Dublin defence and Mary Geaney drove the ball into the net where Sheila Murray blocked the first shot. Earlier, Mary O'Leary had whipped over a point after a fine shot from the left and after 15 minutes Nancy O'Driscoll scored another point to give Cork 3-2 to 0-0 lead.

Patricia Moloney was left off at elbow and palmed an easy goal, then added another in the 30th minute and Mary O'Leary delivered a fine pass to Mary Geaney for the fourth goal before half-time.

Dublin showed greater spirit in the second half and nearly scored just after the break when Noreen Fleming tried to clear from a good position. Three minutes later, however, she was in the right place to deflect a free from Marion Conroy to the net. Miss Fleming added a point from a "50" soon after that, but Miss O'Leary pointed a similar free soon after and then a

---

in outfield positions, was switched to goalkeeper and adapted very well to her new role. Marie Costine controlled her square. Pat Moloney, Mary O'Leary, Cathy Landers, Marion Sweeney and Clare Cronin excelled for Cork.

Dublin made a plucky fight back. Sheila Murray was heroic in goal. Marion Conroy, Barbara Redmond and Mary Mernagh did best for Dublin. but Cork came again to win comfortably by 6–4 to 1–2. Nancy O'Driscoll became the first player to captain her county to All-Ireland victory in two different grades. Nancy and Mary Geaney were the first hockey internationals to win All-Ireland senior medals.

Cork team: Marion McCarthy, Marie Costine, Marie Ryan, Cathy Landers, Patricia Riordan, Clare Cronin, Angela Higgins, Nancy O'Driscoll (captain) (0–1), Mary O'Leary (1–3), Marion Sweeney, Pat Moloney (2–0) and Mary Geaney (3–0).

Dublin team: Sheila Murray (captain), Sheila Wallace, Anne Redmond, Bernie Conway, Catherine Docherty, Anna McManus, Marian Conroy, Barbara Redmond, Evelyn Sweeney, Mary Mernagh, Noreen Fleming (1–1) and Anne Byrne. Subs used: Helen Roche (0–1), Felicity Sutton and Mary Murphy.

Cork's Mary O'Leary is a sister of Seánie O'Leary, who won four All-Ireland senior hurling medals, and an aunt to Tomás O'Leary, Ireland's Grand Slam rugby scrum-half.

1978 All-Ireland Junior Championship

Wicklow appeared in an All-Ireland semi-final for the first time when they met Cork in the semi-final of the junior championship at Páirc Uí Chaoimh. Apart from their three interprovincial players – Kay Barry, Mary O'Loughlin and Kathleen O'Neill – Wicklow were completely unknown to the Munster county. But they were soon to find out. Following a sluggish start, Wicklow set about wiping out Cork's 1–6 to 1–1 advantage and dominated the second-half to finish all square.

Wicklow paraded a goat dressed in county colours around the pitch before the replay in Aughrim. Following a tame first-half which ended level, Cork picked up the pace and the greater accuracy their forwards was the deciding factor. They advanced to the final on the score of 3–5 to 2–2.

Galway travelled to meet Derry in the second semi-final with high expectations. Derry produced some excellent passages of play and gradually began to prise open the Galway defence. Lost opportunities proved costly for Galway and they conceded defeat by 5–2 to 1–2.

Cork played second best to a superior Derry team in the All-

Limerick's Day in the Sun

Ireland junior final at Croke Park. Caroline McWilliams, who played one game on Friday and two on Saturday for the Irish hockey under-23 team, was the star performer, with her two goals early in the second-half putting paid to Cork's chances. While Patricia Fitzgibbon, Martha Kearney, Breda Landers and Eileen Kavanagh worked hard for Cork, they had no answer to a fine Derry side. Sarah Ann Quinn gave an exhibition of great defensive play for Derry and she was well supported by Bridget McLoughlin, Margaret Convery and Bríd McWilliams. Derry secured the title on the score of 3-4 to 1-4

Derry team: Patricia McCloskey, Mary Lee, Brigid McLoughlin (captain), Sarah Ann Quinn (0–1), Eileen McQuillan, Margaret Convery, Bríd McWilliams (0–1), Sharon Loftus, Kathleen Marrion (1–0), Caroline McWilliams (2–0), Brigid McCloskey and Bernadette Deighan (0–2). Sub used: Martina O'Kane.

Cork team: Patricia Fitzgibbon, Mary Maher, Eileen Dineen, Betty Joyce, Breda Landers, Liz Lynch, Martha Kearney (0–1),

Cork – 1978 All-Ireland Minor Champions. Back: Ann Marie Landers, Ger O'Donovan, Fidelma O'Connor, Ann Lee, Imelda Cronin, Helen O'Hea. Front: Sandie Fitzgibbon, Ger McCarthy, Martha Kearney (capt), Claire Kelleher, Lilian Zinkant, Anne O'Shea.

Anne Delaney, Sarah Ryan (1–0), Marie Coughlan (captain), Eileen Kavanagh (0–2) and Annette O'Donovan. Subs used: Ger Murray (0–1) and Noelle O'Driscoll.

1978 All-Ireland Minor Championship

There was plenty of action in the semi-final of the All-Ireland minor championship between Dublin and Roscommon at Russell Park. Edel Murphy, Gráinne Burke and Claire Bolger swapped goals with Mairéad Coyle to leave Dublin slightly ahead at half-time. Dublin tightened their defence and added further goals from Edel Murphy and Jo Holden to make it to the final by 5–2 to 2–0.

Despite the inclement weather, Cork and Down produced an absorbing contest in the second semi-final at Na Piarsaigh Grounds, Cork, with the lead changing hands eight times during the game. The decisive score came three minutes from the end when Sandie Fitzgibbon sent a long ball to the net. Imelda Cronin marshalled the Cork defence to withstand late Down pressure and

Cork won by 3–4 to 3–2.

A large crowd sat on the grassy bank at Na Piarsaigh in brilliant sunshine and enjoyed a camogie classic provided by the minors of Dublin and Cork. Martha Kearney, the Cork captain, was a shining light for Cork. She scored three goals and made a huge contribution to general play, while Ger McCarthy, Sandie Fitzgibbon, Lilian Zinkant, Claire Kelleher and Ann Marie Landers provided great assistance. For Dublin, Edel Murphy was the top player. She got great support from Aileen Redmond, Pauline Lynam and Germaine Noonan, but they were unable to prevent Cork from claiming their third title by 5–1 to 3–4.

Cork team: Helen O'Hea, Ann Lee, Fidelma O'Connor, Anne O'Shea, Ger O'Donovan, Ann Marie Landers, Sandie Fitzgibbon, Imelda Cronin, Ger McCarthy (1–0), Lilian Zinkant (1–1), Martha Kearney (captain) (3–0) and Claire Kelleher.

Dublin team: Yvonne Redmond, Orla Nash, Maria Kerr, Pauline Lynam, Catherine O'Hara, Nora Maguire, Edel Murphy (captain) (2–3), Aileen Redmond, Jo Holden, Gráinne Burke, Germaine Noonan (1–1) and Claire Bolger.

Dublin's Aileen Redmond, now Aileen Lawlor, will take over as President of the Camogie Association at Congress 2012.

1978 All-Ireland Club Championship

Athenry's reign as All-Ireland club champions was short-lived as they failed to match the challenge presented by Buffers Alley (Wexford) in the semi-final at Kenny Park. The Alley were a better balanced side and made good use of the chances that came their way. Margaret Leacy and Deirdre Cousins were unbeatable in defence for the winners, while Teresa Hobbs, Bridie Jacob and Maggie Hearne caused all sorts of problems for the home team. All but a point of Athenry's tally came from the stick of Midge Poniard.

Portglenone made the early running against newcomers, Ballyagran (Limerick), in the second semi-final at Randelstown. They built up a comfortable lead of 2–4 to 0–1 by half-time at which point the Ballyagran selectors made a few astute switches, and their side stormed back to catch Portglenone and win by 4–3 to 2–5.

Buffers Alley took the field in the final at Monamolin without the services of the injured Elsie Walsh, but they had six other Wexford senior players on their team and were strong pre-match favourites. However, Ballyagran, who were given little hope of winning, caused a major shock. Geraldine O'Brien was nothing short of awesome at centre-back and, behind her, Clare girl, Ann Fahy, made an enormous contribution and thwarted many dangerous raids. Buffers Alley never settled to play their normal game. They spurned many good scoring chances and were left wondering where it all went wrong at the final whistle. Ballyagran won by 1–3 to 0–1.

Ballyagran team: Helen Butler, Anne Fahy, Breda Murphy, Geraldine O'Brien, Liz Hayes, Bernadette O'Brien, Pauline McCarthy (captain), Vera Mackey, Margaret Mary O'Keeffe, Marita Murphy, Margaret Carroll and Margo O'Connell.

Buffers Alley team: Kathleen Tonks, Margaret Leacy, Geraldine Duggan, Martina Cousins, Deirdre Cousins, Fiona Cousins, Dorothy Walsh, Teresa Hobbs, Caroline O'Leary, Maggie Hearne, Bridie Jacob and Ann Butler.

Ballyagran Camogie Club was founded in 1968 by Fr Ryan, Eileen Noonan and Mary Foley. Situated close to the Cork border near Charleville, Ballyagran chose black and amber as their club colours. The club has captured all Limerick championship titles from under-10 to senior level. Helen Cagney won the National Féile Skills title and the club was successful in the Under-14 Community Games at Mosney. Three Munster club championships and five Limerick senior championship titles have been claimed by Ballyagran.

1978 Gael-Linn Cup

Leinster overcame Munster in the semi-final and Connacht in the final at Na Fianna to win the Gael-Linn Cup for the 13th time. Bridget Doyle in the unusual position of full-forward scored 2–1 and the superior finishing of the Leinster side earned a 4–9 to 2–2 victory.

Leinster team: Sheila Murray (Dublin) (Capt), Margaret Leacy (Wexford), Ann Downey (Kilkenny), Bridie Martin (Kilkenny), Catherine Docherty (Dublin), Anna McManus (Dublin) (0-2), Dorothy Walsh (Wexford), Mary Fennelly (Kilkenny), Mary Purcell (Kilkenny) (2-0), Mary Mernagh (Dublin) (0-1), Angela Downey (Kilkenny) (0-5) and Bridget Doyle (Wexford) (2-1).

Connacht team: (all Galway) Margaret Killeen, Breda Larkin, Noreen Treacy, Ann Duane, Bridie Glynn, Midge Poniard, Bridie Cunniffe, Una Jordan, (1-2), Catherine Ward, Madge Hobbins, Anne Morris (1-0) and Teresa Duane.

1978 Gael-Linn Trophy

Munster dispatched Leinster by 5–1 to 3–2 in the semi-final and defeated Ulster in the final by 3–2 to 2–1 at Mobhi Road. Early goals from Sarah Ann Quinn and Noreen O'Prey indicated an Ulster win, but Munster roused themselves and hit the front with seven minutes to go. A late Munster goal by Annette O'Donovan sealed a 3–2 to 2–1 victory.

Munster team: Patricia Fitzgibbon (Cork), Mary Maher (Cork), Marie Coughlan (Cork) (captain), Betty Joyce (Cork), Helen O'Sullivan (Limerick), Liz Lynch (Cork), Anne O'Sullivan (Limerick), Anne Delaney (Cork), Martha Kearney (Cork), Sarah Ryan (Cork), Eileen Kavanagh (Cork) and Annette O'Donovan (Cork).

Ulster team: Teresa McDonnell (Monaghan), Margaret Moriarty (Armagh), Brigid McLoughlin (Derry), Sarah Ann Quinn (Derry), Eileen McQuillan (Derry), Una Daly (Tyrone), Deirdre Finnegan (Monaghan), Eileen McGeough (Fermanagh), Kathleen Marrion (Derry), Caroline McWilliams (Derry), Noreen O'Prey (Down) and Noleen McMahon (Monaghan).

Mary Moran Elected President

Born in Limerick, Mary was introduced to camogie at St Aloysius School, Cork. She chaired the Cork County Board

Mary Moran.

and Munster Council and coached Cork teams to win All-Ireland titles at senior, junior and minor grades. Mary had a long involvement with colleges' camogie at Munster and All-Ireland levels.

75th Anniversary

A committee, comprising Sheila McAnulty, Jo Golden, Liz Howard and Brídín Uí Mhaolagáin, was set up to plan events to mark the 75th anniversary of the founding of the Camogie Association, with an official crest and flag being designed for the Association. The first event was staged on Sunday, May 6th, when camogie people all over the country took part in the Association's National Walk. It was held to honour and pay tribute to the patriotism, the pioneering spirit, dedication and courage of the founders and to demonstrate the strength of the Association. At the Dublin walk, 93-year-old Seán O'Duffy took the salute on the steps of Coláiste Mhuire, a building, also known as 25 Rutland Square, that has strong historical links with the founding of the Association.

An Inter-Gaeltacht competition was another way that the Association celebrated its 75th anniversary. The competition was held in Connacht as a tribute to the Pádraig Mac Phiarais centenary and was won by Má Cuilinn.

New All-Ireland senior and junior championship medals were struck. A replica of the Association's crest in gold was awarded to the senior winners and in silver for the junior champions. At the All-Ireland function, a pageant scripted by Sheila McAnulty was staged with Patricia Timmins, Nancy Murray, Brídín Uí Mhaolagáin, Mary Nott, Deirdre White, Brenda Morgan and Bláithin Ní Síocháin acting as performers.

Guest of Honour, actress Siobhán McKenna, is welcomed by Agnes Purcell, Seán Ó Síocháin, Lily Spence, Lil Crowley and Nell McCarthy to the Association's Diamond Jubilee Banquet at the Cill Dara Hotel in 1979.

RTÉ made its contribution on the *Talking Sport* and *Trom agus Eadtrom* programmes and special articles appeared in newspapers and magazines highlighting the progress of the Association. Commemorative match programmes were printed for the All-Ireland finals and the Gael-Linn finals were played at Navan, to forge a link with the first competitive camogie match.

The anniversary celebrations came to a close with a seminar and dinner at the Cill Dara Hotel. The seminar, which was chaired by Sheila McAnulty, comprised lectures by well-known speakers. Journalist, Dave Guiney spoke on 'The Changing Face of Sport'. Anna May McHugh, Manager of the National Ploughing Associa-

Limerick's Day in the Sun

tion and a former Leinster camogie player, covered 'From Playing Field to Committee Room'. 'The Role of the Media in a Changing Lifestyle' was embraced by Maeve Piskorski, Head of Education Programmes in RTÉ. Seán Ó Síocháin, Ard Runaí of the GAA, dealt with 'Ár n-oidhreacht – the Common Bond'. Actress Siobhán McKenna was a special guest at the dinner and entertained the assembly with her delivery of extracts from Seán O'Casey.

Points Bar Dropped

The most significant decision taken at the Special Rules Congress in early March 1979 was to delete the contentious rule that called for the top crossbar. Long-time advocates of the second crossbar were sorry to see it go as they considered it to be a distinctive feature of the game, but they were few and far between as the motion to discontinue its use was all but passed unanimously.

Congress 1979, held in Blarney, decided that, for an initial period of five years, each club would pay an annual affiliation fee of £12, of which £8 would go to Central Council to build up a fund to develop of the organisation further. As the National Senior League was considered to be beyond the scope of most counties, a motion to set up the National Junior League won favour.

1979 All-Ireland Senior Championship

The opening championship tie of the 1979 season was billed as the 'clash of champions'. Kilkenny, the 1977 winners, were paired with Cork, the holders of the O'Duffy Cup, at Ballinlough.

However, events during the days leading up to the game had Cork reeling: midfielder Clare Cronin was nursing a serious leg injury and so was unable to take any part; news that Marie Costine was ill added to the problems; and, then, Pat Moloney dropped a bombshell by announcing her retirement from the game. Junior full-back, Mary Maher, and minor centre-back, Martha Kearney, were thrown in at the deep end. Needless to say, the late changes upset Cork's usual rhythm and Kilkenny advanced by 4–5 to 0–10.

Antrim pulled off the surprise of the camogie year with a spirited 5–5 to 4–3 victory over Kilkenny at Randalstown. With their confidence boosted, they faced visitors, Wexford, at the same

Lily Spence (Antrim) receives a gold necklace as a token of appreciation for twenty-two years of dedicated service in the role of Treasurer of the Camogie Association from President, Mary Moran.

venue a few weeks later. A comprehensive 3–5 to 0–1 win by Antrim proved that they were worthy finalists.

The draw was kind to Tipperary who secured a bye in the opening round. Success over Down and Limerick guaranteed the Premier county a place in the final for the first time since 1965. A goal by Mary Griffin approaching the break was the deciding score in a contest that ended Tipperary 1–6 Limerick 0–6.

At the All-Ireland final in Croke Park on September 9th, the Tricolour flew at half-mast over the Cusack Stand as a mark of respect to the late Paddy Purcell and a minute's silence was observed in his honour. Husband of former camogie president, Agnes Purcell, Paddy was a good friend of camogie and wrote many excellent articles on the game.

The chief contributor to Antrim's success in the final was undoubtedly goalkeeper, Carol Blayney. She brought gasps of amazement from the crowd as she made a string of stunning saves from all angles. An early goal by Siobhán McDonnell settled Tipperary, however, although they enjoyed a generous supply of ball, they were unable to add to their tally.

A rejuvenated Antrim team returned to the field and scored a goal by Ann McAllister to take a lead that they never relinquished. Carol Blayney, Ann McAllister, Siobhán McAtamney and Mairéad Magill outshone all others on the park and secured victory for Antrim by 2–3 to 1–3. Mary O'Brien, Monica Butler, Maura Hackett, Rose Ryan and Siobhán McDonnell toiled relentlessly for Tipperary.

Antrim team: Carol Blayney, Mairéad Donnelly, Mary McMullan, Jo McClements, Jackie McAtamney, Siobhán McAtamney, Mairéad Magill (captain), Rita Moran, Philomena Gillespie, Mairéad Quinn (0–1), Ann McAllister (1–2) and Kathleen McCaughey (1–0). Sub used: Maeve O'Hagan.

Tipperary team: Mary O'Brien, Monica Butler, Maura Hackett, Deirdre Lane (0–1), Rosie Ryan, Maureen Maher (captain), Sheila Delaney (0–1), Mary Griffin (0–1), Mona Quigley, Agnes Brophy, Maolmhuire Tynan and Siobhán McDonnell (1–0). Sub used: Ann Ralph.

Rita Moran (née McAteer) is the wife of Mickey Moran, well-known inter-county football coach and Railway Cup medal holder. Deirdre Lane is a sister of Noel Lane who had won an All-Ireland hurling medal with Tipperary in 1971. Tony McAtamney, a brother of Mairéad Magill, won a Railway Cup medal with Ulster.

Antrim captain, Mairéad Magill, receives the O'Duffy Cup from Camogie President, Mary Moran at Croke Park on September 9th, 1979.

Limerick's Day in the Sun

1979 All-Ireland Junior Championship

It was certainly a game of two halves in the All-Ireland junior semi-final between Galway and Dublin at Ballinderreen. Backed by a gale, Galway opened up a sizeable lead in the first-half that Dublin hauled back in the second period and it took a last-minute point by Una Jordan to separate the sides. Dublin lodged an objection to the condition of the pitch but Central Council did not uphold it. Cavan hunted in packs in their All-Ireland junior semi-final against Cork at Crosskeys. Being used to playing one on one, the Cork players took some time to get used to Cavan's style of play. As Cavan tired, Cork came into their own to secure a place in the final.

Cork started in brilliant fashion in the All-Ireland junior final against Galway. With a 3–0 to 0–2 lead after 20 minutes, they seemed to be on the road to victory - but Galway scored a goal to cut the margin by half-time. Taking up where they left off, Galway assumed control and withstood all attempts at a Cork comeback. Una Jordan, Bridie Cunniffe, Mary Kelly and Bernie Larkin were Galway's top players, whereas Betty Joyce, Noelle O'Driscoll, Claire Kelleher and Anne Delaney stood out for Cork. Galway were ahead by 4–3 to 3–2 at the final whistle.

Galway team: Valerie O'Neill, Ann Poniard, Brenda King, Chris Silke, Bríd Holland, Olive Coady, Bridie Cunniffe, Mary Kelly, Una Jordan (1–3), Bernie Linnane, Mary Mullins and Marion Freaney (captain) (3–0).

Cork team: Patricia Fitzgibbon, Christine Pinfield, Ger Murray, Betty Joyce, Eileen Dineen, Anne Delaney, Liz Lynch, Eileen Kavanagh (captain), Claire Kelleher (0–1), Ger Leahy, Noelle O'Driscoll (2–1) and Sarah Ryan (1–0).

Galway players, Chris Silke and Bernie Linnane are sisters of Seán Silke and Sylvie Linnane respectively, who won All-Ireland senior hurling medals in 1980.

1979 All-Ireland Minor Championship

For the first time it was decided to play the All-Ireland minor semi-finals and final over the same weekend with each province hosting the event in turn. The 1979 minor weekend was held in Ballinasloe with the four provincial winners battling it out for the All-Ireland minor title.

In the semi-finals played on the Saturday, Cork, after a slow start, proved vastly superior to a slow moving Wexford side. In the second match, Cavan surprised everyone by defeating a disappointing Galway team, though Galway did get some compensation when they took the Losers' Shield at the expense of Wexford.

Once again, Cork found Cavan's brand of camogie very difficult to play against. Cavan ran after the ball in numbers and surrounded the Cork girl in possession. The Cork girls had not come up against this style of play and were frustrated. Individually, however, the Cork players were more skilful and that told in the end. The final score was Cork 5–3, Cavan 3–0. Ger McCarthy, Patsy Keniry, Claire McCarthy, Joan Hyde and Sandie Fitzgibbon were most effective for Cork. Cavan had outstanding players in Noreen McGovern, Julie Edwards, Eileen Clarke and Patricia McPhillips.

Cork team: Claire McCarthy, Frances Deasy, Patsy Keniry, Joan O'Riordan, Mary Owens, Joan Hyde, Sandie Fitzgibbon, Paula Goggins, Lilian Zinkant (1–2), Anne Currid, Ger McCarthy (captain) (2–1) and Claire Higgins (2–0). Sub used: Ann Marie Landers.

Cavan team: Ann McKiernan, Margaret Hastings, Lorraine O'Neill, Noreen McGovern, Frances Cahill, Kathleen Smith, Bernie O'Callaghan, Patricia McPhillips, Mairéad Denning, Julie Edwards (1–0), Anne O'Sullivan (1–0) and Eileen Clarke (1–0).

1979 All-Ireland Club Champions

Buffers Alley had their revenge for the previous year when they dethroned the champions, Ballyagran, at the semi-final stage. The Alley attacked the holders from the start and goals from Fiona Cousins and Teresa Hobbs gave them a comfortable half-time lead. Ballyagran threw caution to the wind in an effort to get back into contention, but they could not break down a solid Alley defence. Dorothy Walsh and Bridie Doran hit the back of the Ballyagran net to win a place in the final by 4–2 to 0–1 at Monamolin.

Athenry opened with a flourish and pushed into a lead of 3–1 to 0–0 against Portglenone in the second semi-final on their home grounds. By half-time, Athenry had tightened their grip on the game with a further four goals. Portglenone raised their game in the second-half and were rewarded on the scoreboard, but they were unable to match the scoring exploits of Athenry who won by 10–7 to 3–2.

What a pity that the closing stages of the All-Ireland Club Championship were inevitably played in miserable weather and underfoot conditions. Athenry and Buffers Alley ran out on a sodden pitch at Kenny Park as the muffled up supporters shivered on the sidelines. The Alley adapted better to the heavy conditions, but these skilful sides would surely have produced a camogie spectacle if the game had been played on a dry sod.

It proved to be a tough climb with every score hard-earned. Margaret Leacy, who had previously won an All-Ireland club medal with Eoghan Ruadh, Elsie Walsh, Kathleen Tonks, Fiona Cousins and Bridie Doran caught the eye for. Buffers Alley and they won by 2–6 to 1–2. The people of Monamolin and Kilmuckridge accorded their heroines a champions' home-coming as the cavalcade of cars carrying the team and the Bill Carroll Cup arrived in the parish.

Buffers Alley team: Kathleen Tonks (captain), Margaret Leacy, Geraldine Duggan, Deirdre Cousins, Martina Cousins, Fiona Cousins, Maggie Hearne, Elsie Walsh, Caroline O'Leary, Dorothy Walsh, Teresa Hobbs and Bridie Doran.

Athenry team: Breda Coady, Noreen Treacy, Chris Silke, Anne Duane, Anne Delaney, Olive Coady, Madge Hobbins, Anne Poniard, M. Sweeney, Una Jordan, Anne Morris and Teresa Duane.

Buffers Alley is a crossroads between the townlands of Legnalough and Garrydaniel in north Wexford. The camogie club was founded in 1969 by Tom O'Leary, Tom Butler, John Doyle, Syl Murphy, Bertie Cousins and Peter Kavanagh. They won the Wexford Junior Championship in their first year and the senior title in 1971. They dominated the Wexford scene for years, taking 14 county titles in-a-row. Over the years, the Alley claimed five All-Ireland club titles and were specialists at the seven-a-side game.

1979 Gael-Linn Senior Cup

Leinster overcame Ulster 4–6 to 0–1 at Russell Park and Munster 1–5 to 0–4 at Athboy in typical wet and cold Gael-Linn weather. Munster defeated Connacht at the semi-final stage by 4-8 to 0–2.

Leinster team: Teresa O'Neill (Kilkenny), Anne O'Brien (Dublin), Ann Downey (Kilkenny), Bridie Martin (Kilkenny), Deirdre Cousins (Wexford), Anna McManus (Dublin) Margaret Farrell (Kilkenny), Barbara Redmond (Dublin), Orla Ní Síocháin (Dublin), Angela Downey (Kilkenny), Dorothy Walsh (Wexford) and Helena McCormack (née O'Neill) (Kilkenny).

Munster team: Mary O'Brien (Tipperary), Claire Harrington (Clare), Margie Neville (Limerick), Geraldine O'Brien (Limerick), Maura Maher (Tipperary), Helen Mulcair (Limerick), Angela Higgins (Cork), Bernadette O'Brien (Limerick), Nancy O'Driscoll (Cork), Deirdre Lane (Tipperary), Siobhán McDonnell (Tipperary) and Mary Geaney (Cork).

1979 Gael-Linn Junior Trophy

Munster edged Connacht out by a single point in the semi-final at Páirc Uí Chaoimh, while Ulster proved too strong for Leinster at Russell Park by 5–2 to 1–2. In a very low-scoring final, Ulster inched past Munster by 0–4 to 1–0.

Ulster team: Teresa McDonnell (Monaghan), Margaret O'Prey (Down), Margaret Moriarty (Armagh), Bernie O'Callaghan (Cavan), J. O'Loughlin (Tyrone), Ursula Jordan (Tyrone), Noleen Kiernan (Cavan), Bernie Hasson (Antrim), Mary Ogle (Tyrone), Ann Jordan (Tyrone), Noreen O'Prey (Down) and Eileen Clarke (Cavan).

Munster team: Patricia Fitzgibbon (Cork), Eileen Coffey (Clare), Eileen Dineen (Cork), Betty Joyce (Cork), Ann Gallery (Clare), Helen Clifford (Limerick), Clare Jones (Clare), Anne Delaney (Cork), Eileen Kavanagh (Cork), Noelle O'Driscoll (Cork), Ger McCarthy (Cork) and Mary Lynch (Clare).

Where We're At

Another landmark, the 75th anniversary of the founding of the Association, was reached. The previous decade was one of great change with extensions to the organisation's activities at all levels. The introduction and growth of the game at colleges level was reflected in the changes which occurred in counties formerly regarded as being weak. The rise of the game to its present strength in Kilkenny followed a period of dominance by Mercy, Callan and Presentation, Kilkenny whose past-pupils formed the core of the successful St Paul's side and the Kilkenny senior team.

Progress continued to be made under the heading of coaching. The increased awareness of the necessity to teach the basic skills of the game to all players, which the coaching courses fostered, and the greater ability which those who attended have acquired, are reflected in the ever-strengthening position of the game in areas where it was previously very weak. The publication of the coaching manual and the establishment of coaching grades and badges were other steps forward.

The new National League fulfilled its purpose of providing more games. The additional All-Ireland competitions of the previous decade led to a wider distribution of honours, bringing Limerick, Derry, Down, Galway and Clare into the net for the first time.

How much longer could the Association continue with voluntary staff attending to their duties in their spare time and without a home of its own? The idea of a full-time officer operating from a camogie office was the subject of much discussion.

The attendances at the All-Ireland finals fell well short of what they should have been. The finals received more publicity than ever before but still the crowds did not come in the numbers hoped for. In fact, the 1943 final, which was played in wartime when money was scarce and travel difficult, attracted an attendance of over 9,000 a figure well in excess of the gate returns of the seventies. What was most disappointing, and still is, was the lack of support from our own members. Even if half of our membership came, they would go a long way towards making a sizeable crowd. So many players retire, close that chapter of their lives and do not appear in camogie circles again. Countless players are only interested in playing matches and do not bother to support the game in the role of spectators. People who view top-class camogie for the first are agreeably pleased. Calls to stage camogie matches in conjunction with GAA fixtures, to give the average Gaelic games follower some idea of the standard, were not heeded. Preconceived ideas that the game was not up to much prevailed in some minds. However, a full appreciation of the game itself can come only from attendance at matches.

Chapter Fourteen

FIRST FULL-TIME OFFICIAL

The idea of a full-time official had been in the pipeline for a number of years. On August 11th, 1980, the Camogie Association introduced the appointee, Jo Golden, at a press reception in Croke Park. A maths teacher in the all-Irish Scoil Caitríona, Jo was well-known throughout the country as a player and an administrator. In her new role, she combined the position of Ard Runaí, which she had held on a voluntary basis for five years, with the post of development officer.

The GAA generously made office accommodation available to her in Croke Park and, for the first time, the Camogie Association had an official address. The position was created with the aid of a grant from the Department of Education.

Jo brought a wealth of expertise, knowledge and experience to the job. She set herself the task of raising standards, both on and off the field, through initiating and helping to implement a development plan. Jo saw camogie on an upward curve and it was her ambition to keep it rising.

The Camogie Association's first full-time official, Jo Golden (left), is welcomed to Croke Park by Seán Ó Siocháin, G.A.A. and Camogie President, Mary Moran

Counties were asked to make an assessment of the game in their region and to identify the strengths and weaknesses, problem areas and opportunities for growth, and to set targets within a time frame for expansion and development. The amount of finance needed to put the plan in place was to be identified along with an indication of what funds could be raised locally. Central Council was prepared to assist where possible and the National Walk provided £4,000 for the coffers of the Association to help with this. The question of seeking the services of a professional fundraiser was discussed.

A Game of Our Own

Lily Spence Steps Down

Lily Spence decided not to seek re-election to the position of treasurer of the Camogie Association at Congress 1980 at Castlebar. She had carried out the duties of the office since 1959 in a most careful and efficient manner. Lily was presented with a gold necklace as a token of appreciation for her dedication, hard work and concern for the welfare and advancement of the Camogie Association. Former president, Agnes Purcell, was elected to fill the role.

Cork – All-Ireland Senior Champions 1980. Back: Miriam Higgins, Nancy O'Driscoll, Angela Higgins, Patricia Riordan, Pat Moloney and Mary O'Leary. Front: Cathy Landers, Marian McCarthy, Mary Geaney (Capt), Martha Kearney, Marion Sweeney and Clare Cronin.

Throw In

The method of starting a match has varied from time to time. For many years, the two teams of 12 players faced each other in the centre of the field and, while each player gripped her own stick, she also held the bas of her opponent's hurley. The referee walked around the two lines of players, counting the participants and checking the sticks. She then announced "backs back and centres out" and proceeded to throw in the ball between the four opposing forwards. The forwards who won possession had to work the ball forward rather than strike it ahead. A long ball gave away possession to the defence who were already in place.

Referees had their own customs. The majority rolled the ball in along the ground. Turning her back to the players and throwing the ball over her shoulder was the choice of one referee. Another dropped the ball and scurried backwards while the players ran forward to gain possession.

The tradition existed in parts of the country that it was necessary to score if only one team turned up to ensure victory. The referee lined up and counted the team that was present. She proceeded to throw in the ball and all 12 players scampered off in pursuit of the ball to score the winning goal.

1980 All-Ireland Senior Championship

1980 was Cork's year. A Grand Slam of All-Ireland titles – senior, junior and minor – went to Leeside. As if that was not enough, North Presentation won the All-Ireland Colleges Senior Championship, Killeagh claimed the All-Ireland Club Championship, and

First Full-Time Official

Munster senior, junior and colleges teams won interprovincial titles with a liberal sprinkling of Cork players. Sixteen year-old Claire McCarthy carved a special niche for herself in the camogie record books. She won four All-Ireland medals and two interprovincial medals during the season.

Cork had to fight all the way against Dublin in the All-Ireland senior semi-final at Church Road. The game burst into life in the second-half with two goals apiece within two minutes. The killer blow, a shot by Cathy Landers that went all the way to the net through a ruck of players, helped Cork advance by 5-8 to 3-4. Limerick surprised Kilkenny at Ballyagran. A point ahead at half-time, Limerick drove on with Brigid Darcy, Vera Mackey, Ber O'Brien and Bríd Stokes in fine form. It finished Limerick 4-3, Kilkenny 2-6.

President Paddy Hillery honoured camogie by his presence at the All-Ireland finals at Croke Park on September 14th. Limerick, making their first appearance in the senior final, were not overawed by the occasion. They lifted their game and matched Cork score for score. Mary O'Leary was the only Cork forward to function. Some of her colleagues were error prone and failed to find any kind of form. Limerick grew in confidence as the match progressed. Anne O'Sullivan popped up to snatch a late equaliser and it ended Limerick 3-4 Cork 2-7.

The Cork defence was more secure in the replay at Croke Park on September 28th and were sharper and more organised throughout the field. Cork seemed to be heading towards a comfortable victory when they led by 1-6 to 0-2 with 15 minutes remaining. Then Limerick staged another great fight-back. A 40-metre free by Geraldine O'Brien deceived the Cork defence and dipped into the net. Limerick surged once more and were awarded a 25-metre free. Up stepped Helen Mulcair and crashed the ball through a packed Cork goalmouth. Mary O'Leary steadied a shaky Cork with a fine point to leave the final score Cork 1-8, Limerick 2-2.

Cork team: Marion McCarthy, Patricia Riordan, Miriam Higgins, Catherine Landers, Martha Kearney, Clare Cronin,

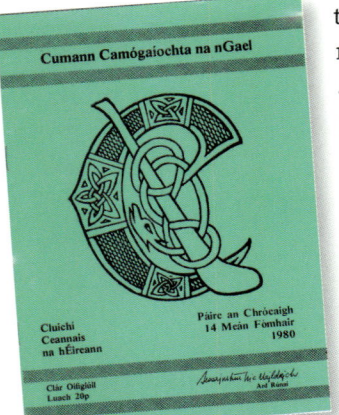

Cork's winning captains 1980. From Left: Betty Joyce (All-Ireland junior), Imelda Cronin (All-Ireland senior colleges), Mary Geaney (All-Ireland senior), Sandie Fitzgibbon (All-Ireland minor) with Camogie President, Mary Moran

Angela Higgins (0–1), Nancy O'Driscoll (0–1), Mary O'Leary (0–3), Marion Sweeney (0–1), Pat Moloney (0–1) and Mary Geaney (captain) (1–1).

Limerick team: Helen Moynihan, Joan O'Shea, Vera Mackey, Geraldine O'Brien (captain) (1–0), Margie Dore (née Neville), Ber O'Brien, Helen Mulcair (1–0), Anne Sheehy, Anne O'Sullivan, Pauline McCarthy (0–2), Betty Conway and Bríd Stokes. Subs used: Bridget O'Brien and Martina O'Donoghue.

Cork – All-Ireland Junior Champions 1980. Back: Noelle O'Driscoll, Christine Pinfield, Helena Fox, Eileen Dineen, Regina O'Brien, Ger O'Donovan and Eileen Barrett. Front: Anne Delaney, Claire McCarthy, Joan O'Sullivan, Betty Joyce, Claire Kelleher, Ger McCarthy, Lilian Zinkant, Ann Currid and Liz Lynch.

1980 All-Ireland Junior Championship

Galway, as winners of the 1979 All-Ireland Junior Championship, had to find a completely new team for the 1980 competition. While the inexperienced newcomers played well in patches, they were unable to cope with a more experienced Cork side at Castlegar and Cork won by 5–8 to 1–2. Tyrone earned a place in the All-Ireland junior final at the expense of Louth at Eglish by 2–7 to 2–1. Ursula Jordan, Bernie Hughes and Sheila Burke picked off scores to leave Tyrone clear-cut winners.

Two great goals in the minutes leading up to half-time and another on the resumption put Cork in an unassailable position against Tyrone in the final at Croke Park. Tyrone rallied but a goal from Lilian Zinkant put paid to their chances. Cork 4–4, Tyrone 1–4 was the final score.

Cork team: Claire McCarthy, Regina O'Brien, Joan O'Sullivan, Eileen Dineen, Liz Lynch, Ger McCarthy (1–0), Betty Joyce (captain), Helena Fox (0–1), Lilian Zinkant (1–0), Anne Delaney (1–0), Claire Kelleher (0–1) and Noelle O'Driscoll (1–2).

Tyrone team: Teresa Kelly, Margaret Haughey, Celia McKay, Pauline Vallelly (captain), Teresa Quinn, Ann Daly, Bernie Hughes (0–3), Anne Jordan, Anna McKenna, Ursula Jordan, Sheila Burke (1–1) and Imelda Fay. Subs used: Kathleen Casey and Celine Gormley.

1980 All-Ireland Minor Championship

Crosskeys, Co. Cavan, was the mecca for camogie followers on August 30th–31st 1980 where the semi-finals and final of the All-Ireland minor championship were played. Cork outclassed Galway

First Full-Time Official

by 2-4 to 0-0 and Cavan got the better of Dublin by 3-1 to 1-3.

Cavan and Cork paraded behind the Tullyvin Accordian Band in front of a large crowd on the final day. The home side started brightly with points from Margaret Carroll and Rosetta Brady. Cork learned from their previous outing against Cavan and played the ball away much faster. Once Cork got into their stride, there was no stopping them. They dominated the game, prevented Cavan from adding to the score and won by 5-5 to 0-2.

Cork forwards, Anne Currid, Claire Higgins, Colette Murphy and Clare Cronin showed delightful touches and picked off some wonderful scores. Margaret Hastings was in tremendous form at full-back for Cavan and got most help from Margaret Carroll and Bernie Callaghan. A special award to the outstanding player of the weekend was donated by Belleek China. Cork forward Anne Currid was a deserving winner. Sandie Fitzgibbon won a third All-Ireland minor medal.

Cork team: Claire McCarthy, Joan O'Riordan, Una O'Connor, Patsy Keniry, Ann Duggan, Finola Broderick, Sandie Fitzgibbon (captain), Joan Hyde (0-1), Anne Currid (1-2), Claire Ronan (1-1), Claire Higgins (2-1) and Colette Murphy (1-0).

Cavan team: Susan Murtagh, Margaret Hastings, Mary McKeon, Mary McMullan, Catherine Nulty, Carol Plunkett, Bernie Callaghan (captain), Frances Cahill, Mary Gillick, Margaret Carroll (0-1), Rosita Brady (0-1) and Anne Sullivan.

1980 All-Ireland Club Championship

Kilkeel, sampling All-Ireland club camogie for the first time, kept in touch with champions, Buffers Alley, in the opening half of the club championship semi-final at Blanchardstown. However, the Alley stepped up the pace and dominated proceedings on the resumption. The experience of Ann Butler, Dorothy Walsh, Teresa Hobbs and Elsie Walsh carried the champions to another final by 2-8 to 0-3. Bonnie McGreevy, Teresa McVeigh, Christine Rooney and Cathy O'Hare did their utmost in the cause of Kilkeel.

A well-prepared Killeagh side outsmarted Oranmore in the second semi-final at Ballyagran. Oranmore were on the defensive from the throw-in and failed to raise a flag in the first-half. Marie Costine and Cathy Landers marshalled the Killeagh defence with Ann-Marie Landers, Betty Joyce, Marion Sweeney and Pat Moloney energising Killeagh. Nono McHugh, Josie Kelly and Mary Keane grafted from start to finish in the interest of Oranmore. Killeagh won by 4-8 to 2-1.

Killeagh brought the Bill Carroll Cup to Cork for the first time when they unseated champions, Buffers Alley, at St John's Park, Kilkenny. Three goals in the opening half, two from Pat Moloney and one from Anne Leahy, paved the way to success for Killeagh. The Alley players tore into their opponents from the restart, but brilliant defensive play from Marie Costine, Cathy Landers, Betty Joyce and Patricia Fitzgibbon curtailed their opportunities. It was a marvellous achievement for Killeagh to win by 4-2 to 1-7. All their players, except Marie Costine, came from the parish of Killeagh.

Killeagh team: Patricia Fitzgibbon, Marie Costine, Mary Spillane, Breda Landers (captain), Cathy Landers, Ann Marie

Landers, Pat Moloney, Barbara Kirby, Betty Joyce, Patsy Keniry, Anne Leahy and Marion Sweeney.

Buffers Alley team: Kathleen Tonks, Ann Butler, Geraldine Duggan, Dorothy Walsh, Deirdre Cousins, Fiona Cousins, Caroline O'Leary, A. Martin, Elsie Walsh, Teresa Hobbs and Mairéad Carty.

Killeagh Camogie Club was formed in 1973 by Tony O'Neill, Sheila Spillane and Eamonn Lenihan. They won Féile na nGael Division 1 in 1977 and have also won five Cork senior and five Munster club championships. All-Ireland referee, Betty Joyce, and Director of Camogie, Mary O'Connor, wore the black and green of Killeagh with distinction.

1980 Gael-Linn Senior Cup

Munster registered a comprehensive 4–8 to 0–2 win over Ulster at Roscrea while Leinster proved too good for Connacht by 6–7 to 1–4 at Castlebar. Munster limited Leinster to a few half-chances in the final at St John's Park. The 2–5 to 2–1 victory wrapped up a fantastic season for Munster.

Munster team: Marion McCarthy (Cork), Claire Harrington (Clare), Vera Mackey (Limerick), Geraldine O'Brien (Limerick), Maura Hackett (Tipperary), Helen Mulcair (Limerick), Cathy Landers (Cork), Martha Kearney (Cork), Mary O'Leary (Cork), Deirdre Lane (Tipperary), Pauline McCarthy (Limerick) and Angela O'Sullivan (Limerick).

Leinster team: Anne Carey (Dublin), Ann Downey (Kilkenny), Anne O'Brien (Dublin), Bridie Martin (Kilkenny), Bernie Conway (Dublin), Margaret Farrell (Kilkenny), Elsie Walsh (Wexford), Barbara Redmond (Dublin), Angela Downey (Kilkenny), Marion Conroy (Dublin), Orla Ní Síocháin (Dublin) and Mary Mernagh (Dublin).

1980 Gael-Linn Junior Trophy

Leinster scored a runaway 10–7 to 0–1 win over Connacht at Castlebar while Munster dispatched Ulster by 7–13 to 1–5 at Roscrea in the semi-finals of the Gael-Linn Trophy. Munster hung on against stiff opposition provided by Leinster in the final at St John's Park and a very close contest ended Munster 1–9, Leinster 3–2.

Munster team: Helen Sheehy (Limerick), Regina O'Brien (Cork), Eileen Dineen (Cork), Joan O'Sullivan (Cork), Carmel Moroney (Clare), Betty Joyce (Cork) (captain), Helena Fox (Cork), Ann-Marie Landers (Cork), Ger McCarthy (Cork), Lilian Zinkant (Cork), Claire Kelleher (Cork) and Noelle O'Driscoll (Cork).

Leinster team: Vivienne Kelly (Louth), Antoinette Merriman (Kildare), Catherine Ledwidge (Dublin), Anna Miggin (Kildare), Joan Naughton (Dublin), Anne Molloy (Offaly), Miriam Malone (Kildare), Mary O'Loughlin (Wicklow), Germaine Noonan (Dublin), Teresa McCann (Dublin), Kay Barry (Wicklow) and Mary Bermingham (Kildare).

Joan Bourke Remembered

Armagh won the inaugural National Junior League by defeating Kildare by 2–5 to 2–3. Members of the Bourke family, Mar-

First Full-Time Official

cus (the GAA historian) and Eileen (winner of five All-Ireland medals), donated a cup for the competition in memory of their sister, Joan. Secretary of Leinster Colleges Council and an Ashbourne medal holder, Joan had gone to her eternal reward.

Jo Golden's Thoughts

Six months into the job of full-time Ard Runaí, Jo Golden penned the following observations as problem areas in the Association: demands on existing administrators out of proportion to the time at their disposal, resulting in the reluctance of many to continue in office and off-putting for potential officers; financial difficulties created by economic recession; poor financial returns from matches and only moderate success with fundraising; apathy of young people towards administration; departure of club players to work in cities; lack of uniformity in interpretation of rules by referees; and a lack of cohesion at all levels in policy making. She posed the question: "Would it be true that our greatest need is enthusiastic, idealistic leadership at every level of the Association?" It would be very difficult to argue with any of the points raised.

Congress 1981 in Newcastle, Co. Down, was a mild affair. The decision to hold the All-Ireland minor championship semi-finals and final over a weekend was reversed and the junior teams of senior counties were allowed to participate in the National Junior League.

Seán Ó'Duffy: quiet, dignified. The tribute by Sheila McAnulty, left, was not read at his graveside in deference to family wishes.

Death of Seán O'Duffy

At the age of 95, Seán O'Duffy fell and broke his hip. Ten days later, October 20th, 1981, he died at Meath Hospital. Mezzo-soprano and All-Ireland medal-holder, Patricia Timmins, sang magnificently at his funeral mass at Mount Argus. For the hundreds of camogie people in the congregation, her rendering of Beethoven's 'Song of Joy', as the coffin was carried from the church, summoned images of Seán marching into Heaven.

The quiet, dignified Mayoman was introduced to camogie through the Crokes Gaelic Club in 1906 and was actively involved in the administration of the Association, its aims, its ideals and its game, for the remainder of his life. He gave unsparingly of his time to the promotion of the game. Dublin benefited most from his labours. Weekend after weekend, Seán spent his time in the Phoenix Park preparing the pitches for Sunday's fixtures and, in his early years, refereeing many of the matches. He was always willing to travel to any corner of Ireland in the hope of forming a new club or aiding one in difficulty. The All-Ireland senior championship cup perpetuates his memory.

Clare Cronin (Cork) solos away from Biddy O'Sullivan (Kilkenny) in the 1981 All-Ireland senior final at Croke Park. Mary O'Leary (Cork) is on left

1981 All-Ireland Senior Championship

Cork qualified for the final of the National Senior League, a title which up to then had eluded them. The Killeagh players did not travel to Dublin with the Cork party on the eve of the final. Instead, they went to Kilkenny and played a friendly match. The Cork selectors were annoyed at their action and dropped Pat Moloney (captain), Cathy Landers and Marion Sweeney from the Cork panel. Nancy O'Driscoll was persuaded to come out of retirement for the semi-final against Galway at St Finbarr's. Cork trailed at the break but a few astute switches brought them into the game and their superior fitness saw them through to the final by 5–10 to 1–7.

Down realised that victory had slipped from their grasp long before the end of the second semi-final against Kilkenny at Nowlan Park. Ahead by 3–4 to 0–2 at the interval, Kilkenny then piled up the scores to win by 4–13 to 1–3.

Controversy raged in Cork. Would the selectors relent and pick the Killeagh girls for the final? There was widespread interest in the impending decision, particularly in Kilkenny. The selectors named the team that defeated Dublin in the semi-final and passed the captaincy to Clare Cronin.

Cork dominated the opening half of the final at Croke Park on September 13th, and were 2–6 to 0–4 ahead at the break. Bridie McGarry was in brilliant form for Kilkenny and prevented a ram-

First Full-Time Official

pant Cork from being further in front. Kilkenny reshaped their team and it worked a treat. Ann Marie Brennan came on as goalkeeper, releasing Teresa O'Neill to take up the full-back duties. Liz Neary moved from full-back to full-forward and planted the ball in the Cork net on her arrival. When a free by Angela Downey was blocked, Liz was on hand to tap the ball into the Cork net for her second goal.

Towards the end of the game, an unwelcome intruder, wearing Kilkenny colours, ran from the Hogan Stand to referee Phyllis Breslin and held up the game for over two minutes while he remonstrated with her. Cork were obviously upset by the disruption. When questioned, Kilkenny denied any knowledge of the man's identity, but it emerged eventually that he was brother of one of the Kilkenny players. Mary Geaney set up Mary O'Leary for what seemed would be the winner, but she drove wide to leave the final score at 3–9 apiece.

Playing in the most appalling weather and underfoot conditions, the replay did not reach the usual heights of Cork v. Kilkenny encounters. Angela Downey was the only forward to rise

Kilkenny – All-Ireland Senior Champions 1981. Back: Margaret Brennan, Geraldine Sutton, Helena O'Neill, Peggy Muldowney, Biddy O'Sullivan, Cathy Dalton, Teresa O'Neill and Ann-Marie Brennan. Front: Anna Whelan, Deirdre Malone, Angela Downey, Bridie McGarry, Liz Neary (Capt), Jo Dunne, Ann Downey, Anne Holden and Margaret Farrell.

above the conditions and was the difference between the sides, though Bridie McGarry's superb positional sense and her ability to catch and clear were also of great benefit to Kilkenny. Mary O'Leary was the lone Cork forward to function. She picked off seven points, mostly from placed balls. Kilkenny regained the O'Duffy Cup by 1–9 to 0–7.

Kilkenny Team: Teresa O'Neill, Liz Neary (captain), Ann Downey, Bridie McGarry, Biddy O'Sullivan, Geraldine Sutton (0–1), Peggy Muldowney, Margaret Farrell (0–1), Helena McCormack (0–1), Angela Downey (1–6), Anna Whelan and Jo Dunne. Sub used: Ann Marie Brennan.

Cork Team: Marion McCarthy, Eileen Dineen, Patricia Riordan, Martha Kearney, Miriam Higgins, Liz Lynch, Nancy O'Driscoll, Angela Higgins, Clare Cronin (captain), Mary O'Leary (0–7), Ger McCarthy and Mary Geaney. Subs used: Joan O'Sullivan, Claire Kelleher and Val Fitzpatrick.

Kilkenny's Geraldine Sutton is a daughter of John Sutton who had won an All-Ireland senior hurling medal in 1957.

A Game of Our Own

1981 All-Ireland Junior Championship

Mary Carey, in the Clare goal, played a major part in her county's win over Kildare in the semi-final of the All-Ireland Junior Championship at Clane. There was little between the sides at any stage and Clare had to withstand a hectic finish before booking a place in the final on the score of 1–5 to 1–4.

The teamwork and accuracy of the Antrim forwards were the deciding factors in the second semi-final against Galway at Tynagh. Elizabeth Traynor put 2–5 on the scoreboard for Antrim and did most to secure a 3–6 to 1–6 win.

Centre-back, Mary Howard, and midfielder, Clare Jones, were most influential in Clare's success over Antrim in the All-Ireland junior final at Croke Park. They blocked the route to goal and kept driving the ball forward to where Lourda Fox, Martina Beegan and Colette Keating added the final touches. Antrim attacked the Clare reargurd for all their worth but danger girl, Elizabeth Traynor, was well marshalled by Carmel Moroney. Bernie Hassan, Joan McAllister, Elizabeth Traynor, Claire McAleese and Maureen McAteer worked tirelessly for Antrim. Clare finished 3–2 to 0–7 in front.

Clare team: Mary Carey, Josie Conlon, Caroline O'Meara, Mary Howard, Carmel Moroney, Veronica Casey, Carmel Wall, Clare Jones (captain), Lourda Fox (2–1), Colette Keating, Martina Beegan (1–0) and Rosemary Fahy (0–1). Sub used: Caroline O'Connell.

Antrim team: Karen Coyles, Anne Kelly, Anne McAtamney, Joan McAllister, Jackie Phillips (captain), Bernie Hasson, Claire McAleese (0–1), Maureen McAteer, Elizabeth Traynor (0–5), Lorraine O'Connor, Doreen Quinn and Margaret McKillop (0–1). Subs used: Brigid McAtamney and Bernadette McAteer.

Catherine O'Loughlin (Clare) shows her skill at a young age as she loses her pursuers

1981 All-Ireland Minor Championship

As it was considered too strenuous for young players to play on two consecutive days, the format for the All-Ireland minor series reverted to the old system of semi-finals and final on separate weekends. Galway fielded a skilful and well-balanced side against Dublin in the semi-final at Tynagh. The home side took control in the first quarter and did not relinquish their grip. Anne Ryan and Margaret Reilly took advantage of a hesitant Dublin defence to slot home goals. Galway advanced by 3–5 to 1–2. A succession of wides together with good goalkeeping by Catherine O'Hara cost Tipperary a place in the final at Randelstown. In the second semi-final, Antrim made better use of their chances to win by 3–4 to 2–5.

Galway and Antrim played at a cracking pace in an entertaining All-Ireland minor final at Tynagh. It was tit-for-tat in a very close first-half with Anne McGarry and Margaret Reilly exchanging goals. A period of Galway dominance put them in a 3–3 to 1–2 lead. Antrim, instead of being down-hearted, came to life with Helen Loughran and Claire Gall shooting a goal apiece. Excitement was high as Galway's Breda Kenny drove several frees wide. She made amends when she popped over the winner to leave the score Galway 3–4, Antrim 3–3.

Galway team: Carmel Briscoe, Lorna Herron, Anne Kennedy, Karen McCormack, Attracta Egan, Anne Briscoe, Breda Kenny (0–4), Maureen Robinson, Martina O'Dowd (1–0), Annette Ryan, Margaret Reilly (2–0) and Anne Ryan.

Antrim team: Catherine O'Hara, Nuala McAtamney, Jean McKinley, Anne McCormack, Siobhán Henry, Margaret Stockman, Eileen Loughman, Anne McGarry (1–2), Geraldine McCann, Brianín Quinn (0–1), Bronagh McIlvenna and Claire Gall (2–0).

1981 All-Ireland Club Championship

Kilkeel lacked a cutting edge in the All-Ireland club semi-final against champions Killeagh at Russell Park. Cathy O'Hare, Teresa Allen, Michelle Morgan and Bonnie McGreevy battled away gamely for Kilkeel but found it nigh impossible to penetrate a splendidly organised defence and Killeagh advanced by 4–6 to 0–3.

Buffers Alley made light work of defeating Oranmore in the second semi-final at Monamolin. Their support play and sharpness in attack had Oranmore on the back foot from the start. The outcome of the game was known long before the finish. The final score was Buffers Alley 6–12, Oranmore 2–4.

The Alley recaptured the All-Ireland club title when they reversed the 1980 result against Killeagh at Gaultier, Co. Waterford. The winners got off to a great start in what was a very competitive game of camogie. Five points in front after ten minutes' play, the Alley benefited hugely from the return of Margaret Leacy who had missed the previous season. Elsie Walsh, Stellah Sinnott, Terri Butler and Kathleen Tonks left an indelible mark on the game. Killeagh's play-maker, Pat Moloney was chased and harried by Stellah Sinnott and was unable to effect her usual influence on the game. The Killeagh defence stood up to the challenge but their attack failed to capitalise on the chances available. The difference between the sides at the finish was 2–6 to 1–4.

Buffers Alley team: Terri Butler, Ann Butler (captain), Geraldine Duggan, Margaret Leacy, Deirdre Cousins, Fiona Cousins, Stellah Sinnott, Elsie Walsh, Gertrude O'Leary, Caroline O'Leary, Dorothy Walsh and Bridie Doran.

Killeagh team: Patricia Fitzgibbon, Marie O'Donovan, Mary Spillane, Cathy Landers, Barbara Kirby, Pat Lenihan, Ann Marie Landers, Fidelma O'Connor, Patsy Keniry, Marion Sweeney and Betty Joyce.

1981 Gael-Linn Senior Cup

Leinster pipped a lethargic Munster side by 3–9 to 2–11 in the semi-final at Russell Park but had plenty to spare over Ulster in the final at the same venue. Capable in defence and always threatening in attack, Leinster finished in front by 3–10 to 2–4.

Leinster team: Kathleen Tonks (Wexford), Anne O'Brien (Dublin), Ann Downey (Kilkenny), Dorothy Walsh (Wexford), Bridie McGarry (Kilkenny), Margaret Farrell (Kilkenny), Elsie Walsh (Wexford), Barbara Redmond (Dublin), Orla Ní Síocháin (Dublin), Angela Downey (Kilkenny), Edel Murphy (Dublin) and Jo Dunne (Kilkenny).

Ulster team: Carol Blaney (Antrim), Stephanie Kelly (Down), Sheila McCartan (Down), Jo McClements (Antrim), Cathy O'Hare (Down), Jackie McAtamney (Antrim), Brigid McLoughlin (Derry), Teresa Allen (Down), Bonnie McGreevy (Down), Phil Gillespie (Antrim), Sarah Ann Quinn (Derry) and Mary McMullan (Antrim).

1981 Gael-Linn Junior Trophy

Connacht scored 5–1 to 3–2 over Ulster at Eglish in the semi-final and shaded the final verdict over Munster by 2–3 to 2–2 at Russell Park.

Connacht team: (all Galway except where stated) Isobel McGee, Breda Kenny, Deirdre Dillon, Ann Gallagher (Capt), Carmel Briscoe, Colette Arnold, Mairéad Coyle (Roscommon), Pauline O'Connor (Roscommon), Jackie Rodgers (Roscommon), Mary Ryan, Angela Manning and Margaret O'Reilly.

Munster team: Mary Carey (Clare), Mary Maher (Cork), Martina O'Donoghue (Limerick), Mary O'Donovan (Cork), Carmel Moroney (Clare), Veronica Casey (Clare), Margo Twomey (Cork), Clare Jones (Clare), Lourda Fox (Clare), Ann Marie Landers (Cork), Stephanie Curtin (Cork) and Colette Keating (Clare).

Mary Fennelly Elected President

From a strong Gaelic games background, Mary Fennelly (Kilkenny) was elected president at Congress 1982 in Wexford. Mary had enjoyed an impressive playing career of which captaining Kilkenny in the 1976 All-Ireland senior championship was the pinnacle. Employed by Callan Wood Limited, Mary served as Secretary of the Kilkenny County Board and Secretary of the Leinster Council.

Liz Howard stepped down from the position of National PRO at the resumed congress in June and was replaced by Mary Moran (Cork). Mary Lynch (Monaghan) was elected to fill the vacant role of director of organisation.

Jo Golden, who availed of a two-year leave of absence from Scoil Caitríona, returned to her teaching post at the start of the school year. Séamus McAleenan, from Leitrim, Co. Down, was appointed Ard Runaí and development officer to succeed her. A graduate of NUU (Coleraine), he came to the Camogie Association from Ogras where he had worked as an organiser. Séamus captained the Fitzgibbon Cup team in college and played hurling and football with Leitrim Fontenoys. Maureen McAleenan, the well-known Down and Ulster player, is a sister of Séamus.

Gradam Tailte

Gradam Tailte, a day of sporting competition involving the top

First Full-Time Official

player from each of the 32 counties, was staged for the first time on May 29th, 1982, at St Patrick's, Drumcondra. The Superstars Competition, devised by Jo Golden, attracted the top names in the game. Liz Neary (Kilkenny), Elsie Walsh (Wexford), Mary O'Leary (Cork), Marion Conroy (Dublin), Nono McHugh (Galway), Jo McClements (Antrim), Ursula McGivern (Armagh), Miriam Malone (Kildare) and Sarah Ann Quinn (Derry) were among the household names that challenged for the prestigious Queen Tailte Trophy.

The competition featured seven events, of which three were compulsory: camogie skills, indoor obstacle race and 100-metre race. Each competitor could choose two further events from 800 metres, basketball, gym tests and an outdoor obstacle course. Run off in glorious sunny conditions, the day's keenly contested competition resulted in Jo McClements (Antrim) being named as winner. She was presented with the impressive Queen Tailte Trophy at a reception in the Gresham Hotel.

The Gradam Tailte competition was staged from 1982 to 1988. The most exciting contest was decided between two highly skilful and supremely fit athletes, Angela Downey (Kilkenny) and Clare Cronin (Cork), in 1983. They pulled away from the field early in the competition and the remaining entrants stood around to watch the top two battle it out. With the camogie skills remaining to be decided, Angela was favourite to lift the trophy. Competition was razor keen and rivalry intense. It came down to penalty-taking, with Marion McCarthy bravely standing in goal. When the dust had settled, Clare was two points in front. Angela more than made up for that slip by taking the next three titles on the trot. Bernie Farrelly (Kildare) won the last two titles. Sadly, interest in the competition waned and it was discontinued.

Cospóir Camogie Day

Tras Honan, Cathaoirleach an tSeanad, and Olympic gold medallist, Ronnie Delany, launched Cospóir Camogie Day, with the day itself taking place on October 10th, 1982 at numerous venues throughout the country. The motto allocated to the day was 'Sport for All – Fun for All'. From dawn to dark, the playing fields were a hive of activity with young and old getting in on the action. Former players returned to try their hands once again.

The day's programme varied from fast-action activities for the fit, young things to more sedate amusement for the 'golden oldies'. Tea and cakes were in plentiful supply and much chat and banter to go with them.

Catherine Ledwidge (Dublin) and Claire Kelleher (Cork) tussle for the ball in the 1982 All-Ireland senior final while Mary Geaney awaits developments at Croke Park.

1982 All-Ireland Senior Championship

Dublin played tidy and composed camogie in the All-Ireland semi-final against Limerick at Na Fianna Grounds. They worked themselves into a good position and seemed to be in no danger. A spirited Limerick rally cut the margin between the sides but Dublin re-established themselves to win by 2-9 to 2-6.

Cork were comfortably positioned 3-5 to 0-6 at the break against Kilkenny in the second semi-final at Nowlan Park. However, with the aid of a strong breeze, Kilkenny ate into Cork's lead with a series of points, many from placed balls. Kilkenny drew level with an exquisite sideline cut by Bridie McGarry from over 30 metres out. Both teams went all out for the winner but were beaten by the referee's whistle. A large crowd lined the bank at Ballinlough for the eagerly awaited replay and they were not disappointed. Ten goals and 21 points, many of them of the highest order, were scored to the delight of the fans. The match went to extra-time. A marvellous goal from Pat Lenihan was met by a thunderous roar. Cork responded to the encouragement and lifted their game even further to take the spoils. Pat Lenihan, Eileen Dineen, Miriam Higgins, Mary O'Leary, Martha Kearney and Ger McCarthy were heroines of an epic match. Angela Downey and Bridie McGarry were in brilliant form for Kilkenny.

Cork full-forward, Mary Geaney, was also captain of the Irish ladies hockey team and a world cup qualifying match clashed with the All-Ireland final. Mary opted for the hockey game. Installed as firm favourites following the Kilkenny games, Cork struggled to survive against a Dublin side that turned up to win at Croke Park on September, 26th. Dublin scored a goal within 20 seconds of the throw-in when Marion Conroy finished off a great pass from Una Crowley. Pat Lenihan raced in to capitalise on the indecision in the Dublin goal and pushed the ball home. Pat was forced to retire with a leg injury and her withdrawal unsettled Cork. Dublin pressurised Cork into errors and worked some good scores to lead by 2-5 to 1-3 at the change-over.

Mary O'Leary led the Cork revival and sent a stinging shot that Dublin goalie, Yvonne Redmond, found too hot to handle. Dublin upped the intensity of their game and had the Cork rearguard under siege. Despite carrying a leg, Pat Lenihan returned to the fray and her reappearance lifted Cork, but the title of match winner was rightly claimed by Mary O'Leary, who calmly stood up to a 45 metre free and struck it sweetly between the posts to

Cork players, Martha Kearney, Marion Sweeney, Mary O'Leary, Pat Lenihan (Capt), Clare Cronin and Miriam Higgins celebrate their All-Ireland win at St. Finbarr's Club in 1982.

First Full-Time Official

Clare Jones (Clare) accepts the All-Ireland Junior Cup from President, Mary Moran

leave the final score Cork 2–7, Dublin 2–6.

Cork team: Marion McCarthy, Eileen Dineen, Miriam Higgins, Cathy Landers, Martha Kearney, Clare Cronin, Val Fitzpatrick, Ger McCarthy, Mary O'Leary (1–6), Pat Lenihan (captain) (1–1), Marion Sweeney and Noelle O'Driscoll. Subs used: Sandie Fitzgibbon and Angela Higgins.

Dublin team: Yvonne Redmond, Anne O'Brien, Frances Murphy, Bernie Toner, Catherine Docherty, Una Crowley (1–1), Mary Mernagh, Edel Murphy (0–2), Anna Condon (0–1), Marion Conroy (1–0), Barbara Redmond and Orla Ryan (0–2). Sub used: Joan Gormley.

1982 All-Ireland Junior Championship

Cork registered a convincing win over a lack-lustre Antrim side in the semi-final of the All-Ireland Junior Championship at St Finbarr's. Sandie Fitzgibbon and Liz Dunphy took a firm grip in midfield and put the Antrim defence under constant pressure. The Cork forwards had the beating of their opponents and reflected their superiority on the scoreboard. Cork won by 6–7 to 0–3.

Vivienne Kelly had a dream game in the Louth goal against Galway in the second semi-final at Dromiskin. She saved shots from all angles as Galway dominated the game. Had they taken points instead of continuously seeking goals, the result would have been different.

Louth survived an appeal by Galway who maintained that the goalposts used were not of regulation size. However, Galway failed to measure the posts in question and were unable to prove their allegation.

Louth won their first All-Ireland camogie title at Croke Park by 1–7 to 1–6 when they edged Cork out in a closely contested game. The result was in doubt up to the final whistle and both sides matched score for score. Noreen Maguire, Eileen Crehan, Kitty Sharkey and Teresa Bates performed well for Louth. Four Crehan sisters – Geraldine, Mary (Connor), Connie and Eileen – stepped up to receive All-Ireland medals.

Louth team: Vivienne Kelly (captain), Anne Harrington, Marion McCabe, Geraldine Crehan, Mary Connor, Colette Tumulty, Anne Currid (0–1), Eileen Crehan, Irene McNamee, Teresa Bates, Kitty Sharkey (0–1), Noreen Maguire (0–5). Sub used: Annette King (1–0).

Cork team: Eileen Barrett, Mary Maher, Joan Shannon, Liz Dunphy, Margo Twomey, Ann Marie Landers (0–1), Patsy Keniry, Mary O'Donovan, Stephanie Curtin (captain) (1–0), Anne Leahy (0–1), Claire Higgins (0–2) and Lilian Zinkant (0–2).

1982 All-Ireland Minor Championship

A scintillating first-half performance was the basis of Dublin's success over Cork in the semi-final of the All-Ireland Minor Championship at Mobhi Road. Cork tried to come to grips with the game in the second-half but the damage had already been done. Carmel O'Byrne, Patsy Murphy and Michelle Sleator heaped misery on Cork and engineered by 6–4 to 1–7 victory. In the second semi-final, title-holders Galway proved too good for Cavan at Drumgoon and won comprehensively by 2–11 to 0–0.

A fast-moving Dublin side, whose direct methods paid dividends, claimed their first All-Ireland minor title at the expense of Galway at rain-soaked Ballinasloe on August 15th. Dublin's ability to do the simple things well made them worthy champions. Galway were in contention for three-quarters of the game, but, in the space of three minutes, three goals were whipped in past an over-worked Galway defence. Galway tried desperately to get back into contention but by then Dublin had secured the outcome by 5–2 to 2–3.

Dublin team: Michelle Sleator, Monica Waters, Lorraine Ormond, Patricia Murphy, Caroline Doyle, Patricia Clinton, Anne Archibold, Suzanne Doyle, Carmel O'Byrne (1–1), Anne Cooper (captain) (1-0), Liz Delaney (3–0) and Adele Campbell (0–1).

Galway team: Angela Laheen, Dolores Hobbins, Anne Kennedy, Attracta Egan, Anne Burke, Martina O'Dowd, Ann Briscoe (captain), Sheila Coen, Claire Harte, Julie Glynn, Deirdre Lawless (2–1) and Anne Ryan (0–2). Subs used: Pauline Madden and Stephanie Coen.

1982 All-Ireland Club Championship

Athenry qualified for the All-Ireland club final at the expense of Portglenone at wind-swept Carrickmacross. Portglenone enjoyed most of the play in the opening half and led by 1–4 to 1–1 at the changeover. Madge Hobbins and Una Jordan took control of midfield on the resumption of play. Teresa Dwane scored two fine goals to erase the deficit and put Athenry ahead and further goals from Anne Morris, Madge Hobbins and Marion Freaney secured victory for the Galway club by 5–3 to 2–7. Bronagh McIlvenna was the top scorer for Portglenone with 2–3 while goalkeeper, Sue Dillon, prevented the margin from being much wider.

The third meeting of Buffers Alley and Killeagh in as many years produced another exhibition of brilliant camogie in the second semi-final at Piltown. Pat Lenihan, Killeagh's star player, was unable to start due to injury. Both goals came under siege as play swung from end to end. The Alley were hanging on precariously to the narrowest of leads as time ticked away. Dorothy Walsh doubled on a high ball from her sister, Elsie, and directed it past Kathleen Costine in the Killeagh goal to give the Wexford club a 2–6 to 1–5 victory.

Torrential rain and a very heavy pitch prevented the final from reaching the standard of the great finals, but there was no question as to which was the better side when Buffers Alley and Athenry met in the final at Birr. Athenry did their scoring in the first six minutes and had to play second best for the remainder of the tie. Goals from Dorothy Walsh and Kathleen Tonks ensured that the Alley brought the cup home again. The final score was

Buffers Alley 3–2, Athenry 0–2.

Buffers Alley team: Terri Butler, Ann Butler, Geraldine Duggan, Margaret Leacy, Stellah Sinnott, Fiona Cousins, Caroline O'Leary, Elsie Walsh (captain), Kathleen Tonks, Gertrude O'Leary, Dorothy Walsh and Bridie Doran.

Athenry team: Breda Coady, Noreen Treacy, Chris Silke, Mary Higgins, Ann Connolly, Sadie Higgins, Olive Molloy, Una Jordan, Teresa Duane, Madge Hobbins, Anne Morris (captain) and Marion Freaney.

1982 Gael-Linn Senior Cup

Leinster met with very little opposition from Ulster in the Gael-Linn semi-final at Eglish and won much as they pleased by 10–17 to 2–4. Munster travelled to Tynagh with high expectations of defeating Connacht and were not disappointed, advancing 2–3 to 0–2. A point in the last minute of normal time by Mary O'Leary secured the Gael-Linn Cup for Munster at Na Fianna Grounds. Mary picked off 2–8 to be the main contributor to Munster's 3–10 to 2–12 victory.

Munster team: Marion McCarthy (Cork), Eileen Dineen (Cork), Miriam Higgins (Cork), Cathy Landers (Cork), Martha Kearney (Cork), Vera Mackey (Limerick) Marion Sweeney (Cork), Ber O'Brien (Limerick), Mary O'Leary (Cork), Deirdre Lane (Tipperary) Ger McCarthy (Cork) and Bríd Stokes (Limerick).

Leinster team: Kathleen Tonks (Wexford), Anne O'Brien (Dublin), Ann Downey (Kilkenny), Bridie McGarry (Kilkenny), Bernie Toner (Dublin), Elsie Walsh (Wexford), Barbara Redmond (Dublin), Edel Murphy (Dublin), Anna McManus (Dublin), Marion Conroy (Dublin), Angela Downey (Kilkenny) and Jo Dunne (Kilkenny).

1982 Gael-Linn Junior Trophy

Ulster struggled to cope with the fitness and teamwork of their Leinster rivals in the semi-final at Eglish and late scores by Leinster added up to a decisive win by 3–11 to 1–4. The Connacht v. Munster semi-final at Na Fianna was won and lost by the respective forward lines. Connacht's attack made their chances count to win by 3–3 to 0–5.

In the final, Leinster signalled their intent from the start and raced into a sizeable lead. They continued to impress with their scoring ability and finished 3–16 to 2–8 in front.

Leinster team: Toni O'Byrne (Dublin), Claire Rainey (Dublin), Antoinette Merriman (Kildare), Mary Duane (Dublin), Anna Miggan (Kildare), Miriam Malone (Kildare), Anne Thorpe (Dublin), Catherine Ledwidge (Dublin), Eithne O'Hehir (Dublin), Anne Colgan (Dublin), Noleen Maguire (Louth) and Noreen Fleming (Dublin).

Connacht team: Carmel Briscoe (Galway), Ann Gallagher (Galway), Deirdre Dillon (Galway), Claire Geraghty (Galway), Kitty Hoey (Galway), Mairéad Coyle (Roscommon), Breda Kenny (Galway), Pauline O'Connor (Roscommon), Jackie Rodgers (Roscommon), Angela Manning (Galway), Deirdre Lawless (Galway) and Margaret O'Reilly (Galway).

A Game of Our Own

Where We're At

The creation of the position of full-time development officer was a momentous decision by the Camogie Association. It was a long-term aim to have a professional organiser who would manage the needs of the Association on a day-to-day basis from a recognised headquarters. With the help of funds from the Department of Education, it became a reality. The GAA generously provided office accommodation and, for the first time, the Camogie Association had a home where members and the general public could make contact.

Voluntary work had been, and continued to be, the mainstay of the Association. Through the efforts of dedicated, unselfish and far-seeing people, camogie had grown from small beginnings to being an organisation catering for 60,000 members. As the expanded, more officials and administrators were required, but there were never enough and the need for a full-time official, to handle the increased workload, became obvious. Jo Golden, who had already proved herself, was an excellent choice. Camogie was on an upward curve and it was Jo's ambition to keep it rising.

An off-shoot of the increased number of competitions, particularly the All-Ireland minor and colleges' championships, was an upward curve in the standard of skill. Brilliant individuals always existed and adorned the game, but with the emphasis on coaching and the introduction of children at a younger age to the game, the overall standard was raised.

A full programme of events was planned to celebrate National Camogie Day. As usual the highlight of the occasion was a 'Golden Oldies' match. Former players were rounded up and turned out in force with the odd grey hair showing. All recognised one and other instantly under their maiden names but were slow to recall the married names of those whom they had not seen for some time. Babies and handbags were placed in the care of others, high-heels discarded and sleeves rolled up.

There was strong competition for goal and full-back positions, but no offers for midfield. Their timing of the ball improved as the game wore on but the poor quality of the modern stick was blamed for short pucks. Anticipation made up for lack of sprinting power. Signs of combination between old team-mates started to appear as players settled into the well-known routine of former days. Husbands, slightly embarrassed at first, vocally supported their wives. Children shouted, 'Come on, Mum', and their mothers responded splendidly. Who won? They were all winners.

Chapter Fifteen

DUBLIN'S RETURN

Delegates clamoured for the implementation of an insurance scheme for players at Congress 1980 and at subsequent meetings. Much time and effort was invested in devising an acceptable scheme. In the first year, the take up of the insurance was a mere one in ten of members. The number dropped from 6,000 to 4,000 in the second year. Efforts to make participation in the scheme compulsory met with opposition, for example, Ulster felt that their members had sufficient cover in alternative schemes and were not prepared to make the Association's scheme mandatory.

The subject of insurance remained a hot potato until 1987 when a motion to make participation compulsory was passed.

Anne Sheehy as Ard Rúnaí

Séamus McAleenan resigned from the position of Ard Runaí to take up a teaching post at St Patrick's, Maghera, and Anne Sheehy, a native of Dublin, was appointed to replace him in November 1983. As a player, she lined out with Holy Faith, Clontarf, Austin Stacks, Dublin and Leinster and had worked for some years in Croke Park as personal assistant to Seán Ó Síocháin. Anne was a member of the small group of enterprising young people who pioneered the Camogie magazine. She brought a depth of knowledge about sport, particularly Gaelic games, with her to the job. Later, Anne married Kerry footballer, Seán Kennedy.

Agnes Purcell

Death of Agnes Purcell

The camogie world was shocked and saddened to learn of the sudden death of Agnes Purcell on November, 25th, 1983. A kind and gracious lady, Agnes had had a great interest in young people and concern for their welfare. Motivated by her love of the game, she had directed her energy to the administration of the Association at various levels. Camogie members grieved at the passing of a warm-hearted friend and colleague.

1983 All-Ireland Senior Championship

Eleven counties entered for the 1983 All-Ireland Senior Championship, the highest number since the separation of senior and junior championships in 1968. Leinster had four counties – Dublin, Kilkenny, Wexford and Louth – and Munster had a similar number – Tipperary, Cork, Limerick and Clare. Antrim, Down and Galway made up the remainder.

Cork's 1982 All-Ireland captain, Pat Lenihan, was working in Bangladesh by the time the championship came around, but Cork had unearthed a new star, teenager Sandie Fitzgibbon, who slotted into midfield. Sharp-shooter Mary O'Leary picked off 1–8 while the Cork defence kept the Wexford attack at bay in the semi-final at Rathnure. Cork had a comfortable win by 1–14 to 0–4.

The Dublin v. Tipperary semi-final opened at a lively pace at Cappawhite. Marion Conroy and Edel Murphy provided the inspiration for their Dublin colleagues while Tipperary faded. Dublin were full value for their 5–9 to 0–9 victory.

With the O'Duffy Cup absent from the sideboard for 17 years, Dublin craved success. The Blues raced into a three-point lead before losing midfielder, Una Crowley, in a freak accident: her dangling earring caught in the collar of her shirt as she fell and tore the lobe of her ear. The two goalkeepers, Yvonne Redmond and Marion McCarthy, were in tremendous form as play swayed from one goalmouth to the other. Dublin had some of the better

Mary O'Leary (Cork) gets ahead of Catherine Ledwidge (Dublin) in the race for the ball at the 1983 All-Ireland senior final at Croke Park.

individuals on view but Cork's teamwork and determination kept them in the hunt. With minutes remaining on the clock, Claire Kelleher secured the decisive score and Cork shaded the verdict by 2–5 to 1–6 at Croke Park on September 25th.

Cork's Marion McCarthy won her eighth All-Ireland senior medal. Her brother, Denis, won an All-Ireland senior hurling medal in 1986. Three Redmond sisters – Yvonne, Anne (O'Brien) and Barbara – played on the Dublin team.

Cork team: Marion McCarthy, Eileen Dineen, Miriam Higgins, Cathy Landers (captain), Martha Kearney, Clare Cronin, Marion Sweeney, Sandie Fitzgibbon, Mary O'Leary (0–4), Val Fitzpatrick (1–0), Claire Kelleher (1–0) and Mary Geaney (0–1). Sub used: Ger McCarthy.

Dublin team: Yvonne Redmond, Anne O'Brien, Catherine Ledwidge, Bernie Toner, Germaine Noonan, Una Crowley (captain,), Edel Murphy (0–4), Barbara Redmond, Anna Condon, Mary Mernagh (1–0), Marion Conroy (captain) (0–2) and Joan Gormley. Subs used: Anne Thorpe and Ann Colgan.

1983 All-Ireland Junior Championship

Dublin dominated the All-Ireland junior semi-final against Down at Russell Park, and had their forwards converted the bulk of the possession provided by midfielders, Eithne O'Hehir and Deirdre Byrne, the winning margin would have been much wider. Down were on the back foot for much of the game and conceded by 3–7 to 1–2.

Cork opened brightly against Galway in the second semi-final at Na Piarsaigh. Goals from Liz Dunphy and Stephanie Curtin and points from the accurate Lilian Zinkant opened a gap on the scoreboard early in the game. Galway came more into the game in the second-half and were close to catching the home side. Cork advanced by 2–9 to 2–7.

Excitement was high as play ebbed and flowed from end to end in the All-Ireland junior final between Dublin and Cork at Croke Park. Cork made the better start but were hauled back before the break. The pattern of play was repeated in the second-half but the Cork defence, superbly marshalled by captain Mary Ring, prevented Dublin from catching up. Ann Marie Landers, Anne Leahy, Lilian Zinkant and Margo Twomey shone for Cork. Dublin's top performers were Geraldine Sutton, Helena Broderick, Carmel O'Byrne, Marie Connell and Noreen Fleming. Cork had two points to spare at the final whistle, 2–5 to 2–3.

Dublin legend, Kathleen Mills, and Dublin coach, Nell McCarthy, inspect the modern sliothar

Cork team: Marie O'Sullivan, Mary Maher, Mary Ring, Liz Dunphy, Margo Twomey (0–1), Mary O'Donovan, Shelley Spillane, Ann Marie Landers, Joan Shannon (1–0), Anne Leahy, Bernie Murphy (captain) and Lilian Zinkant (1–4). Sub used: Patsy Keniry.

Dublin team: Geraldine Sutton, Mairéad Cronin, Anne Tallon, Mary Duane, Helena Broderick, Jo Holden, Eithne O'Hehir, Deirdre Byrne (1–0), Carmel O'Byrne (0–2), Siobhán Cronin, Noreen Fleming, Marie Connell (1–0). Subs used: Bridget Reynolds (0–1) and Claire Rainey.

1983 All-Ireland Minor Championship

Minor specialists, Cork and Galway, met in the semi-final at Na Piarsaigh Grounds. Cork's Paula Carey, Linda Mellerick and Jean Paula Kent took their scoring chances while good defensive work by Paula Morgan and Kathleen O'Keeffe kept Galway scoreless in the second-half. Cork advanced by 3–5 to 2–1.

Derry travelled to meet Dublin at Russell Park in the second semi-final. Dublin's superior sharpness around the goal allowed them to pull away in the second-half and record a 6–1 to 1–3 win.

A thrilling final five minutes saw Cork dethrone the reigning champions, Dublin, in the final at St Finbarr's. After a hectic struggle in hot sunny conditions, it took a late goal from Breda O'Sullivan to give Cork victory. Dublin enjoyed the lion's share of possession. While this yielded goals by Sharon Mullan and Patricia Clinton, much of it was wasted by poor shooting.

Cork were two goals in arrears as they returned from the

dressing room but they lost no time in making amends. Linda Mellerick and Colette O'Mahony wiped out the deficit. From there on it was anyone's game, as the ball sped from end to end. Breda O'Sullivan raced onto a well-directed pass and guided it to the Dublin net to leave the final score Cork 3–3, Dublin 2–3. Linda Mellerick, Colette O'Mahony, Liz Towler, Fiona McCarthy and Jean Paula Kent were in top-class form for Cork. Dublin were well served by Patricia Clinton, Sharon Mullan, Cheryl Whittaker and Pauline Strutt.

Dublin must have been rightly sick of the sight of Cork in 1983. They faced each other in the All-Ireland senior, junior and minor finals and Cork claimed all three titles.

Cork team: Fiona McCarthy, Kathleen O'Keeffe, Diane Deane, Niamh Coughlan, Paula Morgan, Colette O'Mahony (1–2), Liz Towler, Deirdre Christie (0–1), Linda Mellerick (1–0), Jean Paula Kent, Evelyn Healy and Paula Carey. Sub used: Breda O'Sullivan (1–0).

Dublin team: Deirdre Duggan, Cora Hanley, Pauline Strutt, Evelyn Courtney, Fiona McHugh, Cheryl Whittaker,

Clare Cronin (Cork), Rosina McManus (Antrim), Marguerite Guiry (Limerick), Josephine McCuskar (Donegal), Helen Sheehy (Limerick) and Bríd Stokes (Limerick) take a break at the National Coaching Course at Gormanston College in 1983.

Set dancing at the Ceol, Caint and Damhsa Finals

Phyllis Byrne (captain), Patricia Clinton (0–2), Sharon Mullan (2–1), Mary Reagan, Geraldine Dunne and Adele Campbell.

1983 All-Ireland Club Championship

Early chances fell to the Glenamaddy forwards in their semi-final against Croagh-Kilfinny at Glenamaddy and they did not disappoint. Their collective power proved too much for the Limerick side, which included several newcomers since their 1975 success in the competition. Glenamaddy advanced on the score of 3–3 to 1–0.

Buffers Alley remained on course to retain their title despite the very long journey to Swatragh for the semi-final. In a low-scoring game, Swatragh could only manage a point against a splendidly organised defence. While the Alley were not at their best, they did enough to earn a place in the final by 1–5 to 0–1.

Reigning champions, Buffers Alley, were full value for their third successive title when they overcame Glenamaddy in the final at Monamolin. They got down to business from the throw-in and had recorded 1–4 before Glenamaddy threatened their goal. The Galway club came into the game with four points to narrow the gap. Goals

Dublin's Return

by Elsie Walsh, Teresa Hobbs and Caroline Farrington closed out the contest to the delight of the large home following. The Alley were 3–7 to 0–6 in front at the finish.

Buffers Alley team: Terry Butler, Ann Butler, Geraldine Wynne, Margaret Leacy, Stellah Sinnott, Fiona Cousins, Elsie Walsh, Norah Gahan (captain), Caroline Farrington, Gertrude O'Leary, Bridie Doran and Teresa Hobbs.

Glenamaddy team: Chris Divilly, Rita Divilly, Kitty Hoey, Claire Geraghty, Claire Dolan, Teresa Garvey, Mary Kelly, Teresa Rafferty, Catherine Ward, Anne Divilly, Anne Gallagher and Kathleen Garvey.

1983 Gael-Linn Senior Cup

Leinster registered a comprehensive win over Connacht by 5–8 to 1–2 in the semi-final at Mobhi Road and snatched a last-minute win over Munster in the final at Ballinlough with a Joan Gormley special. The final score was Leinster 2–7, Munster 1–7.

Leinster team: Yvonne Redmond (Dublin), Anne O'Brien (Dublin), Geraldine Wynne (Wexford), Bernie Toner (Dublin), Ann Downey (Kilkenny), Biddy O'Sullivan (Kilkenny), Mary Mernagh (Dublin), Edel Murphy (Dublin), Anna Condon (Dublin), Elsie Walsh (Wexford), Angela Downey (Kilkenny) and Joan Gormley (Dublin).

Munster team: Marion McCarthy (Cork), Eileen Dineen (Cork), Miriam Higgins (Cork), Cathy Landers (Cork), Martha Kearney (Cork), Clare Cronin (Cork), Helen Collins (Limerick), Sandie Fitzgibbon (Cork), Mary O'Leary (Cork), Deirdre Lane (Tipperary), Brid Stokes (Limerick) and Mary Geaney (Cork).

Prize-winners at 1983 Gradam Tailte: Patricia Finneran (Roscommon) (3rd), Clare Cronin (Cork) (1st) and Angela Downey (Kilkenny) (2nd).

1983 Gael-Linn Junior Trophy

While Ulster looked the stronger team in the semi-final against Munster at Ballymacward, they were unable to reflect their superiority on the scoreboard and finished 2–12 to 3–5 behind. Leinster had three goals to spare at the close of their contest against Connacht at Mobhi Road. Leinster made the final by 4–6 to 1–4.

The final at Ballinlough was as close a contest as possible with the sides level on 12 occasions before the match went into extra-time. Munster emerged winners by 1–12 to 1–11.

Munster team: Debbie Cleary (Clare), Mary Maher (Cork), Mary Ring (Cork), Liz Dunphy (Cork), Margo Twomey (Cork) (captain), Ann Marie Landers (Cork), Anne Daly (Clare), Mary O'Donovan (Cork), Maura McNicholas (Clare), Anne Leahy (Cork), Helen Cusack (Clare) and Lilian Zinkant (Cork).

Leinster team: Geraldine Sutton (Dublin), Claire Rainey (Dublin), Anne Hyland (Dublin), Mary Duane (Dublin), Anna Dargan (Kildare), Jo Holden (Dublin), Eithne O'Hehir (Dublin), Deirdre Byrne (Dublin), Carmel O'Byrne (Dublin), Miriam

Malone (Kildare), Siobhán Cronin (Dublin) and Linda Forde (Westmeath).

Heavy Agenda at Portrush

Sixty-one motions were listed for discussion at Congress 1984 which was held in Portrush. A 20-motion package from Kilkenny, calling for a 15 a-side game on a full-sized hurling pitch, produced lively argument but drew no support. Limerick sought to make entry in certain events of the waning Ceol, Caint agus Damhsa compulsory, but it met with a similar fate. The meeting did, however, agree: to appoint trustees rather than elect them; to discontinue the post of director of organisation; and increase the width of the playing pitch.

Jo Golden was welcomed back to the top table to fill the vital position of treasurer left vacant by the untimely death of Agnes Purcell. Sheila McAnulty returned to Central Council in the role of trustee where her experience and advice proved to be a great asset.

GAA Centenary

As part of their centenary celebrations, the GAA staged a special exhibition at the RDS. Camogie was very much involved with Anne Sheehy and helpers in attendance at the Association's stand. The programme included matches played under the conditions which prevailed when the two organisations were founded. Camogie rolled back the years when two teams, suitably attired in the dress of the day, re-enacted a 1904 style match. Celtic and Marino supplied the players who really entered into the spirit of the occasion.

The players had reservations about handling the old-fashioned sticks and the much bigger ball before the game, but they adapted excellently. The shape of the sticks ruled out solo-running and the common practice of swapping the ball from hand to stick. With the result, the spectators were treated to an entertaining display of fast and direct camogie. Una Crowley, Orla Ryan, Carmel O'Byrne, Claire Harrington and Evelyn Sweeney had no problems adjusting.

Scéal na Camógaíochta

A short history of the Camogie Association, *Scéal na Camógaíochta*, was published in May 1984. It traced the growth of the game from its foundation in 1904. The research for the booklet was undertaken by Paddy Purcell, GAA correspondent of *The Irish Press*, and the work completed by his wife, Agnes, the former President of the Camogie Association. In welcoming the history, Camogie president, Mary Fennelly, said that: "Reading this short history reinforces our conviction that we are the privileged inheritors of an Association which has very worthy aims and ideals. We are deeply indebted to the pioneers of those early days and to all, who over the years have made a lasting contribution to this success story."

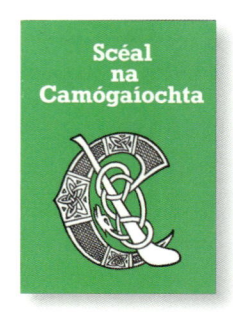

Dublin's Return

The ball sails beyond the reach of Ann Downey (Kilkenny) but is blocked by the stick of Bernie Toner (Dublin) in the 1984 first-round championship match at Parnell Park. Players on left are Breda Holmes (Kilkenny) and Una Crowley (Dublin).

Wasp Stops Match

Kilkenny and Tipperary were going hammer and tongs on the pitch. I had my camera at the ready near the goal hoping to catch a good action shot to go with my next article. Elizabeth, my young niece, had come with me for the spin and sat on the grass behind me munching a chocolate bar. Suddenly, a high-pitched scream rent the air, bringing the match to an immediate halt. A wasp had stung Elizabeth. Players, umpires, referee, supporters and team officials gathered around. Kilkenny's Carmel Savage came to the rescue and, with an old penny, had the sting out in seconds. The match resumed.

1984 All-Ireland Senior Championship

Pipped at the finishing post in 1982 and 1983, Dublin set out with steely determination to bridge the gap from 1966. Excellently prepared by Christy Hayes, Dublin ousted Kilkenny and Limerick en route to the semi-final against the reigning champions, Cork, at Parnell Park. Another cliff-hanger ensued and it took a late goal by Joan Gormley, three minutes from full-time, to give Dublin a place in the final. Cork were over-reliant on Mary O'Leary who scored Cork's total of 1–9 against Dublin's 3–4.

Jenny English snatched a draw for Tipperary with a late goal against Wexford in the second semi-final at Monamolin. First-cousin of All-Star Nicky, Jenny shot nine points in the replay at Borrisokane. Her accuracy together with outstanding goalkeeping by Breda Kennedy saw Tipperary through to their seventh All-Ireland final.

Dublin were full value for their 5–9 to 2–4 win over Tipperary at Croke Park on September 9th, 1984. Club-mates at Celtic, Anne Colgan (Dublin) and Deirdre Lane (Tipperary), led their respective teams in the parade. The game was as good as over when Dublin returned to the dressing room 3–5 to 0–2 in front. To their credit, Tipperary kept toiling away, but their attack only managed a single point from play and was not equal to the challenge. Two brilliantly struck penalties by Deirdre Lane put a more respectable appearance on the scoreboard.

Dublin 1984 All-Ireland senior champions. Back: Marie Connell, Toni O'Byrne, Catherine Ledwidge, Noreen Fleming, Yvonne Redmond, Anne Thorpe and Carmel O'Byrne. **Front:** Una Crowley, Barbara Redmond, Mary Mernagh, Germaine Noonan, Ann Colgan (Capt), Marion Conroy, Joan Gormley, Bernie Toner and Edel Murphy.

It was essentially a team victory for Dublin, but Yvonne Redmond, Edel Murphy, Una Crowley, Germaine Noonan, Marie Connell and Anne Colgan were particularly sharp. Tipperary's teamwork was not on the same level as Dublin's but in Deirdre Lane, Maura Hackett, Mary Sheedy, Anne Gleeson and Jenny English, they had accomplished players. Extended highlights of the match were screened on RTÉ later in the evening, but it was well short of what the game deserved.

Dublin team: Yvonne Redmond, Marian Conroy, Germaine Noonan (1–0), Bernie Toner, Catherine Ledwidge, Una Crowley (1–0), Mary Mernagh (0–1), Barbara Redmond, Joan Gormley (1–1), Anne Colgan (captain), Edel Murphy (0–7) and Marie Connell (2–0). Subs used: Toni O'Byrne and Noreen Fleming.

Tipperary team: Breda Kennedy, Mary Sheedy, Maura Hackett, Siobhán McDonnell, Margaret Madden, Rosie Ryan, Geraldine Ryan, Anne Gleeson, Triona Bonnar (0–1), Deirdre Lane (captain) (2–0), Jenny English (0–2) and Mary Griffin. Subs used: Susan Hickey (0–1), Kirsty McCluskey and Eithne Bonnar.

Marie Connell is a sister of Senan Connell who played senior football with Dublin. Mary Mernagh (Dublin) is a grand-daughter of Tom Mernagh who won three All-Ireland senior football medals with Wexford. Tipperary's Maura Hackett is a daughter of Rose Fletcher who won four All-Ireland medals with Dublin. Mary Sheedy (née O'Brien) and her husband, John, have both kept goal for Tipperary.

1984 All-Ireland Junior Championship

Cavan qualified for the All-Ireland junior final for the first time when they defeated Galway in an entertaining semi-final at Cootehill. The Breffni girls opened at a lightning pace and registered 4–2 in the opening ten minutes. Galway fought back but were unable to make up lost ground and went under by 8–4 to 3–5.

As All-Ireland junior champions, Cork had to field a completely new team for the 1984 competition. There was nothing between Cork and Dublin in the semi-final at St Finbarr's and every score was hard-earned. Josephine Rumley's goal five minutes from the

Dublin's Return

The Cavan team which contested the 1984 All-Ireland junior final at Croke Park. Included are: Anne McKiernan, Margaret Hastings, Elizabeth Fitzpatrick, Ita Brady, Ita Farrelly, Catherine Clarke, Noeleen Kiernan, Frances Smith, Geraldine Martin, Rosita Brady, Pauline Smith, Olive Scorr, Lorraine O'Neill, Bernie Callaghan, Mary McMullen and Margaret Carroll.

end decided the outcome in Cork's favour by 1–7 to 2–2.

Individually, the Cavan players looked impressive in the All-Ireland final against Cork at Croke Park. With a strong wind at their backs, they practically owned the ball but had little to show for it when they turned over at 1–2 to 1–1. Cork got down to the serious business of winning the match on the resumption. They scored three goals in a ten-minute spell and were well on their way to back-to-back titles. Josephine Rumley had the game of her life with four goals and Una O'Connor, Patricia Fitzgibbon, Denise Cotter and Irene O'Leary also impressed for Cork. Margaret Hastings, Ita Brady, Rosita Brady and Frances Smith caught the eye for Cavan. The scoreboard read Cork 5–8, Cavan 2–2 at close of play.

Cork team: Kathleen Costine, Liz Maher, Mary Spillane, Paula Goggins, Una O'Connor, Irene O'Leary (captain), Linda Mellerick, Mary Currid, Regina Scoutts, Josephine Rumley (4–1), Denise Cotter (1–2) and Patricia Fitzgibbon (0–5).

Cavan team: Anne McKiernan (captain), Margaret Hastings (0–1), Lorraine O'Neill, Ita Brady, Ita Farrelly, Catherine Clarke, Noleen McKiernan, Frances Smith, Geraldine Martin (2–0), Rosita Brady (0–1), Pauline Smith and Olive Scorr. Subs used: Bernie Callaghan and Mary McMullen.

Cork's Patricia Fitzgibbon is a grand-niece of Dr Edwin Fitzgibbon, who donated the Fitzgibbon Cup for inter-varsity hurling. Denise Cotter (Cork) is a niece of Joan and Kitty Cotter, the first sisters to win All-Ireland medals.

1984 All-Ireland Minor Championship

Galway got off to a dream start in the All-Ireland semi-final against Dublin at Leopardstown Avenue and had the game well in hand at the break when they led by 3–3 to 0–0. While Dublin improved in the second-half, Galway's route to the final was not threatened. Galway 5–5, Dublin 1–2 was the final score.

Cork held a slender 2–2 to 1–2 lead at the interval against Antrim in the second semi-final at Na Piarsaigh. The home side dominated the remainder of the game as the Antrim girls felt the effects of the long journey. Cork finished in front by 5–6 to 1–3.

A Game of Our Own

The standard of play in the All-Ireland minor final between Galway and Cork at Loughrea was amazing for 16-year-olds. A four-goal spree by Galway before half-time seemed to end Cork's hopes. A great piece of individual skill saw Deirdre Costello waltz past the Cork defence to plant the ball in the net and usher in a period of supremacy for Galway. She created the second goal for Siobhán Maher, devised the third for herself and had a hand in the fourth which was finished by Anne Fahy.

The Cork youngsters, who were without their injured captain Deirdre Christie, showed great character to mount a recovery from such a hammering. They worked very hard to claw their way back into contention. Karen Mellerick and Jean Paula Kent were rewarded with goals while Colette O'Mahony totted up the points. Eventually, Cork got their noses in front. In the dying minute of the game, Deirdre Costello launched a last desperate attack to win the game but she was stopped in her tracks by Niamh Coughlan and Evelyn Healy. In addition to Deirdre Costello, Galway had big performances from Anne Ryan, Maura Kennedy and Sheila Coen. The scoreboard showed Cork 2–12, Galway 5–0 at the finish.

Cork team: Bríd Walsh, Kathleen O'Keeffe, Evelyn Healy, Vivienne O'Brien, Niamh Coughlan, Patricia O'Shea (0–1), Colette Cronin (0–2), Karen Mellerick (1–0), Jean Paula Kent (1–2), Colette O'Mahony (0–6), Ina Leahy (0–1) and Paula Carey. Subs used: Yvonne O'Neill, Deirdre Christie and Helena Barry.

Galway team: Angela Laheen, Angela Cooney, Maura Kennedy, Bríd Stratford, Patricia Finnerty, Deirdre Duffy, Sheila Coen, Siobhán Maher (1–0), Claire Robinson, Deirdre Costello (2–0), Anne Fahy (1–0) and Anne Ryan (1–0). Subs used: Fidelma Hanlon and Mary Coen.

Happy Cork minors with Corn Tailteann after defeating Galway in the 1984 All-Ireland final at Loughrea. From left are Kathleen O'Keeffe, Paula Carey, Colette Cronin, Deirdre Christie (Capt), Colette O'Mahony and Vivienne O'Brien.

1984 All-Ireland Club Championship

Ten points separated Buffers Alley and Glenamaddy in the 1983 All-Ireland club final. When the sides met in the 1984 semi-final, it was a much closer affair. In fact, the Alley had to call on all their ability and experience to see them through. Had St Mary's made better use of the chances that came their way, it could have been a different result. Elsie Cody, Gertrude O'Leary and Bridie Doran found the net for the Alley while Kitty Hoey and Kathleen Garvey did likewise for the home team. Buffers Alley advanced by 3–1 to 2–2.

Killeagh (Cork) carried too much power for newcomers Leitrim in the second semi-final at the Co. Down venue. With Shelly Spillane and Ann Marie Landers commanding midfield, the

Dublin's Return

Killeagh attack was fed with a constant supply of good ball. Marion Sweeney, Patricia Fitzgibbon and Anne Leahy converted their opportunities into goals to see Killeagh advance by 3–3 to 0–2.

Buffers Alley became the first side to claim four All-Ireland club titles in a row when they overcame their great rivals, Killeagh by a single score at Monamolin. The Cork girls led for most of the game, but wilted under severe pressure in the closing minutes. Driven on by the large, vocal home crowd, the Alley launched attack after attack. They were rewarded with a goal from Gertrude O'Leary to seal victory by 2–4 to 1–4. Much credit was due to respective coaches Mick Butler (Buffers Alley) and Fr Bertie Troy (Killeagh) for bringing their players to a very high level.

Buffers Alley team: Kathleen Tonks, Ann Butler, Geraldine Wynne, Dorothy Kenny, Elsie Cody, Fiona Cousins, Stellah Sinnott, Norah Gahan (captain), Caroline Farrington, Gertrude O'Leary, Bridie Doran and Teresa Hobbs.

Killeagh team: Kathleen Costine, Marie O'Donovan, Mary Spillane, Cathy Landers, Breda Landers, Patsy Keniry, Shelley Spillane, Ann Marie Landers, Bernie Costine, Anne Leahy, Patricia Fitzgibbon and Marion Sweeney (captain). Sub used: Betty Joyce.

Donegal camogie team 1984. Back: Ita Blake, Bríd Ronaghan, Mary Hirrell, Noreen McCuskar, Anne McGrath, Josie McCuskar, Gerry Murphy and Andrea McHugh. Front: Anne Marie McCarron, Margaret Curran, Geraldine Kerr, Geraldine Henry, Emer McDonagh, Marie Crawford and Margaret Rooney (Capt).

1984 Gael-Linn Senior Cup

Leinster scored a narrow 2–1 to 1–3 win over Munster at rain-soaked Adare and rounded off a great season for the Dublin players by taking the Gael-Linn Cup with a 3–9 to 1–4 victory over Connacht at Silver Park. Connacht got the better of Ulster in the semi-final by 3–6 to 1–3.

Leinster team: Yvonne Redmond (Dublin), Ann Downey (Kilkenny), Germaine Noonan (Dublin), Tina Fitzhenry (Wexford), Stellah Sinnott (Wexford), Una Crowley (Dublin), Mary Mernagh (Dublin) Biddy O'Sullivan (Kilkenny), Edel Murphy (Dublin), Norah Gahan (Wexford), Angela Downey (Kilkenny) and Joan Gormley (Dublin).

Connacht team: (All Galway) Breda Coady, Noreen Treacy, Anne Briscoe, Chris Silke, Breda Kenny, Claire Geraghty, Anne Gallagher, Mary Kelly, Teresa Raftery, Madge Hobbins, Anne Morris and Una Jordan.

1984 Gael-Linn Junior Trophy

Leinster lasted the pace better in the semi-final against Munster at Adare and were rewarded with a 2–4 to 1–6 win. A strong Ulster side had three goals to spare over Connacht, 4–6 to 1–6, at Castledaly. Leinster overcame the spirited challenge over Ulster to win by nine points, 3–6 to 1–3.

Leinster team: Toni O'Byrne (Dublin), Mairéad Cronin (Dublin), Antoinette Merriman (Kildare), Anna Dargan (Kildare), Patricia Clinton (Dublin), Jo Holden (Dublin), Eunice Keogh (Dublin), Marie Fitzpatrick (Kilkenny), Nuala Smithers (Carlow), Siobhán Cronin (Dublin), Miriam Malone (Kildare) and Adele Campbell (Dublin).

Ulster team: Anne McKiernan (Cavan), Margaret Moriarty (Armagh), Sheila Rafferty (Armagh), Ita Brady (Cavan), Noeleen McKendry (Derry), Siobhán McKeogh (Fermanagh), Sarah Ann Quinn (Derry), Anne Trainor (Down), Pauline Robinson (Derry), Denise McStay (Armagh), Ursula McGivern (Armagh) and Patsy Quinn (Derry).

Mary Lynch Elected President

Mary Lynch (née Kelly) was elected President of the Camogie Association at Congress 1985 at Ballinasloe. A native of Carrickmacross, she brought experience of many years of administration with Monaghan and Ulster to the office. An All-Ireland medal holder with Dublin, Mary was an accomplished referee.

Mary Lynch

London Revival

London camogie lay dormant for almost 30 years. In 1985, a group of people got a team together, aided by a grant from the Greater London Council. Within a year, there were three clubs and by the early nineties, camogie in London had grown to three divisions with 12 clubs, some fielding two teams.

Englishman, Brian Pote-Hunt, a sports manager for the Greater London Council, thought that Irish girls should be playing their own game. He placed an advert in the *Irish Post* which drew an immediate response and, before long, London Irish Camogie Club had 30 members training at Finsbury Park. Rita O'Hanlon trained the players and gave wonderful service to the club.

Etty Kelly, from Ashbourne, Co. Meath, started Newham Gaels at Forrest Gate. She used her vast experience as an inter-county and interprovincial player back in Ireland to improve her team. Mary Noonan, a native of Kildare, established a club south of the River Thames at Croydon. Two years later, Majella and Carmel O'Neill from Kilkenny set up the Tara Camogie Club in northwest London. The camogie scene experienced rapid growth and Islington Irish, Greenwich Gaels and Green Isle were soon added to the growing list of clubs.

Pan Celtic Festival

Pan Celtic, a festival set up to promote and strengthen Celtic languages, culture, music, song and sport, was staged for the first time in Killarney in 1971, though it was several years before camogie participated in the event. Camogie's original involvement saw eight teams play in an under-16 competition. A senior competition was added in 1985. Organiser, Mary Treacy, succeeded in attracting eight clubs to Killarney for the weekend. Éire Óg (Cork) had a facile win over Croagh-Kilfinny (Limerick) in the

Dublin's Return

final at Fitzgerald Stadium.

In all, 38 teams took part in the Pan Celtic camogie competitions, making it one of the biggest sectors of the festival. In 1984, St Finbarr's (Cork) won the under-16A competition while the under-16B was claimed by Croagh-Kilfinny.

The spin-off to hosting the Pan Celtic Camogie Festival was an upsurge of the game in Kerry. Underage teams were formed in Kenmare, Dingle, Tarbert and Cloghane, with a further three in Killarney. A primary schools competition attracted entries from five schools and the county was represented at Féile na nGael.

Mary Cahill Sevens

In 1967, Mary Walsh climbed the steps of the Hogan Stand to accept the O'Duffy Cup, the first Wexford player to do so. The tall, athletic Monageer girl captained Leinster to win the Gael-Linn Cup in 1969. On her marriage to Larry Cahill, she settled in Rathnure. Failing health led to a premature death in September 1985.

The Wexford County Board set up the Mary Cahill Memorial Sevens to perpetuate her memory. It was held first in 1986 when clubs from Connacht, Munster and Leinster travelled to pay tribute to the former star. Her home club, Rathnure, were the first holders of the trophy.

Bridie McGarry, the Kilkenny captain, lifts the O'Duffy Cup and is congratulated by President Mary Lynch at Croke Park in September, 1985.

1985 All-Ireland Senior Championship

In a low-scoring semi-final between Wexford and Kilkenny at Rathnure, Geraldine Wynne's last-minute close-in free sailed inches over the bar to leave Kilkenny advance by 2–6 to 2–5. It looked for a long time like Wexford would hold out but a fabulous goal by Jo Dunne swung the game around.

Cork, who tried to walk the ball into the Dublin goal in the second semi-final at St Finbarr's, paid the price for not taking their points and watched Dublin advance by 1–10 to 3–1. Carmel O'Byrne and Bernie Toner in defence, Edel Murphy and Anna McManus powered the champions to victory.

The combined teams of Dublin and Kilkenny could only manage one goal in the 1985 All-Ireland final at Croke Park on September 15th. However, many of the points scored were top of the range. Defences were to the fore throughout and goal chances were few and far between. That Dublin managed to keep in touch was due to the superb goalkeeping of Yvonne Redmond. As the game progressed, Dublin wilted under Kilkenny's strong challenge. Angela Downey, Margaret Farrell and Breda Holmes struck some classic points to see Kilkenny win by 0–13 to 1–5.

Kilkenny team: Marie Fitzpatrick, Ann Downey, Anne Holden, Bridie McGarry (captain), Biddy O'Sullivan, Liz Neary,

Deirdre Malone, Anna Whelan (0–1), Margaret Farrell (0–5), Angela Downey (0–4), Jo Dunne and Breda Holmes (0–3).

Dublin team: Yvonne Redmond, Marion Conroy, Germaine Noonan, Bernie Toner, Anne Redmond, Una Crowley, Edel Murphy (captain) (0–3), Anna Condon, Joan Gormley, Mary Mernagh, Carmel O'Byrne and Marie Connell (1–2). Subs used: Patricia Clinton and Denise O'Leary.

1985 All-Ireland Junior Championship

Galway delivered a stunning display of skill and fitness in the semi-final against Wexford at Loughrea to earn a place in the final by 3–11 to 1–4. Deirdre Costello, Deirdre Lawless, Anne Ryan and Anne Fahy tore the Wexford defence apart and took delightful scores with ease. Wexford were unable to match the superior play of their Galway opponents.

Armagh seized the initiative from the outset in the second semi-final against Limerick at Lurgan and built up a sizeable 3–8 to 0–2 lead by half-time. Apart from a brief spell that yielded a goal, Limerick were never in the hunt. Armagh's outstanding player, Mary Donnelly, helped herself to 3–3. Armagh finished in front by 5–7 to 1–2.

The speed, accurate passing and clinical finishing of the Galway forwards totally outclassed Armagh in the All-Ireland final at Croke Park. Their ability to play together as an attacking unit was remarkable for junior players. The Armagh girls did not perform badly, but such was the standard of the Galway side that a rift existed between them.

Deirdre Costello, star of so many victories for St Raphael's, Loughrea, amassed four wonderful goals. Galway completed a league and championship double and gave real hope to their supporters of a senior breakthrough. The score stood at Galway 8–7, Armagh 3–7 at the final whistle.

Galway team: Chris Divilly, Eileen Howley, Julie Glynn, Bríd Stratford, Angela Cooney, Ena Cannon (captain), Teresa Rafferty, Claire Dolan, Anne Fahy (1–5), Deirdre Costello (4–0), Deirdre Lawless and Anne Ryan (1–1). Subs used: Patricia Mitchell (1–1) and Mairéad Coyle (1–0).

Armagh team: Bernie McNally, Pat Daly, Sheila Rafferty, Margaret Moriarty (captain), Andrea McAlinden, Fionnuala O'Connor, Denise McStay, Paula Brown, Sally McCone (1–1), Ursula McGivern (0–6), Paula O'Hare and Mary Donnelly (1–0). Sub used: Rita McGuigan (1–0).

Galway's Angela Cooney is a sister of All-Ireland hurling medallists, Joe and Jimmy Cooney. Anne Ryan's brother, Eanna, played corner-forward on the 1988 Galway All-Ireland winning team.

1985 All-Ireland Minor Championship

Cork were on course for a hat-trick of All-Ireland minor titles by virtue of a comprehensive win over Wexford at the semi-final stage in Killeagh. A good first-half display put Cork 3–3 to 1–1 ahead. Wexford were unable to make headway against a very competent defence while Cork added further points to seal the issue by 5–4 to 1–4.

Dublin's Return

Galway looked like a team of all talents as they dismissed Down in the second semi-final at Oranmore. The home side piled on score after score with forwards, Deirdre Costello, Patricia Connors, Imelda Hobbins and Mary Treacy, getting in on the act. Down found their opponents in a different class and conceded by 7–11 to 0–2.

Minor specialists, Galway and Cork, held nine of the 11 titles decided up to the 1985 final between them. A close and exciting game, with some great passages of play, the final saw Cork grab two goals within seconds of the restart to transform a half-time deficit into a four-point lead.

The Galway defence faded under Cork's second-half onslaught, spearheaded by the accurate Jean Paula Kent. Deirdre Ryan, who curtailed danger-girl Deirdre Costello, Aileen Barry, Sheena Morley and Ina Leahy played extremely well for the winners. Galway were best served by Nora O'Rourke, Angela Cooney, Bríd Stratford and Geraldine Kilkelly. Cork won by 3–8 to 2–3 at St Finbarr's Grounds.

Cork team: Bríd Walsh, Deirdre Ryan, Bríd Kelleher, Ina Leahy, Tracy O'Riordan, Aileen Barry, Sheena Morley, Karen Mellerick, Paula Carey (0–1), Jean Paula Kent (1–6), Carmel Currid (1–0) and Bernice Cashman (1–1).

Galway team: Nora O'Rourke, Angela Cooney, Patty Finnerty, Mary Dolphin, Bríd Stratford, Siobhán Maher, Dympna Connell, Geraldine Kilkelly, Deirdre Costello (2–1), Imelda Hobbins (0–2), Mary Treacy and Patricia Connors. Subs used: Pauline Linnane and Carmel Coyne.

Cork's Bríd Walsh is a sister of Denis Walsh who won an All-Ireland senior hurling medal in 1986. Deirdre Ryan is a daughter of Mick Ryan who won three All-Ireland senior hurling medals with Tipperary. Sheena Morley is a daughter of Joan Clancy, who won Gael-Linn medals with Munster.

1985 All-Ireland Club Championship

Three newcomers, Crumlin (Dublin), Éire Óg (Cork) and Eglish (Tyrone), arrived on the All-Ireland club scene in 1985. Crumlin, who fielded half the Dublin team that won the 1984 All-Ireland senior championship, had a close call from the Cork champions in the semi-final at Ovens. It took a last-minute goal by Anna McManus to secure victory for the Dublin side by 2–4 to 1–5. Athenry struggled against Eglish in the semi-final at Kenny Park before pulling clear in the closing stages and securing a place in the final. Eglish showed how they dominated the club scene in Tyrone over many years. They possessed players of no mean ability in Anne Burke, Celia McKay, Pauline Valley, Anne Jordan, Anna McKenna and Maureen Ogle.

Crumlin, who were impressive right through the campaign, were crowned All-Ireland club champions at O'Toole Park, Dublin, at the finish of a well-contested game against Athenry. The Dublin club were particularly strong in defence where Yvonne Redmond, Anne Byrne and Bernie Toner presented a barrier to the Athenry attack. One of the biggest problems presented to Athenry was posed by Galway senior star, Mary Keane, who lined out in the colours of Crumlin. She teamed up with Anna Condon

Crumlin – 1985 All-Ireland Club Champions. Back: Aileen Redmond, Yvonne Redmond, Barbara Redmond, Bernie Toner, Ger Brady, Anne Heavey, Catherine Feehan, Ger Byrne and Joanne Courtney. Front: Anne Byrne, Ann Redmond, Mary Mernagh, Mary Keane, Phyllis Lindsey and Anna Condon.

and Barbara Redmond to open up the Athenry defence. Noreen Treacy, Chris Silke, Madge Hobbins and Ann Coleman did most in the cause of Athenry but could not prevent Crumlin from winning 4–8 to 3–3.

Crumlin team: Yvonne Redmond, Anne Byrne, Ger Brady, Anne Redmond, Bernie Toner, Cathy Walsh, Mary Mernagh, Ger Byrne, Aileen Redmond, Mary Keane, Anna Condon and Barbara Redmond.

Athenry team: Breda Coady, Noreen Treacy, Una Jordan, Chris Silke, Mary Bellew, Olive Molloy, Bríd Holland, Anne Coleman, Madge Hobbins, Teresa Kavanagh, Anne Morris and Marion Freaney.

Founded in 1966 by Phil Barry, Nuala Dunphy and Jeanne Quigley, the Crumlin club was originally known as the Cuchulainns Club. In 1980, the club joined up with the local Crumlin GAA club and, for some time, were known as Crumlin Cuchulainn.

The club drew heavily on the players of the successful Assumption, Walkinstown, winners of Leinster post-primary schools titles. Excellently prepared by two top hurling men, Jimmy Boggan and Billy Maloney, the girls in blue and navy reached their goal.

1985 Gael-Linn Senior Cup

A richly talented Leinster side disposed of Ulster by 5–10 to 0–1 in the semi-final at Cork and proceeded to master Munster in the final by 4–9 to 1–6.

There was much to admire about the Leinster performance as they glided effortlessly past all opposition.

Leinster team: Marie Fitzpatrick (Kilkenny), Marion Conroy (Dublin), Tina Fitzhenry (Wexford) (captain), Bridie McGarry (Kilkenny), Biddy O'Sullivan (Kilkenny), Una Crowley (Dublin), Edel Murphy (Dublin), Ann Reddy (Wexford), Margaret Farrell (Kilkenny), Catherine Murphy (Wexford), Angela Downey (Kilkenny) and Joan Gormley (Dublin).

Munster team: Marion McCarthy (Cork), Eileen Dineen

Dublin's Return

(Cork), Miriam Higgins (Cork), Cathy Landers (Cork) (captain), Vera Mackey (Limerick), Pauline McCarthy (Limerick), Sandie Fitzgibbon (Cork), Clare Cronin (Cork), Bríd Stokes (Limerick), Val Fitzpatrick (Cork), Linda Mellerick (Cork) and Mary Geaney (Cork).

Leinster captain, Tina Fitzhenry, is a sister of All-Star hurling goalkeeper, Damien Fitzhenry.

1985 Gael-Linn Junior Trophy

Munster managed to stay on the right side of the thin line between success and failure. They toiled relentlessly to earn a 1–10 to 1–7 victory over Connacht in the semi-final and made a second-half recovery to earn a 1–7 to 2–3 win over Ulster in the final at Cork.

Munster team: Fiona McCarthy (Cork), Marguerite Guiry (Limerick) (captain), Liz O'Grady (Limerick), Noleen Quinn (Clare), Margaret Barry (Limerick), Mags Finn (Cork), Tina O'Connell (Clare), Maisie Clifford (Limerick), Jean Paula Kent (Cork), Colette O'Mahony (Cork), Maura McNicholas (Clare) and Margo Cassidy (Limerick).

Ulster team: Teresa McVeigh (Monaghan), Margaret Moriarty (Armagh), Sheila Rafferty (Armagh), Sarah Ann Quinn (Derry), Noeleen McKendry (Derry), Fionnuala O'Connor (Armagh), Anne Jordan (Tyrone), Catherine Daly (Tyrone), Sally McCone (Armagh), Denise McStay (Armagh), Patsy Quinn (Derry) and Mary Donnelly (Armagh).

Where We're At

Significant changes took place in Central Council personnel over a few short years: Seán O'Duffy and Agnes Purcell went to their eternal reward; Lily Spence and Sheila McAnulty retired (Sheila was to return in the role of trustee); and Nancy Murray, Nell McCarthy and Rosina McManus, who had served as presidents, returned to their counties to continue their work. Full-time officials came and went. Wise old heads and massive experience were lost to the council. Enthusiastic newcomers came on board with aspirations to progress the Association further.

Increasing the number of counties participating in the All-Ireland Senior Championship has always posed a problem. Because a sizeable gap in standards existed between junior and senior counties. Promotion to the senior ranks was made compulsory, with the winners of the All-Ireland junior championship having to take a considerable step upwards. With the result, 11 names went into the hat for the 1984 All-Ireland Senior Championship – Dublin, Kilkenny, Wexford, Louth, Tipperary, Clare, Limerick, Cork, Down, Antrim and Galway.

Unfortunately, the newcomers were unable to make the grade and, by 1989, the number of senior counties had fallen to six. It often happened that it took so long for a team to make the breakthrough to senior level that the life-span of the team was nearing an end by the time it reached its goal. Every side requires an injection of new blood on an annual basis. If adequate replacements are not available, the standard starts to decline. Nine of the 11 counties that participated in the 1984 Senior Championship fielded inter-county junior sides but, with the exception of the top counties, the standard of the second string was poor. If the newly promoted sides lost players for any reason, they struggled to survive. A succession of decisive defeats led to applications for regrading to a lower level.

Why is it so difficult to get camogie members to adopt something new? They show enthusiasm for a few years and then let it drop. This was the case with the sports days, Ceol, Caint agus Damhsa and Gradam Tailte.

In the first few years, Gradam Tailte, where the top player from each county took part in a series of athletic tests, camogie skills and novelty events, was a great take and created considerable interest. It promoted the game through increased publicity and gave recognition to individual players and their skills. In addition, it increased the finances of the Association. A figure of £2,500 was added to the coffers in the first year, a significant amount in those days. It got off to a great start. Counties held their own competition to find the best player to go forward to Gradam Tailte. The standard was very high with a real competitive edge. After a few years, counties did not bother to hold a contest, but asked a player to turn up on the day to represent the county. Players, who got a late call up, were not properly prepared and did not do themselves justice. Interest in the event waned and, eventually, fizzled out.

Chapter Sixteen

KILKENNY ON A ROLL

In little over five years, the office of Ard Rúnaí and Development Officer of the Camogie Association had seen three occupants, with Anne Sheehy giving notice of her resignation in November 1985. At last, a person was found who was prepared to make a career of the position. Former captain of the Dublin senior team, Sheila Wallace, was appointed to the position in January 1986.

Already knowledgeable in camogie administration from her days as secretary of the Dublin County Board, she slotted in easily and gave great service to the Association over the following 22 years.

Isle of Man Festival

Azaria Limited, whose advertising claimed to be dedicated to the permanent establishment of Gaelic sport in the Isle of Man, were given permission to include camogie in their annual Easter Festival. The festival, which ran from April 17th–19th, had included hurling and football in previous years and was expanded in 1986 to embrace camogie. Croagh-Kilfinny, Avoca, Buffers Alley and St Paul's (Kilkenny) made the short sea trip to the Isle of Man to challenge for Buanchorn na Casca and enjoyed the outing. The number of clubs that entered the competition doubled and trebled in the subsequent years and a junior tournament was added.

Liz Neary, the Kilkenny captain, holds the O'Duffy Cup aloft in September 1986 flanked by Camogie President, Mary Lynch.

Coischéim

The Association undertook a fundraising project featuring a walk from Cork to Dublin in the lead up to the 1986 All-Ireland final. It was aimed at gaining publicity and attracting an increased attendance at Croke Park. The walk was led by Donncha Ó Dúlaing with former president, Nell McCarthy, and Munster chair, Mary O'Callaghan, accompanied Donncha from start to finish. Support was forthcoming from clubs and counties along the route and £6,100 was raised and presented to the Irish Wheelchair Association. The attendance at the camogie finals was boosted as many clubs from around the country joined in the last leg of the walk from the Mansion House to Croke Park and added colour to the occasion.

1986 All-Ireland Senior Championship

Wexford seemed set to reach the All-Ireland final when they were rocked by a four-goal blitz by Dublin's Marie Connell in the semi-final at Monamolin. The full-forward shattered Wexford's dream and secured a place for her team-mates in the final by 5–9 to 3–2.

Cork were leading by five points entering injury time in the second semi-final at Nowlan Park. It seemed that Cork were home and dry when, out of nowhere, Angela Downey pounced and rattled the net. A short puck-out fell to Jo Dunne. She accepted the gift and returned it to the Cork net. Cork, who had led for almost the entire game, were left stunned as the final whistle blew and the scoreboard read Kilkenny 4–11, Cork 3–12.

A slow first-half in the All-Ireland final at Croke Park on September 9th was reflected in the score of Kilkenny 0–5, Dublin 0–2. Edel Murphy careered through the Kilkenny defence almost unchallenged and shot to the net. It was a wake-up call for Kilkenny and Angela Downey responded from the puck-out. She gathered possession, careered past two defenders and crashed the ball past Yvonne Redmond. Kilkenny really started to play and were a class apart from Dublin. Ann Downey did excellent work in midfield and provided good ball for Angela and Jo Dunne to finish over the bar. Angela took a pass from Breda Holmes and drove it

Angela Downey (Kilkenny) shoots for goal past the advancing Bernie Toner (Dublin) in the 1986 All-Ireland senior final at Croke Park. Jo Dunne (Kilkenny) awaits developments.

home with panache to leave the final score Kilkenny 2–12, Dublin 2–3.

Kilkenny team: Marie Fitzpatrick, Liz Neary (captain), Anne Holden, Bridie McGarry, Biddy O'Sullivan, Anna Whelan, Ann Downey (0-2), Clare Jones, Jo Dunne (0–4), Rita Weymes (0–1), Angela Downey (2–4) and Breda Holmes (0–1).

Dublin team: Yvonne Redmond, Marion Conroy, Germaine Noonan, Breda Kenny (0–1), Helena Broderick, Una Crowley (captain), Mary Mernagh, Cathy Walsh, Joan Gormley, Edel Murphy (1–2), Carmel O'Byrne and Marie Connell. Subs used: Bernie Toner, Anna Condon (1-0) and Patricia Clinton.

Kilkenny On a Roll

Waiting for National Anthem

Betty Joyce (Cork) was appointed to referee the 1986 All-Ireland final between Dublin and Kilkenny and was accompanied by four umpires, clad in pale green tracksuits, from her club, Killeagh. By the time Betty and her party took the field, the parade and the preliminaries had already taken place. She received the signal to start the match as Sheila Spillane and Marion Sweeney strolled down to take up their positions at the goalposts. A Dublin attacker raced forward and shot for a point. Betty waited for a signal from her umpires but none was forthcoming. Marion's demeanour as she soaked up the atmosphere led Betty to believe that she had not seen what happened. Betty made her way to Sheila and enquired, "What was it"? A nonplussed Sheila answered "Jaysus, I don't know. I was waiting for the national anthem."

1986 All-Ireland Junior Championship

A large crowd welcomed Clare to sun-drenched Athleague for the semi-final of the 1986 All-Ireland Junior Championship. Roscommon stayed with the visitors on the scoreboard for the first-half. As Clare found their rhythm and pulled away, Roscommon seemed to lose confidence. Clare won impressively by 3–11 to 1–5.

Kildare secured a place in the All-Ireland final at the expense of Derry when the sides met at Bellaghy. The Lilywhites added to their four-point interval lead but were not able to draw clear. Good defensive work saw them through by 3–6 to 0–9.

The 1986 All-Ireland junior final between Clare and Kildare at Croke Park provided two firsts in the history of the game. First, Kathleen Elliott, a Mercy nun, lined out for Kildare. A niece of former Tipperary greats, Terry and Kathleen Griffin, Sr Kathleen had 70 of her pupils at St Mary's College, Naas, cheering in the stands. Second, after 54 years of competition a mother and daughter had won All-Ireland medals. Kitty McNicholas won an All-Ireland junior medal in 1974 and her daughter, Maura, who captained Clare, completed the record.

The final was dominated by four performers: Catherine O'Loughlin and Maura McNicholas for Clare and Miriam Malone and Kathleen Elliott for Kildare. Catherine O'Loughlin displayed speed and control as she cut through the Kildare defence and popped over eight points. Captain, Maura McNicholas, put the finishing touch to 1–5. Miriam Malone donned the Kildare jersey for the first time in 1966 and the best-known Kildare player of

Clare captain, Maura McNicholas, picks her spot watched by Kildare defenders, Phyllis Bambury and Anna Dargan in the 1986 All-Ireland junior final at Croke Park.

all time scored 2–1 from midfield. Kathleen Elliott gave her pupils plenty to shout about as she registered 1–2. When the referee blew the final whistle, Clare were ahead by 1–13 to 3–4.

Clare team: Pauline O'Brien, Helen Cusack, Patricia Ryan, Noeleen Quinn, Siobhán Reidy, Patricia Rynne, Sheila O'Halloran, Noelle Comyns, Catherine O'Loughlin (0–8), Maura McNicholas (captain) (1–5), Catherine Molloy and Carmel Wall.

Kildare team: Rose Merriman, Geraldine Dwyer, Melanie Treacy, Anna Dargan, Antoinette Merriman, Patricia Keatley, Miriam Malone (captain) (2–1), Gemma Cooney, Liz O'Donoghue, Marianne Johnson (0–1), Kathleen Elliott (1–2) and Bernie Farrelly. Subs used: Nuala Kerrigan, Phyllis Bambury and Nora Egan.

1986 All-Ireland Minor Championship

It is the nature of minor teams to change considerably from year to year. Many of the players who wore the Galway and Cork colours in the two previous finals had graduated from the grade. Galway found better replacements as was evident when they met in the All-Ireland semi-final at Castlegar. The Galway attack was more streetwise than their Cork opponents and engineered a 1–5

Clare – 1986 All-Ireland Junior Champions. Back: Maura McNicholas (Capt), Catherine O'Loughlin, Patricia Rynne, Pauline O'Brien, Catherine Molloy and Carmel Wall. Front: Noelle Comyns, Noeleen Quinn, Siobhán Reidy, Sheila O'Halloran, Patricia Ryan and Helen Cusack.

to 0–1 win.

All the scoring in the second semi-final between Wexford and Down was done in the first-half. Comfortably ahead by 4–2 to 0–1, Wexford put up the shutters, ruling out any comeback by Down.

Featuring in the All-Ireland minor final for the first time, Wexford hosted Galway, old hands at the minor game, at Wexford Park. Rated as one of the best teams to wear the maroon and white, the Galway minors stamped their authority on the game and reflected their superiority on the scoreboard. Wexford matched their opponents in certain facets of the game but fell short when it came to scoring. There was no weak link in the Galway side and each girl played her part in the well-deserved victory. The game finished with the score standing at Galway 2–8, Wexford 1–4.

Galway team: Nora O'Rourke, Marlene Linnane, Bronagh Smyth, Ger Fahy, Caroline Linnane, Finola Keane, Mary Cawley (0–4), Suzanne Burke (0–2), Mary Treacy (1–1), Imelda Hobbins, Triona Dolphin (1–1) and Patricia Connors.

Wexford team: Tina Farrell, Deirdre Hearne (captain), Pauline Casey, Deirdre Atkinson (1–2), Eithne Sinnott, Mairéad

Kehoe, Audrey O'Leary, Bríd Lambe, Geraldine Codd (0–2), Clare Cullen, Evelyn Sinnott and Ann-Marie O'Connor.

1986 All-Ireland Club Championship

Eglish stayed with opponents, St Paul's, Kilkenny, in the opening half of the All-Ireland club semi-final at Larchfield, Kilkenny, and trailed by only four points at the break. Kilkenny star, Angela Downey, went on a scoring spree that yielded 7–5 and left the Tyrone girls shattered. St Paul's advanced by 9–7 to 2–5.

Glen Rovers, who had contested the first club championship final in 1964, returned to the All-Ireland stage and made their presence felt. They possessed too much skill for Athenry and proceeded to the final by 5–7 to 2–2.

With both sides littered with All-Ireland senior medal holders and personalities of the game, the meeting of Glen Rovers and St Paul's in the final at Glen Rovers Grounds was eagerly awaited. The match was packed with incident and the lead changed hands regularly. Both sides played great camogie and the scores started to flow. Glen Rovers had the better balanced and more skilful team but in Angela Downey, St Paul's possessed a proven match-winner.

Glen seemed to be heading for an emphatic win when Angela struck with two brilliant goals to wipe out their advantage. In a welter of excitement, Sandie Fitzgibbon burst forward from midfield to put the Glen a point ahead. In the remaining moments, St Paul's threw everything into attack to save the match and the Glen defence had to withstand severe pressure. Angela Downey suffered a nasty injury and had to leave the field. The referee sent Anne O'Donovan off as tension mounted. Glen hung on to achieve a cherished ambition by 4–11 to 5–7. There were many praiseworthy performances on both sides. Val Fitzpatrick, who was named Player of the Match, Therese O'Callaghan, Sandie Fitzgibbon and captain Mary Ring stood out for the Glen. Apart from Angela Downey, Bridie McGarry, Breda Holmes, Ann Downey and Clare Jones impressed for St Paul's.

Glen Rovers team: Fiona McCarthy, Mary Ring (captain), Diana Deane, Marie Ryan, Anne O'Donovan, Sandie Fitzgibbon, Val Fitzpatrick, Mary Currid, Anne Hourigan, Therese O'Callaghan, Ger McCarthy and June Hamill.

Roscommon – 1986 Connacht Junior Champions. Included are: Carmel Cribbins, Martina Waldron, Kathleen Naughton, Teresa Finneran, Patricia Finneran, Geraldine Finneran, Jacqueline Rodgers, Margaret Byrne (Capt), Ann Bevan, Mary Gannon, Ann Walsh and Ann Hynes.

St Paul's team: Maria Lawlor, Liz Neary, Annette Stapleton, Bridie McGarry, Helen Holmes, Clare Jones, Ann Downey, Caroline Holmes, Breda Ryan, Breda Holmes, Angela Downey and Mary Canavan.

1986 Gael-Linn Senior Cup

Munster had no difficulty defeating Ulster by 5–10 to 0–1 in one of the semi-finals at Glenalbyn, Dublin, but found Leinster to be a much tougher nut to crack. Goals from Angela Downey, Jo Dunne and Carmel O'Byrne put Leinster on the road to a 4–6 to 1–6 victory.

Leinster team: Marie Fitzpatrick (Kilkenny), Marion Conroy (Dublin), Tina Fitzhenry (Wexford), Bridie McGarry (Kilkenny), Biddy O'Sullivan (Kilkenny), Cathy Walsh (Dublin), Ann Downey (Kilkenny), Clare Jones (Kilkenny), Jo Dunne (Kilkenny), Carmel O'Byrne (Dublin), Angela Downey (Kilkenny) and Breda Holmes (Kilkenny).

Munster team: Marion McCarthy (Cork), Eileen Dineen (Cork), Mary Spillane (Cork), Helen Clifford (Limerick), Mary Ring (Cork), Anne Gleeson (Tipperary), Val Fitzpatrick (Cork), Sandie Fitzgibbon (Cork), Colette O'Mahony (Cork), Pauline McCarthy (Limerick), Linda Mellerick (Cork) and Anne Leahy (Cork).

Ann Reddy (Rathnure) about to tackle Edel Murphy (U.C.D.) in the final of the Mary Cahill Sevens in 1986.

Prize-winners at the Mary Cahill Sevens in 1986. From left are Gaye Moran (U.C.D.), Bridget Howlin (Rathnure), Bernie Higgins (Rathnure) and Breda Kenny (U.C.D.).

1986 Gael-Linn Junior Trophy

There was little between the four provinces in the Gael-Linn junior competition at Glenalbyn.

Leinster had two points to spare over Connacht in the semi-final and a single point in the final over Munster.

With five minutes remaining, Miriam Malone scored the decisive goal to leave the full-time score at Leinster 1–5, Munster 0–7.

Leinster team: Mary Doyle (Carlow), Geraldine Dwyer (Kildare), Melanie Treacy (Kildare), Anna Dargan (Kildare), Carmel Gray (Dublin), Esther Byrne (Wicklow), Kay Barry (Wicklow) (captain), Miriam Malone (Kildare), Nuala Smithers (Carlow), Geraldine Dunne (Dublin), Marianne Johnson (Kildare) and Valerie Crean (Carlow).

Munster team: Pauline O'Brien (Clare), Helen Cusack (Clare), Patricia Rynne (Clare), Noeleen Quinn (Clare), Niamh Coughlan (Cork), Karen Mellerick (Cork), Carmel Wall (Clare), Sheila O'Halloran (Clare), Catherine O'Loughlin (Clare), Maura McNicholas (Clare), Catherine Molloy (Clare) and Paula Carey (Cork).

Kilkenny On a Roll

Important Decisions

Congress returned to Limerick in 1987 when two important decisions were made.

Insurance had become a regular topic in camogie circles and several efforts had been made to introduce a compulsory scheme. The time was right and delegates voted to make the scheme mandatory.

The whole area of sponsorship was also debated. With ever-increasing costs of organising and promoting the game, congress approved a Dublin motion permitting the acceptance of sponsorship.

The size of the sponsor's logo and lettering allowing on players' jerseys was initially very small.

Wexford sought to have a delegate from each county on the Central Council but the motion was ruled out of order. Roscommon called for the selection of senior and junior All-Stars but the suggestion received little support.

The position of Newtownshandrum received lengthy attention. The club lies inside the Cork border but felt closer to the Limerick scene. Congress granted permission to the club to participate in Limerick competitions.

Leinster – 1986 Gael-Linn Senior Champions, Back: Ann Downey (Kilkenny), Marie Fitzpatrick (Kilkenny), Jo Dunne (Kilkenny), Breda Holmes (Kilkenny), Biddy O'Sullivan (Kilkenny) and Tina Fitzhenry (Wexford). Front: Clare Jones (Kilkenny), Marion Conroy (Dublin), Carmel O'Byrne (Dublin), Bridie McGarry (Kilkenny), Cathy Walsh (Dublin) and Angela Downey (Kilkenny).

Fifteen-a-Side Pilot Scheme

Many players and spectators had suggested that, because of the ever-increasing standard of camogie and players' fitness levels, a larger playing area was necessary and would provide greater scope for the participants and a more entertaining spectacle for supporters. An experiment, sponsored by Kilkenny, was put to the test over a weekend in the end of May. Six senior counties took part in a variety of matches with 12-a-side, 13-a-side and 15-a-side teams on a full-sized hurling pitch. Key people assessed the venture and questionnaires were completed by players, team officials, referees and all interested parties. The process towards a major change in the game was started.

Youth Convention

Seventy delegates in the 16–22 age-group attended the first National Youth Convention organised by the Camogie Association at Croke Park on November 14th 1987. Jo Golden, Treasurer of the Camogie Association; Liam Ó Maolmhichíl, Ard Stiurthóir of the G.A.A.; Mary Hanley, Primary Schools Council; Eoghan Corry, journalist; Donal McCartan, Ulster GAA Council; Angela Downey,

All-Ireland Kilkenny captain; Mary Fennelly, past-president; Bernie Farrelly, Kildare county player; Mary Moran, National PRO; and Deirdre Lane, former Tipperary captain, spoke on a variety of subjects. Lively debate ensued under the chairmanship of Liz Howard with the youthful members airing their views intelligently.

1987 All-Ireland Senior Championship

Two goals, powerfully struck by Irene O'Leary, late in the semi-final against Wexford at Monamolin earned Cork a place in the final by 2-10 to 1-6. Wexford led for much of the game but were overtaken on the run in.

Angela Downey gave a lesson in the art of score-taking from limited opportunities in the second semi-final between Kilkenny and Dublin at O'Toole Park and her sister, Ann, added two magnificent long-range points. Dublin were hard-working but uninspiring. Bridie McGarry and Biddy O'Sullivan dealt capably with what Dublin had to offer. Kilkenny advanced to the final by 3-9 to 0-6.

A number of newcomers had come on the Cork team since their previous visit to Croke Park. It was hoped that a side which

Irene O'Leary (Cork) slips as Rita Weymes (Kilkenny) comes into challenge in the 1987 All-Ireland final at Croke Park.

included Linda Mellerick, Anne Leahy, Mary Ring, Irene O'Leary, Liz Dunphy and Colette O'Mahony could pull it off on the big day. However, it was not to be. Kilkenny's big three – Angela Downey, Liz Neary and Bridie McGarry – dominated the final on September 27th and showed greater alertness, craft and tactical awareness. Kilkenny were a class apart.

Two palmed goals by Breda Holmes left Cork fighting an uphill battle. Angela Downey highlighted Cork's deficiencies at the back by finding time and space to knock over superb points. The selection and placing of Cork players drew criticism from their own supporters. Kilkenny claimed the title with an impressive 3-10 to 1-7 victory.

Christy Ring was marked by Shem Downey in the 1946 All-Ireland senior hurling final. In an amazing coincidence, their daughters, Mary Ring and Angela Downey, faced one another 41 years later.

Kilkenny team: Marie Fitzpatrick, Rita Weymes, Deirdre Malone, Bridie McGarry (captain), Biddy O'Sullivan, Clare Jones, Ann Downey (1-1), Anna Whelan, Jo Dunne, Liz Neary, Angela Downey (1-7), Breda Holmes (1-2).

Cork team: Marion McCarthy, Eileen Dineen, Mary Ring,

Anne Leahy, Linda Mellerick, Sandie Fitzgibbon, Clare Cronin, Liz Dunphy, Irene O'Leary (0–1), Val Fitzpatrick (captain) (0–4), Colette O'Mahony and Noelle O'Driscoll (0–1). Subs used: Mary Geaney (1–1), Cathy Landers Harnedy and Mary Spillane.

1987 All-Ireland Junior Championship

Accurate free-taking by Patricia Keatley, together with goals from Bernie Farrelly and Teresa Hanley, saw Kildare through to the All-Ireland junior final at the expense of Cork at Clane. Midfielders, Liz O'Neill, Karen Mellerick and Paula Carey found the Kildare net but it was not enough. Kildare were full value for their 3–12 to 3–5 victory.

Galway and Armagh had to meet a second time to decide which would go forward to the All-Ireland junior final. In the replay at Derrymacash, Armagh took control as the game wore on. Six well-struck points from Ursula McGivern had a big say in the final result, Armagh 1–9, Galway 2–3.

Nine players from St. Raphael's, Loughrea who won three All-Ireland Colleges senior medals, 1985-87. Back: Caroline Loughnane, Anne Fahy, Claire Robinson, Angela Cooney and Mary Dolphin. Front: Ger Fahy, Imelda Hobbins, Deirdre Costello and Bríd Stratford.

Anna Dargan (Kildare) clears the ball watched by Phyllis Bambury (Kildare) and Anne Donnelly (Armagh) in the 1987 All-Ireland junior final at Croke Park.

Former Limerick hurler, Pat Herbert, had Kildare in fine fettle for the All-Ireland junior final against Armagh in Croke Park. Unlike Armagh, who had some excellent players, Kildare played as a team. They worked the ball into scoring positions and finished the move with accuracy. Ahead by eight points at the interval, Kildare had to withstand a revival sparked by Ursula McGivern, Fionnuala O'Connor, Sally McCone and Mary Donnelly. Having lost the previous year's final, Kildare were not going to let this one slip away.

Miriam Malone, the Kildare number seven, showed why she was a regular for the Leinster team. Melanie Treacy, Marianne Johnson, Antoinette Merriman and Teresa Hanley also shone for the Lilywhites. It was a very proud Geraldine Dwyer who climbed the steps of the Hogan Stand to accept the first All-Ireland cup for Kildare. But spare a thought for Armagh. Since 1970, they had won six Ulster titles and made three All-Ireland final appearances but still awaited an All-Ireland crown. The final score was Kildare 2–10, Armagh 0–7.

Kildare team: Rose Merriman, Anna Dargan, Phyllis Bambury, Melanie Treacy, Geraldine Dwyer (captain), Antoinette Merriman, Miriam Malone (1–6), Patricia Keatley (0–1), Marianne Johnson (1–0), Bernie Farrelly, Teresa Hanley (0–2) and Nuala Kerrigan (0–1). Subs used: Kathleen Elliott and Teresa Farrelly.

Armagh team: Rita McGuigan, Maura Hosty, Fionnuala O'Connor, Sally McCone, Julie McGuinness, Ursula McGivern (0–2), Paula Brown (captain), Patricia Donnelly, Mary O'Hagan (0–4), Denise McStay, Brenda Jordan and Mary Donnelly (0–1). Subs used: Joan Green, Ann Donnelly and Jackie Donnelly.

1987 All-Ireland Minor Championship

Armagh sampled their first taste of All-Ireland minor semi-final fare when they lined out against Cork at Portmore. In the Ulster campaign, Armagh had cruised past Monaghan, Cavan and Down without a single goal being registered against them. A plucky Armagh outfit made Cork work very hard for a 2–6 to 1–2 victory.

Centre-back, Triona Dolphin, was a tower of strength for Galway in the second semi-final against Dublin. She broke up several Dublin attacks and contributed four points from frees to set Galway up for a 2–7 to 0–5 win.

Galway were quickly into their stride against Cork in the All-Ireland minor final at Church Road. Cork, on the other hand, were nervous and made uncharacteristic mistakes. The ability of the Galway attack to convert chances into points was the main difference between the sides. A one-point lead was not going to be enough for Cork as they faced the elements for the second-half. Galway continued to tap over points. A late goal by Fiona O'Driscoll give Cork hope but they ran out of time. The Galway side displayed skill, teamwork and maturity and each time that Mary Treacy, Aileen Brett, Bridget Fahy or Caitríona Finnegan gained possession, a score looked on. Some of the Cork players did not do justice to themselves on the day but were not found wanting for lack of effort. Galway deserved their 1–11 to 3–3 win.

Galway team: Colette Callagy, Caroline Linnane, Martina Dooley, Triona Dolphin (0–3), Siobhán Keane, Imelda Maher, Suzanne Burke, Fionnuala Keane, Caitríona Finnegan, Mary Treacy (captain) (0–2), Aileen Brett (1–2) and Bridget Fahy (0–4).

Cork team: Marie O'Brien, Denise Cronin, Claire Barry, Fiona

Congress 1987 in Limerick. Front: Sheila Wallace (Árd Runaí), Mary Lynch (President) and Jo Golden (Treasurer). Back: Fr. J. Ryan, Helen Sheehy, Eithne Neville, Bríd Stokes, Bernie O'Dea, Carmel O'Driscoll and Tommy O'Brien.

Kilkenny On a Roll

O'Driscoll, Eileen Buckley, Hilda Kenneally, Niamh Cotter, Imelda Leahy, Lynn Dunlea (0–1), Claire O'Regan, Elaine Barry-Murphy (1–0) and Fiona O'Driscoll (2–2). Subs used: Valerie Ellis and Karen Higgins.

1987 All-Ireland Club Championship

St Paul's were always in control against Glenamaddy in the semi-final of the All-Ireland Club Championship. They had the better and more prized set of forwards. Any time Glenamaddy scored, St Paul's immediately tacked on a few points to remain in front and were 2–15 to 2–4 ahead at the finish.

Glen Rovers were made to look very ordinary by Eglish (Tyrone) in front of their own supporters in the second semi-final. The Eglish players exposed all sorts of shortcomings in the Glen team and the visitors were unlucky not to pull off what would have been a major coup. Glen had to call on all their years of experience to extricate themselves from disaster by 3–8 to 4–4.

Good camogie was out of the question as both Glen Rovers and St Paul's had to endure torrential rain, a biting wind and a surface that cut up badly in the final at Ballyragget. The outcome of the game was decided as early as the sixth minute of the second half. Ann Downey dropped a free into the square that was only partially cleared and which was quickly returned to the unmarked Breda Holmes who palmed it to the net. As conditions continued to deteriorate, scores were harder to come by, though the players still worked courageously in the energy-sapping conditions. The Glen forwards were unable to engineer a much-needed goal against heroic defending by the St Paul's rear-guard. The Kilkenny club captured their sixth All-Ireland title by 1–4 to 0–5.

St Paul's team: Maria Lawler, Catherine Neary, Liz Neary, Bridie McGarry, Helen Holmes, Clare Jones, Ann Downey, Geraldine Ryan, Caroline Holmes, Breda Holmes (captain), Angela Downey and Breda Ryan.

Glen Rovers team: Fiona McCarthy, Anne O'Donovan, Mary Ring, Marie Ryan, Diane Deane, Sandie Fitzgibbon, Val Fitzpatrick (captain), Mary Currid, Therese O'Callaghan, Claire McCarthy, June Hamill and Ger McCarthy.

1987 Gael-Linn Senior Cup

In a one-sided semi-final at Clane, Leinster made light work of Munster by 5–6 to 0–7. The four goals and five points scored by Angela Downey paint the story of the game. In the second semi-final, Connacht had nine points to spare over Ulster in a very creditable performance.

The final was a romp in the park for Leinster. Displayed a greater appetite for work, Leinster signalled their intent from the off and won with ease on a score of 8–11 to 0–5 for Connacht at Silver Park, Dublin.

Leinster team: Marie Fitzpatrick (Kilkenny), Rita Weymes (Kilkenny), Mairéad Cronin (Dublin), Bridie McGarry (Kilkenny), Biddy O'Sullivan (Kilkenny), Una Crowley (Dublin), Ann Downey (Kilkenny), Clare Jones (Kilkenny), Carmel O'Byrne (Dublin), Edel Murphy (Dublin) (captain), Angela Downey (Kilkenny) and Breda Holmes (Kilkenny).

Connacht team: (All Galway) Anne Murray, Angela Cooney, Geraldine Heavey, Bríd Stratford, Julie Glynn, Anne Coleman, Mary Kelly, Teresa Raftery, Anne Fahy, Anne Ryan (captain), Deirdre Lawless and Sheila Coen.

1987 Gael-Linn Junior Trophy

Munster had the narrowest of margins 2–5 to 0–10 over Leinster in the semi-final at Clane. In the final against Ulster at Silver Park, they continued to live dangerously and emerged victorious by 2–6 to 2–5.

Munster team: Rose Desmond (Cork) (captain), Mairéad Treacy (Limerick), Patricia Toomey (Limerick), Evelyn Healy (Cork), Orla Flynn (Waterford), Karen Mellerick (Cork), Frances Broderick (Limerick), Patricia Barry (Waterford), Irene O'Keeffe (Cork), Paula Carey (Cork), Therese O'Callaghan (Cork) and Jean Paula Kent (Cork).

Ulster team: Josie McLoughlin (Tyrone), Jean McQuillan (Derry), Anne Daly (Tyrone), Sarah Ann Quinn (Derry), Sally McCone (Armagh), Rosemary Treanor (Down), Margaret Carroll (Cavan), Catherine Daly (Tyrone), Maureen McAleenan (Down), Patsy Quinn (Derry), Sheila Burke (Tyrone) and Denise McStay (Armagh).

Máire Ní Cheallacháin Elected President

From Dripsey in Co. Cork, Máire Ní Cheallacháin was elected President of the Camogie Association at Congress 1988 in Monaghan. Máire had served as chairperson of the Cork County Board and the Munster Council. Her interests stretched beyond camogie to encompass Irish culture, drama, question times and debating.

London Return

Kildare-born Mary Noonan travelled from London to put the case for the inclusion of a London team in the All-Ireland Junior Championship. She was delighted with the warm response to her request and it was felt appropriate that London should enter at the quarter-final stage. A uniform to reflect the four provinces was agreed upon. Green skirts, white jerseys with blue and gold hoops distinguished the London team.

Congress Matters

Kilkenny presented a very detailed report on their pilot scheme for the future of the game. They arrived at the conclusion that the playing strength would require to be increased to 15 to cover the hurling-size pitch. However, due to an oversight, a motion to increase the team numbers to 15 was omitted. They were left with no option but to withdraw the entire scheme.

Congress agreed to extend the time of inter-county senior and junior championship matches to 60 minutes but rejected a motion to permit banding of hurleys. Each county was directed to appoint a youth officer and hold a Youth Convention.

The commission set up by President Mary Lynch presented a detailed report and recommendations to a Special Congress in November 1988. The members saw an obvious weakness in administration from Central Council to county-board level in that the majority of time was taken up by routine matters. Development and promotion of the game suffered as a consequence. Greater use of sub-committees and the appointment of non-Central Council personnel were recommended. A call was made to have a public relations firm carry out a once-off examination of the Association and submit recommendations with a view to: improving the image and increasing match attendances; setting up of county development committees; making a video of camogie skills; establishing a national fundraising committee and an All-Ireland Intermediate Championship; making the use of helmets compulsory; and the upgrading of coaching programmes and county youth seminars.

Millennium Games

Dublin GAA Board's contribution to the celebration of the Dublin Millennium in 1988 was the staging of special games in Croke Park on May 15th. Dublin teams challenged the Rest of Ireland in hurling, camogie and football. The occasion presented an opportunity for camogie players to be selected on a Rest of Ireland team for the first time. In the days prior to the introduction of the Camogie All-Stars, selection on the Rest of Ireland team was considered to be a great honour.

The organisers stipulated that the Rest of Ireland selectors should choose three players from each of the seven senior counties to form a panel of 21. The match proved to be a good advertisement for the proposed 15-a-side game and showed how the top players could effectively display their skills on the full-sized

Rest of Ireland team 1988. Back: Sandie Fitzgibbon (Cork), Noeleen Quinn (Clare), Anne Ryan (Galway), Clare Cronin (Cork), Breda Holmes (Kilkenny), Mary McMullan (Antrim) and Mary Kelly (Galway). **Front:** Elsie Cody (Wexford), Linda Mellerick (Cork), Gertrude O'Leary (Wexford), Pauline O'Brien (Clare), Angela Downey (Kilkenny) (Capt), Ann Downey (Kilkenny), Pauline McCarthy (Limerick) and Catherine O'Loughlin (Clare).

pitch. The Rest of Ireland proved too strong for Dublin and won by 4–6 to 1–5.

Rest of Ireland team: Pauline O'Brien (Clare), Mary McMullan (Antrim), Ann Downey (Kilkenny), Noeleen Quinn (Clare), Elsie Cody (Wexford), Clare Cronin (Cork), Linda Mellerick (Cork), Sandie Fitzgibbon (Cork), Mary Kelly (Galway), Catherine O'Loughlin (Clare), Breda Holmes (Kilkenny), Angela Downey (Kilkenny) (captain), Anne Ryan (Galway), Gertrude O'Leary

(Wexford) and Pauline McCarthy (Limerick). Reserves (all played): Helen Sheehy (Limerick), Mary Lundy (Antrim), Siobhán McAtamney (Antrim), Catherine Murphy (Wexford), Mary Lenihan (Limerick) and Angela Cooney (Galway).

1988 All-Ireland Senior Championship

Kilkenny brushed aside the Galway challenge in the semi-final at Glenamaddy by 3–19 to 1–4. There was no sign of a waning appetite as Kilkenny pushed forward for a four-in-a-row. A multi-talented outfit, they were strong in every sector of the field and excellently prepared by Tom Ryan.

Clare Cronin, Colette O'Mahony and Sandie Fitzgibbon controlled midfield in the second semi-final at Ballinlough and provided the Cork attack with sufficient good ball to beat Wexford by 2–9 to 2–2.

Cork got off to a flying start in the All-Ireland final against Kilkenny at Croke Park on September 14th when Anne Leahy flicked the ball past a hesitant defence. The goal roused the Cats. Goals from Breda Holmes, Clare Jones and Angela Downey left Kilkenny nicely placed at the break. In their efforts to get back into the game, Cork rushed their shots and ended with a total of 17 wides, but they kept trying, and a brace of goals from Mary Geaney and Mary Spillane brought them to within a score of the champions. Once again, Kilkenny lifted their game and drove relentlessly to the finish. But for the brilliance of Marion McCarthy in the Cork goal, the gap would have been much wider than Kilkenny 4–11, Cork 3–8.

Kilkenny goalkeeper, Marie Fitzpatrick, finds her way blocked by Mary Spillane (Cork) in the 1988 All-Ireland senior final at Croke Park. Deirdre Malone (Kilkenny), Mary Geaney (Cork) and Frances Rothwell (Kilkenny) are also in the picture.

Kilkenny team: Marie Fitzpatrick, Biddy O'Sullivan, Helen Holmes, Deirdre Malone, Frances Rothwell, Clare Jones (1–1), Ann Downey (0–4), Anna Whelan, Breda Cahill, Breda Holmes (2–1), Angela Downey (captain) (1–3) and Jo Dunne (0–1). Sub used: Marina Downey (0–1).

Cork team: Marion McCarthy, Mary Ring, Mary Spillane (1–0), Cathy Harnedy, Anne O'Donovan, Sandie Fitzgibbon (0–1), Clare Cronin, Colette O'Mahony (0–1), Anne Leahy (1–0), Linda Mellerick (0–3), Irene O'Leary and Mary Geaney (1–3). Sub used: Liz Dunphy.

The London team which played Limerick in the All-Ireland junior championship quarter-final at Bruff in 1988. Back: Theresa Finneran, Julie Drumm, Majella O'Neill, Christine O'Malley, Emer Duane, Mary Whelan, Triona McKenna, Bernie Lyons, Theresa Aherne and Carmel Dunne. Front: Laura Dolan, Aisling Jenkins, Caroline McNamara, Trisha Ryan, Anne Foudy, Brenda Daffy (Capt), Margo Cassidy, Rita Francis and Liz Roberts.

1988 All-Ireland Junior Championship

London were welcome visitors to Bruff where they surprised Limerick with a fast-moving brand of ground play in the quarter-final of the All-Ireland Junior Championship.

With the influx of Irish girls seeking employment, many of whom had previously represented their native counties, London were in a position to field a strong side. Limerick played with more spirit and urgency in the second-half to win by 2–6 to 0–3.

The fright that Limerick received from London smartened them up for the visit of All-Ireland champions, Kildare, to Ballybrown in the semi-final. Great marksmanship by Pauline McCarthy, who shot 1–8, was a major factor in Limerick's progress to the final by 1–10 to 2–6.

Galway had plenty to spare over Down in the second semi-final at Ballyholland and won comfortably by 4–8 to 1–5.

Galway won the All-Ireland junior final for the fourth time when they defeated Limerick by five points at Croke Park. They owed their victory to the ability of Imelda Hobbins to poach scores together with the efficiency of the defence in which Triona Dolphin, Rita Coen and Geraldine Heavey were magnificent. Limerick had the benefit of a stiff breeze in the opening half but failed to score from play.

Ida Quaid brought Limerick back into contention with a well-worked goal. The decisive score came when Ann Coleman's long, speculative shot rested in the net to leave the final score Galway 3–4, Limerick 1–5.

Galway team: Joan Whoriskey, Rita Coen, Triona Dolphin, Geraldine Heavey (captain), Geraldine Fahy, Suzanne Burke, Anna Carthy, Ann Coleman (1–1), Margaret Greally, Mary Treacy, Hilda Flannery and Imelda Hobbins (2–3). Sub used: Mary Morrissey.

Limerick team: Helen Sheehy, Marguerite Guiry, Elizabeth O'Grady, Mairéad Treacy, Helen Clifford, Mary Lenihan, Frances Broderick, Elizabeth O'Sullivan, Maisie Clifford (0–5), Pauline McCarthy, Ida Quaid (1–0) and Angela O'Sullivan. Sub used: Ann Lenihan.

Marguerite Guiry's mother, Bunty Guiry, had played for Limerick and Munster for many years. Galway's Rita Coen (née

Divilly) married Tommy Coen who played in goal for the Galway senior hurlers.

1988 All-Ireland Minor Championship

Kilkenny qualified for their first All-Ireland minor final when they overcame Cork by 3–3 to 1–8 in a thrilling semi-final at Thomastown. Cork led for most of the game but goals from Bridget Mullally, Orla Ryall and Deirdre Lannon put paid to their chances.

Galway found themselves two goals down before they had settled into their positions in the second semi-final at Portmore. Armagh's ability to score goals was the deciding factor in their progress to the final on a score of Armagh 4–7, Galway 1–3.

The novel pairing of Armagh and Kilkenny met in the All-Ireland final at Portmore. The home side played with great drive and energy to control midfield. Had Armagh's finish been on a par with their approach play, a different result would have ensued.

Kilkenny made the most of limited possession. They brought Gillian Dillon to midfield where she was effective against Armagh's star player, Olive Leonard. Urged on by a huge home following, Armagh took the lead with a classic goal by Deirdre Connolly. Bridget Mullally was put through for a great goal by Sinéad Millea. The seesaw continued and the excitement built to a climax as the final whistle approached. In typical Kilkenny fashion, Deirdre Lannon and Mary McGrath notched goals to leave Kilkenny ecstatic and Armagh shattered. The scoreboard read Kilkenny 5–6, Armagh 2–5.

Kilkenny team: Veronica Wall, Bridget Barnaville, Una Murphy, Esther Kennedy, Gillian Dillon, Tracy Millea, Aisling Cullen, Geraldine Ryan, Bridget Mullally (1–4), Orla Ryall, Mary McGrath (2–0), and Deirdre Lannon (2–1). Sub used: Sinéad Millea (0-1).

Armagh team: Helen Mone, Catherine Browne, Yvonne McKenna, Mairéad Donnelly, Miriam Anderson (captain), Helena Murray, Colette Conway (1–0), Olive Leonard, Deirdre Connolly (0–1), Pauline McCreesh (1–0), Veronica Donnelly and Patricia McAvoy (0–4). Sub used: Donna McCuskar.

Galway – 1988 All-Ireland Junior Champions. Back: Anne Carty, Margaret Greally, Ann Coleman, Susan Burke, Triona Dolphin and Rita Coen. Front: Hilda Flannery, Mary Treacy, Geraldine Heavey (Capt), Imelda Hobbins, Geraldine Fahy and Joan Whoriskey

Kilkenny On a Roll

1988 All-Ireland Club Championship

Glenamaddy (Galway) enjoyed a period of dominance in the first-half of their All-Ireland club semi-final against Swatragh (Derry) and a comfortable lead of 1–5 to 0–1 at the interval. Swatragh stormed back to reduce the deficit but they had left themselves too much to do and ran out of time. Glenamaddy advanced by 2–6 to 2–3.

There was little between St Paul's and Killeagh in the second semi-final at St John's Park until the closing minutes. St Paul's closed with a flurry of scores to secure a place in the final by 4–9 to 4–2. Ann Downey played a major role for the winners, putting 2–6 on the scoreboard. However, all the drama came after the match had finished. In the referee's report, Angela Downey and Breda Kelly (Killeagh) were reported for striking and, following an investigation, both players were suspended for six months. The newspapers highlighted the affair and were critical of the length of the sentence.

St Paul's lined out in the final without the services of Angela Downey. Her team-mates were anxious to fill the void and played with great grit and determination. Glenamaddy, however, put it up to the champions and whittled away at the six-point lead that St Paul's had amassed. The champions had some agonising moments before Ann Downey settled the issue with a fine shot to the top corner of the net to leave the score St Paul's 4–5, Glenamaddy 3–7.

St Paul's team: Maria Lawlor, Catherine Neary, Sarah Russell, Bridie McGarry, Ann Downey, Helen Holmes, Clare Jones (captain), Caroline Holmes, Geraldine Ryan, Breda Ryan, Breda Holmes and Miriam Holland.

Glenamaddy team: Patricia Mitchell, Kathleen Garvey, Rita Coen (captain), Maureen Fahy, Claire Wall, Alva Baxter, Mary Kelly, Teresa Raftery, Margaret Greally, Ann Gallagher, Anne Fahy and Kathleen Comer.

1988 Gael-Linn Senior Cup

Leinster enjoyed a runaway win, 8–9 to 0–2, over Ulster in the semi-final of the Gael-Linn Senior Cup at Ballyholland, Co. Down, and Connacht surprised Munster with a merited 3–10 to 1–7 at Killimor, Co. Galway. Leinster extended their impressive unbeaten run to six years with a 2–9 to 2–4 win over Connacht in the final at Silver Park, Dublin.

Leinster team: Marie Fitzpatrick (Kilkenny), Elsie Cody (Wexford) (captain), Germaine Noonan (Dublin), Mairéad Cronin (Dublin), Biddy O'Sullivan (Kilkenny), Clare Jones (Kilkenny), Ann Downey (Kilkenny), Anna Whelan (Kilkenny), Eileen Kehoe (Wexford), Breda Holmes (Kilkenny), Angela Downey (Kilkenny) and Anne Cooper (Dublin).

Connacht team: (All Galway) Patricia Mitchell, Sheila Coen, Julie Glynn, Bríd Stratford, Kathleen Garvey, Teresa Raftery, Mary Kelly, Ann Coleman, Imelda Hobbins, Deirdre Costello, Anne Ryan and Bridie Cunniffe.

1988 Gael-Linn Junior Trophy

Munster had a rewarding hour against Connacht at Killimor and came away with a 3–7 to 1–2 victory. They then won their third successive Gael-Linn Junior Trophy by a single point, 4–3 to 3–5, against Leinster at Kilmacud, Dublin. Irene O'Keeffe, Mary Lenihan, Fiona O'Driscoll and Pauline McCarthy were the main players for the winners.

Munster team: Maria O'Brien (Cork), Helen Cagney (Limerick), Evelyn Healy (Cork), Frances Broderick (Limerick), Marguerite Guiry (Limerick) (captain), Angela O'Sullivan (Limerick), Breda Kelly (Cork), Liz O'Sullivan (Cork), Mary Lenihan (Limerick), Fiona O'Driscoll (Cork), Irene O'Keeffe (Cork) and Pauline McCarthy (Limerick).

Leinster team: Rose Merriman (Kildare), Anna Dargan (Kildare), Patsy Murphy (Dublin), Melanie Treacy (Kildare), Carmel Gray (Dublin) (captain), Eileen Crehan (Louth), Miriam Malone (Kildare), Esther Byrne (Wicklow), Bernie Farrelly (Kildare), Ger Dunne (Dublin), Margaret Ryan (Carlow) and Adele Campbell (Dublin).

Where We're At

For years, the Camogie Association held a conservative view on the subject of sponsorship and, in particular, the imprinting of sponsor's name on jerseys. Supporters of sponsorship felt that camogie was losing out to other sports by not accepting what was on offer. Sponsors were prepared to put money into sport, but they wanted something in return. The anti-sponsorship camp wondered if pride in the jersey would ever be the same and were loath to accept outside influences. However, with the cost of running club and county teams increasing each year, the majority voted to take the money. Camogie officials were soon to find that Irish companies would queue up to be associated with the glamour of male sport, but were extremely reluctant to take out their chequebooks to support women's sport.

An event that continued to grow and prosper and never lost its magic is that wonderful festival of hurling, camogie and handball, Féile na nGael. It matches, if not surpasses, any other annual occasion on the camogie calendar for excitement, colour and enjoyment. Camogie came on board in 1974 with four teams participating in the competition. Year by year, Féile has evolved and expanded and there is huge competition within counties to secure a place at the national finals.

It is a weekend that young players remember fondly for the rest of their lives. The host clubs do their utmost to ensure that the visiting clubs are warmly welcomed. Lasting friendships are made and return visits planned. Young players get the opportunity to test themselves against their peers from different parts of the country.

The wonderful people who coach these youngsters are passionate about the game and pass on all that is best in camogie. The skill, talent and whole-hearted endeavour of the teams are a pleasure to watch. It is fascinating to attempt to pick out the young stars and note their names for future reference.

Organising such a huge programme of events is a major undertaking. There is incredible voluntary effort from coaches, club officials, parents, referees, administrators and host families to put it all together. It is heartening to know that there is still a great volume of people in our communities willing and ready to give their time to help our young players enjoy their sport and prepare them for sterner tests in the years ahead.

Chapter Seventeen

KILKENNY MOTOR ON

With camogie facing challenges from other activities in winter time, indoor/mini camogie was introduced and provided an enjoyable game for the participants. Where playing pitches were not available or during inclement weather, the modified version of the field game was a boon. Any hall or gym could be adapted to suit, depending on the numbers present.

Lightweight plastic sticks and a soft ball replaced hurleys and sliothar. With no stoppage allowed for balls crossing the endlines or sidelines, the players enjoyed a fast, all-action exercise.

Ashbourne Programme

The main talking point at the Ashbourne Cup weekend at University of Ulster, Jordanstown, was not the action on the playing fields but rather what appeared in the official programme.

Material in the form of pen-pictures of the participating college teams was considered crude and unfit for publication and Central Council judged that the publication brought the Association into disrepute. Following an investigation, 36 members were suspended for three months.

Slow Progress with History

The History Committee – comprising Eilish Redmond, Iney Leonard, Nell McCarthy, Kathleen O'Duffy and Máire Bhreatnach – was appointed in 1985 and requested to research the history of the Camogie Association. Four years later, they reported back advising that research up to 1930 had been completed. They were asked to take it to the next level and write the history of the period that had been studied. However, the project did not advance any further.

A smiling Ann Downey (Kilkenny) with the O'Duffy Cup after her team defeated Cork in the 1989 All-Ireland senior final at Croke Park.

1989 All-Ireland Senior Championship

Kilkenny won as they pleased against a poor Dublin outfit in the semi-final at Nowlan Park. Such was the unrelenting high standard of Kilkenny that Dublin appeared ragged and disorganised. The match was over as a contest long before the end and the final score read Kilkenny 5–14 Dublin 0–2.

Betty Joyce shook Cork out of their lethargy with a brilliant display in midfield against Wexford in the second semi-final at Monamolin. A tremendous second-half display by the Rebels yielded goals from Ger McCarthy, Betty Joyce and Cathy Landers and saw off the Wexford challenge by 4–7 to 2–7.

Cork used a sweeper in a bid to contain the Kilkenny attack when facing the wind in the All-Ireland final at Croke Park on September 24th. The ploy had limited success and left Cork with a lot to do in the second-half. Linda Mellerick raised Cork's hopes with a goal on the resumption. Ann Downey drove a 15-metre free into a crowded goalmouth. The shot was parried but Ann followed up to drive the ball home.

A shot from Angela Downey took a wicked deflection to place it out of the reach of Cork goalie, Marion McCarthy. Angela put a nail in Cork's coffin when she raced in to rob Marion McCarthy of possession. Liz O'Neill made a desperation tackle on Angela but only succeeded in grabbing her skirt. The Kilkenny ace, unperturbed at losing part of her clothing, sprinted past two defenders to plant the ball in the Cork net. She celebrated the goal before retrieving her skirt. The superior stickwork, accuracy and teamwork of the Kilkenny side kept the O'Duffy Cup Noreside for another year. The scoreboard read Kilkenny 3–10, Cork 2–6 at full-time.

Kilkenny team: Marie Fitzpatrick, Biddy O'Sullivan, Deirdre Malone, Bridie McGarry, Frances Rothwell, Clare Jones, Ann Downey (captain) (1–4), Anna Whelan, Marina Downey (0–1), Breda Cahill (0–3), Angela Downey (2–1) and Breda Holmes (0–1).

Cork team: Marion McCarthy, Liz Dunphy, Liz O'Neill, Cathy Harnedy, Mags Finn, Clare Cronin, Therese O'Callaghan, Sandie Fitzgibbon, Linda Mellerick (1–0), Betty Joyce (captain) (0–3), Ger McCarthy (1–1) and Colette O'Mahony. Sub used: Irene O'Leary (0–2).

1989 All-Ireland Junior Championship

Galway and Cork were level on four occasions during the semi-final of the All-Ireland Junior Championship at Bullaun, before Fiona O'Driscoll cut the deficit to the minimum with three

Marina Downey (Kilkenny) and Mags Finn (Cork) strive to gain possession of the ball. Sandie Fitzgibbon watches progress on right.

minutes left. However, Emer Hardiman caught the puck-out, sprinted past the Cork defence and hand passed to the net to give Galway a 4–5 to 2–10 victory.

Kildare continued their unbeaten run but had very little to spare over a keen Down outfit at Ballyholland. A brave young Down side were not far behind at the finish, 4–7 to 3–7.

The Galway selectors relied to a great extent on players who had made history with St Raphael's, Loughrea, to replace the successful 1988 team for the All-Ireland final against Kildare at Croke Park. The credentials of the Kildare team were most impressive. Undefeated in 12 games in the 1989 season, they carried the favourite's tag, but Kildare's reputation counted for nothing in the minds of the young Galway players. They kept their heads and ate away at a Kildare lead that had built up when playing with the aid of a strong breeze. Galway caught Kildare on the line.

Following a mundane first-half, Galway had no answer to the unerring accuracy of Kildare's Miriam Malone in the replay at Birr. Miriam finished with 1–11 to her name. Kildare captain, Bernie Farrelly, Geraldine Dwyer and Teresa Hanley had a major say in the destination of the New Ireland Cup. Imelda Maher was outstanding for Galway. She received good support from Yvonne Larkin, Caitríona Finnegan, Cora Curley, Alice Murphy and Emer

Tipperary full-back, Jovita Delaney pulls first-time on the ball while Sinéad Millea (Kilkenny) comes in to challenge in the 1989 All-Ireland minor final at Semple Stadium.

Hardiman but they could not match the drive of Kildare. The final score was Kildare 3–11, Galway 1–3.

Kildare team: Anna Dargan, Claire Maloney, Phyllis Bambury, Melanie Treacy, Theresa Farrelly, Antoinette Merriman, Miriam Malone, Patricia Keatley, Marianne Johnson, Bernie Farrelly (captain), Teresa Hanley and Rose Merriman.

Galway team: Colette Callaghy, Mary Dolphin, Eilish Kilkenny, Imelda Maher, Bridget Fahy (captain), Caitríona Finnegan, Cora Curley, Fionnuala Keane, Carmel Duane, Aideen Murphy, Alice Murphy and Emer Hardiman.

1989 All-Ireland Minor Championship

In a repeat of the 1988 minor final, Kilkenny faced Armagh in the All-Ireland semi-final at St John's Park. When Kilkenny tacked on two points to the half-time score of 3–5 to 1–1, it seemed that the Cats were about to sail on. However, they had to endure some anxious moments before winning by 3–8 to 1–7.

The respective forward lines were well on top in the second semi-final between Galway and Tipperary at Kilcoleman. The teams registered a combined score of 11 goals 18 points, some of which were beautiful scores. Six Tipperary players got in on the goal-scoring act to propel their side to the final by 8–8 to 3–10.

Some of the most attractive camogie is played by minors. When two traditional counties meet in an All-Ireland minor final, a feast of classic striking, a parade of skills and some great scoring take place. This was the case when Tipperary and Kilkenny met at Semple Stadium in the 1989 decider.

Fifteen-year-old Bridget Mullally etched her name into the history books with a staggering personal tally of 6–7. With such a gifted scorer in their ranks, it was no wonder that Kilkenny defeated Tipperary to take their second title. Apart from Bridget, Kilkenny had top-class players in Aisling Cullen, Gillian Dillon, Sinéad Millea and Brigid Barnaville. Deirdre Hughes, Claire Madden, Marita Tobin and Neasa O'Dwyer tried hard for a gallant Tipperary side. Kilkenny 9–10, Tipperary 3–8 was the final score.

Many links existed between these teams and famous GAA stars. Both Bridget Mullally and her brothers, Richie and Paddy, progressed to win All-Ireland senior medals with Kilkenny. Joe Millea watched his two daughters, Tracy and Sinéad. Pa Dillon was pleased to see his daughter, Gillian, add to the family collection of All-Ireland medals. Orla Ryall is a daughter of Kilkenny GAA historian, Tom Ryall.

Kilkenny – All-Ireland Minor Champions 1989. Back: Áine Dunne, Bridget Wall, Aisling Cullen, Orla Ryall, Bridget Mullally and Gillian Dillon. Front: Siobhán Holden, Anita White, Sinéad Millea, Tracey Millea (Capt), Bridget Barnaville and Una Murphy.

On the Tipperary side, Donie Nealon cheered on his two daughters, Sinéad and Nuala, while Mick Burns encouraged his daughter, Ciara.

Kilkenny team: Siobhán Holden, Brigid Barnaville, Bridget Wall, Una Murphy, Áine Dunne, Aisling Cullen (0–1), Tracy Millea, Gillian Dillon (0–1), Bridget Mullally (6–7), Orla Ryall, Anita White (1–0) and Sinéad Millea (2–1). Subs used: Patricia Treacy, Edel Murphy and Vanessa Butler.

Tipperary team: Sinéad Nealon, Jovita Delaney, Róisín Nash, Claire Madden, Marita Tobin, Orla Hogan (0–5), Lorraine Graham, Deirdre Hughes (2–1), Nuala Nealon, Helen O'Leary (1–0) and Neasa O'Dwyer (0–2). Sub used: Ciara Burns.

1989 All-Ireland Club Championship

Mullagh captured the Galway Senior Championship for the first time backboned by players who won National Féile na nGael titles in 1985 and 1986. In four short years, these players had matured from promising under-14s to serious challengers for the All-Ireland club title. They were pitted against Sixmilebridge in the semi-final at the venue of the Co. Clare club and emerged with one point to spare, 2–6 to 3–2.

Kilkenny Motor On

The old saying "goals win matches" proved very true in Swatragh where the local side took on champions, St Paul's, at the semi-final stage. While Swatragh won a lot of possession and registered more scores than St Paul's, it was goals that made the difference. St Paul's advanced to the final by 5–6 to 1–11.

It was a case of David versus Goliath in the final at Nowlan Park. Newcomers, Mullagh, faced the multi-talented outfit that was St Paul's. Big performances from Ann Downey, Breda Holmes and Angela Downey ensured that Mullagh would have to wait a little longer to make the breakthrough. While not threatening to knock the champions off their perch, Mullagh acquitted themselves quite well. St Paul's retained their title by 6–10 to 4–2.

St Paul's team: Maria Lawlor, Catherine Holmes, Helen Holmes, Bridie McGarry, Catherine Neary, Clare Jones, Ann Downey, Geraldine Ryan, Breda Ryan, Breda Holmes, Angela Downey and Noelle O'Driscoll.

Mullagh team: Kathleen Coen, Eilis Kilkenny, Mary Dolphin, Brigid Fahy, Madge Kennedy, Cora Curley, Triona Dolphin, Emer Hardiman, Aideen Murphy, Alice Murphy and Imelda Hobbins.

1989 Gael-Linn Senior Cup

Munster overwhelmed Ulster in the semi-final of the Gael-Linn Senior Cup by 9–10 to 1–4 at Burren, Co. Down, but failed to deal with Leinster's dangerous forwards and paid the price in the final at Silver Park. Kilkenny players, Angela Downey, Breda Holmes, Ann Downey and Clare Jones, made up the bulk of Leinster's 5–12 to which Munster replied with 3–6.

Leinster team: Marie Fitzpatrick (Kilkenny), Biddy O'Sullivan (Kilkenny), Cathy Walsh (Dublin), Bridie McGarry (Kilkenny), Eileen Kehoe (Wexford), Clare Jones (Kilkenny), Ann Downey (Kilkenny), Stellah Sinnott (Wexford), Anna Whelan (Kilkenny), Ann Reddy (Wexford), Angela Downey (Kilkenny) and Breda Holmes (Kilkenny).

Munster team: Marian McCarthy (Cork), Liz Dunphy (Cork), Irene O'Leary (Cork), Noleen Quinn (Clare), Mags Finn (Cork), Mairéad Toomey (Clare), Therese O'Callaghan (Cork), Siobhán Reidy (Clare), Colette O'Mahony (Cork), Yvonne McInerney (Clare), Betty Joyce (Cork) and Orla Flynn (Waterford).

1989 Gael-Linn Junior Trophy

Leinster were full value for a comfortable 3-12 to 0-14 win over Connacht in the first semi-final at Clane and, in the second semi-final at Burren, Ulster caught Munster on the line to advance by 1–12 to 4–2.

Sarah Ann Quinn and Mary Donnelly were the stars of Ulster's 1–11 to 2–3 victory in the final at Silver Park.

Ulster team: Laura O'Prey (Down), Anne Coyle (Down), Ita McKiernan (Cavan), Sarah Ann Quinn (Derry), Catherine Daly (Tyrone), Bríd Doherty (Derry), Margaret Carroll (Cavan), Olive Leonard (Armagh), Maureen McAleenan (Down), Monica McCartan (Down), Mary Black (Armagh) and Mary Donnelly (Armagh).

Leinster team: Anna Dargan (Kildare), Claire Moloney (Kildare), Phyllis Bambury (Kildare), Melanie Treacy (Kildare), Antoinette Merriman (Kildare), Anne Byrne (Wicklow), Miriam

Malone (Kildare), Esther Byrne (Wicklow), Bernie Farrelly (Kildare), Valerie Crean (Carlow), Nora Maguire (Dublin) and Aileen Redmond (Dublin).

Closer Liaison with GAA

In November 1987, the GAA sought a meeting with the top officials of the Camogie Association with a view to a closer liaison between the two organisations, even though a high level of co-operation already existed: the Camogie Association was almost entirely dependent on the generosity of the GAA in the area of playing pitches and facilities; office accommodation was provided to the Camogie Association in Croke Park; and a growing number of Camogie clubs were integrated with GAA clubs.

President Mick Loftus, Ard Stiurthóir Liam Mulvihill and president elect, John Dowling, sat down with officials of the Camogie Association. Dr Loftus explained that the GAA had sought the meeting with a view to discussing ways and means of involving the ladies to a greater extent in the organisation. They considered that great participation would be to the mutual benefit of all concerned. Both organisations were committed to the same ideals. It was not the intention of the GAA to absorb the Camogie Association or have the Camogie Association lose its identity as an association. It would continue to be completely autonomous in the running of its affairs. It was agreed that both parties would, after discussions with their own associations, present proposals for discussion.

A considerable section of the public and indeed some of our own members were surprised to learn that the Camogie Association was a separate organisation from the GAA. Opinion was divided about what stance should be taken. The majority believed that our autonomy should be preserved irrespective of what form of amalgamation took place. Dublin tabled a motion to Congress 1990 in Navan "That Cumann Camógaíochta na nGael enter into discussions with a view to affiliating with Cumann Luthchleas Gael". However, it was withdrawn on condition that discussions between the two organisations would continue and counties would be kept informed.

A Decade of Growth

A comparison of statistics between 1980 and 1990 showed considerable growth in the number of units affiliated and playing the game. The number of clubs had increased from 370 to 468. Two additional third-level Colleges had affiliated and 28 extra secondary schools were competing in the All-Ireland Colleges' Championships. But the area showing the largest expansion was the

Group pictured on the steps of City Hall, Manhattan during the visit of the Kilkenny and Cork teams to New York in 1990

primary schools. During the 1980s, camogie had been introduced to an extra 194 primary schools.

Kilkenny and Cork Off to U.S.A.

The Young Ireland's Camogie Club, New York, extended an invitation to Kilkenny and Cork teams to travel to New York and play exhibition games as part of their 30th anniversary celebrations in October 1990. This progressive club had promoted Irish culture and Gaelic games in New York. The players did not have to be asked twice and knuckled down to fundraising for the trip.

Kathleen McDonagh, a founder member of the New Ireland's Club, was the driving force behind the organising committee. She had gathered a great team of workers around her, including Bernie Linnane, Breege Lavery, Theresa Goodwin, John Byrne, Noreen Fleming, John Houlihan and the genial Connie Riordan. From the moment the teams landed at Kennedy Airport, the enterprising organising committee looked after their visitors with exceptional care. Warm-up matches against Young Ireland's and a US Selection at Van Cortlandt Park resulted in comfortable victories for the visitors. Temperatures soared in the eighties as Kilkenny and Cork took the field for the first leg of the Helen O'Donnell Cup at Gaelic Park. Buckets of ice and salt tablets were on hand for the wilting players. Kilkenny drew clear to win by 3–8 to 0–5.

A great catch by Wexford's Tina Fitzhenry in the 1990 All-Ireland senior final at Croke Park. Bridget Mullally (Kilkenny) and Elsie Cody (Wexford) are the players on the left.

With the first-round matches over, the holiday aspect of the tour got into full swing. Some players looked up relatives while others visited Boston, Washington or other cities. Broadway shows, the Circle Tour, Ellis Island, the giant department stores and other tourist attractions were fitted in. The social highlight was the Gala Banquet at the Tower View Ballroom.

Action resumed at the weekend. Cork played with great spirit against Kilkenny in the second leg of the Helen O'Donnell Cup and fully deserved their 1–4 to 0–6 win. The destination of the trophy was decided by sudden death. Kilkenny shot three points without reply in the limited time to claim the cup. All too soon time ran out and the moment came to pack the bags. The players headed home with happy memories of a wonderful trip and full of praise for the hospitality of their hosts. The courage, generosity and organisation of the Young Ireland's Club in staging such a huge undertaking were tremendous.

1990 All-Ireland Senior Championship

Kilkenny were lucky to hold on to their All-Ireland crown in the All-Ireland semi-final against Cork at Ballinlough. All the action was packed into the final ten minutes, after a goal by Linda Mellerick had edged Cork in front. The turning point came when Irene O'Leary was pulled to the ground as she broke through on the Kilkenny goal. To the consternation of the large crowd, the Dublin referee awarded the free to Kilkenny. Goalkeeper, Marie Fitzpatrick, drove the ball all the way to the Cork net and Liz O'Neill regained the lead for Cork. However, Marion McCarthy could only parry a dropping ball from Ann Downey. Marina Downey was on hand to tap the ball into the net to see Kilkenny advance by 4–4 to 3–5.

Wexford looked the more competent side in the second semi-final against Dublin at O'Toole Park. Indeed, the difference in the scoreline could have been much greater had Wexford punished Dublin at every opportunity. Siobhán Dunne, Angie Hearne and Paula Rankin got the goals that mattered in Wexford's 4–9 to 3–7 win. Two late goals by Barbara Redmond took the bare look off Dublin's score. Twins, Angela and Ann Downey, scored over two-thirds of Kilkenny's total in the All-Ireland final against Wexford at Croke Park on September 23rd 1990 and finished the day with 20 All-Ireland medals evenly divided between them. Ann had a tremendous game in midfield and made a massive contribution to Kilkenny's sixth title in-a-row. Elsie Cody, the only Wexford player remaining from their 1975 All-Ireland success, curtained Angela Downey to a certain degree. Kilkenny finished 1–14 to 0–7 ahead at the close of a dour contest.

Camogie President, Brídín Uí Mhaolagáin, speaking at the 1990 All-Ireland senior final. Árd Runaí, Sheila Wallace, President Mary Robinson and Kilkenny captain, Angela Downey await the presentation of the cup.

Kilkenny team: Marie Fitzpatrick, Biddy O'Sullivan, Deirdre Malone, Bridie McGarry, Frances Rothwell, Clare Jones, Ann Downey (0–7), Gillian Dillon, Breda Cahill, Breda Holmes (captain) (0–1), Angela Downey (1–2), Bridget Mullally (0–2). Subs used: Marina Downey (0–2), Anna Whelan and Noelle O'Driscoll.

Wexford team: Eilis Kavanagh, Tina Fitzhenry, Elsie Cody, Catherine Murphy (0–3), Stellah Sinnott, Ann Reddy (captain), Christine Harding, Joan O'Leary, Siobhán Dunne (0–4), Eileen Kehoe, Jackie Codd and Angie Hearne. Subs used: Paula Rankin and Ann Marie O'Connor.

1990 All-Ireland Junior Championship

Triona Bonnar, a member of the well-known hurling family from Cashel, arrived late at the All-Ireland junior semi-final between Tipperary and Armagh at Thurles. She joined the fray in the second-half and swung the game around in Tipperary's favour by 3–7 to 1–8.

Kildare had no difficulty in their semi-final against Roscommon at Clane. Roscommon were no match for the vastly experienced Kildare side and conceded by 4–13 to 0–3.

With a nice blend of former seniors and emerging talent from the minor ranks, Tipperary faced Kildare in the All-Ireland junior final at Croke Park. In terms of experience of the big occasion, Kildare had a decided advantage. On the general run of play, Tipperary were not far behind Kildare, but in front of goal, they had shortcomings.

Tipperary turned over with a four-point deficit but expected to make good use of the strong wind. Kildare put in a wholehearted and energetic display to open a gap between the sides. It seemed to be all over when Teresa Hanley goaled but Tipperary put in a storming finish to whittle the margin to four points. However, the clock beat Tipperary and they came up short by 2–14 to 3–7.

Kildare team: Anna Dargan, Geraldine Dwyer, Theresa Farrelly, Melanie Treacy, Phyllis Bambury, Antoinette Merriman, Miriam Malone (captain) (0–7), Bernie Farrelly (0–3), Marianne Johnson, Patricia Keatley (0–1), Teresa Hanley (2–2) and Rose Merriman (0–1). Sub used: Liz O'Donoghue.

Tipperary team: Ann Keeshan, Jovita Delaney, Cora Kennedy, Geraldine Ryan, Claire Madden, Maeve Stokes, Kirsty McCluskey, Kaiffee Moloney, Deirdre Hughes (2–1), Triona Bonnar (0–1), Orla Hogan, Anne Gleeson (captain) (0–4). Subs used: Helen O'Leary (1–1) and Regina O'Meara.

Kilkenny – 1990 All-Ireland Senior Champions. Back: Angela Downey, Ann Downey, Frances Rothwell, Gillian Dillon, Deirdre Malone and Breda Cahill. Front: Bridget Mullally, Bridie McGarry, Breda Holmes (Capt), Marie Fitzpatrick, Biddy O'Sullivan and Clare Jones.

1990 All-Ireland Minor Championship

Bridget Mullally was a highly influential member of the Kilkenny minor team that defeated Galway in the semi-final at Kilkenny. Since her heroics in the 1989 All-Ireland final, she had been called up for duty by the Kilkenny senior team in the National League. She practically beat Galway on her own, scoring 1–9 in Kilkenny's 1–10 to 2–6.

Tipperary were untroubled by Derry in the second semi-final

at Cashel. The home side was superior in all departments and won by 2–14 to 0–1.

The loss of Sinéad Millea, who was recovering from an appendix operation, was a severe handicap to Kilkenny in the final against Tipperary at Nowlan Park. Tipperary dominated midfield when backed by a strong wind during the opening half. Thanks to the accuracy of free-taker Jovita Delaney and a 16th minute goal from Ciara Burns, Tipperary built up a half-time lead of 1–9 to 0–2. Kilkenny put in a huge effort on the resumption which yielded 1–2 and goals from Vanessa Butler and Siobhán Dooley also brought Kilkenny back into contention. Tipperary had to hang on for dear life in the hectic final minutes to win by 2–11 to 3–6.

The final whistle was greeted with great jubilation and rejoicing by Tipperary officials and supporters. Almost seventy barren years had come to an end. Tipperary had, at last, won an All-Ireland crown.

Tipperary team: Chrissie Kennedy, Maria Hogan, Sinéad Nealon, Marita Tobin, Róisín Nash, Neasa O'Dwyer, Lorraine Graham, Caroline Dooley, Helen Kiely (0–1), Jovita Delaney (0–7), Ciara Burns (1–1) and Áine Hogan (1–2). Sub used: Jacqueline Keating.

Kilkenny team: Siobhán Holden, Paula Dowling, Imelda Kennedy, Marie Maher, Bridget Wall, Patricia O'Keeffe (0–1), Áine Dunne, Janet Sweeney, Elizabeth Dermody, Orla Ryall, Vanessa Butler (1–0) and Bridget Mullally (1–5). Subs used: Siobhán Dooley (1–0) and Margaret Comerford.

1990 All-Ireland Club Championship

Glen Rovers made a 300-mile trip to face Swatragh in the semi-final of the All-Ireland Club Championship. Poor shooting by the Glen attack and a superb display by Mairéad McAtamney in the Swatragh goal denied the Munster side on several occasions. At the other end of the pitch, the Glen defence, ably marshalled by Sandie Fitzgibbon, dealt effectively with anything that came their way. The Cork girls advanced by 1–9 to 0–0.

Mullagh showed considerable improvement in 12 months and seriously challenged St Paul's in the second semi-final at Mullagh. Egged on by a large and very vocal home crowd, Mullagh were only a point adrift entering the final quarter. The experienced visitors increased the tempo and match-winning scores followed. Clare Jones had a massive game for Paul's and was well supported

Wexford – All-Ireland senior runners-up 1990. Back: Jackie Codd, Elsie Cody, Catherine Murphy, Tina Fitzhenry and Christine Harding. Front: Angie Hearne, Eilis Kavanagh, Jean O'Leary, Ann Reddy (Capt), Eileen Kehoe, Stellah Sinnott and Siobhán Dunne

by Ann Downey, Helen Holmes and Angela Downey. St Paul's, chasing their ninth national title, entertained fierce rivals, Glen Rovers, in the final at Nowlan Park. It was the third time that the sides had met in a final. With the exception of Liz Neary, who had retired, the St Paul's team had changed little since their previous meeting. The Glen side had lost Marie Ryan, who had retired, and Val Fitzpatrick, who had moved to Boston. Linda Mellerick and Claire McCarthy, two Cork senior players, had joined the team and Denise Cronin had won promotion from the junior team.

Bearing in mind the hectic clashes that these two clubs had in the past, no one predicted a four-goal drubbing for the champions. Glen travelled with massive support. On the day, St Paul's had no answer to the skill and determination of the Cork club. Sandie Fitzgibbon was an inspirational figure at centre-back. Ger McCarthy struck 2–11 in a faultless display and Linda Mellerick added 2–2. The final score was 4–13 to 2–7 in favour of Glen Rovers.

A glorious era in the history of St Paul's had come to an end. A team built around some of the most talented players in the game had brought a record eight All-Ireland Club Championship titles to Kilkenny.

Glen Rovers team: Fiona McCarthy, Mary Ring, Diane Deane, Sandie Fitzgibbon, Mary Currid, Therese O'Callaghan (captain), Deirdre McCarthy, Ger McCarthy, Linda Mellerick, Denise Cronin and June Hamill.

St Paul's team: Maria Lawlor, Caroline Holmes (captain), Clare Jones, Bridie McGarry, Helen Holmes, Ciara Holmes, Ann Downey, Geraldine Ryan, Breda Ryan, Breda Holmes, Angela Downey and Noelle O'Driscoll.

1990 Gael-Linn Senior Cup

It took a last-minute goal by Munster's Patricia O'Grady to snatch victory from Leinster in the Gael-Linn senior semi-final at Farranlea Road. In a match of championship intensity, both teams played fast, lively camogie and kept within touching distance of one another. Ulster overcame the concession of two early goals to dispatch Connacht in the semi-final at Loughrea.

The Gael-Linn final day belonged to Patricia O'Grady. A brilliant solo performance by the Clare girl yielded a personal tally of 9–1 to shatter the hopes of the Ulster side at Ballyholland. The goalkeeper turned full-forward could do no wrong and kept finding the Ulster net right through the game. The match came to a close with the score at Munster 10–10 Ulster 1–2.

Munster team: Marion McCarthy (Cork), Liz Dunphy (Cork) (captain), Paula Goggins (Cork), Breda Kenny (Cork), Siobhán Reidy (Clare), Therese O'Callaghan (Cork), Colette O'Mahony (Cork), Linda Mellerick (Cork), Mairéad Toomey (Clare), Irene O'Leary (Cork), Liz O'Neill (Cork) and Patricia O'Grady (Clare).

Ulster team: Mairéad McAtamney (Antrim), Mary McMullan (Antrim), Olive Scoir (Cavan), Teresa Allen (Down), Donna O'Loughlin (Antrim), Grace McMullan (Antrim), Deirdre O'Doherty (Derry), Elaine McMonagle (Derry), Sinéad O'Kane (Derry), Monica Woolahan (Derry), Mary Devine (Donegal) and Anne McGrath (Donegal).

1990 Gael-Linn Junior Trophy

Paula Carey, Jean Paula Kent and Mary Lenihan hammered home goals for Munster in the Gael-Linn junior semi-final against a Kildare-dominated Leinster side at Farranlea Road. Munster turned the screw with a dozen points to win by 5–12 to 3–6. Ulster proved too good for a disappointing Connacht outfit in the semi-final at Loughrea.

Ulster got nothing easy from Munster in the final at Ballyholland. Every score was hard-earned as two committed sides battled it out to claim the trophy. Maureen McAleenan, Bríd Doherty and Olive Leonard exerted continual pressure to earn a 5–11 to 5–3 victory.

Ulster team: Laura O'Prey (Down), Anne Coyle (Down), Ita McKiernan (Cavan), Sally McCone (Armagh), Bernie McGlone (Derry), Monica McCartan (Down), Margaret Carroll (Cavan), Olive Leonard (Armagh) (captain), Maureen McAleenan (Down), Ellen Donnelly (Armagh), Bríd Doherty (Derry) and Rosita McCabe (Cavan).

Munster team: Ann Keeshan (Tipperary), Marguerite Guiry (Limerick), Mairéad Treacy (Limerick), Evelyn Healy (Cork), Claire Madden (Tipperary), Denise Cronin (Cork), Marie Collins (Clare), Ann Lenihan (Limerick), Jean Paula Kent (Cork), Mary Lenihan (Limerick), Deirdre Hughes (Tipperary) and Paula Carey (Cork).

Brídín Uí Mhaolagáin Elected President

Brídín Uí Mhaolagáin was elected President of the Camogie Association at Congress 1991 in Cork. Educated at St Louis, Monaghan, and UCD, Brídín taught in Ballymun Comprehensive School. Brídín came to the job via Comhairle Camógaíochta Ard-Oideachais.

Group pictured at the Young Irelands, New York victory dinner in October, 1991. Back: Breige Lavery, Noreen Fleming, Immigration Chaplin, Mary O'Dea, Bridie Gregory, Peter Tuohy, Mike Keane, Jackie Salmon, Joe Murphy and Treasa Goodwin. Front: Kathleen McDonagh, Kerry O'Donnell, Danny Healy, Mike Kelly, Bridie O'Neill McManus and John Byrne.

Ashbourne Cup for Queens

Queen's University Belfast entered the Ashbourne Cup for the first time in 1934 and, for 57 years, they gave of their best without success. A side, excellently prepared by Bernie McNally, set the scene alight at Turloughmore in February 1991. They put on an exhibition of direct and highly effective camogie to lower the colours of the three national universities in turn and leave nobody in any doubt that they were worthy champions. Tipperary girl, Joan Tobin, Róisín O'Neill, Deirdre Canning, Monica McCartan, Mary Black and captain, Deirdre O'Doherty made a significant contribution to the historic victory.

Intermediate Championship Introduced

The idea of an All-Ireland Intermediate Championship received the unanimous backing of congress. The new grade was introduced to bridge the gap between senior and junior ranks. The plan was to seed the senior counties in the All-Ireland championship. Teams from the strong or seeded section were drawn against the remaining counties in the first round. The winning teams progressed to the semi-finals of the senior championship. The losing sides entered for the Intermediate Championship together with the All-Ireland junior champions of the previous year. While only five teams went into the hat for the inaugural intermediate championship draw, the competition grew with the annual addition of the All-Ireland junior champions.

Congress decided to allow London enter their champions in the All-Ireland Club Championship but said no to the idea of an All-Ireland Under-14 Championship.

Gillian Dillon (Kilkenny) crashes the ball to the Cork net in the 1991 All-Ireland senior final at Croke Park. Angela Downey (Kilkenny), Bridget Mullally (Kilkenny) and Liz Towler (Cork) are the other players in the picture.

1991 All-Ireland Senior Championship

Cork never looked like losing the All-Ireland semi-final against Galway at Ballinlough, but they were very wasteful, leaving coach, Joe McGrath, with plenty of work to do before the final. Galway fell short of what was required and yielded by 2–13 to 1–4.

In the second semi-final, Wexford were a point ahead at the interval against Kilkenny at Enniscorthy and faced the second-half with optimism.

But they were soon derailed by Ann Downey who took control of midfield. She put eight points on the board and carved openings for Breda Holmes and Gillian Dillon. Kilkenny proceeded to the final by 2–13 to 2–7.

President Mary Robinson lent a certain glamour and colour to All-Ireland day by her presence and the girls were delighted to line up to meet her. Cork had defeated Kilkenny in the National League final in June but that counted for nothing as the teams paraded at Croke Park on September 22nd. Cork won good possession in the opening 20 minutes but a tight-marking Kilkenny defence was unyielding. Breda Holmes and Gillian Dillon scored goals in the run-up to half-time.

Angela Downey drew a magnificent save from Marion McCarthy as play resumed. The Kilkenny ace opened the Cork defence a few minutes later. She palmed the ball into the path of Gillian Dillon who stroked it to the net. Cork continued to win possession in midfield but could not engineer the goals that they so badly needed. Kilkenny extended their impressive run to seven titles by defeating Cork 3–8 to 0–10. Six Kilkenny players had started in all seven All-Ireland finals – Angela Downey, Breda Holmes, Marie Fitzpatrick, Ann Downey, Biddy O'Sullivan and Deirdre Malone.

Down defenders, Anne Coyle and Laura O'Prey, stretch for a high ball in the 1991 All-Ireland junior final at Croke Park.

This Kilkenny side was a truly great combination and among the best ever to grace the camogie fields. They possessed all the ingredients of a team of real quality, superb skill, teamwork and fitness, in abundance. But the special component that set the team apart was their intense will to win. Never satisfied with prior achievements, they united to pursue their aim with unwavering dedication. The panel contained a glittering array of talent. Each player was a star in her own right and exhibited the full range of camogie skills in such fashion that made the team a pleasure to watch. Within the team were a number of superstars who rank with the best that the game has produced. The side was well coached by Tom Ryan, who had the knack of bringing out the best in every player.

Kilkenny team: Marie Fitzpatrick, Biddy O'Sullivan, Una Murphy, Deirdre Malone, Frances Rothwell, Marina Downey, Ann Downey (0–3), Gillian Dillon (2–0), Sinéad Millea, Bridget Mullally, Angela Downey (captain) (0–4) and Breda Holmes (1–1). Sub used: Tracy Millea.

Cork team: Marion McCarthy, Liz Dunphy, Paula Goggins, Breda Kenny, Liz Towler, Colette O'Mahony (0–3), Therese O'Callaghan (captain), Sandie Fitzgibbon (0–1), Linda Mellerick, Ger McCarthy (0–1), Liz O'Neill and Irene O'Leary (0–5). Sub used: Irene O'Keeffe.

1991 All-Ireland Junior Championship

Down put in a great second-half performance to see off the challenge of Galway in the All-Ireland junior semi-final at Loughrea. Maureen McAleenan and Bonnie McGreevy got the scores to book a place in the final by 2–7 to 1–5.

Although Tipperary ran up an impressive score of 5–12 in the second semi-final against Dublin at Blanchardstown, they had had to come from ten points behind. A tremendous rally earned a three-point win, leaving Dublin on the 5–9 mark.

Down bridged a 15-year gap to return to Croke Park. The Ulster county made the early running and went to the dressing room with the considerable advantage of 2–8 to 0–6. It was Tipperary's failure to score for 21 minutes that cost them the match. The break they needed came when a free by Jovita Delaney was deflected off a defender's stick to the net. When Joan Tobin slipped her marker to crack the ball home, Tipperary were in front.

As the seconds ticked away, Tipperary seemed to have done enough and had a hand on the cup. Bonnie McGreevy gathered the ball from the puck-out and burst forward towards the Tipperary goal. She crashed the ball to the net for the most sensational goal of her career. The final whistle sounded with the scoreboard showing Down 3–13, Tipperary 2–14. Teresa Allen, Maureen McAleenan, Bonnie McGreevy, Pauline Green and Nuala McCartan played very well for a team well prepared by Fionnuala McGrady and Bernie McNally.

Down team: Laura O'Prey, Anne Coyle (captain), Pauline Greene, Teresa Allen (0–1), Dolours Smyth, Isabel Oakes (1–0), Nuala McCartan, Bernadette Kelly (0–1), Maureen O'Higgins, Maureen McAleenan (0–8), Noreen O'Prey (0–1) and Bonnie McGreevy (2–2). Sub used: Valerie Hinds.

Tipperary team: Ann Keeshan, Jovita Delaney (1–0), Sinéad Nealon, Cora Kennedy, Claire Madden, Triona Bonnar (0–9), Kaiffee Moloney (captain), Orla Hogan, Deirdre Hughes (0–3), Joan Tobin (1–0), Anne Gleeson (0–1) and Helen O'Leary (0–1). Sub used: Geraldine Ryan-Meagher.

1991 All-Ireland Minor Championship

Kilkenny made light work of Cork in the semi-final of the All-Ireland Minor Championship at Ballincollig. Cork were unable to match the skilful and mature play of the Kilkenny girls. Sinéad Millea, who notched 4–3, proved to be the match-winner for the Noresiders. Kilkenny proceeded to the final by 5–4 to 1–2.

Galway had booked their place in the All-Ireland minor final long before the end of their contest with Antrim at Mullagh. Antrim had nobody to match the class of Sharon Glynn, Olivia Broderick or Dympna Maher and conceded by 6–11 to 0–4.

While no player makes a team on her own, the facts speak for themselves. Sharon Glynn registered 3–9 for Galway in the semi-final against Antrim while Sinéad Millea ran up 4–3 against

Down – 1991 All-Ireland Junior Champions

Cork. The All-Ireland minor final could have been subtitled the "Sinéad v. Sharon Show". As it worked out, both accounted for ten points of their respective scores. It was left to the remaining players to decide where the cup would rest. Imelda Kennedy chipped in with 2–3 while the Kilkenny defence contained the Galway forwards. Kilkenny won their third All-Ireland minor championship title in four years by 4–12 to 3–7. Sinéad Millea, Niamh Phelan, Imelda Kennedy, Paula Dowling and Margaret Hickey played major parts in their success.

Kilkenny team: Michelle Fennelly, Paula Dowling, Niamh Phelan, Margaret Hickey, Mary Brennan, Patricia O'Keeffe (0–2), Maria Maher (0–1), Joanne Dowling, Imelda Kennedy (2–3), Sinéad Costello (0–2), Margaret Comerford and Sinéad Millea (2–4). Subs used: Dolores Lanigan and Janet Sweeney.

Galway team: Ann Broderick (captain), Deirdre Hardiman, Elaine Conroy, Ann Dolan, Emer Doherty, Fiona Ryan, Sharon Glynn (1–7), Helen Ryan, Dympna Maher, Olivia Broderick, Brenda Daniels (2–0) and Martina Haverty. Sub used: Orla Watson.

1991 All-Ireland Club Championship

Mullagh dethroned All-Ireland club champions, Glen Rovers, at the semi-final stage in a cracking game at the Glen. The Galway side made the early running and, despite playing into a strong gale, led by 2–2 to 0–6 at the break. Mary Ring crashed home a 20-metre free to give hope to the Glen. Mullagh were not finished, stormed back and drew level. With time running out, Bridget Fahy pointed to give Mullagh a 2–6 to 1–8 victory.

Eglish celebrated the 25th anniversary of the founding of their club by qualifying for the final of the All-Ireland club championship. Well prepared by Harold Heron, the Eglish players impressed when defeating Dublin champions, Celtic, by 3–7 to 2–4 at Malahide Road.

Only eight years in existence, the Mullagh club achieved the pinnacle of success when Caroline Loughnane lifted the Bill Carroll Cup at the finish of the 1991 final at rain-soaked Ballinasloe. Many of the girls, who won the Galway under-12 final in the first year of the club's history, were now on the senior team. These girls were winners all the way up the ladder, both with the club and in the colours of St Raphael's, Loughrea, in colleges' camogie.

Founded by Dympna Hardiman, Mary Kilkenny, Mary Ferguson, Mrs Fahy and Mrs Dolphin, the Mullagh club achieved their dream in stunning fashion. From the outset, Mullagh took control of the final. Their performance was close to perfect. Eglish were static compared to the movement and stickwork of the win-

Munster Secretary, Rose Malone presenting the Munster Minor Cup to Colette Dennehy in 1991.

ners. Mullagh led by 2–11 to 0–0 at the interval and continued to pick off scores. It was a marvellous team display by Mullagh with every player dominating her sector of the field. The final score was Mullagh 4–13, Eglish 0–2.

Mullagh team: Caroline Loughnane (captain), Sheila Coen, Deirdre Hardiman, Brigid Fahy, Pamela Nevin, Madge Kennedy, Cora Corley, Triona Dolphin, Aideen Murphy, Imelda Hobbins, Alice Murphy and Emer Hardiman.

Eglish team: Mairéad Mason, Anne Mackle, Gráinne Daly, Mary Rose McGready, Nora McGready (captain), Ursula Jordan, Catherine Finnegan, Leona Fay, Una Donnelly, Ann McKenna, Brenda Burke, Anne Jordan.

1991 Gael-Linn Senior Cup

Connacht withdrew from the Gael-Linn semi-finals against Munster scheduled for Tramore. Leinster were not troubled by Ulster in the second semi-final at Navan. Leinster's domination of the interprovincial championship was disrupted by Munster in 1990. In the absence of Angela Downey, Munster had picked up a rare win. Not only was Angela back for the final but so was the work ethic that she demands from those around her. Angela scored 3–4 and Carmel O'Byrne chipped in with 2–1. Leinster regained the cup by 5–12 to 0–7.

Leinster team: Marie Fitzpatrick (Kilkenny), Biddy O'Sullivan (Kilkenny), Elsie Cody (Wexford) (captain), Cathy Walsh (Dublin), Catherine Murphy (Wexford), Ann Downey (Kilkenny), Gillian Dillon (Kilkenny), Marina Downey (Kilkenny), Miriam Malone (Kildare), Angela Downey (Kilkenny), Carmel O'Byrne (Dublin) and Stellah Sinnott (Wexford).

Munster team: Patricia O'Grady (Clare), Liz Dunphy (Cork), Paula Goggins (Cork), Sandie Fitzgibbon (Cork), Liz Towler (Cork), Yvonne McInerney (Clare), Therese O'Callaghan (Cork) (captain), Jean Paula Kent (Cork), Irene O'Leary (Cork), Irene O'Keeffe (Cork), Pauline O'Brien (Clare) and Liz O'Neill (Cork).

1991 Gael-Linn Junior Trophy

With many of Down's All-Ireland winning players in action, Ulster registered an impressive 4–9 to 0–8 win over Leinster in the semi-final at Navan. In the other semi-final, Munster went through in the absence of Connacht. Good approach work set up Ulster for goals by Sarah Ann McNicholl, Mary Black, Rosie Butler and Margaret Carroll in the final at O'Toole Park. Ulster seemed to have that little bit of extra time on the ball and were able to direct their shots accurately. Ulster reclaimed the Gael-Linn Trophy by 4–5 to 0–6.

Ulster team: Laura O'Prey (Down), Anne Coyle (Down) (captain), Nuala McCartan (Down), Teresa Allen (Down), Catherine Daly (Tyrone), Olive Leonard (Armagh), Margaret Carroll (Cavan), Bernadette Kelly (Down), Isabel Oakes (Down), Maureen McAleenan (Down), Bonnie McGreevy (Down) and Sarah Ann McNicholl (Derry).

Munster team: Patricia Toomey (Limerick), Evelyn Healy (Cork), Marguerite Guiry (Limerick), Agnes Sheehy (Limerick), Orla Hogan (Tipperary), Ann Lenihan (Limerick), Claire Madden

(Tipperary), Mary Lenihan (Limerick), Ann Skeahan (Tipperary), Fiona O'Driscoll (Cork), Anne Gleeson (Tipperary) and Deirdre Hughes (Tipperary).

Where We're At

Another decade had been completed in the history of the Camogie Association. What progress had been made in the 1980–1990 period?

In 1980, 370 clubs had been affiliated to the Camogie Association. Considering that the decade was one of high emigration, which forced some small clubs to amalgamate, the figure of 468 clubs on the books in 1990 was pleasing. All three colleges' councils forged ahead which augured well for the future. The primary schools more than doubled the number of affiliations and the second-level colleges welcomed an additional 30 entrants. Steady growth was reported in Britain but the game lost ground in America.

Eleven counties played senior championship early in the decade but four of them reverted to the junior ranks. Louth, Clare and Kildare captured All-Ireland championship honours for the first time. A wide disparity of standards remained within the junior grade. Coaching had become an integral part of the game and the benefits were obvious.

The decade had witnessed: the appointment of the first full-time official and the setting up of a central office; the publication of a short history of the Association; closer ties with the GAA; the holding of administration and development seminars, youth convention and medical/coaching conferences; and the setting up of Gradam Tailte and national camogie day. A start was made on the road to the 15-a-side game and indoor camogie was introduced. The latter provided an opportunity for players to practise their skills and to play the game throughout the entire year. Additional fixtures stretched the resources of referees to the limit.

Kilkenny ruled the roost on the inter-county field. A team of stars marched through the opposition claiming six All-Ireland senior titles. For good measure, they added the national senior league on five occasions. It was a very special Kilkenny side. The artistry and sheer class of Angela Downey, the leadership and silken skills of Bridie McGarry, the cool efficiency of Marie Fitzpatrick, the power play of Ann Downey, the clinical performances of Liz Neary in a variety of roles and the sweeping play of Biddy O'Sullivan made them a pleasure to watch. Cork were in second place and made history by taking a clean sweep of All-Ireland titles in 1980 and 1982. Killeagh, Buffers Alley, Crumlin and Glen Rovers reached the pinnacle of club championship camogie. Yes, good progress had been made but there were more hills to climb.

Chapter Eighteen

CORK ON POINTS SPREE

The Rules Committee presented a comprehensive document to Congress 1992 in Monaghan. With the ever-increasing cost of hurleys, it was no surprise that the use of metallic banding on sticks was permitted, however, the banding was required to be covered with adhesive tape to the referee's satisfaction. A number of motions, including the 'advantage rule' and carrying the ball a fourth step, were rejected, though they have since become part of the game.

Dublin sought to roll in the ball between the opposing number sevens in under-11 matches instead of the usual puck-out as many players in that age group were unable to strike the ball from the hand. Kildare attempted to ban scores from the hand, but there was no support for the idea. Kilkenny reintroduced the subject of the 15-a-side game on the full-sized hurling pitch. By a single vote, it was agreed to play the 1993 and 1994 National Senior League, National Junior League and Gael-Linn competitions as a test series so that all could observe the proposed set up over a period.

P. J. Fulham was elected national PRO. The Westmeath auctioneer holds the distinction of chairing both the GAA County Board and the Camogie County Board. Together with his wife, Maureen, who was Secretary of the Leinster Council, he worked for many years to promote the game in Westmeath and Leinster.

Rosina McManus stood down after 15 years as the hard-working secretary of the coaching committee. The days of a coach drawing from her own experience were gone. All had to comply with the planned requirements of the National Coaching and Training Centre in Limerick.

Former Dublin star, Kathleen Cody is welcomed to Croke Park by Sheila McAnulty (Down).

St Raphael's, Loughrea

St Raphael's, Loughrea, completed an amazing run of seven All-Ireland Colleges Senior championships from 1985–1992. They

277

won the admiration of all for their skilful brand of camogie. Superbly coached by Cyril Farrell and Sr Catherine, the team maintained a very high standard. In the area of skill training, their expertise was exceptional. During that time, the school produced many wonderful exponents of the game – Deirdre Costello, Claire Lynch, Pamela Nevin, Imelda Hobbins, and the Broderick, Hardiman and Maher sisters fall into this category and were a joy to watch, but there were many more.

1992 All-Ireland Senior Championship

For the first time since 1970, Cork took to the field without the familiar figure of Marion McCarthy. She left the scene following a wonderful innings that had yielded eight All-Ireland senior medals. Marion's shoes were filled by Kathleen Costine. Fiona O'Driscoll, Denise Cronin and Irene O'Keeffe were also drafted into the Cork team and a new role was allotted to Breda Kenny. Coach Joe McGrath

Faces in the crowd at the 1992 All-Ireland final. President Mary Robinson and her husband Nick flank Árd Runaí, Sheila Wallace. Mary Fennelly, Miriam O'Callaghan, Catherine Hoare, Rosina McManus and Sheila McAnulty can be seen.

Cork – 1992 All-Ireland Senior Champions. Back: Rose Desmond, Therese O'Callaghan, Paula Goggins, Kathleen Costine, Liz O'Neill, Breda Kenny and Liz Dunphy. Front: Linda Mellerick, Irene O'Keeffe, Colette O'Mahony, Sandie Fitzgibbon (Capt), Liz Towler, Denise Cronin and Fiona O'Driscoll.

invested massive time and effort in skill training.

Seven-in-a-row champions Kilkenny stepped into the lions' den at Ballinlough for the semi-final of the All-Ireland Senior Championship. On this occasion, the lions were ready and waiting and there were few chances in a close first-half. Angela Downey, who had given birth to her daughter a few weeks earlier, did not start but entered the fray shortly before half-time. Kilkenny threw everything at Cork in the first quarter of the second-half and were rewarded with a goal by Breda Holmes. Then, it was Cork's turn. Irene O'Keeffe was on hand to finish when a fierce shot by Denise Cronin was parried. Fiona O'Driscoll and Sandie Fitzgibbon struck points. When Marie Fitzpatrick picked the ball off the ground in a goalmouth melee, Colette O'Mahony stood up and drove the resultant free to the net to leave Cork with a cushion of six points. However, some serious defending had to be done before Cork

Cork On Points Spree

emerged with a 2-11 to 1-8 victory.

Kildare entered the All-Ireland Senior Championship for the first time. While scoring 3-5 against Galway, it was short of what was required. Much was expected from Galway as they faced Wexford in the semi-final at Loughrea. St.Raphael's had been churning out exceptional players and Mullagh held the All-Ireland club title, but they were not good enough on the day. An Ann Reddy goal gave Wexford the lead with the finishing line in sight and they held out for a 2-11 to 1-11 win.

The official referee's uniform came into vogue for the 1992 All-Ireland finals. Áine Derham (senior) and Maria Pollard (junior) stepped out on Croke Park looking very smart in the new design.

Released from the shadow of Kilkenny, the Cork players expressed themselves in the All-Ireland final against Wexford at Croke Park on September 27th, with a brilliant display of camogie. Wexford started brightly but had run their course by half-time when they trailed by four points. It was ten scores to one in the second-half as Cork opened up and took some classic points, particularly those struck on the run by Irene O'Keeffe in full flight along the sideline. Colette O'Mahony's free-taking technique and accuracy earned ten points. For 11 of the Cork 12, it was their first All-Ireland senior medal. Eight years of frustration dissolved for Sandie Fitzgibbon as she high-stepped up the Hogan Stand to receive the O'Duffy Cup. The final score was Cork 1-20 Wexford 2-6.

Cork team: Kathleen Costine, Breda Kenny, Paula Goggins, Therese O'Callaghan, Liz Towler, Linda Mellerick (0-2), Sandie Fitzgibbon (Capt), Denise Cronin, Irene O'Keeffe (0-4), Liz O'Neill (0-2), Colette O'Mahony (0-10) and Fiona O'Driscoll (1-2).

Wexford team: Terri Butler, Tina Fitzhenry, Jean O'Leary, Catherine Murphy (captain) (0-1), Deirdre Hearne, Máire Codd, Stellah Sinnott, Paula Rankin (1-0), Ann Marie O'Connor, Ann Reddy (0-2), Geraldine Codd (1-3) and Angie Hearne. Subs used: Eileen Dillon and Mary Hayden.

1992 All-Ireland Intermediate Championship

Dublin and Antrim, keen rivals for All-Ireland senior honours in

Wexford – 1992 All-Ireland Senior Finalists. Back: Ann Reddy, Geraldine Wynne, Terri Butler, Paula Rankin and Catherine Murphy (Capt). Middle: Eileen Dillon, Deirdre Hearne, Marion O'Leary, Tina Fitzhenry, Angie Hearne and Geraldine Codd. Front: Mary Hayden, Claire Cullen, Stellah Sinnott, Jean O'Leary, Ann-Marie O'Connor and Tina Farrell.

Sandie Fitzgibbon (Cork) was voted Player of the Year for her performances in 1992

past decades, faced one another in the semi-final of the All-Ireland Intermediate Championship at Portmarnock. They provided a gripping encounter that ended Dublin 3–13, Antrim 1–12.

Down and Clare served up a thrill-a-minute game in the second semi-final at Shannon. Neither team was able to affect any real dominance as the play produced score for score to the end. Down had their nose in front at the final whistle.

Down led by 4–3 to 0–10, with six minutes remaining on the clock, in the first All-Ireland intermediate final at Ballygalget. Then, Louise Lynch and Geraldine Dunne struck goals to leave the Down players shattered. Dublin had played poorly for much of the game and only the excellent goalkeeping of Louise Curry kept them in the contest. Cathy Walsh accepted the new Purcell Cup which was presented in memory of the late Agnes Purcell.

Dublin team: Louise Curry, Colette Murphy, Catherine Boyle, Cathy Walsh (captain), Miriam Mulligan, Ruth Lyons, Mary Dwane, Geraldine Dunne (2–7), Louise Lynch (2–1), Christine Lester, Pat Finneran (0–3) and Grace O'Neill.

Down team: Laura Smith, Ann Coyle, Donna Greeran, Teresa Allen, Dolores Smith, Bernie King (1–0) Nuala McCartan, Eileen Magorrian, Isabel Oakes (1–0), Maureen McAleenan (1–1),

Ciara Burns (Tipperary) is presented with the All-Ireland minor cup by Camogie President, Brídín Uí Mhaolagáin, August, 1992.

Coleen Hynes and Bonnie McGreevy (1–3).

1992 All-Ireland Junior Championship

Tipperary's greater craft saw them through against a spirited London side in the quarter-final of the All-Ireland Junior Championship at Ruislip. The Premier County was never in any trouble in the semi-final against Kilkenny at Ballyragget and advanced by 4–7 to 1–7.

Goals from Olivia Broderick and Cora Curley saw Galway defeat Armagh in the second semi-final at Loughrea.

The Tipperary players headed for Croke Park determined to make amends for the losses of the previous two years. With a display of quality camogie, Tipperary overwhelmed Galway. All 12 players made a major contribution to victory but none more than Deirdre Hughes. Galway did not play badly, but they came up against a side that no team would have lived with on the day. Tipperary claimed the New Ireland Cup with the impressive scoreline of 6–13 to 2–7.

Tipperary team: Ailish Delaney, Ann Marie Fitzgerald, Regina O'Meara, Cora Kennedy, Claire Madden, Triona Bonnar (captain), Kaiffee Moloney, Maeve Stokes, Deirdre Hughes (3–4), Joan Tobin (1–0), Sinéad Nealon (0–9) and Jovita Delaney. Subs used: Anne Gleeson (1–0) and Helen O'Leary (1–0).

Galway team: Colette Callaghy, Ursula Hannon, Yvonne Larkin, Bridget Fahy, Deirdre Hardiman, Caitríona Finnegan (1–0), Cora Curley, Dympna Maher, Olivia Broderick (1–6), Madge Kennedy, Teresa Fallon and Emer Hardiman (0–1). Subs used: Fiona Ryan and Catherine Harte.

1992 All-Ireland Minor Championship

Kilkenny and Tipperary needed two bites of the cherry to overcome the challenge of Antrim and Galway respectively. The value of home venues was emphasised as the winners performed much better on their own patch. It took a point from Caitríona Carey to snatch a draw at Casement Park but Kilkenny stamped their authority on the replay by 9–5 to 1–2.

A great second-half performance swept Tipperary to the All-Ireland minor final as the challenge of Galway faded at Holycross in the replay. Galway had the better of things in the opening half. Three goals from Anne Hardiman indicated a win for the visitors. There was only one team in it after the break. Ciara Gaynor, Marie Ryan and Ciara Burns piled on the scores to earn Tipperary a 7–9 to 4–3 passage to the final.

Tipperary knuckled down to the serious business of winning the final straight from the throw-in. Their forwards pounded the Kilkenny goal. Despite the heroic response from Kilkenny goalkeeper, Kathleen Ryan, the scores began to mount up. Ciara Burns showed great individual flair as she opened the Kilkenny defence and in general play around the field. The work rate of Catherine Bourke, Joanne Horgan, Aileen Delaney and Mandy Quigley was a key factor in Tipperary's success. Kilkenny contributed to a fine game but they could not match the fire power of their opponents. The final score was Tipperary 4–9, Kilkenny 1–3.

Tipperary team: Michelle Bulfin, Sheila Coyne, Aileen Delaney, Suzanne Kelly, Joanne Horgan, Alison Lawlor, Therese Brophy, Catherine Bourke, Marie Ryan (2–0), Ciara Burns (captain) (1–6), Mandy Quigley (1–3) and Ciara Gaynor. Sub used: Ann Barry.

Kilkenny team: Kathleen Ryan, Fran Shore, Niamh Phelan, Sinéad Costello (captain), Cora Mackey, Sandra Gleeson, Catherine Butler, Ann Hickey, Caitríona Carey, Margaret Kavanagh (1–0), Louise Slevin and Michelle Fennelly.

Ciara Gaynor is a daughter of All-Ireland Tipperary hurler, Len Gaynor. Caitríona Carey is a sister of All-Star hurler, D. J. Carey.

1992 All-Ireland Club Championship

Portglenone got off to a flying start against Glen Rovers in the semi-final of the All-Ireland Club Championship, delighting their large home following with two early goals. A goal from 45 metres by Sandie Fitzgibbon was the signal to the Glen to get going. Her colleagues responded and quickly got into their stride and the Cork girls raced away to an 8–17 to 4–2 victory.

Both Rathnure and Pearses had an added incentive to make a special effort in the club semi-final. A minute's silence was observed before the game in memory of Pat Reddy, brother of Rathnure midfielder, Ann Reddy. Pearses, on the other hand, wanted to do it for their star, Sharon Glynn who missed the game through suspension. Scores were hard-earned in a low-scoring game. Pearses edged in front at the start of the second-half and kept Rathnure scoreless for a full 30 minutes. Deep into added time, Bernie Higgins struck the vital equaliser. Geraldine Codd and Norma Carty popped over points to leave the score standing Rathnure 2–5, Pearses 1–6.

Fielding five of the players who had helped Cork to win the All-Ireland Senior Championship two months earlier, Glen Rovers were fancied to claim the title at the expense of Rathnure at the Glen Field. The star of the show, however, was not a Cork player but a Galway girl, Ann Coleman, sister of All-Ireland hurler, Michael Coleman. Ann had a magnificent hour in midfield in the most horrendous of weather conditions. Sandie Fitzgibbon, Therese O'Callaghan, Mary Ring and Linda Mellerick were hugely influential for the Glen. On the day, Rathnure were outplayed. They chased and harried to the finish, but were unable to mount a serious challenge to the home side. An exception was goalkeeper, Mary Fleming, who enhanced her reputation and kept the score to Glen Rovers 1–9, Rathnure 0–2.

Glen Rovers team: Mairéad O'Leary, Mary Ring (captain), Deirdre McCarthy, Sandie Fitzgibbon, Diane Deane, Mandy Kennefick, Therese O'Callaghan, Ann Coleman, Linda Mellerick, Denise Cronin, Patricia Murphy and Claire McCarthy.

Rathnure team: Mary Fleming, Catherine Murphy, Anna-Mai White, Mary Hayden (captain), Patricia Dreelan, Norma Carty, Eileen Dillon, Ann Reddy, Geraldine Codd, Lilian Doyle, Bernie Higgins and Bridget Howlin. Subs used: Jackie Codd and Anne English.

Action from Gael-Linn semi-final Ulster v Munster in 1992.

1992 Gael-Linn Senior Cup

Munster were not flattered by a five-point margin against Ulster in the semi-final at Holycross and won comfortably by 2–12 to 2–7. Leinster won as they pleased against a poor Connacht side at Turloughmore. Seven players contributed to the Leinster score of 6–14, to which Connacht replied with 1–3. Leinster surrendered their title in the final at O'Toole Park. Munster's ability to pick off points from far out was the deciding factor and gave them a comfortable 1–18 to 2–9 win.

Munster team: Kathleen Costine (Cork), Liz Dunphy (Cork), Liz Towler (Cork), Therese O'Callaghan (Cork), Denise Cronin (Cork), Linda Mellerick (Cork), Sandie Fitzgibbon (Cork) (captain), Irene O'Leary (Cork), Fiona O'Driscoll (Cork), Colette O'Mahony (Cork) and Catherine O'Loughlin (Clare).

Leinster team: Terri Butler (Wexford), Tina Fitzhenry (Wexford), Una Murphy (Kilkenny), Cathy Walsh (Dublin), Jean

Cork On Points Spree

O'Leary (Wexford), Stellah Sinnott (Wexford), Ann Downey (Kilkenny), Gillian Dillon (Kilkenny), Marina Downey (Kilkenny), Ann Reddy (Wexford), Angela Downey (Kilkenny) and Bridget Mullally (Kilkenny).

1992 Gael-Linn Junior Trophy

Deirdre Hughes was the star of Munster's win in the junior semi-final against Ulster at Holycross. She scored four goals in a one-sided game to see Munster advance by 5-6 to 2-7. Connacht shaded a close encounter with Leinster, 2-5 to 1-6.

The Munster juniors brought off their half of the double in style. They were good value for their 6-11 to 3-3 victory.

Munster team: Ailish Delaney (Tipperary), Marguerite Guiry (Limerick), Ann Marie Fitzgerald (Tipperary), Cora Kennedy (Tipperary), Claire Madden (Tipperary), Mairéad Treacy (Limerick), Bernie Chawke (Limerick), Triona Bonnar (Tipperary) (captain), Sinéad Nealon (Tipperary), Pauline McCarthy (Limerick), Lynn Dunlea (Cork) and Deirdre Hughes (Tipperary).

Connacht team: Maeve Healy (Roscommon), Brigid Fahy (Galway), Elaine Kenny (Galway), Carmel Allen (Galway), Deirdre Connaughton (Roscommon), Dympna Maher (Galway), Margaret Burke (Galway), Teresa Bracken (Roscommon), Olivia Broderick (Galway), Mary Gannon (Roscommon), Caitríona Finnegan (Galway) and Emer Hardiman (Galway).

1993 All-Ireland Senior Championship

Colette O'Mahony and Lynn Dunlea were the heroines of the high-scoring All-Ireland semi-final at Nowlan Park. Colette punished Kilkenny's indiscipline with a remarkable show of free-taking that yielded 3-5. Substitute Lynn shot the ball to the net when completely surrounded by Kilkenny defenders to see Cork win by 5-10 to 2-18.

Galway qualified for their first All-Ireland final since 1962 when they defeated Wexford in a high-scoring game at Duggan Park. Claire Lynch, Anne Ryan and Deirdre Costello, three highly skilled forwards, shot 5-5 between them. The accuracy of Siobhán and Fiona Dunne kept Wexford in touch but the verdict went to Galway by 5-7 to 2-13. Cyril Farrell, who had coached many of the girls at St Raph-

Sandie Fitzgibbon (Cork) and Tracey Millea (Kilkenny) seen in action in the National senior league final.

The crowd on the bank at Ballinlough enjoy the action between Kilkenny and Cork in the 1993 National Senior League

ael's, Loughrea, brought structure to the Galway scene when he took charge. Training was timed for 8 o'clock and players turned up in time whether they were fit, sick or injured. He used the wall at the back pitch in Loughrea before the 'hurling wall' concept was introduced and sharpened the first touch and striking skills of the players.

The final between Cork and Galway at Croke Park on September 26th was played against the backdrop of the partially demolished Cusack Stand. The game was much closer than the scoreline of Cork 3–15 Galway 2–8 suggests. Cork were more proficient at taking their scores. Lynn Dunlea, a lethal finisher, bagged 2–1 and Colette O'Mahony added six points. Kathleen Costine made a match-saving block from Claire Lynch at the key point of the game. This was a very young Galway team with an average age of 21 and playing in an All-Ireland final was a new experience for them.

Cork team: Kathleen Costine, Breda Kenny, Paula Goggins, Therese O'Callaghan, Liz Towler (0–1), Sandie Fitzgibbon (0–2), Denise Cronin (0–1), Linda Mellerick (captain), Irene O'Leary (0–1), Lynn Dunlea (2–1), Colette O'Mahony (0–6) and Fiona O'Driscoll (0–3). Sub used: Irene O'Keeffe (1–0).

Galway team: Tracy Laheen, Sheila Coen, Carmel Allen, Bríd Stratford, Pamela Nevin, Imelda Maher, Sharon Glynn (0–2), Dympna Maher (0–1), Anne Ryan (0–-1), Deirdre Costello (captain), Imelda Hobbins (0–1) and Claire Lynch (1–2). Subs used: Olivia Broderick (0–1) and Brigid Fahy (1–0).

1993 All-Ireland Intermediate Championship

Clare, who had the craftier set of forwards, qualified for the intermediate final by overcoming the strong challenge of Kildare at Ennis by 2–9 to 2–3. In the second semi-final at Bohernabreena, Dublin recorded a convincing win over Tipperary. Tipperary played well in the early part of the contest but, once Dublin got into their stride, there was only going to be one winner and it was Dublin 3–12 Tipperary 1–10 at the finish.

Moira McMahon was the outstanding player on view in the final at Cusack Park, Ennis, and her performance inspired Clare to push forward and claim the trophy. The match produced a high standard of camogie. The Clare side, excellently prepared by Fr Michael McNamara, showed the better teamwork and fully deserved their 1–8 to 1–5 victory. Tina O'Connell, Debbie McDonagh, Sylvia O'Brien and Frances Phelan also had big influences on the outcome. Geraldine Dunne, Una Crowley and Cathy Walsh worked very hard for Dublin.

Clare team: Áine McCormack, Tina O'Connell, Marie Collins, Debbie McDonagh, Marian Costello, Sinéad O'Brien, Sylvia O'Brien (1–1), Frances Phelan (captain) (0–3), Moira McMahon (0–1), Maura McNicholas (0–1), Noelle Comyns and Catherine O'Loughlin (0–2).

Dublin team: Louise Curry, Patsy Murphy, Geraldine Dunne (0–2), Veronica Trehy, Catherine Boyle, Una Crowley, Nora Maguire (captain), Adrienne McGovern, Cathy Walsh (0–2), Ruth Lyons (1–1), Denise O'Leary and Patricia Clinton.

Armagh – 1993 All-Ireland Junior Champions. Back: Tom Monahan (Trainer), Margaret Moriarty, G. Kehoe, Bernie McBride, Margaret McKee, Patricia McEvoy, S. Rice, Colette Byrne, Mary Black and Phil McBride (President of Armagh Co. Board). Front: Mary Donnelly, Áine Lennon, Ursula McGivern (Capt), Celine McGreary, Donna McCuskar, Ann Donnelly and Orlagh Murphy.

1993 All-Ireland Junior Championship

Two Galway goals in the final six minutes of the junior semi-final at Ballincollig ended Cork's challenge. Galway were the better equipped side and deserved to advance to the final.

Armagh had an easy passage in the second semi-final at the expense of Carlow at Myshall. The Leinster side were unable to match the skill and ability of Armagh but they ran up a sizeable score that would have won most games. The final score was Armagh 4–17, Carlow 2–10.

Without reaching the form which brought them the National Junior League earlier in the season, Armagh seemed to have snatched the All-Ireland junior title from Galway with a last-minute goal by Patricia McEvoy – but Galway were not finished. Captain Ursula Hannon slipped her marker and cracked the ball to the net to force a 3–9 to 3–9 draw.

Armagh won their first All-Ireland championship title when the sides renewed acquaintance at Breffni Park on October 10th. Urged on by a large band of supporters, Armagh were sharper in attack and more competent all-round. Galway were denied possession by a strong Armagh rearguard. What ball they did win was not put to the best use. Margaret McKee, in the Armagh goal, was equal to the best that Galway had to offer. Her side won by 2–10 to 0–6.

Armagh team: Margaret McKee, Margaret Moriarty, Sally McCone, Celine McGeary, Orlagh Murphy, Colette Byrne (0–1), Mary Black (0–1), Áine Lennon (0–1), Bernie McBride (0–2), Ursula McGivern (captain) (0–3), Donna McCuskar and Patricia McEvoy (1–2). Sub used: Mary Donnelly (1-0).

Galway team: Anne Broderick, Deirdre Hardiman, Olive Costello, Caitríona Finnegan, Yvonne Larkin, Carmel Hannon (0–2), Geraldine McGrath, Teresa Fallon, Denise Gilligan, Emer Hardiman, Ursula Hannon (captain) and Martina Harkin (0–4).

Margaret Moriarty is a sister of Paddy Moriarty who played football for Armagh and Ulster. Geraldine McGrath, who played hockey for Ireland, is married to All-Ireland hurler, Michael 'Hopper' McGrath.

1993 All-Ireland Minor Championship

Galway had a close shave from Kilkenny in the semi-final at Craughwell. Kilkenny were in front for most of the game but saw a last-minute shot, which would have altered the result, shave the post to leave Galway ahead by 3–5 to 2–6.

A masterly display by Tipperary in the opening half of the second semi-final against Down at The Ragg yielded a score of 4–6 to 0–0. Down improved on the resumption but could only cut the deficit to 7–9 to 2–5.

A pointed free by Anne Hardiman in the last minute of the All-Ireland minor final at The Ragg on July 25th gave Galway a deserved draw against Tipperary. A week later, Tipperary won a third All-Ireland minor title in four years at Ballinasloe. Galway enjoyed the better of the early exchanges and were ahead by 2–3 to 0–4 at the break. Ciara Gaynor blasted two shots to the Galway net to put a different complexion on the game. Both teams gave it everything in a bid to find the winner. When Tipperary half-forward, Anne Barry, found the net, victory was sealed. The game ended with the score at Tipperary 3–10, Galway 2–9.

Tipperary team: Susan Kineally, Sharon Lawton (0–1), Caroline Buckley, Marie White, Joanne Horgan (captain), Nicola Kennedy (0–1), Therese Brophy, Anne Barry (1–1), Mandy Quigley (0–2), Ciara Gaynor (2–4), Mary Looby and Gillian O'Neill (0–1).

Galway team: Erin Dolan, Olivia Coen, Teresa Murphy, Denise Gilligan (0–1), Esther Martyn, Aoife Lynskey, Áine Hillary, Goretta Maher (0–1), Colleen Crowe (2–3), Lorraine Fahy, Anne Hardiman (0–1) and Veronica Curtin (0–3). Subs used: Aisling Ward and Aoife Tannian.

1993 All-Ireland Club Championship

Four players – Ann Downey, Clare Jones, Angela Downey and Noelle O'Driscoll – who had helped St Paul's, Kilkenny, to win several All-Ireland Club Championship titles, made a second coming in the colours of Lisdowney, though their first assault on the club championship did not prove to be a happy one. Sandie Fitzgibbon curtailed Angela Downey to a single score in the semi-final against Glen Rovers at Blackpool. Denise Cronin and Therese O'Callaghan dominated midfield and created excellent opportunities for the Glen sharp-shooters, Lynn Dunlea (4–3), Claire McCarthy (1–2) and Linda Mellerick (0–4). Glen advanced by 6–10 to 2–3.

Mullagh got the better of Antrim champions, Loughgiel, in the second semi-final at Loughrea. Although there was nine points between the sides at the finish, 1–13 to 1–4, Loughgiel made the Galway side fight very hard for their victory.

Glen Rovers overwhelmed Mullagh in the final at Ballinasloe on November 21st. The acquisition of Lynn Dunlea from the Cloughduv club added greatly to the scoring power of the Glen attack. The Mullagh defence was unable to cope with the constant onslaught on their goal. Mary Ring and Sandie Fitzgibbon were key figures in the Glen defence. Denise Cronin dominated midfield and the speedy and skilful forwards ran up a huge score. There was no weak link in the team excellently coached by Noel Lynam. Glen won by 6–10 to 0–2.

Castleblayney – Monaghan County Champions 1993. Included are Marie Hanratty, Mary Kelly, Joanne Kelly, Geraldine Clarke, Caitriona Mulligan, Michelle McArdle, Sinéad Crowe, Marina Flanagan, Rosemary Merry, Mary Murphy, Noelle McGovern, Lisa O'Halloran and Pauleen Devlin.

Glen team: Mairéad O'Leary, Mary Ring, Deirdre McCarthy, Sandie Fitzgibbon, Diane Deane, Mandy Kennefick, Therese O'Callaghan, Ann Coleman, Linda Mellerick, Denise Cronin, Patricia Murphy and Claire McCarthy.

Mullagh team: Caroline Loughnane, Sheila Coen, Deirdre Hardiman, Pamela Nevin (captain), Bridget Fahy, Ruth Cahalan, Alice Murphy, Cora Curley, Aideen Murphy, Emer Hardiman, Imelda Hobbins and Madge Kennedy. Subs used: Anne Hardiman and Geraldine Fahy.

1993 Gael-Linn Senior Cup

Leinster had a convincing 5–7 to 2–10 win over Munster in the semi-final of the Gael-Linn Cup at Clane. Leinster upped the pace in the second-half to leave Munster floundering in their wake. In the other semi-final, Ulster received a walkover from Connacht.

Leinster coasted to the first 15-a-side Gael-Linn senior title when they proved too strong for Ulster at Clane by 6–14 to 1–4.

Leinster team: Louise Curry (Dublin), Cathy Walsh (Dublin) (captain), Catherine Murphy (Wexford), Bridie McGarry (Kilkenny), Stellah Sinnott (Wexford), Clare Jones (Kilkenny), Tracy Millea (Kilkenny), Ann Downey (Kilkenny), Una Murphy (Kilkenny), Fiona Dunne (Wexford), Gillian Dillon (Kilkenny), Sinéad Millea (Kilkenny), Bridget Mullally (Kilkenny), Siobhán Dunne (Wexford) and Angela Downey (Kilkenny).

Ulster team: Imelda Gillon (Antrim) (captain), Marie McAtamney (Antrim), Mary Connolly (Antrim), Donna McLoughlin (Antrim), Monica McCartan (Down), Nuala Magee (Down), Yvonne McKenna (Armagh), Rosemary Merry (Monaghan), Bronagh McCorry (Antrim), Isobel Oakes (Down), Grace McMullan (Antrim), Karen Convery (Antrim), Rosie Butler (Antrim), Noelle McGovern (Monaghan) and Elaine McMonagle (Donegal).

1993 Gael-Linn Junior Trophy

Goals from Irene Kirwan and Annette Heffernan put paid to Munster's chances in the semi-final of the Gael-Linn Trophy against Leinster at Clane. Connacht failed to make an appearance for their semi-final against Ulster.

Adding to their impressive record in this grade, Ulster fought off the challenge of Leinster in the final at Clane by 4–5 to 1–9.

Ulster team: Margaret McKee (Armagh), Pauline Green (Down), Cathy Browne (Armagh), Anne Coyle (Down), Colleen Conway (Armagh), Celine McGeary (Armagh), Orla Murphy (Armagh) (captain), Colette Burns (Armagh), Karen Lee (Derry), Bernie McBride (Armagh), Maureen McAleenan (Down), Deirdre Connolly (Armagh), Eimear Lee (Derry), Patricia McEvoy (Armagh) and Mary Donnelly (Armagh).

Leinster team: Brigid Rosney (Offaly), Sinéad Costello (Kilkenny), Siobhán Aylward (Kilkenny), Mary Smith (Carlow), Ruth Treacy (Kildare), Aisling Treacy (Kildare), Marie Maher (Kilkenny), Valerie Crean (Carlow), Anne Marie Denihy (Meath), Hilda Butler (Kilkenny), Irene Kirwan (Dublin), Geraldine Mahon (Offaly), Michelle Davis (Offaly), Imelda Kennedy (Kilkenny) and Annette Heffernan (Westmeath).

Belle O'Loughlin Elected President

Belle O'Loughlin (née Bannon) was elected President of the Camogie Association at Congress 1994 in Howth. A past pupil of Sacred Heart, Newry, Belle moved to Warrenpoint on her marriage to Arthur O'Loughlin and joined the St Peter's Club. Belle had filled several positions in the Down County Board and on Ulster Council.

Third-Level Expansion

With increasing numbers entering third-level education and the growth in the number of third-level colleges, it was necessary to restructure the Ashbourne Cup and Purcell Cup championships and to introduce additional competitions. Originally, the Ashbourne Cup was confined to universities and the Purcell Cup was decided between non-university colleges. Entry was pertinent on the type of college rather than the standard of the college camogie team.

Under the revised structure, the top camogie colleges qualified to participate in the Ashbourne Cup. Both competitions have grown and developed and are major dates on the camogie calendar. Players have just a few short years to leave their mark and capture one of the most prestigious medals in the game. Add the Higher Education League, the Fr Meachair Shield and the Freshers Cup and the result is a very busy schedule. The

Lynn Dunlea (Cork) picks the ball as Biddy O'Sullivan (Kilkenny) and Deirdre Malone (Kilkenny) advance in the All-Ireland senior semi-final at Ballinlough in 1994.

Belle O'Loughlin

Cork On Points Spree

third-level season was rounded off with the annual challenge between the Combined Universities and the Combined Colleges.

1994 All-Ireland Senior Championship

Angela Downey was coaxed out of retirement, Ann Downey was named as captain and Kilkenny were back in business. Fielding a number of newcomers – Michelle Fennelly, Sinéad Costello, Marie Maher and Una Murphy –, Kilkenny travelled to Ballinlough determined to reverse the previous season's result. Angela Downey, who was approaching the end of a fantastic career, bided her time awaiting real chances. She sprung with telling effect when opportunities presented themselves and struck the back of the Cork net three times. Kilkenny showed great appetite and did not let this one get away. They won by 4-9 to 2-12.

Fiona Dunne gave a tremendous display against Galway in the second semi-final at Wexford Park. Sister of county hurler, Liam, she registered 2-10 and controlled the middle of the field. Galway goalkeeper, Tracey Laheen, scored from a puck-out and Olivia Broderick added a second to lead by 2-2 to 0-3 with only ten minutes elapsed. Thereafter, Wexford took over and ran out easy winners by 3-14 to 2-5.

Fielding a much-changed side since their previous appearance in an All-Ireland final in 1992, Wexford were confident that their young skilful team could recapture the O'Duffy Cup. The new faces included 15-year-old Esme Murphy and Orla Hernan who blended in with the more experienced players.

Ann Downey had a huge influence on the final which was played in Croke Park on September 25th. A general in midfield, she fell back to help the defence and scored three superb long-range points. Wexford were level up to the three-quarter stage. Kilkenny picked up the pace, dug deep into their reserves and scored 1-4 without reply. It was a tough, physically draining encounter that ended Kilkenny 2-11, Wexford 0-8. Wexford matched Kilkenny, except for the Downey twins. Ann climbed the steps of the Hogan Stand to lift the O'Duffy Cup for the second time.

Kilkenny team: Michelle Fennelly, Sinéad Costello, Tracy Millea, Gillian Dillon, Deirdre Malone, Marina Downey (0-1), Ann Downey (captain) (0-3), Marie Maher, Bridget Mullally (0-1), Catherine Dunne, Angela Downey (2-3) and Sinéad Millea (0-2). Sub used: Brigid Barnaville (0-1)

Professor Nellie Lee and U.C.G. captain, Joanne Frost with the Ashbourne Cup in February, 1994.

A Dozen Each – Angela and Ann Downey gets their hands on the O'Duffy Cup for the twelfth time.

Wexford team: Terri Butler, Catherine Murphy, Stellah Sinnott, Paula Rankin (0–1), Mary Hayden, Angie Hearne, Fiona Dunne (0–4), Orla Hernan, Ann Marie O'Connor (0–2), Marion O'Leary, Esme Murphy (0–1) and Ann Reddy (captain). Subs used: Avis Nolan and Geraldine Codd.

Kilkenny's Sinéad Costello and Marie Maher are daughters of twins, Maura and Breda Cassin, who played in the 1970 and 1972 All-Ireland senior finals.

Kilkenny – 1994 All-Ireland Senior Champions. Back: Angela Downey, Bridget Mullally, Marie Maher, Deirdre Malone and Tom Ryan (Trainer). Front: Michelle Fennelly, Marina Downey, Tracey Millea, Ann Downey, Catherine Dunne, Sinéad Costello, Gillian Dillon and Sinéad Millea.

Armagh – 1994 All-Ireland Intermediate Champions. Back: Helen Mone, Bernie McBride, Maggie McKee, Geraldine Haughey, Collette Burns, Denise McCreanor, Celine McGeary, Rosie McCleland, Ursula McGivern, Margaret Moriarty and Tom Monaghan. Front: Deirdre Connolly, Olive McGeown, Mary Black (Capt), Áine French, Orla Murphy, Siobhán Smith, Patricia McEvoy, Mary Donnelly.

1994 All-Ireland Intermediate Championship

Goals by Miriam Malone, Michelle Aspel and Melanie Treacy put Kildare on the road to the All-Ireland intermediate final at the expense of Tipperary at Clane. A tight-marking Kildare defence provided few opportunities to the Tipperary attack and contributed to Kildare's 3–5 to 0–7 victory. Armagh unseated champions Clare in the second semi-final at Portmore. It was a ding-dong battle right up to the final minutes when Armagh put a string of points together to advance by 2–11 to 2–7.

The final of the All-Ireland Intermediate Championship was staged as a curtain-raiser to the under-21 hurling final at Tullamore. Kildare were the superior team in an excellent first-half. Armagh raised their game after the break, becoming more clinical in attack and reaped the rewards. The fleet-footed Armagh forwards opened the Kildare defence and goals started to flow. Armagh collected the Purcell Cup, but the Player of the Match award went to Kildare captain, Melanie Treacy. The final score was Armagh 7–11, Kildare 3–11.

Armagh team: Margaret McKee, Margaret Moriarty, Geraldine Haughey, Celine McGreary, Orlagh Murphy, Áine French

(0-1), Mary Black (Capt) (1-0), Olive McGeown (0-1), Bernie McBride (2-3), Colette Burns (0-3), Ursula McGivern (0-1), Mary Donnelly (3-2). Sub used: Patricia McEvoy (1-0).

Kildare team: Anna Dargan, Geraldine Dwyer, Therese Farrelly, Melanie Treacy (captain), Liz O'Donoghue, Caoimhe Brennan, Claire Moloney, Aisling Treacy, Bernie Farrelly (0-4), Michelle Aspel (0-2), Miriam Malone (2-5) and Elaine Miley (1-0).

1994 All-Ireland Junior Championship

London raised eyebrows when they defeated a fancied Kilkenny side in the quarter-final of the junior championship at Kingsbury. However, they struggled to impose themselves on Galway in the semi-final. The Connacht side was three goals ahead at the break and well on the way to a 6-8 to 2-5 win.

The novel pairing of Limerick and Cavan met in the second semi-final at Ballyhaise. There was little between the sides in the opening half but Limerick pulled away in the closing minutes to win by 5-11 to 0-9.

Galway, who had lost three All-Ireland finals since their previous success, were in no mood to let this one slip. The two Limerick veterans, Pauline McCarthy and Bernie O'Brien, played quality camogie but the Galway youngsters, Veronica Curtin, Martina Harkin, Carmel Hannon, Denise Gilligan and Olive Costello, were skilful and committed performers.

They chased, foraged and harried for every ball and did not let Limerick take control. Galway won their fifth All-Ireland junior title by 2-10 to 1-11.

Galway team: Fiona Earls, Olive Costello, Fiona Ryan, Cora Curley (captain), Denise Gilligan, Gretta Maher, Helen Ryan, Carmel Hannon, Martina Harkin (0-6), Emer Hardiman (0-1), Teresa Fallon (0-1), Veronica Curtin (2-2). Sub used: Yvonne Larkin.

Limerick team: Breda O'Brien (0-1), Helen Clifford, Agnes Sheehy, Bernie O'Brien, Elizabeth Leonard, Elizabeth O'Riordan, Ida Quaide (captain), Mary Bourke, Cecilia McNamara (0-1), Kay Bourke, Pauline McCarthy (1-9) and Marguerite Guiry. Subs used: Mary Lonergan and Michelle McCarthy.

Galway – 1994 All-Ireland Junior Champions. Back: Teresa Fallon, Carmel Hannon, Olive Costello, Helen Ryan and Fiona Earls. Front: Fiona Regan, Martina Harkin, Emer Hardiman, Cora Curley, Veronica Curtin, Denise Gilligan and Goretta Maher.

1994 All-Ireland Minor Championship

Tipperary and Wexford finished all square in the minor semi-final at Monamolin. It was non-stop action from start to finish with some delightful play from the talented youngsters on both sides. Tipperary made better use of their chances in the replay at Templemore. In a brilliant exhibition of camogie, Caitríona Hennessy and Helen Grogan swapped goals with Esme Murphy and Kate Kelly. Tipperary brought on Gráinne Shanahan and she obliged with two cleverly worked goals to seal the match by 4–6 to 2–6.

Veronica Curtin scored an amazing 5–2 as rampant Galway brushed aside the Derry challenge in the second semi-final at Ballinascreen. Derry struggled to exert any dominance and had to concede to the more talented outfit by 10–7 to 2–4.

Star forward, Veronica Curtin scored a whopping 3–5 for Galway as they enjoyed a runaway victory over a disappointing Tipperary side in the All-Ireland minor final at Loughrea. From an early stage, Galway stamped their authority on proceedings and were never in any danger. Apart from Veronica, Galway had stars in Aoife Tannian, Fiona Healy, Áine Hillary and Denise Gilligan. Caitríona Hennessy, Ciara Gaynor, Maeve Corcoran and Helen Grogan did their utmost to stem the tide. Galway were full value for their 7–13 to 3–9 win.

Galway team: Emer Kearney, Esther Martyn, Teresa Murphy, Denise Gilligan (0–2), Alisha McNamara, Aoife Lynskey (0–1), Sandra Farrell (0–1), Goretta Maher (captain) (0–1), Aoife Tannian (2–0), Fiona Healy (1–2), Áine Hillary (1–1) and Veronica Curtin (3–5). Sub used: Fiona Pierce.

Tipperary team: Emily Hayden, Elaine Fitzgerald, Marie Harkin, Jacqueline O'Connor, Maeve Corcoran, Orla Egan, Fiona Hanrahan, Noelette O'Dwyer, Caitríona Hennessy (1–6), Ciara Gaynor (0–3), Helen Grogan (1–0) and Mary Luby (captain) (1–0). Subs used: Gráinne Shanahan and Grace Ormond.

Galway – 1994 All-Ireland Minor Champions. Back: Emer Kearney, A. Winston, M. Glynn, Áine Hillary, S. Roche, Sandra Farrell, Teresa Murphy, H. Huban, Lorraine Linnane, Denise Gilligan, Veronica Curtin and Alisha McNamara. Front: Fiona Pierce, D. Kelly, Sandra Tannian, Aoife Tannian, Esther Martyn, Aoife Lynskey, Goretta Maher (Capt), Rosa Clark, Fiona Healy, Colette Nevin, Shauna Ward and C. O'Rourke.

Cork On Points Spree

1994 All-Ireland Club Championship

Fielding seven members of the Galway senior team, Pearse's travelled to the Glen Field brimful of confidence to tackle Glen Rovers in the club semi-final. The Glen were chasing a hat-trick of titles and can thank goalkeeper Máiread O'Leary that their dream did not end there and then. Pearse's had the lion's share of the play but poor shooting and good goalkeeping cost them dearly. Sharon Glynn, Tracy Laheen, Carmel Hannon and Martina Harkins did not allow Glen Rovers to play their free-flowing game but could not prevent them from winning by 0–12 to 1–4.

Lisdowney, Noel Barnaville's well-drilled team, coasted to victory over Dunloy at Ballyragget in the second semi-final. They imposed themselves on the opposition from the start and ran out comfortable winners. Marina Downey (4–5) and Angela Downey (3–6) got the bulk of the home scores while Sinéad McMullan (1–2) and Majella McMullan (1–1) countered for Dunloy. Lisdowney took a step forward by 7–14 to 2–4.

Lisdowney – 1994 All-Ireland Club Champions. Back: Noel Barnaville (Trainer), Mary Brennan, Deirdre Delaney, Brigid Wall, Olivia Donnelly, Fran Shore, Áine Dunne, Caroline Glendon, Sandra Gleeson, Martina Tallis and Annie Murphy. Front: Ann Marie Hughes, Marina Downey, Angela Downey, Ann Downey, Veronica Wall, Noelle O'Driscoll, Bridget Barnaville and Catherine Dunne (Capt).

Glen Rovers turned over with a lead of 1–10 to 0–6 against Lisdowney in the All-Ireland club final at Ballyragget. The Cork club continued to add to their tally until a seemingly insurmountable margin of ten points separated the sides. The contest seemed to be over.

What followed was an astonishing comeback. In the final minutes, Angela Downey showed what a camogie genius she was. She carved openings and rattled the Glen net on four occasions to snatch victory and leave the Glen Rovers players and supporters shell-shocked. For over three-quarters of the game, Glen Rovers were the better side. But with a talent of Angela Downey's stature on the field, the game is not over until the final whistle and anything can happen in the meantime. The score stood at Lisdowney 5–9, Glen Rovers 1–15 at the finish.

Lisdowney team: Veronica Wall, Caroline Glendon, Brigid Wall, Bridget Barnaville, Fran Shore, Catherine Dunne (captain), Ann Downey, Sandra Gleeson, Marina Downey, Áine Dunne, Angela Downey and Ann Marie Hughes. Subs used: Noelle O'Driscoll and Olivia Donnelly.

Glen Rovers team: Mairéad O'Leary, Deirdre McCarthy, Mary Ring, Stephanie Dunlea, Sandie Fitzgibbon (captain), Denise Cronin, Therese O'Callaghan, Patricia Murphy, Linda Mellerick, Lynn Dunlea, Ger McCarthy and Claire McCarthy. Sub used: Mary Currid.

1994 Gael-Linn Senior Cup

Ulster surprised Leinster in the Gael-Linn semi-finals at Navan when they snatched the verdict by 2–10 to 1–12. Connacht did not field against Munster in the second semi-final. Munster had a convincing win over Ulster in the final at Silver Park by 4–11 to 2–7.

Munster team: Kathleen Costine (Cork), Claire Madden (Tipperary), Breda Kenny (Cork), Liz Towler (Cork), Paula Goggins (Cork), Therese O'Callaghan (Cork) (captain), Stephanie Dunlea (Cork), Eithne Duggan (Cork), Triona Bonnar (Tipperary), Patricia Murphy (Cork), Lynn Dunlea (Cork), Irene O'Keeffe (Cork), Fiona O'Driscoll (Cork), Deirdre Hughes (Tipperary) and Colette O'Mahony (Cork).

Ulster team: Margaret McKee (Armagh), Teresa McNally (Armagh), Donna Greeran (Down), Róisín McCluskey (Derry), Nuala McGee (Down), Colette Byrne (Armagh), Orlagh Murphy (Armagh), Mary Black (Armagh) (captain), Olive McGeown (Armagh), Bernie McBride (Armagh), Maureen McAleenan (Down), Grace McMullan (Antrim), Glenda Fitzpatrick (Fermanagh), Patricia McEvoy (Armagh) and Ursula McGivern (Armagh).

1994 Gael-Linn Junior Trophy

Ulster had two goals to spare over Leinster, 4–8 to 2–8, in the semi-final at Navan. In the second semi-final, Munster got a fright from an all-Roscommon Connacht side and only got on level terms and drew ahead the final quarter. The final score was Munster 1–11, Connacht 2–4.

Three goals from Limerick's Pauline McCarthy decided the outcome of the final between Munster and Ulster at Silver Park. A very entertaining match came to an end with the score at Munster 5–9, Ulster 2–12.

Munster team: Breda O'Brien (Limerick), Colette Cronin (Cork), Evelyn Healy (Cork), Agnes Sheehy (Limerick), Regina O'Meara (Tipperary), Suzanne Kelly (Tipperary), Bernie O'Brien (Limerick), Maeve Stokes (Tipperary), Vivienne Harris (Cork), Kay Burke (Limerick), Helen Kiely (Tipperary), Mary Burke (Limerick), Martha Butler (Waterford), Pauline McCarthy (Limerick) (captain) and Anne Gleeson (Tipperary).

Ulster team: Imelda Gillen (Antrim), Pauline Greene (Down), Mary Rose McGready (Tyrone), Geraldine Haughey (Armagh), Deirdre Cunning (Antrim), Bronagh McCorry (Antrim), Claire McGarry (Antrim), Pauline McGuigan (Derry), Leona Fay (Tyrone), Eimear Brennan (Cavan), Deirdre Savage (Down), Brenda Burke (Tyrone), Rosie Butler (Antrim), Mary Donnelly (Armagh) and Bonnie McGreevey (Down).

Cork On Points Spree

Where We're At

A new approach was needed to develop the game at primary-schools level. No longer was it considered suitable to subject young girls to the same conditions and skills training as older players. The initial learning experience must be an enjoyable one. The newly published *Hurling and Camogie Skills Teaching Manual* provided an excellent resource and was easy to follow by teachers with limited knowledge of camogie. It was important that every beginner was equipped with a hurley of the correct size and weight and a properly fitting helmet. The use of a plastic ball on a hard surface was advocated to give the young player greater satisfaction from her efforts rather than trying to cope with a wet sliothar on a muddy pitch. Practice must be fun, otherwise, the young girls will not return.

A major talking point in camogie circles was Kilkenny's proposal to change camogie to a 15-a-side game on a full-sized hurling pitch. Supporters of the change pointed to the gruelling training schedules that the modern players undertake and the resultant improvement in fitness levels and advocated a larger stage for the players to exhibit their skills. It was suggested that an increased playing area would provide greater scope for the participants and a more entertaining spectacle for supporters. The existing playing pitch was only three-quarters the size of the hurling area and did not figure favourably when compared. Some players felt that they would never be taken seriously while the game was being played on the small pitch.

However, not all camogie followers were in agreement with the proposal. Some saw the emphasis being placed on strength and stamina rather than on skill. Kilkenny had put their proposals to the test in a series of inter-county matches in 1987 and players and supporters had come away from Nowlan Park believing that the senior inter-county players could take the suggested changes in their stride. However, a question mark hung over underage players and those of lesser ability. Would they be lost on the big pitch and, consequently, would they derive less satisfaction from the game? Would clubs find it possible to fill the additional team places with players of the required standard? Would young players be reluctant to play in the big goal? The debate rumbled on.

It was difficult to pinpoint what had gone wrong in Dublin. A lot of hard work went into the 44 clubs that participated in 12 grades of camogie (adding up to over 1,000 matches annually). However, the system was not producing the quality of player who had adorned the game in previous years. With so many players in the county, one would imagine that better teams could be assembled. In previous years, victory was expected but that had changed. Players from Dublin's golden era had great pride in being part of an outstanding team.

Had Dublin grown too big? Was the Dublin players' sense of identity of not as strong as it had been? When all Dublin club matches were played in the Phoenix Park, a community atmosphere prevailed. Players knew those from other clubs and lingered after their own game to watch subsequent matches. An immense air of expectancy awaited the announcement of Dublin teams or even trial selections.

The current fashion of playing several sports lessens the time a player spends with a hurley in her hand. Most of her time is used in competitive situations and very little in skill training. While players are very fit, inadequate ball skills prevents them from reaching great heights.

A Game of Our Own

JUBILATION

Chapter Nineteen

STEP CLOSER TO GAA

When Congress 1995 convened at Waterford, relations with the GAA took a step closer with the unanimous acceptance of the following motion: 'That Cumann Camógaíochta na nGael seek to affiliate to Cumann Luthchleas Gael on the following terms: Cumann Camógaíochta na nGael shall affiliate as a Confederate Body to Cumann Luthchleas Gael. Collective membership of Cumann Luthchleas Gael shall be conferred on Cumann Camógaíochta na nGael.'

Collective membership does not automatically confer individual membership of a Cumann Luthchleas Gael Club. Such membership may only be conferred by a Club in accordance with the Rules of Cumann Luthchleas Gael.

Cumann Luthchleas Gael and Cumann Camógaíochta na nGael shall be autonomous in the running of their own affairs, and each shall be bound by its own Constitution and Playing Rules.'

Post-Match Reception

For many decades, camogie players, both winners and losers, have looked forward to the after-match reception on the night of the All-Ireland final. The hair was done up, make-up applied and the best dress given an airing. With the ever-increasing popularity of alcohol, many players preferred to visit their favourite bar than attend the organised function. Team officials spent time coaxing, pleading and bullying players in an attempt to extract them from the licensed premises and transfer them to the reception, however, players frequently stated that they preferred to remain within their own group on the night of the match. For a trial period of two years, it was decided that

The late Mairéad Meehan, captain of Holy Rosary, Mountbellew, speaking after her side won the All-Ireland junior colleges title in 1997. On the left is Sheila Morgan, All-Ireland Colleges President and, on the right, is Camogie President, Phyllis Breslin.

the post-match function would be discontinued and replaced by a dinner and presentation, hosted by Central Council, the day after the final at a city-centre venue.

Sponsor for All-Ireland Championship

Prior to 1995, camogie had been completely ignored by the commercial world. Bord na Gaeilge became the first sponsor of an All-Ireland camogie championship. Micheál Ó Muircheartaigh, Cathaoirleach of Bord na Gaeilge, said that "in sponsoring the camogie championship, Bord na Gaeilge is underlining the importance of promoting Irish at community level". The organisation was anxious to be associated with something that complemented their aims.

1995 All-Ireland Senior Championship

Wexford remained in the All-Ireland semi-final at Páirc Uí Rinn because of Cork's poor shooting rather than because they played well. With 15 minutes to go, the Cork attack found their range and shot scores from all angles to finish in front of a below-par Wexford outfit by 5–13 to 1–6.

Cork – 1995 All-Ireland Senior Champions. Back: Sandie Fitzgibbon, Eithne Duggan, Kathleen Costine, Paula Goggins and Therese O'Callaghan. **Front:** Mags Finn, Denise Cronin (Capt), Lynn Dunlea, Irene O'Keeffe, Linda Mellerick, Stephanie Dunlea and Fiona O'Driscoll.

Kilkenny left it late to secure a place in the final. Galway led by 1–6 to 0–6 at half-time in the semi-final at Nowlan Park, with Sinéad Millea's immaculate free-taking yielded 11 points. Sinéad sliced through the Galway defence to place Gillian Dillon for the all-important goal to leave the final score Kilkenny 1–14, Galway 1–9.

Angela Downey headed Kilkenny in the pre-match parade with her three-year-old daughter Katie proudly marching beside her at Croke Park on September 24th. Tension in the teams, a strong gale and the constant use of the referee's whistle resulted in a disappointing first-half. However Cork, who had lagged three points behind Kilkenny at the break, picked it up considerably on the resumption. Lynn Dunlea palmed the ball to the Kilkenny net but Angela Downey's bullet-like shot from a free cancelled it out.

Cork called teenager Vivienne Harris from the bench and she made an immediate impact. Once again, Angela Downey ripped the Cork defence open from a placed ball on the 15-metre line. Cork captain, Denise Cronin, took off on a spectacular run through the Kilkenny defence and fired the ball to the net. When

Linda Mellerick gathered a short clearance and sent a speculative ball goalwards, nobody expected it to rest in the Kilkenny net. Cork were in front for the first time in the match. However, they had to endure a third close-in free by Angela Downey before knowing that victory would be theirs on the score of 4–8 to 2–10.

Cork team: Kathleen Costine, Eithne Duggan, Paula Goggins, Sandie Fitzgibbon, Mags Finn, Linda Mellerick (1–0), Denise Cronin (1–0) (captain), Stephanie Dunlea, Fiona O'Driscoll (1–1), Therese O'Callaghan, Irene O'Keeffe and Lynn Dunlea (1–7). Sub used: Vivienne Harris.

Kilkenny team: Michelle Fennelly, Deirdre Malone, Margaret Hickey, Sinéad Costello, Bridget Barnaville, Marina Downey, Ann Downey, Marie Maher, Sinéad Millea (0–5), Breda Holmes, Angela Downey (captain) (2–5) and Gillian Dillon. Sub used: Tracy Millea.

Sisters Lynn and Stephanie Dunlea are grand-nieces of Kate Dunlea who captained Cork to their first All-Ireland success in 1934. Lynn scored 4–20 in the 1995 championship.

President Mary Robinson looks on as Camogie President, Belle O'Loughlin, presents the O'Duffy Cup to Cork captain, Denise Cronin at Croke Park in September, 1995.

Angela Had It All

Born into a hurling environment, it was inevitable that Angela Downey would take up a camogie stick – all of five-foot-one of her. Angela displayed star quality from an early age. Possessing a rich array of skills, she could turn a match around in a few minutes – the 1994 All-Ireland club final between Lisdowney and Glen Rovers is testament to this.

With great hands, wristwork and the speed of a sprinter, Angela saw an opportunity and reacted instantly to gain possession and execute her shot with celerity and pin-point accuracy. An unerring striker of the ball, either from a placed ball or while in full flight, she was powerful and direct. What distinguished Angela from other great players, however, was her fierce competitiveness. Losing was not an option.

After 23 years on the inter-county stage, Angela hung up her boots. Twelve All-Ireland senior medals and cabinets full of awards bear witness to a brilliant career. Angela's name was well known to people who never saw a camogie match and there is no player in today's game to match her star quality. Camogie needs superstars. Roll on the next Angela.

1995 All-Ireland Intermediate Championship

In a thrilling semi-final at Cusack Park in Ennis, Clare got the better of reigning champions, Armagh, by 2–15 to 3–10. With an eight-point cushion, Clare seemed to be cruising to victory. A brace of goals by Armagh's Colette Byrnes had Clare hanging on by the fingertips.

Tipperary had a comfortable passage to the final at the expense of Down at Ballycran. The game was a stop-start event with the whistle sounding incessantly and the majority of scores coming from placed balls. Tipperary went forward by 2–16 to 3–8.

Near neighbours, Clare and Tipperary, knew one another too well for an open game in the final at Toomevara. The thin line between success and failure was emphasised as the lead changed from one team to the other. Catherine O'Loughlin sealed the win for Clare with the last of her eight points and Tipperary fell short by the slimmest margin, 1–10 to 1–9.

Clare team: Áine McCormack, Debbie Kelly, Marion Costello, Debbie McDonagh, Orla Slattery, Clodagh Lennon, Moira McMahon, Sinéad O'Brien (captain), Frances Phelan (0–1), Catherine O'Loughlin (0–8), Anne Keane and Patricia Moloney (1–1).

Tipperary team: Nora Dwane, Therese Bourke, Regina

Clare – 1995 All-Ireland Intermediate Champions. Back: Kitty McNicholas (Manager), Linda Quinn, Sinéad O'Brien (Capt), Patricia Moloney, Debbie McDonagh, Frances Phelan, Áine McCormack, Marian Costelloe and Orla Slattery. Front: Mary Neylon, Moira McMahon, Debbie Kelly, Catherine O'Loughlin, Patricia O'Grady, Noeleen Neylon, Ann Keane, Clodagh Lennon and Joanne Frost.

O'Meara, Cora Kennedy, Claire Madden, Marie Ryan (captain), Kaiffee Moloney, Maeve Stokes, Noelle Kennedy (0–6), Catherine Bourke (0–1), Helen Kiely (0–1) and Deirdre Hughes (1–1).

1995 All-Ireland Junior Championship

Roscommon lived dangerously and took two matches to shake off the attentions of Antrim in the semi-final of the All-Ireland junior championship. The Connacht county was coasting to victory when Margaret McKillop swooped with an equalising goal at Dunloy. Both defences tightened up for the replay at Athleague and left scoring opportunities very scarce. Roscommon coach, Michael Kelly, steered his side to a 1–8 to 1–7 victory.

There was little between Limerick and Kildare when they clashed in the seond semi-final at Mary Immaculate College. Kildare spurned two good chances to level the contest in the closing minutes. Limerick won a place in the final by 2–11 to 2–8.

Disappointed at the outcome of the 1994 final, All-Ireland hurler, Eamonn Cregan, piloted Limerick back to Croke Park in determined mood. It was a massive occasion for Roscommon who were experiencing centre-stage on All-Ireland day for the first time. Two first-half goals from Kay Burke put Limerick on the road to a 2–5 to 0–2 interval lead. Mairéad Coyle spearheaded a Roscommon revival and Limerick's advantage was whittled away. Charmaine Cooney struck what seemed to be the winning goal in injury-time. Roscommon were in the lead for the first time but their joy was short lived. Kay Burke silenced the Roscommon supporters with her third goal to wrench the title back for Limerick by 3–7 to 4–3.

Limerick team: Breda O'Brien, Helen Clifford (captain), Agnes Sheehy, Ann Lenihan, Elizabeth Leonard, Elizabeth O'Riordan, Mairéad Cagney, Mary Burke, Ann Marie Stack (0–1), Kay Burke (3–0), Pauline McCarthy (0–6) and Vera Sheehan. Sub used: Deirdre Sheehan.

Roscommon team: Ursula Hussey, Caroline Connaughton, Emer Farrell, Mary Grehan, Teresa Carty, Charmaine Cooney (1–0), Hillary Hussey (0–1), Karina Jones (captain), Elizabeth Hanley, Mary Gannon (1–0), Geraldine Carr, Maeve Healy (0–1). Subs used: Mairéad Coyle (2–1) and Mary Nagle.

Limerick – 1995 All-Ireland Junior Champions. Back: Helen Clifford-McCarthy (Capt), Elizabeth O'Riordan, Breda O'Brien, Pauline McCarthy, Cecilia McNamara, Bernie O'Brien, Agnes Sheehy, Jean Cullinane, Kathleen O'Connor, Mary Lonergan and Carol Murphy. Front: Kay Burke, Elizabeth Leonard, Vera Sheehan, Mary Burke, Helen Kelliher, Mairéad Cagney, Ann Lenihan, Deirdre Sheehan, Anna Marie Stack, Niamh Cregan and Íde Quaid.

1995 All-Ireland Minor Championship

Galway fought off the vigorous challenge of Tipperary in the semi-final at Semple Stadium. Colette Nevin scored 2–8 from play and placed balls to set her side on the road to a 2–12 to 3–6 victory.

Esme Murphy, with a personal total of 1–12, was the star of the Wexford side that overcame Derry in the semi-final at Monamolin. Derry were a point in front at the change-over but a much-improved second-half performance by Wexford saw them qualify for the final by 2–17 to 2–7.

Wexford got off to a dream start in the final against Galway at Loughrea with goals from Esme Murphy, already an established senior inter-county player, and Rose-Marie Breen. The speedy Wexford forwards continued to create problems for the Galway defence. Galway trailed by 2–8 to 0–4 at the break. However, wind advantage and an increased tempo brought Galway back into the game. A goal by Therese Maher and points from Colette Nevin and Veronica Curtin narrowed the gap, but Galway's tendency to concede frees was their undoing, and all indiscretions were punished by Esme Murphy. Wexford claimed Corn Tailteann by 2–9 to 1–7.

Wexford team: Michelle Hearne, Áine Codd (captain), Claire O'Connor, Emma Carroll, Eileen Hanrick, Sandy Carr, Rose-Marie Breen (1–3), Angela Murphy, Kate Kelly, Michelle O'Leary (0–3), Esme Murphy (1–3) and Marie Butler. Subs used: Tina Bergin and Lizzie Wickham.

Galway team: Emer Kearney, Colette Deeley, Lorraine Murphy, Fiona Healy (captain), Sarah Cullinane, Caroline Murray, Sandra Farrell, Therese Maher (1–1), Sandra Tannian, Aoife Lynskey, Colette Nevin (0–4), Shauna Ward. Sub used: Veronica Curtin (0–2).

Wexford captain, Áine Codd, is a daughter of Kit Codd (née Kehoe), who won All-Ireland senior medals with Dublin and Wexford. Kate Kelly's mother, Peggie Kelly (née Doyle), won an All-Ireland senior medal with Wexford in 1969.

Rathnure – 1995 All-Ireland Club Champions. Back: Bernie Higgins, Elaine Holohan, Jenny Farrell, Claire O'Connor, Michelle O'Leary and Bernie Holohan. Middle: Mary Hayden, Mary Fleming, Ann Reddy, Norma Carty and Orla Brady. Front: Geraldine Codd (Capt), Anna-Mai White, Catherine Murphy, Aoife O'Connor, Margaret Somers and Teddy O'Connor (trainer).

1995 All-Ireland Club Championship

Toomevara needed extra-time to shake off the attentions of Davitt's (Galway) in the semi-final at Craughwell. With three goals to her credit, Deirdre Hughes proved a match winner for Toomevara. Olivia Broderick, Brenda Daniels and Joanne Frost were on the mark for Davitt's but they had to concede by 4–6 to 3–7.

Rathnure booked a place in the final at the expense of Leitrim Fontenoys (Down). The Wexford girls were more clinical in their finish and reaped the rewards. Rathnure's Ann Reddy (4–1) and Geraldine Codd (1–10) kept the score-keeper busy while Maureen McAleenan (0–7) and Nuala McGee (1–2) replied for Fontenoys.

A blow-torch was needed before the deeply frozen section of the pitch at Toomevara was declared playable for the All-Ireland club final between Rathnure and Toomevara. Marguerite Somers' goal lit up an evenly contested first half and saw Rathnure ahead by 1–5 to 0–3 at half-time. The real action came in the third quarter when Bernie Higgins and Ann Reddy struck match-winning goals. Toomevara made an all-out effort to save the match but Mary Fleming in the Rathnure goal was equal to the challenge. Rathnure, coached by Teddy O'Connor, won the title by 4–9 to 1–5.

Rathnure team: Mary Fleming, Catherine Murphy, Anna-Mai White, Mary Hayden, Claire O'Connor, Norma Carty, Aoife O'Connor, Michelle O'Leary, Bernie Higgins, Ann Reddy, Marguerite Somers and Geraldine Codd (captain). Sub used: Lillian Doyle.

Toomevara team: Nora Dwan, Siobhán Cusack, Aileen Delaney, Cora Kennedy, Regina O'Meara, Miriam Maxwell, Siobhán Kelly (captain), Siobhan Maxwell, Josie Browne, Deirdre Hughes, Anne Gleeson and Noelle Kennedy. Subs used: Lena Woods and Gráinne Shanahan.

Rathnure Club: The village of Rathnure is nestled in the Blackstairs Mountains. The camogie club was founded in 1968 by Teddy O'Connor, Larry Cahill, Marcella Redmond, Tish Codd and Syl Barron. Great attention was paid to the underage section and it paid off. Community Games and Féile na nGael titles were won. The late Jim Shiels and his wife Margaret were great workers for the club. Cloughbawn joined forces with Rathnure in 1988 and, in the following year, Rathnure won the Wexford senior championship title.

1995 Gael-Linn Senior Cup

The senior semi-finals provided clear-cut results at Russell Park. Holders Munster overcame Ulster by 3–14 to 2–10 while Connacht got the better of Leinster by 6–10 to 1–10. The final contained some excellent passages of play with the pendulum only swinging towards the champions in the last few minutes. Munster retained the cup on the score of 4–13 to 3–10.

Munster team: Kathleen Costine (Cork), Eithne Duggan (Cork), Paula Goggins (Cork), Sandie Fitzgibbon (Cork), Claire Madden (Tipperary), Regina O'Meara (Tipperary), Therese O'Callaghan (Cork), Stephanie Dunlea (Cork), Irene O'Keeffe (Cork), Linda Mellerick (Cork), Lynn Dunlea (Cork) and Deirdre Hughes (Tipperary).

Connacht team: (All Galway) Louise Curry, Sheila Coen, Tracey Laheen, Carmel Hannon, Pamela Nevin, Olivia Broderick, Sharon Glynn, Martina Harkins, Anne Ryan, Imelda Hobbins, Deirdre Costello and Claire Lynch.

1995 Gael-Linn Junior Trophy

Connacht had a goal to spare over Leinster in the semi-final at Russell Park and Munster outscored Ulster by 3–10 to 1–4 at the same venue. Connacht and Munster provided a display of camogie that ranked with the best. It was score for score as neither side could draw clear. The outcome was decided by an excellent goal by Mairéad Coyle and finished Connacht 1–9 Munster 0–10.

Connacht team: Fiona Earls (Galway), Olive Costello (Galway), Mary Grehan (Roscommon), Cora Curley (Galway), Mary Gannon (Roscommon), Goretta Maher (Galway), Karina Jones (Roscommon), Carmel Hannon (Galway), Martina Haverty (Galway), Mairéad Coyle (Roscommon), Denise Gilligan (Galway) and

Veronica Curtin (Galway).

Munster team: Breda O'Brien (Limerick), Teresa Burke (Tipperary), Colette Cronin (Cork), Evelyn Healy (Cork), Siobhán Cusack (Tipperary), Vivienne Harris (Cork), Alice Deane (Tipperary), Catherine Bourke (Tipperary), Pauline McCarthy (Limerick), Ann Lenihan (Limerick), Marie Ryan (Tipperary), Kay Burke (Limerick), Noelle Kennedy (Tipperary) and Antoinette O'Connell (Cork).

Galway – 1996 All-Ireland Senior Champions. Back: Ann Broderick, Pamela Nevin, Louise Curry, Olive Costello, Sharon Glynn and Olivia Broderick. Front: Carmel Hannon, Veronica Curtin, Imelda Hobbins (Capt), Martina Harkin, Dympna Maher and Denise Gilligan.

£100,000 for Helmets

In 1996, the Minister for Sport made £100,000 available on a one-off basis to the Camogie Association for the provision of helmets. With 480 clubs on the association's books, nine helmets were made available to each club.

The expense incurred in putting out a team with maximum protection was steep and having a supply of helmets available eased the financial burden and allowed newcomers to be introduced to the helmet from the outset.

Congress 1996 in Newcastle, Co. Down, voted to increase the number of All-Ireland medals awarded to the winning side from 16 to 20.

Surviving on a Shoestring

In 1996, treasurer, Jo Golden, set out the sources of the association's income, the areas of expenditure and the relation of each to the total in her annual report. There was no doubt that the association was surviving on a shoestring. Government grants formed a major part (33 per cent) of income. Gate receipts yielded 26 per cent, affiliation fees from clubs delivered 13 per cent and 11 per cent was supplied by sponsors. The total income for the year amounted to £202,075 which included the one-off figure received from the government for helmets.

These figures reveal how dependent the association was on government grants and how poor the returns from gates, affiliation fees and sponsorship were. Every penny was deliberated upon before being spent. A major injection of funds was needed to provide for expansion and initiatives. Of the income received, 20 per cent was allocated in grants to units within the association, 35 per cent was apportioned to running the camogie office, 21 per cent went to the administration of fixtures and 14 per cent covered the travelling expenses of Central Council and sub-committee members. Good housekeeping kept the association afloat.

1996 All-Ireland Senior Championship

Wexford defenders watched a high dropping ball descend near the end-line in the second minute of the All-Ireland semi-final against Galway at Loughrea. In nipped Martina Harkin to flick the ball into the path of Veronica Curtin who pulled first-time to the net. Wexford did not recover. The final score would have looked worse from their point of view had a Galway defender not deflected the ball to her own net. Galway progressed by 1–13 to 1–5.

Cork versus Kilkenny contests over the previous two decades had produced wonderful displays of skilful camogie and fans made their way to Páirc Uí Rínn anticipating more of the same. They were sadly disappointed, not by the players but by a referee who played a constant tune on her whistle. Cork managed to score 1–2 from play to which Kilkenny responded with two points. The rest was left to the two free-takers. The deciding score came late in the game when Cork's Lynn Dunlea caught a perfect pass from Vivienne Harris and struck it out of the reach of Kilkenny goalkeeper, Michelle Fennelly. Cork pressed on to the final by 1–13 to 0–11.

Cork were coasting along nicely in the All-Ireland final at Croke Park on September 22nd when Denise Gilligan ran onto a pass from Sharon Glynn and first-timed the ball to the net. This score was critical to Galway's cause. It narrowed the gap to a very manageable three points as Galway headed for the dressing room and an opportunity to assess the situation. After the break, Carmel Allen was introduced to the half-back line and played with great assurance. Denise Gilligan raced down the left-wing where Sharon Glynn found her with an accurate pass. Denise finished with aplomb. Two minutes later, Denise crossed to Martina Harkin who scored a goal at the second attempt.

When Dympna Maher met an inviting cross and turned it into the net, the Galway supporters could smell victory. They cheered their favourites as they swapped points with Cork. Although Cork brought it back to a two-point margin, they spurned some easy point chances in search of a goal.

Galway hearts beat fast for some moments before they could give vent to their emotions and salute a historic and momentous win. Sixty-three years after their first shot at the title and in their tenth final appearance, Tony Ward's team came good and won by 4-8 to 1-15.

Galway team: Louise Curry, Olive Costello, Ann Broderick, Olivia Broderick, Pamela Nevin, Dympna Maher (1–0), Sharon Glynn (0–5), Carmel Hannon, Martina Harkin (1–1), Imelda Hobbins (captain) (0–1), Denise Gilligan (2–0) and Veronica Curtin (0–1). Subs used: Carmel Allen and Goretta Maher.

Cork team: Kathleen Costine, Eithne Duggan, Paula Goggins, Sandie Fitzgibbon, Mags Finn, Therese O'Callaghan (captain), Vivienne Harris, Linda Mellerick (0–1), Denise Cronin, Mary O'Connor (0–1), Fiona O'Driscoll (0–4) and Lynn Dunlea (1–9). Subs used: Stephanie Dunlea, Miriam Deasy and Irene O'Keeffe.

Imelda Hobbins, the Galway captain, shows the O'Duffy Cup to the fans at Croke Park in 1996.

1996 All-Ireland Intermediate Championship

The Down girls stamped their authority on the semi-final against Clare at Castlewellan from the outset. Five points ahead at the break, they continued to pick off scores and won convincingly. Maureen McAleenan (1–11), Valerie Hynds (2–2) and Jennifer Branniff (1–1) made huge inputs in Down's 4–14 to 1–9 victory.

Limerick's attack had much more to offer than that of opponents Armagh in the second semi-final at Ballymacnab. Eileen O'Brien, Pauline McCarthy and Bernie O'Brien were the main subscribers to Limerick's impressive tally of 4–10. Armagh put 2–4 on the board. Limerick, winners of the 1995 All-Ireland junior title, took the step up to intermediate grade in their stride. They overcame Tipperary, Armagh and Down to take the Purcell Cup.

In the final at the Gaelic Grounds, Limerick always looked in control. Vera Sheehan and Kay Burke scored goals to give Limerick a cushion at the break. A goal from Valerie Hynds gave Down hope, but Limerick's experienced defence staved off any further intrusions on their space. The final score was Limerick 2–10 Down 1–6.

Limerick team: Breda O'Brien, Helen Clifford, Agnes Sheehy, Ann Lenihan, Liz Leonard, Bernie O'Brien, Ida Quaid, Mary Burke, Vera Sheehan (1–0), Pauline McCarthy (0–6), Eileen O'Brien (0–2) and Kay Burke (1–2).

Antoinette O'Connell holds the New Ireland Cup aloft following Cork's victory over Roscommon in the 1996 All-Ireland Junior final at Croke Park. Camogie President, Belle O'Loughlin watches the reaction of the supporters

Down team: Carol Gilmore, Edel Mason, Pauline Green, Nuala Magee, Donna Greeran, Monica McCartan, Colleen Hynds, Deirdre Savage, Jennifer Branniff (0–1), Maureen McAleenan (0–4), Valerie Hynds (1–1) and Bonnie McGreevy.

1996 All-Ireland Junior Championship

Kildare headed Cork by 1–6 to 0–3 following 20 minutes of play in the semi-final at Newbridge. An injury forced Miriam Malone to retire and Kildare lost their grip on the game. Linda O'Sullivan and Antoinette O'Connell struck goals for Cork to carry them through to the final by 2–9 to 1–8.

Once again, Roscommon and Antrim were locked together. They drew in the semi-final, played at Loughgiel, by 2–7 to 1–10. The replay at Athleague was equally close. Roscommon eventually emerged from two hours of combat with a single point to spare, 5–6 to 3–11.

Both Cork and Roscommon enjoyed periods of supremacy in the final at Croke Park. However, Cork ensured a better return from the ball supplied to their attack than the Roscommon forward line did. Cork's Eileen Buckley, Mary Kennefick, Leona Nolan, Sinéad O'Callaghan and Sinéad Cahalane had a significant impact on the outcome of the game. For a county with only six clubs to draw from, reaching Croke Park was a major achievement in itself. It was devastating for the Roscommon girls to lose two finals in succession. In a team that gave their all, Maeve Healy, Caroline Connaughton, Hilary Hussey and Karina Jones caught the eye. Cork won by 6–5 to 2–7.

Cork team: Leona Nolan, Enda Dineen, Alison Dilworth, Colette Cronin, Patricia Doyle, Hilda Kenneally (1–0), Eileen Buckley (1–0), Sinéad Cahalane (0–2), Sinéad O'Callaghan (0–2), Antoinette O'Connell (captain) (1–0), Mary Kennefick (3–0) and Linda O'Sullivan (0–1). Sub used: Evelyn Healy.

Roscommon team: Ursula Hussey (0–1), Caroline Connaughton, Emer Farrell, Cáit Kenny, Teresa Carty, Karina Jones (0–4), Hilary Hussey, Charmaine Cooney, Geraldine Carr (0–1), Mary Grehan (captain), Maeve Healy (2–1) and Mary Gannon.

1996 All-Ireland Minor Championship

It took a last-minute pointed free by Kate Kelly to earn a replay for Wexford in the semi-final against Galway at Wexford Park. Galway came out on the right side of a close encounter in the replay at Loughrea. Once again, the unerring accuracy of Colette Nevin had a major say in the outcome. She

Galway minor captain, Colette Nevin holds Corn Tailteann aloft with President, Belle O'Loughlin after Galway had defeated Tipperary in 1996.

Galway – 1996 All-Ireland Minor (U16) Champions. Back: Aoife Connolly, Lorraine Murphy, Sarah Cullinane, Therese Maher, Colette Deely and Lourda Kavanagh. Front: Cathy O'Rourke, Sandra Tannian, Paula Carrick, Collette Nevin (Capt), Michelle Glynn and Veronica Sweeney.

accounted for 1–11 of Galway's 2–13 total. Wexford responded with 2–10.

The skill and opportunism of Tipperary's Eimear McDonnell and Caitríona Hennessy tore the Antrim defence asunder in the second semi-final at Loughgiel. Ahead by 3–7 to 0–4 at the break, Tipperary moved effortlessly into the final by 5–14 to 0–5.

Galway and Tipperary served up excellent fare in the All-Ireland minor final at Semple Stadium. The Connacht side raced into an early lead and appeared to be heading for an easy victory. Tipperary rallied and threw everything forward in a desperate effort to salvage the game. They reduced the margin considerably. However, in the closing minutes, the Galway defence stood firm to take the trophy for the sixth time by 3–16 to 4–11.

Galway had excellent players in Cathy O'Rourke, Colette Deely, Therese Maher, Michelle Glynn, Sandra Tannian and Colette Nevin. Thirteen-year-old Eimear McDonnell, Caitríona Hennessy, Siobhán Ryan, Emily Hayden and Niamh Dwyer worked extremely hard for Tipperary.

Galway team: Aoife Connolly, Cathy O'Rourke, Colette Deely, Lorraine Murphy, Sarah Cullinane, Paula Carrick (0–1), Michelle Glynn (0–4), Veronica Sweeney (0–1), Sandra Tannian (1–2), Therese Maher, Lourda Kavanagh (0–1) and Colette Nevin (captain) (2–7). Sub used: Ailbhe Kelly.

Tipperary team: Niamh Dwyer, Helena Frawley, Helen Campion, Emily Hayden, Niamh Connolly Jacinta Fahy, Sheena Howard (1–0), Joanne Ryan (1–0), Sinéad Sullivan, Siobhán Ryan (1–0), Eimear McDonnell (0–1) and Caitríona Hennessy (1–10) (captain). Subs used: Sinéad Collins and Helen Collier.

1996 All-Ireland Club Championship

Fourteen-year-old Eileen O'Brien, who had won All-Ireland Colleges senior and sevens medals earlier in the season, scored 11 points for Granagh-Ballingarry (Limerick) in the semi-final against Leitrim Fontenoy's (Down). The gifted teenager caused endless trouble for the Leitrim defence as she waltzed in and out between them to pop the ball over the bar. Despite the best efforts of Leitrim's Maureen McAleenan, who countered with six points, Granagh ran out easy winners by 2–15 to 0–8.

Tipperary - 1996 All-Ireland Minor Finalists. Back: Marion Graham (Selector), Conor Ryan (Selector), Jacinta Fahy, Sheena Howard, Niamh Dwyer, Joanne Ryan, Helena Frawley and Noel Hennessy. Front: Niamh Connolly, Siobhán Ryan, Catherine Hennessy (Capt), Helen Campion, Eimear McDonnell, Emily Hayden and Sinéad O'Sullivan.

All-Ireland club champions, Rathnure, were not able to live with Pearses in the second semi-final at Ballymacward. Powered by the inspirational Sharon Glynn, who scored a massive 1–10 in total, the home side built up a lead of 2–8 to 0–1 by half-time. They continued to turn the screw and finished 3–14 to 3–1 ahead.

Pearses capped a tremendous season for Galway camogie when they lifted the Bill Carroll Cup at the finish of a close, eagerly contested final against Granagh-Ballingarry at the venue of the Limerick club. The respective coaches placed great emphasises on containment. Granagh-Ballingarry's scorer-in-chief, Eileen O'Brien, was restricted to two points by Aisling Ward while Maureen Sheehan confined Sharon Glynn to four scores. It took some excellent performances right through the field by Michael Kennedy's team to emerge as champions by 1–8 to 2–3.

Pearses team: Louise Curry, Aisling Ward, Colette Deeley, Tracey Laheen, Brigid Kilgallon, Michelle Glynn, Martina Harkin, Carmel Hannon, Martina Haverty, Sharon Glynn, Áine Hillary and Anne Forde.

Granagh-Ballingarry team: Breda O'Brien, Patsy McKenna,

Bernie O'Brien, Maureen Sheehan, Ida Quaid, Jean Cullinane, Ber Chawke, Deirdre Sheehan, Kay Burke, Vera Sheehan, Laura Leslie and Eileen O'Brien.

Pearses Club: Founded in 1977 in the Ballymacward and Gurteen areas of Co. Galway by Phil O'Dowd, Valerie Higgins and Jane Beatty, the Pearses Club achieved a lot in its short history, particularly at underage level. Michael Kennedy was a Trojan worker for the club and developed many players from beginners to skilful seniors. The girls in black and white won four National Féile na nGael titles, the Kilmacud Sevens and two All-Ireland club championship titles.

1996 Gael-Linn Senior Cup

The Gael-Linn Interprovincial series were played off on June 16th at Russell Park. Connacht and Ulster were very evenly matched and produced a very entertaining game of camogie. Maureen McAleenan (2-7) and Denise Gilligan (2-6) were the leading lights for their respective provinces. The score stood at Ulster 4-8 Connacht 4-7 at the referee's whistle.

It was sad to see Leinster, a province with a proud record in the Gael-Linn Cup, offer such poor resistance to Munster in the second semi-final. As the final score, 3-16 to 0-6 suggests, Munster won as they pleased.

Ulster stretched Munster all the way in the final. Eight points ahead at the break, Ulster seemed to be on the way to victory. Munster whittled away at the lead and caught them on the line. The match went to extra-time and Munster, the fitter side, lasted the pace better to win by 4-18 to 6-10. Fiona O'Driscoll (Munster) (2-10) and Maureen McAleenan (Ulster) (3-4) had enjoyable outings.

Munster team: Kathleen Costine (Cork), Eithne Duggan (Cork), Miriam Deasy (Cork), Mags Finn (Cork), Triona Bonnar (Tipperary), Catherine O'Loughlin (Clare), Vivienne Harris (Cork), Denise Cronin (Cork) (captain), Lynn Dunlea (Cork), Fiona O'Driscoll (Cork), Irene O'Keeffe (Cork) and Deirdre Hughes (Tipperary).

Ulster team: Margaret McKee (Armagh), Martina Mulholland (Derry), Edel Mason (Down), Pauline Greene (Down), Deirdre Savage (Down), Geraldine Haughey (Armagh), Mary Black (Armagh) (captain), Leona Fay (Tyrone), Bernie McBride (Armagh), Maureen McAleenan (Down), Grace McMullan (Antrim) and Colette Byrne (Armagh).

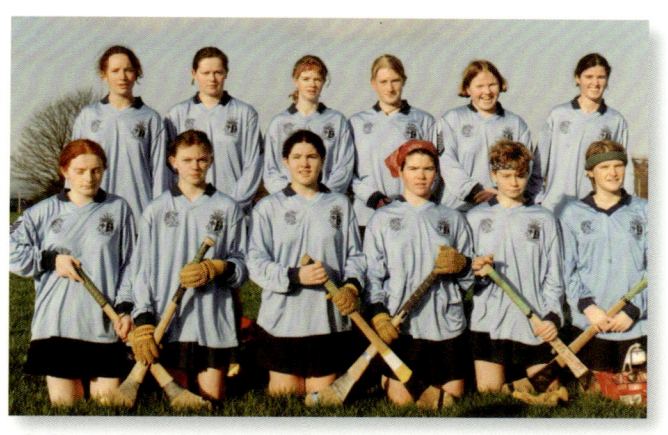

St. Mary's Secondary School, Charleville – 1996 All-Ireland Senior Colleges Champions

1996 Gael-Linn Junior Trophy

Ulster had an easy win over Connacht, 3–12 to 1–3, in the semi-final at Russell Park and Munster proved much too strong for Leinster by 4–13 to 2–7 in the second semi-final. Munster had little trouble in completing the double. They outscored Ulster by 3–17 to 1–7.

Munster team: Breda O'Brien (Limerick), Niamh Bonnar (Tipperary), Paula Bulfin (Tipperary), Claire Madden (Tipperary), Ann Lenihan (Limerick), Hilda Kenneally (Cork), Mary O'Connor (Cork), Maeve Stokes (Tipperary), Noelle Kennedy (Tipperary), Helen Kiely (Tipperary), Pauline McCarthy (Limerick) and Vera Sheehan (Limerick).

Ulster team: Fiona Daly (Tyrone), Donna Greeran (Down), Paula Daly (Fermanagh), Cathy Mulholland (Down), Mary Rose McGrady (Tyrone), Eileen O'Neill (Derry), Denise O'Boyle (Antrim), Ita Brady (Cavan), Michelle Corry (Fermanagh), Mary O'Kane (Derry), Sinéad McGovern (Down) and Elaine Dowds (Antrim).

Phyllis Breslin Elected President

Phyllis Breslin (Dublin) was elected President of the Camogie Association at Congress 1997, which was held in Athlone. Widely known as a referee, Phyllis officiated at All-Ireland senior and junior finals. She had served two terms as chairperson of Leinster Council and had been director of organisation in 1983.

Phyllis Breslin

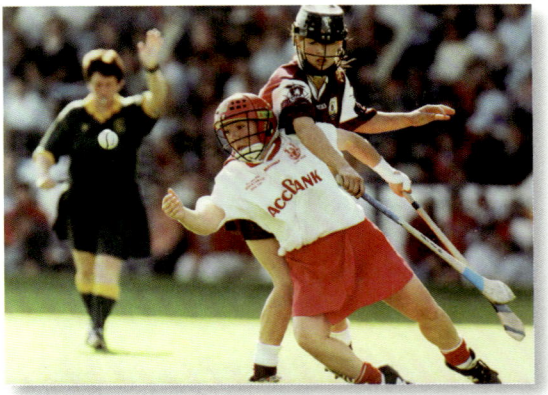

Referee Biddy Phillips signals for a free as Fiona O'Driscoll (Cork) is held back by Galway's Therese Maher in the 1997 All-Ireland senior final at Croke Park.

Coaching Development Programme

The Camogie Association participated in the National Coaching Development Programme in partnership with the National Coaching and Training Centre, Limerick. The first step was to put an effective coaching organisational structure in place. Selecting tutors to be trained in the NCTC, Limerick, was the next action. Brendan Williams, Collette Kennedy, Grace O'Neill, Cathy Hannigan, Bonnie McGreevy and Sarah Russell completed the development programme in 1996. Attention was given to development of syllabi, course content and support material. Foundation and Level 1 courses were developed and organised. A national presentation of Coaching Certificates to Foundation and Level 1 coaches took place on April 26th 1997 to all coaches who had completed the necessary requirements. A calendar of courses was produced and circulated to county boards and councils. Not satisfied to rest on their laurels, the coaching committee pressed ahead to develop the next level and produce tutor manuals.

Step Closer to GAA

Camogie President, Phyllis Breslin, hands the O'Duffy Cup to Cork captain, Linda Mellerick in September, 1997.

1997 All-Ireland Senior Championship

Superbly led by midfielder Sharon Glynn, Galway took a giant step towards retaining their All-Ireland title when they registered a nine-point win over Kilkenny in the semi-final at Loughrea. Sharon came off the field with 2–12 to her name. Ann Downey played herself to a standstill in Kilkenny's cause, but she lacked support to prevent Galway advancing by 4–14 to 2–11.

Wexford were outplayed in almost every area of the field by Cork in the second semi-final at Páirc Uí Rínn. Seven points ahead at the break, Cork did much as they pleased in the second period and kept the scoreboard operator busy to the end. Wexford yielded by 3–22 to 1–7.

Galway and Cork renewed acquaintance for the All-Ireland final at Croke Park on September 7th. Kathleen Costine, Therese O'Callaghan and Paula Goggins had retired and were replaced by Cora Keohane and Sinéad O'Callaghan. Denise Cronin switched from attack to defence. Cork made no mistake this time. They were highly motivated following the previous year's slip-up. Good work by Sandie Fitzgibbon, Vivienne Harris and Lynn Dunlea saw Cork turn-over with a six-point lead.

Denise Gilligan cut Cork's advantage to three points but Lynn Dunlea tapped over two points to redress the situation. The introduction of Veronica Curtin improved the Galway attack. Eithne Duggan and Denise Cronin coped admirably. Cork supporters had to endure five minutes additional time during which a pass from Veronica Curtin to Therese Maher in a most dangerous position was intercepted and Cora Keohane stopped a bullet from Therese Maher. The whistle sounded with the score at Cork 0–15, Galway 2–5.

Cork team: Cora Keohane, Eithne Duggan, Denise Cronin, Sandie Fitzgibbon, Mags Finn, Linda Mellerick (captain), Vivienne Harris (0–4), Mary O'Connor (0–1), Sinéad O'Callaghan, Fiona O'Driscoll, Irene O'Keeffe and Lynn Dunlea (0–10). Sub used: Eileen Buckley.

Officers of Cork Camogie Board 1997. Back: Mary McSweeney, Mary Newman-McCarthy, Marion McCarthy and Kay Dunne. Front: Sheila Golden, Mary Moran and Tracey Sheehan.

Galway team: Louise Curry, Olive Costello, Olivia Broderick, Tracey Laheen, Pamela Nevin, Gretta Maher, Sharon Glynn (0–3), Dympna Maher, Martina Harkin (captain), Imelda Hobbins, Denise Gilligan (1–0) and Anne Forde (0–1). Subs used: Veronica Curtin (1–1) and Therese Maher.

Cliona Meaney (Cork) and Grace McMullan (Antrim) challenge for possession in the 1997 All-Ireland Junior final at Croke Park.

1997 All-Ireland Intermediate Championship

Tipperary survived a real struggle against Armagh in the semi-final for 40 minutes of the match. By then, Armagh had run their course. Tipperary notched several late scores for a clear-cut 4–15 to 3–11 win. Ciara Gaynor (1–5), Jovita Delaney (1–4), Caitríona Hennessy (1–2) and Deirdre Hughes (1–1) were the main contributors. Mary Black registered 1–6 for Armagh.

The Down players jetted into Shannon to face Clare in the second semi-final. Clare reversed the result of the previous year's meeting of these teams in some style, 5–14 to 4–5.

A superb second-half show by Clare left Down in their wake. Sinéad O'Brien shot 4–2 while her Clare colleagues struck points from all angles and distances to win the match convincingly.

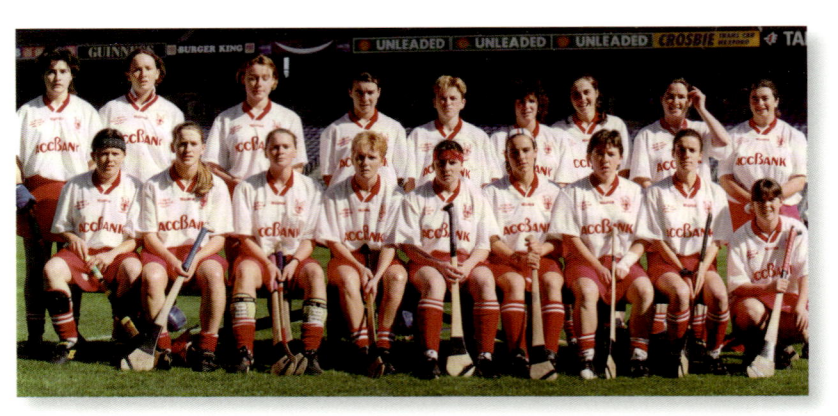

Cork – 1997 All-Ireland Senior Champions. Back: Eithne Duggan, Sinéad O'Callaghan, Stephanie Dunlea, Vivienne Harris, Irene O'Keeffe, Sandie Fitzgibbon, Eileen Buckley, Miriam Deasy and Mary Kennefick. Front: Mags Finn, Mary O'Connor, Cora Keohane, Linda Mellerick (Capt), Denise Cronin, Lynn Dunlea, Fiona O'Driscoll, Hilda Kenneally and Linda O'Sullivan.

Noelle Kennedy contributed a massive 1–18 of Tipperary's total in the All-Ireland final against Clare at The Ragg. Team captain, Deirdre Hughes, also had a huge game for the Premier County. She won regular possession and set up scoring opportunities for the players around her. Ciara Gaynor, Claire Madden, Maeve Stokes and Sinéad Nealon made considerable impacts for the winners. Áine McCormack, Catherine O'Loughlin, Ann Keane, Moira McMahon and Sinéad O'Brien kept Clare in the game which ended Tipperary 2–19, Clare 2–12.

Tipperary team: Nora Dwane, Emily Hayden, Sinéad Nealon (0–1), Suzanne Kelly, Claire Madden, Maeve Stokes, Ciara Gaynor, Therese Brophy, Noelle Kennedy (1–18), Helen Kiely, Jovita Delaney and Deirdre Hughes (captain) (1–0).

Clare team: Áine McCormack, Debbie McDonagh, Marie Collins (1–0), Orla Slattery, Sinéad McMahon, Moira McMahon (captain) (0–5), Sinéad O'Brien, Edel Arthur, Noelle Comyns, Deirdre Murphy, Ann Keane (0–3) and Catherine O'Loughlin (1–4).

1997 All-Ireland Junior Championship

Antrim had a real struggle on their hands when they came face-to-face with Carlow in the semi-final at Casement Park. A Valerie Crean goal saw the Leinster county ahead by 1–3 to 0–4 at the end of a physical first half. Ann McKee and Oonagh Elliott came to Antrim's rescue with goals to secure a place in the final by 2–11 to 1–8.

A new Cork side turned in a top-class display to edge past Galway in the semi-final at Loughrea. The player of the match was Caoimhe Harrington who ran up a personal total of 2–9. Late goals from Caroline Murray and Michelle Glynn cut the deficit but Cork managed to hold out to win by 3–11 to 4–7.

Antrim took the field against Cork in the final at Croke Park wearing the mantle of favourites. Trained by the highly rated hurling coach, Jim Nelson, Antrim were the far more experienced outfit. Grace McMullan raced through the Cork defence to goal with her first taste of action. The signs were ominous even at that early stage of the game. Antrim won the various contests all over the field. Leading by 4–7 to 0–4 at the break, Antrim had the game sewn up. With wind assistance, Cork improved in the second half but they did not seriously trouble Antrim who went on to win by 7–11 to 2–10.

It was an emotional time for the McMullan sisters, Grace and Mary (née Connolly), who, sadly, buried their father at the start of the week. Eighteen years earlier, Mary had been a member of the Antrim team that had won the All-Ireland senior championship. Thus, she became the first player to follow a senior All-Ireland medal with a junior.

Antrim team: Karen Coyles, Brenda McNeill, Mary Connolly, Sinéad McMullan, Maureen Barry, Bronagh O'Neill, Denise O'Boyle (0–2), Claire McGarry, Ann McKee (0–4), Grace McMullan (2–3) Caitríona Higgins (3–2) and Deirdre Heatley (2–0). Subs used: Gráinne Connolly, Oonagh Elliott and Carla Doherty.

Cork team: Sandra Ricken, Cliona Meaney, Sabrina Buckley, Muireann Harrington, Lisa Kelleher, Ursula Troy (0–1), Eimear O'Sullivan, Tina Roche, Eleanor Kenneally (captain), Criona Harte (0–3), Caoimhe Harrington (1–4) and Una O'Donoghue (0–1). Subs used: Nora Aherne (1–1), Helen Kelleher, Elaine Harte and Valerie O'Keeffe.

President Mary McAleese welcomes Sheila Wallace to Árus an Uachtaráin. Micheál Ó Muircheartaigh, Angela Downey-Browne and her daughter, Katie, are also in the picture.

1997 All-Ireland Minor Championship

Cork were much too skilful and streetwise for a disappointing Dublin in the semi-final at Páirc Uí Rínn. The Cork attack had things much their own way and finished ahead by 3–10 to 0–4. In the second semi-final at Loughrea, the Antrim forward-line scored a very respectable 4–2 against Galway, however, their defence leaked scores to the extent that the outcome was obvious long before the end. The final score was Galway 7–19, Antrim 4–2.

The Galway minors showed great appetite for work in the All-Ireland final against Cork at Páirc Uí Rínn. Veronica Sweeney and Therese Maher won most of the ball that entered the midfield area. A good supply of ball was converted into points by Lourda Kavanagh, Elaine Kerins and Mairéad Meehan. When Cork managed to get the ball to their forwards, it was often wasted by poor shooting. Great defending by Donna Burke and Susan O'Regan prevented Cork from closing the gap. Goals by Elaine Kerins and Orla Kilkenny sealed a very deserving win for Galway. An injury-time goal by Elaine Burke put a better complexion on the scoreboard from Cork's point of view. Galway won by 2–14 to 1–6.

Group of former U.C.C. Ashbourne players pictured at presentation to Hannah Dineen. Back: Celine Coakley and Marion Keohane. Front: Sheila Dunne, Emer Hurley, Hannah Dineen and Catherine O'Riordan.

Galway team: Fiona Gahery, Susan O'Regan, Donna Burke, Ailbhe Kelly, Siobhán Hardiman, Therese Maher (0–2), Mairéad Mahoney, Veronica Sweeney, Siobhán Cummins (0–2), Lourda Kavanagh (0–4), Mairéad Meehan (0–3) and Elaine Kerins (1–3). Subs used: Orla Kilkenny (1–0), Colette Glennon and Sherrie Mannion.

Cork team: Geraldine Casey, Amanda O'Regan, Sinéad Buckley, Julie Ann Kingston, Sarah Hayes, Sabrina Buckley (0–1), Elaine Burke (1–1), Mary Enneguess (0–1), Rachel Moloney (0–2), Sinéad Kelly, Una O'Donoghue and Liz Power. Subs used: Ciara Healy (0–1) and Mary O'Connell.

Cork were well beaten in this match. Yet eight of the Cork players listed above went on to win All-Ireland senior medals. On the other hand, none of the Galway girls reached that goal. This raises questions as to how players are managed and developed.

1997 All-Ireland Club Championship

Classed as the camogie game of the year, the All-Ireland club semi-final between Lisdowney and Granagh-Ballingarry at Lisdowney had everything. It served up tremendous entertainment, an array of breathtaking skills, superb scores, brilliant defensive work and a heart-stopping finish. Marina Downey and Kelly Long were top-class while Angela and Ann Downey engineered scores when it did not seem possible. Granagh-Ballingarry lost the game but came off the field with their reputation enhanced. The scoreboard showed Lisdowney 3-15, Granagh-Ballingarry 3-13 at the final whistle.

Sharper in attack and more competent all-round, Pearses proved a handful for Loughgiel in the second semi-final. Once again, Sharon Glynn dictated proceedings and set up scoring opportunities that were gratefully finished by Anne Forde and Áine Hillary. The Co. Galway club marched on to the final by 3-14 to 1-7.

The final offered five members of the Pearses team a perfect opportunity to put the heartbreak of Galway's loss to Cork in the All-Ireland senior decider behind them. They knuckled down and focused on the retention of their All-Ireland title. Playing with passion and skill, Pearses forged a lead of 3-3 to 1-0 by the interval. Lisdowney upped their game and looked very dangerous in front of goal. Ann Downey crashed a free to the net and Marina Downey added three points. With only a score between them, the match was there to be won by either side. Martina Haverty col-

National Player of the Year Imelda Hobbins (Galway) with Camogie President, Phyllis Breslin.

lected a long ball from Michelle Glynn and palmed it to the net. Pearses retained their title by 4-6 to 2-5.

Pearses team: Louise Curry, Aisling Ward, Martina Harkin, Tracey Laheen, Bridget Kilgannon, Veronica Sweeney, Michelle Glynn, Carmel Hannon, Áine Hillary, Sharon Glynn, Martina Haverty and Anne Forde (captain). Sub used: Shauna Ward.

Lisdowney team: Miriam Holland, Fran Shore, Bridget Barnaville, Kelly Long, Olivia Donnelly, Marina Downey, Ann Downey, Catherine Dunne, Ann Marie Hughes, Lizzie Fogarty, Angela Downey, Anna Whelan. Subs used: Áine Dunne and Sandra Gleeson.

1997 Gael-Linn Senior Cup

Thirty-three scores were divided between Leinster and Ulster in the Gael-Linn senior semi-final at Russell Park. The odd score in the split fell to Leinster in a cracking contest and they advanced by 3-14 to 3-13. In the second semi-final, Munster had seven points to spare at the finish of an entertaining contest. Lynn Dunlea notched 2-5 for Munster who won by 3-14 to 2-10.

Leinster were in front by four points with ten minutes remaining in the final against Munster at Russell Park. But Munster managed to rescue the game and added 3-7 in extra-time to lift the title. The final score was Munster 4–18, Leinster 2–11.

Munster team: Cora Keohane (Cork), Eithne Duggan (Cork), Marie Collins (Clare), Jovita Delaney (Tipperary), Mary O'Connor (Cork), Fiona O'Driscoll (Cork), Moira McMahon (Clare), Sinéad O'Callaghan (Cork), Lynn Dunlea (Cork), Pauline McCarthy (Limerick), Linda Mellerick (Cork) and Deirdre Hughes (Tipperary).

Leinster team: Michelle Fennelly (Kilkenny), Avis Nolan (Wexford), Esther Kennedy (Kilkenny), Sinéad Costello (Kilkenny), Kelly Long (Kilkenny), Michelle O'Leary (Wexford), Marina Downey (Kilkenny), Margaret Hickey (Kilkenny), Kate Kelly (Wexford), Catherine Dunne (Kilkenny), Geraldine Codd (Wexford) and Esme Murphy (Wexford).

Tyrone delegates, Bridie McMenamin and Anne Burke at Annual Congress in Roscommon.

Hughes scored 3–1 to place her side on the road to victory.

Munster team: Leona Nolan (Cork), Emily Hayden (Tipperary), Alison Dilworth (Cork), Hilda Kenneally (Cork), Sinéad O'Callaghan (Cork), Helena Frawley (Tipperary), Linda O'Sullivan (Cork), Mary Kennefick (Cork), Enda Dineen (Cork), Jovita Delaney (Tipperary), Deirdre Hughes (Tipperary) and Sinéad Collins (Tipperary).

Leinster team: Mary Henry (Westmeath), Aoife Davitt (Westmeath), Melanie Treacy (Kildare), Derville O'Carroll (Dublin), Claire O'Connor (Wexford), Michelle Davis (Offaly), Ailish Atkinson (Wexford), Christine O'Brien (Meath), Nuala Quirke (Carlow), Annette Heffernan (Westmeath), Miriam Malone (Kildare) and Valerie Crean (Carlow).

1997 Gael-Linn Junior Trophy

Munster led Connacht all the way in the junior semi-final at Russell Park. Connacht finished strongly but left it too late to catch Munster.

The eventual score was Munster 3–14, Connacht 4–6. Leinster shaded a close, low-scoring tussle with Ulster in the second semi-final. Miriam Malone got the only goal of the game which ended Leinster 1–8, Ulster 0–7. Munster did enough to retain their title by 3–11 to 2–10 against Leinster in the final. Tipperary's Deirdre

Where We're At

Discussions on forging a closer relationship between the Camogie Association and the GAA had been ongoing since 1987. The Camogie Association has enjoyed the support of the GAA at various levels over many years, particularly in the provision of playing facilities and at Bunscoileanna level.

The initial move was made by the GAA under the direction of their president, Dr Michael Loftus. The GAA wished it to be known that they took ladies Gaelic games seriously and were willing to give whatever help they could without interfering in the organisations. Discussions continued and problem areas, e.g. voting rights, membership fees, suspensions and club property, were identified and called for further deliberation. Various types of affiliation were considered. The first major step forward was the acceptance of a motion at the 1994 GAA Congress: "That the association shall support the promotion of camogie and ladies football."

It was considered of mutual benefit to work together at club level. The GAA undertook to encourage its clubs to set up camogie sections and to integrate camogie teams into the club and go forward together. They envisaged the club as a family unit catering for all age groups. The Camogie Association approved a motion in 1995 to affiliate as a confederate body to the GAA.

Real progress has been made at club level, where hurling, football, camogie and ladies football run their own affairs under a central committee. All units assist with fundraising schemes on behalf of the club and approved outgoings are met by the central committee. A system covering the use of club facilities is decided upon with all sectors receiving their time slots. This arrangement, where all sports coming under the one umbrella, works at club level. At national level, both associations continued to be autonomous in the running of their own affairs and bound by their own constitution and playing rules.

In her report to the 1996 Congress, Árd Stiúrthóir, Sheila Wallace, gave a breakdown of the winners of the All-Ireland competitions for the previous decade during which time 64 titles were shared by 11 counties: Kilkenny and Cork dominated the senior grade; Clare, Dublin and Armagh shared the intermediate title; Kildare, Galway, Clare, Down, Tipperary, Armagh and Limerick carried off the junior crown; Galway, Kilkenny, Tipperary and Wexford were winners in the minor grade; while the club championship trophy found a home in Cork, Kilkenny, Galway and Wexford. Leinster was the most successful province with 36 titles. They were followed by Munster with 29; Ulster with ten and Connacht with nine titles. The same names were repeated as a handful of counties dominated the scene. The case for lower grade championships, which were to come later, was evident.

Rosina McManus, Sr. Mairéad and Lily Spence having a tea-break at the 1997 All-Ireland Colleges Sevens.

A Game of Our Own

CAMERADERIE

Chapter Twenty

NEW DAWN FOR TIPPERARY

Congress 1998 in Wexford meandered through a long agenda of reports with few decisions of note being taken. However, a further step on the road to the 15-a-side game was made. All competitions under the auspices of Central Council, provincial councils and county boards would be run as a test series for the new format in 1999. Connacht Council sought, unsuccessfully, to confine teams to 13 players.

A working party was set up to examine the structures of all All-Ireland championships with particular reference to the promotion, relegation, grading, marketing and protocol applied to each final. A motion to discontinue the Ceol, Caint agus Damhsa competitions was passed by 32 votes to 6 much to the disappointment of the Ulster delegates. However, interest had been on the wane for some time and only six counties, four from Ulster and two from Connacht, participated in the 1997 event. Wexford were successful in their attempt to have the two All-Ireland senior championship semi-finals played on the same day at a neutral venue.

Life Presidency of the Camogie Association was conferred on Sheila McAnulty, who gave three-quarters of a century of service to camogie, at Congress in Thurles in 1999.

warmly welcomed. A lively and colourful issue, it captured the events, personalities and views of the 1998 season. Máire Ní Cheallaigh, Domhnall Ó Murchú and Máire Uí Scolaí put in a massive effort to make the annual a reality.

The Ragg

The Tipperary County Board showed courage and foresight in undertaking a major development at The Ragg. The first sod was turned on the site of their new grounds on March 7th 1998. A fine pitch was laid out and work commenced on the erection of dressing rooms. Shortage of pitches to play our games has always been a problem in camogie circles. These much-needed facilities proved to be a godsend to the county and their progress coincided with

Camogie Abú

The publication of *Camogie Abú*, the first annual since 1976, was

the advancement and success of camogie in the county. In the years since, Tipperary County Board has added a stand, car-parking facilities and other amenities to the grounds.

1998 All-Ireland Senior Championship

The semi-finals were staged together as a very attractive programme at Nowlan Park. Tipperary, who were on a high following their win over Kilkenny, had to field without star forward, Deirdre Hughes. While their opponents, Galway, were handicapped by the absence of Sharon Glynn. In what was the better of the two contests on view, both counties had their period of supremacy and neither was able to draw clear of the other. A long free by Colette Nevin reached Anne Forde who fired it to the Tipperary net. The score lifted Galway's spirits and they added two further points to finish by 2–11 to 0–14.

While never in any danger of losing the match, Cork gave a below-par performance against Clare. Mary O'Connor, Linda Mellerick and Vivienne Harris won midfield and set up numerous chances that were spurned by their forwards. However, goals by Sinéad O'Callaghan and Irene O'Keeffe placed Cork on the road to a 2-15 to 1-9 victory.

Lynn Dunlea Cork breaks her hurl in a tussle for possession with Olivia Broderick Galway, All Ireland Camogie Final, Croke Park. Pic: SPORTSFILE

In the first All-Ireland camogie final to be televised live, Galway and Cork put on a display worthy of the occasion in Croke Park on September 6th. A storm raged over Dublin which was so violent that RTÉ that enquired on more than one occasion during the morning if the match would go ahead. Playing into the teeth of a gale, Galway made the early running but two well-taken goals by Irene O'Keeffe gave Cork a lead that they never lost. Cork defended heroically for the remainder of the game with huge performances from Linda Mellerick, Denise Cronin, Eithne Duggan and Cora Keohane.

At times, Galway dominated the play thanks to the strength and skill of Sharon Glynn, Colette Nevin and Therese Maher but the Cork defence denied them scoring opportunities. Cork won by 2–13 to 0–15 in what was a victory for grit, determination and never-say-die attitude.

Cork team: Cora Keohane, Eithne Duggan (captain), Denise Cronin, Vivienne Harris, Mags Finn, Ursula Troy, Mary O'Connor (0–1), Linda Mellerick, Sinéad O'Callaghan, Fiona O'Driscoll (0–3), Irene O'Keeffe (2–0) and Lynn Dunlea (0–9). Subs used: Miriam Deasy and Paula O'Connor.

New Dawn for Tipperary

Galway team: Louise Curry, Olivia Broderick (captain), Anne Broderick, Tracey Laheen, Pamela Nevin, Therese Maher (0–3), Sharon Glynn (0–1), Áine Hillary (0–1), Colette Nevin (0–7), Imelda Hobbins (0–1), Veronica Curtin (0–1) and Anne Forde (0–1). Sub used: Denise Gilligan.

Cork captain, Eithne Duggan, is a daughter of Phil Duggan who won a Railway Cup hurling medal with Munster. Ursula Troy is a niece of Fr Bertie Troy who coached Cork senior hurlers to All-Ireland success. This victory for Cork was the sixth success for coach, Tom Nott.

1998 All-Ireland Intermediate Championship

Cork's second string had an easy win over Armagh in the semi-final at Ballincollig. The home side led by 1–10 to 0–4 at the break, leaving the Ulster side with a mountain to climb in the second period. But it was Cork that drove on to win convincingly by 4–16 to 0–6.

There was very little between the two Ulster counties, Down and Antrim, in the second semi-final at Loughgiel. The accuracy of Down's Maureen McAleenan, who struck 1–12, was a major factor in the destination of the trophy. However, Down had to give every ounce of energy to hold off the challenge of Antrim by 2–14 to 3–10.

Down should have had the final against Cork at Páirc Uí Rínn won long before the end. They enjoyed the lion's share of possession but struck 16 wides. Cork were afforded little scope by the tight-marking Down defence. Donna Greeran, Edel Mason and Pauline Green snuffed out any potential threat by the Cork forwards. Jill Hannon, Helen Walsh and Ger Casey performed up to standard for Cork but they had to rely too much on Criona Harte's free-taking for scores. Down were full

Cork – 1998 All-Ireland Senior Champions. Back: Mags Finn, Linda Mellerick, Sinead O'Callaghan, Vivienne Harris, Ursula Troy and Linda O'Sullivan. Front: Irene O'Keeffe, Mary O'Connor, Cora Keohane, Eithne Duggan (Capt), Denise Cronin, Lynn Dunlea and Fiona O'Driscoll. Mascots: Orla Keane and Katie Sheehan.

Down – 1998 All-Ireland Intermediate Champions. Back: Nuala Magee, Cathy Mulholland, Maureen McAleenan, Claire McGrath, Edel Mason, Teresa McGowan and Jennifer Braniff. Front: Ann Morgan, Ciara Cunningham, Pauline Green, Deirdre Savage, Colleen Hynds (Capt), Valerie Hynds, Joan Henderson, Majella Murray and Donna Greeran.

value for their 1–12 to 1–8 win.

Down team: Teresa McGowan, Donna Greeran, Pauline Greene, Edel Mason, Deirdre Savage, Colleen Hynds (captain), Majella Murray, Valerie Hynds (0–1), Jennifer Braniff (0–1), Maureen McAleenan (1–7), Joan Henderson (0–2) and Clare McGrath (0–1).

Cork team: Ger Casey, Enda Dineen, Jill Hannon, Helen Walsh, Caroline Giltenane, Eimear O'Sullivan, Marie Corkery, Tina Roche, Sinéad Cahalane (captain) (0–1), Elaine Burke, Criona Harte (0–7) and Una O'Donoghue (1–0).

1998 All-Ireland Junior Championship

Carlow won their third Leinster title in six years to qualify for the All-Ireland junior semi-final. But once again, they found the next step, the chance to line out in Croke Park, out of their reach. In a keenly contested game against Galway at Carlow, the Connacht county emerged with five points to spare, 3–10 to 1–11.

Bronagh Birt goaled on the stroke of time to earn Derry a replay against Tipperary at The Ragg. Scores were even at the end of a highly entertaining first-half. Tipperary drew seven points clear but were hauled back at the finishing line. Precious goals by Niamh Dwyer and Sheena Howard carried Tipperary past

Galway – 1998 All-Ireland Junior Champions. Back: Caroline Murray, Michelle Glynn, Veronica Sweeney, Ailbhe Kelly, Aoife Connolly and Lourda Kavanagh. Front: Aoife Lynskey, Fiona Healy, Rita Broderick, Ann Dolan, Brenda Daniels and Sandra Tannian.

the challenge of Derry in the replay at Bellaghy. Derry were very much in the game in the first-half but their defiance faded as the game wore on. Tipperary advanced by 2–9 to 0–11.

Tipperary and Galway served up a memorable exhibition of camogie in the All-Ireland junior final. The conditions at Croke Park were appalling. Driving rain and gale-force winds did not deter these skilful exponents of the game. It took a stunning second-half show by Galway to see off the spirited challenge of a gallant Tipperary side. Lourda Kavanagh gave a brilliant display at centre-forward. Michelle Glynn, Brenda Daniels, Ann Dolan and Sandra Tannian stood out on a fine Galway side. Angela McDermott, Alice Deane, Siobhán Cusack, Philly Fogarty and Sheena Howard caught the eye with their accomplished play for Tipperary. Galway claimed the title by 3–11 to 2–10.

Galway team: Aoife Connolly, Ann Dolan (captain), Rita Broderick, Ailbhe Kelly, Fiona Healy, Michelle Glynn, Caroline Murray (0–1), Veronica Sweeney, Aoife Lynskey (0–1), Lourda Kavanagh (1–9), Brenda Daniels (1–0) and Sandra Tannian (1–0). Sub used: Eileen Earls.

Tipperary team: Louise Ryan, Siobhán Cusack, Maeve Corcoran, Tess Bourke, Niamh Connolly, Philly Fogarty (0–2), Alice

New Dawn for Tipperary

Deane (captain) (0–4), Angela McDermott, Joanne Ryan (0–1), Sheena Howard (1–1), Gráinne Shanahan (1–1) and Niamh Dwyer (0–1). Subs used: Mary Looby and Fiona Loughnane.

1998 All-Ireland Minor Championship

Only a hair's-breadth separated Galway and Cork in the semi-final at Loughrea. At the close of a tremendous contest between two very talented teams, Galway's Doreen Kelly bore down on the Cork goal but the referee's whistle sounded before she got in her shot. Cork held out to win by 0–13 to 1–9.

A brilliant team performance by Derry caught Kilkenny in the second semi-final at Castledawson. Derry made the early running and had Kilkenny struggling to keep pace. The home side defended valiantly as the clock ticked on. Susan Kelly set up Paula McCloy for a Derry goal and a ticket to the final on the score of 2–8 to 1–7.

Cork bridged a 13-year gap to extend their collection of All-Ireland minor titles to nine at the expense of Derry at Ballincollig. Derry had no answer to a dynamic Cork outfit. Cork controlled midfield and sent a generous supply of good ball to Ciara Healy, Caitríona Kelly and Rachel Moloney who obliged with some spectacular scores. Cork won comfortably by 3–18 to 1–5.

Group pictured prior to the 1998 All-Ireland minor final at Ballincollig. From left are Cork captain, Catherine Corkery, referee Vera Mulcahy (Limerick), Camogie President, Phyllis Breslin and Derry captain, Sinéad Stephens.

At half-time, the Carrigaline Pipe Band played a lament and the large crowd stood in silence for a minute as a mark of respect to those who had been killed or injured in Omagh the previous Sunday.

Cork team: Aoife Murray, Rosarii Holland, Joanne O'Callaghan, Sarah Hayes (0–2), Amanda O'Regan, Catherine Corkery (0–2), Rachel Moloney (0–6), Bríd O'Neill (0–1), Emer Dillon (0–2), Ciara Healy (1–3), Maria Noonan (0–1) and Caitríona Kelly (2–1). Subs used: Áine Kelleher, Joan Twomey, Liz Bugler, Edel Foley and Jennifer O'Leary.

Derry team: Áine O'Kane, Áine Bradley, Charlene Moore (0–1), Sinéad Stephens, Claire Lagan, Lorna Mulholland (0–2), Susan Kelly, Aisling Kealey (0–1), Paula McCloy, Monica O'Kane (0–1), Claire McColgan (1–0) and Jane Kelly.

1998 All-Ireland Club Championship

Eileen O'Brien, a student at St Mary's, Charleville, was the chief playmaker and scorer for Granagh-Ballingarry against the reigning All-Ireland champions, Pearses, at Ballymacward, Co. Galway. She registered 1–7 while the girls around her fed off her accurate passes. Champions in 1996 and 1997, Pearses failed to find their usual flowing game. When Sharon Glynn had to retire injured, the game was over. Granagh-Ballingarry advanced to the final by

A Game of Our Own

2-11 to 2-4. Maureen McAleenan, Fontenoy's scoring ace, was well shackled by Patsy Murphy, Patricia Clinton and Niamh Cregan in the second semi-final. The Down club suffered big time as a result. Meanwhile Louise Lynch, Denise O'Leary and Denise Smith found their range at the other end and steered St Vincent's to a 3-12 to 1-8 win at Raheny.

Munster Club Champions in 1997 and 1998, Granagh-Ballingarry approached the final against St Vincent's at Ballingarry with steely determination. This one was not going to get away. The arrival of Cork player, Mary O'Connor, boosted their chances.

The Limerick side got down to business from the throw in and left St Vincent's trailing by eight points after 20 minutes. The Granagh-Ballingarry half-forward line of Vera Sheehan, Eileen O'Brien and Mary O'Connor surged forward time and again, picking off delightful points with unerring accuracy. The Dublin side fought back from a poor start and chipped away at the Granagh-Ballingarry lead. Captain Germaine Noonan, Patricia Clinton and Niamh Cregan, daughter of All-Ireland hurler, Eamon Cregan, battled bravely but could not stop Granagh-Ballingarry from taking the title by 1-19 to 1-8.

Granagh-Ballingarry team: Breda O'Brien, Bernie O'Brien, Patricia McKenna, Bernie Chawke, Laura Leslie, Jean Cullinane, Deirdre Sheehan, Kay Burke, Eileen O'Brien, Mary O'Connor, Vera Sheehan (captain) and Ida Quaid.

St Vincent's team: Mary Regan, Patsy Murphy, Niamh Cregan, Patricia Clinton, Germaine Noonan (captain), Ursula Hannon, Denise O'Leary, Róisín Brady, Louise Lynch, Adrienne McGovern, Denise Smith and Emer Brannigan.

President Mary McAleese pictured with three past presidents of the Camogie Association, Nancy Murray, Lily Spence and Rosina McManus.

Granagh-Ballingarry – 1998 All-Ireland Club Champions. Back: Bernie Chawke, Maureen Sheehan, Patricia McKenna, Caroline O'Connor, Marie O'Brien, Sheila Treacy, Bernie O'Brien, Ida Quaid and Claire Lenihan. Front: Jean Cullinane, Breda O'Brien, Eileen O'Brien, Kay Burke, Vera Sheehan (Capt), Deirdre Sheehan, Laura Leslie, Kathryn Leslie and Mary O'Connor.

New Dawn for Tipperary

Granagh-Ballingarry Club: was formed in 1976 when efforts were made to bring camogie to the twin parishes. Michael O'Brien and John O'Connor concentrated on teaching the skills to the youngsters who grew up to be champions. They won all around them from under 12 to senior. Tommy Treacy transformed talented teenagers into highly proficient adult players. The majority of the team went to St Mary's Secondary School, Charleville, where they came under the guidance of top coach, Vincent Harrington. When Mike Chawke took over the senior team in 1992, the Limerick and Munster championships started to roll in. Mike married team member, Bernie O'Brien. The girls in black and white won three All-Ireland club championship titles.

1998 Gael-Linn Senior Cup

Heavy rain acted as a spoilsport and made it hard for the players to produce their best at St Vincent's Grounds. Leinster had a narrow 2–7 to 2–4 win over Connacht while Munster got the better of Ulster in a high-scoring game by 5–19 to 2–13. Munster collected their fourth title on-the-trot with a facile 6–20 to 1–11 win over Leinster. Cork forward, Fiona O'Driscoll, was in rare scoring form and notched 3–9.

Munster team: Cora Keohane (Cork), Eithne Duggan (Cork), Mags Finn (Cork), Ciara Gaynor (Tipperary), Claire Madden (Tipperary), Ursula Troy (Cork), Mary O'Connor (Cork), Catherine O'Loughlin (Clare), Vera Sheehan (Limerick), Fiona O'Driscoll (Cork), Moira McMahon (Clare) and Deirdre Hughes (Tipperary).

Leinster team: Miriam Holland (Kilkenny), Cathy Walsh (Dublin), Tracey Millea (Kilkenny), Germaine Noonan (Dublin), Catherine Boyle (Dublin), Marina Downey (Kilkenny), Áine Codd (Wexford), Patricia Clinton (Dublin), Sonya Byrne (Dublin), Bridget Mullally (Kilkenny), Mag Kelly (Wexford) and Patricia Murphy (Dublin).

1998 Gael-Linn Junior Trophy

Ulster and Munster played a thrilling encounter in the semi-final at St Vincent's Grounds. It was a ding-dong contest from the first whistle to the last with Ulster shading the verdict by 1–13 to 1–11. Connacht lost out to Leinster in the second semi-final by 3–12 to 2–8. Goals from Brenda

Eileen O'Brien, one of the most talented colleges players of all time, pictured with Corn Una, the All-Ireland Colleges Sevens trophy following the victory of St. Mary's, Charleville in 1998

Captains of Ulster counties who brought All-Ireland titles to the province were honoured at the 1999 Ulster final.

Burke, Shauna McCaul and Leona Fay earned Ulster the title by 3–12 to 1–12 for Leinster.

Ulster team: Teresa McGowan (Down), Donna Greeran (Down), Paula Daly (Fermanagh), Nuala Magee (Down), Mary Rose McGrady (Tyrone), Martina Mulholland (Derry), Shauna McCaul (Derry), Majella Murray (Down), Jane Adams (Antrim), Michelle Corry (Fermanagh), Brenda Burke (Tyrone) and Leona Fay (Tyrone).

Leinster team: Niamh Leahy (Dublin), Nuala Kerrigan (Kildare), Bernie Holohan (Wexford), Melanie Treacy (Kildare), Liz O'Donoghue (Kildare), Louise O'Hara (Dublin), Michelle Davis (Offaly), Sarah Weir (Dublin), Nuala Quirke (Carlow), Valerie Crean (Carlow), Miriam Malone (Kildare) and Maggie Lynch (Offaly).

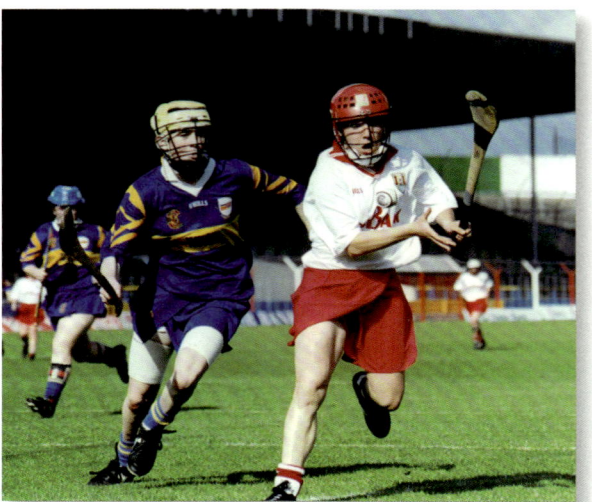

Fiona O'Driscoll (Cork) shoots for a point while Una O'Dwyer (Tipperary) attempts to block at the National League final in Semple Stadium in 1999.

Life Presidency Conferred on Sheila McAnulty

Life Presidency of the Camogie Association was conferred on long-standing administrator, Sheila McAnulty, at Congress 1999 in Thurles. From Warrenpoint, Co. Down, Sheila gave three-quarters of a century of service to camogie, where her qualities of leadership, vision and managerial ability moulded the Association. Under her stewardship, a splintered and divided sport was reunited and placed on a sound footing, solid structures were put in place, and expansion and development supervised.

Sheila's ability was widely recognised both inside and outside the Association, but those who were privileged to know her will remember her for her interest in young people, her willingness to help and encourage, her sense of humour, her flair for telling stories and her ability to view a situation and calmly select the most appropriate path to achieve her goal.

Sheila was taken completely by surprise with the honour bestowed on her. A memento in the form of a copper book bearing the crest of the Camogie Association was presented to her. Many of the officials and delegates present paid personal tributes to Sheila.

Minor B Championship Added

From 1974 to 1999, only seven counties had their names engraved on Corn Tailteann, the All-Ireland minor championship trophy. For many counties, the title lay beyond their wildest dreams as they lacked the necessary resources to mount a serious challenge. The introduction of a Minor B grade presented realistic prospects of success to another bracket of counties.

New Dawn for Tipperary

Jubilee Team Honoured

A further step in the development of All-Ireland day was the invitation extended to the Jubilee Team, the side that had captured the O'Duffy Cup 25 years previously. The first group to be honoured were the Kilkenny team of 1974, led by the captain, Teresa O'Neill. The players, who were delighted to renew acquaintances, were played on to Croke Park by the Artane Band and introduced individually to the attendance. A warm welcome awaited those who marched in 1999, particularly from the many Kilkenny fans in the crowd.

1999 All-Ireland Senior Championship

Winners of the All-Ireland intermediate championship in 1998, Down learned that the difference in standard between the intermediate and senior grades was immense. Their challenge was snuffed out early on in the semi-final against Tipperary at Parnell Park. Tipperary eased their way to the final by 6–22 to 1–3.

The semi-final between Cork and Kilkenny at

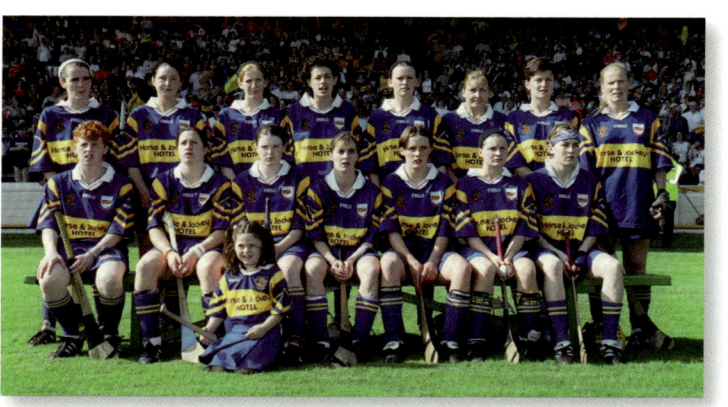

Tipperary - 1999 All Ireland champions. Back: Helen Kiely, Angie McDermott, Therese Brophy, Noelle Kennedy, Suzanne Kelly, Claire Madden, Meadhbh Stokes (captain), Jovita Delaney. Front: Deirdre Hughes, Ciara Gaynor, Niamh Harkin, Sinéad Nealon, Eimear McDonnell, Emily Hayden, Una O'Dwyer. Mascot: Michaela Graham. Pic: Matt Browne/SPORTSFILE

Méadhbh Stokes became the first Tipperary player to receive the O'Duffy Cup. Camogie President, Phyllis Breslin hands over the historic trophy at the post-match reception.

Nowlan Park had everything anyone could wish to see in a camogie contest. Drama, thrills and magnificent play from both sides had the crowd on the edge of their seats. Cork led from the start to seconds from the final whistle. Sinéad Millea stood up to a 55-metre free. She delivered a long looping shot towards the Cork goalmouth. Three Cork defenders rose for the ball, each getting in the others' way. None of them secured possession and the ball dropped into the net. It gave Kilkenny a ticket to the final by 2–12 to 1–13.

It was with a certain degree of apprehension that neutrals approached Croke Park. For the first time, 15-a-side teams would contest the All-Ireland final. No small goalposts were erected. The pitch was not shortened and the sidelines were not taken in. The teams had to perform on the full-sized pitch. Would the game come of age and receive favourable comparison with hurling or would the new format prove too much for players? The sceptics need not have worried. The game of camogie had matured and risen to a new level. The Tipperary and Kilkenny players made the transition effortlessly and displayed their repertoire of skills to great effect on the bigger stage.

Great credit was due to the character and honesty of the Tipperary mentors and players who turned their season around following the humiliating defeat by Cork in the National League. Instead of seeking excuses, they acknowledged that the system they had been using was not good enough. They searched for the best and came up with Michael Cleary and Colm Bonnar. The new coaches honed the skills of the players, increased their confidence, improved their teamwork and gave the team the benefit of their years of experience on the hurling fields.

Fifteen thousand appreciative spectators, including President Mary McAleese, Taoiseach Bertie Ahern and thousands more on live television witnessed the best final in years. A young and eager Tipperary team added a new chapter in camogie history. Seven times in the past, teams in blue and gold had journeyed to Dublin in pursuit of All-Ireland glory. On each occasion, they returned to Tipperary empty-handed. Their joy was unbridled when the final whistle sounded and the barren years were over.

Cork - 1999 All-Ireland Junior Champions. Back: Jill Hannon, Aoife Murray, Karen O'Sullivan, Emer O'Sullivan, Sinéad Buckley, Elaine Burke, Orla O'Sullivan and Lynda O'Connell. **Middle:** Sheenagh Morley, Rosarii Holland, Ger Casey, Rachel Moloney, Muireann Harrington, Helen Walsh (Capt), Ciara Healy, Ruth Cahalan and Criona Harte. **Front:** Marie Corkery, Trisha Murphy, Caroline Giltenane, Cliona Meaney, Áine O'Regan, Ger Collins and Ellen O'Herlihy. **Mascot:** Aileen Corkery.

In an absorbing match, the issue was not decided until well into injury-time. It came down to the last puck of the game. Sinéad Millea was the heroine when her shot dropped into the net in the semi-final. This time the ball fell short and the opportunity to save or win the match was gone. Tipperary won the O'Duffy Cup for the first time by 0–12 to 1–8.

After the match, Kilkenny's Ann Downey announced her retirement following 27 campaigns in the senior grade. Her remarkable career yielded 12 All-Ireland senior, nine National League, seven All-Ireland club and ten Gael-Linn medals. In addition, she represented Ireland at squash and played inter-provincial hockey.

Tipperary team: Jovita Delaney, Suzanne Kelly, Una O'Dwyer, Claire Madden, Méadhbh Stokes (captain), Ciara Gaynor, Sinéad Nealon, Emily Hayden, Angela McDermott, Noelle Kennedy (0–6), Therese Brophy, Helen Kiely, Eimear McDonnell (0–1), Deirdre Hughes (0–3) and Niamh Harkin. Subs used: Caitriona Hennessy (0-2) and Philly Fogarty.

Kilkenny team: Miriam Holland, Tracey Millea, Margaret Hickey, Una Murphy, Sinéad Costello, Gillian Dillon (captain), Mairéad Costello, Kelly Long, Sinéad Millea (0–7), Sandra Gleeson, Bridget Mullally, Marina Downey, Margaret Comerford, Martina Maher (0–1) and Lizzie Lyng (1–0). Sub used: Ann Downey.

1999 All-Ireland Intermediate Championship

Clare reached their fourth All-Ireland intermediate final as a result of a comfortable win over Cork in the semi-final. Fielding a more experienced side, Clare found their way past an overworked Cork defence to slot home four goals and book a place in the final by 4–5 to 1–4.

Antrim had a convincing win over neighbours Armagh in the second semi-final at Dunloy. Armagh failed to find their usual form and conceded by 1–9 to 0–4.

Clare had the forwards capable of creating and finishing chances in the All-Ireland intermediate final against Antrim at Dunloy. This was the key to their victory. On the other hand, Antrim only managed one score from play, which is not good enough for any side seeking All-Ireland honours. Tight-marking kept scores to a minimum. Clare were deserving winners by 1–8 to 1–3.

Clare Team: Áine McCormack, Sinéad Daly, Sinéad McMahon, Anne Keane, Cathy Hally, Marie Collins, Sinéad O'Brien, Moira McMahon (0–3), Deirdre Murphy (0–1), Edel Arthur (0–2),

The Derry panel, 1999 All-Ireland junior finalists, at the post-match reception.

Erica Minogue (0–1), Catherine O'Loughlin, Pauline O'Brien, Patricia O'Grady and Sylvia O'Brien (1–1).

Antrim team: Ciara McKinley, Claire Maguire, Brenda McNeill, Sinéad McMullan, Maureen Duffin, Hannah Healey, Ciara Nelson, Gráinne Connolly, Jane Adams, Ann McKee (captain) (0–3), Elaine Dowds, Oonagh Elliott (1–0), Carla Doherty, Kerri O'Neill and Denise O'Boyle.

Clare defender, Sinéad McMahon, is a sister of All-Ireland hurler, Seánie McMahon.

1999 All-Ireland Junior Championship

An inspired performance by Cork's Rachel Moloney put paid to Offaly's chances of progressing in the All-Ireland junior semi-final at Rath. Rachel recorded 1–8 and had a hand in several other scores. Playing at this level for the first time, Offaly gave a very good account of themselves and were only five points behind, 2–13 to 2–8, at the finish.

Derry gave an exhibition of skill and teamwork against Roscommon in the second semi-final at Athleague. The Ulster county held the upper hand from the outset and were ahead by 4–11 to 1–3 at the final whistle.

A mere point separated Cork and Derry at the end of a pulsating All-Ireland junior final at Croke Park. The teams were level on eight occasions during the hour. Some delightful scores were worked and finished by both sets of forwards. The accurate Rachel Moloney, Ger Casey, Helen Walsh and Rosarii Holland did most to secure a second title in three years for Cork by 1–13 to 2–9.

Cork team: Ger Casey, Muireann Harrington, Rosarii Holland, Sinéad Buckley, Ruth Cahalan, Jill Hannon, Lynda O'Connell, Helen Walsh (captain) (0–1), Sheena Morley, Orla O'Sullivan (1–0), Marie Corkery, Elaine Burke, Criona Harte (0–1), Ciara Healy (0–2) and Rachel Moloney (0–9). Subs used: Valerie O'Sullivan and Caroline Giltenane.

Derry team: Aileen Crilly, Claire Scullion, Grainne Maguire, Paula McKenna, Cathy McDonald, Siobhan Convery, Claire Doherty, Martina Mulholland (0–2), Anna O'Loughlin, Shauna McCaul (0–1), Aileen Tohill (0–1), Paula McAtamney (1–1), Claire McNicholl (0–1), Mary O'Kane (Capt) (1–2) and Karen Rafferty (0–1). Subs used: Aileen O'Kane and Sinéad Stevenson.

1999 All-Ireland Minor Championship

Much-changed Cork and Derry teams met in the semi-final at Ballincollig but the result was the same as the previous year.

Kathleen Timmins, who was made Life President of Leinster Council, receives a presentation from Mary Connor in 1999.

Derry played with great spirit but were up against a side that enjoyed maximum possession. Despite wasting scoring chances, Cork won by 0–11 to 1–0.

Galway scored an excellent win over Kilkenny in the second semi-final at Ardrahan. The players adjusted well to the 15-a-side game and gave an exhibition of the skills of camogie that was enjoyed by the large crowd. Galway advanced by 2–10 to 2–3.

Cork and Galway provided a fabulous game of camogie in the final at Ardrahan. Both teams enjoyed periods of ascendency when they created and rounded off brilliant scores. The match was highlighted by great individual displays. Orla Curtin looked dangerous in possession and found the back of the Cork net on three occasions. Orla Kilkenny, Claire Conroy, Róisín O'Connor and Shauna Murphy did their utmost to swing the game in Galway's favour. Emer Dillon, Caitríona Kelly, Aoife Murray, Niamh Bowles, Gemma O'Connor and Jenny O'Leary were rampant for Cork who captured their tenth minor title by 2–12 to 3–8.

Cork team: Aoife Murray, Joanne O'Callaghan, Joan Twomey, Christine O'Gorman, Jean O'Sullivan, Áine Kelleher, Sinéad Corkery, Orla McCarthy, Niamh Bowles (captain) (0–1), Gemma O'Connor (1–1), Caitríona Kelly (1–0), Emer Dillon (0–6), Jenny O'Leary (0–3), Maria Watson, Sarah O'Donovan. Subs used:

New Dawn for Tipperary

Colette Desmond (0–1) and Karen McCarthy.

Galway Team: Carol Kelly, Claire Linnane, Róisín O'Connor, Louise Linnane, Edel Pierce, Elizabeth Flynn, Darrelle Coen, Regina Glynn, Shauna Murphy, Mary Keogh, Karen Ryan, Brenda Kerins, Claire Conroy (0–5), Orla Curtin (3–0) and Orla Kilkenny (0–3). Subs used: Cathy Bowes and Aislinn Connolly.

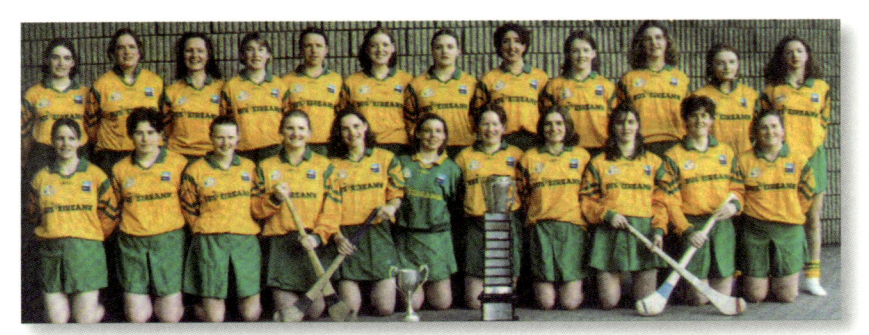

Waterford Institute of Technology – 1999 Ashbourne Cup winners. Back: Mary Walsh, Jackie O'Connor, Aoife Drohan, Ciara Scallan, Mary Ellen Butler, Ursula Walton, T Bergin, Bridget Mullally, Kate Kelly, Marie Butler and Angela Sheehy. Front: Catherine Fitzgerald, U. O'Rourke, Caroline Atkins, Ashling Byrne, K. Long, J. Power, Ciara Moran, B. Davern, Sinéad Nealon, E. Cleary and Esme Murphy.

1999 All-Ireland Club Championship

Leitrim Fontenoy's kept in step with Davitt's until half-time in the semi-final at Leitrim. A goal from Mary Treacy on either side of the break put the game out of the reach of the Down club. Davitt's kept the ball away from Maureen McAleenan, who had shot four points, for the remainder of the game. Doreen Kelly and Mary Treacy added further goals to win by 4–10 to 0–8.

St Lachtain's, Freshford, played all the camogie in the first-half of their semi-final against Granagh-Ballingarry at the Co. Limerick venue and were deserving of their 1–4 to 0–2 advantage. Granagh sprang into life and sent over five points without reply. A superb goal from Jean Cullinane was the deciding score, leaving Granagh 1–10 to 1–9 ahead.

Granagh retained their All-Ireland club title at the expense of Davitt's in what was the first 15-a-side decider at wet and cold Tynagh, Co. Galway. Eileen O'Brien was the star performer and scored 1–3 of Granagh's total. A long-range goal from Caitríona Finnegan kept the margin tight. Granagh drew on their greater experience to fend off the challengers and won by 2–4 to 1–3.

Granagh-Ballingarry team: Breda O'Brien, Patsy McKenna, Bernie O'Brien, Mairéad Cagney, Kay Burke (captain), Bernie Chawke, Maureen Sheehan, Vera Sheehan, Mary O'Connor, Jean Cullinane, Deirdre Sheehan, Eileen O'Brien, Aoifa Sheehan, Kathryn Leslie and Joanne Clifford.

Davitt's team: Fiona Gohery, Orla Watson, Anne Dolan, Fiona Pierce, Anne Broderick, Rita Broderick (captain), Edel Pierce, Caitríona Finnegan, Ailbhe Kelly, Doreen Kelly, Olivia Broderick, Lourda Kavanagh, Lisa Daly, Brenda Daniels and Mary Treacy.

1999 Gael-Linn Senior Cup

The Gael-Linn series was staged at Bohernabreena, where Connacht did what was expected of them against Ulster and won by

1–13 to 1–8. Leinster, on the other hand, fell far short of what was required against Munster and suffered a 7–38 to 0–4 trouncing. Munster showed good clinical finishing in the final against Connacht and earned the trophy by 1–18 to 1–9.

Munster team: Cora Keohane (Cork), Claire Madden (Tipperary), Eithne Duggan (Cork), Mags Finn (Cork), Mary O'Connor (Cork), Moira McMahon (Clare), Vivienne Harris (Cork), Ursula Troy (Cork), Linda Mellerick (Cork), Noelle Kennedy (Tipperary), Fiona O'Driscoll (Cork), Sinéad O'Callaghan (Cork), Lynn Dunlea (Cork) Deirdre Hughes (Tipperary) and Vera Sheehan (Limerick).

Connacht team: (All Galway) Louise Curry, Fiona Ryan, Helen Ryan, Pamela Nevin (captain), Anne Broderick, Olivia Broderick, Rita Broderick, Anne Hardiman, Aoife Lynskey, Tracey Laheen, Áine Hillary, Veronica Curtin, Fiona Healy, Colette Nevin, Caroline Murray, Sandra Tannian, Therese Maher and Michelle Fahy.

1999 Gael-Linn Junior Trophy

Leinster overcame the concession of two early goals to pip Munster by 2–10 to 2–8 at the semi-final stage. Connacht saw off the

Prize-winners in the 1999 National Camogie Golfing outing were: Back: Annette Stapleton, Evelyn Bookle, Mary McCorry and Shauna Doyle. Front: Maeve Gilroy, Helen Fitzharris, Anna Condon, Mary Geaney and Marion Sweeney.

challenge of Ulster by 1–4 to 1–1 in the second semi-final. Leinster bridged a 13-year gap when they defeated Connacht comprehensively by 3–17 to 4–6.

Leinster team: Linda Byrne (Dublin), Dolores Lanigan (Kilkenny), Brigid Barnaville (Kilkenny), Liz O'Donoghue (Kildare), Claire O'Connor (Wexford), Eimear Lyng (Kilkenny), Mary Ellen Butler (Kilkenny), Kathleen Atkins (Kilkenny), Louise O'Hara (Dublin), Aoife O'Connor (Wexford), Michelle O'Leary (Wexford), Noeleen Lambert (Wexford), Olivia Maye (Carlow), Martina Maher (Kilkenny) and Lizzie Lyng (Kilkenny).

Connacht team: (All Galway) Fiona Gohery, Sinéad Kennedy, Tara Keeley, Paula Carrick, Claire Conroy, Doreen Kelly, Donna Burke, Colleen Crowe, Orla Watson, Marguerite Corless, Karen Ryan, Karen Huban, Mairéad Mahony, Elaine Kerins and Aoife Lynskey.

Schwarzkopf came on board to sponsor a Player of the Match Award for both Gael-Linn senior and junior finals. The selected players received a replica of the Gael-Linn Cup together with £1,000 for the recipient's club. Fiona O'Driscoll was voted the Player of the Match in the senior game and brought the cheque home to Fr O'Neill's Club in East Cork. Lizzie Lyng of The Rower-Inistioge was selected as the outstanding player in the junior final.

Tipperary v. the Rest of Ireland

The 1999 season came to a close with newly crowned All-Ireland champions, Tipperary taking on the Rest of Ireland at Nenagh. While Tipperary put up stern resistance, they found the star-laded opposition too much of a handful. Maybe it was the celebrations but Tipperary tended to fade as the contest wore on, allowing the Rest to come out on top by 4–12 to 2–8.

The Rest of Ireland was represented by: Miriam Holland (Kilkenny), Denise Cronin (Cork), Eithne Duggan (Cork), Pamela Nevin (Galway), Olivia Broderick (Galway), Gillian Maher (captain) (Kilkenny), Marie Collins (Clare), Moira McMahon (Clare), Sinéad Millea (Kilkenny), Marina Downey (Kilkenny), Vivienne Harris (Cork), Irene Kirwan (Dublin), Maureen McAleenan (Down), Fiona O'Driscoll (Cork) and Vera Sheehan (Limerick).

Pat Rafferty Elected President

Dubliner Pat Rafferty was elected President of the Camogie Association at Congress 2000 in Cookstown. A member of Eoghan Ruadh, Pat had chaired the Dublin County Board and acted as secretary to Leinster Council. She was a competent referee and an experienced administrator.

P.J. Fulham (Westmeath) stood down following eight years in the role of national PRO. He was succeeded by Máire Uí Scolaí (née McGuirk) from the Cuala Club in Dublin. A past pupil of Coláiste Iosagáin, Máire had studied horticulture in the Botanic Gardens. She served the Dublin County Board as secretary and PRO Máire is married to journalist Niall Scully.

15-A-Side Game Ratified

Kilkenny started the ball rolling to change camogie from 12-a-side played on a small pitch to 15-a-side on the full-size hurling pitch. Thirteen years later, following a pilot scheme, test series, trial periods and much discussion, the 15-a-side format was finally ratified at a Special Congress in October 2000. Among the adjustments made to the game were allowing a player to carry the ball four steps instead of three and increasing the number of substitutes permitted in a match to five.

A Shared Vision

Addressing a camogie audience, President of the GAA, Joe McDonagh, spoke of a shared vision and aspirations, a long history of working together and the common goal of nurturing our Gaelic games and culture in the younger generation. He said he looked forward to the day when a strategic alliance would be formally cemented between the two associations. While there would be formal structures, neither association would lose its own identity. Our unique identities were as important to our future as our shared vision and aspirations. Together we could push the frontiers back even further and could scale any summit. Our coming together would be the enduring story of the century.

Pat Rafferty

A Game of Our Own

In her report to Congress 2000, Ard Stiurthóir, Sheila Wallace, gave the up-to-date position. Following the submission of a Discussion Document, the GAA had invited the Camogie Association to enter discussions regarding a strategic alliance between the associations. Miriam O'Callaghan and Jo Golden had been appointed as representatives of the Camogie Association to attend the talks and progress had been made during the year. Camogie members had been appointed to the following GAA central committees: International Committee, National Féile na nGael Committee, Hurling Development Committee and the committee dealing with the increased participation of women in Gaelic games.

There had always been a high level of co-operation and support from the GAA central committees, particularly in the areas of fixtures, coaching and administration, and the establishment of a more formal link in other areas was a welcome step forward.

Slowdown in Growth

In comparison with the figure of 98 for the eighties, the number of new clubs in the nineties was 38. Munster made considerable progress with 26 new clubs and modest gains were achieved in Leinster (ten) and Connacht (two) but a loss of 21 clubs in Ulster brought the total of clubs affiliated back to 485. A small number of clubs found it difficult to field 15-a-side teams and amalgamated with neighbouring clubs. Expansion continued in the schools and colleges. The advent of indoor camogie significantly boosted the numbers at primary level.

2000 All-Ireland Senior Championship

By the time Wexford registered their first point, seconds before the half-time whistle, in the semi-final at Parnell Park, Cork were already 13 points ahead. Wexford upped the pace in the second-half and put a few scores on the board. The result was known long before Cork finished 3–13 to 1–5 in front.

A crucial goal by Noelle Kennedy proved to be the decisive score in turning the second semi-final in Tipperary's favour. Despite threatening on a number of occasions, Galway failed to get their nose in front. A couple of points by the Tipperary attack sealed the issue to their advantage by 2–11 to 1–8.

Tipperary's star-studded team had Cork in serious trouble as

Tipperary's Angela McDermott in acton against Cork's Ursula Troy in the 2000 All-Ireland final. Pic: Aoife Rice/SPORTSFILE

New Dawn for Tipperary

early as the 17th minute of the All-Ireland final at Croke Park on September 3rd when they led by 2–4 to 0–2. Playing top-class camogie with supreme confidence, Tipperary out-stripped their opponents in all phases of the game. Right through the field, Tipperary had brilliant individuals. Jovita Delaney performed heroics, saving an array of shots from the Cork attack in the second-half. Ciara Gaynor was immense at centre-back. Philly Fogarty and Caitríona Hennessy impressed, whereas Deirdre Hughes with two blistering goals was accountable for Tipperary's dynamic start. Cork, who had to bow to a superior team, were best served by Denise Cronin, Linda Mellerick, Mary O'Connor, Vivienne Harris and Fiona O'Driscoll. Tipperary retained their title by 2–11 to 1–9.

Tipperary team: Jovita Delaney (captain), Suzanne Kelly, Una O'Dwyer, Claire Madden, Sinéad Nealon, Ciara Gaynor, Therese Brophy, Emily Hayden, Angela McDermott, Philly Fogarty (0–1), Noelle Kennedy, Caitríona Hennessy (0–4), Eimear McDonnell (0–2), Deirdre Hughes (2–2) and Claire Grogan (0–2).

Cork team: Cora Keohane, Denise Cronin (0–1), Eithne Dug-

Tipperary - All-Ireland champions in 2000. Back: Therese Brophy, Philly Fogarty, Claire Madden, Noelle Kennedy, Suzanne Kelly, Claire Grogan and Angie McDermott. Front: Deirdre Hughes, Sinéad Nealon, Caitríona Hennessy, Jovita Delaney (captain), Emily Hayden, Eimear McDonnell, Una O'Dwyer and Ciara Gaynor. Mascots: Michaela Graham and Maeve Delaney. Pic: SPORTSFILE

gan, Mags Finn, Sarah Hayes, Mary O'Connor, Vivienne Harris (captain), Ursula Troy, Linda Mellerick, Sinéad O'Callaghan (0–2), Fiona O'Driscoll (0–4), Caoimhe Harrington, Elaine Burke (0–1), Ciara Healy and Una O'Donoghue (1–1). Subs used: Paula O'Connor and Mary Burke.

Fourteen-year-old Claire Grogan is a daughter of former Tipperary hurler, John Grogan. Eimear McDonnell is a niece of Cork All-Ireland footballer, Billy Morgan. Cork's Vivienne Harris is a niece of soccer international, Miah Dennehy.

2000 All-Ireland Intermediate Championship

Cork needed two bites of the cherry to shake off the attentions of Down at the semi-final stage. The sides finished all square at Ballyholland but Cork had nine points to spare, 2–13 to 2–4, two weeks later at Ballincollig.

Sinéad McMullan got an opportunity to rescue Antrim in the second semi-final when she stood up to a 20-metre free at Casement Park. Sinéad's shot sailed over the bar and Limerick went through to the final on the score of 4–5 to 2–10. Some great play was witnessed from both sides during the course of the match.

Cork gained some measure of consolation for the double loss in Croke Park when they won the All-Ireland intermediate title at the expense of Limerick at Bishopstown. With the aid of a stiff breeze, Limerick were two points clear at half-time and were worried that the margin might not be enough. Their worst fears were realised as Cork added 1–7 in the second-half, whereas Limerick could only manage a single point. Cork won by 3–9 to 0–11. Jill Hannon, Emer Dillon, Rachel Moloney, Sheena Morley and Ruth Cahalan played attractive and highly effective camogie for Cork. Eileen O'Brien, Bernie O'Brien and Pauline McCarthy caught the eye for Limerick.

Cork team: Aoife Murray, Joanne O'Callaghan, Rosarii Holland, Caroline Giltenane, Jill Hannon, Ruth Cahalane (0–1), Lynda O'Connell, Emer Dillon (0–1), Sheena Morley (captain), Catherine Corkery (1–1), Helen Walsh (0–3), Jennifer O'Leary, Orla O'Sullivan, Marie Corkery and Rachel Moloney (2–3).

Limerick team: Breda O'Brien, Maeve Nash, Bernie O'Brien, Rose Collins, Kay Burke, Pauline McCarthy (0–1), Marion Neville, Deirdre Sheehan (captain), Mary Lonergan, Eileen O'Brien (0–4), Jean Cullinane (0–4), Michelle Casey, Paula Cronin, Vera Sheehan

Jennifer O'Leary (Cork) carries the ball forward in the All-Ireland junior semi-final against Laois at Mountrath in 2000.

(0–2) and Deirdre Fitzpatrick.

Cork captain, Sheenagh Morley, is a daughter of the Irish soccer international, Jackie Morley, and Joan Clancy, a Cork and Munster camogie player.

2000 All-Ireland Junior Championship

There was no shortage of effort from two committed sides when Derry met Roscommon in the semi-final at Athleague. The difference between the teams was clearly seen in their respective forward lines. The Derry attack was a formidable machine that picked off points from all angles to win by 1–18 to 1–6.

Laois overcame Dublin, Wicklow and Offaly to claim their first Leinster junior championship title. In a thrilling semi-final at Mountrath, they matched Cork in all aspects of the game except the critical area of scoring. Cork's experience and know-how turned half-chances into scores to win by 3–13 to 1–5.

Derry and Cork met in a repeat of the 1999 final at Croke Park. The Ulster county put the lessons learned on that occasion to good use and set about winning the title from the outset. A new Cork team took time to find their feet and did not mount a serious challenge in the first-half. Incessant pressure on the Cork rearguard told and the half-time score of 2–12 to 1–3 was a

New Dawn for Tipperary

true reflection of Derry's superiority. Cork fought back and cut the deficit but Derry came again to complete the job. Derry had superb players in Paula McAtamney, Mary O'Kane, Karen Rafferty, Shauna McCaul, Anna O'Loughlin and Aileen Tohill. Jenny O'Leary, Emer Dillon, Catherine Corkery and Marie Connell did most to reverse the trend of the game for Cork. Derry were clear-cut winners by 3–15 to 1–12.

Derry team: Aileen Crilly, Susan McErlean, Gráinne Maguire, Bláithín McIvor, Cathy McDonald, Claire Doherty, Siobhán Convery, Shauna McCaul (0–1), Anna O'Loughlin (0–1), Aileen Tohill (captain) (0–2), Paula McAtamney (0–8), Aisling Kealey, Claire McNicholl, Mary O'Kane (1–1) and Karen Rafferty (1–2) Subs used: Aileen O'Kane (1–0) and Claire Scullion.

Cork team: Orla O'Callaghan, Sinéad Buckley, Joanne O'Callaghan, Áine Kelleher, Sinéad Corkery, Emer Dillon (0–1), Christine O'Gorman (captain), Valerie O'Keeffe, Marie O'Connell, Catherine Corkery (1–0), Áine O'Regan, Jenny O'Leary (0–11), Eimear O'Friel, Amanda O'Regan and Louise Murphy.

Aileen Tohill is a sister of All-Ireland footballer, Anthony Tohill.

Davitts – Winners of Kilmacud Crokes Sevens in 2000. Back: Lizzie Flynn, Fiona Gohery, Caitríona Finnegan, Ailbhe Kelly and Lourda Kavanagh. **Front:** Anne Broderick, Olivia Broderick, Rita Broderick, Doreen Kelly and Lisa Fahy.

2000 All-Ireland Minor A Championship

Wexford shaded the verdict in a close and tense semi-final against Tipperary at Enniscorthy. Tipperary relied heavily on the free-taking ability of Claire Grogan who accounted for eight points. Josie Dwyer and Marie Mythen slotted home the Wexford goals to advance to the final by 2–7 to 0–12. In the second semi-final at Swatragh, Galway overwhelmed Derry. Once Galway settled, the scores began to flow and they were in front by 6–10 to 1–0 at the close.

Galway's stature in minor camogie grew as they claimed another All-Ireland title at the expense of a disappointing Wexford side at Tullamore. The winners took the initiative early in the game and stayed in front for the duration of the match. Galway were a polished outfit and won with ease by 2–9 to 0–3.

Galway team: Susan Earner, Catherine Moran, Róisín O'Connor (captain), Michelle Raymond, Edel Pierce, Darrelle Carr, Aoife Doherty, Shauna Murphy (1–1), Nicola Galvin, Aislinn Connolly (0–1), Lorraine Lally (0–1), Deirdre Burke, Cathy Bowes (1–2), Emma Kilkenny (0–3), Rebecca Lally. Sub: Sarah Donohoe (0–1).

Wexford team: Ursula Jacob (0–1), Áine Doran, Aisling

Hogan, Marian Hanrick, Caoimhe Fitzpatrick, Mary Leacy, Linda Burke, Jenny O'Leary, Róisín O'Donoghue, Catherine O'Loughlin, Josie Dwyer, Diane Redmond, Marie Mythen, Caroline Murphy (captain) (0–1) and Ciara O'Connor (0–1). Subs used: Louise Codd, Deirdre Codd and Annette Moroney.

Galway midfielder, Aislinn Connolly, is a daughter of All-Ireland hurler, John Connolly. Two former Wexford hurlers, Mick Jacob and Teddy O'Connor, watched their daughters, Ursula and Ciara, play for the county.

2000 All-Ireland Minor B Championship

Tyrone reached the inaugural final of the Minor B Championship by virtue of an emphatic victory over Roscommon in the semi-final at Eglish. Captain Susan McCann was the top player on view and scorer of 3–9. The final score was Tyrone 5–13, Roscommon 2–1.

Clare netted three first-half goals in the second semi-final against Laois at Mountrath, but Laois chipped away at Clare's lead. Goals from a sideline cut by Mary Cleary and a close-range effort from Grace Weston saw Laois through to the final on the score of 2–10 to 3–3.

Laois became the first holders of the Naomh Aoife Cup when they overcame Tyrone in the final at Tullamore. Susan McCann registered the first score of the game for Tyrone but it was not long before Laois took over. Ahead by 3–4 to 1–1 at the break, the Laois players had things much their own way from there to the finish. Eilish Dowling was in lethal form, scoring 5–1. Laois won by 9–14 to 2–1.

Laois team: Elaine Mahony, Caroline Birmingham, Ciara Lanigan, Áine Lawlor, Orla Ryan, Sarah Cuddy, Anna Campion, Aileen O'Loughlin, Emma McEvoy, Eilish Dowling (5–1), Mary Cleary (0–2), Louise Mahony (captain) (0–6), Grace Weston (2–3), Caitríona Phelan and Sinéad Lanham (2–2).

Tyrone team: Lynda McCauley, Gráinne O'Neill, Frances Bigley, Julie Mullan, Madonna Ryan, Sinéad McGroary, Ciara Murtagh, Carolyn Bell, Shauna McGonigal, Laura Heron, Susan McCann (captain) (1–1), Shauna Hagen, Joanne O'Neill, Donna Darcy and Kerry Scullion. Sub used: Cathy McNally (1–0).

2000 All-Ireland Club Championship

Granagh-Ballingarry's hopes of achieving a hat-trick of All-Ireland

Laois – Leinster Junior Champions 2000.

club titles were dashed by Swatragh at the Co. Derry venue. The home side led from start to finish. Two goals in the first six minutes by Aileen Tohill and Paula McAtamney set Swatragh on the road to success. Efficient defending by Swatragh kept Granagh at bay and paved the way for a 2–8 to 1–7 win.

Rathnure got off to a great start with a goal from Geraldine Codd in the second semi-final against Pearses at Ballymacward. Pearses kept in touch with a string of points to leave the sides all square at the break. Sharon Glynn got her side's only goal with time running out. Rathnure were unable to reply and went under by 1–10 to 2–2.

Victory was never in doubt for Pearses in the final against Swatragh at Cusack Park, Mullingar. Swatragh put up stern resistance early on but Pearses, driven on by Sharon Glynn and Áine Hillary, took control. Apart from Gráinne Maguire's goal from a free, it was one-way traffic to the end. Martina Haverty, Tracey Laheen, Martina Harkin and Carmel Hannon contributed handsomely to Pearses' success. The final whistle sounded with the score at Pearses 2–11, Swatragh 1–3.

Pearses team: Louise Curry, Anne Divilly, Aisling Ward, Patricia Burke, Martina Haverty, Tracey Laheen, Martina Harkin, Carmel Hannon, Veronica Sweeney, Michelle Glynn, Áine Hillary (captain), Orla Kilkenny, Shauna Ward, Sharon Glynn and Anne Forde. Sub used: Lorraine Lally.

Swatragh team: Margaret McAtamney, Brenda McGuckin, Claire Scullion, Joanne McKeagney, Nuala O'Hagan, Gráinne Maguire, Paula McKenna, Anna O'Loughlin, Bernie O'Loughlin, Aileen Tohill, Aideen Mullan, Monica O'Kane, Claire McNicholl, Oonagh Mullan and Deirdre O'Doherty.

2000 Gael-Linn Senior Cup

Connacht captured their first Gael-Linn title since 1974 when they proved too strong for Munster in the semi-final by 2–12 to 0–11 and Ulster in the final by 3–10 to 0–3 at St Anne's Grounds, Dublin. Ulster got the better of Leinster by 3–15 to 1–12 in the semi-final.

Connacht team: (All Galway) Fiona Gohery, Tracey Laheen, Anne Broderick, Pamela Nevin, Martina Haverty, Áine Hillary, Olivia Broderick, Michelle Glynn, Carmel Hannon, Orla Kilkenny, Therese Maher, Sandra Tannian, Anne Forde, Colette Nevin and Veronica Curtin.

Ulster team: Maureen Barry (Antrim), Caitríona Higgins (Antrim), Claire Doherty (Antrim), Grace McMullan (Antrim), Jane Adams (Antrim), Patricia McEvoy (Armagh), Olive McGowan (Armagh), Jennifer Braniff (Down), Donna Greeran (Down), Pauline Green (Down), Majella Murray (Down), Mary Black (Armagh), Paula McAtamney (Derry) and Claire McNicholl (Derry).

Siobhán Kelly, captain of St. Patrick's, Shannon, shows the All-Ireland colleges' senior B Cup to her delighted team.

A Game of Our Own

2000 Gael-Linn Junior Trophy

Ulster registered a comfortable 3–9 to 1–8 win over Leinster while Munster had things much their own way in the second semi-final against Connacht and won by 7–18 to 0–8. The final produced a rip-roaring struggle with Ulster shading the verdict by 1–10 to 2–6.

Ulster team: Aileen Crilly (Derry), Susan McErlean (Derry), Gráinne Maguire (Derry), Maureen Duffin (Antrim), Cathy McDonald (Derry), Ciara McKinley (Antrim), Siobhán Convery (Derry), Martina Mulholland (Derry), Aisling Kealey (Derry), Shauna McCaul (Derry), Aileen Tohill (Derry), Áine O'Kane (Derry), Kerrie O'Neill (Antrim) and Karen Rafferty (Derry).

Munster team: Ger Casey (Cork), Áine O'Connell (Limerick), Amanda O'Regan (Cork), Christine O'Gorman (Cork), Lynda O'Connell (Cork), Helen Collins (Limerick), Noelette O'Dwyer (Tipperary), Julie Delaney (Tipperary), Elaine Burke (Cork), Mary Looby (Tipperary), Ciara Healy (Cork), Emer Dillon (Cork), Jenny O'Leary (Cork), Joanne Ryan (Tipperary) and Rachel Moloney (Cork).

Therese Maher (Connacht) and Siobhán Convery (Ulster) were named Schwarzkopf senior and junior players of the tournament.

Action from Féile na nGael 2000, Milford v Carrigaline

Where We're At

Sport continues to grow and occupy a significant portion of our lives. Coverage of sport has expanded in tandem with extra sports channels on television, new magazines devoted to sports and additional sports pages in the daily newspapers.

Is camogie getting its fair share of coverage? Our initial reaction is to shout 'no'. What are we doing to improve matters?

Every sport is competing for space and air time. Those who get it are the ones who show initiative and consistency in supplying the detailed information required. Proper promotion and marketing of the game is essential to ensure the maximum exploitation of all media outlets.

Many players are keen to participate in a variety of sports with each code doing its best to attract players. Sports, with an international outlet, hold special appeal, leaving camogie with a real fight on its hands to maintain, and improve, its present position.

The advent of live television of the All-Ireland camogie finals has boosted the game enormously. The standard displayed came as a revelation to many viewing the game for the first time. The new 15-a-side format has led to an increased level of exposure for our game. It is practical to stage a camogie match as a double-header with a hurling or football match now that the pitch does not require any alterations. Where fixtures are well-signposted and promoted assertively, e.g. the All-Ireland finals, the return is satisfactory, but where little effort is made to sell the competition, e.g. the interprovincial series, the result is little or no coverage, sparse attendance and no atmosphere.

We are let down by our own members who fail to turn out and support our games. We agitate for more coverage but as long as our own members are apathetic why should the national media take us seriously? Greater use of our top players and former stars to promote and increase camogie's profile is called for. Achieving adequate coverage necessitates relentless effort. The arrival of the game's new annual *Camogie Abú* was an important and welcome step in the right direction.

A Game of Our Own

DESPERATE DEFENDING

Chapter Twenty One

PREPARING FOR THE CENTENARY

The first positive step in preparation for the centenary of the Camogie Association in 2004 was put in place. A committee comprising former and current inter-county players was set up to explore the many ways in which to celebrate this historic event in proper style. The high-profile committee consisted of Therese O'Callaghan (Cork), Germaine Noonan (Dublin), Olivia Broderick (Galway), Jane Adams (Antrim), Ann Downey (Kilkenny), Eithne Duggan (Cork) and Jane Monaghan (Armagh).

They sought ideas from all quarters to supplement their own and intended to have a plan in place a year in advance of the centenary.

New Grounds for Croagh-Kilfinny

The Croagh-Kilfinny Club in Co. Limerick had embarked on a Field Development Project in 1996 and on August 26th, 2001, they reaped the rewards of their hard work. When the chance arose for the club to purchase their own field with the help of the GAA, they had grasped the opportunity. Helen Sheehy Fitzgerald was the driving force behind the venture. Development plans were drawn up, fundraising schemes put in place, the land drained and fenced in, car park renovated and dressing rooms revamped. Full credit to the dedicated committee and generous community who saw development targets met and the debt cleared. Camogie president Pat Rafferty officially opened the excellent new facility and an exhibition match between Limerick and Cork marked the occasion.

On a sad note, Helen Sheehy Fitzgerald, the scheme's driving force, had passed away in November 2000. Appropriately, the field was dedicated to her memory and will stand as a reminder of her vision and endeavour.

Core Values in Sport

Both a code of ethics and good practice for youth sport and an anti-doping code were topics that were to occupy time and attention on an increasing scale as the years went by. The Camogie Association has been dedicated to the ideals that, in its games, the spirit of fair play should prevail, that the health of players is paramount and that drugs can have no place in camogie. The welfare of young people has been first priority and the Camogie Association has been committed to co-operating with the Irish Sports Council to advance these values.

Mairéad Ní Mhaoileóin (Cork), Anne O'Brien (Wexford), Marie O'Brien (Roscommon) and Kathleen Woods (Ulster) trained as tutors. Workshops provided training in the implementation of the Code for club representatives and a booklet, *Code of Ethics and Best Practice for Children*, was prepared and issued to all clubs.

Claire Grogan, Tipperary, leads Kilkenny's Maire Maher in the 2001 All-Ireland at Croke Park. Picture: SPORTSFILE

Foot-and-Mouth Outbreak

The restrictions imposed to combat an outbreak of foot-and-mouth disease presented problems to the organisers of competitions. Constraints on travel and sporting events were introduced in February 2001, affecting colleges' competitions more than others. As the weeks went by, the restrictions were relaxed, only to be imposed again as news of fresh outbreaks emerged. The seriousness of a potential outbreak was viewed differently in various parts of the country. As a result, some colleges were prepared to fulfil their fixtures while those in farming areas were reluctant to take the risk. Some competitions fell victim to the outbreak while others were rescheduled for later in the season.

2001 All-Ireland Senior Championship

An injury-time point by Deirdre Hughes saved the day for Tipperary in the semi-final against Cork in Mullingar. A fascinating contest ended Tipperary 2–8, Cork 0–14. Unbelievably, the teams were asked to return to Mullingar for the replay when a more convenient venue would have drawn a larger crowd. Cork were dealt a severe blow before the replay when Lynn Dunlea was ruled out because of a wrist injury. The very close and exciting replay reached its climax with Tipperary slightly in front. Paula O'Connor cut the margin to a single point. Cork pushed forward in search of the winner but left their goal unprotected. Eimear McDonnell and Noelle Kennedy availed of the opportunity to snatch goals in injury-time and leave the final score Tipperary 3–13, Cork 1–12.

Tipperary romped to a three-in-a-row in the All-Ireland final against Kilkenny at Croke Park on September 16th by 4–13 to

1–6. They refused to allow Kilkenny into the game, punished slack defending and opened up an interval lead of 11 points. Kilkenny needed a big start to the second-half to get back into contention but it was not to be. Eimear McDonnell, Claire Grogan and Noelle Kennedy increased Tipperary's margin. Deirdre Hughes, who was a thorn in Kilkenny's side throughout the hour, rattled the net for a second time and put paid to any thoughts of a comeback that Kilkenny may have entertained.

This Tipperary team was endowed with all the attributes necessary to mark them apart as an exceptional camogie side. They were remarkably strong down the middle, had a superb half-back line and a full-forward trio who threatened every time they won possession.

Tipperary team: Jovita Delaney, Paula Bulfin, Una O'Dwyer, Claire Madden, Sinéad Nealon, Ciara Gaynor, Therese Brophy, Suzanne Kelly, Philly Fogarty (0–1), Emily Hayden (captain), Noelle Kennedy (0–5), Joanne Ryan, Eimear McDonnell (1–2), Deirdre Hughes (2–2), Claire Grogan (1–2). Subs used: Gráinne Shanahan (0–1), Niamh Harkin and Sheena Howard.

Kilkenny team: Catherine Ryan, Marie Maher, Sinéad Costello, Mairéad Costello (captain), Esther Kennedy, Kelly Long, Edel Maher, Bridget Mullally (0–1), Lizzie Lyng (0–1), Sinéad Millea (1–2), Martina Maher, Imelda Kennedy (0–1), Catherine Doherty, Aoife Neary and Marina Downey (0–1). Sub used: Gillian Dillon.

2001 All-Ireland Intermediate Championship

Jane Adams was the star of the show for Antrim in the semi-final against Cork at Ballincollig. Time and again, she ghosted past her marker before striking the ball effortlessly over the bar. Cork tried a number of remedies without success and had to concede by 1–13 to 1–6.

Derry looked very impressive when overcoming a disappointing Down side in the second semi-final. Such was Derry's dominance that no fewer than 11 players got their name on the score sheet. Derry advanced by 1–11 to 0–7.

The rivalry was intense as Ulster neighbours lined out in the final at Casement Park. The sides were coached by well-known hurling men, Dominic McKinley (Derry) and Jim Nelson (Antrim). Derry fielded the young side that had captured the 2000 All-Ireland junior title. Antrim, on the other hand, were more experienced. As in the semi-final, Jane Adams excelled both as a creator of chances and a finisher. Grace McMullan, Mairéad Graham, Denise O'Boyle and Ciara Gault played vital roles in Antrim's

Claire Madden, Tipperary, is tackled by Catherine Doherty, Kilkenny. Picture: SPORTSFILE

3–10 to 0–5 victory.

Antrim team: Christine Doherty (0–2), Hannah Healy, Sinéad McMullan, Róisín Duffin, Ciara Gault (captain), Maureen Stewart, Ciara McGinley, Denise O'Boyle, Gráinne Connolly, Jane Adams (0–6), Ann McKee, Kerrie O'Neill, Mairéad Graham (1–0), Grace McMullan (2–1) and Elaine Dowds (0–1).

Derry team: Aileen Crilly, Sinéad Stevenson, Gráinne Maguire, Joanne Carey, Charlene Moore, Siobhán Convery, Anna O'Loughlin, Aisling Kealey (0–1), Sinéad O'Neill, Aileen Tohill, Paula McAtamney (0–2), Claire McColgan, Gráinne McGoldrick (0–1), Mary O'Kane (0–1) and Paula Bell.

The Tipperary team celebrate their 2001 victory over Kilkenny. *Picture: SPORTSFILE*

2001 All-Ireland Junior Championship

Following a listless opening half, Tipperary's second string opened up to book a place in the final at the expense of Galway at The Ragg. Siobhán Ryan, Moira Ryan, sister of hurling star, Declan, Lena Woods and Linda Grogan were excellent for Tipperary who won by 0–12 to 1–4.

Offaly reached the All-Ireland junior final by means of an eight-point win over Derry. The Ulster county had to find a new panel of players as the previous season's successful side had been promoted to the Intermediate Grade. The newcomers gave a very good account of themselves, scoring 4–5 against Offaly's 4–13.

The Tipperary juniors completed the first leg of a historic double when they cruised past Offaly in the final at Croke Park. Offaly got off to a disastrous start, conceding two goals in the first five minutes. They were unable to exert any real pressure on Tipperary whose forwards were sharper. The final score of 4–16 to 1–7 did not flatter Tipperary. It was a fine team effort by the Premier County with each player making a major contribution to victory. Michelle Davis, by far Offaly's best player, Maggie Lynch, Sharron Daly and Jeanette Feighery worked extremely hard for the Leinster county.

Tipperary team: Sarah O'Brien, Sharon Ralph, Helen Breen, Deirdre McDonnell, Maeve Corcoran, Noelette O'Dwyer, Niamh Connolly, Lorraine Bourke, Julie Delaney, Trish O'Halloran (captain) (1–1), Louise Young (1–2), Helen Grogan, Lena Woods (1–3), Siobhán Ryan (0–9) and Linda Grogan (1–1). Subs used:

Paula Ryan, Jenny O'Halloran, Moira Ryan, Deirdre Delaney and Mary Rose Ryan.

Offaly team: Fiona McLeish, Catherine Byrne, Amanda Kelly, Carina Carroll, Mary Molloy, Majella Bergin, Marion Crean, Amanda Glennon, Mary Wyer, Sabrina Carroll, Michelle Davis (0–3), Elaine Dermody (captain), Jeanette Feighery (1–0), Maggie Lynch (0–3) and Sharron Daly (0–1). Subs used: Audrey Hennessy, Orla Carey, Sheila O'Sullivan and Therese Keoghan.

2001 All-Ireland Minor A Championship

Once again, a Cork v. Galway minor clash rose to great heights with both sets of players contributing enormously to the game. The outcome of the match rested on a knife-edge as play swung from end to end. Level five times during the game, it was Cork's determination and willingness to work extremely hard that carried them through by 3–9 to 1–12.

Derry found themselves out of their depth in the second semi-final at Bennettsbridge. Kilkenny worked some exquisite scores as they built up an impressive lead of 5–6 to 1–2 by the break. They continued to motor on with their passage to the final secured long before the end. The final score was Kilkenny 11–8 Derry 2–4.

Camogie President, Pat Rafferty, hands Corn Tailteann to Maria Watson (Cork) in 2001.

Cork looked a classy outfit as they demolished Kilkenny in the final at Nenagh. Coaches John Cronin and Anne Watson had their side in peak condition. A three-goal blitz in the space of three minutes rocked Kilkenny and put Cork firmly on the road to the 11th minor success. Any hope that Kilkenny had of reviving their fortunes were dashed at the start of the second-half when Cork banged in two further goals from close range. Cork had several stars on view. Briege Corkery, Maria Watson, Elaine O'Riordan, Síle Burns and Gemma O'Connor rose to great heights. Aoife Neary, Edel Maher and Therese Muldowney fought hard to turn the tide for Kilkenny but they had to concede by 6–15 to 0–7.

Cork team: Denise Twomey, Marian O'Donovan, Síle Burns, Caitríona Foley, Anna Geary, Sharon Lenihan, Niamh O'Connor, Jacqui O'Keeffe, Gemma O'Connor (0–3), Maria Watson (captain) (2–4), Briege Corkery (0–3), Marie O'Neill (1–1), Emer Watson (2–1), Elaine O'Riordan (0–2), Noelle Collins (1–0). Subs used: Gearóidín Kearney (0–1), Celine Nyhan and Ann Kiely.

Kilkenny team: Jacqui Frisby, Laoighseach Quigley, Susan Kennedy, Gráinne Brennan, Lisa Ryan, Danielle Minogue, Áine Fahy, Mary Love, Edel Maher (0–1), Therese Muldowney (0–1),

Eileen Fitzpatrick, Aoife Neary (0–5), Catherine Kavanagh, Sinéad Corrigan and Marie Ryan. Subs used: Gráinne Daly, Rebecca Phelan and Tara Warren.

Sisters Maria and Emer Watson are daughters of former Limerick and Croagh-Kilfinny player, Anne Sheehy.

2001 All-Ireland Minor B Championship

Down, winners of the first All-Ireland minor title in 1974, were no match for Carlow in the semi-final at Dr Cullen Park. A tally of 2–5 from play by full-forward Eilish Meaney and a brace of goals from Aisling Taylor put Carlow on the road to the final by 4–8 to 0–2.

The Limerick v. Roscommon semi-final was a mismatch. Roscommon had been nominated to represent Connacht without playing a match and were unprepared for the standard of camogie exhibited by Limerick. Sinéad McAuliffe (3–5), Nora Collins (1–11), Aisling O'Brien (3–4) and Aisling O'Connell (0–6) were the main contributors to Limerick's runaway win of 8–34 to 0–1.

Tom D'Arcy saw his Carlow charges account for Westmeath, Offaly, Kildare and Down. But in the All-Ireland final at Nenagh, his team came up against a Limerick side that would have given the Minor A champions more than a rattle. Carlow stayed with Limerick for 20 minutes before Limerick's attack clicked and the scores started to flow. Joanne Clifford was invincible at centre-back for Limerick. Their forward division contained delightfully skilful and talented ball players, none more so than Nora Collins, Sinéad McAuliffe, Maria McGrath and Aisling O'Brien. Coach John Lacey brought his team to a very high level. Carlow battled bravely to the end. Debbie O'Neill, Aisling Taylor, Kelly Dalton and Noreen Coady were most prominent. Limerick wrapped up the title by 3–18 to 1–1.

Contestants in the 2001 National Féile na nGael Skills competition seen in their county colours.

Limerick team: Marie Corkery, Carol Hickey, Marina Cremin, Janice White, Mairéad Sheedy, Joanne Clifford (captain) (1–1), Christine Carroll, Martha O'Connor, Claire Mulcahy, Amanda Sheehan (0–1), Aisling O'Connell (0–3), Sinéad McAuliffe (0–4), Maria McGrath (1–0), Nora Collins (1–7) and Aisling O'Brien (0–2).

Carlow team: Kelly Dalton, Erin Doyle, Ann Marie Kelly, Niamh Kelly, Ann Marie Ralph, Noreen Coady, Anne Comiskey, Elaine Fox, Fiona Byrne, Mary Ellen Doyle, Áine Byrne, Debbie O'Neill (0–1), Aisling Taylor (1–0), Eilish Meaney and Lyndsey Condell.

Preparing for the Centenary

2001 All-Ireland Club Championship

Champions Pearses had little trouble in disposing of Keady (Armagh) in the semi-final at Ballymacward. The Galway side belonged to a higher grade than their spirited opponents and advanced to the final by 4–14 to 1–6.

Cashel made their first appearance in the All-Ireland club championship a winning one. They had six points to spare, 1–15 to 1–9, at the close of an entertaining game against St Ibar's (Wexford) who had also won their provincial title for the first time. Carmel Hannon's point, scored deep into injury-time, ensured that the Bill Carroll Cup remained at Ballymacward. In a tough, exciting encounter, Pearses and Cashel expended every ounce of energy to the delight of the large crowd at Cashel. For most of the game, Pearses maintained a slender advantage. They made better use of their chances and, when it really mattered, were able to engineer the winning score.

The Pearses defence curtailed Cashel to five points from play, making the home side very dependent on Claire Grogan's accuracy from placed balls. For a time, it looked as if Pearses would win comfortably, then Cashel switched Una O'Dwyer to mark Sharon Glynn. Una placed a tight rein on Sharon, allowing Cashel back into contention. When Claire Grogan added a late point, the outcome seemed destined to be a draw. A late, late effort from Carmel Hannon won the day for Pearses by 2–8 to 0–13.

Pearses team: Caroline Cunniffe, Síle Barrett, Aisling Ward, Patricia Burke, Martina Haverty, Tracey Laheen, Martina Harkin, Michelle Glynn, Veronica Sweeney, Orla Kilkenny, Áine Hillary (captain), Carmel Hannon, Shauna Ward, Sharon Glynn and Lorraine Lally.

Cashel team: Sandra Ricken, Michelle Kennedy, Jovita Delaney, Kaiffee Moloney, Helen Breen, Una O'Dwyer, Triona Bonnar, Emily Hayden, Paula Bulfin, Philly Fogarty (0–1), Mairéad Morrissey, Clare Grogan (0–11), Libby Twomey (0–1), Linda Grogan and Helen Grogan.

2001 Gael-Linn Senior Cup

Munster had a convincing 5–16 to 3–7 win over Ulster in the semi-final at St Anne's, Dublin, while Connacht had the narrowest of victories over Leinster, 0–13 to 1–9, in the second semi-final. A star-studded Munster side, dominated by Tipperary players, collected their 15th Gael-Linn Cup by defeating Connacht 1–18 to 1–9.

Munster team: Jovita Delaney (Tipperary), Paula Bulfin (Tipperary), Una O'Dwyer (Tipperary), Claire Madden (Tipperary), Paula O'Connor (Cork), Therese Brophy (Tipperary), Sarah Hayes (Cork), Linda Mellerick (Cork) (captain), Vera Sheehan (Limerick), Eileen O'Brien (Limerick), Philly Fogarty (Tipperary), Fiona O'Driscoll (Cork), Claire Grogan (Tipperary) and Eimear McDonnell (Tipperary).

Connacht team: (All Galway) Louise Curry, Róisín O'Connor, Áine Hillary, Ann Broderick, Pamela Nevin, Olivia Broderick, Cathy Bowes, Therese Maher, Caroline Murray, Stephanie Griffin, Lourda Kavanagh, Elaine Kerins, Orla Kilkenny, Sandra Tannian, Aoife Lynskey.

2001 Gael-Linn Junior Trophy

Munster recorded a good win over Ulster by 2–8 to 0–5 in the semi-final at St– Anne's, Dublin while Leinster edged out Connacht by 3–9 to 1–10. Leinster and Munster were locked together in a compelling final which was finally decided by an Aoife Neary goal, 1–14 to 1–11 in Leinster's favour.

Leinster team: Fiona McLeish (Offaly), Catherine O'Loughlin (Wexford), Carina Carroll (Offaly), Majella Bergin (Offaly), Dervilla O'Carroll (Meath), Orla Bambury (Kildare), Edel Maher (Kilkenny), Gretta Heffernan (Wexford), Michelle Davis (Offaly), Janette Feighery (Offaly), Aoife Neary (Kilkenny), Mary Henry (Westmeath) (captain), Christine Raleigh (Meath), Sharron Daly (Offaly) and Catherine Glynn (Westmeath).

Munster team: Helen Breen (Tipperary), Niamh Connolly (Tipperary), Méadhbh Corcoran (Tipperary), Lorraine Burke (Tipperary), Nora Ahern (Cork), Deirdre McDonnell (Tipperary), Valerie O'Keeffe (Cork), Marie O'Connell (Cork), Sharon Ralph (Tipperary), Jean O'Sullivan (Cork), Siobhán Ryan (Tipperary), Louise Young (Tipperary), Colette Desmond (Cork) and Ger Collins (Cork).

Full-Time Treasurer

A proposal was put before Congress 2002 in Clarinbridge to make the office of treasurer a full-time position. It was felt that with the development of the Camogie Association, the workload of the treasurer at Central Council level had increased to such an extent that it had become virtually impossible for a person working in a voluntary basis to deal with it.

As well as dealing with the normal financial transactions, accounts and budgets of a national organisation, it was imperative that a greater amount of time be given to seeking sponsorship and fundraising. Congress gave the go-ahead to the proposition but no appointment was made until May 2003.

With major development funding required to advance the z, affiliation fees were increased to €100 per club, and while these fees were still modest in comparison with other sports, extracting money from clubs proved an uphill battle in many quarters. The reluctant subscribers frequently questioned what they got in return for the fees they paid.

The title of Ard Runaí was changed to Ardstiurthóir. With the pending appointment of a second full-time official, it was necessary to define the chain of command.

Offaly's bid to introduce an All-Ireland club championship for the junior grade was successful. The Associationlaunched its coaching video using the game's top players to display the skills of the game.

Team Preparation

The days when an ambitious club or county asked a former hurler to give a hand with the training of the team were long gone by 2002. Players no longer parked their bikes, threw off their coats and called for a ball to be pucked.The sport was now at a stage where every move and minute was planned by qualified people.

Players arrive in time to do stretching and warm up. Drills to

Preparing for the Centenary

improve skill and sharpen reflexes come next. The PE trainer works on fitness and knows from constant testing what stage each player is at.

The coach has identified problems in the previous game and seeks to eliminate the cause. Strategies to be incorporated in the game plan of the next fixture receive attention.

The services of specialists are sourced. Early in the season, the dietician charts what the players should eat. Once the matches start, emphasis is placed on recuperation, both from the exertions of the game and any injury that may occur. Ice baths, physiotherapists and doctors are called into action to hasten recovery.

Sports psychiatrists may be needed to get the mind focused, a hurling wall to sharpen the first touch, video analysis to highlight what went wrong and a bonding weekend to create team spirit. What would the players of the thirties or forties think of it all?

Centenary Celebrations

Therese O'Callaghan and Olivia Broderick made a presentation to Central Council on behalf of the Centenary Committee setting out many excellent proposals as a programme of events for

All-Ireland captains, Jacqui Frisby (Kilkenny) and Una O'Donoghue (Cork) pictured with Camogie President, Pat Rafferty and G.A.A. President, Joe McDonagh in September, 2002.

the centenary year. A very attractive schedule of events had been put together, the vast majority of which were carried out. The list included: media launch; celebration at Páirc Tailteann; selection of Team of the Century; Gala Concert; poster competitions for schools; documentary film, calendar, diary and postage stamps; website; camogie exhibition in GAA Museum; special medals/mementos for All-Ireland champions, finalists and referees; international competition and Shinty; selection of All-Stars; county histories; and a centenary banquet. Work immediately started on the planning and preparation of individual events and sponsorship was sought where possible.

Why No Support?

Revived in 1998, the camogie annual *Camogie Abú* grew in size and coverage each year. Events on and off the field were highlighted and illustrated, new developments featured, records and statistics updated, spotlight placed on personalities and a forum offered to those who wished to air an opinion. The annual was an important promotional tool for the Camogie Association and provided a valuable historical record of the events of the year.

It was extremely disappointing, therefore, that the annual was not properly supported by members of the Associationand so disheartening for the producers of the magazine to see bundles of unsold copies lying in the office. Because of losses incurred due to lack of sales, a decision was taken not to publish further issues.

2002 All-Ireland Senior Championship

The three O'Connors, Paula, Mary and Gemma, all unrelated, formed a brick wall across the field as far as Galway were concerned in the semi-final at the Gaelic Grounds. With the result that Ger Casey in the Cork goal did not have a shot to save. The Cork forwards benefited from a constant supply of ball. Fiona O'Driscoll, Jenny O'Leary and Emer Dillon picked off the scores to see Cork through to the final by 4–12 to 0–5.

Kilkenny put in a lot of preparation for the meeting of Tipperary in the second semi-final. They stayed with the champions until the break, turning over just one point behind. However, that was as far as they got. Tipperary put up the shutters, not allowing Kilkenny any further scores. While Tipperary won comfortably by 1–11 to 0–6, their attack did not function as smoothly as usual.

Una O'Donoghue, Cork, holds off against Therese Brophy, Tipperary in the 2002 All-Ireland final. *Pic: Ray McManus / SPORTSFILE*

The Tipperary tide, which had swept all before it over the previous three years, was halted by a suffocating Cork defence in the All-Ireland final at Croke Park on September 15th. Goalkeeper Ger Casey and the line of players in front of her – Joanne O'Callaghan, Eithne Duggan and Stephanie Dunlea –, choked the Tipperary attack from the start. Centre-back, Mary O'Connor, kept Noelle Kennedy scoreless while her flankers, Paula O'Connor and Gemma O'Connor, drove the ball forward. Cork contained Tipperary in the opening half. A three-goal blitz after half-time dethroned Tipperary. Una O'Donoghue took a precision pass from Emer Dillon and finished it to the net. Fiona O'Driscoll raced forward with the ball glued to her stick and hand-passed into the goal. A ball dropped into a group of players on the edge of the square. The diminutive Fiona O'Driscoll made a giant leap, grabbed the ball and, though she appeared to be bottled up, steered the ball out of the reach of Jovita Delaney.

In typical Tipperary tradition, their players fought for every ball but Cork had the bit between their teeth at this stage and were not going to let go. The team, which was well coached by Pa Finn, finished in style by 4–9 to 1–9.

Preparing for the Centenary

Cork team: Ger Casey, Joanne O'Callaghan, Eithne Duggan, Stephanie Dunlea, Paula O'Connor, Mary O'Connor, Gemma O'Connor, Vivienne Harris, Elaine Burke, Linda Mellerick, Emer Dillon (0–3), Jenny O'Leary (0–3), Una O'Donoghue (1–1), Caoimhe Harrington and Fiona O'Driscoll (3–2). Subs used: Rachel Moloney and Orla O'Sullivan.

Tipperary team: Jovita Delaney, Paula Bulfin, Una O'Dwyer, Claire Madden, Sinéad Nealon, Ciara Gaynor (0–1), Therese Brophy, Suzanne Kelly, Angie McDermott, Deirdre Hughes (0–1), Emily Hayden, Noelle Kennedy, Eimear McDonnell (1–1), Philly Fogarty (0–2) and Claire Grogan (0–4). Subs used: Louise Young and Emily Hayden.

Cork's Paula O'Connor is a sister of All-Ireland hurlers, Ben and Jerry O'Connor.

2002 All-Ireland Intermediate Championship

Dublin were very quickly into their stride in the semi-final against Cork at Douglas and built up a five-point lead. Poor shooting cost Cork dearly and their total of wide balls amounted to ten.

The Cork team celebrate winning the 2002 All-Ireland senior championsihp final. Picture: Aoife Rice / SPORTSFILE

Maria and Emer Watson came to Cork's rescue with the sisters finding the Dublin net. Cork advanced by 3–8 to 1–9.

Antrim and Tipperary were locked together in the second semi-final at The Ragg. Chapter two took place at Dunloy where Jane Adams pointed an injury-time free to catapult Antrim to the final by 0–11 to 2–4.

The final at Clan na nGael grounds will be remembered for a fabulous display of goalkeeping by Cork's Denise Twomey. Normally a forward, Denise stopped shots from all angles. Cork had to withstand a late Antrim rally but it was not enough to save the day.

The game produced great camogie. Jean O'Sullivan, Briege Corkery, Regina Curtin, Valerie Maher and Maria Watson were in great form for Cork. Antrim came very close to retaining their title. Had they taken points instead of shooting for goals, the result might have been different. Gráinne Connolly, Jane Adams, Denise Darragh and Carla Doherty did well for Antrim who ended two points behind, 3–6 to 1–10.

Cork team: Denise Twomey, Claire Deasy, Jean O'Sullivan,

Liz Sweetnam, Ann Marie Fleming, Nora Ahern, Joan Twomey, Regina Curtin (0–1), Briege Corkery (0–1), Colette Desmond (0–1), Hilda Kenneally (captain), Linda Dorgan (0–1), Valerie Maher (2–0), Maria Watson (1–2) and Emer Watson.

Antrim team: Christine Doherty, Ciara Gault, Sinéad McMullan, Maureen Duffin (captain), Sheila McCluskey, Maureen Stewart, Ciara McGinley, Róisín Duffin, Jane Adams (1–4), Ann McKee, Denise Darragh, Gráinne Connolly (0–2), Oonagh Elliott, Edel Mason (0–1) and Carla Doherty (0–3).

2002 All-Ireland Junior Championship

In a nail-biting semi-final at Nowlan Park, Kilkenny edged out Galway to qualify for their first All-Ireland junior final. A last-minute goal by Marie Ryan gave the Kilkenny winning margin the comfortable four-point look, 2–10 to 2–6.

Cork showed no signs of fatigue from the long bus journey to Bellaghy where they met Derry in the second semi-final. Maria Watson's early goal settled the Cork side and they motored on to win by 1–13 to 1–3. Derry improved following a poor first-half but they had left themselves too much ground to make up.

A powerful first-half performance set Kilkenny up for their first All-Ireland junior title. Their attack was superbly led by Aoife Neary and built up an impressive half-time lead of 2–9 to 1–4.

Claire Mulcahy, captain of Limerick U16B side which won the 2002 All-Ireland title, seen with Camogie President, Pat Rafferty.

Cork brought on minor Briege Corkery and she made an immediate impact. Her stunning speed and high work rate got Cork moving. The margin was reduced to two points but good defensive work by Kilkenny prevented Cork from catching up. Ann Marie Young, Pauline Aylward, Mairéad Lawlor, Edel Maher and Elaine Aylward provided great back-up to the star of the game, Aoife Neary. The final score was Kilkenny 2–11, Cork 2–8.

Kilkenny team: Caitríona Ryan, Eimear Connery, Ann Marie Young, Eimear Lyng, Pauline Comerford, Mairéad Lawlor, Keira Kinahan, Edel Maher, Elaine Aylward, Marie Ryan, Dolores Lanigan, Jacqui Frisby (captain), Catherine Doherty (1–1), Aoife Neary (1–9) and Marie O'Connor (0–1). Sub used: Ursula Walton and Nora Sutton.

Cork team: Ellen Clifford, Jennifer Browne, Liz Sweetnam, Niamh Bowles, Caitríona Foley, Nora Ahern (captain), Mairéad Holland, Val O'Keeffe, Emer O'Farrell, Colette Desmond (0–3), Caitríona Kelly (0–5), Ger Collins (1–0), Amanda Murphy, Elaine McCarthy and Maria Watson. Subs used: Briege Corkery (1–0), Denise Twomey and Sarah O'Donovan.

Mairéad Lawlor's father, Mick, won All-Ireland senior hurling medals with Kilkenny. Marie O'Connor is a niece of Kilkenny great, Bridie McGarry (née Martin). Eimear Lyng's father, Michael, played senior hurling for Kilkenny.

Preparing for the Centenary

2002 All-Ireland Minor A Championship

Champions Cork had little difficulty in seeing off the challenge of Derry in the semi-final at Lavey. Despite a very good run in the Ulster championship, Derry were unable to provide a serious test for their visitors. Emer Watson (3–6), Denise Twomey (3–2) and Marie O'Neill (1–4) made up the bulk of Cork's total of 9–17. Derry replied with 1–1.

With only four of their 2001 side remaining, Galway did not know what to expect when they took the field against Wexford at Ballinasloe, but they need not have worried. The newcomers were well up to standard. A goal on either side of half-time by Emma Kilkelly set up Galway for a comfortable win over a Wexford team that was over-dependent on Una Leacy for their scores. Galway progressed by 4–12 to 2–8.

A tight defence, high work rate and some good finishing were the ingredients of Cork's 12th All-Ireland minor title at Cashel. Briege Corkery stretched Galway's cover time and again to present scoring opportunities for her team-mates. Galway were unlucky to lose scoring forward Emma Kilkelly with an ankle injury and their attack did not function well in her absence. On the other hand, the opportunism of Emer Watson and Denise Twomey presented a real and constant threat to Galway. Cork won by 1–11 to 1–5.

Cork team: Valerie McCormack, Marguerite Nyhan, Síle Burns, Lisa Healy, Noreen Mulcahy (0–4), Caitríona Foley, Rena Buckley, Elaine O'Riordan (captain), Anna Geary, Briege Corkery, Marie O'Neill, Margaret McCarthy (1–1), Denise Twomey, Emer Watson (0–6) and Mary Coleman. Subs used: Edwina Waters and Marion Murphy.

Galway team: Susan Earner, Anne Coen, Elaine Burke, Triona Byrne, Lorraine Lally, Elaine Tannian, Ann Marie Broderick, Caroline Kelly (captain), Clodagh Glynn (0–1), Susan Keane (0–2), Brenda Hanney (1–1), Marian Geoghegan, Linda Dillon (0–1), Emma Kilkelly and Fiona Hahnefeld. Subs used: Crystal Ruddy, Maureen Finnerty, Colette Hardiman, Ruth Maher and Sarah Dervan.

Cork's Síle Burns is a daughter of All-Ireland hurler, Denis Burns, and Mary Coleman is a daughter of Geraldine O'Brien, the Limerick and Munster star.

2002 All-Ireland Minor B Championship

Champions Limerick had little difficulty in disposing of the Monaghan challenge in the semi-final at St Mellan's Park. The gap in standards was apparent as Limerick skipped past the home side on their way to win by 6–10 to 0–0.

The second semi-final between Offaly and Roscommon was equally one-sided. Roscommon had no answer to Offaly's skill, teamwork and finish. The score stood at Offaly 8–9, Roscommon 0–0 at the final whistle.

Three goals in the opening ten minutes of the final against Offaly at Cashel placed Limerick on the road to victory. Offaly had come a long way in the previous seasons but had not yet reached the standard displayed by Limerick. Indeed, on that display, the Limerick team would not have been out of place in the closing stages of the A championship. Limerick's Claire Mulcahy, Sinéad McAuliffe, Fiona Morrissey, Natalie Heffernan and Christine Carroll were in a different class to their opponents. The Offaly girls kept trying to the very end. Sheila Sullivan, Michelle Murray, Aoife Kelly and Fiona Bermingham put in a huge effort. Limerick's winning margin was 5–7 to 0–2.

Limerick team: Ciara Kelleher, Janice White, Sarah O'Mahony, Fiona Chawke, Fiona Hickey, Claire Mulcahy (captain), Fiona Geary, Natalie Heffernan, Christine Carroll, Sinéad McAuliffe (2–5), Christine O'Shea, Marion O'Connell, Lisa Kelly (1–0), Fiona Morrissey (1–1) and Shannon Brosnan (1–1).

Offaly team: Amy Dolan, Sinead Buckley, Fiona Bermingham, Michelle Murray (captain), Lisa Gardiner, Sheila Sullivan, Anne Digan, Aoife Kelly (0–2), Grace Flynn, Mairéad Bergin, Karen Brady, Lorraine Coughlan, Tanya Coughlan, Jacinta Lyons and Laura Nugent.

2002 All-Ireland Club Championship

Title-holders, Pearses, had to undergo a severe test at the hands of Cashel before qualifying for the final. Two evenly matched teams played with spirit and determination, with the defences dominating at both ends. Once again, Cashel's over-dependence on scores from placed balls was their downfall. Orla Kilkenny was the only player to unlock the barricade to goal and her vital touch gave Pearses passage to the final by 1–9 to 0–10.

St Ibar's qualified for their first final with victory over Keady (Armagh) by 5–8 to 1–9 at Derrynoose. The Wexford side were well on top with goals from Michelle Hearne (two), Mag Kelly, Michelle Murphy and Kate Kelly. Colette McKeever replied for Keady. Jenna Murphy, Edwina Roche, Emma Carroll and Sandy Carr caught the eye for St Ibar's.

Pearses celebrated the 25th anniversary of the founding of the club by joining club championship specialists, St Paul's (Kilkenny) and Buffers Alley (Wexford), as the only clubs to win a hat-trick of All-Ireland titles. The writing was on the wall for St Ibar's at half-time when they trailed by ten points. The Wexford side lacked a cutting edge in attack and only managed 1–2 from play. Pearses, who were never in serious difficulty, had leaders in Sharon Glynn, Tracy Laheen, Martina Harkin and Sile Barrett and won comfortably by 2–13 to 1–5.

Pearses team: Louise Curry, Síle Barrett, Aisling Ward, Patricia Burke, Martina Donnellan, Tracy Laheen, Martina Harkin, Áine Hillary (captain), Carmel Hannon, Orla Kilkenny, Veronica Sweeney, Michelle Glynn, Shauna Ward, Sharon Glynn and Lorraine Lally.

St Ibar's team: Jenna Murphy, Edwina Roche, Emma Carroll, Catherine Doyle, Assumpta Cullen, Sandy Carr, Laura Corrigan, Fiona Cullen, Kate Kelly (0–3), Michelle Murphy (0–1), Jacqui O'Connor, Bridget Curran (0–1), Mag Kelly, Michelle Hearne and Anne Marie Kelly. Sub used: Leona Tector (1-0)

2002 Gael-Linn Senior Cup

Ulster and Connacht served up a sparkling display of camogie in the semi-final at St Anne's, Dublin while Leinster were never

Preparing for the Centenary

a match for Munster and failed to live up to pre-match expectations. Ulster had a one-point win, 3–14 to 2–16, whereas Munster cruised to a 5–13 to 1–10 win. Munster showed their class as they overcame Ulster by 7–23 to 0–11 in the final.

Munster team: Ger Casey (Cork), Joanne O'Callaghan (Cork), Una O'Dwyer (Tipperary), Claire Madden (Tipperary), Sinéad Nealon (Tipperary), Ciara Gaynor (Tipperary) (Capt), Therese Brophy (Tipperary), Jovita Delaney (Tipperary), Philly Fogarty (Tipperary), Colette Desmond (Cork), Vera Sheehan (Limerick), Noelle Kennedy (Tipperary), Eimear McDonnell (Tipperary), Deirdre Hughes (Tipperary) and Eileen O'Brien (Limerick).

Ulster team: Christine Doherty (Antrim), Sinéad Stevenson (Derry), Maureen Duffin (Antrim), Gráinne Maguire (Derry), Edel Mason (Antrim), Ciara Gault (Antrim), Jennifer Braniff (Down), Gráinne Connolly (Antrim), Grace McMullan (Antrim), Gráinne McGoldrick (Derry), Paula McCloy (Derry), Jane Adams (Antrim), Carla Doherty (Antrim), Maureen McAleenan (Down), Paula McAtamney (Derry).

2002 Gael-Linn Junior Trophy

Ulster were well ahead of Connacht, 4–4 to 1–8, at the finish of their semi-final at St Anne's, while Leinster put paid to Munster's chances of advancing with a 2–10 to 1–11 win in the second semi-final. Ulster performed excellently in the final and were full value for their 4–11 to 1–13 win over Leinster.

Ulster team: Claire O'Kane (Derry), Deborah Kelland (Down), Colette Burns (Armagh), Helen Kelly (Derry), Nuala O'Hagan (Derry), Catherine Pickering (Derry), Fionnuala Carr (Down), Katrina Curry (Armagh), Katie McAuley (Derry), Mary Black (Armagh), Patricia McEvoy (Armagh), Paula Bell (Derry), Claire Gormley (Derry), Eilish Doherty (Derry) and Briege Convery (Derry).

Leinster panel: Fiona McLeish, Carina Carroll, Michelle Davis, Jeanette Feighery, Sharron Daly, Maggie Lynch, Majella Bergin, Elaine Dermody, Mary Weir, Amanda Kelly (Offaly), Michelle Jordan, Catherine O'Loughlin, Gretta Heffernan, Una Leacy (Wexford), Mary Burke (Meath), Edel Maher, Aoife Neary (Kilkenny), Louise Conlon (captain) (Kildare) Lenora Lyons and Marguerite Smithers (Laois).

Framework for Integration

Four presidents, Mary McAleese, Seán McCague, Pat Rafferty and Walter Thompson, attended the launch of a pilot scheme at Croke Park on February 25th 2003 that aimed to establish the most appropriate framework for integration of the Camogie Association and the Ladies Football Association with the GAA. The scheme, which ran over an eight-month period in selected counties, endeavoured to highlight the various challenges which integration posed and to provide solutions in advance of closer liaison between the three zs. A report was subsequently prepared and presented to the 2004 Congress of the three bodies.

Miriam O'Callaghan Elected President

The first Offaly lady to hold the office of President of the Camogie

A Game of Our Own

Association, Miriam O'Callaghan (née Casey) was elected at Congress 2003 in Arklow. A founder member of the Tullamore Camogie Club, Miriam had lined out for club and county. She had refereed at all levels and held many positions at club, county and Leinster Council and served as President of the All-Ireland Colleges Council.

There was no election for the post of treasurer as Jo Golden's role had become a full-time paid position. Jo stepped down following almost 30 years of valuable service to the Association as national PRO, Ard Runaí and treasurer.

Kilkenny's motion that the post-match All-Ireland function on the Monday be discontinued was passed. Instead, an informal reception in Croke Park was organised immediately after the senior final. Congress approved a constitution for supporters' clubs which set out the boundaries in which these units had to operate.

'Chicks with Sticks'

The Centenary Committee, with an average age of 27, sought to move camogie forward, electrify its image and make it attractive. While preparing to embark on a massive sponsorship campaign, they came up with the slogan 'Chicks with Sticks'. The media interest was huge and many journalists picked up on the image reflected by the slogan. Getting a more accurate image across of the modern camogie player was the target of the committee. They were at pains to put the message out that camogie is saleable. The modern player is young, attractive and fit, well-educated, highly skilled and dedicated to the game.

CG, the Magazine for the camogie girl, catered exclusively for Ireland's largest female sport and its supporters. With a mixture of camogie and Gaelic games contributors, the first edition was launched in September 2003. Building on the 'Chicks with Sticks' campaign, the publication aimed at encouraging interest in the game from people outside the Association and bringing the latest

Group of Cork players taken at the 2003 Jubilee Lunch on All-Ireland day in Croke Park. Back: Marie Costine-O'Donovan, Cathy Landers-Harnedy, Clare Cronin-Murphy, Marion Sweeney and Mary O'Leary. Front: Pat Moloney-Lenihan, Mary Geaney, Nancy O'Driscoll-O'Donovan and Marian McCarthy.

Preparing for the Centenary

news, reviews, opinions and photos from all over the country and abroad to its supporters.

Financial and Sponsorship Manager

A native of Moycullen, Co. Galway, Sinéad O'Connor was appointed financial and sponsorship manager in June 2003. She graduated with a BS in Accounting from Scranton University in Pennsylvania and obtained a Masters in Accounting from the Smurfit School of Business. She came to the Camogie Association from PricewaterhouseCoopers. A talented musician, Sinéad plays camogie with the Portobello Club in Dublin. With the camogie centenary around the corner, Sinéad had little time to settle into her new surroundings. It was all go from day one.

New Initiatives

The camogie website went live in May 2003, giving immediate access to news, information, fixtures and results. The new medium is user-friendly to the young generation who are much more likely to tap into the web than pick up a newspaper.

Eight counties were invited to participate in the County Development Squad Plan. Talented 13-year-olds formed a panel for special training by qualified tutors with a view to raising the standard of the county teams in the years to come. Coillte came on board with welcome sponsorship. This initiative proved very successful over the following years and was expanded to include a day in Croke Park and an opportunity for all the participating squads to play on the famed sod.

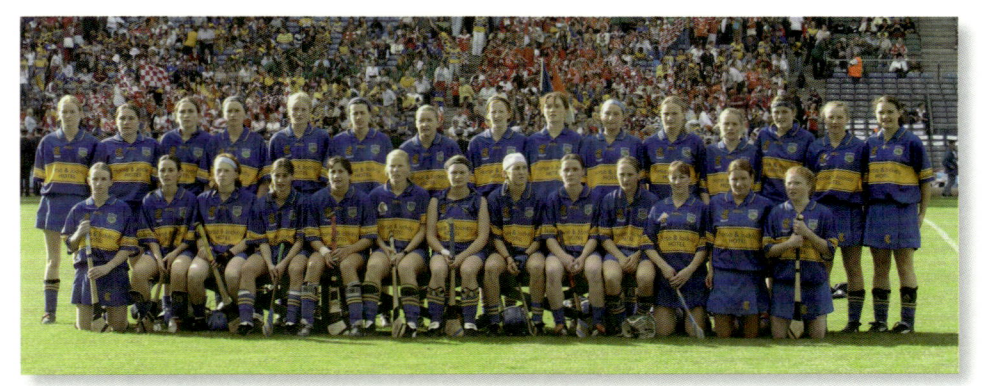

The Tipperary panel at the 2003 Cork v Tipperary All-Ireland final. *Picture: Ray McManus / SPORTSFILE*

2003 All-Ireland Senior Championship

Cork had 3–11 on the scoreboard before Galway registered their opening point in the semi-final at Ennis. Despite the weakness of the opposition, Cork were awesome. Their first touch was immaculate which allowed them to create and finish a host of chances. Cork were ahead by 4–16 to 0–3 when the match was over.

Without reaching their full potential, Tipperary qualified for the final. They scored goals at crucial times of the game. As Limerick ran out of steam towards the end, Tipperary sent over a string of points without reply to win impressively on the score of 4–16 to 0–10.

Tipperary took the field in the final at Croke Park on September 21st determined to prise the O'Duffy Cup out of Cork hands and claim their fourth title in five years. Ultimately, the difference between the sides was the ability of Tipperary's inside forwards, Deirdre Hughes and Eimear McDonnell, to impose themselves and score from play. They continually moved about to create opportunities and kept the Cork defence at full stretch.

There was little between the sides in the opening 25 minutes. Approaching half-time, Eimear McDonnell struck home to the Cork net. The score spurred Tipperary on. Within a minute of the resumption, Deirdre Hughes scored a goal to change the direction of the game. Eimear McDonnell added four points to put Cork in deep trouble. Briege Corkery was introduced and Gemma O'Connor, who earlier retired with a hand injury, returned to the fray. Cork struck a number of bad wides before Gemma O'Connor forced home a consolation goal at the death. Emily Hayden, Philly Fogarty, Joanne Ryan, Una O'Dwyer and Therese Brophy were in scintillating form for a Tipperary side that reclaimed top spot. On a day when Cork struggled in key areas, they lacked a star to ignite the team. Tipperary won by 2–11 to 1–11.

Tipperary team: Jovita Delaney, Suzanne Kelly, Una O'Dwyer (captain), Claire Madden, Sinéad Nealon, Ciara Gaynor, Therese Brophy, Angie McDermott, Philly Fogarty, Joanne Ryan (0–1), Emily Hayden (0–2), Claire Grogan (0–1), Noelle Kennedy (0–2), Deirdre Hughes (1–1) and Eimear McDonnell (1–4). Sub used: Trish O'Halloran.

Cork team: Ger Casey, Joanne O'Callaghan, Eithne Duggan, Stephanie Dunlea (captain), Paula O'Connor, Mary O'Connor (0–2), Gemma O'Connor (1–0), Rachel Moloney, Vivienne Harris, Una O'Donoghue (0–1), Emer Dillon (0–2), Jenny O'Leary (0–2), Orla O'Sullivan (0–1), Caoimhe Harrington and Fiona O'Driscoll (0–3). Subs used: Caitríona Foley, Sarah Hayes, Briege Corkery and Colette Desmond.

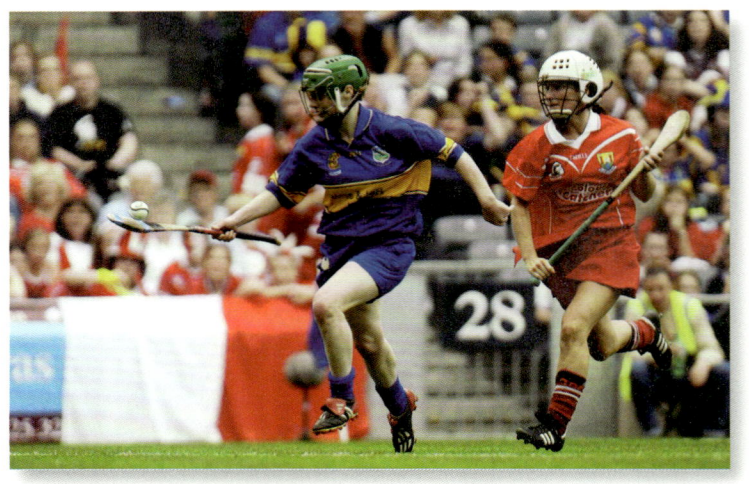

2003 All-Ireland senior final. Eimear McDonnell, Tipperary, beats Cork's Joanne O'Callaghan on her way to scoring her side's first goal.
Pic: Pat Murphy / SPORTSFILE

2003 All-Ireland Intermediate Championship

With six of their senior panel in action in the semi-final at The Ragg, Tipperary made light work of Derry. The Ulster side remained in contention until the break but were unable to match their opponents as the game went on and conceded by 4-13 to 1-4.

A 12-point victory suggests an easy hour's camogie but Antrim did not have it all their own way against Dublin in the second semi-final at Skerries. When Oonagh Elliott scored Antrim's second goal, Dublin saw no way back. Antrim advanced to the final by 3-9 to 0-6.

In a closely contested final at Páirc Tailteann, Antrim enjoyed midfield dominance over Tipperary. They seized an early initiative through Edel Mason's goal. With the wind at their backs for the second-half, Tipperary started promisingly. Their task proved to be an uphill battle and, when Elaine Dowds got through for a second goal, Tipperary's race was run. The match finished Antrim 2-9, Tipperary 0-10.

Antrim team: Christine Doherty, Orla Donnelly, Mairéad Graham, Maureen McAllister, Ciara McGinley, Sheila McCluskey, Ciara McKinley, Jane Adams (0-3), Edel Mason (1-1), Niamh Curry, Gráinne Connolly (0-2), Ann McKee, Oonagh Elliott, Sinéad Lagan (0-1) and Carla Doherty (0-1). Sub used: Elaine Dowds (1-1).

Tipperary team: Paula Ryan, Deirdre McDonnell, Helen Breen, Jenny O'Halloran, Méadhbh Corcoran, Noelette O'Dwyer, Julie Kirwan, Lorraine Burke, Mairéad Morrissey, Áine Mulcahy (0-2), Trish O'Halloran (0-3), Joanne Nolan, Geraldine Kinnane (0-2), Mary Looby (0-2) and Jill Horan (0-1). Subs used: Niamh Connolly, Eimear Ryan, Moira Ryan and Jacqui O'Connor.

Edel Mason was named Player of the Match. She created a bit of history by becoming the first player to win the award with two different counties. She had been the recipient of the award in 1998 when she had fielded with Down.

Tipperary captain Una O'Dwyer lifts the cup after victory over Cork. Picture: Pat Murphy / SPORTSFILE

2003 All-Ireland Junior Championship

Clare emerged jubilant over a brave Armagh side at the end of an hour's pulsating play in the semifinal at Cusack Park. There was nothing between the sides as they built up their tallies score for score. A missed opportunity by Armagh cost them dearly. Clare progressed by 4-7 to 3-8.

Ann Marie Hayes and Emma Kilkelly set up Galway with an interval lead of 2-3 to 0-3 against Wexford in the second semi-final at Portumna. Both teams managed 1-3 in the second-half, allowing Galway to advance to the final by 3-6 to 1-6.

Clare came from behind in dramatic fashion to earn a replay in the final at Croke Park. The Banner County trailed by four points as the game entered injury-time. A point by Deirdre Murphy and a marvellous match-saving goal by Catherine O'Loughlin left the supporters of both sides speechless at the finish. Clare procured a draw by 3-9 to 3-9.

Galway did their homework prior to the replay at Tullamore. They positioned their players with great effect and curtailed the effectiveness of the Clare danger girls. Brenda Kerins moved to centre-forward where she got the Galway attack moving. Deirdre Murphy was held scoreless from play by Roisin O'Connor while Sinéad Cahalan limited the influence of Catherine O'Loughlin. The result was title number seven for Galway by 1–12 to 2–5.

Galway team: Susan Earner, Lizzie Flynn, Sinéad Cahalan, Nicola Lawless, Nicola Gavin, Róisín O'Connor, Sinéad Keane, Caroline Kelly, Colette Glennon, Brenda Hanney (0–1), Cathy Bowes (0–3), Marese Flanagan (0–2), Brenda Kerins (captain) (0–1), Ann Marie Hayes (1–2) and Emma Kilkelly (0–2). Sub used: Catherine Glynn (0–1) .

Clare team: Patricia O'Grady, Jane Scanlon, Denise Lynch, Caitríona McMahon, Marie O'Looney, Noelle Comyns, Marie Whelan, Laura Linnane (0–1), Deirdre Corcoran, Aoife Ryan, Deirdre Murphy (1–2), Áine Keane (0–1), Claire McMahon, Catherine O'Loughlin (captain) (1–1) and Claire Commane. Subs used: Ruth Kaiser and Aileen Martin.

Waterford – 2003 All-Ireland Under16b Champions. Back: Áine Lyng, Orla Heffernan, Aisling O'Brien, Tanya Morrissey, Claire Hartery, Róisín Delahunty, Jenny Simpson, Kate Heneghan and Shelly Keane. Middle: Louise O'Dowda, Amy O'Sullivan, Jenny Houlihan, Vicki Gaffney, Patricia Broderick, Emma Hannon, Patricia Jackman, Róisín Heylin and Susan Finn. Front: Deirdre Walsh, Margo Heffernan, Charlotte Raher, Laura Buckley (Capt), Emma Tallon, Ciara Keogh and Martina Cashin.

2003 All-Ireland Minor A Championship

The difference in class between the Ulster minor champions and the top teams from the remaining provinces was highlighted with a runaway win by Galway over Derry in the semi-final at Ballinasloe. Galway dominated in all sectors of the field to ease their way to the final by 9–14 to 2–2.

Three-quarters of the second semi-final between Kilkenny and Cork at Páirc Uí Rínn was an entertaining contest.

Anna Geary was superb in midfield and supplied the Cork forwards with a constant supply of good ball enabling seven Cork players to get their names on the score sheet. Kilkenny, who were under attack throughout the game, faded in the final quarter. Cork progressed to the final by 3–16 to 2–5.

Mairéad Dunne got Galway off to a great start in the final at Portlaoise when she hit the back of the Cork net with only 20 seconds on the clock.

This upset the Cork girls who struggled nervously throughout the first half. Galway failed to take advantage and allowed many opportunities to pass them by. The teams stood at 1–3 apiece at the break. Cork returned to the field in confident and determined mood and set about winning the match.

Anna Geary, Orla Coughlan and Edwina Waters controlled the middle of the park. Galway were confined to a single point in the second half by an efficient Cork defence. Cork retained the cup by 3-12 to 1-4.

Cork team: Marian Murphy, Emma Dunne, Marguerite Nyhan, Lucy Hawkes, Orla Cotter, Rena Buckley, Edwina Waters, Anna Geary (1-5), Sarah Downing, Orla Coughlan (0-2), Hazel O'Regan, Áine Watson (1-2), Tina Shanahan, Mary Coleman (1-3) and Susan Donovan. Subs used: Deirdre Coomey and Emma Healy.

Galway team: Stephanie Gannon, Julie Brien, Elaine Burke, Colette Gill, Jessica Gill (0-1), Ruth Maher, Clodagh Glynn, Leona Monaghan, Fiona Hahnefeld, Emily Burke, Sarah Noone (0-1), Linda Dillon, Therese Manton, Colette Hardiman (0-1) and Mairéad Dunne (1-1). Subs used: Sarah Dervan, Julie Brien and Martina Conroy.

A group of former Waterford players with Laura Buckley, captain of the All-Ireland U16 team.

2003 All-Ireland Minor B Championship

Fielding a team for the first time at this level, the Kildare youngsters found the more experienced Waterford players a step beyond them in the semi-final at Walsh Park. Waterford made the better use of their chances to win by 5-11 to 2-7.

In the second semi-final against Armagh, Roscommon showed an improvement on their performance at the same stage in 2002. However, the ability of Armagh to create and finish goal opportunities was the difference between the sides. Armagh reached the final by 3-8 to 0-8.

Áine Lyng had the game of her life for Waterford in the final against Armagh at O'Moore Park. The gifted attacker registered 4-3 and inspired her team to realise their dream. Waterford retired to the dressing room with a healthy ten-point lead.

Armagh returned to the field with renewed vigour, but a fourth Waterford goal within five minutes proved to be a major setback to their chances. Róisín Heylin, Jenny Simpson, Charlotte Raher, Aisling O'Brien and Róisín Delahunty all made a big impressions for the winners. Colette McSorley, Charlene Fanthorpe, Ciara Hayes and Michelle Murphy tried very hard to swing the game in Armagh's favour. The final score was Waterford 6–11, Armagh 1–4.

Waterford team: Aisling O'Brien, Patricia Broderick, Orla Heffernan, Margo Heffernan, Laura Buckley (captain), Tanya Morrissey, Róisín Delahunty, Charlotte Raher, Jenny Simpson (1–0), Susan Finn, Emma Hannon (0–3), Róisín Heylin (1–2), Kate Heneghan, Áine Lyng (4–3), Louise O'Dowd (0–2). Sub used: Patricia Jackman (0–1).

Armagh team: Sunniamhna Quinn, Aoibheann McKenna, Ciara Hayes, Danielle McBirney, Emma O'Hare, Charlene Fanthorpe, Shauna McKee, Colette McSorley (1–2), Michelle Murphy (0–1), Angela Clarke, Stephanie McPartland, Aoibheann Murphy (0–1), Dara Collins, Grace Donaghy (captain) and Jolene Rowland.

Waterford's Margo Heffernan is a daughter of Christy Heffernan who won All-Ireland senior hurling medals in the colours of Kilkenny.

A number of former Waterford players sat together in the stand cheering on the county minors. Josie McNamara and Bríd McGrath had played in the 1945 All-Ireland senior final, Lilian Howlett and Geraldine Power had won

Munster senior medals in 1959, while Alicia Browne and Maura Crotty shed tears of joy when Laura Buckley accepted the first All-Ireland championship cup on behalf of Waterford.

2003 All-Ireland Club Senior Championship

Davitt's took some time to adapt to the tight surrounds of Pearse Park, Dunloy, where they met the local side in the semi-final. The small pitch led to much crowding and congested play. Oonagh Elliott and Majella Connolly both scored goals for Dunloy and Mary Kelly replied with a brace of goals for Davitt's, but it was Lourda Kavanagh's 11 points that saw Davitt's to the final. The match ended at Davitt's 2–14, Dunloy 3–4.

Mary O'Connor returned to her native Killeagh and was replaced by Marie Collins of Scariff in the Granagh-Ballingarry midfield since their 1999 success. They were paired with St Lachtain's of Freshford in the semi-final. St Lachtain's gave a good account of themselves but the experience garnered by Granagh over the past five to six years saw them through to the final by 2–11 to 0–10.

Granagh-Ballingarry captured their third All-Ireland club championship title at the expense of Davitt's at Cusack Park, Mullingar. Captain Laura Leslie and Deirdre Sheehan denied possession and territory to the Davitt's attack. Vera Sheehan was at her best in midfield and provided a great service to the forwards. Eileen O'Brien, Joanne Clifford and Maeve Nash put Granagh into a comfortable lead. Lourda Kavanagh posed the main threat to Granagh and her untiring efforts yielded 1–3. Granagh-Ballingarry finished in front by 1–10 to 1–6.

Granagh-Ballingarry team: Breda O'Brien, Aimee McCarthy, Laura Leslie (captain), Maureen O'Gorman, Kay Burke, Ber Chawke, Deirdre Sheehan, Marie Collins, Vera Sheehan, Jean Cullinane, Eileen O'Brien, Aoifa Sheehan, Joanne Clifford, Meadhbh Nash and Fiona Morrissey.

Davitt's team: Michelle Tynan, Orla Watson, Rita Broderick, Lisa Fahy, Fiona Pierce, Anne Broderick, Lizzie Flynn, Ailbhe Kelly, Caroline Kelly, Doreen Kelly, Deirdre Murphy, Caitriona Kelly, Olivia Forde, Lourda Kavanagh and Mary Kelly. Sub used: Anne Marie Broderick.

2003 All-Ireland Club Junior Championship

Drumcullen (Offaly) produced some fine camogie to oust Newmarket-on-Fergus (Clare) by 3–7 to 0–4 in the first semi-final while Crossmaglen (Armagh) proved too good for Ahascragh (Galway) in the second semi-final.

The standard of play in the first junior final was very satisfactory with Crossmaglen coming out on top by 2–5 to 0–7. Crossmaglen became the first holders of the Phil McBride Cup and brought it back to the county where she championed Gaelic Games over several decades.

Crossmaglen team: Leona McShane, Geraldine Daly, Eimear Carragher, Anne McGirr, Donna McShane, Joan Murphy, Pamela Dooey, Alma O'Donnell, Bronagh O'Donnell, Sinéad Lenaghan, Sharon Duncan, Ann Marie Comiskey, Debbie Lundy, Patricia McAvoy and Eilis Short.

Drumcullen panel: Bernie Nugent, Marcella Nugent, Colette Kelly, Leona Gath, Yolanda Spain, Sinéad Colgan, Honor Kinsella, Lorraine Corcoran, Eileen Kinsella, Fiona Stephens, Bríd Fleury, Mary Lyons, Louise O'Brien, Elaine Dermody, Eimear Lyons, Caroline Guinan, Michelle Corcoran, Karen Nugent, Edel Corcoran, Laura Nugent, Maggie Lynch and Pamela Nugent.

2003 Gael-Linn Senior Cup

Munster easily overcame a depleted Connacht side in the semi-final at Portmarnock by 2–20 to 1–3 and Ulster recorded a comfortable 1–20 to 4–2 victory in the second semi-final. Munster did not have things their own way in the final and only pulled away in the closing stages to claim the title by 3–13 to 1–9.

Munster team: Aoife Murray (Cork), Joanne O'Callaghan (Cork), Stephanie Dunlea (captain) (Cork), Sinéad Nealon (Tipperary), Paula O'Connor (Cork), Mary O'Connor (Cork), Angie McDermott (Tipperary), Briege Corkery (Cork), Elaine Burke (Cork), Vera Sheehan (Limerick), Una O'Donoghue (Cork), Joanne Ryan (Tipperary), Eileen O'Brien (Limerick), Ciara Healy (Cork) and Denise Twomey (Cork).

Ulster team: Teresa McGowan (Down), Hannah Healey (Antrim), Pauline Greene (Down), Anna O'Loughlin (Derry), Claire Doherty (Derry), Gráinne Connolly (Antrim), Ciara McGinley (Antrim), Catherine McGourty (Down), Jennifer Braniff (Down), Jane Adams (Antrim), Maureen McAleenan (Down), Paula McAtamney (Derry), Carla Doherty (Antrim), Grace McMullan (Antrim) and Aisling Kealey (Derry).

2003 Gael-Linn Junior Trophy

Ulster had a close call from Leinster in the semi-final and emerged with a goal to spare, 2–7 to 1–7, at the end of an exciting clash, while Munster were not troubled by a weak Connacht side and proceeded to the final by 3–15 to 0–4. A fitter and more competitive Munster side regained the trophy in a one-sided final by 4–7 to 0–5.

Munster team: Paula Ryan (Tipperary), Anna Geary (Cork), Helen Breen (Tipperary), Caitríona Foley (Cork), Méadhbh Corcoran (Tipperary), Amanda O'Regan (Cork), Kate Marie Hearne (Waterford), Val O'Keeffe (Cork), Lorraine Burke (Tipperary), Geraldine Kinnane (Tipperary), Miriam Deasy (Cork), Trish O'Halloran (Tipperary), Michelle Shortt (Tipperary), Elaine O'Riordan (Cork) and Mary Coleman (Cork).

Ulster team: Claire O'Kane (Derry), Deborah Kelland (Down), Jane Carey (Derry), Bernie McKinley (Antrim), Siobhán McCloskey (Antrim), Bernie McBride (Armagh), Orla Smyth (Armagh), Gráinne McGoldrick (Derry), Róisín Duffin (Antrim), Edel Mason (Antrim), Katie McAuley (Derry), Joan Murphy (Armagh), Mary Black (Armagh), Patricia McAvoy (Armagh) and Noelle McCarry (Antrim).

Where We're At

The months leading up to the centenary year celebrations were hectic and exciting. Concentrated planning produced an impressive calendar of events. The young generation, charged with putting the schedule together, came up with the trendy slogan 'Chicks with Sticks'. It was not one that the ladies of Central Council would have come up with, but it did the trick and drew widespread media attention. The goal was to accelerate the transition from a perceived image of the game to that of an attractive and vibrant sport played by athletic, skilful and competitive players.

A number of new developments were already in place. Sponsorship of the All-Ireland senior championship was received from Foras na Gaeilge. A skort, a combination of a skirt and shorts, had been designed for the players. Sinéad O'Connor had taken up her appointment as finance and sponsorship manager. The game had adopted the 15-a-side format. The first issue of *Camogie Girl* magazine and the Association's website had been launched. Efforts were made to stage camogie games alongside inter-county hurling matches to increase the profile of the game and to bring the game to a wider audience. An all-out effort was made to sell camogie to the business community in an attempt to attract much-needed sponsorship for the centenary activities.

It was a similar story at county and club levels. Each unit of the Association put plans in place to celebrate the momentous occasion. There was something to suit all ages: special competitions, fun activities, displays of old photos and nostalgic items and social events. Every effort was made to track down past officers and former players with the intention of bringing all together for a reunion to round off the celebrations.

A common complaint over the years was the lack of information that filtered up and down channels of communication. Those on the ground lamented that delegates did not report back from meetings, leaving them unaware of what was going on. Officials at the top bemoaned the fact that they received few replies to their

Preparing for the Centenary

requests for information. Former players and retired officials were in the dark in regard to what was happening.

Modern technology transformed the scene. The Association moved with the times and launched a website. News and information became available at the press of a button. All members of the camogie family could obtain up-to-date news, details of fixtures, match results and view photos any hour of the day or night. A well-maintained website can be an excellent public-relations tool and the Association's site raised its profile. Prospective members and potential sponsors could learn about the organisation in advance of making contact. As technology developed, further services of benefit to the Camogie Association became available.

2001 was the International Year of the Volunteer. Its aim was to celebrate the achievements and dedication of volunteers who give freely of their time to help others. The Camogie Association depended for almost a century on the voluntary efforts of generations of men and women who gave selflessly of their time. They enriched the girls with a sense of pride in themselves and their community, and helped them to develop through the benefits of sport. For many girls, camogie was the only sport and social outlet available. These wonderful people deserve a huge debt of gratitude. While times have changed, the need for a perpetual supply of volunteers to carry on the vital work of the Association will always remain.

Hurling-shinty internationals between Ireland and Scotland have been an annual fixture on the GAA calendar for some years. It was an obvious place to look when the Camogie Association sought to broaden its horizons and seek an international dimension. The possibility of establishing links with ladies shinty was explored and met with an enthusiastic response. However, while shinty was a long-established and popular male sport, the ladies game was only beginning to get off the ground. Nevertheless, the Scottish girls were willing to put a team together to travel to Ireland for the centenary celebrations.

Anxious to upgrade the standard of the game, the coaching and development committee established guidelines in 2002 for under-14 development squads at county level. The purpose of the squads was to foster long-term interest in camogie among the participants and improve their skill levels. Good coaching is so vital in the formative years of a young player when skills are easily mastered. Coillte came on board as a very welcome partner for the venture and generously supplied the squads with gear and equipment. Kilkenny was the first county to sign up and the phenomenal success of their underage teams in subsequent years underlines the benefits of the system.

A Game of Our Own

GRANDSTAND VIEW

Chapter Twenty Two

LET THE CELEBRATIONS BEGIN

A special year for camogie was set in motion at Croke Park on November 25th, 2003 when the Association launched its centenary logo, designed by Mark Dignam, and a calendar of events to celebrate the 100th anniversary of the founding of the Association. Present to witness the unveiling were John O'Donoghue, Minister for Arts, Sports and Tourism, Seán Kelly, President of the GAA and Miriam O'Callaghan, President of the Camogie Association.

Seán Kelly promised every support saying that the strengthening of the Camogie Association would in turn help strengthen the GAA

A sizeable donation towards the funding of the centenary events underpinned that pledge. With generous sponsorship from the Lynch Hotels Group, the LynchPins Team of 2003 was announced. It was no surprise that Tipperary and Cork, counties that dominated the inter-county scene, claimed the majority of the places on the team. The inaugural All-Stars scheme was warmly welcomed by the players who sought such recognition for some time. The chosen players celebrated with friends and family at a function at the Lynch Green Isle Hotel.

February 2004: An Taoiseach, Bertie Ahern, and Miriam O'Callaghan, Uachtarán, Cumann Camogaíochta na nGael, holding the Team of the Century at the Citywest Hotel, Dublin.

The selected team was: Jovita Delaney (Tipperary), Rose Collins (Limerick), Una O'Dwyer (Tipperary), Stephanie Dunlea (Cork), Mary O'Connor (Cork), Ciara Gaynor (Tipperary), Therese Brophy (Tipperary), Vera Sheehan (Limerick), Jane Adams (Antrim), Emer Dillon (Cork), Claire Grogan (Tipperary), Eileen O'Brien (Limerick), Eimear McDonnell (Tipperary), Deirdre Hughes (Tipperary) and Fiona O'Driscoll (Cork).

Camogie Ambassadors

A team of camogie ambassadors was hand-picked

A Game of Our Own

to raise the profile of the sport and act as role models for young players in their areas during centenary year. Many of these were excellent and attracted positive publicity to the game. The list of ambassadors reads:

Maureen McAleenan (Ulster), Majella Smith-Prior (Cavan), Jane Adams (Antrim), Joan Murphy (Armagh), Claire Doherty (Derry), Janice Rushe (Donegal), Michelle McDermott (Fermanagh), Geraldine Clarke (Monaghan), Julie O'Callaghan (Tyrone), Maureen McAleenan (Down), Eileen O'Brien (Munster), Deirdre Corcoran (Clare), Mary Geaney (Kerry), Fiona O'Driscoll (Cork), Pauline McCarthy (Limerick), Kate Marie Hearne (Waterford), Méadhbh Stokes (Tipperary), Kate Kelly (Leinster), Aoife Davitt (Westmeath), Eilish Mulholland (Louth), Mary Burke (Meath), Sonya Byrne (Dublin), Valerie Crean (Carlow), Tracy Millea (Kilkenny), Ciara Tallon (Kildare) Sarah Duffy (Wicklow), Bernadette Whelan (Laois), Áine Codd (Wexford), Maggie Lynch (Offaly), Lourda Kavanagh (Connacht), Susan Earner (Galway), Noreen Heston (Mayo), Karina Jones (Roscommon), Róisín O'Neill (London), Lucy Clerkin (USA), Claire Harrington (primary schools), Anna Geary (secondary schools) and Deirdre McDonnell (third-level colleges).

The Camogie Team of the Century. Back: Sheila Wallace, Árd Stiúrthóir, Liz Neary, Marie Costine-O'Donovan, Mary Sinnott-Dinan, Bridie Martin-McGarry, Sandie Fitzgibbon, Margaret O'Leary-Leacy, Linda Mellerick, Marion Carolan representing Kathleen Mills-Hill and Mary Fennelly representing Angela Downey. Front: Eileen Duffy-O'Mahony, Mairéad McAtamney-Magill, An Taoiseach, Bertie Ahern, Camogie President, Miriam O'Callaghan, Una O'Connor, Nancy McCarthy, sister of Sophie Brack, Pat Moloney-Lenihan and Deirdre Hughes.

Let the Celebrations Begin

Centenary Banquet

A line of cars and taxis queued up at the entrance to the CityWest Hotel ready to release their glamorous occupants. Inside, the foyer was a buzz of chat and excitement. Players of yesteryear welcomed one another with open arms. Current players looked stunning. Their trim figures, styled hairdos and fashionable gowns gave an air of glamour to the occasion.

The question on everybody's lips was: "Who has been named on the team of the century"? Stars of the past were spotted in the crowd which gave rise to speculation as to their selection. The crowd was ushered into the massive and tastefully decorated hall, with 100 tables to seat the impressive attendance of over a thousand. President Miriam O'Callaghan escorted An Taoiseach, Bertie Ahern, to his seat. The sense of anticipation was almost intolerable. A few probables were on everyone's list but the remaining names varied depending on where one hailed from.

Delegates attending Congress during the centenary celebrations at the Citywest Hotel, Dublin.
Picture: Brendan Moran / SPORTSFILE

The first lady called to the stage was the former Dublin goalkeeper, Eileen Duffy O'Mahony, holder of eight All-Ireland senior medals. Kilkenny's versatile Liz Neary, who had captained her county to All-Ireland honours twice, was next to receive her award. Rated as the most accomplished full-back, Marie Costine O'Donovan (Cork) took her seat. International badminton player, Mary Sinnott Dinan (Wexford), completed the full-back line. Sandie Fitzgibbon (Cork), who had combined camogie at the highest level with an international basketball career, filled the number five spot. One of the great stylists of the game, Kilkenny's Bridie Martin McGarry, was no surprise at centre-back. An outstanding half-back line was completed by the match-winning Margaret O'Leary Leacy.

A classic striker of the ball, Antrim's Mairéad McAtamney Magill won a midfield berth. Kathleen Mills Hill, a legend of the game and holder of 15 All-Ireland senior medals, was chosen in the position she had occupied for Dublin for 21 years. A leader on the field, Cork's Linda Mellerick earned her place for the major contribution she had made to her team. The elusive and intelligent play of Pat Moloney Lenihan (Cork) earmarked her for selection and top player of the fifties and sixties, Una O'Connor (Dublin), was an automatic choice. Queen of full-forwards, Sophie Brack, captained Dublin to six All-Ireland victories. Deirdre Hughes was hugely instrumental in Tipperary's rise to the summit. The team was completed by Angela Downey Browne (Kilkenny), a superb stylist and master of every facet of the game.

Team of the Century

Eileen Duffy O'Mahony

Liz Neary	Marie Costine O'Donovan	Mary Sinnott Dinan
Sandie Fitzgibbon	Bridie Martin McGarry	Margaret O'Leary Leacy
Mairéad McAtamney Magill		Kathleen Mills Hill
Linda Mellerick	Pat Moloney Lenihan	Una O'Connor
Sophie Brack	Deirdre Hughes	Angela Downey Browne

Commemorative Stamps

An Post issued two commemorative stamps on April 25th 2004 to mark the centenary of the Camogie Association. Two 48-cent stamps, with artwork by Corkman Finbarr O'Connor, featured the four counties with the most All-Ireland titles. Wearing the playing uniform of the sixties, Dublin and Antrim players feature on the first stamp against the background of the camogie crest. The O'Duffy Cup is strategically placed between Cork and Kilkenny rivals in modern kit on the second stamp.

From February onwards, county boards, provincial councils and colleges bodies held special events to celebrate the historic year. A Gaelic sports reunion banquet brought graduates from the four corners of the country and beyond back to UCD to renew acquaintances and relive memories of the past. The GAA Museum housed a Camogie exhibition and April 10th was set aside as Lá na gClub, when family and community-oriented events were organised throughout the country.

Let the Celebrations Begin

As in every other season, the competitions were of utmost importance. Added value by way of commemorative and runners-up medals, special programmes and enhanced presentation augmented the occasions.

Twenty-eight counties were represented in the National Féile na nGael finals in the midland counties of Westmeath, Kildare and Meath. Camogie personnel were included for the first time in the primary school visits where star players Bridie McGarry and Miriam Malone proved to be a big hit with the youngsters. A parade was led by the Kilmessan Camogie team through the streets of Navan, 100 years after the first competitive game was played in the town.

Irish captain, Anna Geary, Camogie President, Miriam O'Callaghan and Scottish captain, Lisa Norman pictured after the first international camogie/shinty match at Rathoath in October, 2004

Strategic Plan 2004–2008

The Strategic Plan, based on the proposals of the members, was presented to Congress 2004 at the CityWest Hotel. Based on the four goals of increased and improved participation, quality, management and marketing, it focused priorities for the period ahead. It was deemed vital to the growth of the organisation that the plan should be adopted and that every effort should be made to implement it. Many hours were spent by Sheila Wallace, Jo Golden, Liz Howard and Sinéad O'Connor putting it together.

Sad Loss

The celebrations were temporarily put on hold while the Association mourned the loss of two past-presidents, Nancy Murray and Sheila McAnulty. Nancy's sudden death was a shock to everyone. She had played a very important role in the history of Antrim Camogie.

Nancy Murray

Hundreds of camogie people turned up to pay tribute to Sheila McAnulty who lost the battle to ill-health at the age of 88. Life President of the Camogie Association, Sheila was a legend in her lifetime and will remain so in the memory of all who knew her.

First Match Commemorated

Camogie went back to its roots in Navan on July 17th. The first public match was played at Páirc Tailteann on that day in 1904 between Dublin sides Keatings and Cuchulainns at a Gaelic League Aeridheacht. A commemorative plaque to record this historic event was unveiled by Minister for Education, Noel Dempsey, in the presence of President Miriam O'Callaghan and nine past-presidents. Meath clubs provided teams and referee, dressed in the style of 1904, to enact the original game and primary-school children formed the figure 100 on the pitch.

International Games

Teams from America, Britain and Scotland were welcomed to participate in our first international competitions. An All-Star team, comprised of post-primary-school players, represented Ireland in the camogie-shinty match at Ratoath on October 16th. The rules were adapted to come closer to the Scottish game. Apart from the goalkeeper, players could not handle the ball. Kicking the ball was also prohibited. The talented school players proved much too good for the Scottish girls and won by 6–13 to 0–0.

Irish team: Denise Twomey (Loreto, Fermoy), Elaine O'Riordan (St Mary's, Charleville), Phyllis Hayes (Mercy, Woodford), Deirdre Codd (Col. Bríde, Enniscorthy), Mary Leacy (Col. Bríde, Enniscorthy), Rena Buckley (St Aloysius, Cork), Caroline Kelly (Mercy, Woodford), Katie McAuley (St Mary's, Magherafelt), Anna Geary (captain) (St Mary's, Charleville), Sinéad McAuliffe (St Mary's, Charleville, Ursula Jacob (Col. Bríde, Enniscorthy), Claire McCoy (St Patrick's, Maghera), Brenda Hanney (Portumna CS), Briege Corkery (St Mary's, Macroom) and Cathy Bowes (St Brigid's, Loughrea).

The Irish team composed of Colleges All-Stars who defeated Scotland in the camogie/shinty international at Rathoath in October, 2004. Back: Katie McAuley, Mary Leacy, Deirdre Codd, Anna Geary (Capt), Sinéad McAuliffe, Rena Buckley, Claire McCoy and Brenda Hanney. Front: Caroline Kelly, Briege Corkery, Phyllis Hayes, Denise Twomey, Ursula Jacob and Elaine O'Riordan.

The Irish party returned to their hotel following the reception at approximately 11.30 p.m. It was suggested to the players that they would retire for the night but some of them had other ideas. A night on the town in Dublin seemed much more inviting. The three officers in charge, Lily Spence, Rosina McManus and Mary Moran, took up position on a sofa inside the hall door. While there was no notice saying 'thou shall not pass', the message was clear.

A few players ventured down the stairs but the sight of the trio on duty made them retreat hastily. Then, along came a young Galway lady determined to hit the bright lights. When called to halt, she told the night patrol that she was a woman of the world and would go wherever she wished. Having received an earful, she retreated. Time and again over the next two hours, a figure would tiptoe down the stairs and peer around the corner to see if the night patrol was still in position. Eventually, they gave up and retired to bed.

Ireland won the first-ever International camogie competition when they defeated Britain 10–18 to 1–3 in the final at Croke on October 17th, which was staged as curtain-raiser to the com-

Let the Celebrations Begin

promise rules international between Ireland and Australia. The Purcell Cup combined team represented Ireland and was managed by Michael Cleary. The occasion provided the girls with an opportunity of playing in Croke Park, many of whom would otherwise have no chance of playing there. Therese Maher, the Irish captain, received a cup donated by Eileen Duffy O'Mahony. The American team had been involved earlier in the week but an Irish side drawn from Division Two of the National League had proved too strong for them.

Irish team: Aoife Murray, Gemma Kelly, Susan Kennedy, Claire Conroy, Joanne Clifford, Therese Maher (captain), Aisling Fahey, Orla Carey, Liz Bugler, Eileen O'Brien, Caitríona Ryan, Annette McGeeney, Marese Flanagan, Marie Keating and Emma Kilkelly.

British team: Mary O'Connor, Eileen O'Boyle, Ann-Marie O'Dwyer (captain), Katie Forde, Gráinne Small, Aileen Donnelly, Lisa Woods, Elma Walsh, Róisín O'Neill, Ann Gleeson, Patricia Nihill, Claire Walsh, Suzanne Keatley, Emma Linnane and Edel Reale.

Group of Meath primary school players who took part in the Centenary celebrations at Páirc Tailteann in July, 2004.

Con Hayes and Camogie President, Miriam O'Callaghan pictured at the opening of the Inniscarra camogie club pitch on July 25th, 2004.

New Grounds for Wolfe Tones and Inniscarra

Two Munster clubs, Wolfe Tones (Shannon) and Inniscarra (Cork), opened their own grounds within a few months of each other. Formed in 1967, the Inniscarra Club had set up a committee in 2001 to investigate the possibility of purchasing some land that could be developed into a full-sized playing field. Land was sought adjacent to the Inniscarra Community Centre so that existing arrangements, concerning car parking, changing rooms etc., would continue. The purchase of land signalled the start of fundraising. With the help of lottery funds, the ground was levelled, drained and had grass seed sown. Hedges were planted, fencing, gates and posts erected. Finally, the historic day dawned. President Miriam O'Callaghan performed the official opening. The hard-working committee, spearheaded by Con Hayes and Joan O'Leary, realised their dream. Club members and players looked with pride at a superb facility they could call their own.

A similar story unfolded at Shannon. Thirty-

A Game of Our Own

six years on the go, the Wolfe Tones Camogie Club took the plunge and decided to develop their own facilities. The required land was obtained and plans drawn up for dressing rooms costing €160,000. Fundraising projects were planned, with supporters being asked to help by purchasing two metres of fencing, a brick or a slate to reduce the outlay envisaged. Driven by club chairman, Gus Lohan, father of the famous hurling brothers, the project took shape and was realised in time for a 32-county tournament as the centrepiece of their opening celebrations.

The C100 formed by over 3,000 primary-school children on Centenary All-Ireland day.

Centenary All-Ireland Day

Nights of discussion, drafting and designing went into planning the programme for All-Ireland day to ensure that it was memorable for all followers of the game. The centenary torch, which had been lit in Navan, was carried by inter-county players from Páirc Tailteann to Croke Park and was handed to President Miriam O'Callaghan by Stephanie Gannon (Galway), the Poc Fada Camogie champion. Angela Downey (Kilkenny), member of the Team of the Century, passed on the Golden Hurley to the next generation in the person of Patricia Jackman (Waterford), the All-Ireland Féile na nGael Skills winner.

Primary-school players from the 32 counties played a 16-a-side game between the finals and 3,000 primary-school children formed the centenary C100 on the pitch. Antrim, who had won the All-Ireland title in 1979, the 75th anniversary of the Association, were the jubilee team in 2004 and received a rousing welcome when presented to the crowd. The presence of Mary McAleese, President of Ireland, and her husband, Martin, An Taoiseach, Bertie Ahern, and many other dignitaries added to the occasion.

A Special Milestone

The curtain came down on a memorable year at a banquet in CityWest Hotel on December 4th. The impressive programme of events had brought pride and joy to the members, lifted their spirits and encouraged them to redouble their efforts in promot-

Let the celebrations Begin

ing and developing the Association over the next 100 years. The founders would have been pleased to witness the progress of the sport they started and of the place occupied by camogie in the Ireland of 2004.

The main attraction of the night was the announcement of the first Camogie All-Stars. All-Ireland champions, Tipperary, claimed the lion's share with six awards.

All-Stars 2004: Aoife Murray (Cork), Suzanne Kelly (Tipperary), Una O'Dwyer (Tipperary), Áine Codd (Wexford), Mary Leacy (Wexford), Ciara Gaynor (Tipperary), Therese Brophy (Tipperary), Kate Kelly (Wexford), Gemma O'Connor (Cork), Jenny O'Leary (Cork), Maureen McAleenan (Down), Claire Grogan (Tipperary), Ann Marie Hayes (Galway), Deirdre Hughes (Tipperary) and Sinéad Millea (Kilkenny).

The International Player of the Year was Annette McGeeney (Roscommon) and the Young Player of the Year award went to Stephanie Gannon (Galway).

A telephone call to Liberia informed Gemma O'Connor that she was among the chosen few. Gemma was on a six-month tour of duty with the Irish army and in her absence her award was accepted by her mother, Geraldine. A few weeks later, Gemma received a surprise. President Mary McAleese handed over her All-Star award to Gemma when she visited the Irish troops serving in the UN mission in Liberia.

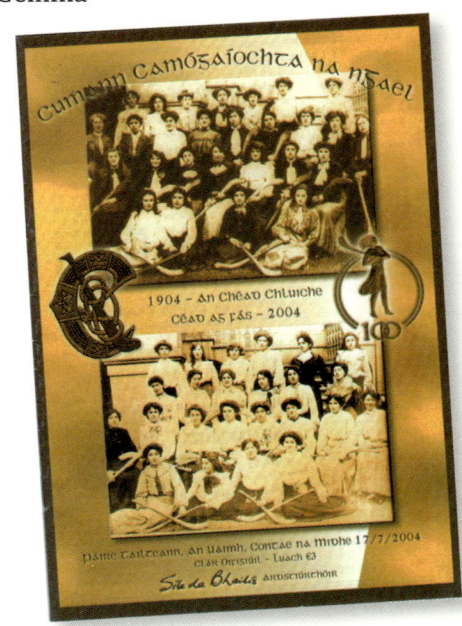

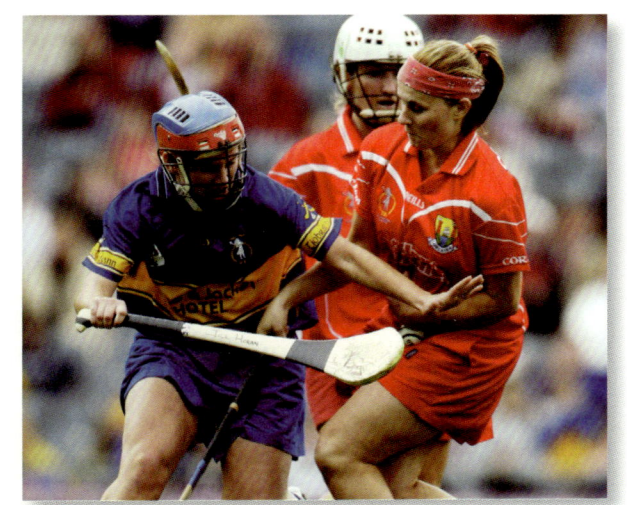

Left: special Centenary programme for the occasion. Above: action from the Centenary final: Cork 'keeper Aoife Murray, supported by Joanne O'Callaghan, is tackled by Tipperary corner forward Jill Horan. *Picture: Ray McManus / SPORTSFILE*

2004 All-Ireland Senior Championship

Live coverage was afforded to the two semi-finals by RTÉ. Cork played poorly against Galway at Nowlan Park. While never looking like losing the game, they fell short of the free-flowing camogie associated with the team. Their scrappy showing left coach, John Considine, with plenty to ponder before the final. Galway gave a gritty performance and considerably reduced Cork's winning margin from the previous year. Cork progressed by 3–9 to 1–4.

Tipperary were put to the test by Wexford in the second semi-final. They had to withstand a staunch Wexford challenge before eventually earning a two-point victory, 1–10 to 2–5. When it appeared that there might have been a shock in store, Deirdre Hughes came to the rescue with an unstoppable shot. The score lifted Tipperary who went on to close out the match.

Twenty-four and a half thousand, the highest number for a camogie- only programme, turned up to see Tipperary defeat arch-rivals Cork by a surprisingly large margin at Croke Park on September 19th. Cork matched their opponents in terms of possession, but Tipperary were clear winners when it came to finishing. Cork's dismal scoring statistics speak for themselves. One point from play from the full-forward line and two from the half-forward line is not sufficient to win an All-Ireland title.

Approaching half-time, Deirdre Hughes pounced on a long pass from Jill Horan. She turned, struck and the Cork net bulged. Midway through the second-half, Eimear McDonnell made an opening for Joanne Ryan to solo through and score. The Tipperary defence was invincible. Una O'Dwyer was a towering figure at full-back. Suzanne Kelly and Julie Kirwan gave tremendous support. The Cork attack was unable to make any progress against this trio. Tipperary won their fifth All-Ireland in six years and the much sought-after centenary title by 2–11 to 0–9.

Tipperary team: Jovita Delaney, Suzanne Kelly, Una O'Dwyer, Julie Kirwan, Sinéad Nealon, Ciara Gaynor, Therese Brophy, Angie McDermott, Philly Fogarty, Joanne Ryan (1–0), Noelle Kennedy, Claire Grogan (0–9), Eimear McDonnell (0–2), Deirdre

Meath players and referee, who staged a replica of the first camogie match at Páirc Tailteann, attired in suitable uniform in July, 2004.

All-Ireland Colleges Centenary All-Stars 2004. Back: Anna Geary, Claire McCoy, Katie McAuley, Briege Convery and Elaine O'Riordan. Middle: Caroline Kelly, Phyllis Hayes, Michelle Tynan, Mary Ryan and Rena Buckley. Front: Ursula Jacob, Sinéad McAuliffe, Briege Corkery, Mary Leacy and Jacqui Frisby.

Let the celebrations Begin

Hughes (1–0) and Jill Horan. Subs used: Paula Bulfin, Emily Hayden and Geraldine Kinnane.

Cork team: Aoife Murray, Joanne O'Callaghan, Stephanie Dunlea, Rosarii Holland, Paula O'Connor, Mary O'Connor, Rena Buckley, Vivienne Harris, Gemma O'Connor (0–2), Rachel Moloney, Emer Dillon (0–2), Jenny O'Leary (0–4), Una O'Donoghue (0–1), Emer Watson and Colette Desmond. Subs used: Elaine Burke and Anna Geary.

2004 All-Ireland Intermediate Championship

Galway made a dream start to the semi-final against Cork at Ballinasloe. A dipping shot from Ann Marie Hayes deceived the Cork goalkeeper and rested in the net. Another Galway goal before half-time had Cork playing catch-up. Galway continued on the offensive to run out easy winners by 4–8 to 0–7.

Tipperary made the long journey to Antrim determined to advance to the final. Great work by Michelle Shortt, Mairéad Luttrell, Julie Kirwan and Julie Delaney saw Tipperary ahead by six points at the break. They dominated the remainder of the game to win by 2–15 to 1–5.

Galway secured their first All-Ireland intermediate title when they overcame Tipperary at Semple Stadium. Playing into a stiff gale, the winners only managed a single point in the first-half. With the wind to their backs, Galway were a different proposition. They wiped out Tipperary's two-point lead and proceeded to build up a winning score while limiting their opponents to a mere point in the second-half. The final score was Galway 1–10, Tipperary 0–4.

Galway team: Susan Earner, Catherine Moran, Sinéad Cahalan, Lizzie Flynn, Róisín O'Connor, Regina Glynn, Sinéad Keane (0–1), Colette Glennon, Lorraine Lally, Brenda Kerins, Brenda Hanney (1–0), Aoife Lynskey (0–2), Caroline Kelly (0–3), Ann Marie Hayes, Emma Kilkelly (0–2). Subs used: Cathy Bowes (0–2), Marese Flanagan and Susan Keane.

Antrim Jubilee team at Croke Park in September, 2004.

Stephanie Gannon (Galway) receives the All-Ireland Puck Fada award from Peter Hoey, former Leinster Council chairman in 2004

Tipperary team: Sarah O'Brien, Deirdre McDonnell, Helen Breen, Mary Looby, Maeve Corcoran, Julie Kirwan, Michelle Shortt, Mairéad Luttrell, Julie Delaney, Geraldine Kinnane (0–1), Eimear Ryan (0–3), Jacqui O'Connor, Mary Ryan, Siobhán Ryan and Denise Ryan. Subs used: Jill Horan, C. Johnston and Caitríona Hennessy.

2004 All-Ireland Junior Championship

Two goals immediately before half-time by Emer O'Farrell and Anna Geary left Cork nicely placed against Wexford in the semi-final at Wexford Park.

Cork continued where they had left off with Miriam Deasy, Síle Burns and Sarah O'Donovan adding further goals in the second-half. Una and Mary Leacy scored goals for the host county but they came too late to affect the outcome. Cork advanced by 5–9 to 2–10.

Down's attack had much more to offer as a unit against Roscommon in the second semi-final at Ballyholland. With Mary McPolin, Maureen McAleenan and Catherine McGourty in scoring form, the task was easy for Down and they won 1–14 to 0–3. Cork coach Lilian Zinkant had her charges in great shape to face

Group pictured at presentation to Mary Moran on her retirement following 32 years as Secretary of Munster Colleges Council. From left: Kathleen Coffey, Rose Malone, Marion Graham, Pat Rafferty, Mary Casey and Eithne Neville.

Down in the final at Croke Park. The level of skill and fitness of the Cork players carried them through a tough test to claim the county's seventh title. The first-half was an enthralling contest with both sides going hammer and tongs. The ball was swept up and down the field with excellent scores being registered at both ends. Cork led by 3–3 to 2–4 at the interval. Their defence was rock solid for the remainder of the game and kept Down scoreless. Ellen Clifford, Elaine O'Riordan, Amanda O'Regan, Valerie O'Keeffe, Liz Bugler and Emer O'Farrell were very visible for the winners who finished in front by 4–5 to 2–4.

Cork team: Ellen Clifford, Gearóidín Kearney, Elaine O'Riordan, Niamh Bowles, Jennifer Browne, Amanda O'Regan, Mairéad Holland, Valerie O'Sullivan, Valerie O'Keeffe (captain) (0–5), Máire O'Connell, Sarah O'Donovan, Liz Bugler (2–0), Emer O'Farrell (1–0), Miriam Deasy and Marian Jagoe (1–0). Subs used: Michelle Hegarty, Janice Duffy and Ger Collins.

Down Team: Teresa McGowan, Claire McGovern, Moya Maginn, Anne Morgan, Deborah Kelland, Pauline Green, Karen Murray, Jennifer Braniff (captain), Lisa McCrickard, Fiona Duff, Maureen McAleenan (1–2), Catherine McGourty (0–2), Fion-

Let the Celebrations Begin

nuala Carr, Cathy Mulholland (1–0) and Karen McGribben. Subs used: Orla Maginn, Brenda Gallagher, Mary McPolin and Angeline Fearon.

2004 All-Ireland Minor A Championship

Clare won the Munster minor championship for the first time, but found the standard set by Galway in the semi-final a step too far and conceded by 5–8 to 1–5. In the second semi-final against Down, Ann Marie Phelan scored 3–4 for Kilkenny, who carried too much scoring power for the Ulster champions and won by 8–12 to 1–2.

Despite playing into a strong breeze, Galway scored two crucial goals in the opening minutes of the final against Kilkenny at Navan on August 7th. Galway built on this advantage and maintained the lead throughout the game. Kilkenny fought back bravely but were unable to make up lost ground. Stephanie Gannon, Jessica Gill, Sarah Noone, Noreen Coen and Fiona Hahnefeld were very conspicuous in Galway's victory. Kilkenny did not reach the same heights as in earlier rounds. But it was no fault of Paula Butler, Anne Dalton, Colette Dormer or Lucinda Gahan that Galway won by 3–16 to 2–6.

Galway team: Stephanie Gannon, Gemma Starr, Mary Ward, Aisling Huban, Aisling Kelly, Jessica Gill (0–1), Julie Brien, Fiona Hahnefeld, Lorraine Ryan (0–1), Niamh Kilkenny (0–1), Sarah Noone (1–1), Caitríona Cormican (0–2), Aisling Tuohy (captain), Martina Conroy (1–8) and Noreen Coen (1–2).

Kilkenny team: Noelle Corrigan, Noreen O'Keeffe, Elaine O'Shea, Sarah Shore, Paula Butler, Carol Phelan, Carol Kavanagh (captain), Marie Murphy, Anne Dalton (0–1), Colette Dormer (1–1), Lucinda Gahan (1–1), Marie Dargan (0–1), Laura Kavanagh, Ann Marie Phelan (0–1) and Orla McCormack (0–1).

2004 All-Ireland Minor B Championship

Roscommon won a closely contested and exciting semi-final against reigning champions Waterford at Woodmount. The Connacht side rose to the occasion and played some fine camogie to qualify for the final by 1–10 to 2–6.

Meath played Antrim in the second semi-final in conjunction with the Centenary celebrations at Páirc Tailteann. Goals from Eilish O'Connor, Orla McCaul, Raquel McCarry and Claire Dallat booked a place in the final for Antrim by 4–7 to 1–5.

Antrim returned to Páirc Tailteann to take on Roscommon in

Camogie President, Miriam O'Callaghan unveiling a plaque at Páirc Tailteann in July, 2004 to commemorate the first competitive match which was played at the ground on July 17th, 1904. Minister, Noel Dempsey, is also in the photo.

the final. The side, well prepared by Aidan McKeown, attacked with pace and purpose. A string of well-taken points placed Antrim in a comfortable position and left Roscommon with a hill to climb. Roscommon were unable to reproduce the form that they displayed in the semi-final. They had to concede to a better side by 1–9 to 0–3.

Antrim team: Shauneen McAuley, Mary McAuley, Róisín O'Boyle, Tammy Pettigrew, Eimear Laverty, Joleen McCarry, Emma Connolly, Claire Dallat, Joanne Campbell (captain) (0–1), Caoimhe Quinn, Michaela Convery (0-1), Orla McCaul (0–1), Raquel McCarry (0–5), Eilish O'Connor (0–1) Claire Laverty. Sub used: Louise McAleese (1–0) .

Roscommon team: Róisín Connaughton, Triona Murray, Fiona Feeley, Laura Mee, Leanne Raftery, Joanne Beattie, Lisa Killeen, Niamh Coyle (captain), Elaine Daly (0–1), Claire Curley, Susan Spillane, Deirdre Sweeney (0–1), Helen Kenny, Jane McDermott (0–1) and Maria Brandon.

2004 All-Ireland Club Senior Championship

Rossa (Belfast) made their All-Ireland club championship debut

Group pictured at Offaly dinner in 2004. Back: Mary Moran, Anne Ryan, Sinéad O'Connor, Margaret Browne, Máire Uí Scolaí, Gráinne McIntyre and Sheila Wallace. Front: Lily Spence, Miriam O'Callaghan and Brídín Uí Mhaolagáin.

in the 40th anniversary of the competition. They were unfortunate to come up against tried and seasoned campaigners, Granagh-Ballingarry, in their first outing. The Limerick club carried too many aces and Rossa had to wait for another day. The match came to a close with the score Granagh-Ballingarry 1–11, Rossa 0–4. Davitt's were unable to cope with the camogie prowess of St Lachtain's when they met in the semi-final. The Kilkenny club carved holes in the Davitt's defence and helped themselves to five goals and a place in the final by 5–6 to 0–5.

A close-range goal from Imelda Kennedy inched St Lachtain's into a half-time lead of 1–3 to 0–4 over Granagh-Ballingarry in the final at Parnell Park. The Limerick side needed to take control after the interval but instead they found themselves on the back foot. Points from St Lachtain's captain, Imelda Kennedy, widened the gap. When Marie O'Connor palmed the ball to the net late in the game, it was all over for the champions. Gillian Dillon and Mairéad Costello thwarted the Granagh forwards and did not allow them to play their normal game. St Lachtain's were crowned champions on the score of 2–8 to 0–7.

St Lachtain's team: Sinéad Costello, Danielle Minogue, Gillian Dillon, Mairéad Lawlor, Deirdre Delaney, Mairéad Costello, Anne Connery, Esther Kennedy, Aoife Fitzpatrick, Margaret Kavanagh, Sinéad Connery, Imelda Kennedy (captain), Anne Dalton, Marie O'Connor and Eileen Fitzpatrick. Sub used: April Purcell.

Granagh-Ballingarry team: Breda O'Brien, Bernie Molloy, Bernie Chawke, Maureen O'Gorman, Kay Burke, Maeve Nash, Deirdre Sheehan (captain), Vera Sheehan, Marie Collins, Joan Cullinane, Eileen O'Brien, Aoifa Sheehan, Fiona Chawke, Fiona Morrissey and Joanne Clifford. Sub used: Aimee McCarthy.

The St Lachtain's Club was founded in the Freshford area of Kilkenny by local teachers, Brian Waldron and Ned Kennedy in 1984. The club has been very successful all the way up from Féile na nGael to All-Ireland club championship. Several St Lachtain's players have lined out with Kilkenny and wear the same colours for club and county. Back in the twenties and thirties, there were two camogie clubs in the parish, St Ita's and St Lachtain's.

2004 All-Ireland Club Junior Championship

Four Roads (Roscommon) led Leitrim Fontenoys (Down) for three-quarters of the final at Parnell Park. The up-to-then dormant Fontenoys sprang to life. In the remaining minutes, they played fantastic camogie to score 4–4 without reply. Caitríona McCrickard, Sinéad Brackenberry, Maureen McAleenan, Rosaleen McCann and Lisa Quinn had much to do with the Phil McBride Cup going to Leitrim. Cáit Kenny had a wonderful opening half for Four Roads. The final score was Leitrim Fontenoys 4–13, Four Roads 0–8.

Leitrim Fontenoys team: Joan Brown, Ann Morgan, Donna Mullan, Sinéad O'Prey, Karen Mullan, Nuala Magee, Claire McGovern, Lisa McCrickard, Rosaleen McCann, Sinéad Brackenberry, Maureen McAleenan, Caitríona McCrickard, Kelly O'Higgins, Ciara McGovern and Lisa Quinn.

Four Roads team: Sharon Finneran, Colette Dowd, Olive Hynes, Catherine Glennon, Orla Hughes, Siobhán Coyle, Maria Hoey, Patricia Lennon, Cáit Kenny, Donna Kelly, Cáit Kenny, Karina Jones, Breda Mannion, Niamh Coyle and Sinéad O'Brien.

2004 Gael-Linn Senior Cup

Connacht edged out Leinster by 3–11 to 3–10 in the semi-final at Glenalbyn. It was a marvellous game of camogie with skill and

Breda Byrne, Leinster Chairperson, Sheila Wallace, Árd Stiúrthóir, and Maureen Fulham, Leinster Secretary photographed at the Westmeath awards dinner.

scores from both sides. Munster had an easier assignment against Ulster. The match ended at Munster 1–20, Ulster 1–9. Player of the match, Mary O'Connor, Deirdre Hughes, Eimear McDonnell and Eileen O'Brien played brilliantly for Munster who won by 1–16 to 1–9.

Munster team: Aoife Murray (Cork), Joanne O'Callaghan (Cork), Una O'Dwyer (Tipperary), Mairéad Kelly (Limerick), Sinéad Nealon (Tipperary), Mary O'Connor (Cork), Therese Brophy (Tipperary), Angie McDermott (Tipperary), Siobhán Ryan (captain) (Tipperary), Jenny O'Leary (Cork), Emily Hayden (Tipperary), Vera Sheehan (Limerick), Eimear McDonnell (Tipperary), Deirdre Hughes (Tipperary) and Eileen O'Brien (Limerick).

Connacht team: (All Galway, except where indicated) Sharon Finneran (Roscommon), Martina Harkin, Sinéad Cahalan, Lizzie Flynn, Colette Glennon, Ailbhe Kelly, Sinéad Keane, Caroline Kelly, Anne Hardiman, Caroline Murray, Áine Hillary, Ann Marie Hayes, Orla Kilkenny, Lourda Kavanagh and Emma Kilkelly.

Eamon Ó hArgáin, Joe McDonagh, President of G.A.A., Miriam O'Callaghan, President of Camogie Association, Micheál Ó Muircheartaigh and Sheila Wallace pictured at launch of Bord na Gaeilge sponsorship.

2004 Gael-Linn Junior Trophy

High-scoring Munster had impressive victories over Ulster, 6–17 to 1–8, and Leinster, 4–16 to 1–4, to retain the Gael-Linn Trophy at Glenalbyn. Catherine O'Loughlin, Áine Lyng, Anna Geary, Deirdre Murphy and Mary Coleman were in rare scoring form over the afternoon.

Munster team: Ellen Clifford (Cork), Joan Scanlon (Clare), Helen Breen (Tipperary), Caitríona Foley (Cork), Méadhbh Corcoran (Tipperary), Amanda O'Regan (Cork), Kate Marie Hearn (Waterford), Elaine O'Riordan (Cork), Julie Kirwan (Tipperary), Áine Lyng (Waterford), Anna Geary (Cork), Deirdre Murphy (Clare), Catherine O'Loughlin (Clare), Miriam Deasy (Cork) and Mary Coleman (Cork).

Leinster team: Emer Butler (captain) (Dublin), Sylvia Hanks (Dublin), Aishling Moran (Wexford), Jenny Codd (Wexford), Eileen Hanrick (Wexford), Louise Conlon (Kildare), Anna Campion (Laois), Therese Keenan (Laois), Orla Bambury (Kildare), Gretta Heffernan (Wexford), Bernie Kennedy (Kildare), Una Leacy (Wexford), Jeanette Feighery (Offaly), Susie O'Carroll (Kildare) and Evelyn Quigley (Wexford).

Let the celebrations Begin

Where We're At

Reaching the centenary was a momentous achievement for those involved in camogie but arriving there in such a healthy and vibrant state was more than significant. Since 1904, camogie has grown beyond the expectations of its founders to become the most popular and widely played female sport in Ireland. From its very formation, and right through its history, the Camogie Association has made a meaningful statement and impacted on the life of Irish women and Gaelic games. With vision and courage, it achieved the position it enjoys today.

The year 2004 was a celebration of a century of achievement and success in the promotion of our native game and of our Irish culture and traditions. Our membership shared the goodwill, pride and joy of an organisation with a century of success, tradition and experience on which to build for the future. An impressive calendar of events to honour the occasion, that reflected on the past, celebrated its achievements and planned for the continued development and promotion of the game, was pieced together. It is true to say that the Association grew in stature and status during centenary year. An attractive image was presented to a wider audience, with increased media coverage, higher match attendances and the goodwill of other organisations, which was acknowledged.

There were many special occasions and highlights as the year unfolded. In excess of 1,000 people were present at the centenary banquet to acclaim 100 years of achievement and to salute the Team of the Century. The re-enactment of the first competitive camogie match in Páirc Tailteann afforded a direct link with the founders of the Association. The All-Ireland finals in Croke Park on September 19th, provided a splendid occasion. Before an attendance of almost 25,000 appreciative supporters, a 16-a-side game was staged with primary-school children from each of the 32 counties, an achievement which would have delighted the founders of the Camogie Association.

The symbolism and pageantry of the occasion provoked a sense of pride in the hearts of the members present, making them believe that they belonged to much more than a sporting organisation. Camogie was displayed at its best in the junior and senior finals. The camogie-shinty compromise game between Scotland and Ireland and the first ever international competition, between teams representing the USA, Britain and Ireland, rounded off the playing season. The curtain came down on a truly remarkable year at a glittering banquet at which the 2004 All-Stars were honoured.

President Miriam O'Callaghan was the public face of the Camogie Association throughout centenary year. Pleasant and articulate, Miriam presented an excellent image and, undoubtedly, raised the profile of the organisation. The work that went into the planning and realisation of the centenary programme was colossal and great credit is due to all involved. As in previous anniversary years, specials events, organised for the occasion, were continued and became part of the annual camogie calendar – for example the All-Star selection, camogie-shinty contest, Poc Fada in the Cooley Mountains and the Féile na nGael school visits.

Camogie members have always been committed to development and it is because of their vision and hard work that the Association reached its centenary in such a strong position. A strategic plan is an essential tool in the development of any organisation. It provides a pathway for future advancement, strengthening and growth. Following widespread consultation with the membership, the views elicited on all aspects of the Association were brought together. Joan O'Flynn, Sheila O'Donohue and Brenda Craig, members of the national development committee, burned the midnight oil and travelled to the four corners of the country to progress the work. Their labour was an investment in the future. With the assistance of a management consultant, the key issues were addressed and priorities identified. A small group of people formulated the plan and presented it to congress where it was approved. The plan identified the requirements necessary to ensure that the Association remained vibrant and was strengthened in the key areas of participation, quality, management and marketing. The successful implementation of the plan was steered by strong leadership and aided by valuable help from the Sports Council.

Chapter Twenty Three

INTO THE SECOND MILLENNIUM

The seemingly unending round of events, special occasions and social functions for centenary year had come to an end and it was time to draw breath. Congress 2005 at Blarney saw the focus return to bread-and-butter issues. The allocation of All-Ireland medals was raised from 20 to 25, though some felt that it lowered the status and value of the medal to hand over so many. Each player on an All-Ireland final panel would, in future, receive four free tickets. Counties were encouraged to formulate their own strategic plans and assistance was offered in this regard.

New Appointees

Up to now full-time staff of the Camogie Association was based in the office at Croke Park. The first efforts to spread out and work throughout the country were made in August 2005 when three full-time officials were added to the staff. Lynn Kelly, a former sports officer at the Limerick Institute of Technology, was installed as national camogie development co-ordinator. Mary O'Connor, one of the game's top players, and Caroline Murray, a Galway county player, took on the role of regional development co-ordinators. These appointments came about thanks to a grant from the Irish Sports Council. Michael McClements was already fulfilling a similar role in Ulster.

Start-up grants of €1,000 were introduced for new clubs. Development programmes were put in place in Kerry, Donegal and Mayo, areas where interest in the game had dwindled. Ten bursaries were made available to third-level camogie playing students.

Competitions Review

Significant changes were made to camogie competitions on the recommendations of the Competitions Review Committee. The committee, chaired by Bernie McNally, with representatives from the four provinces, reported

The Aghabullogue team passes the reviewing stand on Patrick Street, Cork, at the 2005 National Féile na nGael.

on widespread support for change and modernisation.

Key issues emerged during the far-reaching consultation with the membership: the small number of senior counties; grading; the dominance of senior counties; the outdated knockout system; the lack of summer camogie; the lack of competition for developing counties; the league structures; and concern that the intermediate championship had not achieved the desired outcome were the main topics highlighted.

A system that would provide more matches was proposed for all championships: the second teams of senior counties to be accommodated in the intermediate championship; confining the junior championship to junior counties; increasing the age of the minor grade to 18 while retaining the under-16 championship as a separate competition; a revamped league format; a more prestigious interprovincial series and a 'novices' competition to encourage participation of new counties were the main recommendations.

Integration Process

As a practical step on the road to integration with the GAA, Liam O'Neill, Chairman of the Leinster GAA Council and national liaison person appointed to camogie by the GAA under the integration process, met with the members of Central Council and management committee. He posed a number of questions: Where is camogie now? Where should it be? Where do we want it to be? And what role does the GAA have to play in the development of camogie? Each member was asked for their views in relation to these questions. A very worthwhile discussion took place with camogie personnel looking at the issues outside the usual perimeters of their vision.

Camogie President, Miriam O'Callaghan, with the prize-winners at the 2005 National Féile na nGael Skills competition. From left: Louise Walsh (Kildare), Deirdre Ward (Galway) and Racquel McCarry (Antrim).

2005 All-Ireland Senior Championship

Cork were clear favourites going into the All-Ireland semi-final against Limerick at Nowlan Park but nobody anticipated the match being so completely one-sided. Limerick had prepared well for the contest but did not do justice to themselves. Cork dominated all sectors of the field with nine of their players making the scoreboard which read Cork 5–17, Limerick 0–5 at the end.

Tipperary qualified for their seventh consecutive All-Ireland final when they eliminated Wexford by 1–13 to 1–5. Wexford trailed by 1–10 to 1–1 at the break but a tremendous fight back reduced the margin. Late scores by Sheena Howard and Claire Grogan confirmed Tipperary's advancement.

Player of the match in the 2002 All-Ireland final and PE graduate, Fiona O'Driscoll, put what she had learned into practice as trainer of the Cork team. Her refreshing enthusiasm and new ideas drew a great response from the players. She did not panic as Tipperary, in pursuit of a second hat-trick of All-Ireland titles in seven years, pulled ahead in the opening half. A speculative shot by Claire Grogan was misjudged by Aoife Murray in the Cork goal. Jill Horan, Noelle Kennedy and Eimear McDonnell tagged on points to leave Tipperary comfortably ahead by 1–10 to 0–8.

2005 Senior All-Ireland: The Cork squad who took on Tipperary. *Picture: Brendan Moran / SPORTSFILE*

Cork senior captain Elaine Burke lifts the O'Duffy Cup. *Picture: Brendan Moran / SPORTSFILE*

Cork made tactical switches and tweaked the game plan during the interval of the final at Croke Park on September 18th. They burst out of the blocks on the resumption with three points in seven minutes. A long drive from Amanda O'Regan came off the fingers of Una O'Dwyer and was deflected out of the reach of Jovita Delaney for Cork's goal. Tipperary made one last push to save the game but the Cork defence held firm to win by 1–17 to 1–13.

Cork team: Aoife Murray, Rena Buckley, Rosarii Holland, Amanda O'Regan, Briege Corkery (0–1), Mary O'Connor, Anna Geary, Vivienne Harris, Rachel Moloney (0–1), Una O'Donoghue (1–1), Gemma O'Connor (0–3), Jenny O'Leary (0–4), Emer Dillon (0–4), Stephanie Dunlea (0–1), Elaine Burke (0–1). Subs used: Angela Walsh (0–1), Joanne O'Callaghan and Sarah O'Donovan.

Tipperary team: Jovita Delaney, Suzanne Kelly, Una O'Dwyer, Julie Kirwan, Sinéad Nealon, Ciara Gaynor, Therese Brophy, Philly Fogarty (0–1),

Angie McDermott, Joanne Ryan (0–1), Noelle Kennedy (0–1), Claire Grogan (1–5), Eimear McDonnell (0–2), Deirdre Hughes (0–1) and Jill Horan (0–2). Subs used: Michelle Shortt and Emily Hayden.

No All-Ireland Intermediate Championship was played in 2005.

2005 All-Ireland Junior Championship

Starved of success for years, it was easy to understand the delight of the young Dublin juniors when they won their way back to Croke Park after an absence of 18 years. Peter Lucey's team moved too swiftly for Armagh in the semi-final at Parnell Park and reaped the dividends. Dublin 1–15, Armagh 0–7 was on the scoreboard at the finish.

A great second-half performance by Clare ended Galway's interest in the championship at Cusack Park. Claire Commane and Catherine O'Loughlin shared 4–6 between them to ensure an early return to Croke Park for Clare as they won impressively by 4–12 to 2–8.

Dublin opened confidently in the final against Clare at Croke Park and built up a lead of 1–3 to no score in the first quarter. A long-range shot from Deirdre Murphy landed in the Dublin net

Phyllis Breslin, Jo Golden, Sheila Wallace and Lynn Kelly pictured at the Vodafone Player of the Year award luncheon in 2005.

to bring Clare into the game. Scores were scarce as the game progressed. Points from Denise Lynch and Claire McMahon inched Clare ahead as the game headed to a close. Dublin had the last say when Niamh Taylor converted a 50-metre free to send both teams to a replay at 1–7 apiece.

Clare, who had converted only one score from play in the drawn game, knew that they would have to improve considerably on that facet of their play if they were to succeed in the replay at Birr on October 9th. But it was the Dublin girls who stepped up on their previous performance. Ciara Lucey, Louise O'Hara, Ciara Durkan and Caitríona Power were key players in Dublin's first win in the junior championship since 1975. Once again, Clare's lack of finishing power cost them the title and they conceded by 2–9 to 1–4.

Dublin team: Eimear Butler, Sylvia Hanks, Anne McCluskey, Aoife Cullen, Andrea Fitzpatrick, Sinéad Cunnane, Caitríona Power, Ciara Lucey (0–4), Áine Fanning, Niamh Taylor (0–2), Eimear Brannigan (captain) (0–1), Ciara Durkan, Eve Talbot (0–1), Louise O'Hara (1–1) and Emer Lucey (1–0). Sub used: Anne Griffin.

Clare team: Rachel Lynch, Jane Scanlon, Deirdre Corcoran, Caitríona McMahon, Edel Keating, Cathy Halley, Erica Minogue,

Moira McMahon, Deirdre Murphy (captain), Laura Linnane, Áine O'Brien, Fiona Lafferty, Claire McMahon (0–2), Catherine O'Loughlin (1–0), Claire Commane (0–1). Subs used: Marie O'Halloran (0–1) and Siobhán Lafferty.

2005 All-Ireland Minor A Championship

Kilkenny turned the tables on Galway in a most exciting semi-final at Nowlan Park. Both counties have been on the top rung in the minor grade for many years and their meetings are eagerly anticipated. On this occasion, the spirit of Kilkenny shone through as they pressed home their advantage to win in style 5–14 to 3–8.

Tipperary, coached by former county hurler, Pat McLoughney, combined skill and teamwork to move effortlessly into the final. Antrim tried hard but found themselves constantly on the back foot while their attack was starved of possession. Tipperary reached the final by 3–13 to 0–3.

Ten minutes into the final at Parnell Park on August 7th, Kilkenny had two goals to their credit. They held the edge over Tipperary in midfield and were playing confidently. A great goal by Aoife McLoughney gave hope to Tipperary despite trailing 2–6 to 1–3 at the interval. Tipperary started smartly on the resumption but were rocked by a Katie Power goal. An excellent shot by Aoife McLoughney yielded a goal and raised Tipperary's hopes of an equaliser. That ambition was shattered when Marie Dargan guided home goal number four for the winners. Kilkenny won by two clear goals, 4–7 to 2–7.

Kilkenny team: Marie Therese O'Neill, Lydia Phelan, Regina Madigan, Mariga Nolan, Eilish Cantwell, Noreen O'Keeffe, Marie Murphy, Colette Dormer (0–1), Lucinda Gahan (captain) (0–1), Siobhán Fahey (0–1), Edwina Keane (1–2), Marie Dargan (1–1), Katie Power (2–0), Noelle Corrigan (0–1) and Michelle Quilty. Subs used: Anna Farrell and Kate McDonald.

Tipperary team: Kristina Kenneally, Marion Ryan, Sarah Morrissey, Geraldine Stapleton, Niamh O'Connell, Fiona Young (captain), Deirdre Ryan, Therese Shortt, Caitríona Maher, Aoife Shinnors (0–4), Sharon Hayes, Mary Gleeson, Bonnie Kennedy, Siobhán McGrath (0–1) and Aoife McLoughney (2–2). Subs used: Ailish O'Connell, Laura Young and Tracy Flanagan.

2005 All-Ireland Minor B Championship

Armagh, with the backing of a large home following, eased their way past Carlow in the first semi-final. A higher level of skill and teamwork was the key to success for Armagh who won by 10–14 to 2–1.

Offaly had won the Leinster Under-14B title in 2004 and they

Gemma O'Connor (Cork) holds the Vodafone National Player of the Year award for 2005.

built on that success to shape the side that faced Down in the second semi-final. The Offaly girls had made steady progress and it showed as they turned in an excellent display to surpass Down by 9-4 to 4-7.

Offaly captured their first All-Ireland championship title when their under-16 side edged out Armagh in the thrilling finish at Parnell Park on August 7th. A good start was vital if Offaly were to overcome their nerves and mount a serious challenge. They did it in style and raced into a four-point lead. Armagh fought their way back into the game with a goal from Corinna McKee and led by the slimmest of margins at the break. Siobhán Flannery (Offaly) and Colette McSorley (Armagh) matched score for score in a personal duel. Armagh established a five-point lead with three minutes remaining. But Siobhán Flannery was not finished. She netted twice in sixty seconds to snatch the cup and leave luckless Armagh stunned. The winning score was Offaly 2-14, Armagh 3-9.

Offaly team: Claire Birmingham, Sharon Daly, Lee-Ann Scully, Lee-Ann Troy, Kate McCann, Kady McKenna, Alison Dooley, Michaela Morkan (0-2), Aoife Corrigan, Siobhán Flannery (2-5), Natalie McCabe (0-3), Michelle Gleeson, Amy Dooley (0-2), Marcella Maloney (captain) (0-1) and Lorraine Keena (0-1). Subs used: Emma McEniffe, Ann Cordial and Kate Birmingham.

Rachel Moloney on the cat-walk at the Cork Camogie Board's fashion show in 2005.

Armagh team: Catherine Toner, Gráinne Kelly, Sunniamha Quinn, Fionnuala Bradley, Connie Conway, Emma McParland, Colleen McGuigan, Noeleen McKenna (captain) (0-2), Nicole Conway, Colette McSorley (2-5), Laura McGuinness (0-1), Aoibheann Murphy (0-1), Orla O'Hare, Lucy Conway and Corinna McKee (1-0). Subs used: Laura Comiskey and Ciara Donnelly.

Aoife Corrigan is a daughter of Mark Corrigan who won All-Ireland hurling medals in 1981 and 1985.

2005 All-Ireland Club Senior Championship

A goal in the third minute of extra-time earned Davitt's a second chance against Cashel in the semi-final at Tynagh and the County Galway club made sure at the second attempt in New Inn. Caitríona Kelly was the match winner with three well-taken goals. Davitt's secured a place in the final by 3-9 to 1-9.

St Lachtain's welcomed O'Donovan Rossa (Belfast) to Freshford for the second semi-final. The home side fielded a multitalented set of forwards who built up an impressive score whereas Rossa were over-dependent on the attacking skills of Jane Adams. Marie O'Connor and Imelda Kennedy were responsible for ending Rossa's interest in the championship. St Lachtain's were the better side by 4-14 to 2-9.

Into the Second Millennium

There was no case of 'third time lucky' for Davitt's in the final at Cloughjordan. Reigning champions, St Lachtain's, were in no mood to yield, even though captain Margaret Hickey missed the final through injury. As in the semi-final, Imelda Kennedy and Marie O'Connor shared the scoring duties, while Esther Costello, Laura Comerford and Deirdre Delaney provided excellent support. The team prepared by John Lyng and Paul Quigley played with great skill and determination throughout and were very worthy champions. Caroline Kelly, Olivia Forde, Lourda Kavanagh and Karen Power were the pick of the Davitt's players on the day. St Lachtain's had five points to spare, 1–9 to 1–4, at the close of play.

St Lachtain's team: Laura Comerford, Sinéad Cash, Gillian Maher, Fiona Dowling, Margaret McCarthy, Mairéad Costello, Danielle Minogue, Deirdre Delaney, Aoife Fitzpatrick, Sinéad Connery, Esther Costello, Imelda Kennedy, Anne Dalton, Marie O'Connor and Eileen Fitzpatrick.

Davitt's team: Karen Power, Orla Watson, Anne Broderick, Lizzie Flynn, Rita Broderick, Ailbhe Kelly, Linda Gohery, Deirdre Murphy, Phyllis Hayes, Caroline Kelly, Caitríona Kelly, Deirdre Gilchrist, Olivia Forde, Lourda Kavanagh and Mary Kelly. Subs used: Yvonne Donnelly and Aisling Tuohy.

2005 All-Ireland Club Junior Championship

Leitrim Fontenoys (Down) defeated Drumcullen (Offaly) by 3–9 to 1–4 in the semi-final at Drumcullen, while Newmarket-on-Fergus (Clare) had an easy win over Four Roads (Roscommon) in the second semi-final by 2–10 to 0–5 at the Clare venue.

Newmarket led by 0–6 to 0–3 against Fontenoys with 20 minutes to go in the final at Cloughjordan and must have thought that they were on the road to victory. Maureen McAleenan struck a rebound from the post to the net to embark on a scoring spree that yielded 3–2 for the Leitrim sharp-shooter. Lisa and Elaine McCrickard, Anne Morgan and Karen McMullan drew down the shutters, sealing off the Leitrim goal from the Newmarket attack. Moira McMahon, Aimee McInerney and Marie O'Looney put up strong resistance for Newmarket but it was not enough. Victory

Munster Gael-Linn Team 2005. Back: Aoife Murray, Emer Watson, Amanda O'Regan, Caitríona Foley, Una O'Donoghue, Gemma O'Connor, Joanne O'Callaghan, Rachel Moloney, Rena Buckley and Jenny O'Leary. Front: Denise Twomey, Stephanie Dunlea, Anna Geary, Mary O'Connor, Elaine Burke, Suzanne Kelly and Joanne Ryan.

went to Leitrim Fontenoys by 3–7 to 0–8.

Leitrim Fontenoys team: Joan Brown, Anne Morgan, Elaine McCrickard, Sinéad O'Prey, Karen McMullan, Lisa McCrickard (captain), Gráinne O'Higgins, Rosaleen McCann, Ciara McGovern, Caitríona McCrickard, Kelly O'Higgins, Lisa Quinn, Sinéad Brackenbury, Maureen McAleenan and Niamh O'Higgins. Subs used: Denise O'Prey and Corina Cunningham.

Newmarket-on-Fergus team: Trish O'Grady, Mary Higgins, Aileen Kilmartin, Iris Kaiser, Jane O'Leary, Aimee McInerney, Marie O'Looney (captain), Sinéad Cullinan, Moira McMahon, Aoife Ryan, Ruth Kaiser, Áine O'Brien, Claire Arthur, Sharon McMahon and Sinéad Ryan. Sub used: Eleanor McCormack.

2005 Gael-Linn Senior Cup

In the senior semi-final at Ballinteer, Munster recorded a 1–12 to 0–2 win over Ulster while Connacht held off the Leinster challenge by 2–6 to 1–8. Munster were good value for their 3–14 to 2–8 win over Connacht in the final.

Munster Team: Aoife Murray (Cork), Joanne O'Callaghan (Cork), Caitríona Foley (Cork), Rena Buckley (Cork), Mary O'Connor (Cork) Suzanne Kelly (Tipperary), (captain), Anna Geary (Cork), Gemma O'Connor (Cork), Joanne Ryan (Tipperary), Rachel Moloney (Cork), Jenny O'Leary (Cork), Una O'Donoghue (Cork), Stephanie Dunlea (Cork) and Elaine Burke (Cork).

Connacht team: (All Galway) Stephanie Gannon, Regina Glynn, Áine Hillary, Nicola Gavin, Colette Glennon, Sinéad Cahalan, Ailbhe Kelly, Brenda Hanney, Katherine Glynn, Deirdre Burke, Therese Maher, Lourda Kavanagh, Susan Keane, Veronica Curtin and Orla Kilkenny.

2005 Gael-Linn Junior Trophy

Munster edged past Leinster with two points to spare, 2–8 to 2–6, while Ulster had a comfortable passage by 3–10 to 0–7 over Connacht in the semi-finals at Ballinteer. Ulster had no answer to Munster in the final and succumbed by 1–14 to 2–4.

Munster Team: Aisling O'Brien (Waterford), Sinead Scanlan (Clare), Niamh Harkins (Tipperary), Lucy Hawkes (Cork), Michelle Shortt (Tipperary), Cathy Halley (Clare), Edwina Waters

Annette McGeeney (Roscommon) receives the Player of the Match award at the 2005 Camogie/Shinty International at Inverness from Camogie President, Miriam O'Callaghan. Seán Kelly, G.A.A. President is on right.

(Cork), Deirdre Murphy (Clare), Orla Coughlan (Cork), Áine Lyng (Waterford), Áine Watson (Cork), Laura Linnane (Clare), Eimear O'Friel (Cork) (captain), Catherine O'Loughlin (Clare) and Deirdre Twomey (Cork).

Ulster team: Claire O'Kane (Derry), Sinéad Stephenson (Derry), Mairéad Graham (Antrim), Ciara Cushnahan (Derry), Caitríona O'Kane (Derry), Claire Doherty (captain) (Derry), Jane Carey (Derry), Gráinne McGoldrick (Derry), Briege Convery (Derry), Kerrie O'Neill (Antrim), Katie McAuley (Derry), Elaine Dowds (Antrim), Cathy Mulholland (Down), Cathy McGourty (Down) and Sinéad Cassidy (Derry).

The Irish panel for the Camogie/Shinty international photographed at Inverness in 2005

1–3, was named the Player of the Tournament.

Ireland panel: Sandra Greville (Westmeath), Elaine Reilly (Cavan), Orlaith Donnell (Wicklow), Sheila Sullivan (Offaly), Mary Molloy (Offaly), Ann Marie Dennehy (Meath), Susan McCann (Tyrone), Annette McGeeney (Roscommon), Lizzie Glennon (Roscommon), Tanya McDonald (Wicklow), Rosemary Noelle Crowe (Cavan), Angela Lyons (Kildare), Bernie Farrelly (captain) (Kildare), Mary Kennedy (Mayo), Sinéad Muldoon (Mayo), Sharon Raleigh (Meath), Gráinne O'Neill (Tyrone), Pauline Cunningham (Waterford), Dinah Loughlin (Westmeath) and Aisling O'Brien (Waterford).

Camogie-Shinty

The first team of camogie players to travel abroad wearing their country's colours met Scotland in a camogie-shinty tournament at Inverness. The Irish girls proved too good for their Scottish opponents and won by 3–4 to 0–0. Captain Bernie Farrelly accepted the Ceilteach which was the trophy on offer. Selected from the weaker counties, it gave a once in a lifetime opportunity to players to represent their country. Annette McGeeney, who scored

2005 All-Stars

Only in its second year, the All-Star Awards banquet was already established as one of the most prestigious occasions on the camogie calendar. Over 500 people joined President Miriam O'Callaghan and Ossie Kilkenny, chairperson of the Irish Sports Council, to honour the cream of camogie talent at a glittering occasion at the CityWest Hotel. The All-Ireland finalists, Cork and Tipperary, scooped the lion's share of awards, Galway, the National League winners, brought home two awards and Ciara Lucey became the first Dublin recipient.

The Manager of the Year Award went to the victorious Cork manager, John Cronin, and the talented Colette McSorley accepted the Young Player of the Year award.

All-Stars 2005: Jovita Delaney (Tipperary), Sinéad Cahalan (Galway), Catherine O'Loughlin (Wexford), Julie Kirwan (Tipperary), Anna Geary (Cork), Mary O'Connor (Cork), Therese Maher (Galway), Gemma O'Connor (Cork), Ciara Lucey (Dublin), Jennifer O'Leary (Cork), Rachel Moloney (Cork), Claire Grogan (Tipperary), Catherine O'Loughlin (Clare), Eimear McDonnell (Tipperary) and Emer Dillon (Cork).

Liz Howard Elected President

Miriam O'Callaghan, who presented an excellent image of the Camogie Association during the hectic centenary year, stepped down as president at Congress 2006 in Tullamore and was replaced by Tipperary-born, Liz Howard. Steeped in Gaelic games tradition, she had served as the national PRO of the Camogie Association (1979–1982).

New Sponsor

Gala, the convenience retailers, signed a two-year deal

Mary O'Connor and Anna Geary display their All-Star Awards in 2005.

Liz Howard

with the Camogie Association worth a six-figure sum for the sponsorship of the All-Ireland senior championship in May 2006. Considered a natural fit, both are based at the heart of communities across Ireland. Commercial sponsorship was considered essential to develop the sport and the support of Gala was warmly welcomed. The premier championship was renamed the Gala All-Ireland Senior Championship.

St Mary's Charleville

Situated on the Cork-Limerick border, St Mary's, Charleville, were kingpins of second-level camogie for a period of 20 years. The school is surrounded by strong clubs, Granagh-Ballingarry, Milford, Newtownshandrum, Ballyagran, Ballyhea and Charleville. Products of the underage sections of these clubs enrol at the school where, with expert skill training and coaching, they mature into top-class players. In the area of skill training, Vincent Harrington has been exceptional. His ability to manage teams and bring the best out of them has been remarkable.

A camogie pitch beside the school, a strong management team which included Vincent Harrington Anne Marie O'Keeffe, St Margaret, Bríd Mulcahy, Ger O'Donovan, Fr Liam Kelleher and Fr Tim Hazelwood, the backing of

Into the Second Millennium

the school authorities and the support of a large group of parents have been factors in the success enjoyed by St Mary's: 29 All-Ireland titles, seven senior, nine junior and 13 sevens, were captured between 1986 and 2006. Many past pupils became household names in the camogie world, including Eileen O'Brien, Helen Cagney, Claire O'Callaghan, Sinéad O'Callaghan, Vera Sheehan, Caoimhe Harrington, Anna Geary, Elaine O'Riordan and the Watson sisters. The contribution of St Mary's to the promotion of camogie has been tremendous.

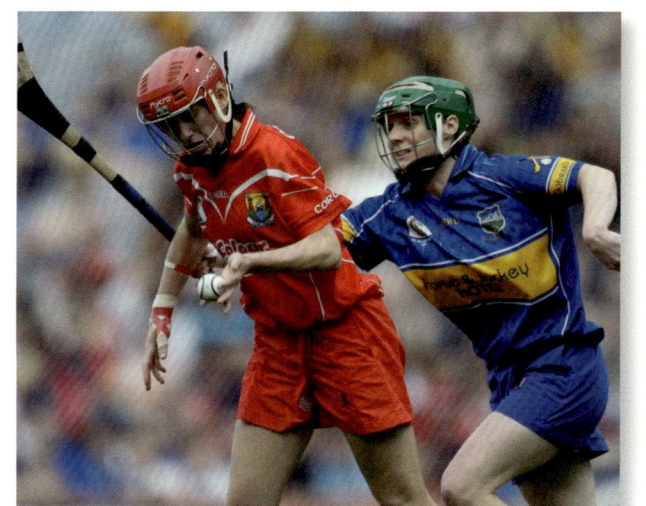

Women in Sport

Women's participation in sport came under the radar of the Ministry of Arts, Sport and Tourism. Funds were provided for schemes to increase women's involvement in sport and recreational activity including coaching, refereeing and decision-making. Anxious to make the best possible use of the funds available, two projects were devised, Spórt agus Spraoi le Coláistí and the TY programme. Under the Spórt agus Spraoi le Coláistí, 800 girls participated in a one-day event which comprised coaching sessions and non-competitive inter-school games. Staged at four venues – UCD, LIT, NUI Maynooth and WIT – it opened lines of communication between second- and third-level colleges. The reaction to these events was phenomenal and the level of participation grew from 800 students from 16 secondary schools in year one to 2,000 pupils from 70 colleges in year two.

2006 All-Ireland Senior final: Mary O'Connor, Cork, in action against Eimear McDonnell, Tipperary.
Picture: David Maher / SPORTSFILE

In the Transition Year (TY) Camogie Project, a 12–14 week transition-year programme, with optional and mandatory modules that covered all aspects of the game, was developed. The programme was self-sustaining and interested teachers were able to deliver the course following an intense one-day induction course and support from the Camogie Association. Schools involved were provided with starter equipment packs and participating girls given six weeks coaching prior to the classroom module. Girls were given an opportunity to coach and referee for locals clubs as part of the practical experience of the module. At the end of a two-year pilot scheme, 16 teachers were trained as foundation level coaches and the TY Camogie programme was delivered to 16 schools. Approximately 400 students were trained to play camogie, to referee, to coach and to handle the administration of a club. Plans to grow these schemes and make them available to the whole country were immediately put in hand.

Gradam Síghle Nic an Ultaigh

The family of the late Sheila McAnulty, Life President, made a donation to the Camogie Association to establish an award in her name. It was decided that the most appropriate manner in which to honour Sheila's unparalleled contribution to the Association would be to make the award, Gradam Síghle Nic an Ultaigh, on an annual basis to administrators. Those honoured would be drawn from all who served or are serving as officers from Central Council, provincial councils, county boards and the three colleges councils. The award would be presented at the All-Stars banquet.

2006 All-Ireland Senior Championship

In a game that did not reach any great heights, Cork made hard work of disposing of Galway's challenge in the semi-final at Nowlan Park. The game was refereed to the letter of the law, with the result that play was stop-start, something that frustrated players and spectators alike. Cork did enough to advance to the final by 1–7 to 0–6.

The Cork senior team celebrate after their win against Tipperary in 2006.
Picture: Matt Browne / SPORTSFILE

Tipperary's Jovita Delaney was in fantastic form against Kilkenny in the second semi-final. She kept the young Kilkenny attackers at bay with a string of saves. Claire Grogan's accuracy from placed balls and good work by the Tipperary defenders weathered the storm and saw Tipperary through to the final by 0–13 to 1–8.

Now in their eighth year on the road in terms of All-Ireland finals, Tipperary had to find replacements for key members of the original team. It is not easy to locate successors for the likes of Ciara Gaynor, Therese Brophy, Noelle Kennedy, Deirdre Hughes or Angie McDermott. Newcomers need time to find their feet and gain experience.

An immaculate display by the Cork defence strangled the Tipperary attack in the final at Croke Park on September 10th. Right from the start, the half-back line comprising Anna Geary, Mary O'Connor and Rena Buckley was impassable. Cork also won the midfield battle where Gemma O'Connor and Briege Corkery took control. The Tipperary forwards were hugely disappointing: four points is a poor return for an hour's camogie. The Tipperary defence battled bravely and kept Jovita Delaney's goal intact. Cork 0–12, Tipperary 0–4 was the first goalless final in the history of the game. The sponsorship of Gala together with the staging of the final on the same bill as the All-Ireland under-21 hurling final made the occasion a financial success for the Camogie Association.

Cork team: Aoife Murray, Joanne O'Callaghan (captain), Caitríona Foley, Amanda O'Regan, Rena Buckley, Mary O'Connor, Anna Geary, Gemma O'Connor (0–2), Briege Corkery (0–1), Rachel Moloney (0–1), Angela Walsh, Jenny O'Leary (0–4), Emer Dillon (0–2), Una O'Donoghue (0–2) and Elaine Burke. Subs used: Sarah O'Donovan and Orla Cotter.

Tipperary team: Jovita Delaney, Suzanne Kelly, Una O'Dwyer, Julie Kirwan, Michelle Shortt, Philly Fogarty (captain), Sinéad Nealon, Claire Grogan, Joanne Ryan (0–1), Jill Horan, Emily Hayden (0–2), Cora Hennessy, Geraldine Kinnane, Louise Young and Eimear McDonnell (0–1). Subs used: Lorraine Bourke and Trish O'Halloran.

2006 All-Ireland Senior B Championship

Cork were in a different class to Tipperary in the semi-final at Kilmallock. Indeed, the match was over as a contest by half-time when Cork held a 3–11 to 0–2 advantage. Marie O'Neill (1–8), Denise Twomey (2–0) and Emer O'Farrell (1–2) were the main scorers for Cork in their facile 4–13 to 0–6 victory.

Two goals from Molly Dunne and a third by Paula Kenny were sufficient to see Galway through to the final at the expense of Kilkenny at Rath. The young Kilkenny players stayed with their more experienced opponents for much of the game but the more clinical finish of the Galway girls won out by 3–8 to 2–7.

Cork added the inaugural All-Ireland Senior B Championship crown to the premier senior title that they had won earlier in the month. Supporters were treated to excellent fare at the Gaelic Grounds as Cork and Galway matched score for score for three-quarters of the contest. The deciding score came when Susan Earner saved a rasper from Marie O'Neill at the expense of a 45. Orla Cotter's resulting shot hit the post and dropped on the edge of the square. Emer Watson was the first to react and she whipped the ball to the net. Orla Cotter tacked on two points to secure the shining new Jack McGrath Cup for Cork by 2–9 to 1–7. The Cork full-back line of Ann Marie Fleming, Sinéad Corkery and Deirdre Hayes were superb and absorbed everything that Galway tried. Susan Earner, Sinéad Keane, Paula Kenny and Emma Kilkelly did most for Galway.

Cork team: Gillian Harrington, Ann Marie Fleming, Sinéad Corkery, Deirdre Hayes, Lynda O'Connell, Jenny Duffy, Eimear O'Sullivan, Orla Cotter (0–6), Linda Dorgan, Marie Corkery (0–1), Marie O'Neill, Emer O'Farrell, Emer Watson (1–2), Miriam Deasy (captain) (1–0) and Maria Watson. Subs used: Lucy Hawkes and Denise Twomey.

Galway team: Susan Earner (0–1), Colette Gill, Sinéad Keane, Lizzie Flynn (captain), Catherine Moran, Fiona Healy, Therese Manton, Paula Kenny (0–1), Phyllis Hayes, Noreen Coen, Martina Conroy, Emma Kilkelly (0–1), Susan Keane (1–4), Sandra Tannian and Molly Dunne. Subs used: C. Conroy, A. Kilkenny and Caitríona Cormican.

2006 All-Ireland Junior Championship

Derry gave a polished performance against Waterford in the semi-final at Páirc Tailteann. They got off to an excellent start and were in control throughout the game. Newcomers to this level, Waterford fought bravely but their lack of experience told.

Dublin and Clare were pitted together in the second semi-final for their third championship meeting in 12 months. With ten minutes remaining on the clock, Dublin were comfortably ahead by 2–11 to 0–8, but Clare put in a storming finish, scoring 1–4 without reply. However, time ran out and Dublin had secured a place in the final by 2–12 to 1–5.

Great disappointment was expressed when it was announced that the All-Ireland junior final would not be played in Croke Park. Derry and Dublin got off to a tentative start in the final at Tullamore. Scores were few and far between but proceedings livened up considerably in the second-half as both sides pushed for victory. A goal by Claire McCloy cut Dublin's margin to two points with six minutes to go. Tension and excitement mounted as Derry went for the winner. Katie McAuley trimmed another point off Dublin's lead but Aisling Jordan sealed victory for Dublin with a late point to leave the final score Dublin 0–12, Derry 1–7.

Dublin team: Eimear Butler, Elaine O'Meara, Ciara Lucey, Jean Murphy, Andrea Fitzpatrick, Anne McCluskey (captain), Caitríona Power, Áine Fanning, Ciara Durkan (0–1), Eimear Brannigan (0–1), Louise O'Hara (0–5), Julie Draper, Niamh Taylor (0–2), Sarah Ryan (0–2) and Aisling Jordan (0–1). Subs used: Muireann O'Gorman and Anne Griffin.

Derry team: Claire O'Kane, Helena Kelly, Catherine Pickering, Jane Carey, Kate Laverty, Claire Doherty, Ceara Cushnahan, Briege Convery, Aisling Diamond, Claire McCloy, Denise McCann, Gráinne McGoldrick, Sinéad Cassidy, Katie McAuley and J Kelly. Subs used: Aileen Lavery and Emma McIvor.

2006 All-Ireland Minor A Championship

Galway signalled their intent from the outset as they raced into a four-point lead against Cork in the semi-final at Glen Rovers' grounds. Jessica Gill and Noreen Coen caused considerable problems for the Cork defence. The Galway players used the ball better than their opponents and took whatever chances that came their way to secure victory by 2–12 to 1–5.

The opportunism of Michelle Quilty around the Tipperary goal was a major factor in Kilkenny's success at Holycross. The Slieverue girl punished the lapses of the home defence and was the difference between the teams. Michelle finished with 3–2 after her name and her team-mate, Laura Kavanagh, chipped in with two goals to book Kilkenny's place in the final by 5–5 to 3–5.

Kilkenny made several positional switches in their team for

the final against Galway at Nenagh. The new placings worked to perfection. With the result, Kilkenny performed clinically and with confidence beyond their years. Galway started well and played great camogie in the first 20 minutes. It began to fall apart for them as Kilkenny came more into the game. Kilkenny had many stars on the day: Sinéad Walsh, Leanne Fennelly and Kate McDonald excelled in defence; Colette Dormer, Anne Dalton and Lucinda Gahan impressed in the middle of the field; and all the forwards raised flags. All of which left the final score Kilkenny 4–10, Galway 2–5.

Kilkenny team: Sinéad Walsh, Leanne Fennelly, Kate McDonald, Eilish Cantwell, Noreen O'Keeffe, Colette Dormer, Sarah Shore, Lucinda Gahan (1-0), Anne Dalton (0–3), Mary Dalton (0–1), Katie Power (0–1), Edwina Keane (0–1), Laura Kavanagh (1–2), Marie Dargan (2–1) and Michelle Quilty (0–1). Subs used: Mariga Nolan, Marie Phelan, Sarah O'Mahony and Carol Phelan (captain).

Galway team: Stephanie Gannon, Emer Haverty, Mary Ward, Aisling Hobbins, Sara Noone, Niamh Kilkenny, Julie Brien, Lorraine Ryan, Paula Kenny, Jessica Gill (0–1), Catríona Cormican, Marian Farragher, Noreen Coen (0–2), Martina Conroy (0-1) and Richelle O'Brien (2–1). Subs used: Gemma Lohan and Michelle Glynn.

2006 All-Ireland Minor B Championship

The inaugural All-Ireland Minor B Championship was decided between Ulster counties, Antrim and Down, at Casement Park. In an exciting end-to-end contest, supporters were treated to an exhibition of individual skills, excellent score-taking and a pulsating finish.

Down were marginally the better team in the opening half and were ahead by 2–2 to 1–4 at the changeover. Three goals inside the first four minutes of the second-half delighted Down supporters. Antrim rallied and closed the gap to a single point with ten minutes remaining. Raquel McCarry and Sara Louise Carr, two of the brightest stars on view, traded spectacular goals as time ran out. Down held on to their slender advantage to win by 5–8 to 6–4.

Down team: Joanna Sloan, Helen McAteer, Corinna Cunningham (captain), Sarah Farnon, Paula Gribben, Carolann Sloan, Gráinne O'Higgins, Karen Tinnelly (0–3), Clare Quinn (1–0), Joanne Fitzpatrick, Lisa McPolin, Lisa Hughes, Stephanie O'Hare (1–0), Sara Louise Carr (1–5) and Aoibhne O'Neill (2–0). Sub used: Claire Malone.

Antrim team: Shaunie McAuley, Lucia Dowds, Róisín O'Boyle, Brianna McDonnell, Sinéad Laverty, Jolene McCarry, Emma Connolly, Joanne Campbell (1–0), Suzanne McKeown, Shannon Graham, Claire Dallat (captain) (0–2), Racquel McCarry (2–1), Cathy Carey (0–1), Aisling McCall and Bronagh Orchin (1–0). Subs used: Aileen Martin (1-0), Michaela Convery (0–1) and Emma McMullan.

2006 All-Ireland Under 16A Championship

Cork had to weather a storm before booking their place in the final. Twenty minutes into the semi-final against Dublin at Nenagh, Cork found themselves a point behind. They rallied and forged ahead by 0–6 to 0–3 at the break. Goals by Niamh Dilworth and Sinéad O'Callaghan cemented victory for Cork by 4–10 to 2–8.

Kilkenny had little difficulty in overcoming the challenge of Clare in the second semi-final. Unfortunately, Clare had to take the field without some key members of their team. On the day, they were unable to exert any dominance and had to yield to a superior Kilkenny side by 6–15 to 1–6.

Kilkenny scored a convincing 2–10 to 0–4 victory over Cork in the final at Portmarnock. The Noresiders were faster to the ball, sharper in their striking and more aware of what was required to win the game. Cork never settled to the pace of the game and were playing catch-up from the beginning. Edwina Keane, Anna Farrell, Michelle Quilty, Katie Power and Marie Dargan showed talent and maturity on the Kilkenny team The Cork girls, who had performed very well in earlier rounds, failed to play to their potential.

Kilkenny team: Ann Marie Lennon, Ciara Lyng, Kate McDonald, Ann Marie Walsh, Aisling Dunphy, Leann Fennelly,

Group pictured at presentation to Mary Casey and Rose Malone on their retirement from Munster Council in 2006. From Left: Séamus O'Sullivan, Marion Graham, Mary Casey, Rose Malone, Jean Hayden, Eamon Browne, Marie Kearney and Morgan Conroy.

Edel Frisby, Karen Duggan, Marie Dargan, Sinéad Kelly, Edwina Keane (captain) (1–2), Katie Power (0–2), Michelle Brennan (0–1), Anna Farrell and Michelle Quilty (1–5). Subs used: Sinéad Long and Róisín Byrne.

Cork team: Dawn O'Keeffe (captain), Christine O'Neill, Rebecca Finn, Eimear Harrington, Leanne O'Shea, Marie Walsh, Mairéad Foley, Ella Kelliher, Fiona O'Connell, Róisín de Faoite, Claire Keohane (0–1), Aisling Thompson, Niamh Dilworth, Catríona Collins (0–2) and Sinéad O'Callaghan (0–1). Subs used: Darina O'Callaghan and Mary Ann Hawkes.

2006 All-Ireland Under 16B Championship

Derry grabbed an early advantage against Waterford in the semi-final at Navan. Their superior skill enabled them to build an impressive lead and see off the challenge of Waterford by 5–12 to 2–4. Meath found themselves out of their depth in the second semi-final against a well-prepared Armagh outfit. With a generous supply of good ball from the outfield players, the Armagh attack could do no wrong and built a winning margin of 5–15 to 1–6.

Derry were the first to settle in the final against Armagh at

Into the Second Millennium

Naomh Mearnóg and held a 1–2 to 0–0 advantage at the break. Armagh upped the pace of the game on the restart and were rewarded with two points. However, they were unable to catch Derry who added to their tally and won comfortably by 3–3 to 1–2.

Derry team: Joni McEldowney, Áine Kelly, Róisín O'Kane, Caoimhe Toner, Ciara O'Kane, Clodagh McPeake, Janine McNeil, Eimear McKenna (captain), Christine McKenna, Maeve McGillen (0–3), Edelle Crossan, Danielle McCrystal (2–0), Michelle Rodgers, Nichole McLaughlin and Keelin Bradley (1–0).

Armagh team: Louise Toner, Shauna Leonard, Paula Mallon, Leon McGuigan, Orla O'Hare, Emma McParland, Laura Comiskey, Nicole Conway, Corinna McKee, Aideen Canavan, Laura McGuinness (captain) (0–1), Noeleen McKenna, Petrina Cosgrove (1–0), L. Lavery and Lucy Conway (0–1).

2006 All-Ireland Club Senior Championship

St Lachtain's goalkeeper, Laura Comerford, was the star of the semi-final against Cashel at Nenagh. Laura saved an array of shots from the talented Cashel forwards. St Lachtain's were fortunate that the winter sun blinded Cashel goalkeeper, Jovita Delaney, enabling Imelda Kennedy's speculative shot to drop under the bar for the only goal of the game. Imelda Kennedy, Marie O'Connor and Aoife Fitzpatrick for St Lachtain's and Claire Grogan, Jill Horan and Libby Twomey for Cashel struck some fine points. The score at full-time was St Lachtain's 1–8, Cashel 0–10.

Athenry ended two decades in the wilderness when they ousted Pearses in the final of the Galway Senior Championship and returned to challenge for the All-Ireland club title. They met Rossa in a very entertaining game at Drumlane, Co. Cavan. Both sides played brilliant camogie before the final whistle blew with Rossa a point ahead, 3–11 to 2–11.

The All-Ireland club final between Rossa and St Lachtain's was fixed for O'Moore Park much to the annoyance of Rossa who, having travelled to Co. Cavan for the semi-final, did not consider it fair that they should be asked to make the journey to Portlaoise. St Lachtain's joined the three in-a-row club at the finish of a close, low-scoring game. Rossa did not take full advantage of the gale in the first-half and were only a point in front on the changeover. Imelda Kennedy opened the Rossa defence and placed Marie O'Connor for a fine goal. Strong play by Rossa worked the ball forward for Orla McCall to reply. Rossa were not to score again. St Lachtain's picked off points by Imelda Kennedy, Sinéad Connery and Anne Dalton to put the Kilkenny club in front. Lashing rain, high winds and even hail stones kept scores to a premium. It was a hard dogged struggle to the end with both teams giving everything and ended St Lachtain's 1–5, Rossa 1–3.

St Lachtain's team: Laura Comerford, Sinéad Cash, Gillian Maher, Fiona Dowling, Margaret McCarthy, Mairéad Costello, Áine Connery, Esther Costello, Aoife Fitzpatrick, Deirdre Delaney, Sinéad Connery, Imelda Kennedy, Anne Dalton, Marie O'Connor and Eileen Fitzpatrick. Sub used: Mary Dalton.

Rossa team: Teresa McGowan, Pauline Green, Hannah Healy, Shauneen McGourty, Ciara Gault, Maureen Stewart, Aisling

McCall, Colleen Doherty, Seáinín Daykin, Mairéad Rainey, Gráinne Connolly, Fiona Kennedy, Mairiosa McGourty, Jane Adams and Orla McCall. Sub used: Sinéad O'Neill.

2006 All-Ireland Club Junior Championship

From the Cullohill/Durrow area of Co. Laois, The Harps eased past Gaultier (Waterford) in the semi-final to set up a final date with Keady, who had conquerored Athleague by 6–8 to 2–6, at O'Moore Park. The weather on final day ensured that free-flowing camogie was out of the question. Instead defences were on top and opportunities few and far between. Louise Mahony, Denise Quigley and Elaine Mahony were influential players for The Harps as they built up a half-time lead of 0–6 to 0–3. The critical score came nine minutes into the second-half when Elaine Mahony got the only goal of the game. Keady pushed very hard for the remainder of the match but were unable to raise a flag. The Harps won by 1–7 to 0–5.

The Harps team: Áine Mahony, Joan Dollard, Michelle Fitzpatrick, Laura Mahony, Denise Quigley (captain), Caitríona Phelan, Catríona Phelan, Aoife Donohue, Louise Mahony, Angela Hanlon, Erinne Dunne, Elaine Cuddy, Elaine Mahony, Aisling Phelan and Teresa Bennett.

Camogie President, Liz Howard, Gerry Fahy, Vodafone, and Mary O'Connor (Cork) who received the award for her performances in 2006.

Keady team: Eileen McCrory, Brenda McQuade, Catherine Doyle, Patrice Murphy, Colleen Comiskey, Katrina Kinsella, Róisín Murray, Helena Murray, Colleen Conway, Kathy Ann Hughes, Annie O'Farrell, Patricia McCabe, Claire Kinsella, Collette McKeever and Michelle Murray.

2006 Gael-Linn Senior Cup

Páirc Tailteann, venue for the first Gael-Linn interprovincial championship in 1956, housed the 50th anniversary with a single senior match Leinster v. Munster. In a low-scoring game, two late points enabled Leinster to claim their 25th title and deny Munster.

Leinster clinched victory by 2–7 to 1–8.

Leinster team: Caitríona Ryan (Kilkenny), Keira Kinahan (Kilkenny), Catherine O'Loughlin (captain) (Wexford), Bronagh Furlong (Wexford), Áine Fanning (Dublin), Elaine Aylward (Kilkenny), Andrea Fitzpatrick (Dublin), Kate Kelly (Wexford), Rose-Marie Breen (Wexford), Lizzie Lyng (Kilkenny), Louise O'Hara (Dublin), Marie Dargan (Kilkenny), Bridget Curran (Wexford), Eimear Brannigan (Dublin) and Aoife Neary (Kilkenny).

Munster team: Ellen Clifford (Cork), Joanne O'Callaghan (Cork), Suzanne Kelly (Tipperary), Amanda O'Regan (Cork), Rena Buckley (Cork), Mary O'Connor (Cork), Anna Geary (Cork),

Gemma O'Connor (Cork), Joanne Ryan (Tipperary), Angela Walsh (Cork), Deirdre Murphy (Clare), Jenny O'Leary (Cork), Áine Lyng (Waterford), Deirdre Twomey (Cork) and Rachel Moloney (Cork).

2006 Gael-Linn Junior Trophy

The junior final was a nail-biting affair which ended in a one-point win for Connacht, 3–12 to 1–17 over Ulster. Ulster had led 1–13 to 2–4 at the interval but Connacht fought back heroically and snatched victory with a last-gasp point from Veronica Curtin.

Connacht team: Maeve Healy (Roscommon), Emer Farrell (Roscommon), Fiona Connell (Roscommon) Lizzie Flynn (Galway), Serena Brien (Galway), Claire Conroy (Galway), Julie Brien (Galway), Annette McGeeney (Roscommon), Brenda Hanney (Galway), Emma Kilkelly (Galway), Veronica Curtin (Galway), Susan Keane (Galway), Rachel O'Brien (Galway), Ann Marie Hayes (Galway) and Lisa Smith (Galway).

Ulster team: Claire O'Kane (Derry), Jacinta Dixon (Antrim), Catherine Pickering (Derry), Jane Carey (Derry), Bernie McBride (Armagh), Claire Doherty (Derry), Fionnuala Carr (Down), Gráinne McGoldrick (Derry), Colette McSorley (Armagh), Denise McCann (Derry), Maureen McAleenan (Down) (captain), Briege Convery (Derry), Elaine Dowds (Antrim), Katie McAuley (Derry) and Aileen Laverty (Derry).

2006 Nancy Murray Cup

Armagh registered a convincing win over Laois in the final of the Nancy Murray Cup (All-Ireland Junior Shield) by 0–7 to 0–1 at Drogheda. Armagh did what was expected of them and took the chances that came their way.

Armagh team: Bronagh Keenan, Gráinne Kelly, Marie Larkin, Laura Gribben, Katrina Kinsella, Bernie McBride (captain), Michelle Murray, Helena Murray, Colleen Conway, Colette McSorley, Kelly Ann Hughes, Julie O'Neill, Catríona Curry, Andrea McAlinden and Colette McKeever.

Laois team: Marion O'Grady, Emma Cuddy, Emer Moynan, Caitríona Phelan, Denise Quigley, Laura Mahony, Louise Mahony, Catríona Downey, Eimear Delaney, Sharon Moylan, Aoife Donoghue, Karen Cuddy, Therese Keenan, Elaine Mahony and Teresa Bennett.

Camogie-Shinty

The selectors of the Irish team were restricted to five counties – Louth, Westmeath, Monaghan, Mayo and Donegal – for

Pictured at the Launch of the Ashbourne Cup at NUI Galway were from left Denise Twomey, Geraldine McGrath, Claire McMahon, Iognaid Ó Muircheartaigh, President of NUI Galway, Colette Gill and Neasa O'Donnell, President of the CCIA.

their choice of players. With the result the standard of the Irish team was not on a par with previous years. Scotland travelled to Ratoath, Co. Meath, and played Ireland on the same bill as the under-21 hurling–shinty international on November 4th. Showing a higher level of skill than in previous years, the Scottish players were full value for their 4–8 to 3–0 win. Indeed, the margin of victory would have been much wider but for the excellent play of Irish goalkeeper, Sandra Greville who denied the visitors on numerous occasions. Yvonne Byrne (two) and Marie Grennan were the Irish goal scorers. The four teams enjoyed a night of Irish and Scottish music and dancing.

Irish team: Sandra Greville (captain) (Westmeath), Clare Campbell (Donegal), Jemma Egan (Westmeath), Mairéad McCarron (Monaghan), Julie Finnegan (Louth), Eilish Mulholland (Louth), Ciara Cullen (Donegal), Pamela Greville (Westmeath), Maeve Murphy (Mayo), Mary Henry (Westmeath), Kevina Kenny (Louth), Avril Flannery (Mayo), Yvonne Byrne (Mayo), Marie Grennan (Monaghan) and Eleanor McQuaid (Monaghan), Donna Ferguson (Donegal), Helen Hughes (Monaghan) and Ann Marie Kane (Louth).

2006 All-Stars Awards

Tadhg Kennelly, Kerry Gaelic football and Aussie Rules player, was the special guest at the 2006 All-Star Awards night at the CityWest Hotel. Once again, the All-Ireland finalists, Cork and Tipperary, were the big winners. Peter Lucey (Dublin) was named Manager of the Year and the Young Player of the Year award went to Marie Dargan (Kilkenny).

All-Stars 2006: Jovita Delaney (Tipperary), Regina Glynn (Galway), Suzanne Kelly (Tipperary), Rena Buckley (Cork), Philly Fogarty (Tipperary), Mary O'Connor (Cork), Anna Geary (Cork), Gemma O'Connor (Cork), Kate Kelly (Wexford), Joanne Ryan (Tipperary), Briege Corkery (Cork), Jenny O'Leary (Cork), Imelda Kennedy (Kilkenny), Louise O'Hara (Dublin) and Veronica Curtin (Galway).

Where We're At

The centenary year reminded one and all of the significant contribution that camogie has made to the shaping of Irish society over the past 100 years and showed the huge amount of goodwill that exists towards the Association. Camogie was placed on a pedestal in 2004 and carried along on a high throughout the year. It was vital, as it turned into the second century, that the Association did not sit back but moved forward from that position and built on the gains achieved.

Two factors were critical in making the right choice. The path laid out in the Strategic Plan pointed the way and the appointment of a national development co-ordinator and two regional development co-ordinators was the key to driving the programme forward. A concentrated effort to tackle areas where the game was weak, through a series of well-planned projects, drew excellent results. The availability of full-time staff allowed a much more structured approach to be made regarding the formation of new clubs. In the past, a county-board officer attended a meet-

Into the Second Millennium

ing of the proposed new club, outlined the level of organisation required, handed over a rule book and departed. A team was put together and entered for competition. Players, who were not properly prepared, found themselves out of their depth and, often within a short time, the new club found itself in difficulties.

The RDO was able to provide a service equal to the task: she mobilised the primary schools in the area; provided training for club officials and prospective coaches; and organised fun days, blitzes and small-sided games to ease the players into the game and give them a chance to learn it. A start-up grant from Central Council helped to equip the club. The new club knew that the RDO was at the end of the phone should any difficulty arise.

A point that jumped out from the Competitions Review Report was the overall dominance of the strong senior counties. One would naturally expect them to control the senior grade but the report showed that they also monopolised the intermediate and junior grades. With the result that the latter grades were not doing the job that they were set up to do. A competition which was designed to help the junior counties had become dominated by the second-string teams of the senior counties. The existing system did not provide a second chance. Therefore, half the junior teams ended their inter-county season after one match. This arrangement called for radical overhaul.

Within the junior grade, a disparity of standards existed. Two or three junior competitions were called for to allow each county find its own level and encounter comparable opposition. There was strong support for a new under-18 championship and welcome for the recently introduced All-Ireland Junior Club Championship.

A Game of Our Own

Forward Momentum

Chapter Twenty Four

GROWING STAFF

2007 opened on a sad note with the untimely death of Mairéad Meehan, at the age of 25, in her home at Caltra, Co. Galway. Máiréad had battled with illness for seven years with great dignity and courage. The heartfelt grief felt at her passing was reflected in the large number, estimated at 10,000, who attended her home and funeral over the course of three days.

She had achieved a great deal in her short life. Captain of Holy Rosary team that won the All-Ireland Colleges Championship, she won two All-Ireland minor medals with Galway and All-Ireland club medal with Pearses. A highly talented player at both camogie and ladies football, Máiréad is a sister of the famous Meehan brothers who brought the All-Ireland club football title to the village of Caltra.

Later in the year, a true gentleman of camogie, Michael Kennedy, was called suddenly from this life. He was the driving force behind the Pearses camogie club which won five All-Ireland club titles between 1996 and 2002 and was chairman of the Galway camogie board when the county won its only All-Ireland senior title. Father of colleges' official, Colette Walsh, Michael spent countless hours coaching the skills of the game to young players.

Mairéad Meehan

Before the year was out, camogie had lost three significant contributors to the promotion of the game. Past-president, Eilish Redmond, Kathleen Timmins of Naomh Aoife, and Leinster Council and Tyrone's Bridie McMenamin all went to their heavenly reward.

Director of Camogie

Mary O'Connor, who had been on the payroll since 2005 as a regional development co-ordinator, was appointed the Camogie Association's director of camogie in February 2007. Her new role involved: driving the development of the game; maximising

A Game of Our Own

participation at all levels; and developing effective coaching and refereeing structures in line with the Association's Strategic Plan. She started with a staff of two but, by the end of the year, five more full-time officials had come on board.

With funding from the Irish Sports Council, the Association appointed four additional RDCs – Jenny Duffy (Cork), Eve Talbot (Dublin), Gerard Gribben (Armagh) and Deirdre Murphy (Clare) – as well as a second-level development co-ordinator, Jennifer Steede (Galway). Mary's focus and energy led the team with great effect.

With the season's calendar catering for 18 competitions, the fixtures workload was beyond the capacity of a voluntary official. Bronagh Gaughan (Meath) took over the role of fixtures administrator where her cheerful manner was very suited to the task.

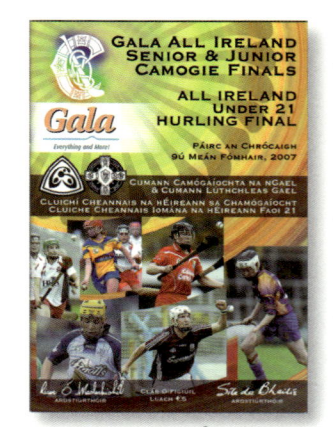

2007 - Una Leacy, Wexford, in action against Amanda O'Regan, Cork, on the way to scoring her side's second goal in the Gala All-Ireland Senior Camogie final. Picture: Brian Lawless / SPORTSFILE

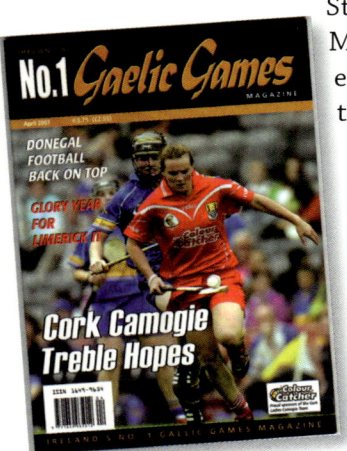

Cover girl, Briege Corkery (Cork) followed by Joanne Ryan (Tipperary) on Gaelic Games Magazine 2007.

No to Membership Fees

The first motion on the agenda at Congress 2007 in Armagh sought the introduction of a membership fee in lieu of the existing affiliation fees. The amount requested was €20 per adult member and €10 for juveniles. The proposal involved long and, at times, vigorous discussion. Finance manager, Sinéad O'Connor, highlighted the need for increased income and spelled out how the funds would be spent in some detail. However, when the votes were counted, there were 29 for and 45 against the motion.

Congress accepted the idea of a president-elect and approved an extra year for the outgoing president as a non-voting member of the Central Council. The appointment of a children's officer to each unit of the Association also met with approval.

2007 All-Ireland Senior Championship

Cork reached the All-Ireland final by doing the simple things well. Their

Growing Staff

2007 - Wexford players celebrate at the final whistle. Right: Wexford captain Mary Leacy lifts the O'Duffy Cup. *Pictures: Brian Lawless / SPORTSFILE.*

defence afforded minimum opportunities to the Tipperary attack in the semi-final at Nowlan Park and stood firm when the Premier County attempted a fight-back. Apart from Claire Grogan, who rifled over six points, Tipperary were limited in attack. Cork took their chances to win by 2–11 to 0–9.

Wexford players and officials went wild with excitement at the final whistle in the second semi-final against Galway at Nowlan Park. Winning a place in the All-Ireland final meant so much to them. Kate Kelly capped a great individual display by scoring 1–11. Wexford cemented a place in the final by 2–18 to 0–14.

Wexford's greater hunger and passion, driven by a 32-year title famine, played a big part in their success over Cork in the All-Ireland final at Croke Park on September 9th. Two early goals by Una Leacy meant that Cork were fighting an uphill battle for most of the game. To Cork's credit, they fought back to cut the gap to the minimum. Playing with guts and skill, the superbly fit Wexford side were not going to allow Cork to take the O'Duffy Cup.

Wexford pressed home their advantage and tagged three points without reply. Cork came again but superb defending by Noeleen Lambert, Avis Nolan, Deirdre Codd and Mary Leacy kept Cork at bay. Wexford's phenomenal work rate managed to contain Cork's threat. Kate Kelly, Bróna Furlong, Caroline Murphy, Una Leacy and Ursula Jacob were hugely influential for Wexford. Gemma O'Connor, Briege Corkery, Orla Cotter and Rena Buckley did most to turn the tide for Cork. Croke Park erupted at the final whistle, as Wexford players, officials and fans gave vent to their unbridled joy. The scoreboard read Wexford 2–7, Cork 1–8.

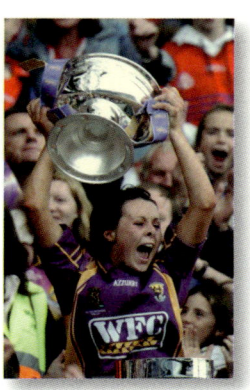

Wexford team: Mags D'Arcy, Noeleen Lambert, Catherine O'Loughlin, Avis Nolan, Áine Codd, Mary Leacy (captain), Deirdre Codd, Kate Kelly (0–3), Caroline Murphy, Bróna Furlong, Rose-Marie Breen (0–1), Michelle O'Leary, Una Leacy (2–0), Michelle Hearne and Ursula Jacob (0–2). Subs used: Katrina Parrock (0–1), Aoife O'Connor and Claire O'Connor.

A Game of Our Own

Cork team: Aoife Murray, Joanne O'Callaghan, Caitríona Foley, Amanda O'Regan, Rena Buckley, Mary O'Connor, Anna Geary, Briege Corkery (0–1), Gemma O'Connor (captain) (0–3), Una O'Donoghue, Angela Walsh (0–1), Jenny O'Leary (0–1), Emer Dillon (1–1), Orla Cotter (0–1) and Síle Burns. Subs used: Emer Watson and Sarah O'Donovan.

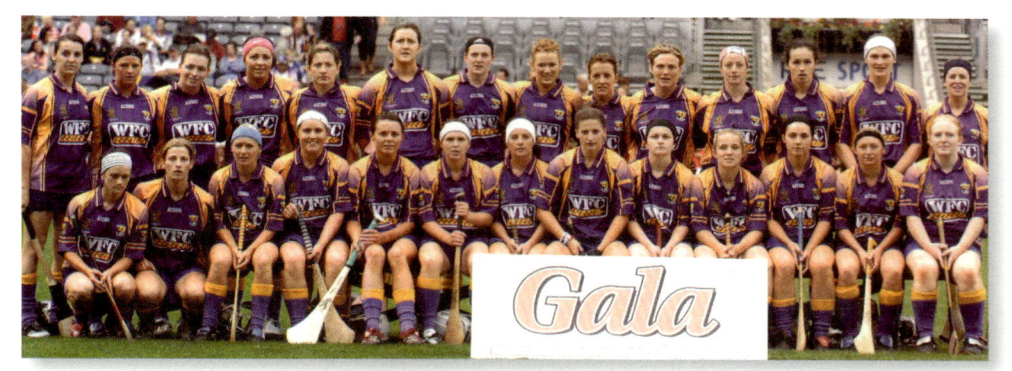

Wexford – 2007 All-Ireland Senior Champions. Back: Síona Nolan, Karen Atkinson, Ursula Jacob, Una Leacy, Deirdre Codd, Catherine O'Loughlin, Caroline Murphy, Louise Codd, Kate Kelly, Michelle Hearne, Rose-Marie Breen, Bróna Furlong, Áine Codd and Avis Nolan. Front: Stacey Redmond, Bridget Curran, Bernie Holohan, Colleen Atkinson, Mary Leacy (Capt), Michelle O'Leary, Claire O'Connor, Mags D'Arcy, Noeleen Lambert, Katrina Parrock, Aoife O'Connor, Lenny Holohan and Helena Jacob.

The All-Ireland senior championship commenced in 1932. In 76 years of competition, no mother and daughter had won All-Ireland senior medals. Wexford's victory put three pairs into that category. Margaret O'Leary (1968, 1969 and 1975) is the mother of Mary and Una Leacy, Kit Kehoe (1965, 1966 and 1975) is the mother of Áine Codd and Peggie Doyle (1969) is the mother Kate Kelly.

2007 All-Ireland Senior B Championship

Cork's pride was hurt when Wexford relieved them of the All-Ireland Senior A Championship title. Six days later, the counties clashed again in the semi-final of the senior B championship at Templemore. A very determined Cork side took the field and immediately got down to business. Four points ahead at the break, Cork stayed in front for the duration of the match although the issue was in the balance up to the final whistle when the score stood at Cork 1–8, Wexford 1–6.

Limerick were well on top over Galway in the second semi-final at the Gaelic Grounds. A fine goal by Mairéad Kelly and six points by Eileen O'Brien set Limerick on the road to the final. The Limerick defence coped efficiently with what the Galway attack had to offer. The final score was 1–10 to 0–4 in Limerick's favour.

Limerick had re-established themselves as a force to be reckoned with since All-Star hurler Ciarán Carey took over the coaching of the side. He improved every facet of their game. They faced Cork with confidence in the final at the Gaelic Grounds. Cork looked to be on target to retain their title with a goal in each half, but a storming finish by Limerick, including a goal from Aoifa

Sheehan, from a 21-metre free, caught Cork on the line, Limerick 1–10 Cork 2–7.

The sides renewed acquaintance on the following Sunday at Páirc Uí Rínn. This time there was no disputing which was the better side. The Limerick forward-line fired whereas the Cork attack failed to ignite. Seeing the winning post ahead, Limerick pressed ahead and claimed the prize. The final score was Limerick 2–9, Cork 0–6.

Limerick team: Síle Moynihan, Aideen McNamara, Rose Collins, Janet Garvey, Grace McNamara, Aoifa Sheehan (captain), Claire Mulcahy, Vera Sheehan, Deirdre Fitzpatrick, Eileen O'Brien (1–4), Moira Dooley, Niamh Mulcahy (0–2), Dympna O'Brien, Meadhbh Nash (0–1), Orla Curtin (1–1). Sub used: Marie Keating (0–1).

Cork team: Gillian Harrington, Deirdre Hayes, Noreen Mulcahy, Lucy Hawkes, Lynda O'Connell (captain), Regina Curtin, Tina Roche, Lynda Dorgan, Aisling Thompson, Eimear O'Sullivan (0–5), Marie Corkery, Marian Jagoe, Deirdre Twomey (0–1), Maria Watson and Rachel Myers. Subs used: Michelle Browne, Denise Cronin, Kathleen O'Brien and Ann Marie Fleming.

2007 All-Ireland Junior Championship

Clare started at a blistering pace against Waterford in the semi-final at Templemore and laid the foundations for victory in the opening 20 minutes. Waterford, who had won the National Junior League, struggled to get into the game. Clare's commitment on the day secured a place in the final by 2–14 to 1–6.

Neighbours, Derry and Antrim, met in the second semi-final. Derry's superior skill and sharpness, particularly around the goal, allowed them to pull away from their opponents. Their place in the All-Ireland final was secured well before the final whistle. Derry won by the comfortable margin of 5–19 to 2–6.

Much to the delight of the finalists, the All-Ireland junior final returned to Croke Park, where there was an emotional finish to the game when the Derry girls realised their dream and were ecstatic. For Clare, who suffered their third final defeat since 2003, it was sheer heartbreak and desolation. Six minutes into injury-time, the score stood at 2–12 apiece. Clare pressed for the winner and Claire Commane responded with two points. It looked good for the Banner County. The referee gave a throw-in on the Clare 21-metre line. The ball broke to the unmarked Aisling Diamond who accepted the gift and planted it in the Clare net. Time was up and the cup was in Derry hands. The appreciative crowd applauded great camogie from both sides. The successful Derry side was coached and managed by husband and wife, Pádraig and Susan Ó Mianáin.

Derry team: Claire O'Kane, Catherine Pickering, Helena Kelly, Ciara Cushnahan, Kate Laverty, Claire Doherty (captain),

Marian McStay, President of Armagh Camogie Board seen with deputy Lord Mayor, Cllr. Thomas O'Hanlon at 2007 Annual Congress in Armagh.

A Game of Our Own

Jane Carey, Gráinne McGoldrick (1-3), Bríd Convery, Katie McAuley, Aisling Diamond (1-3), Edelle Henry, Sinéad Cassidy (0-3), Paula McAtamney (0-3) and Aileen Laverty (1-0). Sub used: Maeve McGoldrick.

Clare team: Denise Lynch, Helen McMahon, Deirdre Corcoran, Amy Colleran, Kathy Hally, Deirdre Murphy (captain) (1-0), Aimee McInerney, Kate Lynch, Jane Scanlon, Carina Roseingrave (0-2), Catherine O'Loughlin, Aoife Ryan (0-2), Claire Commane (1-6), Sharon McMahon (0-3) and Sharon O'Loughlin. Subs used: Fiona Lafferty (0-1), Stephanie Maloney and Áine O'Brien.

Sharon O'Loughlin is a sister of Ger 'Sparrow' O'Loughlin who won All-Ireland senior hurling medals with Clare in 1995 and 1997.

2007 All-Ireland Minor A Championship

The efficiency of the Cork defence kept their chances of advancing to the minor A final alive against Tipperary at the Gaelic Grounds. The hard-working Maria Walsh, Leah Weste and Áine Moynihan held firm against the best efforts of Tipperary. Meanwhile, the

Ger Dullea (St. Mary's, Nenagh) and Ārd Stiúrthóir, Sheila Wallace seen at the 2007 G.A.A. President's Awards function.

Cork forwards squandered several good chances or were foiled by the excellent goalkeeping of Kristine Kenneally. Cork did enough to progress by 1-10 to 1-5.

Antrim, winners of the minor B championship, entered the minor A competition at the quarter-final stage where they accounted for Clare. They came up against the reigning champions, Kilkenny, in the semi-final, but found the goal-scoring Cats a step too far.

Cork had no answer to Kilkenny in the final at Clonmel. They lacked the scoring ability and killer instinct of their opponents. Kilkenny's Marie Dargan and Michelle Quilty were way above what the Cork forward line had to offer. They registered 3-7 between them. The Cork forwards found it very difficult to advance beyond the highly efficient Kilkenny half-back line of Leann Fennelly, Colette Dormer and Kate McDonald. Kilkenny were impressive winners by 3-12 to 0-7.

Kilkenny team: Emma Staunton, Mariga Nolan, Ann-Marie Walsh, Paula Butler, Leann Fennelly, Colette Dormer, Kate McDonald (0-1), Maria Murphy, Lucinda Gahan, Sinéad Long, Katie Power (0-3), Catherine Walsh (1-0) Noreen O'Keeffe (0-1), Marie Dargan (0-4) and Michelle Quilty (2-3). Subs used: Eilish

Cantwell, Georgina Culleton and Aisling Dunphy.

Cork team: Denise Leahy, Leah Weste, Áine Moynihan, Christine O'Neill, Carolyn Motherway, Maria Walsh, Róisín de Faoite, Bríd Twomey, Aisling Thompson (0–2), Kathleen O'Brien, Niamh Dilworth (0–2), Deirdre Twomey (0–2), Erin Corkery, Denise Cronin and Sinéad O'Callaghan. Subs used: Juanita Brennan, Sharon Whelton, Lydia Cunningham and Siobhán Gleeson.

Leann Fennelly is a daughter of Liam Fennelly who captained Kilkenny to All-Ireland hurling glory.

2007 All-Ireland Minor B Championship

The semi-finals of the minor B championship were non-events. Down and Antrim demolished Roscommon and Waterford respectively (10–25 to 0–3 and 5–27 to 0–2) to raise more questions about the grading than anything else.

A power-packed opening half by Antrim in the final against Down at Páirc Esler (Newry) yielded 3–12. Three second-half goals for the home side were not sufficient to reverse the damage done. Down depended far too much on Sara Louise Carr, daughter of All-Ireland footballer, Ross Carr, who provided the only threat to Antrim. Shannon Graham, Emma Connolly and Roisín O'Boyle as well as the entire forward division performed very well for Antrim to leave the final score 3–18 to 5–3 in their favour.

Antrim team: Shaunie McAuley, Caitríona Hannon, Róisín O'Boyle, Brianna McDonnell (captain), Sinéad Laverty, Emma Connolly, Sarah McNicholl, Claire Laverty, Shannon Graham (0–3), Joanne Campbell (0–2), Michaela Convery (0–2), Racquel McCarry (2–4), Orla McCall (0–2), Louise McAleese (0–4) and Cathy Carey (1–1).

Down team: Jordan Hynds, Laura Brennan, Suzelle Johnston, Stephanie O'Hare, Paula Gribben, Carol-Ann Sloan, Joanne Fitzpatrick, Karen Tinnelly (captain) (0–1), Jenny Fowler, Nicola Braniff, Lisa McPolin (1–0), Lisa Hughes (0–1), Sabrina McCullogh, Sara Louise Carr (3–1) and Nicola O'Hagan. Subs used: Niamh Mulhern, Amy McCarthy (1-0) and Megan O'Reilly.

2007 All-Ireland Under-16 A Championship

Cork did not have it all their own way in the semi-final against Dublin at Nenagh. At times, they seemed to be headed for victory, only to be hauled back again by an energetic Dublin side. Cork were in front, however, when it mattered most and advanced by 1–13 to 1–8.

At the same venue, Kilkenny had a close call from Clare in the second semi-final. The Clare girls set the pace of the game and were six points clear after 25 minutes. Kilkenny cut the margin to a point by half-time and had the better of the exchanges from there on and won by 2–12 to 1–10.

Kilkenny gave a master class in the final against Cork at Nenagh on August 5th. Cork were shell-shocked by the speed, combination and scoring ability of the Noresiders. All over the field, Cork were outplayed by a Kilkenny side that played above their grade.

Cork could only manage two points from play over the hour as a tight-marking Kilkenny defence put up the shutters. Kilkenny controlled midfield but it was in attack that they produced something really special. All their forwards had the ability to create and finish chances at pace. Cork had no answer to this brand of play. The gulf between the teams on the day made each and every one of the Kilkenny players look star quality. The final score of Kilkenny 8–11, Cork 0–6 says it all.

Kilkenny team: Emma Staunton, Caoimhe Shiels, Kate McDonald (captain), Alison Walsh, Niamh Kelly, Edel Frisby, Nicola Butler, Ruth Jones, Aisling Dunphy (0–1), Denise Gaule (0–4), Áine Curran (0–2), Niamh Byrne, Michelle Brennan (3–2), Anna Farrell (2–2) and Michelle Farrell (3–0). Sub used: Laura Wall.

Cork team: Mary Ellen O'Donovan, Moira O'Donovan, Rebecca Finn, Pamela Mackey, Orlaith O'Mahony, Mary Ann Hawkes, Emma Kingston, Jennifer Lynch, Catríona Collins (0–3), Joanne Casey, Julia White (0–1), Katrina Mackey, Denise Luby (0–1), Sinéad O'Neill (0–1) and Aileen O'Donovan. Subs used: Michelle Healy, Claire Keohane, Catherine O'Brien (captain), Aoife McCarthy and Mariah Reidy.

2007 All-Ireland Under-16 B Championship

Derry had a facile win over Kildare in the semi-final. Kildare found themselves out of their depth against a free-flowing Derry side that took scores without difficulty and won by 7–13 to 1–5.

The second semi-final produced a better contest with Waterford ending four points ahead, 4–9 to 1–14, against Down.

The decider between Derry and Waterford ended in draw, 2–7 to 3–4, at St Peregrine's, Blakestown. Patricia Jackman scored the goals and the equalising point for Waterford. Derry captured the title in the replay at the same venue. The sides were level 1–4 to 2–1 following an entertaining opening half. Derry were the stronger side in the second-half and goals from Emma Mullally and Siobhán McKeague ensured their win by 3–14 to 2–2.

Derry team: Joni McEldowney, Oonagh Devlin, Gráinne O'Kane, Mary Brigid McGilligan, Áine Kelly (captain), Keelin Bradley, Mary Jo McCullagh, Michelle Rodgers (0–2), Siobhán McKeague (1–2), Eilis Ní Chaiside (0–1), Eimear Mullan (0–2), Rachel Bradley, Danielle McCrystal (0–2), Rachel Kelly (0–1) and Emma Mullally (2–4).

Waterford team: Tracy Kiely, Jenny McCarthy, Jackie Forbes, Caoimhe Fitzgerald, Rachel Murphy, Shauna Kiernan, Mary Claire Dunphy, Jessica Gleeson, Marie Russell, Michelle Tobin, Patricia Jackman, Sarah Fenton, Jessica Johnston, Sarah Smith, Rachel Whelan.

2007 All-Ireland Club Senior Championship

Cashel scored 1–7 against Rossa (Belfast) in a devastating ten-minute spell early in the first-half of the semi-final at Páirc Esler. The Tipperary girls continued to push ahead and had the match won by half-time when they led by 2–10 to 1–3. Rossa never looked capable of catching Cashel. Claire Grogan with 2–5 was scorer-in-chief for Cashel while Jane Adams (1–2) and Mairéad Rooney (1–0) were on target for Rossa. The score stood at Cashel 2–13, Rossa 2–3 when play finished.

St Lachtain's (Freshford) saw their three-year reign as All-Ireland club champions come to an abrupt end at Ballinasloe when Athenry claimed a final spot with five points to spare. Teenager Jessica Gill made a vital contribution of 2–6. A late brace of goals by Anne Dalton cut the deficit but the final whistle sounded before St Lachtain's could save the match.

Fielding eight All-Ireland senior medal-holders, including Kilkenny sharp-shooter Sinéad Millea, Cashel proved much too good for a young and inexperienced Athenry side. They showed how much they had matured since the one-point defeat in their first final in 2001. Playing with power, pace and skill, they racked up a huge total to make victory seem easy at Cashel 1–18, Athenry 0–9.

Every member of the Cashel side played her part in bringing the Bill Carroll Cup back to Tipperary after an absence of 40 years. Una O'Dwyer moved to centre-back where she held Therese Maher scoreless. Philly Fogarty and Jill Horan did great work in midfield. Up front Claire Grogan, Emily Hayden and Cora Hennessy figured prominently. Athenry struggled throughout the field and had to concede to a better team. In 1977, Midge Poniard was in midfield when Athenry won the All-Ireland club title. On this occasion, she was directing operations from the sideline while her daughter, Regina Glynn, played at number five.

Cashel team: Helen Breen, Sarah Morrissey, Noelette O'Dwyer, Julie McGrath, Paula Bulfin, Una O'Dwyer, Sinéad Millea (captain), Philly Fogarty, Jill Horan, Linda Grogan, Mairéad Morrissey, Cora Hennessy, Alison Lonergan, Emily Hayden and Claire Grogan. Subs used: Libby Twomey, Deirdre Ryan and Kaiffee Moloney.

Athenry team: Stephanie Gannon, Katherine Glynn, Alice Poniard, Darelle Coen, Regina Glynn, Krystel Ruddy, Emma Costello, Sarah Donohue, Laura Linnane, Jessica Gill, Therese Maher, Sharon Quirke, Mary Keogh, Nicola Nally and Noreen Ruddy. Subs used: Deirdre Ward and Katie O'Dwyer.

Cashel Club: Camogie was revived in Cashel in the early seventies in the Presentation Convent by Willie Prendergast, Sr Mary Brennan and Sr Maureen McGrath. The school enjoyed successful years, winning Munster and All-Ireland colleges' titles. This sparked off fresh interest in the Cashel club. Six Tipperary titles in-a-row were won in the late eighties and early nineties. Julia O'Dwyer, Anne Moloney and Geraldine Ryan Meagher worked hard over the years to build up the club and T.J. Connolly coached the present team.

2007 All-Ireland Club Junior Championship

Keady (Armagh) defeated Clare champions, Kilnamona, 5–6 to 3–7 while The Harps (Laois) overcame Athleague (Roscommon) 3–19 to 1–3 in the semi-finals.

The Harps and Keady were level with four minutes to go in the final at Stabannon, Co. Louth. The outcome hung in the balance until the final whistle as both sides vied for scores. The minutes went by without yielding a score to either side. Well into injury time, Áine Mahony made the vital connection and the ball sailed over the bar for the winner.

Keady made the early running in this game and opened up a

six-point lead. Harps stormed back to take a slight lead into the break. It was tit-for-tat in the second-half with players working very hard to earn scores. Play came to an end with the score at The Harps 2–8, Keady 2–7.

The Harps team: Maeve Brophy, Elaine Cuddy, Denise Quigley, Patricia Dunphy, Aoife Donohue, Caitríona Phelan, Laura Mahony, Louise Mahony, Joanne Prior, Theresa Bennett, Erinne Dunne, Claire Walsh, Áine Mahony, Elaine Mahony and Angela Hanlon. Sub used: Linda Byrne.

Keady team: Laura Comiskey, Brenda McQuade, Eileen McGrory, Michelle Murray, Colleen Comiskey, Katrina Kinsella, Ciara Keenan, Colleen Conway, Mairéad Doyle, Claire Kinsella, Áine O'Farrell, Noeleen McKenna, Michelle Murphy, Colette McKeever and Patricia McCabe. Sub used: Helena Murray.

2007 Gael-Linn Senior Cup

Ulster came through a tough semi-final against Munster by 4–9 to 2–10 at Russell Park while Leinster received a walkover from Connacht. Ulster ended a 40-year wait for their second Gael-Linn senior title. Jane Adams, Fionnuala Carr, Moya Maginn, Gráinne McGoldrick and Sinéad Cassidy were in excellent form as they deposed the holders, Leinster, by 2–12 to 3–8.

Ulster team: Claire O'Kane (Derry), Ciara McGovern (Down), Moya Maginn (Down), Kate Laverty (Derry), Karen McMullan (Down), Claire Doherty (captain) (Derry), Maureen Stewart (Antrim), Gráinne McGoldrick (Derry), Fionnuala Carr (Down), Karen Gribben (Down), Jane Adams (Antrim), Bríd Convery (Derry), Sheila Cassidy (Derry), Katie McAuley (Derry) and Aisling Diamond (Derry).

Leinster team: Eimear Butler (Dublin), Elaine Aylward (Kilkenny), Catherine O'Loughlin (Wexford), Aoife O'Connor (Wexford), Eimear Brannigan (captain) (Dublin), Aoife Cullen (Dublin), Mary Leacy (Wexford), Bróna Furlong (Wexford), Rose-Marie Breen (Wexford), Kate Kelly (Wexford), Louise O'Hara (Dublin), Michelle O'Leary (Wexford), Una Leacy (Wexford), Katie Power (Kilkenny) and Aoife Neary (Kilkenny).

2007 Gael-Linn Junior Trophy

Munster had a runaway victory over Ulster in the semi-final by 5–23 to 1–7 but went under to Leinster by 3–16 to 0–11 in the final.

Leinster team: Eimear Moynan (Laois), Eimear O'Connor (Wexford), Pauline Comerford (Kilkenny), Orla Banbury (captain) (Kildare), Sharon Moylan (Laois), Máire Griffith (Carlow), Liz Shaw (Westmeath), Jacinta Goonery (Westmeath), Elizabeth Lynch (Meath), Frances Lynch (Meath), Aileen Donnelly (Meath), Elaine Mahony (Laois), Catríona Phelan (Laois) and Louise Mahony (Laois).

Munster team: Aisling O'Brien (Waterford), Denise Lynch (Clare), Mary Ann Hawkes (Cork), Sally Ann O'Grady (Clare), Deirdre Murphy (Clare), Fiona Lafferty (Clare), Aisling Kelly (Waterford), Charlotte Raher (Waterford), Bríd Twomey (captain) (Cork), Deirdre Corcoran (Clare), Jane Scanlon (Clare), Kate Lynch (Clare), Sharon McMahon (Clare), Gráinne Kenneally (Waterford) and Áine Lyng (Waterford).

2007 Nancy Murray Cup

The final of the Nancy Murray Cup between Laois and Meath at Leixlip was an extraordinary affair. Meath played some great camogie to lead by 1–9 to 0–3 at the break. From a position of total dominance in the first-half, Meath conceded an unanswered 1–12 and allowed Laois to dictate the trend of the game to the finish. The final score was Laois 1–15, Meath 1–9.

Laois team: Laura Dunne, Denise Quigley, Eimear Moynan, Caitríona Downey, Laura Mahony, Caitríona Phelan, Brigie Cuddy, Louise Mahony, Lynn O'Callaghan, Elaine Mahony, Amy O'Callaghan, Eimear Delaney, Sharon Moylan, Teresa Bennett and Elaine Cuddy.

Meath team: Emily Mangan, Edel Guy, Sharon Raleigh, Margarita Stephens, Frances Lynch, Aileen Donnelly, Louise Donoghue, Laura Flynn, Katie Mullen, Elizabeth Lynch, Dearbhla O'Carroll, Stephanie Horan, Christine O'Brien, Ann Marie Dennehy and Jane Dolan.

2007 Máire Ní Chinnéide Cup

Carlow claimed their first national title when they defeated Monaghan in the final at Toureen, Co. Mayo, by 0–10 to 1–3 on September 1st. Valerie Crean was the star of the Carlow team with an accurate display of point-taking that yielded nine points. Isobel Kiernan and Mary Coady were prominent throughout.

Camogie-Shinty

Scotland and Ireland met in the fourth Camogie-Shinty Tournament at Fort William, Scotland, on October 14th. Drawn from Louth, Monaghan, Mayo, Westmeath, Carlow and Donegal together with a representative from the Brussels Club, Ireland narrowly failed to regain the title.

Irish team: Maeve Murphy (Mayo), Yvonne Byrne (Mayo), Sinéad Muldoon (Mayo), Maria Coyne (Mayo), Eleanor McQuaid (captain) (Monaghan), Marie Greenan (Monaghan), Mairéad McCarron (Monaghan), Helen Hughes (Monaghan), Sandra Greville (Westmeath), Pamela Greville (Westmeath), Ann Marie Kane (Louth), Julianne Finnegan (Louth), Patricia Marmion (Louth), Ciara Cullen (Donegal), Ciara McMenamin (Donegal), Aisling Newton (Donegal), Valerie Crean (Carlow), Mary Coady (Carlow), Margaret Coady (Carlow) and Margaret Francois (Brussels).

2007 All-Stars

All-Ireland champions, Wexford, scooped five of the prestigious All-Star awards at the CityWest Hotel on November 10th. Mary and Una Leacy became the first sisters to be honoured with All-Star awards. Derry and Limerick were on the list for the first time with Aisling Diamond and Rose Collins getting the nod. The Young Player of the Year award went to Niamh Mulcahy (Limerick) and Stellah Sinnott (Wexford) was named Manager of the Year. The inaugural Síghle Nic an Ultaigh Award was given to Rose Malone (Munster). International rugby player, Gordon D'Arcy, was the special guest on the night.

A Game of Our Own

All-Stars 2007: Mags D'Arcy (Wexford), Eimear Brannigan (Dublin), Catherine O'Loughlin (Wexford), Rose Collins (Limerick), Rena Buckley (Cork), Mary Leacy (Wexford), Caitríona Foley (Cork), Gemma O'Connor (Cork), Philly Fogarty (Tipperary), Veronica Curtin (Galway), Aisling Diamond (Derry), Jenny O'Leary (Cork), Kate Kelly (Wexford), Claire Grogan (Tipperary) and Una Leacy (Wexford).

All-Ireland junior captains, Moira Caldwell (Down), Kathleen Henry (Derry), Vera Feely (Dublin), Sheila Wallace (Dublin), Nono McHugh (Galway), Nancy O'Driscoll (Cork) and Margaret O'Toole (Clare) being introduction to the crowd at the 2008 All-Ireland finals at Croke Park.

Joan O'Flynn Voted President Elect

A native of Ladysbridge, Co. Cork, Joan O'Flynn became the first President-Elect of the Camogie Association at Congress 2008 in Athlone. She took a seat at Central Council to familiarise herself with the workings of the Association in preparation for stepping up to the premier job.

Strategic Review

A sports management firm was commissioned to carry out a strategic review of the structure, image and organisation of camogie. The purpose of the exercise was to: review the leadership and administrative structure; identify the role of the provincial councils; assess communication and information systems; and evaluate the Association's marketing and branding.

The findings of the review highlighted the sound structure and many positive developments which had been achieved by the Association. The positives far outweighed the negatives and formed the focus of propelling the Association into the future. Some areas required attention to meet the challenges presented by a sport which had reached the milestone of more than 100,000 members and was in transition from a volunteer-driven organisation to one that combines volunteers and full-time staff. The functions and workload were continually growing. New technology needed to be embraced, modern management systems adopted, provincial councils revitalised, future leaders earmarked and trained and the image and marketing improved.

Media Awards

To give recognition to the excellent work being done to promote Camogie and keep it in the public eye, media awards were inaugurated. RTÉ sponsored the Mick Dunne Memorial Awards. A native

Growing Staff

of Clonaslee, Co. Laois, Mick Dunne was a Gaelic Games journalist and broadcaster. Four awards bear his name as a tribute to his contribution towards promoting camogie. The winners of both 2006 and 2007 awards were honoured at a function in Croke Park on May 13th.

	2006	2007
PRO of the Year:	Séamus Massey, Dublin	Mary Burke, Meath
Broadcaster of the Year:	RTÉ	RTÉ
Photo of the Year:	Michael Harpur, Wexford	Richie Lyng, Waterford
Published article:	'Fantastic Final' Antrim	Meath
Camogie Association Media Awards:		
Best match programme:	Wexford Co. Final	Wexford Co. Final
Best provincial newspaper:	The People, Wexford	The People, Wexford
Best Local Radio	Seven FM Ballymena	South East Radio
Gradam Speisialta,	Raidió na Gaeltachta	Alan Aherne for Camogie Queens

Sheila Wallace Retires

In 22 years of dedicated service as Ard Runaí and later Ard Stiúrthóir, Sheila Wallace saw the Camogie Association develop and expand under her direction. Year by year, her workload increased as membership grew and new competitions and events were added to the camogie calendar. For most of her time, she operated single-handedly. Eventually, she got help of a personal assistant in the person of Phil Clarke. Development plans, funding applications, congress papers, schedules for training programmes, fixture lists and correspondence from the four corners of the country crossed her desk and were dealt with in a very capable way. No matter how busy she was, she received each caller with a friendly greeting and an offer of help. The large attendance at her farewell function demonstrated the high esteem in which she was held by camogie people all over the country and beyond.

Sheila Wallace, retired.

2008 All-Ireland Senior Championship

Jessica Gill scored a stunning goal for Galway in injury-time of the semi-final at Nowlan Park to strip Wexford of their All-Ireland crown. Wexford came from four points behind to draw level and seemed to have done enough to earn a replay at least. Galway made the early running against a Wexford team that failed to reach their own high standards of 2007 and conceded by 1–13 to 1–10.

A Game of Our Own

Cork trailed by two points at the interval of the second semi-final but blew Tipperary away with a power-packed display on the resumption. Gemma O'Connor led the Cork charge and was ably supported by Rachel Moloney, Briege Corkery and Orla Cotter. Tipperary played encouragingly in the first half but were unable to contain Cork when they upped the pace. Cork advanced to the final by 3–14 to 0–10.

Two goals by Síle Burns and three marvellous saves by Aoife Murray were key factors in Cork's win over Galway in the final at Croke Park on September 14th. Cork made a slow start to the game and allowed Galway to race into a four-point lead.

Síle Burns came to Cork's rescue with a brace of goals. Galway played skilful and, at times, brilliant camogie but the fact that they only managed one score from play underlined their problem. However, the very efficient Cork defence must take considerable credit for their containment.

Cork stood up and were counted in every line of the field. The side was well managed by Denise Cronin, who captained Cork to All-Ireland success in 1995, and was prepared by Jim McCarthy. The tireless Briege Corkery, Aoife Murray, Joanne O'Callaghan, Caitríona Foley, Gemma O'Connor, Síle Burns and Rachel Moloney returned Cork camogie to the top rung of the ladder. The final score was Cork 2–10 to Galway 1–8.

Cork team: Aoife Murray, Lynda O'Connell, Caitríona Foley, Joanne O'Callaghan, Gemma O'Connor, Mary O'Connor, Sarah Hayes, Orla Cotter (0–1), Briege Corkery (0–1), Amanda O'Regan, Una O'Donoghue, Eimear O'Sullivan (0–1), Síle Burns (2–0), Rachel Moloney (0–7) and Elaine O'Riordan. Subs used: Emer O'Farrell, Rena Buckley and Linda Dorgan.

Galway team: Susan Earner, Sandra Tannian, Ailbhe Kelly, Therese Manton, Ann-Marie Hayes, Sinéad Cahalan, Niamh Kilkenny, Áine Hillary (1–0), Sarah Noone, Molly Dunne, Therese Maher, Veronica Curtin, Orla Kilkenny, Jessica Gill (0–8) and Brenda Kerins. Subs used: Lourda Kavanagh, Catríona Cormican and Deirdre Burke.

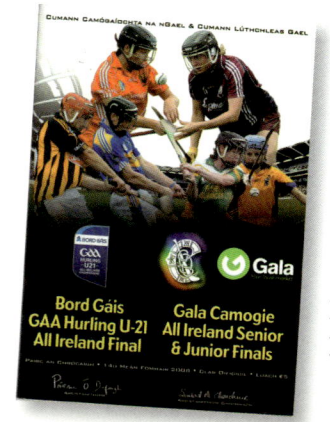

2008: Ailbhe Kelly, Galway, is tackled by Sile Burns, Cork in the All-Ireland Senior Championship Final. *Picture: Ray McManus / SPORTSFILE*

2008 All-Ireland Senior B Championship

Cork came from behind to oust Derry in the semi-final at Mullingar. Charlotte Kearney and Marian Jagoe contributed goals to cancel Katie McAuley's fine effort. Four points separated the sides at the finish, Cork 2-8, Derry 2-4.

Kilkenny fought back from a slow start to force a draw with Galway in the second semi-final at Thurles. Kilkenny and Galway met for the third time in the competition in the replay at Templemore. Although held scoreless for the opening 18 minutes, Kilkenny battled their way back into contention and edged in front when it mattered most to win by 2-5 to 0-9.

Statistics showed that there was little between the finalists, Kilkenny and Cork. On the way to the final at Nenagh, Kilkenny scored 14 goals and 63 points whereas opponents, Cork, put 13 goals and 70 points on the scoreboard. Teams that could build up such impressive totals were bound to produce a gripping game when they were face to face. That is how it turned out.

Kilkenny caught Cork on the hop by placing their classy centre-back, Colette Dormer, at full-forward. The free-scoring Kilkenny attack peppered the Cork goal with shots. The Cork defence was unable to cope with the onslaught that yielded 4-5 by half-time. The Cork attack saw little of the ball and relied too much on the accuracy of Michelle Browne from frees. Cork returned to the field with a mountain to climb but they knuckled down to the task and showed a marked improvement. With seven minutes remaining, Cork drew level with Kilkenny. Chances were missed by both sides before Colette Dormer got her stick to the ball to

Cork – 2008 All-Ireland Senior Champions. Back: Linda Dorgan, Rena Buckley, Aoife Murray, Julia White, Margaret O'Herlihy, Síle Burns, Lynda O'Connell, Jenny Duffy, Emer O'Farrell, Gemma O'Connor, Sarah Hayes, Amanda O'Regan, Lucy Hawkes, Emer White, Orla Cotter and Rosarii Holland. **Front:** Marion Murphy, Michelle Browne, Denise Cronin, Mary O'Connor, Joanne O'Callaghan, Briege Corkery, Caitríona Foley (Capt), Una O'Donoghue, Elaine O'Riordan, Emer O'Sullivan, Rachel Moloney and Regina Curtin.. *Picture: Ray McManus / SPORTSFILE*

Deirdre Burke, Galway, shows her disappointment after the game. *Picture: Pat Murphy / SPORTSFILE*

deflect it to the Cork net for the winner. The score stood at Kilkenny 5-5 Cork 1-14 at the final whistle.

Kilkenny team: Ann Marie Lennon, Lisa Phelan, Elaine O'Shea, Áine Fahy, Leann Fennelly, Sinéad Long, Ann Marie Phelan (0-1), Jenny Reddy, Lucinda Gahan (1-0), Claire Ryan, Denise Gaule (1-1), Michelle Farrell, Michelle Brennan, Colette Dormer (1-0) and Claire Aylward (2-3). Subs used: Laura Kavanagh, Sinéad Kelly and Hannah Maher.

Cork team: Gillian Harrington, Ann Marie Fleming, Siobhán Gleeson, Christine O'Neill, Maria Walsh, Lucy Hawkes, Regina Curtin, Jennifer Lynch, Marie Corkery (captain), Julia White (0-1), Niamh Dilworth (1-1), Maria Watson (0-1), Charlotte Kearney (0-1), Michelle Browne (0-10) and Marian Jagoe. Subs used: Katrina Mackey, Leah Weste and Aisling Thompson.

Sheila Wallace photographed at her retirement function with ten camogie presidents. Back: Belle O'Loughlin, Mary Fennelly, Lil O'Neill, Mary Moran, Miriam O'Callaghan and Phyllis Breslin. Front: Mary Lynch, Lily Spence, Sheila Wallace, Liz Howard and Brídín Uí Mhaolagáin.

2008 All-Ireland Junior Championship

A powerful second-half performance by Offaly booked a place in the final when they ran out clear winners over Waterford at Cashel. The teams had been all square at half-time but Offaly increased their work-rate and the pace of the game on the resumption. Michaela Morkam (0-6) and Natalie McCabe (1-2) led the charge to victory for the Faithful County and they pressed ahead to win by 1-14 to 0-3.

Rookies Laois gave Clare a good fright in the second semi-final at Banagher. All-Ireland finalists in 2007, Clare had to fight every inch of the way to shake off the attentions of a gallant Laois side by 1-9 to 1-8.

Joachim Kelly, winner of All-Ireland senior hurling medals in 1981 and 1985, prepared Offaly and took them to the final at Croke Park. There they met Clare who had suffered more than their share of heartbreak since 2003. Brothers Eoghan and Colm Hanley instilled a steely determination in the Clare players. This time, there was no room for error. But it was so close. Offaly led by 1-7 to 1-3 at the break. They weathered something of a storm by Clare and looked to be on course to record a historic victory. Amid a welter of excitement, they were caught at the death when Shonagh Enright hand passed the ball to the net. Offaly played great camogie and were desperately unlucky to lose by 2-8 to 1-10. Sheila O'Sullivan, Michaela Morkan, Linda Sullivan and Tina Hannon were top class. Deirdre Murphy was heroic for Clare.

Not far behind were Kate Lynch, Denise Lynch, Fiona Lafferty and Carina Roseingrave.

Clare team: Denise Lynch, Cathy Hally, Siobhán Lafferty, Aimee McInerney, Kate Lynch, Dee Corcoran, Jean Scanlon, Chloe Morey, Deirdre Murphy (captain), Carina Roseingrave (1–1), Sharon McMahon (0–1), Laura Linnane (0–4), Shonagh Enright (1–1), Claire McMahon and Claire Commane (0–1). Subs used: Fiona Lafferty and Shonagh Enright.

Offaly team: Audrey Kennedy, Aoife Kelly, Elaine Dermody, Karen Brady, Sheila O'Sullivan, Michaela Morkan (0–2), Linda Sullivan, Marion Crean (captain), Karen Nugent, Siobhán Flannery (0–2), Tina Hannon (0–4), Michelle Davis, Fiona Stephens (0–1), Natalie McCabe and Arlene Watkins (1–1). Subs used: Lorraine Keena, Jean Brady and Aoife Corrigan.

2008 All-Ireland Minor A (Under-18) Championship

A score of 3–15 would be more than adequate to win most camogie matches but it was not enough to enable Cork defeat Kilkenny in the semi-final at the Gaelic Grounds. In a rip-roaring contest, both teams played brilliant camogie in awful weather conditions. Great defending and fantastic scores delighted the attendance. Kilkenny shaded the verdict by 5–10 to 3–15.

A hat-trick of goals from the lethal Carina Roseingrave secured a place in the final for Clare at the expense of Tipperary at the Gaelic Grounds. Shauna Enright added 11 points to put the outcome beyond Tipperary's reach. Clare 4–15, Tipperary 0–9 was the final score.

Clare failed to reach the heights that they achieved in previous matches when they met Kilkenny in the final at Athy. This Clare team had improved considerably under the guidance of former Clare hurling goalkeeper, Davy Fitzgerald, but they found the experienced champions a bridge too far. Kilkenny married tight defensive work with skilful and accurate attacking play to demonstrate why they were kingpins of underage camogie. Edwina Keane, Anna and Shelly Farrell, Aisling Dunphy and Claire Phelan turned in five-star performances for Kilkenny. A Clare side that went down by 3–15 to 1–7 had fine players in Susan Vaughan, Kate Lynch, Carina Roseingrave and Chloe Morey.

Kilkenny team: Emma Staunton, Leann Fennelly, Ann-Marie Walsh, Róisín Byrne, Mariga Nolan, Edwina Keane, Nicola Butler, Aisling Dunphy, Anna Farrell (0–1), Denise Gaule (0–1), Katie Power (0–3), Claire Phelan (1–1), Michelle Farrell (1–2), Marie Dargan (0–1) and Michelle Quilty (1–6). Subs used: Sinéad Long, Ruth Bergin, Ciara Lyng and Georgina Culleton.

Clare team: Susan Vaughan, Sarah Reidy, Kate Lynch, Carol O'Leary, Aiveen O'Shea, Róisín McMahon, Carol Kaiser, Niamh Corry, Chloe Morey, Áine O'Brien, Shonagh Enright (0–4), Stephanie Moloney (0–2), Aoife Griffin, Carina Roseingrave (1–1) and Róisín O'Brien. Subs used: Niamh Martin, Eimear Considine, Mary Clune and Louise Woods.

2008 All-Ireland Minor B (Under-18) Championship

Based on the results of the previous year's competition, the under-18 B teams were divided into two groups. Offaly, Waterford, Laois, Armagh and Down remained in the under-18 B grade and played each other for Corn Aoife. Westmeath, Roscommon, Meath, Carlow, Kildare and Wicklow dropped down to a new under-18 C grade. These counties participated in a one-day blitz that was won by Kildare.

Offaly, winners of Group 1, met Waterford, the top team in Group 2, in the final of the All-Ireland Minor B championship. Offaly led by 2–4 to 1–5 at the close of a low-scoring first half. They upped the pace on the resumption and outscored Waterford by 2–9 to 1–2. Kerry McLeish, Shauna Flynn and Jean Brady netted for the Faithful County. Patricia Jackman and Sarah Fenton replied for Waterford. Joint-captains Michaela Morkan and Alison Dooley lifted Corn Aoife on behalf of a well-deserving Offaly team. The final score was Offaly 4–13, Waterford 2–7.

Offaly team: Claire Beatty, Sandra Walsh, Leanne Scully, Shauna Flaherty, Alison Dooley, Michaela Morkan, Sarah Cleary, Ailsa Hughes, Emma Fogarty, Siobhán Flannery, Serena Keena, Shauna Flynn, Kerry McLeish, Michelle Gleeson and Jean Brady.

Westmeath - All-Ireland U16C Champions. Back: Linda Heffernan, Tammy Commins, Niamh Lynch, Alannah Nash, Chloe Kelly, Louise O'Connor, Sarah Purcell, Grace Mulvanney, Nicola Fagan, Róisín Scally, Orla Lynch, Ellen Taite, and Nadina Grace. **Front:** Eimear Flynn, Sarah Jackson (captain), Aisling Boyhan, Lorna Daly, Debbie Ennis, Emma Kincaid, Saoirse O'Neill, Avril Fagan, Sinéad Connell and Catríona Murtagh.

Waterford team: Tracy Kiely, Deirdre Nugent, Clare Dunne, Caoimhe Fitzgerald, Siobhán Kavanagh, Shauna Kiernan, Mary Claire Dunphy, Marie Russell, Shona Curran (captain), Sarah Fenton, Patricia Jackman, Deirdre Foley, Kate Rockett, Gemma Tobin and Caitríona McGlone.

2008 All-Ireland Under 16A Championship

A fine team effort saw Cork overpower Dublin in the semi-final at Cloughjordan. Playing against a strong breeze, Cork dominated the game and had built up a lead of 2–9 to 0–3 at the break. Dublin found it very difficult to make headway against the Cork defence and had to concede victory by 3–17 to 1–3. Four-in-a-row-chasing Kilkenny had to fight to the finish to get the better of Galway at Cloughjordan. The Galway girls matched their opponents in approach play but their finish let them down on several occasions. Kilkenny ran up 1–15 against 3–8 for Galway.

Kilkenny realised their dream of four successive under-16 A titles when they outscored Cork by 3–7 to 2–5 in the final at Semple Stadium. Bearing in mind that Kilkenny scored eight goals against them in the 2007 final, the Cork selectors deployed seven defenders. The tactic was not a success. Five Cork forwards were unable to compete with six Kilkenny backs. Meanwhile, the free Kilkenny player, Laura Fennelly, had time to place long, accurate clearances to her team's advantage.

Aisling Dunphy was very effective in midfield for Kilkenny. Forwards Michelle Farrell, Ciara Holden, Claire Phelan, Eimear Mulholland and Michelle Maher made significant contributions to Kilkenny's win. The tremendous work put into this group by Kilkenny coaches, Liam Dunne, Stephen Dormer, Brendan Williams and Ted Browne was well rewarded.

Kilkenny team: Laura Walker, Jane Cullen, Ruth Jones, Grace Walsh, Margaret Simpson, Laura Fennelly, Davina Tobin, Eimear Mulhall, Aisling Dunphy, Niamh Byrne, Claire Phelan (0–5), Michelle Maher (1–0), Emma Comerford, Ciara Holden (1–1) and Michelle Farrell (captain) (1–1). Subs used: Maeve Mansfield, Noelle Maher and Yvonne McGrath.

Cork team: Tessa Hawkes, Sarah Harrington, Alison Coughlan, Katie McCarthy, Pamela Mackey (captain) (0–1), Rosie O'Mahony, Katrina Mackey (0–2), Emma Kingston, Miriah Reidy (0–1), Joanne Casey, Aileen O'Donovan (0–1), Kate Harrington (1–0), Finola Neville, Katie Buckley (1–0) and Sinéad O'Halloran. Sub used: Fiona Cotter.

2008 All-Ireland U16B Championship

The format of the All-Ireland Under-16 B Championship was altered to two groups with the winners playing off in the final. Derry emerged from Group 1, which had contained Down, Waterford and Carlow, to contest the final against Offaly at Ashbourne. Offaly surfaced from Group 2, which had contained Laois, Armagh and Meath.

Karen Kielt had a day to remember as Derry captured the Ann Naughton Cup for the third successive time. In a flawless display, Karen scored an incredible 2–13 as Derry ran out easy winners against outclassed Offaly. Gráinne McNicholl, daughter of former Derry star, Sarah Ann Quinn, notched a brace of goals. Derry were superior in all divisions of the fields and proved worthy winners by 6–18 to 0–6.

Derry team: Niamh McQuillan, Grace Kelly, Gráinne O'Kane, Maria Mooney, Danielle McCrystal (captain), Mary Jo McCullagh, Kelly Marie Hegarty, Rachel Kelly, Eilis Cassidy, Karen Kielt, Eimear Mullan, Dania Donnelly, Mary Kelly, Gráinne McNicholl and Teresa McEvoy.

Offaly team: Shauna Carroll, Mary Bergin, Katie Hand, Emily Quinlan, Sinéad Kelly, Róisín Coughlan, Jane McCarthy, Julie Stephens, Debbie Flynn, Orla Murray, Niamh Scully, Mary Nevin, Mary Nevin, Claire Nevin and Laura Dooley.

2008 All-Ireland Club Senior Championship

Ballyboden St Enda's learned a harsh lesson on their visit to Casement Park to meet Rossa in the semi-final of the club championship. It takes an outstanding team to lift the Bill Carroll Cup. On the day, only Rossa were serious contenders. Jane Adams, with a personal tally of 2–11, was the player of the hour and steered her side to a 3–18 to 0–6 win.

Drom & Inch (Co. Tipperary) qualified for their first final by virtue of a narrow and hard-earned win over Athenry at Cloughjordan. Excellent play from Therese Maher and accurate stick work from Jessica Gill saw Athenry 0–7 to 0–4 in front at the interval. Therese Shortt reduced arrears for Drom & Inch. The Tipperary side looked more threatening as the game proceeded. Their tight-marking defence denied space to the Athenry attack. Joanne Ryan struck a long ball into the Athenry danger zone and it was flicked to the net by Siobhán McGrath for the winner. Athenry tasted disappointment for the third year running. The final score was Drom & Inch 1–8, Athenry 0–10.

There was a massive buzz in both camps in the lead up to the final between Rossa and Drom & Inch at Ashbourne. Whatever the outcome, a new name would be engraved on the cup. The game was a personal triumph for Rossa captain, Jane Adams. The newly crowned All-Star scored 2–9 and inspired those around her. Drom & Inch made a great match of the occasion and placed Rossa under constant pressure. Therese Shortt, Mary Looby, Joanne Ryan and Geraldine Kinnane showed up well for the Tipperary side. Seáinín Daykin, Kerrie O'Neill and Bronagh Orchin performed very well for Mickey McCullough's team but Jane Adams was unquestionably the Player of the Match. Rossa were worthy winners by 2–15 to 1–12.

Rossa team: Teresa McGowan, Teresa Adams, Pauline Green, Maureen Quinn, Aisling McCall, Natalie McGuinness, Bronagh Orchin, Colleen Doherty, Seáinín Daykin, Kerrie O'Neill (0–1), Gráinne Connolly (0–2), Orla McCall, Maorisa McGourty (0–2), Jane Adams (capt) (2–9) and Maureen Stewart (0–1).

Drom & Inch team: Rosie Kennedy, Caitríona Kennedy, Niamh Harkin, Patricia McGrath, Sinéad O'Meara, Michelle Shortt, Triona Butler, Therese Shortt (0–7), Norma Harrington, Joanne Ryan (0–3), Mary Looby (1–2), Geraldine Kinnane, Catríona Shortt, Emer Shanahan and Siobhán McGrath.

2008 All-Ireland Club Junior Championship

The Harps (Laois) had a close call from Lavey (Derry), 1–10 to 1–8, while Kilmaley (Clare) sailed past Four Roads (Roscommon), 4–11 to 0–3, in the semi-finals.

The Laois club became the first side to attain a hat-trick of All-Ireland club junior titles when they edged past Kilmaley at Nenagh. Both teams enjoyed a period of supremacy in the opening half before retiring to the dressing room all square. However, Kilmaley regretted squandering two good goal chances from close range. Harps picked off four points over the course of the second-half while Kilmaley, encouraged by a large vocal following, went for goals and were foiled time and again. Harps, who made use of the opportunities that came their way, deserved to win by 1–11 to 3–2.

The Harps team: Maeve Brophy, Elaine Cuddy, Aoife Donohoe, Catríona Phelan, Denise Quigley, Michelle Fitzpatrick, Claire Walsh, Caitríona Phelan, Louise Mahony (0–3), Joanne Prior (0–1), Barbara Hosey, Laura Mahony, Angela Hanlon, Aisling Phelan (0–4) and Áine Mahony (1–3). Subs used: Laura Saunders and Denise Cuddy.

Kilmaley team: Dympna Killeen, Lisa Kennedy, Denise Lynch, Orla Keane, Eimear Considine, Sarah Reidy, Sinéad O'Halloran, Siobhán Maher, Aida Griffey, Helen McMahon, Emma O'Driscoll, Shonagh Enright, Maria Hehir (1–0), Claire McMahon (2–2) and Katie Cahill. Subs used: Lorna Higgins and Aisling O'Halloran.

2008 Gael-Linn Senior Cup

Connacht scored a runaway 1–28 to 0–7 win over Ulster in the semi-final at Ashbourne while Munster had a narrow, 3–14 to 2–14, victory over Leinster in the second semi-final.

Connacht bridged an eight-year gap from their previous Gael-Linn success with a hard-earned 1–14 to 2–10 win over Munster. Jessica Gill and Veronica Curtin were the stars of the Connacht side which hung on for glory in a gripping finish.

Connacht team: (All Galway) Susan Keane, Sandra Tannian, Elaine Burke, Therese Manton, Ann Marie Hayes, Sinéad Cahalan (captain), Niamh Kilkenny, Lorraine Ryan, Áine Hillary, Jessica Gill, Therese Maher, Lourda Kavanagh, Brenda Kerins, Orla Kilkenny and Veronica Curtin.

Munster team: Aoife Murray (Cork), Suzanne Kelly (Tipperary), Rosarii Holland (Cork), Joanne O'Callaghan (Cork), Gemma O'Connor (Cork), Trish O'Halloran (Tipperary), Vera Sheehan (Limerick), Briege Corkery (Cork), Mairéad Morrissey (Tipperary), Emer O'Farrell (Cork), Philly Fogarty (Tipperary), Orla Cotter (Cork), Emily Hayden (Tipperary), Claire Grogan (Tipperary) and Síle Burns (Cork).

2008 Gael-Linn Junior Trophy

Munster had a narrow win, 4–6 to 1–12, over Leinster while Ulster recorded an easy 2–11 to 1–6 victory over Connacht in the semi-finals at Ashbourne. A determined Munster side made short work of Ulster and won comprehensively by 3–17 to 0–3.

Munster team: Denise Lynch (Clare), Aimee McInerney (Clare), Caroline Motherway (Cork), Aisling Kelly (Waterford), Jenny O'Grady (Waterford), Fiona Lafferty (Clare), Leah Weste (Cork), Ruth Kaiser (Clare), Louise Hayes (Clare), Róisín O'Brien (Clare), Áine Lyng (Waterford) (captain), Evelyn Ronayne (Cork), Carina Roseingrave (Clare), Denise Luby (Cork).

Ulster team: Bronagh Keenan (Armagh), Laura Gribben (Armagh), Maura McAuley (Derry), Gráinne Kelly (Armagh), Kelly Maybin (Antrim), Katrina O'Kane (Derry) (captain), Louise Loughran (Armagh), Danielle McBirney (Armagh), Michelle McGuigan (Armagh), Karen Tinnelly (Down), Cathy Mulholland (Down), Suzi Devlin (Antrim), Cathy Carey (Antrim), Joanne Mallon (Armagh) and Aisling Carr (Tyrone).

2008 Nancy Murray Cup

Five second-half points enabled Meath to get the better of Roscommon in the final of the Nancy Murray Cup at Drumlane, Co. Cavan. Jane Dolan, Elizabeth Lynch and Sinéad Hackett were on target to leave Meath in front by 0–10 to 1–6 at the end of a very close and exciting match.

Meath team: Emily Mangan, Margarita Stephens, Laura Donegan, Karen Ward, Edel Guy, Aileen Donnelly (captain),

Louise Donohue, Ann Marie Fagan, Laura Flynn, Elizabeth Oakes, Frances Lynch, Sinéad Hackett, Elizabeth Lynch, Jane Dolan and Stephanie Horan.

Roscommon team: Caroline Connaughton, Eimear Farrell, Niamh Connolly, Siobhán Coyle, Carmel Killeen, Donna Kelly, Catríona Morris, Caitríona Regan, Kellie Hopkins, Ciara Moran, Annette McGeeney, Elaine Daly, Fiona Connell, Claire Curley and Clodagh Rogers.

2008 Máire Ní Chinnéide Cup

Tyrone claimed the Máire Ní Chinnéide Cup with a convincing win over Wicklow, 4–11 to 0–3, in the final at Ardboe. Tyrone, Cavan, Wicklow, Monaghan and Donegal participated in the blitz and Monaghan goalkeeper, Róisín McKenna, was named Player of the Tournament.

Tyrone team: Paula Neill, Siobhán Hughes, Maeve McKearney, Colette Donnelly, Frances Begley, Julie Lagan (captain), Ríonach Laverty, Aisling Carr, Emma McAliskey, Emma McErlean, Susan McCann, Maeve McGurk, Shona Hagan, Leona Gallagher and Annette Jordan.

2008 Camogie-Shinty

In a close and exciting contest at Nowlan Park on October 19th, Scotland shaded the verdict over Ireland by 2–2 to 2–1.

Irish panel: Róisín McKenna (Monaghan), Emma McErlean (Tyrone), Ciara Rocks (Tyrone), Róisín Martin (Cavan), Leanne Lifely (Wicklow), Orla Sheerin (Monaghan), Helen Hughes (Monaghan), Isobel Kiernan (Monaghan), Pamela Maher (Wicklow), Aisling Corr (Tyrone), Anne Donnellan (Cavan), Sinéad Byrne (Wicklow), Maria Coyne (Mayo), Majella Smith (Cavan), Eileen McElroy (Monaghan), Emma Fitzgerald (Tyrone), Emma McAliskey (Tyrone), Maeve McGuirk (Tyrone), Sinéad Muldoon (Mayo) and Margaret McCabe (Cavan).

2008 All-Star Awards

All-Ireland senior champions, Cork, collected seven All-Star Awards while Offaly and Antrim picked up their first awards. Carina Roseingrave was named Young Player of the Year. Liam Dunne and Stephen Dormer (Kilkenny) shared the Manager of the Year award. Tipperary hurling goalkeeper, Brendan Cummins, was guest speaker and presented the awards.

All-Stars 2008: Aoife Murray (Cork), Caitríona Foley (Cork), Catherine O'Loughlin (Wexford), Trish O'Halloran (Tipperary), Michaela Morkan (Offaly), Sinéad Cahalan (Galway), Gemma O'Connor (Cork), Briege Corkery (Cork), Orla Cotter (Cork), Jessica Gill (Galway), Therese Maher (Galway), Aoife Neary (Kilkenny), Síle Burns (Cork) Rachel Moloney (Cork) and Jane Adams (Antrim).

Where We're At

Additional Sports Council funding facilitated the appointment of five new regional development co-ordinators. The extra manpower gave impetus to the advancement and expansion outlined in the Strategic Plan. A second-level development officer under-

Growing Staff

took the heavy workload of: increasing the number of secondary schools participating in competition; establishing transition year coaching and refereeing modules; and delivering the already successful Women in Sport initiatives. Mary O'Connor was promoted to the position of Director of Camogie where her dynamism and commitment guided the team of RDOs. With the result, considerable inroads were made in the targets of the Strategic Plan.

This was all new to the senior people in the Association, some of whom wondered if we were running too fast. It is easy to understand their point of view as they administered in very different times. Personally, I have witnessed dramatic changes in the management of the Association since I sat on the Central Council for the first time in the late sixties. It was usual for an incoming officer to fill the shoes of her predecessor and continue to do what she had done. In those days, the council was concerned with operational day-to-day matters and reacted to situations rather than plan for the future.

Plans are all very fine but it takes money to implement them. There was no money for sport prior to 1970. Neither the government nor the business community had come around to supporting it. The Association generated very meagre funds and it took top-class housekeeping to record a credit balance at the end of the year. The ladies excelled themselves at balancing the books.

Society placed women in a supporting role. Men filled the positions of authority and were the decision-makers. As women became better educated, they secured more responsible positions in the workplace and carried their newly acquired authority and confidence to their leisure time activities. The government came to realise the long-term benefits of supporting sport and set up the Sports Council. With money available to fund a well thought-out plan, it was a case of get on-board or be left behind.

With a busy office, staff in the regions, a membership approaching 100,000 and a calendar of fixtures and events to organise, the Camogie Association required to be run on business lines. The role of president took on a much greater relevance. The days when one pondered on who might be the next occupant of the post, glanced around the Central Council table and said 'Ah, its Mary's turn' were long gone. To prepare the next incumbent of the office with a first-hand view of the workings of the Association, the post of president-elect was introduced. The job of president is very demanding in terms of time and energy. The list of meetings, events, matches and social occasions, which must be attended, is continually on the increase, making it very difficult to marry the position with a full-time job.

A Game of Our Own

TENACIOUS TACKLING

Chapter Twenty five

CHANGING OF THE GUARD

Within a few short months of each other, two former presidents, Rosina McManus and Nell McCarthy, passed to their eternal reward. Both ladies made an enormous contribution to the development of the Camogie Association. Rosina collapsed at the Ulster final in company of her many friends. A new trophy bearing her name has been presented for the Ulster senior championship. Nell, the former Dublin supremo, had been in failing health for some time.

Joan O'Flynn Steps Up

At Congress 2009 in Nenagh, Liz Howard stepped down at the end of three very busy years in the role of president. She invested a massive amount of time and energy in a hectic schedule. Joan O'Flynn, who had served her apprenticeship as president-elect, moved to the centre chair at the top table and set about putting her imprint on the scene.

The Central Council sub-committees were reviewed. Some received a make-over from a change of name to a tweaking of their terms of reference. New sub-committees were established including ones for player welfare headed up by Stellah Sinnott (Wexford), and volunteer and officer support and development chaired by Máire Ní Cheallaigh (Dublin). New faces and expertise were brought on board. Joan set out to visit all county boards to listen to the issues, concerns and aspirations at local level. Among the decisions taken at congress was the awarding of 30 medals to the winners of All-Ireland championships.

Some believed that this move lowered the status of the medal as it is most unlikely that all 30 panel members would have reached the required standard. In an effort to increase the attendance at the All-Ireland senior and junior finals, clubs were obliged to purchase two All-Ireland tickets. The position of the national PRO was discontinued and the outgoing president was no longer allowed an extra year on Central Council.

New Initiatives

The busy communications and web committee produced a camogie ezine and a magazine *On the Ball*. The Association appointed

Claire Egan (Mayo) as Director of Communications and Marketing. Live television coverage of the All-Ireland junior final was procured. A 'Night at the Dogs' was organised as a fundraiser at Shelbourne Park. The top players in the junior grade were recognised with 'Soaring Stars' awards. Much work was done in preparing a new rule book and putting a new Strategic Plan together.

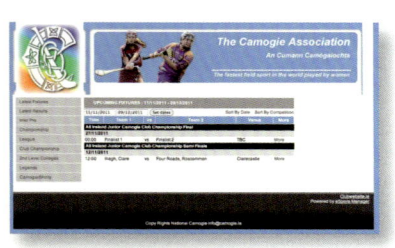

Camogie ezine

Media Awards

The 2008 Media Awards recognised the expertise of the following: Orla Considine (Clare), PRO of the Year; Stephen McCarthy (Sportsfile), Photo of the Year; Séamus McAleenan (Down), Published Article of the Year; Best Match Programme, Wexford county final; Best Provincial Coverage, *Connacht Tribune*; Best Local Radio, Clare FM, and Best Broadcaster, – RTÉ.

Cathal Goan, RTE Director General, left, presents the award for Camogie Photo of the year to Stephen McCarthy, *Sportsfile,* **far right, with Lilly Dunne, wife of the late Mick Dunne, and Liz Howard, President, during the Mick Dunne Memorial Awards 2008, sponsored by RTE. Croke Park, Dublin. Stephen's photographs also feature on these pages.** Picture: Ray Lohan / SPORTSFILE

2009 All-Ireland Senior Championship

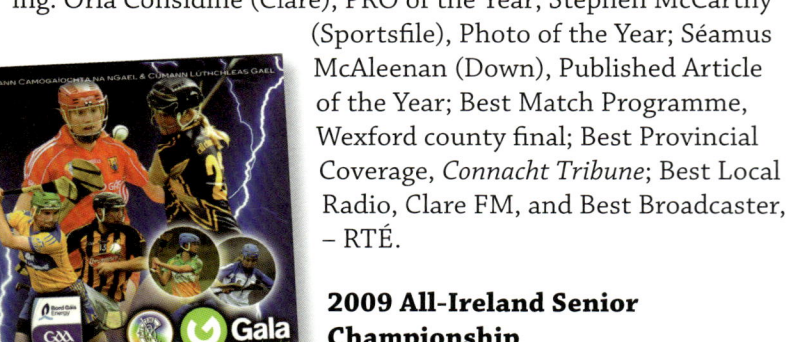

It looked promising for Wexford at half-time in the semi-final against Cork at Nowlan Park. Having played into the stiff breeze, they led by two points and their prospects of making the final looked better than Cork's. However, Cork moved up a gear on the resumption and, surprisingly, Wexford did not come with them. Gemma O'Connor put Briege Corkery through for a Cork goal. Minutes later, substitute Julia White hand passed to Emer Farrell for Cork's second major. Wexford's heads dropped as Cork advanced to the final by 2–13 to 1–10.

Changing of the Guard

Ann Downey's young charges seemed to be heading for a championship exit when an injury-time goal by Marie O'Connor saved the day. Up to that point, it looked like Galway had done enough to qualify for the final. The Kilkenny youngsters battled gamely and grabbed whatever opportunities that came their way. Their defence was outstanding in the last 20 minutes and coped with everything that Galway threw at them. Kilkenny booked their place in the final by 1–13 to 1–11.

On the previous occasion that Cork and Kilkenny met in an All-Ireland final, Ann Downey and Denise Cronin both wore the number seven jersey in their respective county colours. On this occasion, they patrolled the sideline directing proceedings as the respective managers of Kilkenny and Cork. Fielding a side which had enjoyed unprecedented success at underage level, Kilkenny were facing a team figuring in their eighth successive final.

The Cork defence was magnificent. They suffocated the Kilkenny attack and confined them to two points from play over the hour. Briege Corkery, Orla Cotter and Gemma O'Connor gave Cork a decided pull in the middle of the field. The accuracy of Rachel Moloney from frees kept edging Cork ahead. Cork's experience was a huge factor. They had been in this situation so many times. The score stood at Cork 0–15, Kilkenny 0–7 when the final whistle blew.

Cork team: Aoife Murray, Joanne O'Callaghan, Caitríona Foley, Rena Buckley, Jenny Duffy, Mary O'Connor, Sarah Hayes, Briege Corkery, Orla Cotter, Eimear O'Sullivan (0–3), Gemma O'Connor (0–2), Una O'Donoghue (0–1), Síle Burns, Rachel Moloney (0–7) and Emer Farrell (0–1). Subs used: Katrina Mackey (0–1), Emer Dillon, Amanda O'Regan (captain) and Lynda O'Connell.

Kilkenny team: Caitríona Ryan, Leann Fennelly, Catherine Doherty, Jacqui Frisby, Lizzie Lyng, Amy Butler, Elaine Aylward, Colette Dormer, Ann Dalton (0–1), Therese Muldowney, Katie Power, Edwina Keane, Michelle Quilty (0–1), Denise Gaule and Aoife Neary (0–5). Subs used: Aisling Dunphy, Deirdre Delaney,

2009 All-Ireland senior final: Síle Burns, Cork, bears down on goal watched by Jacqui Frisby, left, and Elaine Aylward, Kilkenny. Picture: Stephen McCarthy / SPORTSFILE

Marie O'Connor and Keeva Fennelly.

2009 All-Ireland Intermediate Championship

A great second-half performance from Galway, in which they held Tipperary scoreless, was the key to them winning a place in the final. Martina Conroy and Caroline Murray tapped over 11 points between them to ensure Galway's passage by 0–16 to 0–7 at Thurles.

Derry, fielding their first-choice team, registered 18 points in the semi-final against Cork at St Peregine's grounds. That tally would win most matches. Opponents Cork shot four goals in a determined effort to reach their third successive final. Mary Coleman (two), Maria Walsh and Emer Watson were Cork's goalscorers in their 4–10 to 0–18 victory.

A draw was a fair result at the Gaelic Grounds, giving both Galway and Cork another chance to amend for misses and mistakes. The teams were level many times in the game. An Emer Watson goal gave Cork the edge, 1–7 to 0–7, at the break. Galway upped their game and forged ahead. With both sides scrambling for scores, Niamh Dilworth found Maria Walsh who slotted home the equaliser. There was no argument as to which was the better side in the replay at Nenagh. Galway totally outplayed and outclassed a disappointing Cork side. Hungry for victory, they were first to the ball and used it intelligently. Cork were unable to lift their game and wipe out a four-point deficit. It was Galway that took over as the game progressed. Goals from Aoife Lynskey and Caroline Murray put the game out of Cork's reach and it stood Galway 3–10, Cork 1–5 at the finish.

Galway team: Deirdre Ward, Jennifer Coone, Nicola Lawless, Karen Brien, Colette Gill, Sarah Dervan, Caroline Kelly (captain), Heather Cooney, Paula Kenny, Aoife Lynskey (1–2), Cathy Bowes (0–1), Caroline Murray (1–2), Martina Conroy (0–4), Tara Rutledge, Gemma Kelly. Subs used: Claire Conroy (0–1), Louise Mitchell (1–0) and Lorraine Pardy.

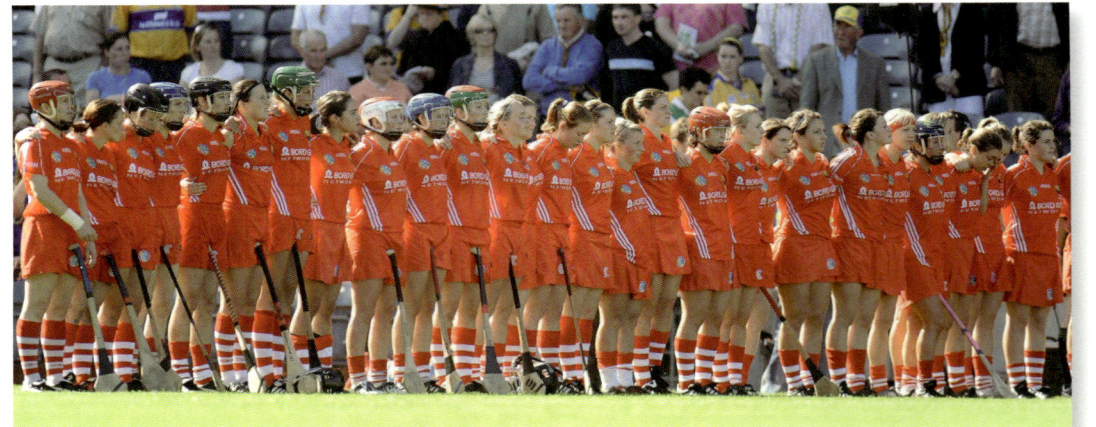

The Cork squad standing for the National Anthem. *Picture: Stephen McCarthy / SPORTSFILE*

Changing of the Guard

Cork team: Jessica Kavanagh, Ann Marie Fleming, Christine O'Neill, Pamela Mackey, Leah Weste, Carolyn Motherway, Áine Watson, Maria Walsh, Helen O'Mahony, Maria Watson, Mary Coleman, Liz Power, Niamh Dilworth (0–2), Emer Watson (1–0) and Michelle Browne (0–3). Subs used: Sarah Buckley, Miriah Reidy, Denise Luby, Regina Curtin and Marion Jagoe.

2009 All-Ireland Junior Championship

Memories of three semi-final defeats were put to bed as Waterford advanced to the All-Ireland final at the expense of Laois at Nowlan Park. A good start, in which they put 1–4 on the scoreboard, was the winning of the match for Waterford. The Laois girls put up a defiant and brave display but fell short by 1–13 to 1–7.

Offaly returned to Croke Park to finish the job that they came so close to completing in 2008. A Meath side, which had made considerable strides in recent times, was unable to halt their progress. Michaela Morkan (0–6) and Siobhán Flannery (0–4) had a big say in Offaly's progress to the final. Offaly 0–16, Meath 1–8

Cork senior captain Amanda O'Regan is presented with the O'Duffy Cup by Joan O'Flynn, Association President. *Picture: Pat Murphy / SPORTSFILE*

was the final score.

The All-Ireland final at Croke Park was a huge game for Offaly and Waterford. Both counties had witnessed positive results of a concerted investment in development and coaching. They were ready to step up another rung of the ladder. Offaly hit the ground running and, by half-time, they were in the happy position of being 1–11 to 0–4 in front. They did not panic when Waterford cut the deficit to six points. Superb defending by Lorraine Keena, Michaela Morkan and Sheila Sullivan kept Waterford at bay. Goals by Siobhán Flannery and Arlene Watkins ensured that there was no way back for Waterford.

Croke Park nerves upset Waterford. By the time they had settled into the game, Offaly were well ahead. Waterford played some great camogie in the second-half which was appreciated by the large crowd. Mary O'Donnell, Charlotte Raher, Nicola Morrissey, Karen Kelly, Patricia Jackman and Áine Lyng won admirers for their stylish play. But it was Offaly's day, and they celebrated their 3–14 to 2–8 win in style. The county had made massive strides in a few short years.

A Game of Our Own

Offaly team: Audrey Kennedy, Karen Brady, Lorraine Keena, Fiona Stephens, Linda Sullivan, Marion Crean (captain), Sheila Sullivan, Karen Nugent, Michaela Morkan, Aoife Kelly, Tina Hannon (0–2), Michelle Davis (0–3), Siobhán Flannery (1–1), Elaine Dermody (1–7), Arlene Watkins (1–1). Subs used: Jean Brady, Aoife Corrigan and Emma Dunne.

Waterford team: Aisling O'Brien, Vicky Gaffney, Sally O'Grady (Capt), Kate Marie Hearne, Gráinne Kenneally, Mary O'Donnell, Shauna Kiernan, Mairéad Murphy, Charlotte Raher, Shona Curran, Áine Lyng (1–3), Nicola Morrissey (0–1), Patricia Jackman (1–1), Karen Kelly (0–3) and Áine Breathnach. Subs used: Jenny Simpson, Aisling Kelly and Marie Russell.

Offaly forward, Aoife Kelly, is a daughter of All-Ireland hurler, Joachim Kelly, who coached the side.

Aoife Corrigan is a daughter of Mark Corrigan who had won an All-Ireland hurling medal with Offaly in 1985.

Dublin – 2009 Jubilee Team. Back: Marie Connell, Noreen Fleming, Toni O'Byrne, Catherine Ledwidge, Yvonne Redmond, Bernie Toner and Germaine Noonan. Front: Una Crowley, Carmel O'Byrne, Barbara Redmond, Mary Mernagh, Ann Colgan (Capt), Joan Gormley and Edel Murphy.

2009 All-Ireland Minor A Championship

Very little divided Clare and Cork at any stage of the semi-final at Kilmallock. The teams battled bravely in pursuit of a place in the final. When the final whistle blew, Clare were a point in front, 1–9 to 0–11. It was a different story in the second semi-final. Kilkenny's slick and skilful minors motored past Tipperary in style at Kilmallock. Scorer-in-chief, Denise Gaule, bagged 3–7 and was ably assisted by Aoife Murphy with 2–3 to her credit. Tipperary worked very hard but, like other sides, they found this Kilkenny side to be a very special talent. Kilkenny advanced by 5–15 to 3–4.

Kilkenny had monopolised the All-Ireland Minor A Championship title since the start of the competition in 2006. Clare sought to break their dominance in the 2009 final at Semple Stadium, but their fate was sealed in a stunning spell before half-time that produced four goals to put Kilkenny in an unassailable lead. Clare fought back bravely.

Changing of the Guard

They outscored Kilkenny in the second-half but the damage had already been done. Huge performances from Denise Gaule, Claire Phelan, Kate McDonald, Aisling Dunphy and Michelle Farrell enabled Kilkenny win by 5–10 to 3–8.

Kilkenny team: Emma Staunton, Caoimhe Shiel, Alison Walsh, Nicola Butler, Niamh Kelly, Kate McDonald, Mairéad Power, Aisling Dunphy (0–1) Niamh Byrne, Áine Curran, Karan Duggan, Anna Farrell (0–1), Claire Phelan (2–3), Denise Gaule (2–4) and Michelle Farrell (1–1). Subs used: Davina Tobin, Grace Walsh, Aoife Murphy and Stacey Quirke.

Clare team: Ailish Considine, Anne Marie McMahon, Chloe Morey (0–2), Carol O'Leary, Aiveen O'Shea, Eimear Considine, Christina Glynn, Róisín McMahon (1–0), Louise Woods, Orlaith Duggan, Niamh Corry, Aisling Hannon, Shonagh Enright (1–5), Róisín O'Brien (1–1) and Katie Cahill. Subs used: Carol Kaiser, Susan Fahy and Niamh Martin.

Kilkenny's Áine Curran is a daughter of Nuala Jennings who had won All-Ireland medals with Cork.

2009 All-Ireland Minor B Championship

Derry ran Waterford very close in the semi-final at Ashbourne and stayed within touching distance throughout the game. However, Waterford were a goal in front, 1–9 to 0–9, when the final whistle blew. In the second semi-final, Limerick and Wexford provided a fascinating contest with some excellent camogie. The point-taking ability of Limerick yielded a 3–16 to 3–9 victory.

The final at Mallow produced as dramatic a finish as one could imagine. Waterford looked the better team throughout and had built up what everyone in the grounds considered a winning lead. Two minutes into injury-time, Waterford led by 1–15 to 1–10. Parents and friends of the Waterford players moved down to the gate to be ready to run onto the field and congratulate their players. However, they will remember the name Naomi Carroll for a long time. Twice in a minute, she leaped in the air, grabbed the ball and struck it to the net to leave Waterford stunned. Initially, silence greeted the final whistle. It took a moment for Limerick to realise that they had won by 3–10 to 1–15.

Limerick team: Patricia Kerins, Lisa Scanlon, Niamh Power, Aisling Enright, Niamh Richardson, Sarah Carey, Judith Mulcahy, Tara Hurley, Mary O'Callaghan, Claire Casey, Caroline Scanlon (0–1), Kerrie Brosnan, Rachel Carmody, Naomi Carroll (3–5) and Annette McAuliffe (0–2). Subs used: Kristy Carroll (0–2), Mairéad Ryan and Aisling Russell.

Waterford team: Tracy Kiely, Sarah Smith, Lorna Behan, Mary Claire Dunphy, Jenny McCarthy, Shauna Kiernan, Sarah Fenton, Marie Russell (captain) (0–2), Jessica Gleeson, Katie Hannon, Patricia Jackman (1–8), Rachel Whelan (0–3), Caitríona McGlone (0–1), Deirdre Fahy and Kate Rockett (0–1). Subs used: Niamh Rockett, Michelle Tobin and Caoimhe Fitzgerald.

Sarah Carey is a daughter of All-Star hurler, Ciarán Carey.

2009 All-Ireland Minor C Championship

Laois proved too good for Roscommon in the semi-final of the minor C championship and won much as they pleased by 8–12 to

1–1. Laois were joined by Carlow, who advanced at the expense of Cavan, in the final. Laois captain, Sarah Ann Fitzgerald, led the way in the final against Carlow at Clane. She scored 2–2 to leave her side nicely positioned. There was much to admire in the play of both sides. Laois held on to their advantage to win by 3–5 to 2–3.

Laois team: Yvonne O'Neill, Marie Bourke, Mairéad Burke, Michelle Fitzpatrick, Claire Walsh, Rosemarie Birmingham (0–1), Aisling Burke, Alison McEvoy, Sarah Anne Fitzgerald (captain) (2–2), Síle Burke (0–1), Niamh Dollard, Ciara Carroll, Dawn Mortimer (0–1), Emma Hogan (1–0) and Maria Fitzpatrick.

Carlow team: Katie Byrne, Shauna Barcoe, Maria Kehoe, Kate Nolan, Emma Kelly, Tara Wilson, Michelle Kelly, Ann Murphy, Mary Ellen Doyle, Edel Fenlon, Margaret Murphy (1–0), Olivia McDonald, Lorraine Bible, Niamh Quirke (1–3) and Ciara Quirke.

2009 All-Ireland Under-16 A Championship

Kilkenny's great run in the All-Ireland Under-16 A Championship came to an end at the hands of Galway in the semi-final at Templederry, Co. Tipperary. Playing with great attitude and spirit, Galway attacked from the throw-in and were 1–7 to 0–5 ahead at half-time. They continued to pick off points and booked their place in the final by 1–13 to 0–10.

Clare and Tipperary played a highly competitive and entertaining semi-final at LIT. The standard of play was very good as two talented teams went all out for victory. Orla McEniry had an outstanding game in goal for Tipperary and saved her team time and again. Tipperary went forward to the final by 1–7 to 1–5.

Play swung from end to end in an enthralling final between Galway and Clare at the Gaelic Grounds. The sides traded points before Aoife Ryan reacted quickly to a rebound and slotted the ball to the Galway net. Rachel Monaghan was brought down as she bore down on the Tipperary goal. Rebecca Hennelly held her nerve to drive home the resultant penalty. The teams returned to the dressing rooms with the score at 1–5 apiece. The introduction of Orlaith McGrath and some positional switches improved the Galway performance. The Tipperary challenge faded as Galway grew in confidence. Orlaith McGrath gathered a ball and placed it past Orla McEniry for a Galway goal. The Connacht side added points before Ciara McGrath claimed an injury-time goal for Galway to win 2–11 to 2–7.

Galway team: Olivia Lane, Tara Kenny, Mairéad Linnane, Laura Donnellan, Noreen Murphy (captain), Nicola Muldoon, Chantel Muldoon, Clodagh McGrath, Laura Mitchell (0–2), Tracey Murray, Rebecca Hennelly (1–2), Aoibhin Kenny, Marie Brehony (0–1), Niamh McGrath (0–5) and Rachel Monaghan. Sub used: Orlaith McGrath (1–1).

Tipperary team: Orla McEniry, Moira Ryan, Sheila Ryan, Louise McLoughlin, Bríd Quinn, Caoimhe Maher, Mairéad Barry, Theresa Ryan, Aisling Carroll, Niamh O'Donoghue, Alice Fogarty, Claire Kennedy, Nicole Walsh (0–5), Michaela Graham (0–1) and Aoife Ryan (1–1).

Sisters Niamh, Clodagh and Orlaith McGrath had huge roles in Galway's win. They are daughters of All-Ireland hurler, Michael

'Hopper' McGrath, and his wife, Geraldine, who played camogie for Galway and hockey for Ireland.

2009 All-Ireland Under-16 B Championship

The All-Ireland Under-16 B Championship continued to be played on a round-robin basis but it was adjusted to include semi-finals. Wexford went on a scoring spree against Kildare at Bagenalstown and, led 5–6 to 0–1 by half-time, well on their way to their 7–14 to 1–1 victory.

The Waterford v. Armagh semi-final was much more competitive. In a large spread of scores, 14 players got their names on the score sheet with Ruth Geoghegan making the greatest impact with three goals. Waterford's ability to score goals resulted in a 4–10 to 2–10 win.

Neighbours Waterford and Wexford met in the final at Piltown. At the close of a very exciting contest, Wexford claimed their third national camogie title of the season. Inside the first minute, Shannon Byrne, daughter of All-Ireland winner, Billy, opened the scoring for Wexford with a well-taken goal. Waterford gained parity on a few occasions but were never able to go in front. The game ended in a welter of excitement as both teams went flat out for the winner. Victory went to Wexford by 2–11 to 1–12.

Wexford team: Kate Flynn, Siobhán O'Regan, Shannon O'Connell, Clara McGuinness, Fiona Donnellan, Shauna Sinnott (captain), Niamh Murphy, Laura Warren (0–1), Louise Sinnott (0–5), Susie McGovern (1–1), Mairéad Sheehan (0–2), Emma Walsh, Shannon Byrne (1–0), Marie-Claire Morrissey (0–2) and Tara Somers.

Waterford team: Helen O'Donnell, Shauna Prendergast, Clara Hogan, Sarah McGlone, Shannon Denton, Niamh Prendergast, Gemma Burke, Niamh Rockett, Michelle Tobin (captain) (1–7), Aoife Hannon (0–2), Ciara Moore, Valerie O'Brien, Caroline Farrelly (0–1), Ruth Geoghegan (0–2) and Una Jackman.

2009 All-Ireland Under-16 C Championship

Tyrone and Westmeath met in the inaugural All-Ireland Under-16 C Championship final at St Tiernach's Park, Clones, on May 9th. Open play led to a high-scoring game and an exciting end-to-end contest. The Tyrone side, which was very good at backing the player in possession, came out on top by 6–9 to 5–3.

Tyrone team: Seana O'Hagan, Simone McKiver, Cara Fitzgerald, Áine Donnelly, Larissa O'Neill, Rebecca Barker, Róisín Jordan, Caoimhe Rafferty, Aoife Molloy (captain), Aisling Jordan, Jane Canavan, Lauren Fitzgerald, Caoimhe O'Callaghan, Orla Foley and Alanna Mellon.

Westmeath team: Alana Nash, Sarah Purcell, Lorna Daly, Tammy Commons, Emer Flynn, Aishling Boyhan, Saoirse O'Neill, Sarah Jackson, Nadina Grace, Niamh Lynch, Louise O'Connor, Chloe Kelly, Emma Kincaid, Caitríona Murtagh and Grace Mulvanney.

2009 All-Ireland Club Senior Championship

The 2007 champions, Cashel, had to come from behind before

pulling off a memorable 1–14 to 2–7 win over first-time semi-finalists, Oulart The Ballagh, at the County Wexford venue.

Loughgiel had their hopes dashed by the very impressive Athenry side at Ballinasloe. Strong in defence and deadly up front, Athenry progressed by 1–15 to 0–3.

Cashel and Athenry served up an enthralling contest in atrocious weather conditions in the final at Clarecastle. The superb full-back play of Una O'Dwyer and the accuracy of Claire Grogan kept Athenry's half-time advantage to a single point despite thwe fact that the Galway side were backed by a stiff breeze. Conditions deteriorated as play progressed. The high winds and torrential rain absorbed the energy of the players as they struggled to make progress. Scores were hard to come by and neither team was able to draw clear. In the last throw of the dice, Athenry sprung Jessica Gill. Sidelined since September with cruciate ligament damage, she caused consternation in the Cashel defence and lifted the spirits of her side. She shot a point and lessened the impact of Una O'Dwyer. Cashel held out under fierce pressure to win by 0–11 to 0–9. Therese Maher, Noreen Coen, Brenda Kerins and Stephanie Gannon were the pick of the Athenry players.

Cashel team: Helen Breen, Claire Ryan, Una O'Dwyer (captain), Noelette Dwyer, Paula Bulfin, Philly Fogarty, Julie McGrath, Jill Horan, Linda Grogan, Cora Hennessy, Mairéad Morrissey, Claire Grogan, Alison Lonergan, Emily Hayden and Cliona Dwyer. Subs used: Sharon Hayes and Danielle O'Connell.

Athenry team: Stephanie Gannon, Katherine Glynn, Alice Poniard, Darelle Coen, Ciara Cunniffe, Regina Glynn, Krystle Ruddy, Sarah Donohue, Laura Linnane, Natalie Jordan, Therese Maher, Noreen Coen, Brenda Kerins, Katie O'Dwyer and Mary Keogh. Sub used: Jessica Gill.

2009 All-Ireland Club Junior Championship

St Anne's, Dunhill, Co. Waterford, caused a shock by ousting three times champions, The Harps (Laois), in the semi-final at Portlaoise by 3–10 to 0–16 on November 29th. In contrast, Four

6 December 2009; Cashel captain Una Dwyer, front centre, with Bill Carroll Cup, celebrates with team-mates after victory over Athenry in All-Ireland Senior Camogie Club Championship Final in Clarecastle, Co. Clare. Picture: Diarmuid Greene / SPORTSFILE

Changing of the Guard

Roads (Roscommon) were brushed aside, 3–12 to 0–2, by classy Lavey (Derry).

An hour's camogie plus extra-time failed to separate St Anne's and Lavey in the final at Ashbourne. The sides were dead-locked at 1–11 apiece. High winds and driving rain made it a match of two halves, one side pressing ahead and then being hauled back. Excellent weather conditions awaited the teams on their return to Ashbourne for the replay. Massive performances from Attracta McPeake, Ceara Cushnahan and Siobhán Convery ensured that the Phil McBride Cup returned to Ulster. Charlotte-Marie Raher, Carolyn Ahearn and Karen Kelly played very well for the Waterford side but could not prevent Lavey from winning by 1–13 to 0–7.

Lavey team: Ciara Boyle, Aedin McVeigh, Kathleen Taggart, Ciara Mullan, Alana McMullan, Ceara Cushnahan, Siobhán Convery, Attracta McPeake, Edelle Henry, Teresa McIlroy, Clare McCoy, Denise McShane, Paula McCloy, Mary O'Kane and Helen O'Neill.

St Anne's team: Carolyn Ahearn, Emma Fitzgerald, Lorena Mooney, Lorna Behan, Claire Whyte, Annette Raher, Siobhán Kavanagh, Charlotte-Marie Raher, Ailish Dunphy, Mairéad Murphy, Jenny Simpson, Kate Rockett, Zoe O'Donoghue, Karen Kelly and Niamh Rockett.

2009 Gael-Linn Senior Cup

Ulster did not participate in the 2009 interprovincial series. With the result, the competition was played on a round-robin basis with Munster and Connacht meeting in the final. In a low-scoring tie at Ashbourne, Munster did not allow Connacht the same freedom which they enjoyed in earlier rounds. Orla Cotter, Emer Dillon, Emily Hayden and Carina Roseingrave raised white flags to earn Munster victory by 0–7 to 0–2.

Munster panel: Denise Lynch (Clare), Suzanne Kelly (Tipperary), Amanda O'Regan (Cork) (captain), Joanne O'Callaghan (Cork), Trish O'Halloran (Tipperary), Fiona Lafferty (Clare), Jen-

Clare McCoy, Lavey, celebrates with the cup. All-Ireland Junior Camogie Club Championship Final Replay, Lavey, Derry, v St. Anne's Dunhill, Waterford, Donaghmore, Ashbourne, Co. Meath. Picture: Brian Lawless / SPORTSFILE

ny Duffy (Cork), Emily Hayden (Tipperary), Orla Cotter (Cork), Laura Linnane (Clare), Deirdre Murphy (Clare), Geraldine Kinnane (Tipperary), Emer Dillon (Cork) Una O'Donoghue (Cork) and Carina Roseingrave (Clare).

Connacht panel: (All Galway) Susan Earner, Sandra Tannian, Ailbhe Kelly, Therese Manton, Regina Glynn, Sinéad Cahalan, Áine Hillary, Ann-Marie Hayes, Lorraine Ryan, Jessica Gill, Brenda Hanney, Laura Kavanagh, Niamh Kilkenny, Therese Maher, Brenda Kerins, Clodagh Glynn, Orla Kilkenny, Niamh McGrath, Sarah Noone, Aislinn Connolly, Emma Kilkelly, Veronica Curtin, Catríona Cormican and Sarah Donohue.

erine Glynn (Galway), Caroline Murray (Galway), Paula Kenny (Galway), Caroline Kelly (Galway), Annette McGeeney (Roscommon), Sarah Dervan (Galway), Susan Keane (Galway), Aoife Lynskey (Galway) and Claire Curley (Roscommon).

Munster team: Jessica Kavanagh (Cork), Sarah Sherlock (Clare), Sally O'Grady (Waterford), Pamela Mackey (Cork), Kate Marie Hearne (Waterford), Chloe Morey (Clare), Helen O'Mahony (Cork), Louise Hayes (Clare), Katrina Mackey (Cork), Patricia Jackman (Waterford), Áine Lyng (Waterford), Áine Breathnach (Waterford), Mary Coleman (Cork), Denise Luby (Cork) and Carol Kaiser (Clare).

Three Cork presidents, Lil O'Neill, Joan O'Flynn and Mary Moran, seen at Congress in 2009.

2009 Gael-Linn Junior Trophy

Connacht, Leinster and Munster played a round-robin series with Connacht and Munster qualifying for the final. In their third match of the day, Connacht had more in reserve and won comfortably by 4–4 to 0–2.

Connacht team: Sharon Finneran (Roscommon), Róisín Callanan (Galway), Darelle Coen (Galway), Niamh Connolly (Roscommon), Molly Dunne (Galway), Mairéad Linnane (Galway), Cath-

Nancy Murray Cup

With a goal on either side of half-time, Colette McSorley placed Armagh in a happy position in the final against Roscommon at Breffni Park. Roscommon, who started sluggishly, came back into contention with a brace of goals from Claire Curley. The pendulum swung back again as Niamh McGeown grabbed a late equaliser to leave the final score Armagh 3–5, Roscommon 2–8. In the replay at Drumlane, Co. Cavan, Roscommon made the early running. Kelly Hopkins, Claire Curley, Donna Kelly and Annette McGeeney laid the foundations of victory. A single score, 1–7 to 0–7, divided the teams in Roscommon's favour in the end.

Roscommon team: Caroline Connaughton, Marie Glennon, Niamh Connolly, Caitríona Morris, Catherine Rogerson, Donna Kelly (captain), Gráinne Egan, Patricia Lennon, Niamh Coyle, Kelly Hopkins, Annette McGeeney, Caitríona Regan, Sinéad O'Brien, Cáit Kenny and Claire Curley.

Armagh team: Colleen Comiskey, Michaela King, Ann McGuigan, Patrice Murphy, Emma Farrell, Laura Gribben, Caoimhe McKenna, Bernie Murray, Niamh McGeown, Ciara Donnelly, Gráinne Kelly, Joanne Mallon, Cathy Smith, Colette McSorley and Paula Mallon.

2009 Máire Ní Chinnéide Cup

Louth, Cavan, Wicklow, Monaghan, Mayo and Donegal entered for the Junior Championship Blitz which was staged at Monaghan on August 29th. Cavan and Wicklow qualified for the final. In a close exciting decider, Cavan edged in front to win by 0–5 to 0–4.

Cavan team: Emer Brady, Aisling Smith, Lorraine Day, Carmel McBride, Jenny O'Rourke, Lisa McGaurahan, Marie Brady, Sinéad Coyle, Angela O'Reilly, Rosie Crowe, Niamh Brady, Josephine Maguire, Margaret McBride, Anne Donnellan (captain), Philomena Cundellan, Geraldine Mulvanney and Mairéad McCabe.

Wicklow team: Lynsey Walsh, Kellie Byrne, Mary O'Neill, Rosie Keogh, Lindsey Quinlan, Leanne Lifely, Eve Whyte, Laura Hogan, Ann-Marie Doran, Clare Byrne, Sinéad Byrne, Karen Walsh, Mary Whelan, Pamela Maher and Sinéad Fisher.

2009 Camogie-Shinty

Ireland travelled to Inverness to face Scotland in the annual camogie-shinty contest. A goal in either half scored by Margaret McBride and Aisling Corr earned victory for the Irish girls. Collette McSorley was voted Player of the Match.

Irish panel: Caroline Connaughton (Roscommon), Niamh Connolly (Roscommon), Sandra Greville (Westmeath), Karen Walsh (Wicklow), Niamh Breen (Kildare), Bernie Murray (Armagh), Róisín O'Connell (Kildare), Margaret McBride (Cavan), Frances Bigley (Tyrone), Lorraine Day (Cavan), Valerie Crean (Carlow), Ann Marie Doran (Wicklow), Claire Curley (Roscommon), Colette McSorley (Armagh), Pamela Greville (Westmeath), Róisín McKenna (Monaghan), Rosie Crowe (Cavan), Aisling Corr (Tyrone), Margaret Coady (Carlow) and Sharon McQuillan (Monaghan).

2009 All-Star Awards

Cork's Gemma O'Connor was awarded a sixth successive All-Star award at the annual banquet in the CityWest Hotel. Testament to her great versatility, Gemma has won All-Star awards in defence, midfield and attack. On duty with the Irish army in Chad, she was unable to accept the award in person but her mother Geraldine acted on her behalf. Five players, Jacqui Frisby, Elaine Aylward, Anne Dalton, Katie Power and Gráinne McGoldrick, were honoured for the first time.

The Young Player of the Year went to Denise Gaule (Kilkenny) and Denise Cronin (Cork) was named Manager of the Year. Minister Mary Hannafin was the guest speaker at the function.

All-Stars 2009:
Aoife Murray (Cork), Regina Glynn (Galway), Caitríona Foley (Cork), Jacqui Frisby (Kilkenny), Ann Marie Hayes (Galway), Mary O'Connor (Cork), Elaine Aylward (Kilkenny), Briege Corkery (Cork), Anne Dalton (Kilkenny), Katie Power (Kilkenny), Gemma O'Connor (Cork), Therese Maher (Galway), Aoife Neary (Kilkenny), Gráinne McGoldrick (Derry) and Rachel Moloney (Cork).

The 2009 Camogie All-Star team. Back row from left: Anne Dalton, Kilkenny, Aoife Murray, Cork, Regina Glynn, Galway, Cathriona Foley, Cork, Jacqui Frisby, Kilkenny, Anne Marie Hayes, Galway, Mary O'Connor, Cork, Elaine Aylward, Kilkenny, Briege Corkery, Cork, Rachel Moloney, Cork, and Grainne McGoldrick, Derry. Front row from left; Katie Power, Kilkenny, Geraldine O'Connor, who collected the award on behalf of her daughter Gemma O'Connor, Cork, Sinead O'Connor, Ard Stiurthóir of the Camogie Association, Mary Hannifin T.D., Minister for Social Welfare, Joan O'Flynn, President of the Camogie Association, Tony Towell, MD of O'Neills, and Paul Brady, World Handball Champion, Therese Maher, Galway, Aoife Neary, Kilkenny, at the 2009 Camogie All-Stars Awards, in association with O'Neills. Citywest Hotel, Conference, Leisure & Golf Resort, Dublin. *Picture: Pat Murphy / SPORTSFILE*

2009 Soaring Stars

The inaugural Soaring Stars recognised the talent and flair of the players who compete in the junior divisions.

Those honoured were: Audrey Kennedy (Offaly), Fiona Stephens (Offaly), Eimear Moynan (Laois), Karen Brady (Offaly), Karen Tinnelly (Down), Michaela Morkan (Offaly), Louise Donoghue (Meath), Louise Mahony (Laois), Niamh Coyle (Roscommon), Arlene Watkins (Offaly), Catherine McGourty (Down), Áine Lyng (Waterford), Susie O'Carroll (Kildare), Karen Kelly (Waterford) and Elaine Dermody (Offaly).

Feast of Camogie

CIT played host to Ashbourne and Purcell Cup competitions over

Changing of the Guard

the weekend of February 20th–21st, 2010. The magnificent facilities at the Bishopstown Campus ensured that both competitions could be staged together. The organising committee, spearheaded by Keith Ricken (the GAA's development officer) and Miriam Deasy (CIT's sports officer), saw to it that the visitors enjoyed a special weekend on and off the field. Sixteen teams and their mentors converged on Cork to decide the destiny of the cup and shield competitions.

Many of the players on view were already established on the inter-county scene, thus ensuring a very high standard of play. For once, the weather was kind to the third-level events. Four pristine pitches saw lively action over the two days before WIT retained the Ashbourne Cup with two points to spare over UCC. UL claimed the Ashbourne Shield by defeating CIT by 1–10 to 1–4. The Purcell Cup was brought home by DIT while the Purcell Shield went north with Queen's University. The Ashbourne and Purcell weekends are much more than the closing stages of two competitions. Friendships are made and renewed; ambitions to secure a coveted medal before graduation cemented and images of the weekend stored in the memory forever.

The 2009 Camogie Soaring Stars team. Back row, from left; Audrey Kennedy, Offaly, Fiona Stephens, Offaly, Eimear Moynan, Laois, Karen Brady, Offaly, Karen Tinnelly, Down, Michaela Morkan, Offaly, Louise Donoghue, Meath, Louise Mahony, Laois, Niamh Coyle, Roscommon. Front row, from left; Arlene Watkins, Offaly, Catherine McGourty, Down, Aine Lyng, Waterford, Joan O'Flynn, President of the Camogie Association, Susie O'Carroll, Kildare, Karen Kelly, Waterford, and Elaine Dermody, Offaly. Picture: Pat Murphy / SPORTSFILE

Our Game, Our Passion

The Camogie Association's Strategic Plan 2010–2015, titled 'Our Game, Our Passion', was unveiled at Congress 2010 at Newbridge. The plan is aimed at maximising the potential of camogie and branding the Association as a confident, modern, community-based organisation. The Association aspired to increase its membership base by 40 per cent over five years, grow the number of clubs to 750 and attract an attendance of 60,000 at the 2015 All-Ireland final. The roadmap for camogie concentrates on five strategic priorities of: growing participation; improving performance; supporting volunteer development and leadership; enhancing camogie's profile; and achieving excellent governance and organisational development.

President Joan O'Flynn described these goals as 'achievable and realistic'. The key, she continued, is to ensure that all elements of the Association – full-time team, voluntary committees, provincial councils and county boards – get behind the plan and work to achieve the goals that have been set.

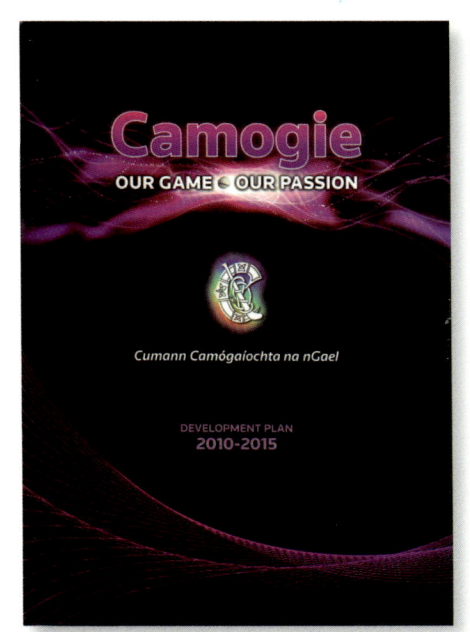

The Camogie Association's Strategic Plan 2010–2015, titled 'Our Game, Our Passion', which was unveiled at Congress 2010 in Newbridge.

Media Awards

The fourth annual Media Awards were presented at the Congress banquet. Those honoured were: Tom Allen (Limerick), PRO of the Year; Michael Kelly (*Wicklow People*), Photo of the Year; Dave Devereux (*Wexford People*), Published Article of the Year; *C'mon Caman*; National Broadcast of the Year; Armagh, Best Match Programme; Roscommon Herald, Best Provincial Newspaper Coverage; KFM, Best Local Radio; and Paul Rouse, author of *Pride and Passion*, won a special category.

Constitution and Rules Updated

A constitution and set of rules geared for an association run by volunteers was updated to reflect the modern fast-changing organisation of 2010. With 540 clubs, 13 full-time staff and a turnover in excess of €1 million, a new approach was required. E-voting was used for the first time at the Special Congress on May 22nd to vote on the 40-odd motions tabled in the new document. The experiment was a great success. Time spent in counting votes and working out the figure for a two-thirds majority was eliminated and progress through the long agenda was rapid.

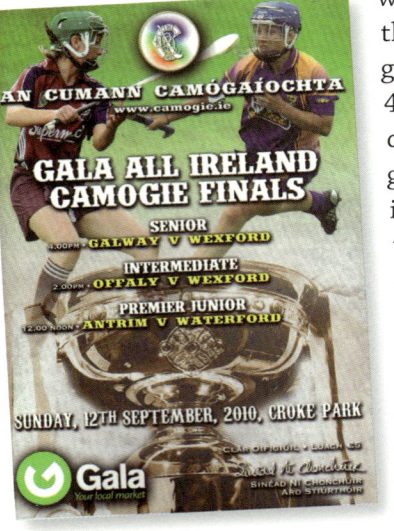

Among the new rules agreed were: a commitment to work in partnership with the wider Gaelic games family; a limiting of

Changing of the Guard

All-Ireland senior final 2010: President Mary McAleese and Joan O'Flynn, President of the Camogie Association, meet the Wexford captain, Una Leacy, before the start of the game. Right: Katrina Parrock, Wexford, tries to evade Regina Glynn, Galway.
Pictures: SPORTSFILE

an elected officer's term; granting of voting rights to those over 16 years of age; designating a player's home club; legislating for transfers, player grading and disciplinary issues; introducing age bands for underage competitions, and age restrictions on under-15s and under-16s playing in adult competitions; adopting child-centred, small-sided games for under-12 players; giving power to Annual Congress to elect three members of the Central Council; specifying the role of president; permitting official correspondence to be signed in Irish or English; introducing new penalties for reported late starts to matches and requiring umpires at inter-county matches to be over 15.

The Irish name of the Association reverted to An Cumann Camógaíochta, the original name chosen in 1904.

2010 All-Ireland Senior Championship

Galway and Cork produced a thrilling and entertaining tussle in the semi-final at Nowlan Park on August 14th. Opportunity beckoned for Galway as Cork carried little threat in the opening 25 minutes. However, the momentum swung towards the champions in the ten minutes leading up to half-time when they struck six

A Game of Our Own

points to take the lead for the first time. Galway reorganised their attack during the break and two well-taken points on the resumption signalled their intent. End-to-end play had the appreciative audience on the edge of their seats. Cork fought to equalise but a Veronica Curtin goal pushed Galway ahead. Síle Burns struck two placed balls accurately to level the game. With time almost up, Galway mounted one last attack. The referee signalled a free to Cork when Galway supporters believed that Therese Maher had been fouled. A terrific encounter ended all square, Galway 3–11, Cork 1–17.

The replay at Semple Stadium on August 22nd failed to live up to expectations. The stop-start nature of the game, in which 34 frees were awarded, did nothing to excite the attendance. Galway's defence were on top of Cork's limited attack and they restricted the Cork players to three points from play. Susan Earner, Regina Glynn, Ann Marie Hayes and Niamh Kilkenny were magnificent for the Connacht side. As usual, the defence was the most efficient sector of the Cork team and little room was afforded to

The Wexford team who defeated Galway in the 2010 All-Ireland Senior Championship. *Picture: Oliver McVeigh / SPORTSFILE*

the Galway attack. With the game in injury-time, Cork worked a free 60 metres from the Galway goal but the chance to level the game drifted wide to leave the result Galway 0–10, Cork 0–9.

The second semi-final between Kilkenny and Wexford at Nowlan Park was nip and tuck in the first half. Wexford's greater physical presence curtailed the young Kilkenny side and Ursula Jacob's accuracy from placed balls saw Wexford a point ahead at the interval. Club-mates, Katrina Parrock and Kate Kelly shot to the Kilkenny net in a two-minute spell to leave Kilkenny with a mountain to climb. A second major from Kate Kelly sealed the verdict for Wexford. Denise Gaule's injury-time goal came too late in influence the result which stood at Wexford 3–12, Kilkenny 1–11.

Galway gambled on Jessica Gill, who had cruciate surgery some months previously, for their meeting with Wexford in the All-Ireland final at Croke Park on September 12th. The reshuffled attack failed to ignite and had only three points from play to show for their efforts. Scoring opportunities were few and

Changing of the Guard

far between as the teak-tough Wexford defenders, particularly Catherine O'Loughlin, Mary Leacy and Claire O'Connor, did not concede an inch.

Wexford fielded more lethal of forwards. Una Leacy and Ursula Jacob were powerful on the ball and the exciting skills of Kate Kelly and Katrina Parrock put the Galway goal at risk when they got possession. Aislinn Connolly's accuracy from placed balls kept the gap between the sides to reasonable proportions and, when her 35-metre free dropped into the Wexford net, Galway were thrown a lifeline. In the remaining moments, Galway tried all they knew to breakdown the splendid Wexford defence but it was not to be. The final score was Wexford 1–12, Galway 1–10.

Wexford team: Mags D'Arcy, Claire O'Connor, Catherine O'Loughlin, Karen Atkinson, Noeleen Lambert, Mary Leacy, Aoife O'Connor, Caroline Murphy, Deirdre Codd, Kate Kelly (0–2), Una Leacy (captain) (0–1), Michelle O'Leary (0–1), Katrina Parrock

2010 All-Ireland Intermediate champions: Offaly players from left, Shelia Sulivan, Karen Nugent, Emma Dunne, Karen Brady and Linda Sullivan celebrate after the game. Picture: Oliver McVeigh / SPORTSFILE

(1–2), Ursula Jacob (0–6) and Josie Dwyer. Subs used: Ciara Storey and Lennie Holohan.

Galway team: Susan Earner, Sandra Tannian, Sarah Dervan, Regina Glynn, Niamh Kilkenny, Ann-Marie Hayes, Therese Manton, Brenda Hanney, Orla Kilkenny (0–1), Caroline Murray, Therese Maher (captain), Aislinn Connolly (1–6), Tara Rutledge, Jessica Gill (0–1) and Veronica Curtin (0–1). Subs used: Lorraine Ryan, Emma Kilkelly (0–1), Heather Cooney, Niamh McGrath and Aoife Lynskey.

2010 Intermediate Championship

Offaly secured a place in Croke Park on All-Ireland Day for the third year running when they overcame the strong challenge of Derry by 2–12 to 1–13 at Clones on August 21st. Goals from Elaine Dermody and Karen Nugent forged a two-point win at the end of a thrilling tussle.

Limerick, who fielded their first-choice players, were surprisingly turned over by Wexford's second string in the second semi-

451

final at Ardfinnan on August 21st. A resolute Wexford defence kept their goal intact despite being under constant pressure. Injury-time points from Ciara O'Connor and Louise Codd secured a final spot for Wexford by 1–9 to 0–11.

Offaly took another step up the camogie ladder with a 2–12 to 2–10 victory over Wexford in the All-Ireland final at Croke Park on September 12th. One year after leaving the junior ranks, they earned admission to the senior grade for 2011. A brace of goals from Elaine Dermody had Offaly nicely placed at 2–7 to 0–4 at the interval.

Wexford battled back admirably with well-taken scores, including a couple of goals from Fiona Rochford, to level the match. Siobhán Flannery and substitute Ailsa Hughes pointed to end an entertaining game.

Offaly team: Audrey Kennedy, Fiona Stephens, Lorraine Keena, Karen Brady, Sheila Sullivan, Michaela Morkan (captain), Linda Sullivan, Arlene Watkins (0–1), Marion Crean, Jean Brady (0–2), Aoife Kelly, Siobhán Flannery (0–4), Karen Nugent, Elaine Dermody (2–3) and Tina Hannon. Subs used: Ailsa Hughes (0–1), Emma Dunne (0–1) and Michelle Davis.

Wexford team: Helena Jacob, Jean Hayden, Louise O'Leary, Colleen Atkinson, Frances Doran, Louise Codd, Shelley Kehoe, Emma Moran, Lorraine O'Connor, Fiona Rochford (2–1), Síona Nolan, Stacey Redmond (0–1), Stacey Kehoe, Ciara O'Connor (captain) (0–5) and Lisa Bolger (0–2). Subs used: Eimear O'Connor, Bridget Curran and Linda Bolger (0–1).

All-Ireland Premier Junior Championship – Kay Mills Cup

Waterford powered past Meath in the All-Ireland semi-final at Dr Cullen Park to book a place in the final by 2–14 to 1–9. It was a very different story in the second semi-final at Casement Park. Antrim chiselled out a one-point victory over a fine Down side by 3–10 to 3–9.

Defences dominated in the All-Ireland final between Antrim and Waterford at Croke Park on September 12th. The half-time scoreline of Antrim 0–4, Waterford 0–3 indicates how few chances fell to the respective attackers. Jane Adams and Racquel McCarry found their range on the resumption to put the Ulster side in a commanding position. However, accurate point-taking by Waterford narrowed the gap and set up an exciting finish. Waterford's Karen Kelly had the last say with an equalising point to leave the score Antrim 1–9, Waterford 1–9.

The sides resumed the chase at Ashbourne on October 3rd. With the aid of a stiff breeze, Waterford built up a comfortable 0–9 to 0–3 lead. Antrim put the elements to good use on the changeover. With Rhona Torney dominating midfield, the Antrim forwards were well supplied with good ball. Michaela Convery and Laura Connolly finished goals which were to be the deciding factor of the game. Waterford found it very difficult to make headway against a resolute Antrim defence and were unable to create goal chances. Antrim were full value for their 2–10 to 0–12 win.

Antrim team: Mairéad Graham, Colleen Doherty, Aisling Jackson, Muirinn Quinn, Bronagh Orchin, Aisling McCall, Emma Connolly, Rhona Torney (0–1), Kerrie O'Neill (0–1), Michaela

Convery (1–1), Natalie McGuinness, Shannon Graham (0–1), Racquel McCarry (0–4), Katie McAleese and Jane Adams (captain) (0–2), Subs used: Charlene Hamill, Bernie McKinley and Laura Connolly (1–0).

Waterford team: Aisling O'Brien, Emma Hannon, Shona Curran, Kate Marie Hearne, Pauline Cunningham, Patricia Jackman (0–1), Jenny Simpson, Charlotte Raher, Shauna Kiernan, Nicola Morrissey, Áine Lyng (0–8), Jenny McCarthy, Niamh Rockett (0–2), Aisling Kelly and Karen Kelly (0–1). Subs used: Deirdre Fahy, Mairéad Murphy (captain) and Mary O'Donnell.

All-Ireland Junior A Championship – Nancy Murray Cup

Kildare had a comfortable victory over London while Armagh got the better of Westmeath in the semi-finals.

Armagh opened brightly in the final against Kildare, at Ashbourne on August 28th, with goals from Andrea McAlinden and Joanne Mallon. However, a goal by Orla Mullally and some carefully judged points by Róisín O'Connell brought Kildare back into contention. Armagh, who were ahead by 2–5 to 1–6 at the break, only managed three points in the second half. The sun blinded their goalkeeper, allowing Mary Murtagh's speculative shot to drop into the net. When Louise Walsh rifled home a goal in the dying moments, it was all over for Armagh. Kildare had bridged a 20-year gap to their previous All-Ireland success on the scoreline of 3–10 to 2–8.

Kildare team: Bríd Byrnes, Niamh Breen (captain), Regina Gorman, Niamh Concannon, Gillian O'Hurley, Carol Nolan, Lorraine Bowes, Clodagh Flanagan, Clodagh Farrell, Mary Murtagh, Ciara Tallon, Susie O'Carroll, Róisín O'Connell, Orla Mullally and Siobhán Hurley. Sub used: Louise Walsh.

Armagh team: Catherine Toner, Emma Farrell, Ann McGuigan, Caoimhe McKenna, Mairéad Shortt, Laura Gribben, Gráinne Kelly, Bernie Murray (captain), Niamh McGeown, Joanne Mallon, Ciara Donnelly, Katie O'Brien, Andrea McAlinden, Colette McSorley and Bríd O'Hagan.

2010 All-Ireland Junior B Championship – Máire Ní Chinnéide Cup

Kildare's second string found Cavan too hot to handle in the semi-final at Ashbourne on August 8th and conceded by 6–19 to 1–2. In a much tighter contest, Monaghan had a goal to spare over Meath at the same venue.

A late goal by substitute Aoishe O'Reilly gave Cavan a second bite of the cherry against Monaghan in the final at Ashbourne. Monaghan fell five points behind in the opening quarter and would have been further adrift but for poor shooting by the Cavan forwards. Another close and exciting contest was witnessed when the sides returned to Ashbourne on August 22nd. Both teams were guilty of wasting chances as the match came to an exciting finish. Monaghan captain, Eileen McElroy swung the result in Monaghan's way by 0–12 to 1–8.

Monaghan team: Róisín McKenna, Mary Meehan, Sharon McQuillan, Orla McMeel, Edel Kieran, Angela Kerr, Isobel Kieran, Siobhán McKenna, Eleanor McQuaid (0–2), Karen Boyle (0–1),

Helen Hughes, Shauna Finnegan (0–1), Rosita Finnegan, Mary McElroy and Eileen McElroy (captain) (0–7). Subs used: Lizzie McConnon (0–1).

Cavan team: Geraldine O'Reilly, Sinéad Brady, Niamh Brady, Siobhán Reynolds, Lisa Bennett, Sinéad Coyle, Rosie Crowe (captain), Andrea Lynch, Josephine Maguire, Majella Prior (0–4), Lorraine Day, Bríd Boylan (0–1), Aoishe O'Reilly, Róisín O'Keeffe (1–3) and Marie Brady. Subs used: Aileen Smith, Sinéad McKenna and Caroline Larkin.

2010 All-Ireland Minor A (Under-18) Championship

Three goals and two points from Susan Fahy powered Clare in the direction of the All-Ireland minor final. Naomi Carroll and Chloe Morey rowed in with three points apiece to dismiss Tipperary in the semi-final at Kilmallock.

The Galway captain, Laura Donnellan, lifts the cup after their 2010 All-Ireland Minor A Camogie Championship victory against Clare at Semple Stadium, Thurles. Picture: Matt Browne / SPORTSFILE

With a good spread of scorers, Galway eked out a narrow win over four-in-a-row champions, Kilkenny at the same venue. Kilkenny only managed 1–3 from play and relinquished their title by 1–14 to 2–10.

Excellent defensive play by both Galway and Clare had a huge impact in the final at Nenagh on August 7th. The hooking, blocking and intercepting of the ball by the respective backs kept the scoring low and prevented either side from drawing clear. All the excitement was packed into the closing minutes. Rebecca Hennelly took a pass from Shauna Healy and drove it to the Clare net. Clare battled back with well-taken points. As time ran out, Rebecca stood up to a vital free and tapped it over the bar to give Galway a second chance.

Galway raced into a four-point lead in the replay at Semple Stadium on August 21st. Laura Mitchell, Siobhán Coen, Tara

Changing of the Guard

Kenny and Lorraine Farrell put in great work for Galway. Marie Breheny sealed Clare's fate when she connected with a speculative ball from Rebecca Hennelly and turned it past Suzie O'Shea in the Clare goal. Clare kept trying and secured a goal deep into injury-time from Susan Fahy but it was too late to prevent Galway winning by 2–12 to 2–8. It was very hard luck on Chloe Morey, one of Clare's top players, to be on the losing side for the third year in succession.

Galway team: Olivia Lane, Tara Kenny, Karen Brien, Siobhán Coen, Noreen Murphy, Laura Donnellan (captain), Lorraine Farrell, Laura Mitchell, Shauna Healy, Rebecca Hennelly (0–6), Clodagh McGrath (0–1), Ailish O'Reilly (1–1), Finola Keely (0–1), Maria Brehony (1-1) and Aoife Donohue. Subs used: Niamh McGrath (0–2) and Maria Cooney.

Clare team: Suzie O'Shea, Joanne Walsh, Marie McGrath, Jessica O'Neill, Louise Woods, Chloe Morey (captain) (0–5), Christina Glynn, Lisa Loughnane, Niamh O'Dea, Regina O'Brien, Katie Cahill, Niamh Corry, Naomi Carroll (0–1), Susan Fahy (1–1) and Sinéad Tuohy. Subs used: Rachel O'Halloran, Ailish Considine and Laura McMahon.

2010 All-Ireland Minor B (Under-18) Championship

Offaly were overwhelmed by a rampant Derry side in the semi-final at Ashbourne. They had no answer to the classy play of the Ulster girls and finished 5–17 to 0–5 behind. Waterford, who have been knocking on the door of this championship for the past few seasons, were disappointed once again. Antrim's accurate shooting earned them victory by 2–14 to 2–6 at Ashbourne.

Neighbours, Derry and Antrim, clashed in the final at Celtic Park on August 29th. Experience played a big part in Derry's 3–10 to 0–9 win. Established players, Karen Kielt, Eilís Ní Chaiside and Gráinne McNicholl took a firm grip on proceedings and allowed little scope to the Antrim girls. Goals from Mary Jo McCullagh, Mary Kelly and Gráinne McNicholl sealed the verdict in Derry's favour. Laura Connolly, Una McNaughton, Samantha McKillen and Aimee McAtamney were prominent on the Antrim side.

Derry team: Niamh McQuillan, Sarah McAllister, Eimear Mullan, Mairéad Walsh, Aoife Ní Cháiside, Danielle McCrystal, Maria Mooney, Karen Kielt (0–7), Eilís Ní Chaiside, Rachel Kelly, Gráinne McNicholl (1–1), Niamh Boylan, Mary Jo McCullagh (1–1), Mary Kelly (1–1), Gráinne O'Kane. Subs used: Shauna Quinn, Shauneen Donaghy and Elizabeth Corbett.

Antrim team: Cathy McCarry, Áine Connolly, Laura Connolly (captain), Aoife Laverty, Shauna Devlin, Una McNaughton, Michaela Beattie, Rebecca Walsh (0–1), Maeve Connolly, Samantha McKillen (0–3), Aimee McAtamney (0–2), Hannah Devlin, Aisling McFadden, Chloe Drain (0–2), Ruby Marie Rice (0–1). Subs used: Niamh Donnelly, Dervla O'Neill and Anna Kelly.

2010 All-Ireland Minor C (Under-18) Championship

Carlow capped a great season with a notable underage double. In a fantastic game of camogie at Ashbourne on September 4th, they added the under-18 title to the under-16 crown captured earlier in the season. The standard of play was of the highest quality as they dispatched final opponents, Armagh, by a margin of ten points.

Two goals by Eleanor Treacy had left Carlow well-positioned as they returned to the dressing room and a thrilling second-half saw the total number of scores rise to 28 shared by 15 players. The ability of the Carlow girls to turn five of their chances into goals was the difference between the teams. Carlow won by 5–10 to 1–12.

Carlow team: Niamh Curran, Amy Skelton, Maria Kehoe, Jillian English, Shauna Barcoe (0–1), Michelle Kelly (captain), Emma Kelly, Margaret Murphy (1–3), Lorraine Bible (1–0), Olivia McDonald (0–1), Ann Murphy, Ciara Quirke (0–1), Collette Malone, Eleanor Treacy (2–2), Sarah Jane Burke. Subs used: Kate Nolan, Katie O'Byrne (0–1), Michelle Nolan (0–1), Rebecca O'Dwyer (1–0) and Chloe Kenny.

Armagh team: Cliodhna McAteer, Gemma McKeown, Amy Lavery, Michelle McPartland, Caoimhe Smith, Hannah McGeown, Aoife Murphy, Petrina Cosgrove (0–4), Orlagh Kearns (captain) (0–1), Kirsty Sheridan, Eadaoin Murphy (0–1), Joanne Mullin (0–4), Cáit McGivern, Megan McKensie and Meabh Leneghan (0–1). Subs used: Laura Smith (1–1), Aisling Murphy and Megan Grimley.

2010 All-Ireland Under-16 A Championship

From the throw-in, Galway were in total command and brushed aside the inadequate challenge of Cork in the semi-final at The Ragg. Superior in all aspects of the game, this talented Galway outfit had secured their place in the final by 1–20 to 1–0 long before the end.

Tipperary captain, Aoife Ryan led from the front with an impressive tally of nine points against Kilkenny in the semi-final at The Ragg. Tipperary held the edge all through and were deserving winners by 0–13 to 1–3.

In a repeat of the 2009 All-Ireland final, Galway and Tipperary produced the same result and the same score, Galway 2–11, Tipperary 2–7 at Tullamore. The standard of camogie was excellent with two skilful sides giving of their best. Galway led from Rebecca Hennelly's first-minute free and could have had the game wrapped up long before the finish had they availed of all their chances. Maria Cooney was majestic at centre-back for the winners and had great support from Rebecca Hennelly, Aoibhinn Kenny, Orlaith McGrath, Catríona Daly, Clodagh McGrath and Ailish O'Reilly. Tipperary did not let Galway have it all their own way. Far from it, they kept Galway under pressure but were unable to find the scores necessary for victory.

Galway team: Catríona Daly, Sarah Keenan, Sinéad Cormican, Michelle Dunleavy, Lorraine Farrell, Maria Cooney, Áine Dervan, Clodagh McGrath (captain), Rebecca Hennelly (0–6), Ailish O'Reilly (1–1), Rachel Monaghan, Aoibhin Kenny (0–2), Sara Skehill, Maria Brehony (1–0) and Orlaith McGrath (0–2). Sub used: Aoife Dolan.

Tipperary team: Orla McEniry, Julienne Bourke, Caoimhe Maher, Louise McLoughlin, Rachel Kennedy, Clodagh Quirke, Mary Walsh, Teresa Ryan (1–0), Sarah Fryday, Ciara McGrath

(0–2), Anne Eviston (0–1), Tara Kennedy (1–0), Aoife Ryan (captain) (0–1), Michaela Graham (0–1) and Andrea Loughnane (0–2). Subs used: Cliodhna Ryan and Megan Ryan.

Maria Cooney and Katie Forde are daughters of All-Ireland senior hurling medal winners, Joe Cooney and Bernie Forde. Andrea Loughnane is a grandniece of legendary Tipperary hurler, Jimmy Doyle.

2010 All-Ireland Under-16 B Championship

Elaine Mullane (2–1) and Martina McMahon (1–6) caught the eye in the colours of Limerick against Antrim in the semi-final at Ashbourne. Their ability to put scores on the board put Limerick firmly on the road to the final. The game ended at Limerick 6–8, Antrim 2–8. In the second semi-final at Ashbourne, the accuracy of Shannon Kearney was instrumental in Derry's 0–12 to 2–4 win over Waterford. Waterford kept in touch but were unable to secure victory.

There was little between Derry and Limerick at the close of a well-contested first-half in the final at St Peregrine's. The half-back trio of Noeleen McKenna, Aoife Cassidy and Bronagh McGillian formed a barrier to the Derry goal in the second-half and drove the ball forward to where Michaela Mullan, Rachel Mulholland and Mairéad McNicholl put it to good use. A fine team performance by Derry earned a 3–9 to 1–6 win.

Derry team: Una Bradley, Megan Kerr, Maeve Quinn, Paula McElwee, Noeleen McKenna, Aoife Cassidy (captain), Bronagh McGillian, Shauna Quinn (0–3), Catherine McColgan, Michaela Mullan (1–1), Shannon Kearney (0–3), Mairéad McNicholl (1–0), Aneica Duffy (0–1), Rachel Mulholland (1–1) and Sinéad Donnelly.

Limerick team: Claire Keating (1–1), Grace Lee, Katherina White, Emma Quaid, Katie Hurley (captain), Lisa Scanlon, Kate Brislane, Niamh Ryan (0–1), Tahlia Fitzgerald, Niamh Cagney, Martina McMahon (0–2), Muireann Creamer, Kristy Carroll (0–1), Elaine Mullane (0–1) and Rebecca Delee.

2010 All-Ireland Under-16 C Championship

Carlow and Meath swept through to the All-Ireland final following decisive victories over Roscommon and Tyrone. Three goals from Ciara Quirke set Carlow up for a 5–8 to 0–0 win at Tullamore. Meath had sharpshooters in Adrienne McCann, Lauren Patterson and Shona White and won comfortably by 7–4 to 1–2 at Truagh.

The final was a day to remember for Carlow's Eleanor Treacy who scored 3–2 to see her county defeat Meath at Blakestown by 4–8 to 1–3. While Eleanor put the finishing touches to some well-worked chances, it was far from a one-girl show. Carlow were the better team right through the field and had excellent players in Lorraine Bible, Michelle Nolan, Ann Marie Kelly, Katie O'Byrne and Chloe Kenny. Meath struggled to exert authority. In the dying moments, full-back Ellan Burke moved up field to score a consolation goal.

Carlow team: Niamh Curran, Ann Marie Kelly, Katie O'Byrne, Chloe Kenny (captain), Shauna Barcoe (0–2), Kate Nolan, Emma

A Game of Our Own

Kelly, Lorraine Bible (1–1), Michelle Nolan, Olivia McDonald, Ciara Quirke (0–2), Shauna Daly, Maria Carroll, Eleanor Treacy (3–2), Rebecca O'Dwyer (0–1). Subs Used: Casey Tobin, Laura Quirke and Megan McDonald.

Meath team: Ellan Duigan, Ciara Donoghue, Ellan Burke, Mollie Duigan, Cheyenne O'Brien, Lauren McCann (captain), Ailbhe Lynch, Lisa Carroll, Maggie Randell, Susie Gartland, Adrienne McCann, Laura Irwin, Lauren Patterson, Shona White and Caoimhe McDermott. Subs used: Áine Kirby, Aoibhinn Leahy, Cathy Collins and Emma Gill.

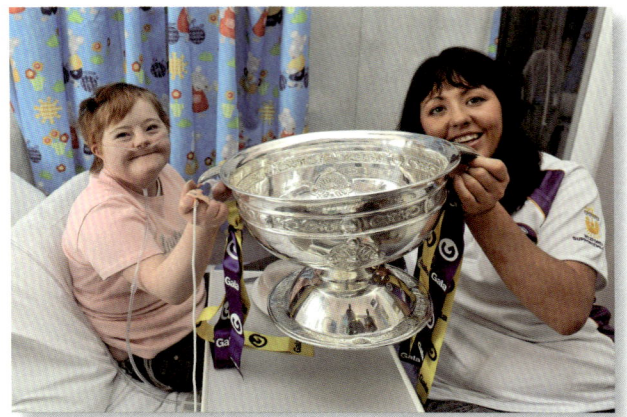

Wexford senior camogie captain Una Lacey pictured with Aine Gibbons, from Prosperous, Co. Kildare, during a team visit at Our Lady's Hospital for Sick Children, Crumlin, Dublin. Picture: *David Maher / SPORTSFILE*

2010 Gael-Linn Cup

The Gael-Linn interprovincial championships were restricted to one competition in 2010. A fall-off in the interest shown in the series with players declining to participate led to this action. Senior teams only took part in 2010 with the junior sides scheduled to return in 2011. Eleven Munster players scored in a rout of Connacht in the semi-final at Trim on May 16th. The Munster attack was well on top against a porous Connacht defence and paved the way for a 9–17 to 0–12 win. Leinster had a comfortable hour against Ulster in the second semi-final and were ahead by 4–7 to 1–4 in the end.

A mainly Kilkenny-Wexford combination playing under the Leinster banner possessed better teamwork and understanding than the Munster side which was drawn from five counties. Leinster moved the ball well and were fully deserving of their nine-point win, 3–17 to 1–14.

Leinster team: Catríona Ryan (Kilkenny), Michaela Morkan (Offaly), Catherine Doherty (Kilkenny), Jacqui Frisby (Kilkenny), Catherine O'Loughlin (Wexford), Mary Leacy (Wexford), Elaine Aylward (Kilkenny), Denise Gaule (Kilkenny), Arlene Watkins (Offaly), Anne Dalton (captain) (Kilkenny), Katie Power (Kilkenny), Michelle Quilty (Kilkenny), Kate Kelly (Wexford), Una Leacy (Wexford), Elaine Dermody (Offaly). Subs used: Shelley Kehoe (Wexford) and Ciara Burgess (Dublin).

Munster panel: Aoife Murray (Cork), Gráinne Kenneally (Waterford), Caitríona Foley (Cork), Jenny Duffy (captain) (Cork), Mary Ryan (Tipperary), Sabrina Larkin (Tipperary), Julie McGrath (Tipperary), Orla Cotter (Cork), Anna Geary (Cork), Marie Walsh (Cork), Niamh Mulcahy (Limerick), Jill Horan (Tipperary), Áine Lyng (Waterford), Deirdre Murphy (Clare), Noreen Flanagan (Tipperary), Susan Flanagan (Clare), Gemma O'Connor

Changing of the Guard

(Cork), Jenny O'Leary (Cork), Patricia Jackman (Waterford) and Fiona Lafferty (Clare).

2010 All-Ireland Club Championships

A decision was taken to defer the closing stages of the 2010 All-Ireland senior and intermediate club championships to spring 2011.

Senior Club Championship

Galway champions, Killimor, survived a stern test in heavy conditions at the hands of Oulart The Ballagh (Wexford) in the semi-final of the All-Ireland Club Championship at Ballinasloe. With the sides evenly matched and the marking tight, scores were hard to come by. Every ball was pursued relentlessly as torrential rain cut up the playing surface. Killimor had their noses in front by 0–5 to 0–4 at the interval and held the slender advantage to the finish. Martina Conroy's accuracy from placed balls, together with the never-say-die attitude of her team-mates, secured a place in the final by 0–9 to 0–8.

The semi-final between Inniscarra (Cork) and Rossa (Antrim) fell victim to a water-logged St Conleth's Park at Newbridge. Inniscarra contained Rossa for 45 minutes of the rescheduled match in Nowlan Park and, then, opened up to take control of the game. With the Inniscarra supporters in full voice, the Cork girls struck some sublime points to draw away from their opponents and win by 1–14 to 1–6.

The All-Ireland club championship final returned to Croke Park for the first time since 1973. Before a sizeable crowd on March 6th, Killimor produced a stunning display of skilful camogie to leave Inniscarra devastated. The Galway side got into the game from the throw-in whereas the play appeared to pass Inniscarra by. Twenty-three minutes elapsed before Niamh Dilworth opened the scoring for Inniscarra. By then, Killimor were motoring at full throttle and had the game won, barring a dramatic comeback, when they led by 2–4 to 0–1 at the break.

The Inniscarra resurgence did not materialise. If anything, Killimor upped their performance. They opened up the Inniscarra defence, ran through and picked off delightful scores. It was a wonderful display of the top class camogie by Killimor. They defended with determination and discipline and attacked with skill and flair, giving one of the best performances ever witnessed in this competition. Killimor claimed the title by 3–18 to 1–4. Brenda Hanney (Player of the Match), Ann Marie Hayes, Susan Keane and Martina Conroy stood out in a team of stars. For luckless Inniscarra side, who had taken their supporters on a wonderful journey, it was a step too far.

Killimor team: Helen Campbell, Niamh Hanney, Nicola Lawless, Julie Brien, Karen Brien, Ann Marie Hayes, Marie Duane, Emer Haverty (0–2), Ann Marie Starr, Susan Keane (0–4), Brenda Hanney (captain) (0–4), Martina Conroy (1–6), Helen Quinn (1–0), Claire Conroy (0–1) and Lorraine Donnelly (1–0). Subs used: Anna Maria Lagana, Serena Brien (0–1), Nicola Donnelly, Niamh Connolly and Ciara Brien.

Inniscarra team: Sinéad Ní Riain, Aileen Sheehan, Liz Hayes,

Mary Buckley, Emma Kingston (0–1), Rosie O'Mahony, Karen Jones, Rena Buckley (0–1), Orla Healy, Joanne Casey (0–1), Margaret Noelle O'Sullivan (captain), Katie O'Mahony, Margaret Cosgrove, Fiona O'Connell and Niamh Dilworth (1–1). Subs used: Laura Burke, Treasa McCarthy and Liz Buckley.

Intermediate Club Championship

It took a stunning late goal from substitute Katie Mullan to book a place in the final for Eoghan Rua (Derry) when they met Lismore (Waterford) in the semi-final of the All-Ireland Intermediate Club Championship at Cloughjordan. The Coleraine girls got off to a great start and built up a five-point lead but they allowed Lismore back into the game. It took a gritty second-half show by Eoghan Rua to grind out a 2–6 to 1–6 victory.

The experienced Laois side, The Harps, who had won three All-Ireland junior club titles between 2006 and 2008, carried too much power for Sarsfields (Galway) in the second semi-final at Ballinasloe. Sarsfields made The Harps fight hard for victory but, in the end, they had to conceded to a better side by 2–12 to 1–7.

Playing an attractive brand of camogie, Eoghan Rua won the inaugural All-Ireland Intermediate Club Championship title at the expense of The Harps in Croke Park on March 6th, 2011. By no means did Eoghan Rua have an easy passage. The Harps fought every inch of the way to make it a great contest. Eoghan Rua team captain, Méabh McGoldrick, gave a commanding performance at centre-back and drove her side forward at every opportunity. The ability of the very experienced Grace McMullan to turn chances into goals was the deciding factor. The Harps attack received a plentiful supply of ball but their accuracy left them down. Eoghan Rua delighted their huge following with a well-deserved 3–8 to 2–3 victory.

Eoghan Rua team: Aileen Moore, Aisling Carey, Kelly Maybin, Maureen Heneghan, Éilis McNamee, Méabh McGoldrick (captain), Maria Mooney, Megan Kerr, Jane Carey, Maeve Dillon, Gráinne McGoldrick (0–7), Sinéad Boyle, Hannah Eastwood, Grace McMullan (3–1), Rosanna McAleese. Subs used: Katie Mullan and Adelle Archibald.

The Harps team: Teresa Bennett, Elaine Cuddy (captain), Denise Quigley, Patricia Dunphy, Claire Walsh, Caitríona Phelan, Michelle Fitzpatrick, Louise Mahony, Joanne Prior, Áine Mahony, Angela Hanlon, Elaine Mahony, Joan Dollard, Ashling Phelan and Laura Saunders.

Junior Club Championship

Claire Commane was the star of the show for Corofin (Clare) in the All-Ireland club junior semi-final against Tír na nÓg (Antrim). An impressive 2–9 by the talented forward went a long way to seeing off the challenge of the Ulster side. The final score was Corofin 2–10, Tír na nÓg 1–8. In the second semi-final, Four Roads (Roscommon) proved much too slick and experienced for Kilmessan (Meath) and won comfortably by 2–13 to 0–6.

Four Roads and Corofin braved arctic conditions in the final at Ballinasloe on November 28th. Scores were hard to come by in a close and exciting opening-half. A two-point advantage, 0–4

Changing of the Guard

President of the Camogie Association Joan O' Flynn with 2010 Camogie All-Star nominees, Soaring Stars, Intermediate Soaring Stars, and Young Players of the Year at the 2010 Camogie All-Stars in association with O'Neills. Citywest Hotel, Saggart, Co. Dublin. *Picture: Stephen McCarthy / SPORTSFILE*

to 0–2, was a poor return for the possession enjoyed by the Four Roads attack. Both teams had good scoring opportunities in the second-half, some taken and others spurned. A well-taken goal by Gráinne Egan sealed the outcome in favour of Four Roads by 1–9 to 0–6. Lizzie Glennon-Tully, Orla Hughes, Donna Kelly and Marie Glennon-Kelly turned in match-winning performances for Four Roads. Carmel Tierney, Lisa Clancy, Niamh O'Dea and Claire Commane kept Corofin in the picture.

Four Roads team: B. Mannion, C. Glennon, Orla Hughes, Marie Glennon-Kelly, Aoife Fallon, Siobhán Coyle, Donna Kelly, Gertie Dowd, Catherine Rogerson, Niamh Coyle, Gráinne Egan, Sinéad O'Brien, Lizzie Glennon-Tully, Patricia Lennon and Edel Treacy. Sub used: Aisling Rogers.

Corofin team: Carmel Tierney, Neasa Carkill, Lisa Clancy, Donna Courtney, Brenda O'Donoghue, Muireann Kelleher, Niamh Shannon, Edel Keating, Niamh O'Dea, Linda McMahon, Marie Raftery, Aislinn Kelleher, Aoife Davoren, Claire Commane and Siobhán Kelleher.

2010 Camogie-Shinty

Ireland registered a comprehensive win over Scotland in the seventh annual camogie-shinty contest held at Ratoath on October 30th. Susie O'Carroll, Róisín O'Keeffe and Colette McSorley mastered the heavy-underfoot conditions to score goals in the opening 20 minutes. A sweetly struck ball by Joanne Gillanders reduced the margin before further goals by Jemma Egan, Aisling Corr and Colette McSorley sealed victory for the home side. The final score was Ireland 6–9, Scotland 2–2.

Irish panel: Róisín McKenna (Monaghan), Niamh Breen (Kildare), Regina Gorman (Kildare), Clodagh Byrne (Carlow), Rosie Crowe (Cavan), Isabel Kiernan (Monaghan), Laura Gribben (Armagh), Bríd Grennan (London), Bernie Murray (Armagh), Róisín O'Keeffe (Cavan), Pamela Greville (Westmeath), Susie O'Carroll (Kildare), Jemma Egan (Westmeath), Colette McSorley (Armagh), Shauna Jordan (Tyrone), Bríd Boylan (Cavan), Áine Charlton (Mayo), Bronagh McLernon (London), Claire Coffey (Meath) and Aisling Corr (Tyrone).

The *Irish Daily Star*/Gala Performance Awards

A new initiative was introduced to the senior championship in 2010. A player of the match was chosen from a selected game in the seven rounds of the championship and the All-Ireland semi-finals and featured in the *Irish Daily Star* on the Monday after the match. Match-winning performances by the top players were rewarded and their fantastic skills levels highlighted. The players

Group pictured at Stormont Castle, Belfast in 2010. Back: Sheila Wallace, Catherine Neary, Brighidin Heenan, Peadar de Barra and Liz Howard. Front: Catherine O'Hara, Phyllis Breslin, Sinéad O'Connor and Mary Herald.

honoured were: Brenda Hanney (Galway), Gemma O'Connor (Cork), Mary Leacy (Wexford), Aoife O'Connor (Wexford), Regina Glynn (Galway), Anna Geary (Cork), Jenny O'Leary (Cork) and Aislinn Connolly (Galway).

2010 All-Star Awards

All-Ireland senior champions, Wexford, and runners-up, Galway, scooped the bulk of the 2010 All-Star awards with eight and five respectively. The occasion was honoured by the presence of President Mary McAleese, who was very complimentary to the recipients. Two pairs of sisters, Mary and Una Leacy (Wexford), and Niamh and Orla Kilkenny (Galway), collected awards.

2010 All-Stars: Mags D'Arcy (Wexford), Claire O'Connor (Wexford), Catherine O'Loughlin (Wexford), Niamh Kilkenny (Galway), Regina Glynn (Galway), Mary Leacy (Wexford), Anna Geary (Cork), Orla Kilkenny (Galway), Ann Dalton (Kilkenny), Kate Kelly (Wexford), Una Leacy (Wexford), Brenda Hanney (Galway), Katrina Parrock (Wexford), Ursula Jacob (Wexford) and

Changing of the Guard

Aislinn Connolly (Galway).

2010 Soaring Stars Awards

All-Ireland premier junior finalists, Antrim and Waterford, were the main recipients of the 2010 Soaring Stars awards. Winners Antrim collected five positions while Waterford captured four. Jane Adams, the Antrim captain, won an All-Star award in 2008 and became the first player to be named on both selections.

Those honoured were: Caroline Connaghton (Roscommon), Rhona Torney (Antrim), Shona Curran (Waterford), Regina Gorman (Kildare), Fionnuala Carr (Down), Patricia Jackman (Waterford), Jenny Simpson (Waterford), Bernie Murray (Armagh), Kerrie O'Neill (Antrim), Michaela Convery (Antrim), Áine Lyng (Waterford), Shannon Graham (Antrim), Sarah Ann Fitzgerald (Laois), Jane Adams (Antrim) and Jane Dolan (Meath).

Three intermediate Soaring Stars were chosen: Michaela Morkan (Offaly), Elaine Dermody (Offaly) and Ciara O'Connor (Wexford) picked up the awards in this new category. Laura Mitchell (Connacht) was crowned Young Player of the Year with Sarah Carey (Munster), Aisling Dunphy (Leinster) and Danielle McCrystal (Ulster) in the runner-up positions. Former Offaly hurler, Joachim Kelly, who guided his charges to the 2009 All-Ireland Junior and the 2010 All-Ireland Intermediate titles, was named Manager of the Year.

Media Awards

The Media Awards for the 2010 season honoured the outstanding work of those who keep camogie in the public eye and recognise the huge contribution made by national, provincial press and our own voluntary workers in promoting and enhancing the profile of the game.

The recipients of the Camogie Association Media Awards were: Armagh, Best Match Programme; Clare FM, Local Radio Station; *Offaly Express*, Best Provincial Newspaper; and Dublin Camogie Board, Best Website). The RTÉ Mick Dunne Memorial Awards were claimed by Barbara Ryan (Wexford), PRO of the Year; Caroline Quinn, Photo of the Year; *I Gotta Feeling* by Dean Goodison (Wexford), Best Published Work); and *Irish Examiner*, Best National Coverage.

Claire O'Connor, Wexford, in action against Ann Marie Starr, right, and Tara Ruttledge, Galway in the 2011 All-Ireland Senior Championship Final. Picture: Brian Lawless / SPORTSFILE

2011 All-Ireland Senior Championship

Shortcomings in attack and the retirement of key defensive players left Cork vulnerable in the semi-final against Wexford at Nowlan Park on August 13th. The All-Ireland champions capitalised on these frailties and outscored Cork by five points, 2-11 to 1-9, to advance to the final. Kilkenny kept in touch with Galway until the final minutes of the second semi-final at the same venue. A late goal by Tara Ruttledge sealed victory for Galway by 2-13 to 2-7. The brilliant Kilkenny minors, who dominated their age-group for several seasons, had not yet come of age in the senior ranks.

Conditions were perfect for good camogie as Wexford and Galway lined up for the eightieth All-Ireland senior final at Croke Park on September 11th. A stop-start opening half-hour yielded very little entertainment, particularly to the neutral spectator. The ever-dangerous Kate Kelly was hauled-down as she descended on goal and Una Leacy converted the subsequent penalty to see the champions off to a good start. Despite failing to score from play, Wexford headed for the half-time break 1-2 to 0-3 in front.

A fired-up Galway side returned to the fray and quickly wiped out the deficit. When Tara Ruttledge sent an unstoppable shot to the Wexford net, Galway looked to be on the road to victory. Therese Maher, Niamh Kilkenny and Ann Marie Starr played brilliant camogie and drove the ball forward but the Galway attack was unable to build of their advantage and apply the killer blow. Wexford played with real conviction in the closing minutes. A magnificent goal from captain, Ursula Jacob, lifted the team. She added two points to seal victory and earn the right to lift the O'Duffy Cup. Galway will regret nine wides and shots which dropped short as they reflect on the final score of Wexford 2-7 Galway 1-8.

Wexford Team: Mags D'Arcy, Claire O'Connor, Catherine O'Loughlin, Karen Atkinson, Noeleen Lambert, Mary Leacy, Aoife O'Connor, Deirdre Codd, Josie Dwyer (0-1), Kate Kelly, Una Leacy (1-0), Michelle O'Leary, Lenny Holohan (0-1), Ursula Jacob (Capt) (1-5), Katrina Parrock. Subs used: Fiona Kavanagh, Evelyn Quigley, Ciara Storey.

Galway Team: Susan Earner, Therese Manton, Sinéad Cahalan, Lorraine Ryan, Ann-Marie Hayes, Therese Maher, Heather Cooney, Niamh Kilkenny (0-1), Ann Marie Starr, Noreen Coen (0-1), Martina Conroy (0-1), Aislinn Connolly (0-2), Tara Ruttledge (1-1), Brenda Hanney (Capt), Veronica Curtin (0-1). Sub used: Orla Kilkenny (0-1).

2011 All-Ireland Intermediate Championship

The All-Ireland semi-finals produced exciting fare. Wexford edged in front of Derry, 3-8 to 2-10, while Antrim shaded the verdict against Limerick, 2-11 to 2-9, at Páirc Tailteann.

Wexford got off to a brilliant start with two goals inside the opening ten minutes of the All-Ireland final against Antrim at Croke Park on September 11th. Ciara O'Connor and Fiona Rochford took advantage of poor defending to ease Wexford into a comfortable lead. Antrim fought back heroically with the accurate Jane Adams reducing the deficit to three points by half-time.

Changing of the Guard

Waterford players, from left, Deirdre Fahey, Ruth Geoghegan, Mairead Murphy, and Asling O'Brien celebrate after their All-Ireland Premier Junior Championship Final victory over Down. Picture: Brian Lawless / SPORTSFILE

Wexford stretched their lead to seven points and seemed destined for a facile victory. But Antrim were not finished. Jane Adams' accuracy from placed balls whittled away at Wexford's surplus to create an exciting climax to the contest. A last minute free, which could have yielded an equalising goal, was blocked and cleared to leave Wexford champions by 2-12 to 0-15.

Wexford Team: Helena Jacob, Colleen Atkinson, Bernie Holohan, Frances Doran, Louise O'Leary, Áine Codd, Lisa Bolger, Shelly Kehoe, Síona Nolan (0-2), Louise Codd (0-2), Bridget Curran, Stacey Redmond, Ciara O'Connor (1-3), Fiona Rochford (1-1), Linda Bolger (0-2). Subs used: Tracey Nolan (0-2), Stacey Kehoe.

Antrim Team: Mairéad Graham, Cathy Carey, Aileen Martin, Ashling McCall, Bronagh Orchin, Emma Connolly, Ashling Jackson, Colleen Doherty, Rhona Torney, Michaels Convery (0-1), Natalie McGuinness, Charlene Hamill (0-1), Katie McAleese, Jane Adams (Capt) (0-13), Louise McAleese. Subs used: Máiríosa McGourty, Orlagh O'Hara, Louise McMullan.

2011 All-Ireland Premier Junior Championship

Waterford proved too good for Laois in the semi-final at Nowlan Park by 2-17 to 2-3 while Down qualified for the final at the expense of Meath by 1-17 to 1-13 at Clontibret. Waterford and Down served up a hugely-entertaining game of camogie when they met in the All-Ireland final at Croke Park on September 11th. The standard of play was very pleasing and belied the fact that it was the third level of adult camogie. Ruth Geoghegan and Karen Kelly contributed goals to Waterford's half-time lead of 2-8 to 0-5.

Down battled back admirably and trimmed Waterford's advantage with eight unanswered points. Spurred on by the memory of previous final defeats, Niamh Rockett put a stop to the Down charge with a well-taken point to leave four points between the sides. Down's Nicola Braniff goaled in injury time to the delight of the Ulster following. The referee's whistle was sweet music to the Waterford players who had brought the first adult All-Ireland title to the county. The final score was Waterford 2-11 Down 1-13.

Waterford Team: Aislinn O'Brien, Emma Hannon, Jennie Simpson, Kate-Marie Hearne, Shauna Kiernan, Charlotte Raher, Gráinne Kenneally, Patricia Jackman (0-2), Deirdre Fahey, Niamh Rockett (0-2), Nicola Morrissey (Capt), Aoife Hannon, Ruth Geoghegan (1-1), Karen Kelly (1-5), Zoe O'Donoghue (0-1). Sub used: Jenny McCarthy.

Down Team: Kitty Fegan, Orla Maginn, Ciara McGovern, Emma McCormick, Paula Gribbin, Fionnuala Carr (0-2), Karen Tinnelly, Lisa McPolin (0-1), Karen McMullan (0-1), Catherine McGourty (0-5), Lisa McCrickard (Capt), Kelly O'Higgins (0-1), Karen Gribbin, Sarah-Louise Carr, Niamh Mallon (0-3). Subs used: Laura Hughes, Nicola Braniff (1-0).

2011 All-Ireland Junior B Championship – Máire Ní Chinnéide Cup

Considering that Wicklow were unable to field an adult team in 2010, they did very well to reach the final of the All-Ireland Junior B Championship in 2011. However, they found the greater strength and experience of Monaghan too much to cope with in the final at Ashbourne on August 28th. Marie Grennan, Michelle Morgan and Eleanor McQuaid stamped their authority on the game to see Monaghan run out winners by 1-12 to 1-7.

Monaghan Team: Róisín McKenna, Louise O'Connell, Aisling Greenan, Joanne McSkeane, Edel Kieran, Isobel Kieran, Mary Meehan, Michelle Morgan, Siobhán McKenna, Mairéad McCarron, Shauna Finnegan (0-1), Eleanor McQuaid (0-2), Nicola Morgan (1-1), Marie Greenan (0-7), Karen Boyle (0-1).

Wicklow Team: Nicky Keddy, April Dickenson, Mary O'Neill, Nora O'Neill, Róisín Mulford, Teresa Keogh, Claire Whelan, Laura Manley (0-5), Karen Walsh, Claire Byrne, Sinéad Byrne (0-1), Amanda Waters (0-1), Mary Whelan (0-1), Síle Whelan (0-1), Kellie Byrne.

2011 All-Ireland Minor (U18)A Championship

Tipperary earned their place in the All-Ireland final by virtue of a one-point win over Clare, 3-9 to 1-14, in the semi-final at Kilmallock. Kilkenny emerged from the second semi-final at Nenagh with a comfortable seven-point winning margin, 3-16 to 3-9. In what was a truly-remarkable contest, Tipperary staged a stunning comeback to wipe out the half-time deficit of 2-6 to 1-0 in the final at Semple Stadium on July, 31st. With eight minutes remaining, Nicole Walsh raced through the Kilkenny defence and struck the ball to the net to bring the sides level. The same player converted a last minute free to earn Tipperary a 4-4 to 2-9 victory.

Tipperary Team: Orla McEniry, Julie Ann Burke, Sheila Ryan, Louise McLoughlin, Clodagh Quirke, Aisling Cremin, Mairéad Barry, Bríd Quinn (Capt) (0-1), Caoimhe Maher, Andrea Loughnane, Ereena Fryday, Nicole Walsh (1-1), Sarah Fryday (2-0), Michaela Graham (1-0), Ciara McGrath. Subs used: Anne Eviston, Theresa Ryan, Tara Kennedy (0-1), Alice Fogarty (0-1), Mairéad Teehan.

Changing of the Guard

Kilkenny Team: Áine Kinsella, Niamh Phelan, Jennifer Cunningham, Laura Norris, Meighan Farrell, Grace Walsh, Noelle Maher, Kate Holland, Kelly Hamilton, Lydia Fitzpatrick (0-2), Claire Phelan (1-1), Miriam Walsh (0-2), Aisling Curtis (0-2), Orla Hanrick (1-1), Aoife Murphy. Sub used: Emma Kavanagh (0-1).

2011 All-Ireland Minor (U18)B Championship

Limerick proved too strong for Wexford when the sides met in the semi-final at De la Salle, Gracedieu. The Shannonsiders came away with a comfortable 2-12 to 1-5 victory. Antrim controlled the second semi-final against Waterford at Trim and finished in front by 4-8 to 2-7. One point ahead, 2-6 to 2-5, at the interval of the final against Antrim at Ashbourne on July 31st, Limerick drove on to force a 4-10 to 2-8 win.

Limerick Team: Claire O'Riordan, Emma Quaid, Grace Lee, Aisling Enright, Michelle Browne, Lisa Scanlon (0-1), Patricia Liston, Elaine Kennedy, Rebecca Delee, Bríd Hannon (0-1), Martina McMahon (1-7), Kristy Carroll (Capt), Caoimhe Costello (1-1), Niamh Ryan (2-0), Claire Keating.

Antrim Team: Danielle McMichael, Nuala Kelly, Maria Donnelly, Shauna O'Neill, Shannon Woulahan, Michaela Beattie, Colleen Patterson, Shauna Devlin (Capt), Laura Connolly, Orlagh O'Hara (1-1), Chloe Drain (0-2), Meabh Laverty (0-3), Ursula McCotter (0-2), Ruby Marie Rice (1-0), Niamh Donnelly. Subs used: K. Donnelly, Lauren Elliott, Maeve McCouaig, N. Adams, Lucia McNaughton.

2011 All-Ireland Minor (U18) C Championship

Armagh and Meath, two evenly-matched sides, produced a thrilling final at Drogheda on August 28th. Play swung from end to end, with both teams enjoying a period of dominance. The deciding score came when Armagh's Eadaoin Murphy connected sweetly with the ball to steer it out of the reach of Meath goalkeeper, Aoife Flynn. Armagh claimed victory by 3-5 to 1-10.

Armagh Team: Róisín Hughes, Claire Garvey, Emer Hayes, Orla Fox, Catherine McCooney, Hannah McGeown, Aoife Murphy, Laura Smyth (0-1), Caoimhe Smith, Kirsty Sheridan (0-1), Eadaoin Murphy (1-0), Michelle Morgan, Joanne Mullen (2-1), Nicole Nugent, Rachel Merry (0-2).

Meath Team: Aoife Flynn, Susie Gartland, Hazel Coleman, Ellen Burke, Ailbhe Lynch, Adrienne McCann, Lisa Carroll, Kristina Troy (0-5), Cheyanne O'Brien (0-1), Anna Fagan, Stacey Duigan, Tara Murphy, Lauren McCann (0-1), Niamh Kirby, Maggie Randle (1-3).

2011 All-Ireland Under 16A Championship

Tipperary required a second day to shake off the attentions of Cork at the semi-final stage at Kilmallock but found their scoring touch in the replay to advance by 5-6 to 1-6. In the second semi-final, Kilkenny blitzed a Clare side, 5-17 to 0-8, which had performed well in the earlier rounds. Five points behind Kilkenny at the interval in the final at the Gaelic Grounds on May 7th, Tipperary appeared to be in some difficulty. But they made a magnificent fight-back and whittled away at Kilkenny's lead. Tipperary edged in front in a thrilling finish to win by 2-8 to 0-13.

Tipperary Team: Sarah Coonan, Julie Ann Burke, Jenny Logue (Capt), Alana Morris, Ciannah Walsh, Anne Eviston, Laura Loughnane, Caoimhe Maher (0-2), Mairéad Teehan (1-0), Megan Ryan, Leah McKeogh (0-2), Tara Kennedy (0-4), Gillian McKenna, Jenny Grace (1-0), Cliodhna Ryan.

Kilkenny Team: Noelle Murphy, Deirdre Walsh, Catherine Foley, Katie Doheny, Meighan Farrell, Mary O'Connell, Rachel Lynch (Capt), Miriam Walsh (0-6), Niamh Leahy, Lydia Fitzpatrick (0-2), Michaela Kenneally (0-1), Julie Ann Malone (0-4), Áine Gannon, Niamh Dermody, Mary Corcoran.

2011 All-Ireland Under 16B Championship

In a double-header at The Ragg, Limerick readily disposed of Waterford, 3-18 to 2-7, while Offaly scrapped past Wexford by 2-5 to 1-7 to qualify for the final.   Playing an excellent brand of camogie in front of their home supporters at the Gaelic Grounds on May 7th, Limerick proved much too strong for Offaly and won by 3-12 to 0-9.   Martina McMahon, Deborah Murphy, Claire Keating, Katie Hennessy and Rebecca Delee performed very well for the winners and will be in the higher ranks in the years to come.

Limerick Team: Áine Bresnihan, Katrina White, Helena Fitzpatrick, Miren O'Grady, Aoife Doyle, Muireann Creamer, Jane Wilson, Katie Hennessy, Rebecca Delee, Leona McCarthy, Martina McMahon (0-6), Deborah Murphy (0-3), Aoife Wilson (1-1), Caoimhe Costello (0-1), Claire Keating (Capt) (2-1).   Subs used: Rosemary Hanafin, Elaine Murphy.

Offaly Team: Tara Dooley, Laura Hogan, Edel O'Meara, Aisling Brennan, Kelly Sammon, Ann Marie Guinan (Capt) (0-1), Paula Kinnearney, Eimear Mooney, Laura Keenahan, Gráinne Egan (0-1), Helen Dolan, Christine Cleary (0-1), Rachel Brennan (0-1), Cailín Fitzgerald, Mairéad Jennings (0-4). Sub used: Lisa Gorman (0-1).

2011 All-Ireland Under 16C Championship

Down secured a two-goal victory over Westmeath, 4-6 to 2-6, in the semi-final at Inniskeen while Carlow finished in front of Meath by 1-6 to 0-5 at Rathcoole on April 23rd.   In a low-scoring but none-the-less exciting final at Ashbourne on May 7th, Down emerged victorious by the smallest of margins, 1-3 to 1-2.

Down Team: Olivia Boyle, Anthea Trainor, Paddi Hawkins, Catherine Rocks (Capt) (0-1), Caitlin McCartan, Jenna Boden, Aoife McKeown (0-1), Ciara Gibson, Deirbhle Savage, Jane McAleenan, Aimee McAleenan, Monica McKay (0-1), Róisín Mulholland (1-0), Tierna Rooney.

Carlow Team: Niamh Doyle, Breege Nolan, Katie O'Byrne, Becky O'Dwyer, Eimear Byrne, Kate Nolan (Capt), Maria Kinsella, Michelle Nolan, Alison Ruschitzko, Ruth Foley, Eleanor Treacy, Miriam O'Brien, Laura Regan, Niamh Canavan, Danielle Jordan.

2011 Gael-Linn Junior Trophy

Built around the Waterford side that contested the 2010 All-Ireland Premier Junior final, Munster caught Leinster at the death in the final of the Gael-Linn Junior series at St. Judes, Dublin on

Changing of the Guard

May 15th. Leinster dominated the contest but Munster had the last say to edge in front by 1-15 to 2-11.

Munster Team: Aisling O'Brien (Waterford), Emma Hannon (Waterford), Jennie Simpson (Waterford) (0-1), Aideen McNamara (Limerick), Kate Marie Hearne (Waterford) (0-1), Charlotte Raher (Waterford), Pauline Cunningham (Waterford), Gráinne Kenneally (Waterford), Deirdre Fahy (Waterford), Niamh Rockett (Waterford) (0-4), Niamh Mulcahy (Limerick) (0-3), Orla Curtin (Limerick) (0-1) Nicola Morrissey (Waterford), Patricia Jackman (Waterford) (0-2), Karen Kelly (Waterford) (1-3).

Leinster Team: Emily Mangan (Meath), Regina Gorman (Kildare), Aoife Thompson (Meath), Āine Keogh (Meath), Aoife Tarrant (Kildare), Kristina Troy (Meath), Louise Donoghue (Meath), Louise Mahony (Laois) (0-1), Elaine Mahony (Laois), Paula Gribben (Meath), Siobhán Hurley (Kildare) (0-1), Jane Dolan (Meath) (0-3), Āine Mahony (Laois) (2-1), Susie O'Carroll (Kildare) (0-5), Fiona Trant (Kildare).

Where We're At

The Camogie Association invited 200 families and 50 leaders from different ethnic and cultural backgrounds, who live and work in Ireland, to the 2010 All-Ireland finals in Croke Park. Sport is a powerful medium through which all are brought together and our guests were happy to be included in this initiative to celebrate inclusion and diversity in Ireland. Camogie has been an important facet of Irish life for decades, and it is important that this tradition be shared with the new communities. This initiative was inspired by camogie's aim to increase participation in our game. How many of the young visitors will return in the years to come to represent their county on the field of play?

Camogie's underage sector was the subject of lively debate

2011 Camogie All-Star team. Back row, from left, Brenda Hanney, Galway, Ursula Jacob, Wexford, Katrina Parrock, Wexford, Jennifer O'Leary, Cork, Una Leacy, Wexford, Kate Kelly, Wexford, Jill Horan, Tipperary, Niamh Kilkenny, Galway, and Susan Earner, Galway. Front row, from left, Anna Geary, Cork, Therese Maher, Galway, Ann-Marie Hayes, Galway, Tony Towell, Managing Director of O'Neills, Joan O'Flynn, President of the Camogie Association, Guest of honour Brian Cody, Kilkenny hurling manager, Sinead O'Connor, Ard Stiúrthoir of the Camogie Association, Lorraine Ryan, Galway, Catherine O'Loughlin, Wexford, and Anne O'Connor, Wexford, accepting the award on behalf of her daughter Claire O'Connor. Picture: Stephen McCarthy / SPORTSFILE

with major changes being envisaged in the updating the Rule Book. The pertinent question, whether underage games should be based on participation or competition, occupied the minds of administrators. Advice emanating from experts in childcare, stressed the importance of participation rather than the winning of competitions. Children play sport to have fun and enjoy themselves, to be with their friends, to become proficient at the skills of the game, and to find games exciting and challenging.

Concerns were expressed in regard to the selection of underage players on adult teams. Was damage being caused to the young players by intense training? Was it right to place competitive expectations on young players and expose them to the attention that adult players receive? The new thinking was that games for under-12s should be small-sided, with modified rules to suit the developmental stages of the children, and organised in a non-competitive way. The spirit behind the games should be one of full participation, where every player gets to play the entire match and in a number of positions. The emphasis should be on improving skills in an enjoyable atmosphere. Age restrictions were introduced with regard to when an underage player could commence playing with a particular team. The new rule raised concerns in many clubs. With players limited to an age range and not permitted to play above that point, a shortage of players to make up a team could be a reality. It will be interesting to see how the new system works out in the years ahead. Will it produce skilful players who wish to continue their involvement in camogie into adulthood?

The setting-up of sub-committees for transfers, hearings and disciplinary matters, to hear and adjudicate on objections and investigate irregularities and have power and autonomy to suspend, fine or disqualify clubs or individuals for breaches of the rules, was considered radical in some quarters. The tricky issue of transfers also comes within their remit. This reflects a considerable shift of power from the parent body to the sub-committee, leaving the county board or provincial council with little or no say in these important matters. Finding people, with a sound knowledge of the rules and the capacity to apply them fairly and sensibly to a particular case, will be the making or breaking of this new rule.

The point was frequently made that the Camogie Association was over-reliant on Irish Sports Council funding. Because of the economic climate, it was vital that increased income should be generated within the Association. Two fundraising initiatives – 'A Night at the Dogs' and a golf classic – were organised to redress the balance. The increased affiliation fee of €300 per club made a positive impact on the income of the Association. Together, they provided additional self-generated income and were a step in the right direction.

Strategic planning had become part and parcel of the Camogie Association. Before the previous plan had run its course, an in-depth consultation process commenced to identify priority areas for developing the Association into the future. Opinions of players, administrators and units were obtained. The findings and recommendations of the strategic review carried out by a sports

Changing of the Guard

management firm in 2008–2009 framed much of the work which went into the new plan. An Ard Chomhairle sub-committee headed by Louise Byrne oversaw the drafting of the national development plan. Geraldine McGrath, Joan O'Flynn, Sinéad O'Connor, Liz Howard, Brighidin Heenan, Eamonn Browne, Susan Malone and Sarah O'Connor (from the Federation of Irish Sport) acted on the committee.

The new plan, titled 'Our Game Our Passion', set its vision at providing an inclusive, enjoyable and lifelong involvement in camogie, as Ireland's leading female sport, and a vibrant part of the Gaelic games family, at home and internationally. Its mission was to expand opportunities to participate in and enjoy camogie through building a professional, dynamic and inclusive Association. The plan touched every area of the Association's activities. Clearly defined and obtainable targets were set out in the document to bring the Association: to the next level of its development; to a position where there are sufficient camogie clubs to ensure that all females have the opportunity to play camogie; that coaches, referees and administrators will have sufficient training; that camogie will be well represented in all media; and that its structures and governance will reflect best practice. Driven by president, Joan O'Flynn, Ard Stiúrthóir, Sinéad O'Connor, director of camogie, Mary O'Connor, the full-time team and hundreds of hard-working volunteers throughout the country, implementation of the plan led to good progress being achieved in its first year.

A Game of Our Own

Modern Game

Chapter Twenty Six

WE'VE COME A LONG WAY

What would Máire Ní Chinnéide and the co-founders of the Camogie Association have thought if they had been present at the 2010 All-Ireland finals? The sight of a stand-alone programme of camogie matches in a world-class stadium featuring six superbly fit and highly skilled teams playing with passion and enthusiasm; a woman President of Ireland as guest of honour; a game that has developed out of all recognition to what they started; an enthusiastic attendance in excess of 17,000; a link with the past with the jubilee team; an attachment to the future with the mini-games and the hand of welcome to the new ethnic communities would surely have impressed the pioneers.

Camogie has travelled a long, difficult road to reach the stage it is at right now. The impediments to progress far outweighed the advantages in the early years. People today would find it almost impossible to appreciate the difficulties that confronted the founders.

Opposition to women's participation in sport was strong in the early years of the 20th century. The belief existed: that women were physiologically unsuited to sporting activity and could be damaged by it; that women taking part in sport presented an unattractive spectacle; and that the actions and conduct associated with sport were inconsistent with femininity. Women were denied equal access to sport and progress was very slow in the face of opposition.

Máire Ní Chinnéide: what would she have thought of a modern camogie All-Ireland final?

Attitudes to women playing the game were hostile and forced the players to go against public opinion. It is true to say that the founding of the Camogie Association was another step on the road to the emancipation if Irish women.

The tiny number of women with any degree of independence and free time to participate; lack of playing facilities; difficulty in mastering the game; transport problems; the indifference of the media; absence of support from state, commercial world and general public; the demands of a woman's role at work and in the home and officials, at club and county levels, with little training in organisation and who, in their working lives, were more used to taking orders than giving them, all thwarted advancement. Internal splits and divisions undid headway made. It is true to say that the Camogie Association encountered more obstacles in its first 20 years than any other sports organisation.

On the plus side, there were girls demanding a game of their own and willing to go against public opinion to form a team. As members of the Gaelic League, they were already enthusiastic and committed to the new Irish-Ireland and anxious to contribute to the culture and traditions of the nation. The Gaelic League network of branches provided a platform for the expansion of the game. In the new Association, all classes of women rubbed shoulder to shoulder. A poor or uneducated background has never been an impediment to playing camogie. The game itself proved to be an excellent product and exhilarating to those who sampled it. Volunteers to organise and administer the sport were forthcoming.

Class

Class has never been an issue in camogie circles. All are welcome to join irrespective of background or occupation. I have played on teams with girls and sat on committees with ladies without knowing what they did for a living. The subject did not come up. Everyone is accepted at face value.

Clubs attract players from all walks of life. The Cork teams of the thirties comprised office clerks, shop assistants, university graduates and factory workers. An article on an All-Ireland winning team of the mid-sixties lists the occupations as: teachers (three), civil servants (three), machinists (two), a college secretary, a office clerk, a youth leader and a cashier.

The considerable increase in the number of females entering third-level education and the opening-up of a range of professions and careers to women is reflected in the occupations recorded in the 2009 All-Ireland programme for the Cork team. The business activities documented are physiotherapists (two), a quantity surveyor, a biochemist, a business development representative, a regional development officer, a national director of camogie, a laboratory analyst, a stone mason, a university student, a pharmacist, a member of defence forces, a food analyst, a marketing executive and a nutritionist. Camogie mirrors the social changes in Ireland as women are better educated and branch out into new areas of employment.

Uniform

The uniform worn by camogie players reflects the attire and custom of the day. Leisure wear was unheard of in the early days of the 20th century, but the ladies of the Gaelic League would have found a long-sleeved blouse and a full-length skirt in their wardrobes. Boots, suitable for physical activity, did not come in women's sizes, so it was a case of whatever footwear a player possessed. A lady was not considered dressed without a hat at outdoor events, leading to a variety of headgear being displayed. To distinguish teams, a coloured tie or sash was added. As the years wore on, the hems of the skirts inched upwards and the hats were dispensed with.

The gym frock came into vogue as the camogie uniform

We've Come a Long Way

Camogie across the ages. Different eras but the same game and the same spirit.

around 1930. It was the standard uniform in most secondary schools. The sash or girdle was worn around the hips in the beginning but it soon moved to a more comfortable position around the waist. Long black stockings, black underwear and a long- or short-sleeved blouse completed the outfit. Dunlops introduced a canvas boot with a rubber toe-cap and sole which became the choice of players from the late thirties.

While never described as a fashion item, the gym frock suited all figures and covered a multitude. Dublin and Cork teams lined out in summertime in gym frocks made of heavy serge. The choice of fabric had more to do with economics than practicality. Some commentators are prone to ridicule the gym frock and black stockings ensemble. As one who togged out in it for many years, I must say that when the east wind blew in from the sea across the Phoenix Park on a Sunday morning in January or February, I was mighty glad to have the comfort of the old-style uniform. The gym frock was highly rated by goalkeepers. Many a shot at goal got trapped in the skirt and saved the embarrassment of conceding a score. The arrival of tights to replace the black stockings was welcome as they proved to be much more comfortable.

Helmets for camogie players made an appearance in 1970. The initial helmets did not have a face-guard and only a minority of players chose to wear them. In time, the helmets became popular as clubs insisted that beginners and underage players adopt them. The gym frock was finally assigned to the bin in 1972 when the short skirt, sports shirt and bobby socks, which were more suitable for athletic activity, were voted in. Light-weight boots, in a variety of colours, sponsors' logo on jerseys and the arrival of the skort followed. A debate on whether to replace the skort with shorts is ongoing.

Religious Orders

Religious orders played a major part in the spread and development of camogie. The playing of the game in the schools stretches back to the early days of the Association. Dominican College, Muckross Park, Dublin, where founder member, Máire Ní Chinnéide, was educated, was the first school to respond to the founding of the Camogie Association. Within months of the formation of the rules of the game, the girls of this famous college had hurleys in their hands. In the absence of schools competition, Muckross Park participated in the Dublin league, lining out against adult sides. When the Dublin colleges' leagues commenced in 1917, it was Dominican College, Eccles Street, that monopolised the competition.

The Brigidine, Holy Faith, Mercy, Presentation, St Louis, Cross and Passion and Loreto orders made a valuable contribution to the advancement of the game. A sporting attitude to the game was advocated by the nuns. Players were expected to give of their best, take pride in representing the school and uphold the traditions and values of their alma mater. If attention to these objectives did not lead to victory, so be it. It was a different story when the nuns were replaced by lay teachers. A greater emphasis on winning became the norm as they sought a return for the time invested in preparing the team.

Many Changes

Much has altered in Ireland since the foundation of the Camogie Association and the pace of change has quickened, particularly so in the past decade. For camogie, the important elements in the changing process have included: the transformation in the role of women; the opening up of education to women; married women working; the scope of opportunities available in the workplace and in leisure time; the drift from the land; emigration; greater mobility; a shorter working week; a move away from the extended family; the advent of new technology; increased disposable income; increased media coverage particularly at local level; and competition from other sports and leisure activities.

The Camogie Association has undergone a marked change in

We've Come a Long Way

the past decade. Like other national governing bodies, camogie is required to produce business plans to ensure state funding. With an increasing number of full-time staff, employed to develop and promote the sport, a professional approach is essential. Camogie is no longer a pastime, organised and run by amateurs, it is a business that competes for scarce resources and requires a business attitude to its management.

Strategic planning, human resources strategies and marketing plans have led to improvements in the organisation. Good management practice is necessary for survival. The introduction of tight financial controls; the emphasis on achieving defined goals and the importance of selecting staff with good management and people skills have played a big part in the transformation.

Sponsors and spectators have great expectations of the major events on the camogie calendar. It is not enough to simply stage the match. Entertainment must be organised between the games and at half-time. Comfortable conditions and catering outlets are required to keep the fans happy. A massive amount of work behind the scenes is carried out prior to the All-Ireland finals. Successful staging of the event raises the profile of the Association. It is vital to make the most of these opportunities, gain maximum exposure and attract the largest audience possible. Camogie is changing from being a low-interest sport with little coverage to becoming better recognised but there is a long way to go.

Close to Hurling

By and large, camogie has prospered in hurling areas. Exceptions, of course, have existed. Mayo contested the 1959 All-Ireland senior final and Darver (Louth) ranked among the elite clubs in the country in the thirties. On the other hand, one may well ask where the Kilkenny camogie players were before 1970. Camogie players have been influenced by how hurling has developed and have been inclined to copy the tactics and innovations of the men.

The game itself has developed considerably over the years. Early exponents were individuals who did their own thing. The fundamentals of teamwork came later. Ground-play was the order of the day with players striking the ball as far as they could. For the majority, the ball remained on the ground for several decades. Great strides were made in the thirties when the top exponents from Dublin, Cork, Louth and Galway brought the game to a new level. Teams concentrated on scoring goals. Points almost exclusively came from placed balls.

The Dublin teams of the fifties and sixties perfected teamwork and were unbeatable by sides which neglected this vital aspect of the game. Cork, Kilkenny, Tipperary and Wexford added new skills and innovations and facilitated the evolvement of the play. Higher levels of fitness were required for players wishing to run with the ball at every opportunity. The introduction of the 15-a-side game brought camogie closer to hurling.

Today's top exponents are accomplished athletes, who demonstrate amazing levels of skill, fitness, ball control and technique. They represent their club and county with passion and pride and aim at the highest standards.

A Game of Our Own

If the Keating Branch of the Gaelic League had not devised the game of camogie and established the Camogie Association, would girls today be playing with hurley sticks? I believe that they would. In the intervening years, women have tried all sports, even those of a very physical and confrontational nature like rugby and boxing. No doubt, a game based on hurling would have been fashioned and played. However, it would have been no more than a game. Camogie, with its roots in the Gaelic League, was born of a spirit of national resurgence and an awakening of the women of Ireland to a realisation of their destiny in the shaping of a Gaelic nation. Over the years, girls and women have been attracted to the Association and motivated by the ideals and aim of its founders. Many remained on after their playing days were over and worked enthusiastically because they wished to see the Association continue and prosper.

Camogie Abroad

For many years, Irish communities in Britain and North America promoted Gaelic games. In times of high unemployment, when thousands travelled abroad in search of work, camogie clubs were formed in cities where the Irish congregated, and provided a healthy pastime and a social outlet for the newcomers. When economic conditions improved, many of the Irish returned home and, subsequently, the game declined abroad. It became obvious that if the clubs in foreign parts were to survive, they would have to look beyond Irish girls who came for a few years and then departed. The Asian Gaelic Games Championships in Seoul included camogie for the first time in 2011.

Second-generation Irish, the daughters of those who had settled in the area, were introduced to the game but the numbers were small and inadequate to sustain the clubs. Attracting non-Irish girls to join was another option. However, the situation called for a more organised approach. A concerted effort to develop the game at underage level is underway in London, where six clubs already support underage sections, and in North America. Both areas have development plans to grow the game.

Camogie continues to flourish in Europe and Australia where there has been an upsurge of activity as girls leave our shores, once again, in search of work. The European championship was organised at four venues in 2010, The Hague, Brussels, Zurich and Paris, alongside the European hurling championship, with Belgium emerging as winners. News emanating from Western Australia and New South Wales is positive as numbers participating and skills levels continue to rise.

Volunteers

The Camogie Association was built by the selfless work and generosity of volunteers. People – both men and women – gave of their time to provide a healthy pastime for the girls of the country. These willing workers are to be found in every club and county. Coaching teams, attending meetings, collecting gates, organising competitions, refereeing matches and fundraising are but a few of the chores that they take on. The Association must support its volunteers and provide the backing and recognition that they deserve. Without the dedication of these workers, the Association would have folded years ago. It is vital that the Association retains the services of volunteers in the future.

Media Coverage

Like all women's sports, camogie struggled over the years to gain adequate coverage in the national media. The difference in the quality and quantity of reporting male and female sport in significant. Treatment has always had an overwhelming masculine bias, with women's sport receiving only a tiny fraction of that afforded to male sport and with women's sport only being reported at the top level. The way in which camogie is portrayed by the media can affect its value and limit its appeal.

The media presents the message that male sport is more important and of greater intrinsic value than women's sport. The lack of focus on top-class camogie players undermines their efforts and prevents them from being instantly recognisable and portrayed as role models as is the case with the male counterparts. All areas of the sports media are male dominated and a masculine ethos permeates through sport. Any effort to promote gender equality is resisted.

Definite inroads have been achieved in recent times. Camogie fares well in the provincial press where accurate reports and intelligent comment are to be found. New communication channels have opened up through technology, in particular web and social media. These have increased awareness of the game and make information on fixtures and events available to the public. Colourful and informative match programmes and the arrival of *On the Ball* magazine further enhance the profile of the association. The appointment of a director of communications and marketing is a step in the right direction.

Camogie Development Initiatives

Many innovative projects and initiatives have been launched to transform the aims of the current strategic plan into reality. Director of camogie, Mary O'Connor, and RDO, Caroline Murray, have pioneered the 'Player Pathway' which describes the opportunities to play camogie from beginner to elite player. It is aimed at giving everyone, at every age and stage, the chance to maximise their potential, whatever their level, and to stay involved in camogie throughout their lifetime.

The target audience of the 'Mum and Me' initiative is mothers and daughters currently not playing the game. The purpose of the course is to increase the involvement of parents helping out with underage coaching and to provide each participant with proper coaching information and technique to coach the basic skills of the game.

Mothers, whose daughters play camogie but never played themselves, are the object of the camóg-aerobics scheme. 'Come and Try It' day invites primary-school children to sample what camogie has to offer. 'Sport agus Spraoi le Coláistí', summer camps, the Social Inclusion Project and the Gaisce Programme are further initiatives on the road to achieving a more vibrant Association which will go from strength to strength in the future.

A Game of Our Own

One Club Model

Camogie, the GAA and ladies football are in the process of exploring the development of a 'One Club Model'. The aim is to oversee the organisation and promotion of all Gaelic games under a single administration unit at club level. There are so many interests, so many activities, so many development objectives, common to the three organisations that a joint approach to these would seem logical, desirable and indeed inevitable.

The 'One Club Model' is already in existence across the country. Club unity is stronger because people are working together on allocation of pitches, coaching, fundraising and social events. Camogie is represented on the club central committee and has a say in decision-making while running its own affairs through the sub-committee structure. The three associations will continue to have separate administrative structures at county, provincial and national levels. No doubt, this concept will be advanced and refined in the years to come.

Our National Game

The Camogie Association has been the leading women's sports organisation in Ireland for 107 years. It is the first organisation to have promoted Gaelic games for women, a sport which has developed to be the most skilful and attractive available. It embraces all of Ireland and units abroad and provides for all age groups through its national, provincial, county, club, primary-school, second-level colleges and third-level colleges structures.

The aims and objects of the Camogie Association have altered little since its inception. The 2010 Rule Book brought them in line with modern Ireland. The core values of the association are detailed as inclusiveness, voluntarism, equality and fair play, openness, anti-racism, anti-sectarianism, accountability, professionalism and respect. The objects of the Association are: to promote, develop and manage camogie in Ireland and internationally; to promote the active participation of women in sport, to work in partnership with the wider Gaelic games family; to foster an awareness of the richness of our national culture, including the Irish language; to support Irish industries; to create a safe environment for our members and supporters; and to promote community development and community spirit.

In 1943, the President of Ireland, Dr Douglas Hyde, stated: "Camogie is our national game for women, and its increasing popularity affords proof of its wide appeal. Besides being good in itself, it is of more value to Irish girls than any foreign game can be, because it appeals to what is instinctive and hereditary in Irish blood. Camogie has been developed on our own soil in our time, in spite of obvious difficulties, and there is every reason to believe that it will expand greatly in the years to come."

Camogie is played in the 32 counties of Ireland, as well as in England, Scotland, Wales, North America, Australia, Asia and many parts of Europe. The number of clubs affiliated is being upwardly revised on a constant basis. New initiatives, under an array of headings, are being driven by a full-time team as the Association continues to grow and fan out in several directions. The Camogie Association may face the future with confidence.

Roll of Honour

Legends of the Game

Kay Mills

Holder of an amazing haul of 15 All-Ireland senior medals, Kay Mills is a true camogie legend and merits a special place in the history of the game. Born of a Dublin mother and a Cork father, she was a natural athlete. Tall, slight and fair-haired, Kay possessed a devastating turn of speed that never seemed to diminish as years went by. She had a competitive spirit that was roused to its greatest when defeat threatened.

Raised in South Square, Inchicore, Kay was educated at Goldenbridge Convent. She played her club camogie with GSR (Great Southern Railways – later renamed CIÉ). Her father was employed at the company's Inchicore Works and, in his free time, helped out at the company's sports club which was set up for the workers and their families. Kay made her debut for Dublin in 1941 and owned the left-wing midfield position until her retirement in 1961.

She had a particularly neat style of play. Frequently, she sprinted forward, rose and struck the ball in one movement sending it marginally under the opposing crossbar. A left-handed player, she scored more long-range goals than any other player in camogie.

Always pleasing to watch Kay struck up a great partnership with her GSR and Dublin colleague, Kathleen Cody. Excellent to distribute the ball, Kay instructed Una O'Connor, when she joined the Dublin team, to "sprint towards the goal when you see me getting the ball". Invariably, the ball was at Una's feet as she arrived on the edge of the square.

Kay played in the golden era of Dublin camogie. She was surrounded by a galaxy of stars including Íde O'Kiely, Peg Griffin, Doreen Rogers, Kathleen Cody, Sophie Brack, Eileen Duffy and Una O'Connor. Moulded and guided by Nell McCarthy, the greatest coach in the history of the game, Dublin reigned supreme.

Kay was an automatic choice for the Team of the Century and was inducted into the Cuchulainn Hall of Fame. On her retirement in 1961, she was presented with a replica of the O'Duffy Cup by the Dublin County Board. Kay married George Hill but, in camogie circles, was always known as Kay Mills. Sadly, Kay passed to her eternal reward in 1996 but her memory lives on through the Kay Mills Cup, trophy of the All-Ireland Premier Junior Championship.

Peggy Hogg

Peggy was an inspirational figure on the Cork teams of the late thirties and early forties. She made her debut for Cork while a pupil in sixth class at St Aloysius Junior School. There was a real touch of class about everything she did. Widely recognised as one of the greatest goalkeepers to play camogie, she was frequently compared to the Clare and Munster hurling goalkeeper, Tom Daly.

Tall and athletic, Peggy covered the whole goal and attacked the ball. Match reports of her time include the following quotations: "only luck got a ball past Peggy"; "every save and clearance was sheer class" and "she was untroubled by shots from all angles".

Peggy finished her schooling at the French Convent, Holyhead, and travelled by boat to Dublin when Cork had important matches in Croke Park. A Cork captain, she played a massive role in bringing four All-Ireland titles to the county and may have won more but for the dispute which kept Cork out of the All-Ireland championship for eight years. In 1964, she was voted into the Cuchulainn Hall of Fame and also received a Stars of the Past award.

An all-rounder, she represented Munster

in tennis on many occasions. Peggy married John Fitzgerald, brother of her Old Aloysians and Cork colleague, Mary Fitzgerald, and son of Cork All-Ireland hurling goalkeeper, Andy Fitzgerald.

Kathleen Cody

Kathleen rarely appeared in an arena that she did not adorn and have the crowd talking. Her name spelt a kind of magic to camogie followers. An individual player, she could work wonders with the ball but wanted to do it all herself. Great wristwork, spectacular overhead play, skilful technique and general mastery of all aspects of the game, coupled with uncommon speed, marked her apart for true greatness.

Daughter of Michael Cody of Kells, Co. Kilkenny, and Mary Morkan of Templemore, Co. Tipperary, Kathleen had hurling in her veins. Jimmy Langton, the famous Kilkenny hurler, is her cousin. As a young child, she spent her summers with her granny in Tipperary where she played in hurling matches with the boys. In later years, she was to be seen training with members of the garda, Mick Gill, Mattie Power, Fowler McInerney and Garrett Howard, in the Phoenix Park. On another occasion, Mick Mackey, Jack Lynch and Jim Young remained on after their hurling match to watch Kathleen play a camogie game. They were so impressed that they presented their hurleys to her and said that they were honoured that she accepted them.

At the age of 11, Kathleen played senior championship for Celtic but in was in the colours of CIÉ that she was best known. She wore the blue of Dublin from 1941 to 1951 and finished her career with seven All-Ireland medals. She popularised the quick lift, solo run and powerful shot. Kathleen always managed to execute her stroke even when surrounded by a circle of opponents. She is fondly remembered by those who had the privilege of seeing her play.

Una O'Connor

The top camogie player of her era, Una was born in Marino, Dublin, to a Kildare father and a Carlow mother. The youngest of a family of seven, she was the only one to show an interest in sport. She played with the boys on the road where her talent was spotted. Celtic invited her to join them and she quickly moved up the grades. By the time she was 15, she had won a place on the Dublin senior team. Una possessed great ability. She was a supreme forward. She read the play at a glance and was always able to make room for herself Roaming from the full-forward position, she distributed the ball with telling effect. Una proved elusive to defenders. Endowed with an exceptional body swerve, which immediately created space between herself and her opponent, she was able to get in her shot without being hooked or blocked. She took her scores with rare accuracy and built up a tremendous understanding with her Dublin teammate, Judy Doyle.

Witty and good humoured, Una always played with a short, light stick. She was the first camogie player to be honoured with a coveted Caltex (Texaco) Award. Her inter-county career stretched from 1953 to 1967 and concluded with 13 All-Ireland senior medals including a never to be equalled ten-in-a-row. Una's father was a huge supporter throughout her career and was so proud of her achievements.

Una, who captained Dublin to glory in successive years, loved the 'inquest' after the match. She was sorry to see the end of the 12-a-side game and good ground play. The modern game, she feels, has become too close to hurling. Una, who was employed throughout her working life by bakers and confectioners,

Johnson, Mooney & O'Brien was more than handy at tennis and table tennis.

Margaret O'Leary

From an early age, Margaret was very focused on improving as a player. She continually practised her skills, studied top-class hurlers and set very high fitness levels for herself. Peerless at centre-back, she dominated the majority of matches in which she played. Margaret attacked from whatever position of the field she occupied and could score goals from her own half of the field.

Always exceptionally fit and equally proficient off the right and the left, she was outstanding at catching and delivering the ball. Margaret was utterly dedicated and never gave up. Her single-minded approach paid off allowing her to collect a host of trophies and honours throughout her career. A place on the Team of the Century was a fitting reward for her talent and dedication.

From Monamolin in north Wexford, Margaret is one of a family of 13. Under the watchful eye of her father, she joined the children of the locality in a nearby field to practise the skills of the game. She quickly progressed to competitive camogie with St Ibar's club. When she took up a position with the ESB in Dublin, she threw in her lot with Eoghan Ruadh and helped them win the All-Ireland Club Championship. Margaret returned to Wexford and became the inspirational leader of her home club, Buffers Alley, guiding them to five All-Ireland club and fourteen Wexford championship titles. She played a huge role in Wexford's All-Ireland victories.

In 2007, camogie saw the first daughters of All-Ireland senior medal holders step up to repeat the feat. Not alone did Margaret's girls, Mary and Una Leacy, win coveted All-Ireland medals but they both captained Wexford on the big occasion, Mary (2007) and Una (2010). Margaret's enthusiasm for camogie remains as strong as ever and she is regularly seen at matches all over the country.

Liz Garvan

Liz played camogie with the grace and poise of a ballet dancer. Her play was marked by sheer brilliance and exuberance for the game which was a delight to watch. She perfected the skills of the game to a very high degree and displayed them effortlessly. It seemed so easy to Liz who had all the qualities of a star athlete.

Liz was seen on the national stage for the first time in the inaugural All-Ireland colleges' final between St Aloysius, Cork, and Presentation, Kilkenny, in 1969. The duel between herself and Liz Neary was out of the top drawer. Energised by young players like Liz, Pat Moloney and Rosie Hennessy, Cork bridged a 27-year gap to claim the All-Ireland senior title in 1970. In a truly remarkable performance, Liz scored three goals and six points from play in the final against Kilkenny.

Liz had the qualities to make it to the top in any sport. Without ever taking a tennis lesson, she won the South of Ireland tennis championship and reached the final of the Irish Close Championship. Her father, Peadar, hurled with Sarsfields and had the occasional outing with Cork. Liz was joined on the Old Aloysians side by her sisters, Marie, Deirdre and Bernice. In an all-too-short career, Liz won three All-Ireland senior and Ashbourne medals and was named National Player of the Year in 1970.

Gentle, ladylike and reserved, Liz was a reluctant star. She shunned media attention. On graduating from UCC, Liz went to Zambia where she took up a teaching position at the age of 21. One may speculate what heights she would have reached if she continued her camogie career. The memory of her silken skills will remain with those who were privileged to have seen her play.

Roll of Honour

Brigid Doyle

Brigid hails from one of the most remarkable families in camogie history – the Kehoes of Clonleigh, Co. Wexford. Nine girls and eight boys, all skilled in handling a hurley, make up the family of Edward and Josephine Kehoe. When the farm work was finished for the day, the children of the family headed for a field at the back of the house, picked teams and the match got underway. It was a great way to learn the skills of the game.

Brigid was a natural leader and an excellent all-round player. She controlled the game from the centre-back position. Whether it was a match or just training, Brigid loved to get out and hurl. Always focused on getting the ball, she was a steadying influence on the players around her. An outstanding captain, Brigid was seen at her best when under pressure.

Four of her sisters, Josie, Annie, Kit and Gretta, won All-Ireland senior medals. Brigid collected three All-Ireland senior medals during an impressive career and was named National Player of the Year in 1975. She captained Wexford to success in 1969 and won Gael-Linn honours with Leinster. A classic striker of the ball, it was no surprise that she mastered golf when her camogie days were over.

Marie Costine

Marie gave little indication in the early days of her camogie career that she would grow and develop into a most accomplished defender. She took to the game later than most and played her first competitive match at the age of 17. Born within a stone's throw of the home of Christy Ring in the east Cork village of Cloyne, Marie was inspired by the deeds and achievements of the hurling legend.

She brought her hurley along to the local pitch on Saturday mornings where Christy hurled and passed on tips to all-comers. He advised Marie to develop good wristwork, a recommendation which she acted upon to great effect. When Cloyne formed a camogie club, Marie threw in her lot with them. Seven Costine sisters, Marie, Bunnie (mother of All-Star hurler, Donal Óg Cusack), Bernie, Kathleen, Rita, Geraldine and Ashlin were on the field when Cloyne claimed the Cork intermediate championship in 1973.

Always willing to learn and improve, she moved quickly up the ladder and found her best position at full-back. Marie read the game intelligently and had great positional sense. She was excellent to catch the ball and clear at speed even when completely surrounded. Tall, strong and mobile, she had superb ball control and with her long reach, she intercepted passes destined for the opposition. Frequently called up the pitch when selectors felt a goal might be on from a close-in free, she would duly oblige and shake the net with a powerful shot. Marie always had a word of encouragement for her team-mates, particularly one who had made a mistake or a newcomer to the team.

There are many outstanding performances which come to mind when reflecting on Marie's career. Countless times in the 1973 All-Ireland final against Antrim, Marie's hand, covered as usual with a black glove, went up through a thicket of sticks, took down the ball and dispatched it to the other end of the field. Five years later, she played as if she could keep Dublin at bay on her own in the 1978 All-Ireland final. When the Cloyne club folded, Marie joined neighbours, Killeagh, and produced a heroic exhibition of skill and courage in the All-Ireland club final against Buffers Alley.

Following 20 years at the top, Marie retired. She was honoured with a place on the Team of the Century. Married to Edmond O'Donovan, she has two children, Edmond Junior and Joanne.

Sandie Fitzgibbon

One of a very select band of sportswomen to marry top class careers in two different sports, Sandie deserved the title 'superstar'. Six All-Ireland senior medals, a place on the Team of the Century together with 64 appearances for the Irish basketball team gives a picture of her sporting life.

Sandie joined Glen Rovers as a diminutive nine-year-old and became, in the opinion of many, the greatest camogie player Cork ever produced. It was usual for Sandie to run a mile and a half from her home to training at the Glen. She progressed quickly and was the first player to win three All-Ireland minor medals. Promotion to the Cork senior team was immediate.

A special talent with an exceptional work rate, Sandie was invaluable to her team whether placed in midfield or centre-back. Excellent to read the game, she was extremely fast to cover the ground. She always went for the ball and controlled it superbly. Sandie regularly played her opposite number out of the game, helped the defence and supporter the attack.

Although small in size, Sandie could wreak havoc on the basketball court. She accommodated both games in an unbelievable busy schedule. In an eight-day period in October 1990, Sandie played in an All-Ireland club semi-final against Swatragh in Co. Derry on the Sunday beforeflying to Boston and playing in three international basketball games with the Irish team during the week. She returned to Ireland on the Friday and was the star of the Glen Rovers team in the All-Ireland club final against St Paul's (Kilkenny) on the Sunday.

Good humoured and friendly, Sandie gave of her best to the Cork senior team for 16 years. Dedicated to sport, she stepped off the stage with a multitude of awards from both sports which she richly deserved.

Sophie Brack

A pioneer of full-forwards, Sophie opened up the play for her attacking colleagues and was constantly taking up astute positions. An intelligent forward who distributed the ball brilliantly, she scored her share of goals as well. Very difficult to mark, Sophie mastered the knack of being in the right place at the right time. She hugged the square but was exceptionally fast over a few yards if an opportunity presented itself.

From Ballybrack in the foothills of the Dublin mountains, Sophie wore the colours of Slieve Bloom, CIÉ and Austin Stacks. Sophie's leadership qualities were recognised by the Dublin selectors who named her captain for six All-Ireland campaigns. Each time, she carried O'Duffy Cup home. She won eight All-Ireland titles in all from 1948 to 1955 and represented Leinster in the Jubilee Exhibition in 1954. A place on the Team of the Century was well deserved.

Sophie's interest in camogie stretched way beyond the playing of the game. She was a virtual encyclopaedia as regards past players, scores and scorers, records and competition winners. Employed by the ESB, Sophie gave her time to Dublin County Board and Leinster Council as registrar and selector over lengthy periods.

Liz Neary

Liz Neary's name was one of the first to be written on the team sheet. Her versatility made her an invaluable member of the side. She was equally proficient in any role from full-back to full-forward and her mastery of the skills of the game enabled her to play camogie with elegance. An excellent ground hurler, she was never beaten on a 50–50 pull.

From Dunbell, Co. Kilkenny, Liz was a very intelligent player. She sized up the situation at a glance and reacted to the advantage of her team with the minimum of fuss. An outstanding team player, she created space and opportunities for those around her.

Liz caught the eye in the colours of Presentation, Kilkenny, and was a key figure in their success. She afforded wonderful service to St Paul's, Austin Stacks (Dublin), Kilkenny and Leinster. Liz won seven All-Ireland senior, seven All-Ireland club medals, was twice named as the National Player of the Year and was honoured with a place on the Team of the Century.

Shy by nature, Liz was well regarded by opponents for her sporting approach to the game. She spent her working life in the nursing profession and finished as sister-in-charge of the intensive care unit at St Luke's Hospital.

Pat Moloney

A right-hand-below-left-hand player, Pat's speed, style and skill made her elusive and a delight to watch. Her incisive solo runs outstretched opposing defences and provided the opportunity to get in a telling shot. Pat was a motivator on the field. Equally at home in midfield or attack, Pat did not take things as face value but questioned if they could be done better.

Daughter of Maurice and Nell Moloney of Killeagh, Co. Cork, Pat learned the game at Presentation, Youghal and came to the notice of the Cork selectors while a student at UCC. She was one of a new breed of young players who brought confidence and belief to the Cork team which resulted in a four-in-a-row of All-Ireland titles (1970–1973).

Pat won seven All-Ireland senior medals and captained Cork to glory in 1982. She played a significant role in bringing the All-Ireland club title to Killeagh. National Player of the Year in 1978, she was named on the Team of the Century.

Pat married Eamonn Lenihan, who trained the Killeagh side to win the Bill Carroll Cup. When Pat retired following the 1982 All-Ireland final, they both went to Bangladesh to work as volunteers for a two-year period. Pat lectures in Applied Social Science at UCC.

Angela Downey

Angela had a massive impact on the camogie scene and enjoyed an immense innings. Small in stature but immeasurable on skill and determination, Angela was a one-off. In terms of pure skill, she equalled any hurler and was far better than most. Fiercely competitive, she did not entertain thoughts of losing.

Daughter of All-Ireland hurler, Shem Downey, she grew up in the hurling stronghold of Ballyragget, Co. Kilkenny. Nine-year-old Angela took up camogie and quickly made her mark. She lined out for St Brigid's, Callan, in the final of the 1975 All-Ireland Colleges' senior final against Presentation, Athenry. In a welter of excitement and drama tried all she knew to work a winning score. It was not to be and the match went to extra time. While racing through the Athenry defence in search of a goal, Angela's knee gave away under her and she was forced to leave the field. Without their star, Callan collapsed and lost by five goals.

Angela broke into the Kilkenny senior team in 1972. She contested 14 All-Ireland finals, winning 12. Master of the complete array of camogie skills, she was virtually unstoppable. She struck terror in the hearts of opponents.

A deadly striker of the ball, whether stationary or moving, her accuracy was unerring. She could unleash a powerful shot while running at top speed from any angle. But Angela was not just a taker of scores. She saw herself as the first line of defence. By harrying, hassling and blocking, she regularly disposed her opponent and won possession. Angela could turn a match around in minutes and often did. There was no such thing as a comfortable margin while she was on the field. The 1994 All-Ireland club final between Lisdowney and Glen Rovers is a case in point. Trailing by ten points as the final minutes ticked by, any other player would have believed that the game was beyond recovery, but not Angela. She blitzed the Glen goal to achieve one of the greatest comebacks ever seen.

Her brilliance was acknowledged by friend and foe. A never-say-die spirit saw a career strewn with trophies and awards. Angela's honours include 12 All-Ireland senior; six All-Ireland club; ten Gael-Linn and 22 Kilkenny championship titles. Individual awards came thick and fast. Four times named as National Player of the Year, she was honoured with a Texaco Award in 1986. Her twin sister, Ann, a star in her own right, was with Angela every step of the way. Fittingly, they both received a Lifetime Achievement award in 2009.

Angela, who teaches at Vocational School, Thomastown, is married to Ted Browne.

Mairéad McAtamney

A great exponent of overhead play, Mairéad could double on a ball as it flew above her and drive it effortlessly 60 or 70 metres. She was a master of midfield play. Her style and artistry were admired throughout the country. A very polished performer, Mairéad could dictate the trend of a game.

Mairéad's career started at the Dominican Convent, Portstewart. Her family were steeped in Gaelic games. She was joined on the Portglenone club side by her sisters, Frances, Theresa and Sheena and her five brothers played Gaelic football. Mairéad wore the colours of Antrim from 1958 to 1983 winning two All-Ireland senior and 15 Ulster senior medals. She captained Antrim to glory in the 1979 All-Ireland final. Named National Player of the Year in 1965 and 1979 and acclaimed by the Team of the Century, Mairéad adorned the game. A commerce teacher, she gave of her time to pass on her skills to the next generation. Mairéad married Liam Magill. Their daughter, Clare, plays for Tír na Óg, the Ulster junior club champions.

Bridie Martin

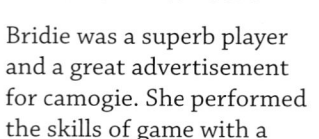

Bridie was a superb player and a great advertisement for camogie. She performed the skills of game with a high degree of expertise and in a very attractive style. Very quick to get the ball into her hand, she distributed it intelligently. Bridie had an uncanny positional sense which allowed her to be in the right place at the right time.

From Freshford, Co. Kilkenny, Bridie started her career with Dicksboro. She progressed to St Paul's with whom she won four All-Ireland club titles. Bridie made the centre-back position her own on the Kilkenny team for two decades. A leader on the field, she captained Kilkenny to All-Ireland success in 1985 and 1987.

Winner of many awards, she was named as National Player of the Year in 1976 and chosen on the Team of the Century. Bridie stepped off the inter-county stage with nine All-Ireland senior and eight Gael-Linn medals.

An accomplished soccer player, she was selected to play for the Republic of Ireland on one occasion but withdrew as it clashed with a camogie fixture. Bridie served as registrar of the Kilkenny County Board and was a very capable referee. Married to Benny McGarry, they have two sons, Shane and Cormac.

ADMINISTRATORS

SERVANTS OF THE GAME

A Game of Our Own

Cāit O'Donoghue

Cáit was born in Carrignavar, Co. Cork, daughter of Donncha O'Donoghue, an Irish speaker and farmer. She had three brothers, Tadhg ('Torna'), Eamonn and Donncha and sisters, Ciss and Nora. The family was well-known in Gaelic circles and the children grew up fluent in the Irish language.

Her early memories include travelling to Cork City by horse and trap; threshings, gatherings around the fire when her father would read the paper for the neighbours, walking barefoot to school in the summer months, stories of fairies and banshees and lively dances in the kitchen.

When her brother Tadhg took up a teaching position at St. Patrick's, Drumcondra, Cáit followed him to Dublin and acted as his housekeeper at his residence near Santry. She helped to entertain their many and varied visitors. Cáit invited the distinguished guests to write in her autograph book. The pages include offerings by Douglas Hyde, Pádraig Ó Duinin, Eoin MacNeill, George Russell (A.E.), Standish O'Grady and Máire de Buitléir.

Both Tadhg and Cáit were very active in the Gaelic League. Cáit was one of the girls who pushed for an Irish game for women. When the Keating Branch of the Gaelic League responded and drew up rules for the new game, Cáit was named as captain and played in the first competitive match at Navan on July 17th, 1904.

Appointed the first organiser of the Camogie Association, Cáit worked enthusiastically to spread the word and encourage girls to take up the game. She used her contacts in the Gaelic League to promote camogie and wrote letters to the papers to draw attention to it. When the initial interest started to wane, she welcomed the offer of help from the Crokes Gaelic club and worked closely with Seán O'Duffy over the next few years to advance development of the Association.

In 1916, her brother, Tadhg, returned to Cork to take up the position of Professor of Irish Studies at U.C.C. Cáit followed him. She founded the Cara Cliodhna club in the Glasheen Road area of the city. Years later, a member of Cara Cliodhna was suspended for playing hockey. Several members of the club turned to hockey in sympathy with the culprit. The club floundered and Cáit withdrew from the camogie scene. By this time, her brother, Eamonn, had become Professor of Celtic Studies at U.C.C. and Canon Donncha had been appointed parish priest of Bandon.

Seān O'Duffy

For seventy-five years, Seán O'Duffy gave his time unsparingly to promote the national game of camogie and, in particular, its aims and ideals. He organised, refereed, administered and guided those who sought his help. Seán had nothing to gain from his labours but the satisfaction of seeing the game develop and expand. His contribution to the growth of the Association is immeasurable.

As a young lad Seán came to Dublin in 1900 from Cill an Bhaile, near Westport, where his father was a member of the R.I.C. His mother was a native Irish speaker who encouraged Seán to appreciate the wealth of his Irish heritage. He continued his schooling in Dublin at St. James' where he counted nationally-minded students among his friends. Seán joined Crokes, a club with strong tradition and ideals.

Seán was a freedom fighter and a Trade Union leader. In the 1913 strike, he played his part and fought under Commandant Ned Daly in the 1916 Rising in North King Street. He spent some time in Stafford Gaol. When peace was restored, Seán redoubled his efforts to spread and promote camogie.

Tall, broad-shouldered, dignified and soft-spoken, Seán filled the role of national organiser for much of his camogie life. A practical man, he watched the financial outgoings of the Association with great care in his role of trustee. Seán married Kathleen McKeown, a native of Omeath, in 1939. They had no family. Kathleen was in great demand as a referee and coach.

Seán supplied camogie copy to the Irish Press under the pen-name 'Tír na nÓg' for many years. The O'Duffy Cup, trophy of the All-Ireland senior championship, commemorates his name. For Seán, no journey was too long, no task too difficult, no job too small. He cycled from his home in Harold's Cross to the Phoenix Park to put down the side-line flags and hang up the goal nets so that the Sunday fixtures could proceed with everything in order. At the age of ninety-five, Seán died on October 20th, 1981 having rendered a lifetime of service to camogie.

Dr. Agnes O'Farrelly

Born on June 24th, 1874 at Raffony, Virginia, Co. Cavan, Agnes O'Farrelly was a daughter of Peter and Ann O'Farrelly. One of five daughters and three sons, the family had a traditional interest in the Irish language. Agnes became a noted Gaelic scholar, educationist, writer and champions of women's rights. An executive member of the Gaelic League, she was a close friend of Douglas Hyde, first President of Ireland, and other leading personalities in the Irish Ireland movement.

Cáit O'Donoghue, the first Organiser of the Camogie Association, wrote to Agnes O'Farrelly, then lecturer in Modern Irish Poetry at U.C.D., inviting her to become involved in camogie and to use her influence to set up teams in the universities. Agnes presided over the inaugural meeting of the U.C.D. Camogie Club and became its first President, a position she held until her death in 1951. She prevailed on her friend, Edwin Gibson, Lord Ashbourne, to donate the impressive Ashbourne Cup for intervarsity competition.

By 1932, Agnes was one of the most prominent women of her time. She was appointed Professor of Modern Irish Poetry at U.C.D., elected to the Senate, held a seat on the Governing Body of U.C.D. and was an established writer. Under the pen name 'Una Uladh', she wrote two novels and books of poetry in the Irish language. With Mary Hayden, she campaigned for women's rights in the universities. Together, they founded the Irish Association of Women Graduates. She chaired the inaugural meeting of Cumann na mBan but withdrew at the time of the 'Volunteer Split'.

She became more deeply involved in camogie affairs. Her voice carried weight. When she spoke, delegates listened, when she spoke in public, the newspapers picked up and gave her words prominence. At a time when the Camogie Association struggled for recognition and acceptance, Agnes lent credence and status. She guided the Association through difficult times and was made Life President of the Association in 1935. During the split-ridden forties, Agnes sought to bring all sides together.

She established an Irish language college in Glangevin, West Cavan and was actively involved with the Irish language summer school at Cloghaneely, Co. Donegal. Very hospitable, she entertained regularly at the house in the Donegal Gaeltacht and at her residence in Brighton Road, Dublin. In recognition of her services, the National University conferred upon her an honorary D. Litt.

Intelligent, generous and an achiever, Agnes saw what needed to be done and did something about it. Alphonsus O'Farrelly, Professor of Science at U.C.D. was a brother of Agnes and her sister, Sr. M. Athanasius, was Rev. Mother of the Holy Faith Convent at Clontarf. It is an indication of the esteem in which she was held that the President of Ireland, Seán T. O'Kelly, and the Taoiseach, Eamon de Valera, attended her funeral in November, 1951.

Sheila McAnulty

Daughter of Hugh and Rose McAnulty, and sister of Moya, Rosaleen and Terry, Sheila McAnulty was the leading administrator in the Camogie Association for several decades. She made reference to the fact that two events of monumental importance took place in 1916 – the Easter Rising and her birth. She joined the Betsy Gray camogie club in Warrenpoint, called after the insurgent heroine who was killed at Ballinahinch in 1798.

Sheila's first administrative role in camogie was secretary of the Betsy Gray club. She moved quickly up the ladder serving the Newry and District League, Down County Board and Ulster Council, leaving her mark on all of them. Sheila's qualities were recognised at national level and she was elected President of the Camogie Association in 1949. She made an immediate impact bringing a splintered Association together. Under her leadership, the Association consolidated and expanded and she was rewarded with a fourth year in the top post.

On completion of her term of office, she became Árd Runaí, a role she filled with astuteness, foresight and expertise from 1953 to 1975. Held in high regard by all, Sheila launched new ideas and encouraged others to do likewise. She passionately pursued the ideals of the Association throughout her life. Sheila lent a sympathetic ear to inexperienced officials who sought help and guidance when they found themselves in difficulty. She listened to their tale of woe and placed them on the right path without any reproach.

Managing Director of a motor factors company, Sheila reached the top of her profession. An ardent follower of Down football, Sheila wrote Ó Shíol go Bláth, a history of Down G.A.A. Recognised outside the Association as a leading sports administrator, she was appointed to COSAC, the sports advisory council in 1970.

An articulate speaker, Sheila could hold her own in any company. Well read, she possessed a deep pool of general knowledge which she put to good use in winning the All-Ireland Scór Question Time in 1996. When Sheila retired from business, she enrolled as a student at Queen's University and graduated with distinction.

Lil O'Neill, who served as President while Sheila was Árd Runaí, penned the following lines: "To me, Sheila is Camogie and she is the best ambassador camogie has ever had. She will be remembered for her kindness, thoughtfulness and help at all times, her sense of humour, her interest in young people and the encouragement she gave them, and her ability to sort out any problem".

In 1999, Sheila was honoured with the title of Life President in recognition of her unique contribution to the Camogie Association. Sadly, she died on July 7th, 2004 at the age of 88.

Elizabeth, Countess of Fingall

Daughter of George E. Burke of Danesfield, Moycullen, Co. Galway, Elizabeth married Arthur Plunkett, the 11th Earl of Fingall, at the age of seventeen, and lived in Killeen Castle. A notable figure in Irish society, she served as President of the United Women of Ireland (later renamed the Irish Countrywomen's Association) from 1912-1942 and was prominent in assisting the home industries movement. She sat on numerous charitable committees. In 1927, she published her memoirs "Seventy Years Young".

She greeted everyone with genuine friendship and took a keen interest in their concerns. Endowed with a quick mind and ready wit, she summed up people instantly and was seldom wrong. Those in trouble always received her sympathy and, if needed, her ready help.

Elizabeth did not attend meetings and filled the role of patron rather than president in the Camogie Association. She died in October, 1944 at the age of seventy-eight.

Mollie Gill

The longest serving president in the history of the Association, Mollie Gill was born to James and Jane Gill in 1891. She resided with her parents, brothers James and Michael, and sister, Margaret, at Murphystown, Sandyford A member of the Crokes camogie club, she had an impressive playing career. Captain of Dublin for many years and the Leinster Tailteann teams of 1928 and 1932, she possessed a neat style of play which proved most effective and, at times, spectacular. Mollie, who always wore a soft felt hat on the field, was the first player to accept the O'Duffy Cup. She captained Dublin to win the All-Ireland title in 1932 and, again, in 1933.

She chaired the Dublin County Board from 1917 to 1935 and was already an experienced official when she was elected President of the Camogie Association in 1923. She opposed the introduction of the ban on hockey in the late thirties.

Nationalistic in outlook, she worked for the Irish Republican Prisoners' Dependent Fund. A member of Inghinidhe na hÉireann, she later joined Cumann na mBan. She was employed as an artist by the Yeats sisters at the Cuala Press which specialised in publishing the work of Irish writers. In May, 1923, she was arrested at her place of work together with Āine Ní Riain, Rúnaí of the Camogie Association and interned in Kilmainham jail. Mollie never married and lived her adult life in Rialto. She died on March, 15th 1977, at the age of 86.

Lil Kirby

Lil enjoyed a distinguished playing career. Winner of several Cork schools' championship medals with St. Aloysius School, she captained U.C.C. to win the Ashbourne Cup. Regular on the Cork team from 1934 to 1941, Lil collected six All-Ireland medals, leading Cork to success in 1940. She joined Cara Cliodhna on graduation from U.C.C. but transferred to Old Aloysians when the past pupils club was formed in 1937.

Lil was the first woman to chair the Cork County Board and the county reaped the benefits of her firm and capable leadership. In 1941, she was elected President of the Camogie Association.

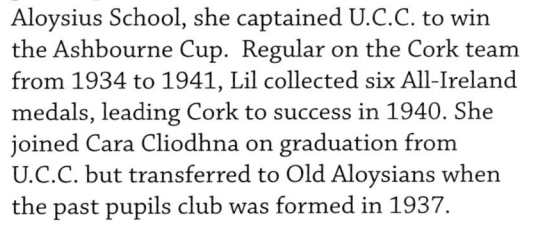

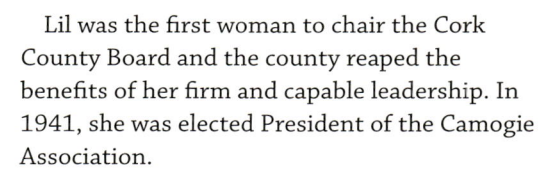

A commerce graduate, she worked in the family business, Kirby & Kirby, auditors and accountants. Lil was a top class swimmer. In 1931, she swam across Cork Harbour from White Bay to Graball Bay, a distance of over two miles.

She was the first lady to finish and the second overall. She received a letter from the bishop rebuking her for allowing herself to be photographed with the male winner while wearing a swimming costume.

Lil sat listening at Congress while a motion to ban Old Time waltzes was discussed. It was too much for Lil when she heard a Leinster delegate pronounce that no self-respecting girl would allow herself to be whirled around a room in that fashion. She jumped to her feet and announced that she enjoyed being swung around a hall in the arms of a man.

In the spring of 1942, Lil married David Crowley and settled in Bandon. She immersed herself in the local activities through the I.C.A. and faded from the camogie scene.

Anne Hennessy

A native of Drumgoon, near Cootehill, Co. Cavan, Anne Hennessy defeated Esther Ryan (Dublin) by twenty-two votes to thirteen to become President of the Camogie Association in 1945. A founder member and first secretary of the O'Leary's camogie club in Drumgoon in 1933, she served the Cavan County Board for thirteen years, 1935-1948. She performed the duties of vice-chairman from 1935 to 1940 when she was promoted to chairman, a post she held until 1948. Anne served Ulster Council and was sought-after referee throughout the province.

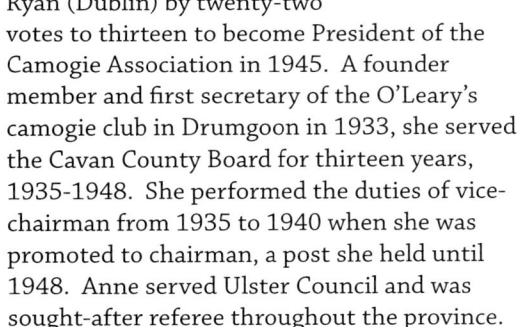

Married to James J. Hennessy, town clerk of Cootehill, she had four sons and three daughters. Shortly after her election as President, her husband died suddenly and she did not seek re-election in 1946.

Sheila Horgan

Of farming stock in Ballinora, Co. Cork, Sheila was unopposed for the position of President in 1946. She kept Mid-Cork faithful to the Camogie Association during the years that the Cork County Board was on the outside. She organised the Mid-Cork (Muskerry) divisional board providing competition for the teams involved. She was vice-chairman of the Cork County Board prior to Cork's abstention and served as secretary of Munster Council for two years.

A quiet, soft-spoken and hard-working woman, Sheila was a key player on the Ballinora team which won the Cork junior championship in 1934. Her brother, Jim, played full-back for the Cork senior hurling team. She married Dan Connolly and they had one son, Tim. Sheila was very prominent in the I.C.A. and Macra na Tuaithe.

Lucy Byrne

Daughter of Larry Cullen, the first treasurer of the Wicklow G.A.A. Board, Lucy came from a strong gaelic games background. She moved from Ashford to Glenealy on her marriage to Christy ('C.M.') Byrne, who chaired the Wicklow G.A.A. Board from 1910 to 1947. Lucy was the guiding light in Wicklow camogie circles over a thirty year period.

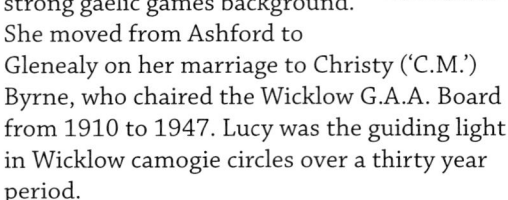

She spoke out when the Wicklow players and officers were suspended for participating in the 1924 Tailteann Games by the Dublin-based steering committee of the Camogie Association. Elected as President of the Association in 1953, Lucy was held in high respect. An enthusiastic and whole-hearted worker for the Association, she possessed a good knowledge of camogie administration.

Fluent in Irish, she was a member of the Gaelic League and Cumann na mBan. A strikingly handsome woman, she did not enjoy the best of health during her presidency and died in November, 1956, a few months after completing her term of office.

Lily Spence

A member of the St. Teresa's camogie club in Belfast, Lily was elected President of the Camogie Association in 1956. Indeed, Belfast provided both presidents of the G.A.A. and the Camogie Association at the same time as Séamus McFerran was her opposite number. A North of Ireland civil servant, Lily was never afraid to air her views, irrespective of whether they were popular or not.

She was introduced to camogie at St. Dominic's School and made the playing panel in her first year. While still a schoolgirl, she joined St. Teresa's. With players of the calibre of Deirdre

Administrators

and Marie O'Gorman, Kathleen Rainey and Claire Marshall lining out for the club, success came easily. Lily collected a coveted All-Ireland medal in 1947.

Sent as a delegate of her club to the Antrim County Board, she questioned any matter that she was not happy with. The officials recognised her interest and brought her the other side of the top table where she looked after the Board's financial affairs with the utmost care.

Long-serving secretary of Ulster Colleges Council, Lily headed the new All-Ireland Colleges' Council when it was formed in 1969. Throughout the Troubles in Northern Ireland, Lily travelled with her great friend, Rosina McManus, to oversee colleges' fixtures over the length and breadth of the country. Ignoring the danger, they arrived in time to collect at the gate, sell programmes and, more often than not, one of them refereed the match.

When Lily's term of office as President was complete, she was voted treasurer of the Camogie Association, a role she filled with great efficiency for twenty years. Lily excelled at refereeing and took charge of four All-Ireland senior finals. Talkative and entertaining, she has always been a champion of the underdog and numbers no enemies in her scores of camogie acquaintances. Lily loves camogie company and has many friends all over the country.

Eilish Redmond

Eilish Keegan and her sisters were founder members of the Celtic club in 1928. She had a life-long attachment to the club which grew to be one of most successful and famous clubs in the county. She filled the position of club chairman for many years. Eilish gave her time and talents to Dublin through the roles of Chairman of the Dublin County Board and selector of Dublin teams.

Elected to the post of President of the Camogie Association in 1959, she presented the O'Duffy Cup to captains from her own county on three occasions. Secretary to a firm of accountants, she always did what was expected of her in a ladylike way. Sincere and concerned, Eilish worked for camogie with enthusiasm. She married John Redmond and resided in Beaumont, Dublin.

Crios O'Connell

Limerick lady, Crios O'Connell was elected President of the Camogie Association in 1962. A fluent Irish speaker and a member of the Gaelic League, she had great interest in Irish culture. She belonged to St. Patrick's camogie club, with whom she won a Limerick championship medal in 1947. Quick to grasp the situation and get people to accept her authority, Crios was a very able official.

Crios chaired the Limerick County Board for many years before moving to Munster Council. She guided Munster affairs from 1952 to 1958.

A fine singer, particularly of Irish songs, Crios ran a bakery at her home in Pennywell. Her brothers, Mick, Seán and Matt, served the Limerick City G.A.A. Board. Crios was appointed to chair the Munster Colleges' Council when it was formed in 1969. Generous, confident and affable, Crios oversaw the Diamond Jubilee celebrations of the Camogie Association in 1964. She died on May 3rd, 1985.

Lil O'Grady

Lil O'Grady (Old Aloysians, Cork) succeeded Crios O'Connell as President of the Camogie Association in 1965. A very efficient official, she served the Cork Board in several positions including chairman and led Munster Council for twelve years. Ladylike, sincere and dedication, Li chaired meetings with complete impartiality. As a player she lined out for St. Aloysius School, Old Aloysians and the Cork Schools team, winning several championship medals. Born in Sligo, Lil comes from a gaelic games family. Her father, Michael, played football for Leitrim and was vice-chairman of Sligo County Board. Her uncle, Standish O'Grady, played for Cavan and Monaghan. Lil's sister, Jo, was a regular for Cork and Munster. Much in demand as a referee, Lil officiated at the 1969 All-Ireland senior final.

An employee of P. J. Carroll & Company throughout her working life, she married John O'Neill and lives in Ballinlough, Cork. Following a break from the game, Lil returned to camogie administration, firstly as chairman of Munster Colleges' Council and, later, as President of the All-Ireland Colleges' Council. She maintains a lively interest in camogie affairs.

Rosina McManus

A native of Kilkeel, Co. Down, Rosina McManus (nee Hughes) was elected President of the Camogie Association in 1968. Rosina was a highly-respected official who made a massive contribution to the game under several headings. A pioneer in the area of coaching, she was instrumental in setting up the inaugural courses at Orangefield, Belfast. Rosina's enthusiasm and light-hearted approach, as secretary of the National Coaching Committee, was one of the main reasons for the success of the courses at Gormanston College. She took a hurley in her hand at St. Louis, Kilkeel and learned to enjoy the game. Rosina moved to Belfast to join the N.I. Civil Service and made a huge contribution to her adopted county in camogie terms. She served Antrim and Ulster in many roles but her real passion was working for and with underage players. She organised the Ulster Intermediate schools for many years before they were absorbed into the Ulster Colleges. Coach to the Antrim minors, she led them to an All-Ireland final. But the dedication she gave to the youngsters of her beloved Connolly's was way above the call of duty.

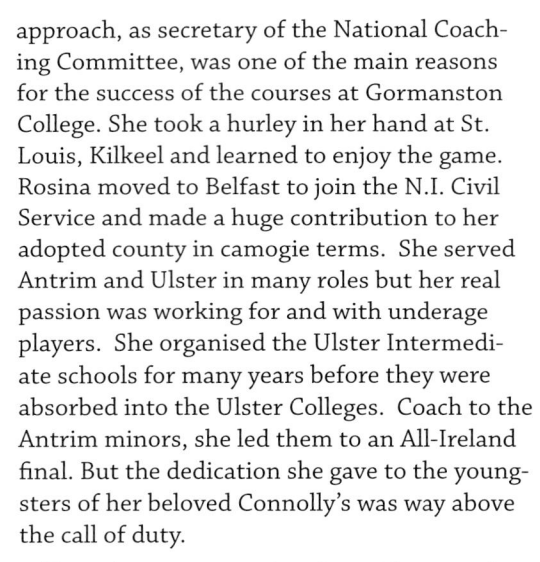

Her value was appreciated outside camogie and she was appointed to the North of Ireland Sports Council and Cospóir. A knight of the whistle, she officiated at hundreds of games including the 1980 All-Ireland senior final. As President of the All-Ireland Colleges' Council, she saw real progress being made.

Married to Fermanagh man, Frank McManus, Rosina was a great talker and could keep the party going for hours. She collapsed at the 2008 Ulster final in Dunloy, surrounded by many friends, and died two days later on June, 17th.

Nell McCarthy

Nell was born into a hurling family in Carrigtwohill, Co. Cork. Jimmy 'Major' Kennedy, who captained Cork to the 1919 All-Ireland senior hurling title, was an uncle of Nell. Her brother, Dan, wore the famed red jersey. From an early age, Nell listened to the men folk analyse hurling matches and learned how to read the game; how to place a team to the best advantage and how to counteract the opposition.

She was educated at South Presentation Convent, Cork, and headed for Dublin to join the civil service. She was attached to the Department of Education for many years and, later, worked in the National College of Art.

She played for Craobh an Cheitinnigh and Cuchulainns before joining Celtic. Nell made Celtic into a great club which challenged for top honours every season. The club attracted many players from the country who came to Dublin to work and Nell took a personal interest in their welfare. In 1936, she became secretary of the Dublin Junior Board and moved to chairman a few years later. From 1952 to 1970, Nell chaired the Dublin County Board and always commanded respect.

Best known for her coaching ability, she

Administrators

guided the great Dublin teams of the Fifties and Sixties. Adept at spotting talent and reading the game, she brought out the best in her players. She realised the importance of starting young players the right way and spent much time coaching schoolgirls at Holy Faith, Glasnevin and Sisters of Charity, George's Hill.

Nell was elected President of the Camogie Association in 1971 but only served two years of her term of office. She made a huge contribution to the game. Always happy to talk hurling or camogie and she possessed a depth of knowledge on both subjects. Nell died on February 18th, 2009 and was brought back to Carrigtwohill to be buried.

Nancy Murray

Born Nancy Milligan, she served the Camogie Association in many capacities. She had a distinguished playing career with club and county, went on to be a successful coach and referee and proved to be an administrator of the highest calibre.

She will always be associated with the Deirdre club and was full-back on the team which reached two All-Ireland club finals. She was on the first Antrim side to capture the O'Duffy Cup in 1945. Antrim retained the title for the next two seasons with Nancy playing a leading role. When marriage shortened her playing career, she returned to coaching with great success and guided Antrim to All-Ireland victories in 1956 and 1967. A very capable referee, Nancy officiated at four All-Ireland senior finals.

As an administrator, Nancy rose up through the ranks from South Antrim Board to Antrim County Board; Ulster Council to President of the Camogie Association in 1973. Knowledgeable and experienced, Nancy was held in high respect. Warm-hearted and caring, she had an excellent singing voice. Nancy married Seán Murray and had two sons, Donal and Seán. Two weeks before her death on May 16th, 2004, she travelled to Portglenone to join in a tribute to Mairéad Magill, who had been named on the Team of the Century.

Agnes Purcell

A lady who gave devoted service to the game she loved, Agnes Hourigan, was born in Ballingarry, Co. Limerick. Agnes took up the game at the age of twelve and, three years later, was named captain of the Limerick team. She enrolled at U.C.D. and, while there, won four Ashbourne Cup medals. She fielded on the right wing where her speed was seen to good effect. In 1938, she won an All-Ireland medal with Dublin. While a student at U.C.D., she met Pádraig Purcell, the G.A.A. writer and historian, and they were married in 1943.

For many years, Agnes supplied camogie copy for the national newspapers. In dealing with players, she boosted the morale and was much too gentle a soul to hurt by criticism even when a player's performance left a lot to be desired. Agnes had a long association with U.C.D. camogie club; Leinster and All-Ireland Colleges; the C.C.I.A and Leinster Council. In 1976, the Association paid tribute to her by electing her national President. She brought a new dimension to the job. She travelled to matches and meetings all over the country, sparing no effort to promote the game. When her term of office was over, she was not allowed to rest. The post of treasurer was vacant and she was persuaded to don that hat. Enthusiastically, she set about building up the funds of the Association so that it could shortly embark on the momentous step of appointing a full-time development officer.

A kind and generous lady, she made her home at Kenilworth Park an open house where camogie folk enjoyed the best of Irish hospitality. Mother of daughter, Anne, sons, Dick,

John and Pádraig, she died unexpectedly on November 25th, 1983 at the age of 64. Always willing to tackle any task, no job was too big or too small for her to tackle. She gave herself unsparingly to the game she loved.

Mary Moran

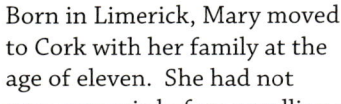

Born in Limerick, Mary moved to Cork with her family at the age of eleven. She had not seen camogie before enrolling at St. Aloysius School. She took to the game immediate and it became a lifetime addiction. As a player, Mary won Cork and Dublin championship medals with Old Aloysians and Celtic respectively. She collected an All-Ireland senior medal with Cork and was a member of the Celtic team that won the first All-Ireland club championship.

Mary chaired the Cork Camogie Board from 1968 to 1978 and coached Cork teams to win All-Ireland minor, junior and senior titles. She served Munster Council as treasurer and chairperson. In 1979, she was elected President of the Camogie Association. The appointment of the first full-time officer and the 75th anniversary celebrations took place under her watch.

Mary was secretary of Munster and All-Ireland Colleges' Councils for thirty-two years and served as President of the All-Ireland Colleges' Council. She also filled the roles of national coach, national P.R.O., inter-county referee and trustee of the Association. She has written the history of Munster Colleges, All-Ireland Colleges, Cork and Munster camogie. An avid collector of camogie material and memorabilia, she has built up a considerable stockpile over the past fifty years. Mary was employed by Allied Irish Banks and served in Enniscorthy, Dublin and Cork.

Mary Fennelly

Kilkenny took over the two top posts in gaelic games on the same weekend when Mary Fennelly was elected President of the Camogie Association and Paddy Buggy was installed as President of the G.A.A. From a strong gaelic games family, Mary is a first-cousin of All-Star hurlers, Liam and Ger Fennelly. John Fennelly, Mary's father, chaired the Kilkenny Camogie Board while her sister, Bríd, played alongside her.

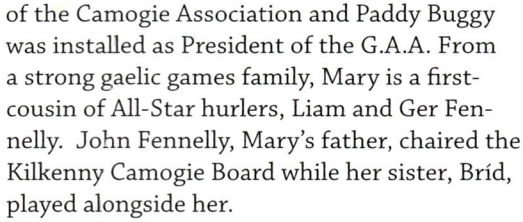

Carrickshock was Mary's first club but she moved to St. Paul's and, later, to Celtic while working in Dublin. In keeping with the Fennelly name, Mary excelled on the camogie field. She captained Kilkenny to win the All-Ireland senior championship in 1976 and finished her playing career with three All-Ireland senior; two All-Ireland club championship with St. Paul's; two Gael-Linn with Leinster; Kilkenny and Dublin championship medals. A left-handed player, she read the game well and had a very accurate shot.

Mary learned the ropes as secretary of the Kilkenny County Board and Leinster Council. Attracting more players, improving the image of the Association and bringing the concerns of the grassroots to the notice of top administrators were issues in her manifesto as she sought the top post. Mary was a strong advocate of the fifteen-aside game but it took some years before the idea was sold to the country.

Mary Lynch

The first Monaghan lady to hold the prestigious office, Mary Lynch was elected President of the Camogie Association at the 1985 Congress in Ballinasloe. As Mary Kelly, she learned the basics of the game at St. Louis, Carrickmacross and made the county team while still a schoolgirl. She accepted an appointment in the Office of the Land Commission in Dublin and joined the Celtic club. The Dublin selectors recognised Mary's playing ability and she was named in midfield on the

Administrators

Dublin team which claimed the All-Ireland honours in 1949.

On the occasion of her marriage to Willie Lynch, Mary returned to Carrickmacross. Family commitments curtailed her camogie involvement for the next few years. Mary passed on her love of gaelic games to her three boys, Brendan, Bill and Tony, who hurled for Monaghan and her daughter, Marion, who played Ashbourne Cup with U.C.C.

In 1962, Mary made a determined effort to revive the game in Co. Monaghan and place it on a sound footing. She stepped forward to fill the role of county chairperson and guided the revival. Mary held each position on Ulster Council in turn, sat on the national fixtures and referees committees and was a member of the All-Ireland Primary Schools' Council.

It is, perhaps, as a referee that Mary was best known. She officiated at minor, junior and senior All-Ireland finals. Mary was a trustee of the Association from 1994 to 2004. She set up a commission to examine all aspects of camogie during her presidency which led to many initiatives being introduced. Anxious to help her community, Mary gave her time to the local Social Services, Care of the Aged, youth and recreational organisations.

Máire Ní Cheallachán

A well-known and colourful character, Máire was elected President of the Camogie Association in 1988. Daughter of Edmund and Ellen O'Callaghan, Máire came from a republican background. Her uncle, Danny O'Callaghan, was executed by the British in 1921 for his part in the Dripsey ambush. As a player, Máire fielded with Lee Valley but joined Inniscarra when the club was formed in her parish.

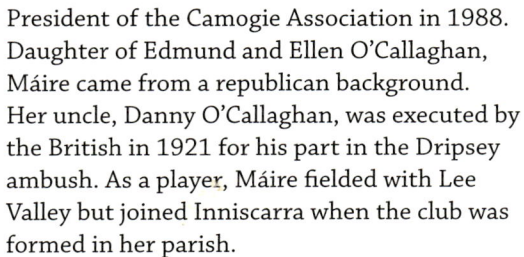

She chaired the Cork Camogie Board (1980-1985) and Munster Council (1985-1987) and was a member of successful Cork selection committees. Máire's interests stretched beyond camogie. She was an active member of the Gaelic League and a Cathaoirleach of Dáil na Mumhan. She played a prominent part in the Dripsey Gaelic League Players one-act play, An Bunán Buidh which won first place at an Oireachtas. Her portrayal of Frau Crantz in the play 'Out of the Darkness' with the successful Berrings I.C.A. drama group of the early seventies, will live long in the memory of those who witnessed it. She won All-Ireland honours with the Muskerry Gaelic League debating team in 1976 and helped Inniscarra camogie club to win the CCD Question Time in 1984 and 1986. Máire died on April 10th, 1992.

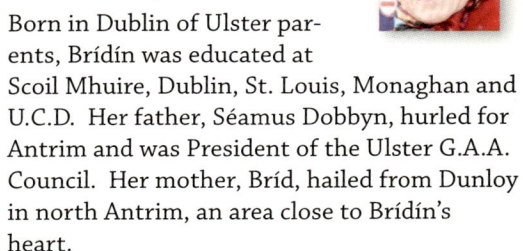

Brídín Uí Mhaolagáin

Born in Dublin of Ulster parents, Brídín was educated at Scoil Mhuire, Dublin, St. Louis, Monaghan and U.C.D. Her father, Séamus Dobbyn, hurled for Antrim and was President of the Ulster G.A.A. Council. Her mother, Bríd, hailed from Dunloy in north Antrim, an area close to Brídín's heart.

Brídín won five Ashbourne medals with U.C.D. and captained the winning team in 1958. She has retained her links with the club in the capacity of President for many years. Many years of work for third level colleges was rewarded with the title of Uachtarán Saoil, Comhairle Camógaíochta Ard-Oideachais. In 1991, Brídín was elected President of the Camogie Association at Congress in Cork.

Brídín left her mark on the handball and racquetball scene. She represented Ireland in both codes and filled the role of President of the Ladies Handball Association. Brídín had always maintained a great interest in drama, particularly in the Irish language. She played the part of 'Brigette' in Rós na Rún on TG4. Brídín taught in Ballymun Comprehensive School for over thirty years. With her husband, Aidan Mulligan, she shares an interest in the Special Olympics.

Belle O'Loughlin

Belle Bannon from Home Avenue, Newry developed her love and enthusiasm for camogie from Sister Mary de Sales at the Sacred Heart School. She polished the skills of the game in the Ulster Colleges' competitions. A member of the St. Bridget's club, Belle soon attracted the attention of the Down selectors and made a significant contribution to the county's success in the 1968 Ulster junior championship.

She married Arthur O'Loughlin and settled in Warrenpoint. She took a keen interest in the local St. Peter's Club, both as a player and coach. She immersed herself in camogie administration and serve Down and Ulster in several positions. A highly regarded referee, she officiated at the All-Ireland senior finals in 1982 and 1988. In 1994, Belle was elected President of the Camogie Association at Congress in Howth.

Belle's other great love was tennis. She won many tournaments at local level and around the province. A member of the Newry and Mourne Sports Development Committee, she was keen to see youth enjoy and gain the benefits of sport. Belle has three sons, Damian, Mark and Barry and a daughter, Nicola.

Phyllis Breslin

From a very young age, Phyllis Breslin has been involved in camogie. Born into a strong G.A.A. family, she followed family members to the Eoghan Ruadh club on Dublin's northside where her uncle, Bill North was the first captain and her father, Thomas Breslin, was president. Starting with underage competitions and culminating with an All-Ireland club championship victory in 1967, Phyllis gave wonderful service to Eoghan Ruadh. Wearing the blue of her beloved Dublin, she collected All-Ireland junior championship in 1975 and a national senior league medal in 1979. But it was at refereeing that Phyllis was best known. A firm and fair official, she travelled the country with her whistle. She officiated at two All-Ireland senior and two All-Ireland junior finals.

At the tender age of thirteen, Phyllis attended the Dublin County Board as an Eoghan Ruadh delegate. Her administrative experience led eventually to becoming Leinster Council chair and delegate to Central Council. In 1997, she was elevated to President of the Camogie Association at Congress in Athlone. Phyllis presided over the introduction of the fifteen-aside game; live television of the All-Ireland senior final; the All-Star awards; coaching development programmes; the publication of 'Camogie Abú' magazine and the invitation of the Jubilee teams to All-Ireland day. An occasion that she will always remember was the bestowing of the title Life President to Sheila McAnulty.

On a historical note, Peadar Breslin, grandfather of Phyllis, fought in the Four Courts in 1916 alongside Seán O'Duffy.

Phyllis continues to work for camogie in the roles of trustee and treasurer at national level. A member of Naomh Bríd club, she was employed by the Irish Dairy Board for most of her working life. Phyllis loves the social side of camogie and keeps in touch with her many friends around the country. Sincere and considerate, Phyllis is a keen photographer and golfer.

Administrators

Pat Rafferty

Pat Rafferty came to the post of President with a wealth of experience and knowledge of camogie affairs. She had served a long apprenticeship with the Dublin Junior Board, Dublin Senior Board and Leinster Council. Pat chaired and acted as secretary in both Dublin and Leinster and came within a single vote of taking the Árd Runaí position in 1975. She became leader of the Camogie Association at Congress in Cookstown in 2000.

Educated by the Irish Sisters of Charity at Mountjoy Street and Trinity College, Pat lined out for Eoghan Ruadh winning Dublin and All-Ireland club championship medals. A member of the successful Dublin junior team in 1971, she fielded with the Dublin senior team. She joined Naomh Aoife and participated in the club's sixtieth anniversary celebrations.

Later, Pat moved to County Fermanagh and immersed herself in camogie affairs. She holds the unique distinction of having served as provincial secretary in two different provinces, Leinster and Ulster. A concerned person, she had devoted much time to anti-doping and childcare issues. Pat worked as a librarian.

Miriam O'Callaghan

Miriam O'Callaghan was the first Offaly lady to be elected President of the Camogie Association. She was the public face of the Association during the hectic Centenary year of 2004 and portrayed an excellent image. A founder member of the Tullamore camogie club, she fielded for club and county. A very capable official, Miriam served Offaly and Leinster camogie in several positions. She was much sought after as a referee and regularly obliged. She officiated at all levels including the All-Ireland senior finals of 1991 and 1993.

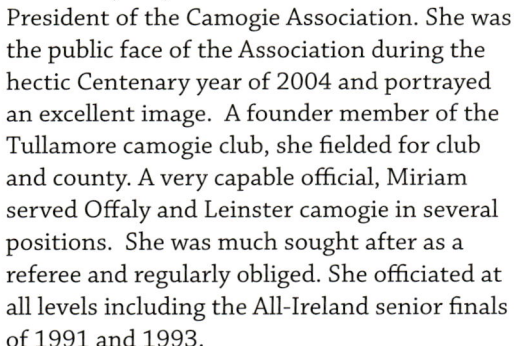

Interested in politics from a young age, Miriam has served her community in several capacities. She has sat on the Tullamore Town Council, Offaly County Council and the Offaly VEC committee. She chaired the Offaly Sports Partnership and was a member of the National Sports Campus Development Authority. Her excellent work for these bodies, together with her impressive leadership of the Camogie Association, was recognised and she was honoured with the Offaly Person of the Year in 2004.

An interest in youth drew her to colleges' camogie and she served as President of the All-Ireland Colleges' Council for four years. Miriam continues to work for the Association as a member of the Management committee. She is employed by the HSE as an administrator. She resides in Tullamore with her husband, Liam, and daughters, Áine and Orla.

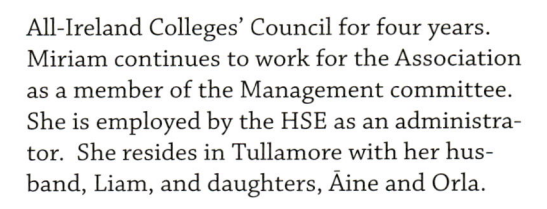

Liz Howard

Liz Howard, the first Tipperary lady to hold the top post, was elected President of the Camogie Association at the 2006 Congress in Tullamore. Born in Carrick-on-Suir to a family steeped in gaelic games tradition, it was no surprise that Liz grew up with a passion for camogie and hurling. Her father, Garrett, a Limerick native, won All-Ireland hurling medals with both Dublin and Limerick. She moved to County Clare at the age of eight, where her parents set up the Feakle camogie club. In her playing days, Liz wore the colours of Feakle (Clare), Roscrea and Knockshegowna (Tipperary), Celtic and Phoenix (Dublin). She won a national senior league medal with Tipperary, an All-Ireland junior medal with Dublin and Dublin championship and league medals.

Liz was appointed National PRO of the Camogie Association in 1979 but switched codes to fill a similar role with the Tipperary

GAA Board. Never shy to air her views, she was a hurling analyst on RTE and chaired 'The Sunday Game'. Liz spent her working life in Dublin with the Civil Service, Aer Lingus and the Public Appointments Service.

She returned to the camogie scene and played a major part in the preparations for the Centenary celebrations. In 2006, she was elected President of the Camogie Association. An increase in clubs and playing membership; implementation of goals in the Strategic Plan; a review of the Association by a sports management firm and additional full-time staff were achievements under her watch. Her efforts were rewarded with a Tipperary Personality of the Year award and the National Administrator of the Year award at the Volunteers in Irish Sport Awards 2009. Liz continues to be involved in camogie administration in the role of trustee.

Joan O'Flynn

A native of Ladysbridge, Co. Cork, Joan O'Flynn became the first President Elect of the Camogie Association at Congress 2008 in Athlone. Joan grew up in a gaelic games environment. Her father, Séamus Ó Floinn, was a well-known administrator with the Imokilly divisional board and the Cork GAA Board. Joan joined the Fr. O'Neill's camogie club in Ballymacoda and helped them to win the Cork junior championship.

Joan was educated at St. Mary's, Midleton, U.C.C. and U.C.D., graduating with a master's degree in Equality Studies. She worked with young Irish emigrants in London and for Combat Poverty in Dublin before becoming a civil servant in the Department of Community Equality and Gaeltacht affairs. On her return from London, she settled in Celbridge and immersed herself in camogie administration at club, county and provincial levels. Joan documented the history of camogie in Kildare in her book 'Soaring Sliothar'. She continued her playing career and was a member of the Celbridge side that won the first county title for the club.

Proficient at forward planning, Joan chaired the Strategic Plan committee which drew up plans to maximise the potential of the Association in a document entitled 'Our Game, Our Passion' (2010-2015). At Congress 2009 in Nenagh, Joan hit the ground running as she took over as President. She established new sub-committees, including Player Welfare and Volunteer and Officer Support and Development, and spread the net to draw in new faces and expertise. She visited every county to listen to the concerns of the grassroots and appointed a working group to update the constitution and rules of the Camogie Association.

Jo Golden

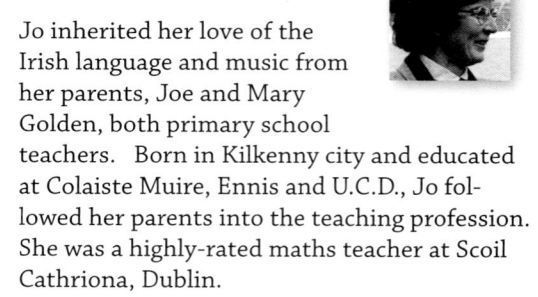

Jo inherited her love of the Irish language and music from her parents, Joe and Mary Golden, both primary school teachers. Born in Kilkenny city and educated at Colaiste Muire, Ennis and U.C.D., Jo followed her parents into the teaching profession. She was a highly-rated maths teacher at Scoil Cathriona, Dublin.

As a player, Jo won two Ashbourne Cup medals with U.C.D.; All-Ireland club championship medals in 1968 and 1969 with St. Paul's and two Gael-Linn medals with Leinster. Jo featured in goal for Kilkenny in the 1970 All-Ireland final.

Appointed National P.R.O. in 1974, she edited the first 'Camogie' magazine. She stepped up to fill the demanding Árd Rúnaí post in 1975. It was a daunting task to fill the shoes of Sheila McAnulty but Jo handled it very capably and left her own imprint on the job. In August 1980, the Camogie Association decided to make the role a full-time post. Jo accepted the job and moved to her office in Croke Park where she set about developing the game. Two years later, having broken new ground and set the template of the post, Jo returned to her teaching job.

In 1984, Jo was elected Treasurer of the Camogie Association. For nineteen years, she carefully managed the finances. She sought to make the Association financially independent by increasing the amount of income produced internally. Jo looked to increase membership fees and gate receipts so that the Association would have the funds to develop and expand.

Jo made a sizeable contribution to the Camogie Association in different roles. Intelligent and professional, Jo was in charge of the situation and saw what needed to be done. An avid reader, she loves to travel and explore areas off the beaten track.

Sheila Wallace

For twenty-two years, 1986-2008, Sheila Wallace guided the Camogie Association in the capacity of Árd Runaí and, later, as Ardstiúrthóir. Presidents came and went but Sheila remained constant driving the growth and expansion of the Association under several headings. A genuine camogie person, love of the game and the idealism attached to it motivated her to unrelenting efforts. It was never a nine to five job with Sheila. She remained on to see that everything was looked after.

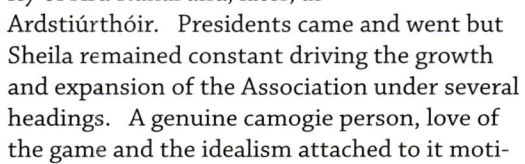

For much of her time, Sheila operated the camogie office single-handedly. Frequently, the work load was massive but she did not complain. In later years, she was happy to welcome additional full-time staff whom she led and supported in their work. Sheila saw camogie's profile rise, funding and sponsorship increase, playing membership grow, new competitions added and progress made in the area of coaching and refereeing. She fostered good relations with the G.A.A. during her years in Croke Park.

Sheila came to the job with a sound knowledge of camogie administration. She served her apprenticeship as secretary of the Dublin junior board and gained valuable experience in a similar role with the Dublin senior board. Sheila was the first Cuala club player to wear the blue of Dublin. She captained the Dublin senior team and led them to success in the national senior league. She won an All-Ireland junior medal in 1971 and refereed the 1985 All-Ireland junior final.

Sheila was well-respected by the camogie community throughout her time in office. Good humoured and friendly, she made herself readily available and was always prepared to listen and offer help.

The Wallace name was well-known in Croke Park. Sunday after Sunday, for many years, Sheila's father acted as a stile man and counted the gate takings. Outside camogie, Sheila's passion is gardening. Endowed with green fingers, her garden in Dalkey makes quite a picture. Sheila is still making a contribution to the game through coaching the Cuala youngsters.

A Game of Our Own

Officials of the Association

Life Presidents

1935–51	Professor Agnes O'Farrelly (Cavan)
1999–04	Sighle Nic an Ultaigh (Sheila McAnulty) (Down)

Presidents

1905	Máire Ní Chinnéide (May Kennedy) (Dublin)
1911	Elizabeth, Countess of Fingal (Meath)
1923	Mollie Gill (Dublin)
1942	Lil Kirby (Cork)
1945	Agnes Hennessy (Cavan)
1946	Sheila Horgan (Cork)
1949	Sighle Nic an Ultaigh (Sheila McAnulty) (Down)
1953	Lucy Byrne (Wicklow)
1956	Lily Spence (Antrim)
1959	Eilish Redmond (Dublin)
1962	Crios O'Connell (Limerick)
1965	Lil O'Grady (Cork)
1968	Rosina McManus (Antrim)
1971	Nell McCarthy (Dublin)
1973	Nancy Murray (Antrim)
1976	Agnes Purcell (Dublin)
1979	Mary Moran (Cork)
1982	Mary Fennelly (Kilkenny)
1985	Mary Lynch (Monaghan)
1988	Máire Ní Cheallacháin (Mary O'Callaghan) (Cork)
1991	Brídín Uí Mhaolagáin (Dublin)
1994	Belle O'Loughlin (Down)
1997	Phyllis Breslin (Dublin)
2000	Pat Rafferty (Dublin)
2003	Miriam O'Callaghan (Offaly)
2006	Liz Howard (Tipperary)
2009	Joan O'Flynn (Kildare)

Secretaries

1905	Nora Roche (Dublin)
1911	Tomás MacAodha
1923	Áine Ní Riain (Dublin)
1932	Esther Ryan (Dublin)
1941	Jean McHugh (Antrim)
1953	Sighle Nic an Ultaigh (Sheila McAnulty) Down
1975	Seosaimhín Nic Uaildrich (Jo Golden) (Kilkenny)

Secretary–Development Officers (Full-time)

1980	Seosaimhín Nic Uaildrich (Jo Golden) (Kilkenny)
1982	Séamus Mac Giolla Fhinnéin (Seamus McAleenan) (Down)
1983	Anne Sheehy (Dublin)
1986	Sheila Wallace (Dublin)

Ard Stiúrthóir

2002	Sheila Wallace (Dublin)
2008	Sinéad O'Connor (Galway)

Treasurers

1911	George Hughes (Dublin)
1914	Tomás MacAodha (Dublin)
1923	Áine Ní Riain (Dublin)
1932	Esther Ryan (Dublin)
1941	Jean McHugh (Antrim)
1946	Mary Montayne (Waterford)
1948	Joan Cosgrove (CIÉ-Dublin)
1949	Iney O'Kelly (Dublin)
1951	Kathleen Cody (Dublin)
1952	Iney O'Kelly (Dublin)
1956	Noreen Murphy (Cork)
1959	Lily Spence (Antrim)
1980	Agnes Purcell (Dublin)
1984	Seosaimhín Nic Uaildrich (Jo Golden) (Kilkenny)
2003	Sinéad O'Connor (Galway) (full-time)
2009	Paula Bruen (Dublin) (full-time)

Trustees

1952–93	Iney O'Kelly Leonard (Dublin)
1952–53	Paddy Higgins (Galway)
1953–81	Seán O'Duffy (Dublin)
1982–83	Agnes Purcell (Dublin)
1984–04	Sighle Nic an Ultaigh (Sheila McAnulty) (Down)
1994–04	Mary Lynch (Monaghan)
2005-	Phyllis Breslin (Dublin)
2005–10	Mary Moran (Cork)
2010–	Liz Howard (Tipperary)

National PRO

1974	Seosaimhín Nic Uaildrich (Jo Golden) (Kilkenny)
1975	Kitty Murphy (Clare)
1977	Liz Howard (Tipperary)
1982	Mary Moran (Cork)
1992	P. J. Fulham (Westmeath)
2000	Máire Uí Scolaí (Dublin)

Third-Level Colleges Officers

Presidents

1973	Agnes Purcell (UCD)
1977	Brídín Uí Mhaolagáin (UCD)
1982	Freda Carroll (Queen's)
1983	Mary Rose O'Connor (Maynooth)
1987	Bernie McNally (Queen's)
1991	Sheila O'Donoghue (WIT)
1995	Marcella Leonard (UUC)
1996	Fiona O'Driscoll (UL)
2000	Susan Malone (UUC)
2002	Carla Doherty (St Mary's)
2003	Susan Vaughan (UCD)
2005	Louise Byrne (UCD)
2007	Neasa O'Donnell (UL)
2009	Lynn Kelly (UL)
2010	Shane Darcy (DIT)

Secretaries

1973	Jane Beatty (UCG)
1975	Mary Matthews (Queen's)
1977	Breda Larkin (Maynooth)
1978	Ann O'Hanlon (Maynooth)
1979	Una Carroll (St Pats)
1981	Toni O'Byrne (St Pats)
1983	Gaye Moran (UCD)
1985	Patricia McAllister (Queen's)
1987	Bríd Kilpatrick (UUJ)
1989	Sheila O'Donoghue (WIT)
1991	Marcella Leonard (UUC)
1995	Camillus King (AIT)
2001	Susan Vaughan (UCD)
2002	Camillus King (AIT)
2004	Damien Young (WIT)
2006	Lizzie Flynn (WIT)
2010	Rena Buckley (UCD)

Appendix

All-Ireland Senior Championship

Year	Date	Venue	Result				Referee
1932	July 30, '33	Sportsfield, G'way	Dublin	3–02	Galway	0–02	Stephen Jordan (Galway)
1933	Dec. 17	Killester	Dublin	9–02	Galway	4–0	Julian McDonnell (Meath)
1934	Oct. 28	Croke Park	Cork	4–03	Louth	1–04	Tommie Ryan (Tipperary)
1935	Nov. 24	Cork Athl. Gnds.	Cork	3–04	Dublin	4–00	Tommie Ryan (Tipperary)
1936	Oct. 11	Croke Park	Cork	6–04	Louth	3–03	Peg Morris (Galway)
1937	Nov. 28	Croke Park	Dublin	9–04	Galway	1–00	Lil Kirby (Cork)
1938	Oct. 30	Cork Athl. Gnds.	Dublin	5–00	Cork	2–03	Peg Morris (Galway)
1939	Nov. 12	Croke Park	Cork	6–01	Galway	1–01	Vera Campbell (Tyrone)
1940	Oct. 12	Croke Park	Cork	4–01	Galway	2–03	Vera Campbell (Tyrone)
1941	Oct. 12	Croke Park	Cork	7–05	Dublin	1–02	Peg Morris (Galway)
1942	Oct. 25	Mardyke, Cork	Dublin	1–02	Cork	1–02	Seán Gleeson (Tipperary)
	Nov. 15	Croke Park	Dublin	4–01	Cork	2–02	Seán Gleeson (Tipperary)
1943	Oct. 17	Croke Park	Dublin	8–00	Cork	1–01	Vera Campbell (Tyrone)
1944	Nov. 5	Corrigan Park	Dublin	5–04	Antrim	0–00	Vera Campbell (Tyrone)
1945	Sept. 30	Cappoquin	Antrim	5–02	Waterford	3–02	Seán Gleeson (Tipperary)
1946	Sept. 29	Corrigan Park	Antrim	4–01	Galway	2–03	Michael Hennessy (Clare)
1947	Nov. 9	Corrigan Park	Antrim	2–04	Dublin	2–01	Celia Mulholland (Galway)
1948	Oct. 23	Croke Park	Dublin	11–04	Down	4–02	James Byrne (Waterford)
1949	Oct. 30	Roscrea	Dublin	8–06	Tipperary	4–01	Celia Mulholland (Galway)
1950	Dec. 3	Croke Park	Dublin	6–05	Antrim	4–01	Celia Mulholland (Galway)
1951	Aug. 19	Croke Park	Dublin	8–06	Antrim	4–01	Celia Mulholland (Galway)
1952	Aug. 10	Croke Park	Dublin	5–01	Antrim	4–02	Celia Mulholland (Galway)
1953	Aug. 2	Croke Park	Dublin	8–04	Tipperary	1–03	Lily Spence (Antrim)
1954	Aug. 22	Croke Park	Dublin	10–04	Derry	4–02	Noreen Murphy (Cork)
1955	Aug. 28	Croke Park	Dublin	9–02	Cork	5–06	Lily Spence (Antrim)
1956	Sept. 30	Croke Park	Antrim	5–03	Cork	4–02	Kathleen O'Duffy (Dublin)
1957	Oct. 6	Croke Park	Dublin	3–03	Antrim	3–01	Noreen Murphy (Cork)
1958	Aug. 10	Croke Park	Dublin	5–04	Tipperary	1–01	Nancy Murray (Antrim)
1959	Sept. 13	Croke Park	Dublin	11–06	Mayo	1–03	Nancy Murray (Antrim)
1960	Nov. 13	Croke Park	Dublin	6–02	Galway	2–00	Eithne Neville (Limerick)
1961	Oct. 8	Croke Park	Dublin	7–02	Tipperary	4–02	Maeve Gilroy (Antrim)
1962	Aug. 12	Croke Park	Dublin	5–05	Galway	2–00	Maeve Gilroy (Antrim)
1963	Sept. 8	Croke Park	Dublin	7–03	Antrim	2–05	Gloria Lee (Kildare)
1964	Oct. 4	Croke Park	Dublin	7–04	Antrim	3–01	Vera McDonnell (Mayo)
1965	Sept. 19	Croke Park	Dublin	10–01	Tipperary	5–03	Nuala Kavanagh (Sligo)
1966	Sept. 18	Croke Park	Dublin	2–02	Antrim	0–06	Bernie Byrne (Monaghan)
1967	Sept. 17	Croke Park	Dublin	4–02	Antrim	4–02	Eithne Neville (Limerick)
	Oct. 15	Croke Park	Antrim	3–09	Dublin	4–02	Eithne Neville (Limerick)
1968	Sept. 15	Croke Park	Wexford	4–02	Cork	2–05	Nancy Murray (Antrim)
1969	Sept. 21	Croke Park	Wexford	4–04	Antrim	4–02	Lil O'Grady (Cork)
1970	Sept. 20	Croke Park	Cork	5–07	Kilkenny	3–02	Nancy Murray (Antrim)
1971	Sept. 19	Croke Park	Cork	4–06	Wexford	1–02	Lily Spence (Antrim)
1972	Sept. 17	Croke Park	Cork	2–05	Kilkenny	1–04	Lily Spence (Antrim)
1973	Sept. 16	Croke Park	Cork	2–05	Antrim	3–01	Phyllis Breslin (Dublin)
1974	Sept. 15	Croke Park	Kilkenny	3–08	Cork	4–05	Jane Murphy (Galway)
	Oct. 6	Croke Park	Kilkenny	3–03	Cork	1–05	Jane Murphy (Galway)
1975	Sept. 21	Croke Park	Wexford	4–03	Cork	1–02	Jane Murphy (Galway)
1976	Sept. 19	Croke Park	Kilkenny	0–06	Dublin	1–02	Jane Murphy (Galway)
1977	Sept. 18	Croke Park	Kilkenny	3–04	Wexford	1–03	Mary Lynch (Monaghan)
1978	Sept. 17	Croke Park	Cork	6–04	Dublin	1–02	Helena O'Neill (Kilkenny)
1979	Sept. 9	Croke Park	Antrim	2–03	Tipperary	1–03	Sheila McNamee (Dublin)
1980	Sept. 14	Croke Park	Cork	2–07	Limerick	3–04	Rosina McManus (Antrim)
	Sept. 28	Croke Park	Cork	1–08	Limerick	2–02	Rosina McManus (Antrim)
1981	Sept. 13	Croke Park	Kilkenny	3–09	Cork	3–09	Phyllis Breslin (Dublin)
	Oct. 4	Croke Park	Kilkenny	1–09	Cork	0–07	Phyllis Breslin (Dublin)
1982	Sept. 26	Croke Park	Cork	2–07	Dublin	2–06	Belle O'Loughlin (Down)
1983	Sept. 25	Croke Park	Cork	2–05	Dublin	1–06	Kathleen Quinn (Galway)
1984	Sept. 9	Croke Park	Dublin	5–09	Tipperary	2–04	Kathleen Quinn (Galway)
1985	Sept. 15	Croke Park	Kilkenny	0–13	Dublin	1–05	Miriam Higgins (Cork)
1986	Sept. 14	Croke Park	Kilkenny	2–12	Dublin	2–03	Betty Joyce (Cork)
1987	Sept. 27	Croke Park	Kilkenny	3–10	Cork	1–07	Anne Redmond (Dublin)
1988	Sept. 14	Croke Park	Kilkenny	4–11	Cork	3–08	Belle O'Loughlin (Down)
1989	Sept. 24	Croke Park	Kilkenny	3–10	Cork	2–06	Kathleen Quinn (Galway)
1990	Sept. 23	Croke Park	Kilkenny	1–14	Wexford	0–07	Miriam Murphy (Cork)
1991	Sept. 22	Croke Park	Kilkenny	3–08	Cork	0–10	Miriam O'Callaghan (Offaly)
1992	Sept. 27	Croke Park	Cork	1–20	Wexford	2–06	Áine Derham (Dublin)
1993	Sept. 26	Croke Park	Cork	3–15	Galway	2–08	Miriam O'Callaghan (Offaly)
1994	Sept. 25	Croke Park	Kilkenny	2–11	Wexford	0–08	Maria Pollard (Waterford)
1995	Sept. 24	Croke Park	Cork	4–08	Kilkenny	2–10	Áine Derham (Dublin)
1996	Sept. 22	Croke Park	Galway	4–08	Cork	1–15	Áine Derham (Dublin)
1997	Sept. 7	Croke Park	Cork	0–15	Galway	2–05	Biddy Phillips (Tipperary)
1998	Sept. 6	Croke Park	Cork	2–13	Galway	0–15	John Morrissey (Tipperary)
1999	Sept. 5	Croke Park	Tipperary	0–12	Kilkenny	1–08	Áine Derham (Dublin)
2000	Sept. 3	Croke Park	Tipperary	2–11	Cork	1–09	Áine Derham (Dublin)
2001	Sept. 16	Croke Park	Tipperary	4–13	Kilkenny	1–06	Áine Derham (Dublin)
2002	Sept. 15	Croke Park	Cork	4–09	Tipperary	1–09	Aileen Lawlor (Westmeath)
2003	Sept. 21	Croke Park	Tipperary	2–11	Cork	1–11	Úna Kearney (Armagh)
2004	Sept. 19	Croke Park	Tipperary	2–11	Cork	0–09	John Pender (Kildare)
2005	Sept. 18	Croke Park	Cork	1–17	Tipperary	1–13	Fintan McNamara (Clare)
2006	Sept. 10	Croke Park	Cork	0–12	Tipperary	0–04	John Morrissey (Tipperary)
2007	Sept. 9	Croke Park	Wexford	2–07	Cork	1–08	Eamonn Browne (Tipperary)
2008	Sept. 14	Croke Park	Cork	2–10	Galway	1–08	Úna Kearney (Armagh)
2009	Sept. 13	Croke Park	Cork	0–15	Kilkenny	0–07	Karl O'Brien (Dublin)
2010	Sept. 12	Croke Park	Wexford	1–12	Galway	1–10	Karl O'Brien (Dublin)
2011	Sept. 11	Croke Park	Wexford	2-7	Galway	1-8	Mike O'Kelly (Cork)

All-Ireland Senior Medal Holders Roll of Honour 1932-2011

15 Medals
Kathleen Mills (Dublin)

13
Una O'Connor (Dublin)

12
Angela Downey (Kilkenny) and Ann Downey (Kilkenny)

10
Kay Ryder

9
Betty Hughes (Dublin), Kay Lyons (Dublin), Bridie McGarry (Kilkenny) and Deirdre Malone (Kilkenny)

8
Sophie Brack (Dublin), Eileen Duffy (Dublin), Eithne Leech (Dublin), Marian McCarthy (Cork), Jo Dunne (Kilkenny) and Biddy O'Sullivan (Kilkenny)

7
Kathleen Cody (Dublin), Annette Corrigan (Dublin), Pat Moloney (Cork), Liz Neary (Kilkenny), Anna Whelan (Kilkenny), Breda Holmes (Kilkenny), Marie Fitzpatrick (Kilkenny) and Mary O'Connor (Cork)

6
Lil Kirby (Cork), Kitty Buckley (Cork), Nancy Caffrey (Dublin), Brid Reid (Dublin), Ally Hussey (Dublin), Doreen Rodgers (Dublin), Mary Ryan (Dublin), Marion McSweeney (Cork), Sandie Fitzgibbon (Cork), Noelle O'Driscoll (Cork/Kilkenny), Linda Mellerick (Cork), Fiona O'Driscoll (Cork) and Denise Cronin (Cork)

5
Doretta Blackton (Dublin), Eileen Bourke (Dublin), Annie Donnelly (Dublin), Judy Doyle (Dublin), Patricia Timmins (Dublin), Mary Sherlock (Dublin), Concepta Clarke (Dublin), Brid Keenan (Dublin), Marie Costine (Cork), Clare Jones (Kilkenny), Frances Rothwell (Kilkenny), Anne Holden (Kilkenny), Marina Downey (Kilkenny), Irene O'Keeffe (Cork), Sinead Nealon (Tipperary), Therese Brophy (Tipperary), Una O'Dwyer (Tipperary), Jovita Delaney (Tipperary), Suzanne Kelly (Tipperary), Philly Fogarty (Tipperary), Eimear McDonnell (Tipperary), Emily Hayden (Tipperary), Ciara Gaynor (Tipperary), Deirdre Hughes (Tipperary), Vivienne Harris (Cork), Noelle Kennedy (Tipperary), Aoife Murray (Cork), Joanne O'Callaghan (Cork), Stephanie Dunlea (Cork), Gemma O'Connor (Cork), Rachel Moloney (Cork), Jennifer O'Leary and Una O'Donoghue (Cork)

4
Joan Cotter (Cork), Josie McGrath (Cork), Peggy Hogg (Cork), Sheila Donnelly (Dublin), Doreen Brennan (Dublin), Josie Kelly (Dublin), Carmel Walsh (Dublin), Nuala Murney (Dublin), Brid Kenny (Dublin), Patty Kenny (Dublin), Jean Hannon (Dublin), Peggy Griffin (Dublin), Rose Fletcher (Dublin), Rose Martin (Dublin), Hannah Dineen (Cork), Sheila Dunne (Cork), Betty Sugrue (Cork), Anne McAuliffe (Cork), Anne Comerford (Cork), Rosie Hennessy (Cork), Nuala Guilly (Cork), Mary O'Leary (Cork), Angela Higgins (Cork), Cathy Landers (Cork), Clare Cronin (Cork), Teresa O'Neill (Kilkenny), Helena O'Neill (Kilkenny), Rita Weymes (Kilkenny), Breda Cahill (Kilkenny), Peggy Carey (Kilkenny), Siobhan Ryan (Kilkenny), Lynn Dunlea (Cork), Mags Finn (Cork), Eithne Duggan (Cork), Claire Madden (Tipperary), Angela McDermott (Tipperary), Claire Grogan (Tipperary), Joanne Ryan (Tipperary), Emer Dillon (Cork), Sarah Hayes (Cork), Amanda O'Regan (Cork), Anna Geary (Cork), Briege Corkery (Cork) and Rena Buckley (Cork)

3
Mary Walsh (Dublin), Ita McNeill (Dublin), Emmy Delaney (Dublin), Eva Moran (Dublin), Nuala Sheehan (Dublin), Kathleen Kearns (Dublin), Maura Moore (Dublin), Mona Walsh (Dublin), Nan Mahon (Dublin), Joan Cosgrave (Dublin), Sheila Sleator (Dublin), May Kavanagh (Dublin), Mary O'Sullivan (Dublin), Sheila Ware (Dublin), Orla Ní Síocháin (Dublin), Kathleen Coughlan (Cork), May McCarthy (Cork), Renee Fitzgerald (Cork), Eileen Casey (Cork), Mary Fitzgerald (Cork), Essie Stanton (Cork), Lena Delaney (Cork), Maura Cronin (Cork), Mary Vallelly (Cork), Kathleen Barry-Murphy (Cork), Celia Quinn (Antrim), Kathleen Rainey (Antrim), Marjorie Griffin (Antrim), Sue McKeown (Antrim), Mavis Madden (Antrim), Nancy Milligan (Antrim), Ita O'Reilly (Antrim), Kit Kehoe (Dublin/Wexford), Margaret O'Leary (Wexford), Bridget Doyle (Wexford), Mary Fennelly (Kilkenny), Carmel Doyle (Kilkenny), Margaret Farrell (Kilkenny), Mary Canavan (Kilkenny), Gillian Dillon (Kilkenny), Bridget Mullally (Kilkenny), Liz Garvan (Cork), Deirdre Sutton (Cork), Mary Whelton (Cork), Miriam Higgins (Cork), Mary Geaney (Cork), Eileen Dineen (Cork), Martha Kearney (Cork), Kathleen Costine (Cork), Paula Goggins (Cork), Therese O'Callaghan (Cork), Colette O'Mahony (Cork), Rose Desmond (Cork), Niamh Harkin (Tipperary), Sheena Howard (Tipperary), Louise Ryan (Tipperary), Paula Bulfin (Tipperary), Louise Young (Tipperary), Elaine Burke (Cork), Orla Cotter (Cork), Caitriona Foley (Cork), Elaine O'Riordan (Cork) and Emer O'Farrell (Cork). The following all Wexford - Mags D'Arcy, Noeleen Lambert, Catherine O'Loughlin, Mary Leacy, Deirdre Codd, Kate Kelly, Michelle O'Leary, Una Leacy, Ursula Jacob, Helena Jacob, Aoife O'Connor, Lenny Holohan, Katrina Parrock, Claire O'Connor and Colleen Atkinson

Appendix

All-Ireland Senior Records

Players who won All-Ireland senior medals with two counties

Kit Kehoe (Codd)
1965 and 1966 with Dublin; 1975 with Wexford

Noelle O'Driscoll
1980, 1982 and 1983 with Cork; 1989, 1990 and 1991 with Kilkenny

Ann Keane (Colgan)
1972 and 1973 with Cork; 1984 with Dublin

Players who captained the most All-Ireland winning teams

Sophie Brack captained Dublin to win six All-Ireland titles

Angela Downey captained Kilkenny to win three All-Ireland titles

Mollie Gill captained Dublin to win two All-Ireland titles

Peggy Griffin captained Dublin to win two All-Ireland titles

Doreen Rogers captained Dublin to win two All-Ireland titles

Betty Hughes captained Dublin to win two All-Ireland titles

Una O'Connor captained Dublin to win two All-Ireland titles

Kay Ryder captained Dublin to win two All-Ireland titles

Liz Neary captained Kilkenny to win two All-Ireland titles

Ann Downey captained Kilkenny to win two All-Ireland titles

Bridie McGarry captained Kilkenny to win two All-Ireland titles

Linda Mellerick captained Cork to win two All-Ireland titles

Highest scorers in an All-Ireland final

6–7 (25 points)	Kathleen Cody (Dublin)	1949
6–0 (18 points)	Kitty Buckley (Cork)	1941
5–0 (15 points)	Judy Doyle (Dublin)	1965
3–6 (15 points)	Liz Garvan (Cork)	1970
4–2 (14 points)	Sophie Brack (Dublin)	1951
4–1 (13 points)	Una O'Connor (Dublin)	1953
4–0 (12 points)	Ita McNeill (Dublin)	1933
4–0 (12 points)	Jean Hannon (Dublin)	1937
4–0 (12 points)	Renee Fitzgerald (Cork)	1939
1–9 (12 points)	Lynn Dunlea (Cork)	1996

Most consecutive All-Ireland medals

10 medals in a row	Una O'Connor (Dublin)
9 medals in a row	Kay Ryder (Dublin)
8 medals in a row	Eithne Leech (Dublin)
7 medals in a row	Betty Hughes (Dublin)
	Angela Downey (Kilkenny)
	Breda Holmes (Kilkenny)
	Marie Fitzpatrick (Kilkenny)
	Ann Downey (Kilkenny)
	Biddy O'Sullivan (Kilkenny)
	Deirdre Malone (Kilkenny)

Players who won an All-Ireland senior medal and refereed an All-Ireland senior final

Lil Kirby (Crowley) (Cork)
Lily Spence (Antrim)
Kathleen McKeown (O'Duffy) (Dublin)
Nancy Milligan (Murray) (Antrim)
Eithne Neville (Limerick)
Maeve Gilroy (Antrim)
Mary Kelly (Lynch) (Monaghan)
Miriam Higgins (Murphy) (Cork)
Helena O'Neill (McCormack) (Kilkenny)

Players who won an All-Ireland senior medal and became President of Camogie Association

Mollie Gill (Dublin)
Lil Kirby (Crowley) (Cork)
Lily Spence (Antrim)
Nancy Milligan (Murray) (Antrim)
Agnes Hourigan (Purcell) (Limerick/Dublin)
Mary Moran (Cork)
Mary Fennelly (Kilkenny)
Mary Kelly (Lynch) (Monaghan)

All-Ireland senior medal winners who played at senior international level for Ireland

Monica Hegarty (Cotter) (Cork) Golf
Mary Sinnott (Dinan) (Wexford) Badminton
Mary Geaney (Kerry)   Hockey

A Game of Our Own

National Player of the Year Award

Year	Player	Sponsor
1970	Liz Garvan (Cork)	Elvery's
1971	Pat Morrissey (Dublin)	
1972	Rosie Hennessy (Cork)	Elvery's
1973	Marie Costine (Cork)	Elvery's
1974	Helena O'Neill (Kilkenny)	Family Building Society
1975	Bridget Doyle (Wexford)	B & I
1976	Bridie Martin (Kilkenny)	B & I
1977	Angela Downey (Kilkenny)	B & I
1978	Pat Moloney (Cork)	B & I
1979	Mairéad Magill (Antrim)	B &I
1980	Marion McCarthy (Cork)	B & I
1981	Liz Neary (Kilkenny)	B & I
1982	Mary O'Leary (Cork)	B & I
1983	Clare Cronin (Cork)	B & I
1984	Yvonne Redmond (Dublin)	B & I
1985	Liz Neary (Kilkenny)	B & I
1986	Angela and Ann Downey (Kilkenny)	B & I
1987	Breda Holmes (Kilkenny)	B & I
1988	Biddy O'Sullivan (Kilkenny)	B & I
1989	Angela and Ann Downey (Kilkenny)	B & I
1990	No Award	
1991	Angela Downey (Kilkenny)	National Irish Bank
1992	Sandie Fitzgibbon (Cork)	National Irish Bank
1993	Linda Mellerick (Cork)	National Irish Bank
1994	Angela and Ann Downey (Kilkenny)	National Irish Bank

National Player of the Year Award

Year	Player	Sponsor
1995	Sandie Fitzgibbon (Cork)	National Irish Bank
1996	Imelda Hobbins (Galway)	National Irish Bank
1997	No Award	
1998	Linda Mellerick (Cork)	Eircell
1999	Deirdre Hughes (Tipperary)	Eircell
2000	Jovita Delaney (Tipperary)	Eircell
2001	Ciara Gaynor (Tipperary)	Eircell
2002	Fiona O'Driscoll (Cork)	Vodafone
2003	Eimear McDonnell (Tipperary)	Vodafone
2004	Una O'Dwyer (Tipperary)	Vodafone
2005	Gemma O'Connor (Cork)	Vodafone
2006	Mary O'Connor (Cork)	Vodafone
2007	Kate Kelly (Wexford)	Vodafone
2008	Aoife Murray (Cork)	Vodafone
2009	Ann Dalton (Kilkenny)	Vodafone

All-Ireland Second-Level Colleges Officers

President
- 1969 Lily Spence (Antrim)
- 1973 Rosina McManus (Antrim)
- 1977 Carmel Desmond (Cork)
- 1981 Lil O'Neill (Cork)
- 1985 Sr Máiréad (Armagh)
- 1989 Sheila Morgan (Cork)
- 1993 Kathleen Henry (Derry)
- 1997 Miriam O'Callaghan (Offaly)
- 2001 Mary Moran (Cork)
- 2005 Donal Burke (Galway)
- 2009 Cathy Mulholland

Secretary
- 1969 Mary Moran (Cork)
- 2001 Sr Máiréad (Armagh)
- 2005 Prionsias Creedon (Cork)

All-Ireland Primary Schools Officers

President
- 1974–1989 Sighle Nic an Ultaigh (Sheila McAnulty) (Down)
- 1989– Mary Hanley (Clare)

Secretary
- 1974–1989 Mary O'Brien-Hanley (Clare)
- 1989–2004 Claire Harrington (Dublin)
- 2004– Alison McCormack (Westmeath)

Appendix

All-Ireland senior medal winners who played at senior international level for Ireland (continued)

Nancy O'Driscoll (O'Donovan) (Cork) — Hockey
Sandie Fitzgibbon (Cork) — Basketball
Vivienne Harris (Cork) — Kick-Boxing
Liz Towler (Cork) — Ladies Soccer
Paula Goggins (Cork) — Ladies Soccer
Ann Downey (Kilkenny) — Squash
Bronagh Furlong (Wexford) — Athletics.
Maeve O'Hagan (Antrim) — Basketball (Northern Ireland)
Amanda O'Regan (Cork) — Basketball

Players who won All-Ireland senior medals in camogie and ladies football

Mary O'Connor — Cork
Briege Corkery — Cork
Rena Buckley — Cork
Catriona Foley — Cork
Angela Walsh — Cork
Elaine O'Riordan — Cork
Regina Curtin — Cork

Brothers and sisters with All-Ireland senior medals

John Quirke (1941–1944) and Dolly Quirke (1935) (Cork)
Matt Fletcher (1942) and Rose Fletcher (1937–1938, 1942–1944) (Dublin)
Mick Jacob (1968) and Bridie Jacob (1975) (Wexford)
Kevin Heffernan (1958) and Claire Heffernan (1966) (Dublin)
Bill Casey (1963) and Mary Casey (1964) (Dublin)
Mickey Whelan (1958, 1963) and Fran Whelan (1965–1966) (Dublin)
Dave Geaney (1959) and Mary Geaney (1978, 1980, 1983) (Kerry)
Sean McCarthy (1990) and Marion McCarthy (1970–1973, 1978, 1980, 1982–1983) (Cork)
Sean O'Leary (1976–1978, 1984) and Mary O'Leary (1978, 1980, 1982–1983) (Cork)
Willie Purcell (1982–1983) and Mary Purcell (1977) (Kilkenny)
Paddy Mullally (2003), Richie Mullally (2002–2003) and Bridget Mullally (1990–1991, 1994) (Kilkenny)
Kevin Murray (1999) and Aoife Murray (2002, 2005–2006, 2008–2009) (Cork)
Ben and Jerry O'Connor (1999, 2004–2005) and Paula O'Connor (1998, 2002, 2005) (Cork)
Enna Ryan (1988) and Anne Ryan (1996) (Galway)

Husbands and wives with All-Ireland senior medals

Jimmy Cooney (Tipperary) (1937) and Angela Egan (Dublin) (1937–1938)
Tomás Ryan (Cork) (1970) and Anne McAuliffe (Cork) (1970–1972)
Brian Cody (Kilkenny) (1975, 1982–1983) and Elsie Walsh (Wexford) (1975)
Brian McEvoy (Kilkenny) (2000, 2002) and Tracey Millea (Kilkenny) (1991, 1994)
Declan Ruth (Wexford) (1996) and Aoife O'Connor (Wexford) 2006, 2010)

Mothers and daughters with All-Ireland senior medals

Kit Kehoe (1965–1966, 1975) and Áine Codd (2007) (Wexford)
Margaret O'Leary (1968–1969, 1975) and Mary and Una Leacy (2007 and 2010) (Wexford)
Peggie Doyle (1969) and Kate Kelly (2007, 2010, 2011) (Wexford)

Fathers and daughters with All-Ireland senior medals

Pat and Kathleen Coughlan (Cork)
Mick and Eithne Neville (Limerick, won with Dublin)
Paddy and Ursula Grace (Kilkenny)
Shem, Angela and Ann Downey (Kilkenny)
John and Geraldine Sutton (Kilkenny)
Con and Mary Geaney (Kerry) (Mary won with Cork)
Joe, Tracey and Sinéad Millea (Kilkenny)
Pa and Gillian Dillon (Kilkenny)
Donie and Sinéad Nealon (Tipperary)
Len and Ciara Gaynor (Tipperary)
Martin and Ciara Storey (Wexford)
Denis and Síle Burns (Cork)
Dan and Evelyn Quigley (Wexford)

A Game of Our Own

All-Ireland Intermediate/Senior B Championship

Year	Date	Venue	Result				Referee
1992	Aug .23	Ballygalget	Dublin	4–11	Down	4–04	Mary Connor (Louth)
1993	Aug. 29	Ennis	Clare	1–08	Dublin	1–05	Colette Kennedy (Galway)
1994	Aug. 28	Tullamore	Armagh	7–11	Kildare	3–11	Miriam O'Callaghan (Offaly)
1995	Sept.10	Toomevara	Clare	1–10	Tipperary	1–09	Mary Connor (Louth)
1996	Sept. 8	Gaelic Grounds	Limerick	2–10	Down	1–06	Maria Pollard (Waterford)
1997	Sept.21	The Ragg	Tipperary	2–19	Clare	2–12	Áine Derham (Dublin)
1998	Sept.20	Páirc Uí Rinn	Down	1–12	Cork	1–08	Biddy Phillips (Tipperary)
1999	Sept.19	Dunloy	Clare	1–08	Antrim	1–03	Áine Derham (Dublin)
2000	Sept.17	Bishopstown	Cork	3–09	Limerick	0–11	John Morrissey (Tipperary)
2001	Sept.29	Casement Park	Antrim	3–10	Derry	0–05	Úna Kearney (Armagh)
2002	Nov. 17	Clan na nGael	Cork	3–06	Antrim	1–10	Áine Derham (Dublin)
2003	Oct. 3	Navan	Antrim	2–09	Tipperary	0–10	Úna Kearney (Armagh)
2004	Oct.3	Semple Stadium	Galway	1–10	Tipperary	0–04	Áine Derham (Dublin)
2005	Not Played						
2006	Sept.30	Gaelic Grounds	Cork	2–09	Galway	1–07	John Morrissey (Tipperary)
2007	Oct. 6	Gaelic Grounds	Limerick	1–10	Cork	2–07	Ciarán Quigley (Kildare)
	Oct.13	Páirc Uí Rinn	Limerick	2–09	Cork	0–06	Ciarán Quigley (Kildare)
2008	Oct. 5	Nenagh	Kilkenny	5–05	Cork	1–14	Alan Lagrue (Kildare)
2009	Sept.19	Gaelic Grounds	Galway	0–15	Cork	2–09	Alan Lagrue (Kildare)
	Oct. 10	Nenagh	Galway	3–10	Cork	1–05	Karl O'Brien (Dublin)
2010	Sept.12	Croke Park	Offaly	2–12	Wexford	2–10	Owen Elliott (Antrim)
2011	Sept 11	Croke Park	Waterford	2-11	Down	1-13	Walter Coyle (Cork)

All-Ireland Junior Championship

Year	Date	Venue	Result				Referee
1968	Sept.15	Croke Park	Down	2–03	Cork	1–01	Phyllis Breslin (Dublin)
1969	Sept.21	Croke Park	Derry	4–02	Cork	2–04	Anne Ashton (Dublin)
1970	Sept.20	Croke Park	Dublin	4–02	Armagh	3–03	Vera Mannion (Mayo)
1971	Sept.19	Croke Park	Dublin	2–02	Cork	1–02	Nancy Murray (Antrim)
1972	Sept. 17	Croke Park	Galway	3–06	Wexford	2–01	Lil O'Grady (Cork)
1973	Sept.16	Croke Park	Cork	4–04	Galway	2–01	Teresa Byrne (Wicklow)
1974	Sept.15	Croke Park	Clare.	3–02	Dublin	3–00	Mary Lynch (Monaghan)
1975	Sept.21	Croke Park	Dublin	5–00	Down	0–03	Eithne Neville (Limerick)
1976	Sept.19	Croke Park	Down	3–04	Wexford	3–03	Phyllis Breslin (Dublin)
1977	Sept.18	Croke Park	Limerick	2–07	Wexford	3–01	Miriam Higgins (Cork)
1978	Sept.17	Croke Park	Derry	3–04	Cork	1–04	Phyllis Breslin (Dublin)
1979	Sept. 9	Croke Park	Galway	4–03	Cork	3–02	Carrie Clancy (Limerick)
1980	Sept.14	Croke Park	Cork	4–04	Tyrone	1–04	Kathleen Quinn (Galway)
1981	Sept.13	Croke Park	Clare	3–02	Antrim	1–04	Belle O'Loughlin (Down)
1982	Sept.26	Croke Park	Louth	1–07	Cork	1–06	Kathleen Quinn (Galway)
1983	Sept.25	Croke Park	Cork	2–05	Dublin	2–03	Brid Stokes (Limerick)
1984	Sept. 9	Croke Park	Cork	5–08	Cavan	2–02	Rita Whyte (Dublin)

All-Ireland Junior Championship

Year	Date	Venue	Result				Referee
1985	Sept.25	Croke Park	Galway	8–07	Armagh	3–07	Síle Wallace (Dublin)
1986	Sept.14	Croke Park	Clare	1–13	Kildare	3–04	Rose Ryan (Dublin)
1987	Sept.27	Croke Park	Kildare	2–10	Armagh	0–07	Kitty McNicholas (Clare)
1988	Sept.14	Croke Park	Galway	3–04	Limerick	1–05	Rose Merriman (Kildare)
1989	Sept.24	Croke Park	Kildare	0–15	Galway	2–09	Áine Derham (Dublin)
	Oct. 8	Birr	Kildare	3–11	Galway	1–03	Áine Derham (Dublin)
1990	Sept.23	Croke Park	Kildare	2–14	Tipperary	3–07	Miriam O'Callaghan (Offaly)
1991	Sept.22	Croke Park	Down	3–13	Tipperary	2–14	Mary Connor (Louth)
1992	Sept.27	Croke Park	Tipperary	6–13	Galway	2–07	Maria Pollard (Waterford)
1993	Sept.26	Croke Park	Armagh	3–09	Galway	3–09	Biddy Phillips (Tipperary)
	Oct.10	Breffni Park	Armagh	2–10	Galway	0–06	Biddy Phillips (Tipperary)
1994	Sept.25	Croke Park	Galway	2–10	Limerick	1–11	Catherine McAllister (Antrim)
1995	Sept.24	Croke Park	Limerick	3–07	Roscommon	4–03	Maria Pollard (Waterford)
1996	Sept.22	Croke Park	Cork	6–05	Roscommon	2–07	Fiona McKenna (Armagh)
1997	Sept. 7	Croke Park	Antrim	7–11	Cork	2–10	Mary Connor (Louth)
1998	Sept. 6	Croke Park	Galway	3–11	Tipperary	2–10	Catherine McAllister (Antrim)
1999	Sept. 5	Croke Park	Cork	1–13	Derry	2–09	John Morrissey (Tipperary)
2000	Sept. 3	Croke Park	Derry	3–15	Cork	1–13	John Pender (Kildare)
2001	Sept.16	Croke Park	Tipperary	4–16	Offaly	1–07	Aoife Woods (Armagh)
2002	Sept.15	Croke Park	Kilkenny	2–11	Cork	2–08	Úna Kearney (Armagh)
2003	Sept.21	Croke Park	Galway	3–09	Clare	3–09	Eamonn Browne (Tipperary)
	Oct. 11	Tullamore	Galway	1–12	Clare	2–05	Eamonn Browne (Tipperary)
2004	Sept.19	Croke Park	Cork	4–05	Down	2–04	Aileen Lawlor (Westmeath)
2005	Sept.18	Croke Park	Dublin	1–07	Clare	1–07	Úna Kearney (Armagh)
	Oct. 8	Birr	Dublin	2–09	Clare	1–04	Úna Kearney (Armagh)
2006	Aug.19	Tullamore	Dublin	0–12	Derry	1–07	Cathal Egan (Cork)
2007	Sept. 9	Croke Park	Derry	3–12	Clare	2–14	Cathal Egan (Cork)
2008	Sept.14	Croke Park	Clare	2–08	Offaly	1–10	Úna Kearney (Armagh)
2009	Sept.13	Croke Park	Offaly	3–14	Waterford	2–08	Pat Walsh (Armagh)
2010	Sept 12	Croke Park	Antrim	1–09	Waterford	1–09	Donal Leahy (Tipperary)
	Oct 3	Ashbourne	Antrim	2-10	Waterford	0-12	Killian Loney (Cork)
2011	Sept 11	Croke Park	Waterford	2-11	Down	1-13	Walter Cole (Cork)

All–Ireland Minor A (Under-18) Championship

Year	Date	Venue					Result
2006	Oct. 15	Nenagh	Kilkenny	4–10	Galway	2–05	John Pender (Kildare
2007	Oct. 14	Clonmel	Kilkenny	3–12	Cork	0–07	Damien Noble (Dublin)
2008	Aug. 31	Athy	Kilkenny	3–15	Clare	1–07	Rosemary Merry (Monaghan)
2009	Aug. 8	Semple Stadium	Kilkenny	5–10	Clare	3–08	Julie O'Neill (Armagh)
2010	Aug. 7	Nenagh	Galway	1–08	Clare	0–11	John O'Leary (Cork)
	Aug. 21	Thurles	Galway	2–12	Clare	2–08	Killian Looney (Cork)
2011	July 31	Thurles	Tipperary	4–04	Kilkenny	2–09	Mike O'Kelly (Cork)

Appendix

All-Ireland Minor B (Under-18) Championship

Year	Date	Venue	Result				Referee
2006	Sept. 1	Casement Park	Down	5–08	Antrim	6–04	Rosemary Merry (Monaghan)
2007	Aug. 12	Park Esler, Newry	Antrim	3–18	Down	5–03	Julie O'Neill (Armagh)
2008	Aug. 31	Athy	Offaly	4–13	Waterford	2–07	Paddy McQuillan (Antrim)
2009	Aug. 11	Mallow	Limerick	3–10	Waterford	1–15	Dermot Connolly (Galway)
2010	Aug. 28	Celtic Park	Derry	3–10	Antrim	0–09	Donal Ryan (Dublin)
2011	July 31	Ashbourne	Limerick	4–10	Antrim	2–08	Con Ó Céadaigh (Wicklow)

All-Ireland Under-16 A Championship

Year	Date	Venue	Result				Referee
1974	Oct. 6	Croke Park	Down	3–00	Cork	0–01	Mary Ryan (Dublin)
1975	Sept. 14	Na Piarsaigh Cork	Cork	6–02	Galway	0–03	Helena O'Neill (Kilkenny)
1976	Aug. 29	Mayobridge	Cork	4–06	Down	2–01	Rose Ryan (Dublin)
1977	Aug. 28	Croke Park	Galway	5–04	Dublin	2–01	Helena O'Neill (Kilkenny)
1978	Aug. 27	Na Piarsaigh Cork	Cork	5–01	Dublin	3–04	Elsie Walsh (Wexford)
1979	Aug. 5	Ballinasloe	Cork	5–03	Cavan	3–00	Jane Beatty (Galway)
1980	Aug. 31	Crosskeys, Cavan	Cork	5–05	Cavan	0–02	Catherine McErlean (Derry)
1981	Aug. 30	Tynagh, Galway	Galway	3–04	Antrim	3–03	Rose Ryan (Dublin)
1982	Aug. 15	Ballinasloe	Dublin	5–02	Galway	2–03	Mary Lynch (Monaghan)
1983	Aug. 14	St Finbarr's, Cork	Cork	3–03	Dublin	2–03	Brid Stokes (Limerick)
1984	Aug. 5	Loughrea	Cork	2–12	Galway	5–00	Belle O'Loughlin (Down)
1985	Aug. 4	St Finbarr's, Cork	Cork	3–08	Galway	2–03	Miriam O'Callaghan (Offaly)
1986	Aug. 3	Wexford Park	Galway	2–08	Wexford	1–04	Betty Joyce (Cork)
1987	Aug. 9	Blackrock, Cork	Galway	1–11	Cork	3–03	Brid Stokes (Limerick)
1988	Aug. 7	Portumna	Kilkenny	5–06	Armagh	2–05	Fionnuala McGrady (Down)
1989	July 30	Semple Stadium	Kilkenny	9–10	Tipperary	3–08	Kathleen Quinn (Galway)
1990	July 29	Nowlan Park	Tipperary	2–11	Kilkenny	3–06	Miriam O'Callaghan (Offaly)
1991	Aug. 4	Nowlan Park	Kilkenny	4–12	Galway	3–07	Betty Joyce (Cork)
1992	July 26	Holycross, Tipp.	Tipperary	4–09	Kilkenny	1–03	Áine Derham (Dublin)
1993	July 25	The Ragg, Tipp.	Tipperary	1–05	Galway	1–05	Catherine McAllister (Antrim)
	Aug. 2	Ballinasloe	Tipperary	3–10	Galway	2–09	Catherine McAllister (Antrim)
1994	Aug.14	Loughrea	Galway	7–13	Tipperary	3–09	Betty Joyce (Cork)
1995	Aug. 7	Loughrea	Wexford	2–09	Galway	1–07	Biddy Phillips (Tipperary)
1996	Aug.11	Semple Stadium	Galway	3–16	Tipperary	4–11	Áine Derham (Dublin)
1997	Aug. 7	Páirc Uí Rinn	Galway	2–14	Cork	1–06	Biddy Phillips (Tipperary)
1998	Aug. 22	Ballincollig	Cork	3–18	Derry	1–05	Vera Mackey (Limerick)
1999	Aug. 22	Ardrahan	Cork	2–12	Galway	3–08	Celine Doody (Limerick)
2000	Aug. 5	Tullamore	Galway	2–09	Wexford	0–03	Aoife Woods (Armagh)
2001	Aug. 5	Nenagh	Cork	6–15	Kilkenny	0–07	John Morrissey (Tipperary)
2002	Aug. 4	Cashel	Cork	1–11	Galway	1–05	Eamonn Browne (Tipperary)
2003	Aug. 3	Portlaoise	Cork	3–12	Galway	1–04	Eileen Hamill (Down)
2004	Aug. 7	Páirc Tailteann	Galway	3–16	Kilkenny	2–06	Liam Davitt (Westmeath)
2005	Aug. 7	Parnell Park	Kilkenny	4–07	Tipperary	2–07	Fintan McNamara (Clare)

All-Ireland Minor C (Under-18) Championship

Year	Date	Venue	Result				Referee
2009	Aug. 9	Clane	Laois	3–05	Carlow	2–03	Rita Coen (Galway)
2010	Sept.4	Ashbourne	Carlow	5–10	Armagh	1–12	Justin Heffernan (Wexford)

All-Ireland Under-16 A Championship

Year	Date	Venue	Result				Referee
2006	Aug. 6	Portmarnock	Kilkenny	2–10	Cork	0–04	Morgan Conroy (Waterford)
2007	Aug. 5	Nenagh	Kilkenny	8–11	Cork	0–06	Rita Coen (Galway)
2008	Aug. 2	Semple Stadium	Kilkenny	3–07	Cork	2–05	Eadhmon MacSuibhne (Dub)
2009	May 9	Gaelic Grounds	Galway	2–11	Tipperary	2–07	Fintan McNamara (Clare)
2010	May 8	Tullamore	Galway	2–11	Tipperary	2–07	Mike O'Kelly (Cork)
2011	May 7	Gaelic Grounds	Tipperary	2–8	Kilkenny	0–13	Karl O'Brien (Dublin)

All-Ireland Under-16 B Championship

Year	Date	Venue	Result				Referee
2000	Aug. 6	Tullamore	Laois	9–14	Tyrone	2–01	Liam Davitt (Westmeath)
2001	Aug. 5	Nenagh	Limerick	3–18	Carlow	1–01	Rita McGrath (Westmeath)
2002	Aug. 4	Cashel	Limerick	5–07	Offaly	0–02	Una Kearney (Armagh)
2003	Aug. 3	Portlaoise	Waterford	6–11	Armagh	1–04	Noeleen Cormican (Galway)
2004	Aug. 7	Páirc Tailteann	Antrim	1–09	Roscommon	0–03	Damien Noble (Dublin)
2005	Aug. 7	Parnell Park	Offaly	2–14	Armagh	3–09	Áine Derham (Dublin)
2006	Aug. 6	Portmarnock	Derry	3–03	Armagh	1–02	Ciarán Quigley (Kildare)
2007	Aug. 5	St Peregine's	Derry	2–07	Waterford	3–04	Joe Kennedy (Louth)
	Sept.15	St Peregine's	Derry	3–14	Waterford	2–02	Joe Kennedy (Louth)
2008	May 11	Ashbourne	Derry	6–18	Offaly	0–06	Mike O'Kelly (Cork)
2009	May 9	Pilltown	Wexford	2–11	Waterford	1–12	Donal Leahy (Tipperary)
2010	May 8	St Peregine's	Derry	3–09	Limerick	1–06	Killian Looney (Cork)
2011	May 7	Gaelic Grounds	Limerick	3–12	Offaly	0–9	John Dolan (Clare)

All-Ireland Under 16C Championship

Year	Date	Venue	Result				Referee
2010	May 8	Blakestown	Carlow	4–08	Meath	1–03	Gerry McGough (Dublin)
2011	May 7	Ashbourne	Down	1–03	Carlow	1–02	Ger O'Dowd (Limerick)

All-Ireland Club Intermediate Championship

Year	Venue	Result				Referee
2010	Croke Park	Eoghan Rua, Derry	3–08	The Harps, Laois	2–03	Mike O'Kelly (Cork(

A Game of Our Own

All-Ireland Club Senior Championship

Year	Venue	Result				Referee
1964	Croke Park	Celtic, Dublin	5–02	Deirdre, Belfast	1–00	Lil O'Grady (Cork)
1965	Casement Pk	St Patrick's, Tipp	3–03	Deirdre, Belfast	2–03	Kathleen O'Duffy (Dublin)
1966	St John's Park	St Patrick's, Tipp	5–05	St Paul's, Kilk	2–01	Nancy Murray (Antrim)
1967	Parnell Park	Eoghan Ruadh	3–04	Oranmore, Galway	4–01	Nancy Murray (Antrim)
	Ballinasloe	Eoghan Ruadh	7–03	Oranmore, Galway	1–00	Nancy Murray (Antrim)
1968	St John's Park	St Paul's, Kilk	7–02	Ahane, Limerick	1–02	Nancy Murray (Antrim)
1969	Castleconnell	St Paul's, Kilk	3–07	Ahane, Limerick	2–01	Kathleen O'Duffy (Dublin)
1970	Bellaghy	St Paul's, Kilk	6–05	Bellaghy, Derry	2–00	Mary Lynch (Monaghan)
1971	Croke Park	Austin Stacks	5–04	Thurles	2–01	Nancy Murray (Antrim)
1972	Croke Park	Austin Stacks	4–02	Portglenone, Antrim	2–00	Mary Moran (Cork)
1973	Nowlan Park	Oranmore	3–02	St Paul's, Kilk	2–03	Mary Ryan (Dublin)
1974	Ballindereen	St Paul's, Kilk	3–03	Oranmore, Galway	1–01	Mary Lynch (Monaghan)
1975	Athenry	Croagh–Kilfinny	4–06	Athenry	4–05	Phyllis Breslin (Dublin)
1976	Nowlan Park	St Paul's, Kilk	6–03	Athenry	1–03	Anne Ashton, Dublin
1977	Athenry	Athenry	10–05	Portglenone, Antrim	1–01	Sheila Murray (Dublin)
1978	Monomolin	Ballyagran, Limk	1–03	Buffers Alley, Wexf.	0–01	Jane Beatty (Galway)
1979	Athenry	Buffers Alley,	2–06	Athenry	1–02	Marie Cribben (Kildare)
1980	St John's Park	Killeagh, Cork	4–02	Buffers Alley, Wexf	1–07	Phyllis Breslin (Dublin)
1981	Gaultier	Buffers Alley, Wx	3–02	Killeagh, Cork	1–04	Belle O'Loughlin (Down)
1982	Birr	Buffers Alley,	3–02	Athenry	0–02	Rose Ryan (Dublin)
1983	Monomolin	Buffers Alley,	3–07	Glenamaddy	0–06	Rita Whyte (Dublin)
1984	Monomolin	Buffers Alley,	2–04	Killeagh, Cork	1–04	Kathleen Quinn (Galway)
1985	O'Toole Park	Crumlin, Dublin	4–08	Athenry	3–02	Bridie McGarry (Kilkenny)
1986	Glen Rovers	Glen Rovers, Cork	4–11	St Paul's, Kilk	5–07	Kathleen Quinn (Galway)
1987	Ballyragget	St Paul's, Kilk	1–04	Glen Rovers, Cork	0–05	Kitty McNicholas (Clare)
1988	Glenamaddy	St Paul's, Kilk	4–05	Glenamaddy	3–07	Betty Joyce (Cork)
1989	Nowlan Park	St Paul's, Kilk	6–10	Mullagh	4–02	Betty Joyce (Cork)
1990	Nowlan Park	Glen Rovers, Cork	4–13	St Paul's, Kilk	2–07	Áine Derham (Dublin)
1991	Ballinasloe	Mullagh, Galway	4–13	Eglish, Tyrone	0–02	Betty Joyce (Cork)
1992	Glen Rovers	Glen Rovers, Cork	1–09	Rathnure, Wexford	0–02	Jane Beatty (Galway)
1993	Ballinasloe	Glen Rovers, Cork	6–10	Mullagh, Galway	0–02	Áine Derham (Dublin)
1994	Ballyragget	Lisdowney, Kilk	5–09	Glen Rovers, Cork	1–15	Áine Derham (Dublin)
1995	Toomevara	Rathnure, Wex	4–09	Toomevara, Tipp	1–05	Maria Pollard (Waterford)
1996	Ballingarry	Pearses, Galway	1–08	Granagh–Ballingarry	2–03	Áine Derham (Dublin)
1997	Ballymacward	Pearses, Galway	.4–06	Lisdowney, Kilk	2–05	Áine Derham (Dublin)
1998	Ballingarry	Granagh-Ballingarry	1–19	St Vincent's, Dublin	1–08	Biddy Phillips (Tipperary)
1999	Tynagh	Granagh-Ballingarry	2–04	Davitt's, Galway	1–03	Biddy Phillips (Tipperary)
2000	Mullingar	Pearses, Galway	2–11	Swatragh, Derry	1–03	Áine Derham (Dublin)
2001	Cashel	Pearses, Galway	2–08	Cashel, Tipp	0–13	Jack O'Brien (Wexford)
2002	Ballinasloe	Pearses, Galway	2–13	St Ibar's, Wexford	1–05	Eamonn Browne (Tipperary)
2003	Mullingar	Granagh-Ballingarry	1–10	Davitt's, Galway	1–06	Áine Derham (Dublin)

All-Ireland Club Senior Championship

Year	Venue	Result				Referee
2004	Parnell Park	St Lachtain's, Kilk	2–08	Granagh-Ballingarry	0–07	Liam Davitt (Westmeath)
2005	Cloughjordan	St Lachtain's, Kilk	1–09	Davitt's, Galway	1–04	Jack McGrath (Cork)
2006	O'Moore Park	St Lachtain's, Kilk	1–05	Rossa, Belfast	1–03	Cathal Egan (Cork)
2007	Gaelic Grounds	Cashel, Tipperary	1–18	Athenry	0–09	Frank McDonald (Armagh)
2008	Ashbourne	Rossa, Belfast	2–15	Drum-Inch, Tipp	1–12	Eadhmonn MacSuibhne (Dublin)
2009	Clarecastle	Cashel, Tipperary	0–11	Athenry	0–09	Fintan McNamara (Clare)
2010	Croke Park	Killimor, Galway	3–18	Inniscarra, Cork	1–04	Owen Elliott (Antrim)

All-Ireland Club Junior Championship

Year	Venue	Result				Referee
2003	Mullingar	Crossmaglen	2–05	Drumcullen, Offaly	0–07	Liam Davitt (Westmeath)
2004	Parnell Park	Leitrim Fontenoys	4–13	Four Roads, Rosc	0–08	Eamonn Browne (Tipperary)
2005	Cloughjordan	Leitrim Fontenoys	3–07	Newmarket-on-Ferg	0–08	John Pender (Kildare)
2006	Portlaoise	The Harps, Laois	1–07	Keady, Armagh	0–05	Oliver Webb (Cork)
2007	Stabannon	The Harps, Laois	2–08	Keady, Armagh	2–07	Cathal Egan (Cork)
2008	Nenagh	The Harps, Laois	3–02	Kilmaley, Clare	3–02	Dermot Connolly (Galway)
2009	Ashbourne	Lavey, Derry	1–11	St Anne's, Dunhill	1–11	Mike O'Kelly (Cork)
	Ashbourne	Lavey, Derry	1–13	St Anne's, Dunhill	0–07	Mike O'Kelly (Cork)
2010	Ballinasloe	Four Roads, Rosc	1–09	Corofin, Clare	0–06	Cathal Egan (Cork)

Gael-Linn Senior Interprovincial Championship

Year	Venue	Result				
1999	St Anne's, Dublin	Munster	1–18	Connacht	1–09	
2000	St Anne's Dublin	Connacht	1–10	Ulster	0–03	
2001	St Anne's, Dublin	Munster	1–18	Connacht	1–09	
2002	St Anne's, Dublin	Munster	7–23	Ulster	0–11	
2003	Portmarnock	Munster	3–13	Ulster	1–09	
2004	Glenalbyn, Dublin	Munster	1–16	Connacht	1–09	
2005	Ballinteer, Dublin	Munster	3–14	Connacht	2–08	
2006	Páirc Tailteann, Navan	Leinster	2–07	Munster	.1–08	
2007	Russell Park, Dublin	Ulster	2–12	Leinster	3–08	
2008	Ashbourne, Co. Meath	Connacht	1–14	Munster	2–10	
2009	Ashbourne, Co. Meath	Munster	0–07	Connacht	0–02	
2010	Trim, Co. Meath	Leinster	3–17	Munster	1–14	

Appendix

Gael-Linn Senior Interprovincial Championship

Year	Venue	Result			
1956	Knockbridge	Leinster	7–01	Ulster	3–01
1957	Cahir	Leinster	5–01	Munster	3–01
1958	Russell Park	Leinster	8–02	Ulster	3–03
1959	Casement Park	Leinster	6–00	Ulster	1–03
1960	Cahir	Leinster	4–01	Munster	3–02
1961	Pearse Park, Galway	Munster	5–02	Connacht	1–00
1962	Casement Park	Leinster	7–02	Ulster	5–03
1963	Gorey	Munster	3–02	Leinster	2–02
1964	Cahir	Munster	2–06	Leinster	3–02
1965	Casement Park	Leinster	4–03	Ulster	4–01
1966	Ballinlough, Cork	Munster	4–02	Leinster	1–03
1967	Parnell Park	Ulster	5–04	Leinster	.5–01
1968	Croke Park	Leinster	7–00	Ulster	.2–05
1969	Cahir	Leinster	5–04	Munster	2–02
1970	Carrickmacross	Leinster	12–02	Ulster	4–01
1971	Parnell Park	Leinster	5–04	Ulster	0–05
1972	Ballinasloe	Leinster	7–07	Connacht	4–02
1973	Parnell Park	Connacht	4–04	Leinster	3–03
1974	Ballinasloe	Connacht	3–07	Munster	3–00
1975)					
1976)	Not Played				
1977)					
1978	Na Fianna, Dublin	Leinster	4–09	Connacht	2–02
1979	Athboy, Meath	Leinster	1–05	Munster	0–04
1980	St John's Park, Kilk	Munster	2–05	Leinster	2–01
1981	Russell Park, Dublin	Leinster	3–10	Ulster	2–04
1982	Na Fianna, Dublin	Munster	3–10	Leinster	.2–12
1983	Ballinlough, Cork	Leinster	2–07	Munster	1–07
1984	Silver Park, Dublin	Leinster	3–09	Connacht	1–04
1985	St Finbarr's, Cork	Leinster	4–09	Munster	1–06
1986	Glenalbyn, Dublin	Leinster	4–06	Munster	1–06
1987	Silver Park, Dublin	Leinster	8–11	Connacht	0–05
1988	Silver Park, Dublin	Leinster	2–09	Connacht	2–04
1989	Silver Park, Dublin	Leinster	5–12	Munster	3–06
1990	Ballyholland, Co. Down	Munster	10–10	Ulster	.1–02
1991	O'Toole Park, Dublin	Leinster	5–13	Munster	0–07
1992	O'Toole Park, Dublin	Munster	1–18	Leinster	2–09
1993	Clane, Co. Kildare	Leinster	6–14	Ulster	1–04
1994	Silver Park, Dublin	Munster	4–11	Ulster	2–07
1995	Russell Park	Munster	4–13	Connacht	3–10
1996	Russell Park	Munster	4–18	Ulster	6–10
1997	Russell Park	Munster	4–18	Leinster	2–11
1998	St Vincent's, Dublin	Munster	6–20	Leinster	1–11
1999	St Anne's, Dublin	Munster	1–18	Connacht	1–09
2000	St Anne's Dublin	Connacht	1–10	Ulster	0–03
2001	St Anne's, Dublin	Munster	1–18	Connacht	1–09
2002	St Anne's, Dublin	Munster	7–23	Ulster	0–11
2003	Portmarnock	Munster	3–13	Ulster	1–09
2004	Glenalbyn, Dublin	Munster	1–16	Connacht	1–09
2005	Ballinteer, Dublin	Munster	3–14	Connacht	2–08
2006	Páirc Tailteann, Navan	Leinster	2–07	Munster	.1–08
2007	Russell Park, Dublin	Ulster	2–12	Leinster	3–08
2008	Ashbourne, Co. Meath	Connacht	1–14	Munster	2–10
2009	Ashbourne, Co. Meath	Munster	0–07	Connacht	0–02
2010	Trim, Co. Meath	Leinster	3–17	Munster	1–14

Gael-Linn Junior Interprovincial Championship

Year	Venue	Result			
1975	Adare, Co. Limerick	Munster	5–01	Ulster	2–00
1976	Adare, Co. Limerick	Leinster	2–06	Munster	2–03
1977	Adare, Co. Limerick	Munster	3–07	Connacht	3–01
1978	Na Fianna, Dublin	Munster	3–02	Ulster	2–01
1979	Athboy, Co. Meath	Ulster	0–04	Munster	1–00
1980	St John's Park, Kilkenny	Munster	1–09	Leinster	3–02
1981	Russell Park, Dublin	Connacht	2–03	Munster	2–02
1982	Na Fianna, Dublin	Leinster	3–16	Connacht	2–08
1983	Ballinlough, Cork	Munster	1–12	Leinster	1–11
1984	Silver Park, Dublin	Leinster	3–06	Ulster	1–03
1985	St Finbarr's, Cork	Munster	1–07	Ulster	2–03
1986	Glenalbyn, Dublin	Leinster	1–05	Munster	0–07
1987	Silver Park, Dublin	Munster	2–06	Ulster	2–05
1988	Silver Park, Dublin	Munster	4–03	Leinster	3–05
1989	Silver Park, Dublin	Ulster	1–11	Leinster	2–03
1990	Ballyholland, Down	Ulster	5–11	Munster	5–03
1991	O'Toole Park, Dublin	Ulster	4–05	Munster	.0–06
1992	O'Toole Park, Dublin	Munster	6–11	Connacht	3–03
1993	Clane, Co. Kildare	Ulster	4–05	Leinster	1–09
1994	Silver Park, Dublin	Munster	5–09	Ulster	2–12
1995	Russell Park, Dublin	Connacht	1–09	Munster	0–10
1996	Russell Park, Dublin	Munster	3–17	Ulster	1–07
1997	Russell Park, Dublin	Munster	3–11	Leinster	2–10
1998	St Vincent's, Dublin	Ulster	3–12	Leinster	1–12
1999	St Anne's, Dublin	Leinster	3–17	Connacht	4–06
2000	St Anne's, Dublin	Ulster	.1–10	Munster	2–06
2001	St Anne's, Dublin	Leinster	1–14	Munster	1–11
2002	St Anne's, Dublin	Ulster	4–11	Leinster	1–13
2003	Portmarnock	Munster	4–07	Ulster	0–05
2004	Glenalbyn, Dublin	Munster	4–16	Leinster	1–04
2005	Ballinteer, Dublin	Munster	3–14	Connacht	2–08
2006	Páirc Tailteann, Navan	Connacht	3–12	Ulster	1–17
2007	Russell Park, Dublin	Leinster	3–16	Munster	0–11
2008	Ashbourne, Co. Meath	Munster	3–17	Ulster	0–03
2009	Ashbourne, Co. Meath	Connacht	4–04	Munster	0–02
2010	Not played				
2011	St Judes, Dublin	Munster	1–15	Leinster	2–11

A Game of Our Own

National League Division 1

Date	Venue	Result				Referee
6/3/77	Thurles	Tipperary	4–02	Wexford	1–03	Helena O'Neill
5/3/78	Clonroche	Wexford	2–05	Cork	0–04	Helena O'Neill
12/11/78	Adare	Kilkenny	2–04	Limerick	1–05	Marie Cribben
18/11/79	Russell Park	Dublin	0–06	Limerick	0–00	Elsie Walsh
29/6/80	Roscrea	Kilkenny	3–08	Tipperary	1–03	Miriam Higgins
21/6/81	Russell Park	Dublin	1–07	Cork	1–04	Belle O'Loughlin
22/5/82	St John's Park	Kilkenny	2–05	Cork	1–04	Phyllis Breslin
22/5/83	Russell Park	Dublin	4–08	Wexford	1–06	Kathleen Quinn
17/5/84	Ballinlough	Cork	1–08	Dublin	0–04	Bríd Stokes
2/6/85	Parnell Park	Kilkenny	4–07	Dublin	3–06	Miriam Higgins
18/5/86	O'Toole Park	Cork	3–08	Dublin	1–10	Bríd Farrell
7/5/87	Nowlan Park	Kilkenny	4–08	Dublin	1–06	Betty Joyce
12/5/88	O'Toole Park	Kilkenny	3–10	Dublin	2–04	Kathleen Quinn
18/6/89	Nowlan Park	Kilkenny	6–07	Cork	1–11	Gerry Mullen
10/6/90	Enniscorthy	Kilkenny	1–10	Wexford	2–04	Miriam O'Callaghan
30/5/91	Ballinlough	Cork	2–13	Kilkenny	2–06	Miriam O'Callaghan
14/6/92	Enniscorthy	Cork	2–17	Wexford	0–11	Idwal Cooper
6/6/93	Ballyragget	Kilkenny	4–07	Cork	1–13	Miriam O'Callaghan
12/6/94	Ballinasloe	Galway	1–13	Tipperary	1–08	Áine Derham
21/6/95	St Finbarr's	Cork	5–16	Armagh	3–04	Biddy Phillips
2/6/96	Páirc Uí Rinn	Cork	3–16	Galway	1–07	Miriam O'Callaghan
8/6/97	Páirc Uí Rinn	Cork	4–12	Kilkenny	0–09	Biddy Phillips
31/5/98	Ballinasloe	Cork	1–16	Galway	2–09	Áine Derham
22/5/99	Thurles	Cork	9–19	Tipperary	2–04	Áine Derham
20/5/00	Tullamore	Cork	3–07	Tipperary	1–10	Áine Derham
27/10/01	Nenagh	Cork	6–09	Galway	0–11	John Morrissey
24/5/02	Ennis	Galway	6–06	Limerick	1–07	Eamonn Browne
11/5/03	Páirc Uí Rinn	Cork	3–13	Tipperary	2–12	Seán O'Brien
22/5/04	Nowlan Park	Tipperary	3–10	Wexford	2–09	Jack McGrath
29/5/05	Thurles	Galway	2–10	Cork	2–07	Aileen Lawlor
14/5/06	Thurles	Cork	2–07	Tipperary	2–05	John Pender
6/5/07	Nowlan Park	Cork	3–08	Wexford	2–10	John Pender
26/4/08	Nowlan Park	Kilkenny	3–11	Galway	0–17	Ciarán Quigley
25/4/09	Parnell Park	Wexford	2–12	Tipperary	0–11	Frank McDonald
24/4/10	Thurles	Wexford	1–07	Kilkenny	1–06	Alan Lagrue
17/4/11	Thurles	Wexford	3–10	Galway	0–10	Mike O'Kelly

National League Division 2

Date	Venue	Result				Referee
11/5/80	Cappagh	Armagh	2–05	Kildare	2–03	Phyllis Breslin
31/5/81	Cootehill	Cavan	0–04	Louth	0–02	Kathleen Quinn
22/5/82	Eglish	Dublin	6–09	Tyrone	0–02	Bríd Stokes
29/5/83	Mullingar	Dublin	3–09	Westmeath	2–05	Miriam O'Callaghan
8/7/84	Glenalbyn	Dublin	2–04	Armagh	1–03	Helena McCormack
7/7/85	Bullaun	Galway	3–10	Kildare	3–03	Miriam Higgins
18/5/86	Glenalbyn	Kildare	2–03	Dublin	1–04	Miriam O'Callaghan
2/8/87	Clane	Dublin	6–04	Kildare	1–07	Susan McGuinness
3/7/88	Leitrim	Armagh	1–09	Down	0–06	Áine Derham
23/7/89	Clane	Kildare	2–14	Armagh	3–08	Miriam O'Callaghan
26/8/90	Kilkenny	Kildare	2–13	Kilkenny	1–03	Miriam O'Callaghan
21/7/91	Athleague	Limerick	3–13	Roscommon	3–04	Miriam O'Callaghan
12/7/92	Mary Immaculate	Limerick	4–13	Down	2–06	Maria Pollard
20/6/93	StVincent's	Armagh	3–08	Dublin	2–01	Maria Pollard
3/7/94	Ballincollig	Armagh	1–10	Cork	1–10	Biddy Phillips
17/7/94	Portmore	Armagh	1–18	Cork	1–02	Biddy Phillips
16/7.95	Loughrea	Galway	.4–13	Down	2–09	Áine Derham
30/5/96	An Ríocht	Limerick	5–10	Down	3–07	Mary Connor
25/5/97	Casement Park	Antrim	5–12	Down	3–16	Fiona McKenna
31/5/98	Ballincollig	Down	0–20	Cork	0–12	Biddy Phillips
16/5/99	Gorey	Derry	3–07	Wexford	0–07	Celine Doody
20/5/00	Tullamore	Cork	2–1	2	Kildare	0–04
3/11/01	Tallaght	Cork	3–14	Derry	4–03	Áine Derham
26/5/02	Portlaoise	Offaly	3–18	Laois	2–06	John Pender
25/5/03	Portmore	Galway	2–10	Armagh	1–08	Mary Connor
22/5/04	Nowlan Park	Kildare	2–11	Laois	2–06	Una Kearney
29/5/05	Templemore	Cork	2–10	Galway	2–07	John Pender
13/5/06	St Peregine's	Kilkenny	2–08	Dublin	2–07	Declan Magee
6/5/07	Nowlan Park	Limerick	1–14	Cork	0–05	Ciarán Quigley
26/4/08	St Peregine's	Clare	4–08	Derry	3–09	Damien Noble
25/4/09	Parnell Park	Wexford	2–09	Antrim	0–11	Ciarán Quigley
24/4/10	Thurles	Wexford	2–09	Offaly	1–09	Karl O'Brien
17/4/11	Ashbourne	Waterford	0–16	Antrim	2–9	Aidan O'Brien

Appendix

National League Division 3

Date	Venue	Result				Referee
7/5/06	Páirc Tailteann	Derry	1–14	Clare	3–07	Aileen Lawlor
30/4/07	O'Moore Park	Waterford	1–18	Down	2–13	Damien Noble
13/4/08	St Peregine's	Antrim	6–11	Offaly	3–07	Dermot Connolly
13/4/09	Ashbourne	Down	0–15	Laois	2–08	Joe Kennedy
11/4/10	Tullamore	Laois	2–10	Meath	2–05	Eoghan Elliott
24/4/11	Ashbourne	Meath	3–09	Kildare	2–11	Malachy Toal

National League Division 4

Date	Venue	Result				Referee
7/5/06	Páirc Tailteann	Waterford	5–12	Roscommon	1–10	Cathal Egan
29/4/07	O'Moore Park	Westmeath	3–07	Meath	2–08	Frank McDonald
13/4/08	St Peregine's	Meath	5–07	Roscommon	1–05	Malachy Toal
12/4/09	Ashbourne	Kildare	3–07	Westmeath	1–10	Donal Ryan
11/4/10	Omagh	Tyrone	3–12	Westmeath	1–09	Eoghan Elliott
24/4/11	Ashbourne	Westmeath	4–06	Cavan	2–08	Donal Ryan

Purcell Cup – Third Level Colleges

Year	Winners	Year	Winners
1977	Mary Immaculate, Limerick	1994	University College, Cork
1978	Mary Immaculate, Limerick	1995	Athlone RTC
1979	Ulster Polytechnic, Belfast	1996	St Patrick's College, Maynooth
1980	Ulster Polytechnic, Belfast	1997	Queen's University, Belfast
1981	Thomond/NIHE, Limerick	1998	Mary Immaculate, Limerick
1982	St Mary's, Belfast	1999	Limerick Institute of Technology
1983	Mary Immaculate, Limerick	2000	University of Ulster, Jordanstown
1984	Ulster Polytechnic, Belfast	2001	Cork Institute of Technology
1985	Thomond College, Limerick	2002	Carlow Institute of Technology
1986	Thomond College, Limerick	2003	University of Ulster, Jordanstown
1987	Thomond College, Limerick	2004	Athlone Institute of Technology
1988	Thomond College, Limerick	2005	Garda College, Templemore
1989	Mary Immaculate, Limerick	2006	University of Ulster, Jordanstown
1990	Waterford RTC	2007	Athlone Institute of Technology
1991	Thomond College, Limerick	2008	Queen's University, Belfast
1992	Waterford RTC	2009	Athlone Institute of Technology
1993	Waterford RTC	2010	Dublin Institute of Technology
		2011	Queen's University, Belfast

Ashbourne Cup – Third-Level Colleges

Year	Winners	Year	Winners	Year	Winners
1915	UCD	1947	UCC	1979	UCG
1916	UCD	1948	UCG	1980	UCD
1917	UCG	1949	UCG	1981	UCD
1918	UCD	1950	UCD	1982	UCD
1919	UCC	1951	UCC	1983	UCD
1920	UCG	1952	UCD	1984	UCD
1921	UCD	1953	UCD	1985	UCC
1922	UCC	1954	UCD	1986	UCD
1923	UCC	1955	UCD	1987	UCD
1924	UCC	1956	UCG	1988	UCD
1925	UCC	1957	UCG	1989	UCG
1926	UCC	1958	UCD	1990	UCG
1927	UCC	1959	UCD	1991	Q.U.B.
1928	UCG	1960	UCD	1992	UUJ
1929	UCC	1961	UCD	1993	UUJ
1930	UCG	1962	UCD	1994	UCG
1931	UCC	1963	Unfinished	1995	UL
1932	UCC	1964	UCG	1996	UCC
1933	UCD	1965	UCC	1997	UUJ
1934	UCC	1966	UCD	1998	UCC
1935	UCD	1967	UCC	1999	WIT
1936	UCC	1968	UCG	2000	UCC
1937	UCD	1969	UCD	2001	WIT
1938	UCD	1970	UCD	2002	UCC
1939	UCD	1971	UCD	2003	UCC
1940	UCD	1972	UCC	2004	U.L.
1941	UCD	1973	UCC	2005	U.L.
1942	UCD	1974	UCC	2006	U.L.
1943	Not Played	1975	UCC	2007	UCD
1944	UCC	1976	UCC	2008	UCD
1945	UCC	1977	UCC	2009	WIT
1946	UCD	1978	UCG	2010	WIT
				2011	WIT

Corn Sceilg – All-Ireland Post-Primary Senior A Championship

Year	Venue	Winners	Score	Runners-up
1969	Croke Park	Presentation, Kilkenny	3–02 to 1–02	St Aloysius, Cork
1970	Croke Park	Presentation, Kilkenny	2–03 to 1–01	Sacred Heart, Newry
1971	Croke Park	Sacred Heart, Newry	3–02 to 2–01	Presentation, Mountmellick
1972	Croke Park	Pres. Oranmore	6–01 to 4–04	St Louis, Kilkeel
1973	Croke Park	Pres. Mountmellick	4–02 to 1–02	Presentation, Athenry
1974	Croke Park	Pres. Athenry	3–01 to 1–00	St Louis, Kilkeel
1975	Croke Park	Pres. Athenry	7–04 to 2–04	StBrigid's, Callan
1976	Croke Park	St Aloysius, Cork	2–02 to 0–02	Pres. Athenry
1977	Croke Park	Scoil Mhuire, Cashel	2–02 to 1–03	Pres. Athenry
1978	Croke Park	Pres. Athenry	2–03 to 2–02	Loreto, Coleraine
1979	Croke Park	Scoil Mhuire, Cashel	3–03 to 1–03	Pres. Athenry
1980	Croke Park	North Pres. Cork	4–07 to 1–01	Assumption, Walkinstown
1981	Croke Park	St Patrick's, Cork	1–03 to 0–05	Assumption, Walkinstown
1982	Croke Park	St Patrick's, Shannon	1–07 to 1–04	St Raphael's, Loughrea
1983	Belfield	St John of God, Artane	2–06 to 2–01	St Patrick's, Cork
1984	Croke Park	Maryfield College	2–05 to 0–05	North Presentation, Cork
1985	Cashel	St Raphael's, Loughrea	4–07 to 3–03	St Patrick's, Cork
1986	Croke Park	St Raphael's, Loughrea	3–05 to 0–04	FCJ., Bunclody
1987	Ennis	St Raphael's, Loughrea	3–08 to 0–04	St Mary's, Charleville
1988	Nowlan Park	St Raphael's, Loughrea	2–13 to 1–05	FCJ, Bunclody
1989	Donagh	St Raphael's, Loughrea	5–09 to 2–10	St Patrick's, Keady
1990	O'Toole Park	St Raphael's, Loughrea	3–11 to 2–00	Scoil Mhuire, Cashel
1991	Tullamore	St Raphael's, Loughrea	3–06 to 0–00	Vocational, Thomastown
1992	Tullamore	St Raphael's, Loughrea	7–07 to 2–04	St Brigid's, Callan
1993	Tullamore	St Brigid's, Callan	3–07 to 1–02	St Mary's, Charleville
1994	Tullamore	St Mary's, Nenagh	1–10 to 1–02	St Patrick's, Maghera
1995	Tullamore	Pres. Kilkenny	3–04 to 2–04	St Mary's, Charleville
1996	Tullamore	St Mary's, Charleville	1–15 to 3–03	St Raphael's, Loughrea
1997	Tullamore	St Mary's, Charleville	2–16 to 4–02	St Brigid's, Loughrea
1998	Tullamore	St Mary's, Charleville	1–11 to 1–04	Col. Bríde, Enniscorthy
1999	Nenagh	St Mary's, Charleville	3–10 to 0–05	Col. Bríde, Enniscorthy
2000	Ballinasloe	St Mary's, Nenagh	3–06 to 0–07	Seamount, Kinvara
2001	Moycarkey	St Mary's, Charleville	4–07 to 0–03	Loreto, Kilkenny
2002	Nenagh	St Mary's, Charleville	4–16 to 1–09	Portumna Comm. College
2003	Kilbeggan	Col. Bríde, Enniscorthy	5–07 to 1–05	St Patrick's, Maghera
2004	Cashel	Col. Bríde, Enniscorthy	4–07 to 1–04	St Mary's, Charleville
2005	Carrick-on-Suir	Col. Bríde, Enniscorthy	1–08 to 2–03	St .Mary's, Charleville
2006	Doíla, Co. Tipp.	St Mary's, Charleville	2–05 to 2–05	Presentation, Athenry
	Meelick	St Mary's, Charleville	1–09 to 0–04	Presentation, Athenry
2007	Nenagh	St Mary's, Magherafelt	0–11 to 3–02	Presentation, Athenry
	Drom-Inch	St Mary's, Magherafelt	2–09 to 2–06	Presentation, Athenry
2008	Clonmel	St Brigid's, Callan	3–07 to 0–06	St Mary's, Charleville
2009	Drom-Inch	St Brigid's, Callan	1–11 to 1–06	Portumna Comm. College
2010.	Ardfinnan	Loreto, Kilkenny	2–05 to 1–07	Blackwater S.C. Lismore
2011	Trim	Loreto, Kilkenny	4–10 to 1–05	St Patrick's, Maghera

All-Ireland Post-Primary Senior B Championship

Year	Venue	Winners	Score	Runners-up
1999	Nenagh	Sacred H. Clonakilty	3–13 to 2–05	Kilcormac Voc. School
2000	Ballinasloe	St Patrick's, Shannon	3–05 to 1–00	St Cuan's, Castleblayney
2001	Borrisoleigh	St Brigid's, Callan	2–05 to 1–04	Mercy, Woodford
2002	Nenagh	Mercy, Waterford	2–08 to 1–05	Mercy, Ballinasloe
2003	Kilbeggan	Coachford Comm	1–05 to 0–07	Presentation, Athenry
2004	Cashel	St Rynagh's, Ban	2–07 to 0–07	St Raphael's, Loughrea
2005	Nenagh	Mercy, Woodford	2–07 to 0–04	Ursuline, Thurles
2006	Mullingar	St Fergal's, Rathdowney	2–09 to 2–04	St Patrick's, Keady
2007	Drom-Inch	St Mary's, Nenagh	3–06 to 1–08	Castlecomer C.S.
2008	Feenagh	Christ the King, Cork	2–12 to 3–06	St Killian's, New Inn
2009	Rathoath	Blackwater, Lismore	4–05 to 3–04	St MacNissi's, Garron Tower
2010.	Cahir	Col. Colm, B'collig	3–09 to 2–05	Borris. VS
2011	Trim	Grennan College	4–09 to 3–03	St Louis, Ballymena

All-Ireland Post-Primary Senior C Championship

Year	Venue	Winners	Score	Runners-up
2006	Mullingar	Col. Colm, B'collig	1–06 to 1–02	Gort CS, Co. Galway
2007	Drom-Inch	Scoil Muire, C-on-Suir	4–09 to 1–04	St Brendan's, Birr
2008	Feenagh	Blackwater, Lismore	3–03 to 1–07	Sacred Heart, Tullamore
2009	Rathoath	St Colm's, Draperst	1–07 to 0–09	Grennan Coll. Thomastown
2010.	Toomevara	Pres. Thurles	3–09 to 1–01	St Rynagh's, Banagher
2011	Trim	Castlecomer CS	4–02 to 2–05	St Pius, Magherafelt

Appendix

All-Ireland Post-Primary Junior A Championship

Year	Venue	Winners	Score	Runners-up
1974	Croke Park	Pres., Athenry	3–00 to 0–00	North Presentation, Cork
1975	Croke Park	Scoil Mhuire, Cashel	4–00 to –00	Presentation, Terenure
1976	Croke Park	Pres. Athenry	4–02 to 3–02	Scoil Mhuire, Cashel
1977	Croke Park	Pres. Athenry	4–01 to 1–03	Sacred Heart, Cork
1978	Croke Park	Scoil Mhuire, Cashel	2–03 to 0–01	Vocational, Bawnboy
1979	Croke Park	Mercy, Roscommon	1–02 to 0–01	Scoil Pól, Kilfinane
1980	Croke Park	Maryfield College	2–03 to 1–05	Pres de la Salle, Hospital
1981	Croke Park	St John of God, Artane	4–00 to 0–02	St Patrick's, Cork
1982	Croke Park	Maryfield College	3–09 to 4–00	St Raphael's, Loughrea
1983	Belfield	Mercy, Roscommon	7–01 to 1–03	St Paul's, Kilrea
1984	Croke Park	St Raphael's, Loughrea	6–08 to 2–01	St Patrick's, Shannon
1985	Cashel	St Raphael's, Loughrea	3–04 to 1–00	Colaiste Muire, Ennis
1986	Croke Park	St Mary's, Charleville	2–06 to 0–03	F.C.J. Bunclody
1987	Ennis	St Mary's, Charleville	2–03 to 1–04	St Raphael's, Loughrea
1988	Nowlan Park	St Raphael's, Loughrea	5–07 to 1–00	St Mary's, Macroom
1989	Donagh	St Raphael's, Loughrea	5–00 to 0–01	St Patrick's, Maghera
1990	O'Toole Park	St Brigid's, Callan	5–08 to 1–04	St Patrick's, Maghera
1991	Tullamore	St Mary's, Nenagh	3–09 to 1–10	St Cuan's, Castleblakeney
1992	Tullamore	St Mary's, Nenagh	2–06 to 0–08	St Mary's, Magherafelt
1993	Tullamore	F.C.J. Bunclody	2–07 to 1–04	St Mary's, Charleville
1994	Tullamore	St Mary's, Charleville	3–06 to 1–05	St Mary's, Magherafelt
1995	Tullamore	St Mary's, Charleville	2–12 to 1–01	St Mary's, Magherafelt
1996	Tullamore	St Mary's, Magherafelt	1–10 to 0–04	F.C.J. Bunclody
1997	Tullamore	Holy Rosary, M'bellew	2–04 to 1–05	St Mary's, Charleville
1998	Tullamore	Seamount, Kinvara	3–08 to 1–02	St Mary's, Magherafelt
1999	Nenagh	St Mary's, Charleville	2–08 to 0–06	Seamount, Kinvara
2000	Tullamore	Col. Bríde, Enniscorthy	3–05 to 0–08	Seamount, Kinvara
2001	Moycarkey	St Mary's, Charleville	7–16 to 1–02	St Mary's, Magherafelt
2002	Nenagh	St Mary's, Charleville	4–10 to 4–08	Col. Bríde, Enniscorthy
2003	Kilbeggan	St Mary's, Charleville	9–09 to 0–03	Portumna Community Sch.
2004	Cashel	Col. Bríde, Enniscorthy	8–06 to 0–04	Presentation, Athenry
2005	Rathoath	Presentation, Athenry	3–10 to 2–03	St Mary's, Magherafelt
2006	Dolla, Co. Tipp	St Mary's, Charleville	1–11 to 0–05	Portumna Comm. Sch.
2007	Drom-Inch	Loreto, Kilkenny	0–07 to 0–05	Portumna Comm. Sch.
2008	Ballyhaise	C & P. Ballycastle	2–08 to 2–05	St Brigid's, Loughrea
2009	Rathoath	Loreto, Kilkenny	2–07 to 0–09	St Patrick's, Maghera
2010.	Toomevara	Loreto, Kilkenny	1–16 to 2–07	St Brigid's, Loughrea
2011	Trim	Loreto, Kilkenny	3–11 to 0–07	St Patrick's, Maghera

All-Ireland Post-Primary Schools Junior B Championship

Year	Venue	Winners	Score	Runners-up
1999	Ballinasloe	Colaiste Muire, Ennis	2–10 to 1–02	Loreto, Mullingar
2000	Tullamore	Presentation, Kilkenny	2–06 to 0–05	Holy Rosary, Mountbellew
2001	Ballyboden	Mercy, Woodford	4–09 to 3–06	St Patrick's, Keady
2002	Cashel	Loreto, Fermoy	7–12 to 2–07	Mercy, Ballinasloe
2003	Nenagh	St Fergal's, Rathdowney	4–08 to 3–05	Holy Rosary, Mountbellew
2004	Mountmellick	Scariff Comm. Co. Clare	5–02 to 1–05	Castlecomer Comm
2005	Rathoath	Colaiste Muire, Ennis	1–09 to 1–07	Borris Voc. Sch., Carlow
2006	The Ragg	Borris Voc. Sch. Carlow	2–06 to 0–04	Gort, Co. Galway
2007	Drom-Inch	Coachford Comm. Cork	3–05 to 2–05	St Dominic's, Cabra
2008	Freshford	St Mary's, Nenagh	5–06 to 0–4	Loreto, Wexford
2009	Ashbourne	St Joseph's, Borrisoleigh	5–07 to 1–02	St Patrick's, Keady
2010.	Rathoath	St Flannan's, Ennis	2–17 to 2–03	St Louis, Ballymena
2011	Fermoy	Presentation, Thurles	3–06 to 2–05	Coachford C.S. Cork

All-Ireland Post-Primary Schools Junior C Championship

Year	Venue	Winners	Score	Runners-up
2006	Virginia	St Joseph's, Tulla	1–03 to 0–00	St Patrick's, Dungannon
2007	Nowlan Park	Col. Colm, Ballincollig	4–12 to 0–03	Pres. Bagnelstown
2008	St Peregine's	St Mary's, New Ross	3–04 to 2–02	St MacNissi, Garron Tower
2009	Rathoath	Hazelwood, Drumcollogher	5–15 to 0–00	St Paul's, Kilrea
2010.	Nowlan Park	Presentation, Thurles	6–11 to 1–03	Grennan College, Kilkenny
2011	Ellistown	Maryfield College, Dublin	2–07 to 1–07	Col. Dun Lascaigh, Cahir

Féile na nGael – Division 1

Year	Venue	Winners	Score	Runners-up
1974	Gaelic Grounds	Rathnure (Wexford)	5–00 to 0–01	Ahane (Limerick)
1975	St Finbarr's	Knockananna (Wicklow)	4–10 to 1–00	Croagh-Kilfinny (Limerick)
1976	Páirc Uí Chaoimh	Na Piarsaigh (Cork)	2–01 to 2–00	Thomastown (Kilkenny)
1977	Walsh Park	Killeagh (Cork)	4–03 to 1–00	Enniskillen (Fermanagh)
1978	Nowlan Park	Croagh-Kilfinny (Limk.)	3–01 to 3–00	Marino (Dublin)
1979	Nowlan Park	Woodville (Dublin)	1–01 to 0–00	Blackrock (Cork)
1980	Pearse Stadium	Woodville (Dublin)	3–02 to 1–01	Black and Whites (Kilkenny)
1981	Pearse Stadium	Marino (Dublin)	1–04 to 1–03	Bishopstown (Cork)
1982	Croke Park	Marino (Dublin)	3–00 to 1–03	St Finbarr's (Cork)
1983	Croke Park	Sarsfields (Galway)	3–00 to 1–01	St Dominic's (Roscommon)
1984	Wexford Park	An Caisleáin (Dublin)	3–02 to 2–00	Shamrocks (Kilkenny)
1985	Wexford	Mullagh (Galway)	4–05 to 1–01	Marino (Dublin)
1986	Cusack Park	Mullagh (Galway)	1–02 to 0–04	Bishopstown (Cork)
1987	Cusack Park	Bishopstown (Cork)	2–03 to 1–02	St Monica's (Dublin)
1988	Birr	Pearses (Galway)	4–05 to 1–01	Killeagh (Cork)
1989	Portlaoise	St Lachtain's (Kilkenny)	1–05 to 1–02	Pearses (Galway)
1990	Thurles	St Lachtain's (Kilkenny)	4–01 to 0–07	Killeagh (Cork)

A Game of Our Own

Féile na nGael – Division 1

Year	Venue	Winners	Score	Runners-up
1991	Thurles	Granagh-Ballingarry (Lim.)	2–02 to 0–02	Ballyboden St Enda's (Dublin)
1992	Athenry	Clara (Kilkenny)	6–01 to 3–00	Drom-Inch (Tipperary)
1993	Athenry	Craughwell (Galway)	0–05 to 0–01	Ardrahan (Galway)
1994	Gaelic Grounds	Pearses (Galway)	1–09 to 0–04	St Ibar's (Wexford)
1995	Gaelic Grounds	Pearses (Galway)	1–06 to 0–03	Drom-Inch (Tipperary)
1996	Walsh Park	Templemore (Tipperary)	2–10 to 1–03	Courcey Rovers (Cork)
1997	Walsh Park	Athenry (Galway)	2–05 to 0–04	Rathnure (Wexford)
1998	Bellfield	Oulart The Ballagh (Wexf.)	4–06 to 4–05	Templemore (Tipperary)
1999	Bellfield	Oulart The Ballagh (Wexf.)	2–03 to 0–00	Milford (Cork)
2000	Casement Park	Oulart The Ballagh (Wexf.)	1–08 to 1–01	Davitt's (Galway)
2001	Cork	Oulart The Ballagh (Wexf.)	4–03 to 3–04	Harps (Laois)
2002	Casement Park	Oulart The Ballagh (Wexf.)	2–05 to 0–01	Davitt's, (Galway)
2003	Mullingar	St Vincent's, (Dublin)	2–09 to 0–04	Douglas, Cork
2004	Navan	Douglas (Cork)	3–04 to 2–01	Thomastown (Kilkenny)
2005	Cork	Douglas (Cork)	6–09 to 0–00	St Vincent's (Dublin)
2006	Cork	Douglas (Cork)	2–03 to 1–02	Inniscarra (Cork)
2007	Kilkenny	Sarsfields (Galway)	2–08 to 1–03	Milford (Cork)
2008	Portlaoise	Lucan Sarsfields (Dublin)	2–03 to 1–03	Mullagh (Galway)
2009	Tullamore	Douglas (Cork)	1–07 to 2–02	St Vincent's, (Dublin)
2010	Ennis	Lucan Sarsfields (Dublin)	6–04 to 0–02	Burgess-Duharra (Tipperary)
2011	Galway	Cahir (Tipperary)	4–10 to 1–07	St Martin's (Wexford)

Féile na nGael – Divisions 2, 3 & 4

Year	Division 2 Winners	Divisions 3 Winners	Division 4 Winners
1996	Granagh-Ballingarry (Limerick)	Ballyholland Harps, (Down)	Drumcullen (Offaly)
1997	St Lachtain's, (Kilkenny)	Kinnity (Offaly)	Wolfe Tones (Clare)
1998	Wolfe Tones (Clare)	The Harps (Laois)	Butlerstown (Waterford)
1999	Ballyboden St Enda's (Dublin)	Granagh-Ballingarry (Limerick)	Kiltegan, (Wicklow)
2000	The Harps, (Laois)	St Lachtain's (Kilkenny)	Johnstownbridge (Kildare)
2001	Kilnamona (Clare)	Ballymacnab (Armagh)	No competition
2002	Newmarket-on-Fergus (Clare)	Bellaghy (Derry)	No competition
2003	Ballinascreen (Derry)	St Brenda's, (Armagh)	No competition
2004	Camross (Laois)	Ballycastle (Antrim)	Oran (Roscommon)
2005	Ballycastle (Antrim)	Killeagh (Cork)	No competition
2006	Ballycran (Down)	Lismore (Waterford)	Sarsfields (Cork)
2007	Ballinascreen (Derry)	Rower Inistigue (Kilkenny)	Rathoath (Meath)
2008	Michael Davitt's (Derry)	Rathoath (Meath)	Kerry
2009	St Brenda's (Armagh)	Kerry	Na Brideoga (Mayo)
2010	Eire Óg (Clare)	Celbridge (Kildare)	Cillard (Kerry)
2011	St Killian's (Offaly)	Knockananna (Wicklow)	St Coleman's (Galway)

Féile na nGael – Divisions 2, 3 & 4

Year	Division 2 Winners	Divisions 3 Winners	Division 4 Winners
1978	Johnstown (Kilkenny)		
1979	Avoca (Wicklow)		
1980	Oran Roscommon)		
1981	Na Piarsaigh (Cork)		
1982	Oran (Roscommon)		
1983	Crumlin (Dublin)	Parke (Mayo)	
1984	Annacurra (Wicklow)	Leitrim Fontenoy's, Down	
1985	Carbury (Kildare)	Rasharkin (Antrim)	
1986	Keady (Armagh)	Eire Óg (Clare)	
1987	Keady (Armagh)	Wolfe Tones (Clare)	Tubberclair (Westmeath)
1988	Wolfe Tones (Clare)	Burgess (Tipperary)	Ardagh (Mayo)
1989	Wolfe Tones (Clare)	Oran (Roscommon)	Lismore, (Waterford)
1990	Granagh-Ballingarry (Limerick)	Portaferry (Down)	Toomevara (Tipperary)
1991	Pearses (Galway)	Naomh Moling (Carlow)	Roscrea (Tipperary)
1992	Davitt's (Galway)	Oran, (Roscommon)	Cullion (Westmeath)
1993	Bunclody (Wexford)	Mountbellew (Galway)	Teemore, Fermanagh)
1994	Drom-Inch (Tipperary)	Teemore (Fermanagh)	Na Piarsaigh (Limerick)
1995	Teemore (Fermanagh)	O'Donovan Rossa (Antrim)	Camross (Laois)

National Féile na nGael Skills Winner

Year	Winner	Year	Winner
1978	Deirdre O'Shea (Cork)	1995	Liz Fowler (Waterford)
1979	Deirdre O'Shea (Cork)	1996	Niamh Harkin (Tipperary)
1980	Marie Fitzgibbon (Kilkenny)	1997	Nikki Keddy (Wicklow)
1981	Anne Ryan (Galway)	1998	Aoife Sheehan (Limerick)
1982	Ann Wolfe (Dublin)	1999	Cathy Bowes (Galway)
1983	Jean Paula Kent (Cork)	2000	Charlene Fanthrope (Armagh)
1984	Yvonne McInerney (Clare)	2001	Sarah Dervan (Galway)
1985	Helen Cagney (Limerick)	2002	Gráinne O'Higgins (Down)
1986	Michelle Cameron (Dublin)	2003	Claire Coulter (Down)
1987	Claire Lynch (Galway)	2004	Patricia Jackman (Waterford)
1988	Bridget Mullally (Kilkenny)	2005	Racquel McCarry (Antrim)
1989	Nora O'Connell (Cork)	2006	Caroline Scanlon (Limerick)
1990	Triona Maher (Tipperary)	2007	Emma Quaid (Limerick)
1991	Vivienne Harris (Cork)	2008	Vera Loughnane (Clare)
1992	Mary Kearns (Limerick)	2009	Gráinne Sheehy (Cork)
1993	Michelle Casey (Limerick)	2010	Caoimhe Costelloe (Limerick)
1994	Emma Galvin (Waterford)	2011	Laura Twomey (Clare)

Appendix

Provincial Senior Champions

Year	Ulster	Munster	Leinster	Connacht
1934	Antrim	Cork	Louth	Galway
1935	Antrim	Cork	Dublin	Galway
1936	Antrim	Cork	Louth	Galway
1937	Antrim	Cork	Dublin	Galway
1938	Antrim	Cork	Dublin	Galway
1939	Antrim	Cork	Dublin	Galway
1940	Cavan	Cork	Dublin	Galway
1941	Cavan	Cork	Dublin	Galway
1942	Antrim	Cork	Dublin	Galway
1943	Antrim	Cork	Dublin	Galway
1944	Antrim	Clare	Dublin	Galway
1945	Antrim	Waterford	Dublin	Galway
1946	Antrim	Clare	Dublin	Galway
1947	Antrim	Tipperary	Dublin	Galway
1948	Down	Tipperary	Dublin	Galway
1949	Down	Tipperary	Dublin	Galway
1950	Antrim	Tipperary	Dublin	Galway
1951	Antrim	Tipperary	Dublin	Galway
1952	Antrim	Cork	Dublin	Mayo
1953	Down	Tipperary	Dublin	Mayo
1954	Derry	Cork	Dublin	Mayo
1955	Antrim	Cork	Dublin	Mayo
1956	Antrim	Cork	Dublin	Mayo
1957	Antrim	Cork	Dublin	Mayo
1958	Antrim	Tipperary	Dublin	Mayo
1959	Antrim	Waterford	Dublin	Mayo
1960	Antrim	Tipperary	Dublin	Galway
1961	Antrim	Tipperary	Dublin	Galway
1962	Antrim	Cork	Dublin	Galway
1963	Antrim	Cork	Dublin	Galway
1964	Antrim	Tipperary	Dublin	Galway
1965	Antrim	Tipperary	Dublin	Galway
1966	Antrim	Tipperary	Dublin	Galway
1967	Antrim	Cork	Dublin	Mayo
1968	Antrim	Cork	Wexford	Galway
1969	Antrim	Tipperary	Wexford	Galway
1970	Antrim	Cork	Kilkenny	
1971	Antrim	Cork	Wexford	
1972	Antrim	Cork	Kilkenny	
1973	Antrim	Not Played	Wexford	
1974	Antrim	Cork	Wexford	
1975	Antrim	Cork	Dublin	
1976	Not Played	Cork	Kilkenny	
1977	Antrim	Tipperary	Kilkenny	
1978	Down	Cork	Wexford	
1979	Antrim	Cork	Dublin	
1980	Down	Cork	Kilkenny	
1981	Down	Cork	Dublin	
1982	Antrim	Cork	Dublin	
1983	Down	Cork	Dublin	
1984	Down	Cork	Dublin	
1985	Antrim	Cork	Dublin	
1986	Antrim	Cork	Dublin	
1987	Down	Cork	Dublin	
1988	Down	Cork	Kilkenny	
1989	Derry	Cork	Kilkenny	
1990	Derry	Cork	Kilkenny	
1991	Down	Cork	Wexford	
1992	Armagh	Not Played	Kilkenny	
1993	Armagh	Not Played	Kilkenny	
1994	Armagh	Cork	Wexford	
1995	Down	Cork	Wexford	
1996	Down	Cork	Kilkenny	
1997	Antrim	Cork	Kilkenny	
1998	Down	Cork	Kilkenny	
1999	Derry	Cork	Wexford	
2000	Antrim	Not Played	Wexford	
2001	Derry	Cork	Wexford	
2002	Antrim	Cork	Kilkenny	
2003	Derry	Tipperary	Wexford	
2004	Derry	Tipperary	Wexford	
2005	Down	Tipperary	Kilkenny	
2006	Not Played	Cork	Kilkenny	
2007	Not Played	Cork	Wexford	
2008	Antrim	Cork	Kilkenny	
2009	Derry	Cork	Kilkenny	
2010	Antrim	Tipperary	Wexford	
2011	Antrim	Cork	Wexford	

Provincial Junior Champions

Year	Ulster	Munster	Leinster	Connacht
1968	Down	Cork	Wexford	Galway
1969	Derry	Cork	Kildare	Galway
1970	Armagh	Cork	Dublin	Roscommon
1971	Armagh	Cork	Dublin	Roscommon
1972	Armagh	Limerick	Wexford	Galway
1973	Armagh	Cork	Wexford	Galway
1974	Antrim	Clare	Dublin	Galway
1975	Down	Limerick	Dublin	Roscommon
1976	Down	Limerick	Wexford	Galway
1977	Monaghan	Limerick	Wexford	Galway
1978	Derry	Cork	Wicklow	Galway
1979	Cavan	Cork	Dublin	Galway
1980	Tyrone	Cork	Louth	Galway
1981	Antrim	Clare	Kildare	Galway
1982	Antrim	Cork	Louth	Galway
1983	Down	Cork	Dublin	Galway
1984	Cavan	Cork	Dublin	Galway
1985	Armagh	Limerick	Wexford	Galway
1986	Derry	Clare	Kildare	Roscommon
1987	Armagh	Cork	Kildare	Galway
1988	Down	Limerick	Kildare	Galway
1989	Down	Cork	Kildare	Galway
1990	Armagh	Tipperary	Kildare	Roscommon
1991	Down	Tipperary	Dublin	Galway
1992	Armagh	Tipperary	Kilkenny	Galway
1993	Armagh	Cork	Carlow	Galway
1994	Cavan	Limerick	Kilkenny	Galway
1995	Antrim	Limerick	Kildare	Roscommon
1996	Antrim	Cork	Kildare	Roscommon
1997	Antrim	Cork	Carlow	Roscommon
1998	Derry	Tipperary	Carlow	Galway
1999	Derry	Cork	Offaly	Roscommon
2000	Derry	Cork	Laois	Roscommon
2001	Derry	Tipperary	Offaly	Roscommon
2002	Derry	Cork	Kilkenny	Galway
2003	Armagh	Clare	Wexford	Galway
2004	Down	Cork	Wexford	Roscommon
2005	Armagh	Clare	Dublin	Galway
2006	Derry	Cork	Kilkenny	Galway
2007	Derry	Waterford	Laois	Roscommon
2008	Tyrone	Cork	–	Galway
2009	Tyrone	Tipperary	Meath	Galway
2010	Cavan	Tipperary	Kildare	Galway

Provincial Club Senior Champions

Year	Ulster	Munster	Leinster	Connacht
1964	Deirdre, Belfast	Glen Rovers, Cork	Celtic, Dublin	Newport, Mayo
1965	Deirdre, Belfast	St Patrick's, Glengoole	St Ibar's, Wexford	St Rita's, Galway
1966	Deirdre, Belfast	St Patrick's, Glengoole	St Paul's, Kilkenny	Oranmore, Galway
1967	Deirdre, Belfast	Glen Rovers, Cork	Eoghan Ruadh, Dublin	Oranmore, Galway
1968	Deirdre, Belfast	Ahane, Limerick	St Paul's, Kilkenny	Ballinasloe, Galway
1969	Aghohill, Antrim	Ahane, Limerick	St Paul's, Kilkenny	Oranmore, Galway
1970	Bellaghy, Derry	South Pres. P.P. Cork	St Paul's, Kilkenny	Breffy, Mayo
1971	Portglenone	Thurles, Tipperary	Austin Stacks, Dublin	Ballinasloe, Galway
1972	Portglenone	Ahane, Limerick	Austin Stacks, Dublin	Oranmore, Galway
1973	Creggan, Antrim	Thurles, Tipperary	St Paul's, Kilkenny	Oranmore, Galway
1974	Portglenone	UCC	St Paul's, Kilkenny	Oranmore, Galway
1975	Newry, Down	Croagh-Kilfinny, Limk.	Buffers Alley, Wexford	Athenry, Galway
1976	Creggan, Antrim	Ahane, Limerick	St Paul's, Kilkenny	Athenry, Galway
1977	Portglenone	Ballyagran, Limerick	St Paul's, Kilkenny	Athenry, Galway
1978	Portglenone	Ballyagran, Limerick	Buffers Alley, Wexford	Athenry, Galway
1979	Portglenone	Ballyagran, Limerick	Buffers Alley, Wexford	Athenry, Galway
1980	Kilkeel, Down	Killeagh, Cork	Buffers Alley, Wexford	Oranmore, Galway
1981	Kilkeel, Down	Killeagh, Cork	Buffers Alley, Wexford	Oranmore, Galway
1982	Portglenone	Killeagh, Cork	Buffers Alley, Wexford	Athenry, Galway
1983	Swatragh, Derry	Croagh-Kilfinny, Limk.	Buffers Alley, Wexford	Glenamaddy,
1984	Leitrim Fonten.	Killeagh, Cork	Buffers Alley, Wexford	Glenamaddy
1985	Eglish, Tyrone	Eire Óg, Cork	Crumlin, Dublin	Athenry, Galway
1986	Eglish, Tyrone	Glen Rovers, Cork	St Paul's, Kilkenny	Athenry, Galway
1987	Eglish, Tyrone	Glen Rovers, Cork	St Paul's, Kilkenny	Glenamaddy
1988	Swatragh, Derry	Killeagh, Cork	St Paul's, Kilkenny	Glenamaddy
1989	Swatragh, Derry	Sixmilebridge, Clare	St Paul's, Kilkenny	Mullagh, Galway
1990	Swatragh, Derry	Glen Rovers, Cork	St Paul's, Kilkenny	Mullagh, Galway
1991	Eglish, Tyrone	Glen Rovers, Cork	Celtic, Dublin	Mullagh, Galway
1992	Portglenone	Glen Rovers, Cork	Rathnure, Wexford	Pearses, Galway
1993	Loughgiel, Antr.	Glen Rovers, Cork	Lisdowney, Kilkenny	Mullagh, Galway
1994	Dunloy, Antrim	Glen Rovers, Cork	Lisdowney, Kilkenny	Pearses, Galway
1995	Leitrim Fonten.	Toomevara, Tipp.	Rathnure, Wexford	Davitt's, Galway
1996	Leitrim Fonten.	Granagh-Ballingarry, Limk.	Rathnure, Wexford	Pearses, Galway
1997	Loughgiel, Antr.	Granagh-Ballingarry, Limk.	Lisdowney, Kilkenny	Pearses, Galway
1998	Leitrim Fonten.	Granagh-Ballingarry, Limk.	St Vincent's, Dublin	Pearses, Galway
1999	Leitrim Fonten.	Granagh-Ballingarry, Limk.	St Lachtain's, Kilkenny	Davitt's, Galway
2000	Swatragh, Derry	Granagh-Ballingarry, Limk.	St Lachtain's, Kilkenny	Pearses, Galway
2001	Keady, Armagh	Cashel, Tipperary	St Ibar's, Wexford	Pearses, Galway
2002	Keady, Armagh	Cashel, Tipperary	St Ibar's, Wexford	Pearses, Galway
2003	Dunloy, Antrim	Granagh-Ballingarry, Limk.	St Lachtain's, Kilkenny	Davitt's, Galway
2004	Rossa, Belfast	Granagh-Ballingarry, Limk.	St Lachtain's, Kilkenny	Davitt's, Galway
2005	Rossa, Belfast	Cashel, Tipperary	St Lachtain's, Kilkenny	Davitt's, Galway

APPENDIX

Provincial Club Senior Champions

Year	Ulster	Munster	Leinster	Connacht
2006	Rossa, Belfast	Cashel, Tipperary	St Lachtain's, Kilkenny	Athenry, Galway
2007	Rossa, Belfast	Cashel, Tipperary	St Lachtain's, Kilkenny	Athenry, Galway
2008	Rossa, Belfast	Drom-Inch, Tipperary	Ballyboden St Enda's	Athenry, Galway
2009	Loughgiel, Antr.	Cashel, Tipperary	Oulart-The Ballagh, Wexf..	Athenry, Galway
2010	Rossa, Belfast	Inniscarra, Cork	Oulart-The Ballagh, Wexf.	Killimor, Galway

Provincial Club Junior Champions

Year	Ulster	Munster	Leinster	Connacht
2003	Crossmaglen	Newmarket-on-Fergus	Drumcullen, Offaly	Aghascragh, Galway
2004	Leitrim Fonten	Kilnamona, Clare	St Laurence's, Kildare	Four Road, Roscommon
2005	Leitrim Fonten	Newmarket-on-Fergus	Drumcullen, Offaly	Four Road, Roscommon
2006	Keady, Armagh	Gaultier, Waterford	The Harps, Laois	Athleague, Roscommon
2007	Keady, Armagh	Kilnamona, Clare	The Harps, Laois	Athleague, Roscommon
2008	Lavey, Derry	Kilmaley, Clare	The Harps, Laois	Four Roads, Roscommon
2009	Lavey, Derry	Dunhill, Waterford	The Harps, Laois	Four Roads, Roscommon
2010	Tir na nOg, Antr.	Corofin, Clare	Kilmessan, Meath	Four Roads, Roscommon

Kilmacud Crokes All-Ireland Sevens

Year	Winners	Year	Winners
1974	Buffers Alley (Wexford)	1992	Mullagh (Galway)
1975	St Paul's, (Kilkenny)	1993	Rathnure (Wexford)
1976	Celtic (Dublin)	1994	Pearses (Galway)
1977	Drom-Inch (Tipperary)	1995	Marino (Dublin)
1978	St Paul's, (Kilkenny)	1996	Drom-Inch (Tipperary)
1979	St Paul's, (Kilkenny)	1997	Toomevara (Tipperary)
1980	St Paul's, (Kilkenny)	1998	Lisdowney (Kilkenny)
1981	Killeagh (Cork)	1999	Pearses (Galway)
1982	St Paul's, (Kilkenny)	2000	Davitt's (Galway)
1983	St Paul's, (Kilkenny)	2001	Pearses (Galway)
1984	Buffers Alley (Wexford)	2002	Granagh-Ballingarry (Limerick)
1985	Buffers Alley (Wexford)	2003	O'Donovan Rossa (Antrim)
1986	Buffers Alley (Wexford)	2004	Athenry (Galway)
1987	Celtic (Dublin)	2005	Milford (Cork)
1988	Buffers Alley (Wexford)	2006	Oulart-The Ballagh (Wexford)
1989	Buffers Alley (Wexford)	2007	Athenry (Galway)
1990	Glen Rovers (Cork)	2008	O'Donovan Rossa (Antrim)
1991	Marino (Dublin)	2009	Cashel (Tipperary)
		2010	Cashel (Tipperary)
		2011	Toomevara (Tipperary)

An Poc Fáda

Year	Winner
2004	Stephanie Gannon (Galway)
2005	Denise Lynch, (Clare)
2006	Mary Henry (Westmeath)
2007	Lyndsey Condell (Carlow)
2008	Lyndsey Condell (Carlow)
2009	Patricia Jackman (Waterford)
2010	Patricia Jackman (Waterford)
2011	Patricia Jackman (Waterford)

Players Who Changed Their Name During Their Inter-county Career

Maiden Name	County	Married Name	Maiden Name	County	Married Name
Mary Black	Armagh	Rafferty	Carol Blayney	Antrim	McAllister
Rose-Marie Breen	Wexford	O'Loughlin	Olivia Broderick	Galway	Forde
Helen Butler	Limerick	Moynihan	Peggy Carey	Kilkenny	Muldowney
Olive Coady	Galway	Molloy	Bernie Conway	Dublin	Toner
Anne Comerford	Cork	Phelan	Sinéad Costello	Kilkenny	Cash
Marie Costine	Cork	O'Donovan	Mel Cummins	Cork	Clinton
Veronica Curtin	Galway	Coleman	Anne Delaney	Cork	O'Donovan
Marion Delaney	Armagh/Down	McGarvey	Jovita Delaney	Tipp.	Heaphy
Gillian Dillon	Kilkenny	Maher	Hannah Dineen	Cork	Cotter
Angela Downey	Kilkenny	Browne	Carmel Doyle	Kilkenny	Savage
Geraldine Duggan	Wexford	Wynne	Ann Duane	Galway	Connolly
Sheila Dunne	Cork	Morgan	Emer Farrell	Cork	Fennell
Bernie Farrelly	Kildare	Kennedy	Terry Griffin	Tipp.	Geaney
Ann Graham	Tipp.	Ralph	Martina Harkin	Galway	Carr
Martina Haverty	Galway	Donnellan	Eileen Hawkins	Wexford	O'Gorman
Michelle Hearne	Wexford	Martin	Angela Higgins	Cork	Sheehan
Maura Hogan	Tipperary	Hackett	Lilian Howlett	Waterford	O'Sullivan
Chris Hughes	Antrim	O'Boyle	Bridie Jacob	Wexford	Doran
Ann Keane	Cork/Dublin	Colgan	Marion Kearns	Antrim	McFetridge
Teresa Kearns	Antrim	Cassidy	Buffers Kehoe	Wexford	Doyle
Bridget Kehoe	Wexford	Doyle	Gretta Kehoe	Wexford	Quigley
Kit Kehoe	Wexford	Codd	Mary Kennedy	Kilkenny	Canavan
Cathy Landers	Cork	Harnedy	Olive Leonard	Armagh	McGeown
Susan Lively	Down	Hynes	Sally Long	Tipp.	Kelly
Marie Mackey	Cork	Ryan	Bridie Martin	Kilkenny	McGarry
Miriam Miggan	Kildare	Malone	Nancy Milligan	Antrim	Murray
Tracey Millea	Kilkenny	McEvoy	Pat Moloney	Cork	Lenihan
Bernie Moloney	Tipperary	O'Dowd	Jane Murphy	Galway	Beatty
Helen Mulcair	Limerick	Collins	Sheila Murray	Dublin	McNamee
Mairéad McAtamney	Antrim	Magill	Rita McAteer	Antrim	Moran
Ann McAuliffe	Cork	Ryan	Anna McManus	Dublin	Condon
Mary McMullan	Antrim	Connolly	Orla Ní Síocháin	Dublin	Ryan
Ciara Nelson	Antrim	Gault	Margie Neville	Limerick	Dore
Bernie O'Brien	Limerick	Chawke	Geraldine O'Brien	Limerick	Coleman
Nancy O'Driscoll	Cork	O'Donovan	Margaret O'Leary	Wexford	Leacy
Helena O'Neill	Kilkenny	McCormack	Mairéad Quinn	Antrim	Diamond
Sarah Ann Quinn	Derry	McNicholl	Anne Redmond	Dublin	O'Brien
Cally Riordan	Cork	O'Donovan	Ann Ryan	Galway	Forde
Mary Jo Ryan	Cork	Daly	Monica Ryan	Tipp	Butler
Bridie Scully	Tipp.	Conroy	Betty Sugrue	Cork	McCarthy
Siobhan Tynan	Tipp.	McDonnell	Dorothy Walsh	Wexford	Kenny
Elsie Walsh	Wexford	Cody	Sue Ward	Antrim	Cashman

INDEX

Ashbourne Cup
22, 24
Ashbourne, Lord
21, 22, 48
Barry, Margaret
158
Bourke, Joan
210
Breslin, Phyllis
297, 310, 311, 315, 327, 500
Burke, Elaine
389
Burns, Ciara
280
Byrne, Lucy
30, 77, 90, 94, 494

Camogie
All Ireland Colleges' Council, inaugural colleges' championship 144;
- and the Irish Revolution 24, 26;
ban on hockey 60, 72;
ban on foreign dances 49, 62, 149;
ban on foreign games 44, 46, 72;
BBC coverage 107;
Camogie ezine 433;
Camogie magazine 154, 155, 358, 433;
Centenary year 369;
coaching 147, 150, 187, 295;
Competitions Review 387; 407;
Constitution and rules updated 449;
Diamond Jubilee 121;
dropping the 'points' bar 199;
fifteen a side game 247, 295, 319; 333;
Financial and Sponsorship Manager 359;
first set of rules 5;
first goal in competitive Camogie 7;
first match in Dublin 7;
first match in Cork 10;
first Tipperary club 19;
first inter county match 19;
first match programme 67;
first Radio Éireann broadcast 67;
first Trustees 86;
first inter provincial match 92;
first All Ireland Club Championship 127;
first All Ireland Junior championship 147;
first rule on substitutions 149;
first government grant 150;
first administration course 169;
first national PRO 170;
first All Ireland minor championship 174;
first full time officer 193, 205;
first national PRO 170;
first All Ireland minor championship 174;
first full time officer 193, 205;
first youth convention 247;
first sponsor 298;
first live TV broadcast 320;
first website 359;
first shinty international 367;
first media awards 420;
full time Treasurer 350;
first Soaring Star Awards 446;
first All Ireland Intermediate club championship 460;
Golden Jubilee 92;
helmets 304; 476;
inclusion and diversity initiative 469;
London revival 234;
marriage ban 59;
membership fees 411;
men's exclusion 49;
new National League 188;
new playing uniform 157;
North American Board 188;
playing uniform 157; 475;
President Elect 411;
Primary Schools' Council 169;
Provincial Councils' establishment 46;
75th anniversary 198;
revised rules 17;
rules updates 449;
Scéal na Camógaíochta (history) 228;
Special Policy Commission 139;
Strategic Plan 2004-2008 373; Review 420; Strategic Plan 2010-2015 447, 471;
Ulster, first colleges' council 66.

Camóguidheacht
6
An Cumann Camóguidheachta
8, 16
Camogie abroad
478
Ceol, Caint and Damhsa Programme
170, 187, 319
Coaching Development
310, 479
Coltas Camógaíochta na hÉireann, An
77
Cody, Kathleen
277, 483
Connor, Mary
330
Costine, Marie 485
Cotter-Hegarty, Monica
48
Council for Colleges of Higher Education
158
Crokes club 11-13, 15, 23, 28
Cronin, Denise
299
Cuchulainns
2, 7, 8, 11
Culacht Camógaíocht na hÉireann
88
Dennehy, Colette
274
Donnellan, Laura
454
Downey, Angela
227, 242, 247, 266, 276, 289, 299, 313, 487-8
Downey, Ann
229, 259, 276, 289, 343
Doyle, Brigid 485
Duffy, Eileen
105
Emer's club
9, 11, 12, 19
Fág an Bealach club
6
Farrell, Cyril
278
Féile na nGael
193, 258, 348
Fennelly, Mary
216, 228, 498
Fingal, Elizabeth, Countess of
15, 16, 17, 18, 492-3
Fitzgibbon, Sandie
279, 283, 486
GAA, closer links
264, 297, 317, 333, 334, 357, 388, 480
Gaelic League
2, 13, 17, 23
Garvan, Liz 484
Gill, Mollie
25, 28, 33, 36, 40, 64, 65, 493
Golden, Jo
170, 176, 187, 205, 211, 228, 304, 334, 358, 373, 502

522

Index

Gradam Táilte
  216
Hennessy, Anne 494
Hobbins, Imelda
  305, 315
Hogg, Peggy 482-3
Horgan, Sheila
  75, 494
Howard, Liz
  373, 396, 404, 433, 501-2
Hyde, Dr. Douglas
  4, 17, 480
Hynes, Ita
  49
Irish Women's National Athletic and Camóguidheachta Association
  32
Jones, Clare
  219
Jones' Road
  18, 23
Keatings Branch of the Gaelic League, club
  2, 3, 6, 7, 8, 11, 15, 478
Kilmacud Sevens
  170
Kirby Lil
  57, 64, 65, 493
Ladies hurling
  11
Leacy, Mary
  411, 412
Lynch, Mary
  234, 235, 241, 252, 498-9
Magill, Mairéad (McAtamney)
  200, 488
Malone, Rose
  274, 402
McAleenan, Seamus
  223
McAnulty, Sheila (Nic an Ultaigh, Síghle)
  83, 88, 90, 91, 92, 97, 106, 115, 162, 169, 176, 211, 228, 277, 319, 326, 373, 398, 492
McCarthy, Nell
  92, 96, 97, 108, 123, 154, 162, 225, 259, 433, 496-7
McGarry, Bridie (Martin)
  235, 276, 488
McGarvey, Marian
  181
McGeeney, Annette
  394
McHugh, Jean
  72, 91
McManus, Rosina
  133, 138, 149, 150, 154, 187, 277, 317, 324, 433, 496
McQuaid, John Charles
  47
McStay, Marian
  413
Meehan, Mairéad
  297, 409
Mellerick, Linda
  311
Mills, Kathleen (Kay)
  70, 112, 113, 149, 225, 482
Moloney, Pat 487
Moran, Mary
  144, 163, 176, 187, 198, 199, 200, 205, 219, 311, 498
Morrissey, Pat
  158
Mulcahy, Claire
  354
Murray, Nancy
  136, 162, 324, 373, 497
National Camógaíocht Association, The
  60
Neary, Liz
  241, 276, 486-7
Nevin, Colette
  307
Nic an Ultaigh, Síghle (see McAnulty)
Ní Cheallacháin, Máire (O'Callaghan, Mary)
  252, 499
Ní Chinnéide, Máire
  2, 7, 8, 9, 14, 133, 134, 473, 476
Ó Braonáin, Séamus
  3, 5
O'Brien, Eileen
  325
O'Callaghan, Miriam
  334, 357, 394, 501
O'Connell, Antoinette
  306
O'Connell, Crios
  94, 115, 495
O'Connor, Gemma
  391
O'Connor, Mary
  387, 396, 404, 409, 471
O'Connor, Sinéad
  359, 373, 411, 471
O'Connor, Una
  129, 483-4
Ó Donnachadha, Tadhg (Torna)
  2, 3, 7
O' Donoghue, Cáit
  7, 15, 17, 18, 19, 31, 490
O'Donoghue, Tadhg (Torna)
  3, 4, 7
O'Donovan Rossa's funeral
  21
O'Duffy, Kathleen
  117, 169, 259
O' Duffy, Seán
  12, 17, 23, 28, 31, 34, 36, 39, 40, 41, 60, 63, 64, 88, 92, 94, 115, 121, 169, 198, 211, 490-1
O'Dwyer, Una
  361
O'Farrelly, Agnes
  17, 21, 31, 32, 40, 45, 47, 49, 50, 56, 57, 64, 69, 76, 88, 491-2
O'Flynn, Joan
  420, 433, 437, 449, 471, 502
O'Leary, Margaret 484
O'Grady, Lil
  124, 133, 495-6
O'Loughlin, Belle
  288, 299, 306, 307, 500
O'Regan, Amanda
  437
Ó Siocháin, Seán
  198, 199, 205, 223
Pan Celtic Festival
  234
Phoenix Park
  7, 18, 28, 40, 45
Purcell, Agnes
  158, 181, 200, 206, 223, 228, 497-8
Rafferty, Pat
  333, 347, 354, 501
Redmond, Eilish
  106, 113, 409, 495
Sheehy, Anne
  223, 241
Spence, Lily
  99, 116, 144, 145, 187, 199, 206, 317, 324, 494-5
Stokes, Méadhbh
  327
Team of the Century
  372
Timmins, Kathleen
  330
Ua (Ó) Ceallaigh, Seán (Sceilg)
  2, 4, 37, 144
Uí Mhaolagáin, Bridín
  266, 270, 280, 499-500
Wallace, Sheila
  241, 313, 317, 334, 373, 414, 421, 424, 503
Ward, Sue
  133
Watson, Maria
  347